PREFACE

To compile a dictionary of quotations is a daunting but fascinating experience. One must allow a huge range of statements, observations and conceptions, drawn from the many traditions of human thought, to filter through the mind, while at the same time attempting to select from among them those that may justifiably be defined as 'quotations'. When I started to collect items for this dictionary, I assumed that the ultimate criterion of quotability lay in the form, in the acuteness of the thought's phrasing. Although I still regard formal qualities as crucial, it was happily early in my labours that I was forced to broaden this perspective by a friend to whom I showed a small selection of what I thought were the wittier contributions. He frowned over the first quotation, and then said thoughtfully, 'Yes, I suppose that might be true.' I hope that this collection will from time to time provoke in its readers similarly critical reflections, and that as well as providing accurate reference to the men and women who have created such memorable expressions, it will also bear witness to the marvellous multiplicity of conceptions of truth that humankind has generated.

In this volume, quotations are arranged according to authorship, in alphabetical order, except for such material as ballads, nursery rhymes, and the many memorable utterances of anonymous people; these are placed together alphabetically under those headings. Quotations from each author are presented in alphabetical order by the title of each work. With major authors, the leading mode of writing is dealt with before minor ones (thus, Milton's poems come before his prose works); where such definitions are difficult or obviously tendentious, the writings are simply presented in alphabetical order by title. These may be followed by other sources such as letters and speeches (both in chronological order), remarks, attributed quotations ('Attr.') and those found in biographical or other works, and finally, 'last words'. (In speeches, letters, etc., each quotation is drawn from a separate occasion unless 'Ib.' is employed; 'Ib.' indicates that the quotation comes from the same source as the previous one.)

Citations from the Bible, which is quoted in the King James Version, are presented in sequence under the title of each book; the Vulgate, the Prayer Book and the Latin Mass are also arranged sequentially. Quotations from foreign languages have generally been provided with recent, literal, prose translations, except where it would be a pity to omit a celebrated traditional rendition. Index entries are provided for both the original language version and the translation. With Greek and the less well-known modern languages, quotations are given only in English versions, this is also done when the phrasing of the original quotation is thought unlikely to be recalled by English-speaking readers.

References have been made as compact as possible while still allowing the reader to find the context reasonably easily in the original work. 'Ib.' appearing alone refers to the previously cited source and location, while 'Ib.' followed by a reference number refers to the last-cited title.

The index, which has been assembled with the aid of a computer, was of course designed by and for the human brain. Keywords head up an alphabetical listing of phrases in which that word appears, and each phrase is followed by the page number and the number of the relevant quotation on that page. With an average of three keywords per quotation, it should be possible to find out who actually uttered a well-remembered quotation by searching for the most obvious word; half-remembered quotations may be traced if one of the more striking words can be recalled; and something apposite on all the great topics of human experience can be discovered by looking up an appropriate word.

I should like to thank all those friends and colleagues who, while giving me information and advice, also insisted on thrusting me their favourite quotations, many of which I have used. My editor, Ian Crofton, has been a steady source of advice, support, and additional quotations. My ultimate debt of gratitude is owed to my wife, Alison.

Donald Fraser

THE QUOTATIONS

Accius, Lucius (170–90 B.C.)

1 *Oderint dum metuant.* Let them hate so long as they fear. [*Atreus*]

Acheson, Dean (1893–1971)

2 Great Britain has lost an Empire and not yet found a role. [Speech, 1962]

Acton, First Baron (1834–1902)

3 Power tends to corrupt and absolute power corrupts absolutely. [Letter, *Life of Mandell Creighton*]

4 Every class is unfit to govern. [Quoted in Auden, *A Certain World*]

Adams, Henry (1838–1918)

5 Every one carries his own inch-rule of taste, and amuses himself by applying it, triumphantly, wherever he travels. [*Education of Henry Adams*]

6 They know enough who know how to learn. [Ib.]

7 Simplicity is the most deceitful mistress that ever betrayed man. [Ib.]

8 All the steam in the world could not, like the Virgin, build Chartres. [Ib.]

Adams, Sarah Flower (1805–1848)

9 Nearer, my God, to Thee, / Nearer to Thee! [Hymn]

Addison, Joseph (1672–1719)

10 And, pleas'd th' Almighty's orders to perform / Rides in the whirlwind, and directs the storm. [*The Campaign*]

11 'Tis not in mortals to command success, / But we'll do more, Sempronius; we'll deserve it. [*Cato*, I]

12 A day, an hour of virtuous liberty / Is worth a whole eternity in bondage. [Ib. II]

13 The woman that deliberates is lost. [Ib. IV]

14 From hence, let fierce contending nations know / What dire effects from civil discords flow. [Ib. V]

15 Poetic fields encompass me around, / And still I seem to tread on classic ground. ['Letter from Italy']

16 A painted meadow, or a purling stream. [Ib.]

17 Music, the greatest good that mortals know, / And all of heaven we have below. ['Song for St. Cecilia's Day']

18 Nothing which is a phrase or saying in common talk, should be admitted into a serious poem. ['Essay on Virgil's Georgics']

19 [Of Virgil] He delivers the meanest of his precepts with a kind of grandeur, he breaks the clods and tosses the dung about with an air of gracefulness. [Ib.]

20 [The Georgics] The most complete, elaborate, and finisht piece of all antiquity. [Ib.]

21 Themistocles, the great Athenian general, being asked whether he would choose to marry his daughter to an indigent man of merit, or to a worthless man of an estate, replied, that he would prefer a man without an estate to an estate without a man. [*The Fortune Hunter*]

22 The truth of it is, learning, like travelling, and all other methods of improvement, as it finishes good sense, so it makes a silly man ten thousand times more insufferable, by supplying variety of matter to his impertinence, and giving him an opportunity of abounding in absurdities. [*The Man of the Town*]

23 It was said of Socrates that he brought philosophy down from heaven to inhabit among men; and I shall be ambitious to have it said of me that I have brought philosophy out of closets and libraries, schools and colleges, to dwell in clubs and assemblies, at tea-tables and in coffee-houses. [*Spectator*, 1]

1 Thus I live in the world rather as a spectator of mankind than as one of the species. [Ib. 1]

2 A perfect tragedy is the noblest production of human nature. [Ib. 39]

3 Sir Roger told them, with the air of a man who would not give his judgement rashly, that much might be said on both sides. [Ib. 122]

4 I have often thought, says Sir Roger, it happens very well that Christmas should fall out in the Middle of Winter. [Ib. 269]

5 Our language sunk under him [Milton], and was unequal to that greatness of soul which furnished him with such glorious conceptions. [Ib. 297]

6 These widows, Sir, are the most perverse creatures in the world. [Ib. 335]

7 We have in England a particular bashfulness in every thing that regards religion. [Ib. 458]

8 The spacious firmament on high, / With all the blue ethereal sky, / And spangled heavens, a shining frame, / Their great Original proclaim. [Ib. 465]

9 Forever singing as they shine, 'The Hand that made us is divine.' [Ib.]

10 I value my garden more for being full of blackbirds than of cherries, and very frankly give them fruit for their songs. [Ib. 477]

11 'We are always doing,' says he, 'something for Posterity, but I would fain see Posterity do something for us.' [Ib. 583]

12 When I read the several dates of the tombs, of some that died yesterday, and some six hundred years ago, I consider that great day when we shall all of us be contemporaries, and make our appearance together. [*Thoughts in Westminster Abbey*]

13 I consider woman as a beautiful, romantic animal, that may be adorned with furs and feathers, pearls and diamonds, ores and silks. [*Trial of the Petticoat*]

14 Arguments out of a pretty mouth are unanswerable. [*Women and Liberty*]

15 See in what peace a Christian can die. [Dying words]

Aeschylus (525–456 B.C.)

16 Things are where things are, and, as fate has willed, / So shall they be fulfilled. [*Agamemnon*; trans. Browning]

17 Make not my path offensive to the gods / By spreading it with carpets. [Ib.]

18 The wisest of the wise may err. [*Fragments*]

19 It is always the season for the old to learn. [Ib.]

20 Words are the physicians of a mind diseased. [*Prometheus Bound*]

21 His resolve is not to seem the bravest, but to be it. [*Seven against Thebes*]

Agathon (c. 448–400 B.C.)

22 This only is denied to God: the power to change the past. [Aristotle, *Nicomachean Ethics*, VI]

Ainger, A. C. (1841–1919)

23 God is working His purpose out as year succeeds to year, / God is working His purpose out and the time is drawing near; / Nearer and nearer draws the time, the time that shall surely be, / When the earth shall be filled with the glory of God as the waters cover the sea. [Hymn]

Alain (1868–1951)

24 There are only two kinds of scholars; those who love ideas and those who hate them. [Quoted in Mackay, *The Harvest of a Quiet Eye*]

Albertano of Brescia (c. 1190–c. 1270)

25 The angry man always thinks he can do more than he can. [*Liber Consolationis*]

26 *Qui omnes despicit, omnibus displicet.* Who despiseth all, displeaseth all. [Ib.]

Alcott, Amos Bronson (1799–1888)

27 Civilization degrades the many to exalt the few. [*Table Talk*, 'Pursuits']

1 A sip is the most that mortals are permitted from any goblet of delight. [Ib. 'Habits']

Alcuin (735–804)

2 *Vox populi, vox dei.* The voice of the people is the voice of God. [Letter to Charlemagne]

Albee, Edward (1928–)

3 Who's Afraid of Virginia Woolf? [Play title]

Aldrich, Henry (1647–1710)

4 If all be true that I do think, / There are five reasons we should drink; / Good wine — a friend — or being dry — / Or lest we should be by and by — / Or any other reason why. ['Five Reasons for Drinking']

Alexander the Great (356–323 B.C.)

5 Heaven cannot brook two suns, nor earth two masters. [Plutarch, *Apothegms*]

6 [At Achilles' tomb] O fortunate youth, to have found Homer as the herald of your glory. [Cicero, *Pro Archia*]

7 If I were not Alexander, I would be Diogenes. [Plutarch, *Life*]

8 I assure you I had rather excel others in the knowledge of what is excellent, than in the extent of my power and dominion. [Ib.]

Alexander, Cecil Frances (1823–1895)

9 All things bright and beautiful, / All creatures great and small, / All things wise and wonderful — / The Lord God made them all. [Hymn]

10 Jesus calls us! O'er the tumult / Of our life's wild restless sea. [Hymn]

11 There is a green hill far away, / Without a city wall, / Where the dear Lord was crucified, / Who died to save us all. [Hymn]

Alexander, Sir William, Earl of Stirling (c. 1567–1640)

12 Yet with great toil all that I can attain / By long experience, and in learned schools, / Is for to know my knowledge is but vain, / And those that think them wise are greatest fools. [*The Tragedy of Croesus,* II]

Alfonso X (1221–1284)

13 [On the Ptolemaic system of astronomy] If the Lord Almighty had consulted me before embarking upon Creation, I should have recommended something simpler. [Attr.]

Ali, Muhamad (1942–)

14 I am the greatest. [Catchphrase]

15 Float like a butterfly, sting like a bee. [Ib.]

Alison, Richard (fl. c. 1606)

16 There cherries grow, that none can buy / Till cherry-ripe themselves do cry. ['An Hour's Recreation in Music']

Allainval, Léonor Jean D' (c. 1700–1753)

17 *L'Embarras de Richesse.* The embarrassment of riches. [Title of play]

Allen, Woody (1935–)

18 [Of masturbation] Don't knock it, it's sex with someone you love. [*Annie Hall*]

19 [Of God] The worst that can be said is that he's an under-achiever. [*Love and Death*]

20 I'm really a timid person — I was beaten up by Quakers. [*Sleeper*]

21 Not only is there no God, but try getting a plumber on weekends. [*Getting Even*, 'My Philosophy']

22 I don't want to achieve immortality through my work...I want to achieve it by not dying. [Attr.]

Allingham, William (1824–1889)

1 Up the airy mountain, / Down the rushy glen, / We daren't go a-hunting, / For fear of little men. ['The Fairies']

2 Four ducks on a pond, / A grass-bank beyond, / A blue sky of spring, / White clouds on the wing: / What a little thing / To remember for years — / To remember with tears. ['A Memory']

Ambrose, St. (c. 340–397)

3 *Si fueris Romae, Romano vivito more; / Si fueri alibi, vivito sicut ibi.* If you are in Rome, live in the Roman way; if you are elsewhere, live as they do there. [Jeremy Taylor, *Ductor Dubitantium*]

Amery, Leo (1873–1955)

4 Speak for England, Arthur! [Interjection in House of Commons, 1939]

Amiel, Henri-Frédéric (1828–1881)

5 Action is but coarsened thought — thought become concrete, obscure, and unconscious. [*Journal,* 1850]

6 The age of great men is going; the epoch of the ant-hill, of life in multiplicity, is beginning. [Ib. 1851]

7 Every life is a profession of faith, and exercises an inevitable and silent influence. [Ib. 1852]

8 A belief is not true because it is useful. [Ib. 1876]

Amis, Kingsley (1922–)

9 More will mean worse. [*Encounter,* 1960]

Andersen, Hans Christian (1805–1875)

10 'But the Emperor has nothing on at all!' said a little child. ['The Emperor's New Clothes']

11 Every man's life is a fairy-tale written by God's fingers. [*Works,* Preface]

Andrews, Bishop Lancelot (1555–1626)

12 The nearer the Church the further from God. [Sermon]

13 A cold coming they had of it, at this time of the year; just, the worst time of the year, to take a journey, and specially a long journey, in. [Ib.]

Anonymous

14 [Of Dr. Temple, Headmaster of Rugby] A beast, but a just beast.

15 A rainbow in the morning / Is the Shepherd's warning; / But a rainbow at night / Is the Shepherd's delight. [Old Weather Rhyme]

16 A very gallant gentleman. [Inscription on grave of Capt. Oates]

17 *Ad majorem Dei gloriam.* To the greater glory of God. [Motto of the Society of Jesus]

18 All present and correct. [Queen's Regulations]

19 [A lie] An abomination unto the Lord, but a very present help in time of trouble.

20 An army marches on its stomach. [Attr. to Napoleon]

21 An Austrian army, awfully arrayed, / Boldly by battery besieged Belgrade. ['Siege of Belgrade', progressive alliterative rhyme]

22 An intelligent Russian once remarked to us, 'Every country has its own constitution; ours is absolutism moderated by assassination.' [Munster, *Political Sketches of Europe*]

23 Appeal from Philip drunk to Philip sober. [*Valerius Maximus,* VI]

24 Are we downhearted? No! [Slogan of World War I, based on remark of Joseph Chamberlain]

25 Be happy while y'er leevin, / For y'er a lang time deid. [Scottish Motto]

26 Begone, dull Care! I prithee begone from me! / Begone, dull Care! Thou and I shall never agree. [Song, 17th century]

1 *Caveant consules ne quid res publici detrimenti caperet.* Let the consuls see to it that no harm come to the state. ['Ultimate decree' of the Senate of Rome]

2 *Cet animal est très méchant, / Quand on l'attaque il se défend.* / This animal is very wicked, / When it is attacked it defends itself. [*La Ménagerie*, 1868]

3 [Of Bayard] *Chevalier sans peur et sans reproche.* Knight without fear and without blame. [*Chronicles*, 1476–1524]

4 Christmas is coming, the geese are getting fat, / Please to put a penny in the old man's hat; / If you haven't got a penny, a ha'penny will do, / If you haven't got a ha'penny, God bless you! [Beggar's Rhyme]

5 Conduct...to the prejudice of good order and military discipline. [Army Act]

6 *Cras amet qui nunquam amavit, quique amavit cras amet!* Let those love now, who never loved before; / Let those who always loved, now love the more. [Pervigilium Veneris]

7 Dear Sir, Your astonishment's odd: / I am always about in the Quad. / And that's why the tree / Will continue to be, / Since observed by Yours faithfully, God. [Reply to Ronald Knox, 'There once was a man']

8 Difficult things take a long time; / the impossible takes a little longer. [Sometimes attr. to Nansen, and others]

9 Early one morning, just as the sun was rising, / I heard a maid sing in the valley below: / 'Oh, don't deceive me; Oh, never leave me! / How could you use a poor maiden so?' [Song, 'Early One Morning']

10 *Ein Reich, Ein Volk, Ein Führer.* One realm, one people, one leader. [Nazi Party slogan, 1934]

11 Esau selleth his birthright for a mess of potage. [*Geneva Bible* (heading to Genesis 25)]

12 *Et in Arcadia ego.* And I too in Arcadia. [Variously attr.]

13 Everyman, I will go with thee, and be thy guide, / In thy most need to go by thy side. [*Everyman*]

14 For so long as but a hundred of us remain alive, we will in no way yield ourselves to the dominion of the English. For it is not for glory, nor riches, nor honour that we fight, but for Freedom only, which no good man lays down but with his life. [Declaration of Arbroath, 1320]

15 From ghoulies and ghosties and long leggety beasties / And things that go bump in the night, / Good Lord, deliver us! [Cornish prayer]

16 *Gaudeamus igitur, / Juvenes dum sumus / Post jucundam juventutem, / Post molestam senectutem, / Nos habebit humus.* Let us be happy while we are young, for after carefree youth and careworn age, the earth will hold us also. [Students' song, traced to 1267]

17 God be in my head, / And in my understanding; / God be in my eyes, / And in my looking; / God be in my mouth, / And in my speaking; / God be in my heart, / And in my thinking; / God be at my end, / And at my departing. [Sarum Missal]

18 [Of America] God's own country. [First found in this form, 1921]

19 *Honi soit qui mal y pense.* Evil be to him who evil thinks. [Motto of the Order of the Garter]

20 Here's tae us; wha's like us? / Gey few, and they're a' deid. [Scottish toast]

21 How different, how very different from the home life of our own dear Queen! [Remark by woman at performance of Cleopatra by Sarah Bernhardt]

22 I sing of a maiden / That is makeles; / King of all kings / To her son she ches. [Carol]

23 If all the world were paper, / And all the sea were ink; / If all the trees were bread and cheese / How should we do for drink? [17th century]

24 I'll sing you twelve O / Green grow the rushes O. [Traditional song]

25 In your heart you know he's right. [Slogan for Goldwater Presidential campaign, 1964]

26 In England, justice is open to all, like the Ritz Hotel. [Variously attr.]

1 Is your journey really necessary? [Railway poster, World War II]

2 It is good to be merry and wise, / It is good to be honest and true, / It is best to be off with the old love, / Before you are on with the new. [Song]

3 It's the same the whole world over, / Ain't it all a blooming shame, / It's the rich wot gets the pleasure, / It's the poor wot gets the blame. [Song of World War I (many variants)]

4 *Laborare est orare.* Work is prayer. [Unknown origin]

5 *Liberté! Egalité! Fraternité!* Liberty! Equality! Brotherhood! [Revolutionary slogan, 1793]

6 Lizzie Borden took an axe / And gave her mother forty whacks; / When she saw what she had done / She gave her father forty-one. ['Lizzie Borden']

7 Love me little, love me long, / Is the burden of my song. [Song, 16th century]

8 Matthew, Mark, Luke, and John, / The Bed be blest that I lie on. / Four angels to my bed, / Four angels round my head, / One to watch, and one to pray, / And two to bear my soul away. [Ady, *A Candle in the Dark*]

9 Monday's child is fair of face, / Tuesday's child is full of grace, / Wednesday's child is full of woe, / Thursday's child has far to go, / Friday's child is loving and giving, / Saturday's child works hard for its living, / And a child that's born on the Sabbath day / Is fair and wise and good and gay. [Bray, *Traditions of Devon*]

10 Multiplication is vexation, / Division is as bad; / The rule of three doth puzzle me, / And practice drives me mad. [Elizabethan]

11 *Nemo me impune lacessit.* Wha daur meddle wi' me. [Motto of the Scots Crown]

12 *Nous n'irons plus aux bois, les lauriers sont coupés.* We'll to the woods no more, / The laurels all are cut. [Nursery rhyme; trans. Housman]

13 Now I lay me down to sleep; / I pray the Lord my soul to keep. / If I should die before I wake, / I pray the Lord my soul to take. [Traditional]

14 O Death, where is thy sting-a-ling-a-ling, / O Grave, thy victoree? / The bells of Hell go ting-a-ling-a-ling / For you but not for me. [British Army song, World War I]

15 Once a clergyman always a clergyman. [Attr. ruling in trial of Horne Tooke]

16 Overpaid, overfed, oversexed, and over here. [Remark on GIs in Britain during World War II]

17 Oxford gave the world marmalade and a manner, / Cambridge science and a sausage. [Traditional]

18 Please to remember / The Fifth of November, / Gunpowder, treason and plot; / We know no reason / Why gunpowder treason / Should ever be forgot. [Rhyme]

19 *Plus royaliste que le roi.* More royalist than the King. [Phrase invented under Louis XVI]

20 *Post coitum omne animal triste.* After intercourse every animal is sad. [Traditional saying]

21 *Quidquid agas, prudenter agas, et respice finem.* Whatever you do, do it warily, and take account of the end. [*Gesta Romanorum*]

22 Rest in peace — until we meet again. [Widow's epitaph for husband; quoted in Mitford, *The American Way of Death*]

23 *Revenons à nos moutons.* Let us go back to the subject. (*lit.* Let us return to our sheep). [*Maistre Pierre Pathelin*]

24 *Se non è vero, è molto ben trovato.* If it is not true, it is a happy invention. [16th century]

25 See the happy moron, / He doesn't give a damn, / I wish I were a moron, / My God! perhaps I am! [*Eugenics Review*, 1929]

26 Seven wealthy Towns contend for Homer Dead / Through which the living Homer begged his Bread. [*Aesop at Tunbridge*, 1698]

1 [Of Ireland] She's the most distressful country that iver yet was seen / For they're hangin' men an' women there for the wearin' o' the Green. ['The Wearin' o' the Green']

2 Since wars begin in the minds of men, it is in the minds of men that the defences of peace must be constructed. [Constitution of UNESCO]

3 *Solvitur ambulando.* It is solved in walking. [Quoted as epigraph by Clough, *Amours de Voyage*]

4 Summer is icumen in, / Lhude sing cuccu! / Groweth sed, and bloweth med, / And springeth the wude nu. ['Cuckoo Song', c. 1250]

5 *Tempora mutantur, et nos mutamur in illis.* The times are changing, and we are changing in them. [Harrison, *Description of Britain*]

6 That this house will in no circumstances fight for its King and country. [Motion passed at Oxford Union, 1933]

7 The almighty dollar is the only object of worship. [*Philadelphia Public Ledger*, 1860]

8 The best defence against the atom bomb is not to be there when it goes off. [*The British Army Journal*, quoted in *Observer*, 'Sayings of the Week', 1949]

9 The eternal triangle. [*Daily Chronicle*, 1907]

10 The King over the Water. [18th-century Jacobite toast]

11 The nature of God is a circle of which the centre is everywhere and the circumference is nowhere. [Attr. to Empedocles (quoted in *Roman de la Rose*)]

12 There is so much good in the worst of us, / And so much bad in the best of us, / That it hardly becomes any of us / To talk about the rest of us. [Variously attr.]

13 Time wounds all heels. [Sometimes attr. to Jane Ace]

14 *Totus mundus agit histrionem.* The whole world plays the actor. [Motto of Globe playhouse]

15 Turn again, Whittington, / Lord Mayor of London. [Refrain of Bow Bells heard by Dick Whittington]

16 *Vox et praeterea nihil.* A voice and nothing more. [Description of the nightingale]

17 We hold these truths to be self-evident, that all men are created equal, that they are endowed by their Creator with certain unalienable rights, that among these are life, liberty and the pursuit of happiness. [American Declaration of Independence, 1776 (originally drafted by Jefferson)]

18 'Well, what sort of sport has Lord —— had?' / 'Oh, the young Sahib shot divinely, but God was very merciful to the birds.' [G.W.E. Russell, *Collections and Recollections*]

19 Western wind, when wilt thou blow, / The small rain down can rain? / Christ, if my love were in my arms / And I in my bed again! [*Oxford Book of 16th-Century Verse*]

20 Wha hes gud malt and makis ill drink, / Wa mot be hir werd! / I pray to God scho rot and stink, / Sevin yeir abone the erd. [G.F. Maine, *A Book of Scotland*]

21 What did you do in the Great War, Daddy? [Caption on recruiting poster, World War I]

22 What is our life? a play of passion, / Our mirth the music of derision, / Our mothers' wombs the tiring houses be, / Where we are dressed for this short comedy. ['On the Life of Man']

23 Only we die in earnest, that's no jest. [Ib.]

24 Whaur's yer Wully Shakespeare noo? [Cry from audience after opening night of Home's *Douglas*, 1756]

25 When Adam delved, and Eve span, / Who was then a gentleman? [Attr. John Ball, 1381]

26 Would you like to sin / With Elinor Glyn / On a tiger-skin? / Or would you prefer / to err / with her / on some other fur? [Quoted in A. Glyn, *Elinor Glyn*]

27 You pays your money and you takes your choice. [V. S. Lean, *Collectanea*]

1 You too can have a body like mine. [Advertising slogan for Charles Atlas body-building courses]

2 Your King and Country need you. [Caption on recruiting poster, World War I]

Antiphanes of Macedonia (fl. 360 B.C.)

3 Idly inquisitive tribe of grammarians, who dig up the poetry of others by the roots...Get away, bugs that bite secretly at the eloquent. [*Greek Anthology*, 11]

Arabian Nights

4 Who will change old lamps for new ones?...New lamps for old ones? ['The History of Aladdin']

5 Open Sesame! ['The History of Ali Baba']

Arbuthnot, John (1667–1735)

6 [Biography] One of the new terrors of death. [Carruthers, *Life of Pope*]

7 Here continueth to rot the body of Francis Chartres. [First line of epitaph]

Archimedes (287–212 B.C.)

8 Give me a firm place to stand, and I will move the earth. [Pappus Alexander, *Collectio*]

9 *Eureka!* I've got it! [Vitruvius Pollio, *De Architectura*]

Archpoet of Cologne (fl. c. 1205)

10 *Meum est propositum in taberna mori: / Vinum sit appositum sitienti ori: / Ut dicant cum venerint angelorum chori / 'Deus sit propitius isti potatori.'* I have resolved to die in a tavern; let the wine be close to my parched lips, so that the band of angels may say when they come: 'May God be gracious to this drinker.' [*The Confession of Golias* (also attr. to Walter Map and others)]

Ariosto, Ludovico (1474–1533)

11 *Natura il fece, e poi roppe la stampa.* Nature made him, and then broke the mould. [*Orlando furioso*, X]

Aristophanes (c. 444–380 B.C.)

12 A man may learn wisdom even from a foe. [*The Birds*]

13 How do you like 'Cloudcuckooland'? [Ib.]

14 Old men are children for a second time. [*The Clouds*]

15 Brekekekex, koax, koax. [*The Frogs*]

16 You cannot make a crab walk straight. [*The Peace*]

Aristotle (384–322 B.C.)

17 The roots of education are bitter, but the fruit is sweet. [Diogenes Laertius, *Life*]

18 What is a friend? A single soul dwelling in two bodies. [Ib.]

19 I count him braver who overcomes his desires than him who overcomes his enemies. [Stobaeus, *Florilegium*]

20 The whole is more than the sum of the parts. [*Metaphysics*]

21 All men by nature desire knowledge. [Ib.]

22 Piety requires us to honour truth above our friends. [*Nicomachean Ethics*, I]

23 If one way be better than another, that you may be sure is Nature's way. [Ib.]

24 Where we are free to act, we are also free to refrain from acting, and where we are able to say No, we are also able to say Yes. [Ib. III]

25 Our characters are the result of our conduct. [Ib.]

26 What we have to learn to do, we learn by doing. [Ib.]

27 A tragedy, then, is the imitation of an action that is serious, has magnitude, and is complete in itself...with incidents arousing pity and fear, wherewith to accomplish its catharsis of such emotions. [*Poetics*, 6]

28 The poet's function is to describe, not the thing that has happened, but the kind of thing that might happen, i.e. what is possible as being probable or necessary. [Ib. 9]

29 Revolutions are not about trifles, but spring from trifles. [*Politics*]

1 Man is by nature a political animal. [Ib.]

Armin, Robert (fl. 1610)

2 A flea in his ear. [*Foole upon Foole*]

Armistead, Lewis (1817–1863)

3 Give them the cold steel, boys! [Remark at Gettysburg, 1863]

Armstrong, Neil (1930–)

4 That's one small step for a man, one giant leap for mankind. [On stepping on to the moon]

Arnold, Matthew (1822–1888)

5 And we forget because we must / And not because we will. ['Absence']

6 The Sea of Faith / Was once, too, at the full, and round earth's shore / Lay like the folds of a bright girdle furl'd. ['Dover Beach']

7 Ah, love, let us be true / To one another! [Ib.]

8 And we are here as on a darkling plain / Swept with confused alarms of struggle and flight, / Where ignorant armies clash by night. [Ib.]

9 Is it so small a thing / To have enjoy'd the sun, / To have liv'd light in the spring, / To have lov'd, to have thought, to have done? [*Empedocles on Etna*, I]

10 Come, dear children, let us away, / Down and away below. ['The Forsaken Merman']

11 Children dear, was it yesterday / (Call yet once) that she went away? [Ib.]

12 But as on some far northern strand, / Thinking of his own Gods, a Greek / In pity and mournful awe might stand / Before some fallen Runic stone — / For both were faiths, and both are gone. ['The Grand Chartreuse']

13 Wandering between two worlds, one dead, / The other powerless to be born. [Ib.]

14 Years hence, perhaps, may dawn an age, / More fortunate, alas, than we, / Which without hardness will be sage, / And gay without frivolity. [Ib.]

15 Yes! in the sea of life enisled, / With echoing straits between us thrown, / Dotting the shoreless watery wild, / We mortal millions live *alone*. ['To Marguerite - Continued']

16 The unplumb'd, salt, estranging sea. [Ib.]

17 Creep into thy narrow bed, / Creep, and let no more be said. ['The Last Word']

18 So Tiberius might have sat, / Had Tiberius been a cat. ['Poor Matthias']

19 Strew on her roses, roses, / And never a spray of yew. / In quiet she reposes: / Ah! would that I did too. ['Requiescat']

20 Yet they, believe me, who await / No gifts from Chance, have conquer'd Fate. ['Resignation']

21 Friends who set forth at our side, / Falter, are lost in the storm, / We, we only are left. ['Rugby Chapel']

22 Go, for they call you, Shepherd, from the hill. ['The Scholar-Gypsy']

23 Tired of knocking at Preferment's door. [Ib.]

24 Waiting for the spark from heaven to fall. [Ib.]

25 Light half-believer in our casual creeds. [Ib.]

26 This strange disease of modern life. [Ib.]

27 Still nursing the unconquerable hope, / Still clutching the inviolable shade. [Ib.]

28 Others abide our question. Thou art free. / We ask and ask: Thou smilest and art still, / Out-topping knowledge. ['Shakespeare']

29 Rustum, my father; who I hoped should greet, / Should one day greet, upon some well-fought field, / His not unworthy, not inglorious son. [*Sohrab and Rustum*]

30 Truth sits upon the lips of dying men. [Ib.]

31 But now in blood and battles was my youth, / And full of blood and battles is my age; / And I shall never end this life of blood. [Ib.]

32 Still standing for some false impossible shore. ['A Summer Night']

1 Too quick despairer, wherefore wilt thou go? ['Thyrsis']

2 Who saw life steadily, and saw it whole. ['To a Friend']

3 Culture being a pursuit of our total perfection by means of getting to know, on all the matters which most concern us, the best which has been thought and said in the world. [*Culture and Anarchy*]

4 The pursuit of perfection, then, is the pursuit of sweetness and light. [Ib.]

5 The great aim of culture is the aim of setting ourselves to ascertain what perfection is, and to make it prevail. [Ib.]

6 The men of culture are the true apostles of equality. [Ib.]

7 One has often wondered whether upon the whole earth there is anything so unintelligent, so unapt to perceive how the world is really going, as an ordinary young Englishman of our upper class. [Ib.]

8 Our society distributes itself into Barbarians, Philistines, and Populace. [Ib.]

9 [Oxford] Beautiful city! so venerable, so lovely, so unravaged by the fierce intellectual life of our century...Home of lost causes, and forsaken beliefs, and unpopular names, and impossible loyalties. [*Essays in Criticism*, Preface]

10 My own definition of criticism; a disinterested endeavour to learn and propagate the best that is known and thought in the world. [Ib. 'Functions of Criticism at the Present Time']

11 A beautiful and ineffectual angel, beating in the void his luminous wings in vain. [Ib. 'Shelley']

12 Miracles do not happen. [*Literature and Dogma*]

13 When we are asked further, what is conduct? — let us answer: Three fourths of life. [Ib.]

14 The grand style arises in poetry, when a noble nature, poetically gifted, treats with simplicity or with severity a serious subject. ['On Translating Homer']

15 Dryden and Pope are not classics of our poetry, they are classics of our prose. ['The Study of Poetry']

Arnold, Thomas (1795–1842)

16 My object will be, if possible, to form Christian men, for Christian boys I can scarcely hope to make. [Letter, 1828]

17 Rather than have Physical Science the principal thing in my son's mind, I would rather have him think that the Sun went round the Earth, and the Stars were merely spangles set in a bright blue firmament. [Quoted in Mackay, *The Harvest of a Quiet Eye*]

Ascham, Roger (1515–1568)

18 *Inglese Italianato, è un diavolo incarnato*, that is to say, you remain men in shape and fashion, but become devils in life and condition. [*The Schoolmaster*]

Asquith, Herbert Henry (1852–1928)

19 We shall never sheathe the sword which we have not lightly drawn until Belgium receives in full measure all and more than she has sacrificed, until France is adequately secured against the menace of aggression, until the rights of the smaller nationalities of Europe are placed upon an unassailable foundation, and until the military domination of Prussia is wholly and finally destroyed. [Speech, 1914]

Asquith, Margot (1865–1945)

20 [Of Lloyd George] He couldn't see a belt without hitting below it. [Attr.]

Astley, Sir Jacob (1579–1652)

21 O Lord, thou knowest how busy I must be this day; if I forget thee, do not thou forget me. [Prayer before Battle of Edgehill, 1642]

Attlee, Clement (1883–1967)

22 Russian Communism is the illegitimate child of Karl Marx and Catherine the Great. [*Observer*, 'Sayings of the Week', 1956]

Aubrey, John (1626–1697)

1 How these curiosities would be quite forgot, did not such idle fellows as I am put them down. [*Brief Lives*, 'Venetia Digby']

2 Sir Walter, being strangely surprised and put out of his countenance at so great a table, gives his son a damned blow over the face. His son, as rude as he was, would not strike his father, but strikes over the face the gentleman that sat next to him and said 'Box about: 'twill come to my father anon.' [Ib. 'Sir Walter Raleigh']

Auden, W. H. (1907–1973)

3 To save your world you asked this man to die: / Would this man, could he see you now, ask why? ['Epitaph for an Unknown Soldier']

4 When he laughed, respectable senators burst with laughter, / And when he cried the little children died in the streets. ['Epitaph on a Tyrant']

5 He disappeared in the dead of winter: / The brooks were frozen, the airports almost deserted, / And snow disfigured the public statues. ['In Memory of W.B. Yeats']

6 You were silly like us: your gift survived it all. [Ib.]

7 Earth, receive an honoured guest: / William Yeats is laid to rest. [Ib.]

8 In an upper room at midnight / See us gathered on behalf / Of love according to the gospel / Of the radio-phonograph. ['The Love Feast']

9 Lay your sleeping head, my love, / Human on my faithless arm. ['Lullaby']

10 About suffering they were never wrong, / The Old Masters. ['Musée des Beaux Arts']

11 This is the Night Mail crossing the Border / Bringing the cheque and the postal order. ['Night Mail']

12 Private faces in public places / Are wiser and nicer / Than public faces in private places. [*The Orators*]

13 New styles of architecture. A change of heart. ['Sir, no man's enemy']

14 Hunger allows no choice / To the citizen or to the police; / We must love one another or die. ['September 1, 1939']

15 History to the defeated / May say Alas but cannot help nor pardon. ['Spain 1937']

16 Out on the lawn I lie in bed, / Vega conspicuous overhead. ['A Summer Night']

17 Most people enjoy the sight of their own handwriting as they enjoy the smell of their own farts. [*The Dyer's Hand*, 'Writing']

Augier, Émile (1820–1889)

18 *La nostalgie de la boue.* Homesickness for the gutter. [*Le Mariage d'Olympe*, I]

Augustine, St. (354–430)

19 To Carthage I came, where all about me resounded a cauldron of unholy loves. [*Confessions*, III]

20 In love with loving. [Ib.]

21 *Da mihi castitatem et continentiam, sed noli modo.* / Give me chastity and continence, but not yet. [Ib. VIII]

22 *Tolle lege, tolle lege.* / Take up and read, take up and read! [Ib.]

23 *Securus indicat orbis terrarum.* The judgement of the world is sure. [*Contra Epistolam Parmeniani*, III]

24 *Salus extra ecclesiam non est.* There is no salvation outside the church. [*De Bapt.*, IV]

25 *Audi partem alteram.* Hear the other side. [*De Duabus Animabus*, XIV]

26 *Nisi credideritis, non intelligitis.* If you don't believe it, you won't understand it. [*De Libero Arbitrio*]

27 Will is to grace as the horse is to the rider. [Ib.]

28 *Ama et fac quod vis.* Love and do what you like. [*In Joannis*, VII (popular variant)]

29 *Roma locuta est; causa finita est.* Rome has spoken; the matter is settled. [*Sermons*, 1]

30 We make a ladder of our vices if we trample those same vices underfoot. [Ib. 3]

1 There is one case of death-bed repentance recorded, that of the penitent thief, that none should despair; and only one that none should presume. [Quoted by Samuel Beckett]

Augustus, *see* CAESAR, AUGUSTUS.

Aurelius, Marcus (A.D. 121-180)

2 Everything that happens, happens as it should, and if you observe carefully, you will find it to be so. [*Meditations*, IV]

3 That which is not good for the bee-hive, cannot be good for the bees. [Ib. VI]

Austen, Jane (1775-1817)

4 Matrimony, as the origin of change, was always disagreeable. [*Emma*, 1]

5 One half of the world cannot understand the pleasures of the other. [Ib. 9]

6 Drinking too much of Mr. Weston's good wine. [Ib. 15]

7 Human nature is so well disposed towards those who are in interesting situations, that a young person, who either marries or dies, is sure to be kindly spoken of. [Ib. 22]

8 Perfect happiness, even in memory, is not common. [Ib. 27]

9 Why not seize the pleasure at once? How often is happiness destroyed by preparation, foolish preparation! [Ib. 30]

10 One has no great hopes from Birmingham. I always say there is something direful in the sound. [Ib. 36]

11 Emma denied none of it aloud, and agreed to none of it in private. [Ib. 42]

12 The stain of illegitimacy, unbleached by nobility or wealth, would have been a stain indeed. [Ib. 55]

13 It is happy for you that you possess the talent of flattering with delicacy. [*Mansfield Park*, 14]

14 You must try not to mind growing up into a pretty woman. [Ib. 21]

15 There seems something more speakingly incomprehensible in the powers, the failures, the inequalities of memory, than in any other of our intelligences. [Ib. 22]

16 We all talk Shakespeare, use his similes, and describe with his descriptions. [Ib. 34]

17 Let other pens dwell on guilt and misery. [Ib. 48]

18 A family of ten children will always be called a fine family, where there are heads, and arms, and legs enough for that number. [*Northanger Abbey*, 1]

19 'And what are you reading, Miss ——?' 'Oh! it is only a novel!' replies the young lady; while she lays down her book with affected indifference, or momentary shame. It is only *Cecilia*, or *Camilla*, or *Belinda*; or, in short, only some work in which the greatest powers of the mind are displayed, in which the most thorough knowledge of human nature, the happiest delineations of its varieties, the liveliest effusions of wit and humour, are conveyed to the world in the best chosen language. [Ib. 5]

20 A woman, especially if she have the misfortune of knowing anything, should conceal it as well as she can. [Ib. 14]

21 One does not love a place the less for having suffered in it, unless it has all been suffering, nothing but suffering. [*Persuasion*, 20]

22 All the privilege I claim for my own sex...is that of loving longest, when existence or when hope is gone. [Ib. 23]

23 It is a truth universally acknowledged, that a single man in possession of a good fortune, must be in want of a wife. [*Pride and Prejudice*, 1]

24 Happiness in marriage is entirely a matter of chance. [Ib. 6]

25 A lady's imagination is very rapid; it jumps from admiration to love, from love to matrimony in a moment. [Ib.]

26 You have delighted us long enough. [Ib. 18]

1 What is the difference in matrimonial affairs, between the mercenary, and the prudent motive? [Ib. 26]

2 Lord, how ashamed I should be of not being married before three and twenty! [Ib. 39]

3 You ought certainly to forgive them as a Christian, but never to admit them in your sight, or allow their names to be mentioned in your hearing. [Ib. 57]

4 For what do we live, but to make sport for our neighbours, and laugh at them in our turn? [Ib. 57]

5 [Mr. Darcy] I have been a selfish being all my life, in practice, though not in principle. [Ib. 58]

6 An annuity is a very serious business; it comes over and over every year, and there is no getting rid of it. [*Sense and Sensibility*, 1]

7 On every formal visit a child ought to be of the party, by way of provision for discourse. [Ib. 6]

8 'I am afraid,' replied Elinor, 'that the pleasure of an employment does not always evince its propriety.' [Ib. 13]

9 I do not want people to be very agreeable, as it saves me the trouble of liking them a great deal. [Letter, 1798]

10 The little bit (two inches wide) of ivory on which I work with so fine a brush as produces little effect after much labour. [Letter, 1816]

11 History tells me nothing that does not either vex or weary me; the men are all so good for nothing, and hardly any women at all. [*Letters*]

12 In nine cases out of ten, a woman had better show more affection than she feels. [Ib.]

Austin, Alfred (1835–1913)

13 Flash'd from his bed, the electric tidings came, / 'He is no better, he is much the same.' [Attr., 'On the Illness of the Prince of Wales']

Babbage, Charles (1792–1871)

14 Every minute dies a man, / And one and one-sixteenth is born. [Letter to Tennyson; see Tennyson, *The Vision of Sin*]

Bacon, Francis (1561–1626]

15 If a man will begin with certainties, he shall end in doubts; but if he will be content to begin with doubts, he shall end in certainties. [*Advancement of Learning*, I]

16 [Knowledge is] a rich storehouse, for the glory of the Creator and the relief of man's estate. [Ib.]

17 Silence is the virtue of fools. [Ib.]

18 Riches are a good handmaid, but the worst mistress. [Ib.]

19 They are ill discoverers that think there is no land, when they can see nothing but sea. [Ib. II]

20 A man must make his opportunity, as oft as find it. [Ib.]

21 Fortunes...come tumbling into some men's laps. [Ib.]

22 Antiquities are history defaced, or some remnants of history which have casually escaped the shipwreck of time. [Ib.]

23 Words are the tokens current and accepted for conceits, as moneys are for values. [Ib.]

24 We are much beholden to Machiavel and others, that write what men do, and not what they ought to do. [Ib.]

25 All good moral philosophy is but an handmaid to religion. [Ib.]

26 Hope is a good breakfast, but it is a bad supper. [*Apothegms*, 36]

27 One of the Seven was wont to say: 'That laws were like cobwebs; where the small flies were caught, and the great brake through.' [Ib. 181]

28 What is Truth? said jesting Pilate; and would not stay for an answer. [*Essays* 1, 'Of Truth']

29 This same Truth is a naked and open daylight, that doth not show the masques and mummeries and triumphs of the world half so stately and daintily as candlelights. [Ib.]

30 Doth any man doubt, that if there were taken out of men's minds, vain opinions, flattering hopes, false valuations, imaginations as one would, and the like; but it would leave the minds of a number of men poor shrunken things. [Ib.]

1 The inquiry of Truth, which is the love-making, or wooing of it, the knowledge of Truth, which is the presence of it, and the belief of Truth which is the enjoying of it, is the sovereign good of human nature. [Ib.]

2 But it is not the lie that passeth through the Mind, but the lie that sinketh in, and settleth in it, that doth the hurt. [Ib.]

3 To say that a man lieth, is as much to say, as that he is brave towards God, and a coward towards Men. [Ib.]

4 Men fear Death as children fear to go in the dark; and as that natural fear in children is increased with tales, so is the other. [Ib. 2, 'Of Death']

5 Revenge triumphs over Death; Love slights it; Honour aspireth to it; Grief flieth to it. [Ib.]

6 It is as natural to die as to be born; and to a little infant, perhaps, the one is as painful as the other. [Ib.]

7 All colours will agree in the dark. [Ib. 3, 'Of Unity in Religion']

8 Revenge is a kind of wild Justice, which the more man's nature runs to, the more ought Law to weed it out. [Ib. 4, 'Of Revenge']

9 Prosperity is not without many fears and distastes; and Adversity is not without comforts and hopes. [Ib. 5, 'Of Adversity']

10 Prosperity doth best discover Vice, but Adversity doth best discover Virtue. [Ib.]

11 Wives are young men's mistresses, companions for middle age, and old men's nurses. [Ib. 8, 'Of Marriage and Single Life']

12 He that hath wife and children, hath given hostages to fortune; for they are impediments to great enterprises, either of Virtue or Mischief. [Ib.]

13 But the most ordinary cause of a single life, is Liberty; especially in certain self-pleasing and humorous minds, which are so sensible of every restraint as they will go neare to think their girdles and garters to be bonds and shackles. [Ib.]

14 Certainly, wife and children are a kind of Discipline of Humanity. [Ib.]

15 They do best who, if they cannot but admit Love, yet make it keep quarter; and sever it wholly from their serious affairs and actions of life: for if it check once with Business, it troubleth Men's Fortunes, and maketh Men, that they can no ways be true to their own ends. [Ib. 10, 'Of Love']

16 Men in Great Place are thrice Servants: Servants of the Sovereign or State; Servants of Fame; and Servants of Business...It is a strange desire to seek Power and to lose Liberty. [Ib. 11, 'Of Great Place']

17 All rising to Great Place is by a winding stair. [Ib.]

18 If the Hill will not come to Mahomet, Mahomet will go to the Hill. [Ib. 12, 'Boldness']

19 If a man be gracious and courteous to strangers, it shows he is a citizen of the world. [Ib. 13, 'Goodness, and Goodness of Nature']

20 And Money is like muck, not good except it be spread. [Ib. 15, 'Of Seditions and Troubles']

21 It is true, that a little Philosophy inclineth Man's Mind to Atheism; but depth in Philosophy bringeth Men's Minds about to Religion. [Ib. 16, 'Atheism']

22 There is a superstition in avoiding superstition. [Ib. 17, 'Of Superstition']

23 Travel, in the younger sort, is a part of Education; in the elder, a part of Experience. He that travelleth into a country before he hath some entrance into the language, goeth to school, and not to travel. [Ib. 18, 'Of Travel']

24 Books will speak plain when counsellors blanch. [Ib. 20, 'Of Counsel']

25 In things that are tender and unpleasing, it is good to break the ice by some whose words are of less weight, and to reserve the more weighty voice to come in as by chance. [Ib. 22, 'Of Cunning']

1 I knew one that when he wrote a letter he would put that which was most material in the postscript, as if it had been a bymatter. [Ib. 22]

2 And he that will not apply new Remedies, must expect new Evils; For Time is the greatest innovator. [Ib. 24, 'Of Innovations']

3 I knew a wise man that had it for a by-word, when he saw men hasten to a conclusion, 'Stay a little, that we may make an end the sooner.' [Ib. 25, 'Of Dispatch']

4 Whosoever is delighted in solitude, is either a wild Beast, or a God. [Ib. 27, 'Of Friendships']

5 This communicating of a Man's Self to his Friend works two contrary effects; for it redoubleth Joys, and cutteth Griefs in halves. [Ib.]

6 Some in their Discourse, desire rather Commendation of Wit, in being able to hold all Arguments, than of Judgement in discerning what is true. [Ib. 32, 'Of Discourse']

7 I knew One, was wont to say in scorn; He must needs be a wise man, he speaks so much of Himself. [Ib.]

8 Of great Riches, there is no real use, except it be in distribution; the rest is but Conceit. [Ib. 34, 'Of Riches']

9 Nature is often hidden; sometimes overcome; seldom extinguished. [Ib. 38, 'Of Nature in Men']

10 A Man that is young in years, may be old in hours, if he have lost no Time. But that happeneth rarely. [Ib. 42, 'Of Youth and Age']

11 There is no Excellent Beauty, that hath not some strangeness in the proportion. [Ib. 43, 'Of Beauty']

12 God Almighty first planted a Garden. And indeed, it is the purest of human Pleasures. [Ib. 46, 'Of Gardens']

13 To spend too much Time in Studies, is Sloth; To use them too much for Ornament, is Affectation; To make Judgement wholly by their rules is the humour of a Scholar. [Ib. 50, 'Of Studies']

14 Crafty men contemn Studies; simple men admire them; and wise men use them. [Ib.]

15 Some Books are to be tasted, others to be swallowed, and some few to be chewed and digested; that is, some Books are to be read only in parts; others to be read but not curiously; and some few to be read wholly, and with Diligence and Attention. [Ib.]

16 Reading maketh a full man; conference a ready man; and writing an exact man. [Ib.]

17 Light gains make heavy purses. [Ib. 52, 'Of Ceremonies and Respects']

18 It was prettily devised of Aesop, 'The fly sat upon the axletree of the chariot-wheel and said, what a dust do I raise.' [Ib. 54, 'Of Vain-Glory']

19 Fame is like a river, that beareth up things light and swollen, and drowns things weighty and solid. [Ib. 53, 'Of Praise']

20 The ill and unfit choice of words wonderfully obstructs the understanding. [*Novum Organum*]

21 Opportunity makes a thief. [Letter to the Earl of Essex, 1598]

22 I have as vast contemplative ends, as I have moderate civil ends; for I have taken all knowledge to be my province. [Letter, 1592]

23 I have rather studied books than men. [*Works*, II]

24 *Nam et ipsa scientia potestas est.* Knowledge itself is power. [*Religious Meditations*, 'Of Heresies']

25 The world's a bubble: and the life of man / Less than a span. ['The World']

26 What then remains, but that we still should cry, / Not to be born, or being born, to die? [Ib.]

Bagehot, Walter (1826–1877)

27 A constitutional statesman is in general a man of common opinions and uncommon abilities. [*Biographical Studies*]

28 The Crown is, according to the saying, the 'fountain of honour'; but the Treasury is the spring of business. [*The English Constitution*, 1]

29 *The Times* has made many ministries. [Ib.]

1 Women — one half the human race at least — care fifty times more for a marriage than a ministry. [Ib. 2]

2 The best reason why Monarchy is a strong government is, that it is an intelligible government. The mass of mankind understand it, and they hardly anywhere in the world understand any other. [Ib. 2]

3 So long as the human heart is strong and the human reason weak, Royalty will be strong. [Ib.]

4 Of all the nations in the world the English are perhaps the least a nation of pure philosophers. [Ib.]

5 The Sovereign has, under a constitutional monarchy such as ours, three rights — the right to be consulted, the right to encourage, the right to warn. [Ib. 3]

6 A Parliament is nothing less than a big meeting of more or less idle people. [Ib. 4]

7 Writers, like teeth, are divided into incisors and grinders. ['The First Edinburgh Reviewers']

8 The habit of common and continuous speech is a symptom of mental deficiency. [*Literary Studies*, 1]

9 A man who has not read Homer is like a man who has not seen the ocean. There is a great object of which he has no idea. [Ib.]

10 Poverty is an anomaly to rich people. It is very difficult to make out why people who want dinner do not ring the bell. [Ib. 2]

11 Nothing is more unpleasant than a virtuous person with a mean mind. [Ib.]

12 So long as there are earnest believers in the world, they will always wish to punish opinions, even if their judgement tells them it is unwise, and their conscience that it is wrong. [Ib.]

13 The whole history of civilization is strewn with creeds and institutions which were invaluable at first, and deadly afterwards. [*Physics and Politics*]

14 One of the greatest pains to human nature is the pain of a new idea. [Ib.]

15 The most melancholy of human reflections, perhaps, is that, on the whole, it is a question whether the benevolence of mankind does most good or harm. [Ib.]

Baillie, Joanna (1762-1851)

16 What custom hath endeared / We part with sadly, though we prize it not. [*Basil*, I]

17 But woman's grief is like a summer storm, / Short as it violent is. [Ib. V]

Bairnsfather, Charles Bruce (1888-1959)

18 Well, if you knows of a better 'ole, go to it. [*Fragments of France*]

Baker, H.W. (1821-1877)

19 The King of Love my Shepherd is, / Whose goodness faileth never; / I nothing lack if I am His / And He is mine for ever. [Hymn]

20 Perverse and foolish oft I strayed; / But yet in love He sought me. [Ib.]

21 Lord, Thy word abideth, / And our footsteps guideth; / Who its truth believeth / Light and joy receiveth. [Hymn]

Baldwin, Stanley (1867-1947)

22 [Of the House of Commons, 1918] A lot of hard-faced men who look as if they had done very well out of the war. [Attr.]

23 My lips are sealed. [Speech, 1935]

Balfour, Lord Arthur (1848-1930)

24 Nothing matters very much, and very few things matter at all. [Attr.]

25 This is a singularly ill-contrived world, but not so ill-contrived as all that. [Attr.]

26 His Majesty's Government views with favour the establishment in Palestine of a national home for the Jewish people. ['The Balfour Declaration', 1917]

Ballads

N.B. Most ballads are of uncertain date and exist in many versions.

1 'Annan water's wading deep, / And my love Annie's wond'rous bonnie; / And I am laith she should weet her feet, / Because I love her best of ony.' ['Annan Water']

2 O cherry, cherry was her cheek, / And golden was her hair; / But clay-cauld were her rosy lips — / Nae spark of life was there. ['Annie of Lochryan']

3 In Scarlet town, where I was born, / There was a fair maid dwellin', / Mack every youth cry *Well-a-way!* / Her name was Barbara Allen. ['Barbara Allen']

4 It fell about the Lammas tide, / When the muir-men win their hay, / The doughty Douglas bound him to ride / Into England, to drive a prey. ['Battle of Otterbourne']

5 'But I hae dream'd a dreary dream, / Beyond the Isle of Skye; I saw a dead man win a fight, / And I think that man was I.' [Ib.]

6 There were twa sisters lived in a bower — / *Binnorie, O Binnorie!* / There came a knight to be their wooer, / *By the bonnie mill-dams o' Binnorie.* ['Binnorie']

7 He courted the eldest wi' glove an' ring, / But he loved the youngest above a' thing. [Ib.]

8 Ye Highlands and ye Lawlands, / O where hae ye been? / They hae slain the Earl of Murray, / And hae laid him on the green. ['The Bonny Earl of Murray']

9 O lang will his Lady / Look owre the Castle Doune, / Ere she see the Earl of Murray, / Come sounding through the toun. [Ib.]

10 He strack the top-mast wi' his hand, / The fore-mast wi' his knee; / And he brake that gallant ship in twain, / And sank her in the sea. ['The Daemon Lover']

11 O are ye come to drink the wine, / As ye hae doon before, oh? / Or are ye come to wield the brand, / On the bonny banks o' Yarrow? ['The Dowie Houms o' Yarrow']

12 Why does your brand sae drap with bluid? / Edward! Edward! / Why does your brand sae drap with bluid, / And why sae sad gang ye, O? ['Edward! Edward!']

13 Goodman, you've spoken the foremost word! / Get up and bar the door. ['Get Up and Bar the Door']

14 A ship have I got in the North Country / And she goes by the name of the Golden Vanity. ['The Golden Vanity']

15 I wish I were where Helen lies / Night and day on me she cries; / O that I were where Helen lies / On fair Kirkconnell lea! ['Helen of Kirkconnell']

16 I lighted down my sword to draw, / I hacked him in pieces sma', / I hacked him in pieces sma', / For her sake that died for me. [Ib.]

17 'Oh, it's Hynde Horn fair, and it's Hynde Horn free; / Oh, where were you born, and in what countrie?' / 'In a far distant countrie I was born; / But of home and friends I am quite forlorn.' ['Hynde Horn']

18 O Johnny was as brave a knight / As ever sailed the sea, / An he's done him to the English court, / To serve for meat and fee. ['Johnny Scott']

19 There was a May, and a weel-far'd May, / Lived high up in yon glen; / Her name was Katherine Janfarie / Weel loved by mony men. ['Katherine Janfarie']

20 O is my basnet a widow's curch? / Or my lance a wand of the willow tree? / Or my arm a lady's lily hand, / That an English lord should lightly me? ['Kinmont Willie']

21 The Laird o' Drum is a-wooing gane, / It was on a morning early, / And he has fawn in wi' a bonny may / A-shearing at her barley. ['The Laird o' Drum']

22 'For an' I war dead, and ye war dead, / And baith in ae grave laid, O, / And ye and I war tane up again, / Wha could distain your moulds frae mine, O?' [Ib.]

23 'Where hae ye been hunting Lord Randal, my son? / Where hae ye been hunting, my handsome young man?' / 'In yon wild wood, O mither; so make my bed soon, / For I'm weary wi' huntin', and fain wad lie doun.' ['Lord Randal']

1 There liv'd a lord on yon sea-side, / And he thought on a wile, / How he would go o'er the salt-sea, / A lady to beguile. ['Lord Thomas and Fair Annie']

2 This ae nighte, this ae nighte, / — *Every nighte and alle*, / Fire and fleet and candle-lighte, / *And Christe receive thy saule.* ['Lyke-Wake Dirge']

3 When captains couragious whom death could not daunte, / Did march to the seige of the city of Gaunt. ['Mary Ambree']

4 The ane was buried in Marie's kirk, / The other in Marie's quire; / And out of the ane there sprang a birk, / And out of the other a brier. ['Prince Robert']

5 Marie Hamilton's to the kirk gane, / Wi' gloves upon her hands; / The king thought mair o' Marie Hamilton / Than the Queen and her lands. ['The Queen's Maries']

6 Yestreen the Queen had four Maries, / The night she'll hae but three; / There was Marie Seaton, and Marie Beaton / And Mary Carmichael and me.
O little did my mother ken, / The day she cradled me, / The lands I was to travel in / Or the death I was to dee! [Ib.]

7 She sought him east, she sought him west, / She sought him braid and narrow; / Sine, in the lifting of a craig, / She found him drown'd in Yarrow. ['Rare Willie Drowned in Yarrow']

8 There are twelve months in all the year, / As I hear many men say, / But the merriest month in all the year / Is the merry month of May. ['Robin Hood and the Widow's Three Sons']

9 The king sits in Dunfermline town, / Drinking the blude-red wine; / 'Oh, where will I get a gude skipper / To sail this ship of mine?' ['Sir Patrick Spens']

10 'I saw the new moon late yestreen / Wi' the auld moon in her arm; / And if we gang to sea, master, / I fear we'll come to harm.' [Ib.]

11 Then she has kilted her green kirtle / A little abune her knee; / And she has braided her yellow hair / A little abune her bree. ['Tamlane']

12 True Thomas lay on Huntly bank; / A ferlie he spied with his e'e; / And there he saw a ladye bright, / Came riding down by the Eildon tree. ['Thomas the Rhymer, Part 1']

13 'O, see ye na that braid, braid road, / That lies across the lily leven? / That is the path of wickedness, / Tho' some call it the road to heaven.

And see ye not yon narrow road, / Sae thick beset with thorns and briars? / That is the path of righteousness, / Tho' after it but few inquires.' [Ib.]

14 When seven years were come and gane, / The sun blink'd fair on pool and stream; / And Thomas lay on Huntly bank, / Like one awaken'd from a dream. [Ib. Part 2]

15 There were three ravens sat on a tree, / They were as black as they might be. / The one of them said to his make, / 'Where shall we our breakfast take?' ['The Three Ravens']

16 As I was walking all alane, / I heard twa corbies making a mane: / The tane unto the tither did say, / 'Whaur sall we gang and dine the day?'

'— In behint yon auld fail dyke / I wot there lies a new-slain knight; / And naebody kens that he lies there / But his hawk, his hound, and his lady fair.

'His hound is to the hunting gane, / His hawk to fetch the wild-fowl hame, / His lady's ta'en anither mate, / So we may make our dinner sweet. ['The Twa Corbies']

17 There lived a wife at Usher's Well, / And a wealthy wife was she; / She had three stout and stalwart sons, / And sent them o'er the sea. ['The Wife of Usher's Well']

Balzac, Honoré de (1799–1850)

18 *L'ironie est le fond du caractère de la Providence.* / Irony is the essence of the character of Providence. [*Eugénie Grandet*]

19 *Penser, c'est voir.* To think is to see. [*Louis Lambert*]

1 *Je préfère la pensée à l'action, une idée à une affaire, la contemplation au mouvement.* I prefer thought to action, an idea to an event, reflection to activity. [Ib.]

2 *Que signifie adieu, à moins de mourir? Mais la mort serait-elle un adieu?* What does farewell mean, if not death? But will death itself be a farewell? [Ib.]

3 *La fin est le retour de toutes choses à l'unite qui est Dieu.* The final aim is the reversion of everything to the unity which is God. [Ib.]

4 *Elles doivent avoir les défauts de leurs qualités.* They must have the defects of their qualities. [*Le Lys dans la vallée*]

5 To kill the emotions and so live to old age, or to accept the martyrdom of our passions and die young is our doom. [*La Peau de Chagrin*]

Bangs, Edward (fl. 1775)

6 Yankee Doodle came to town / Riding on a pony; / Stuck a feather in his cap / And called it Macaroni. ['Yankee Doodle']

Bankhead, Tallulah (1902–1968)

7 There is less in this than meets the eye. [Attr.]

8 Cocaine isn't habit-forming. I know, because I've been taking it for years. [Attr.]

Barbour, John (c. 1316–1395)

9 A! fredome is a noble thing! / Fredome mayss man to haiff liking; / Fredome all solace to man giffio: / He levys at ess that frely levys! [*The Bruce*, 1]

10 Na he that ay hass levyt free, / May nocht knaw weill the propyrté, / The angyr, na the wrechyt dome, / That is cowpyt to foule thyrldome. [Ib.]

11 And suld think fredome mar to pryss, / Than all the gold in warld that is. [Ib.]

12 [Of loyalty] / For quhar it failyeis, na vertu / May be of price, na of value, / To mak a man sa gud, that he / May symply gud man callyt be. [Ib.]

13 For certis, I trow, thar is no man / That he ne will rew up-on woman. [Ib.]

Barham, Rev. Richard Harris (1788–1845)

14 There, too, full many an Aldermanic nose /Roll'd its loud diapason after dinner. [*The Ingoldsby Legends*, 'The Ghost']

15 A servant's too often a negligent elf; / — If it's business of consequence do it yourself! [Ib. 'The Ingoldsby Penance. Moral']

16 His eye so dim, / So wasted each limb, / That, heedless of grammar, they all cried, 'That's him!' [Ib. 'The Jackdaw of Rheims']

17 The Jackdaw sat on the Cardinal's chair! [Ib.]

18 So put that in your pipe, my Lord Otto, and smoke it! [Ib. 'Lay of St. Odille']

Baring-Gould, Sabine (1834–1924)

19 Onward! Christian soldiers, / Marching as to war, / With the Cross of Jesus / Going on before. [Hymn]

20 Like a mighty army / Moves the Church of God; / Brothers, we are treading / Where the saints have trod. [Ib.]

21 Onward, then ye people! / Join our happy throng; / Blend with ours your voices / In the triumph song. [Ib.]

Barnfield, Richard (1574–1627)

22 King Pandion, he is dead, / All thy friends are lapp'd in lead. ['An Ode']

23 My flocks feed not, / My ewes breed not, / My rams speed not, / All is amiss. / Love is dying, / Faith's defying, / Heart's denying, / Causer of this. ['A Shepherd's Complaint']

Barnum, Phineas T. (1810–1891)

24 There's a sucker born every minute. [Attr.]

Barrie, James Matthew (1860–1937)

25 As Dr. Johnson never said, is there any Scotsman without charm? [Address, Edinburgh University]

1 His Lordship may compel us to be equal upstairs, but there will never be equality in the servants' hall. [*The Admirable Crichton*, I]

2 I'm a second eleven sort of chap. [Ib. III]

3 I do loathe explanations. [*My Lady Nicotine*]

4 You canna expect to be baith grand and comfortable. [*The Little Minister*, III]

5 When the first baby laughed for the first time, the laugh broke into a thousand pieces and they all went skipping about, and that was the beginning of fairies. [*Peter Pan*, I]

6 Every time a child says 'I don't believe in fairies,' there is a little fairy somewhere that falls down dead. [Ib.]

7 To die will be an awfully big adventure. [Ib. III]

8 Do you believe in fairies?...If you believe, clap your hands! [Ib. IV]

9 But the gladness of her gladness / And the sadness of her sadness / Are as nothing, Charles, / To the badness of her badness when she's bad. ['Rosalind']

10 [Charm] It's a sort of bloom on a woman. If you have it, you don't need to have anything else; and if you don't have it, it doesn't much matter what else you have. [*What Every Woman Knows*, I]

11 A young Scotsman of your ability let loose upon the world with£300, what could he not do? It's almost apalling to think of; especially if he went among the English. [Ib.]

12 You've forgotten the grandest moral attribute of a Scotsman, Maggie, that he'll do nothing which might damage his career. [Ib. II]

13 There are few more impressive sights in the world than a Scotsman on the make. [Ib.]

14 The tragedy of a man who has found himself out. [Ib. IV]

Barrington, George (1755–c. 1835)

15 True patriots we; for be it understood, / We left our country for our country's good. ['Prologue' for the opening of the Playhouse, Sydney, N.S.W., 1796]

Barrow, Isaac (1630–1677)

16 Poetry is a kind of ingenious nonsense. [Spence, *Anecdotes*]

Barth, John (1930–)

17 If you are a novelist of a certain type of temperament, then what you really want to do is re-invent the world. God wasn't too bad a novelist, except he was a Realist. [Attr.]

Baruch, Bernard (1870–1965)

18 Let us not be deceived — we are today in the midst of a cold war. [Speech, 1947]

Bateman, Edgar (fl. 19th cent.)

19 Wiv a ladder and some glasses, / You could see to 'Ackney Marshes, / If it wasn't for the 'ouses in between. [Music hall song]

Baudelaire, Charles (1821–1867)

20 *Hypocrite lecteur, — mon semblable, — mon frère!* Hypocrite reader, my likeness, my brother. [*Les Fleurs du Mal*, 'Au Lecteur']

21 *L'air est plein du frisson des choses qui s'enfuient, / Et l'homme est las d'écrire et la femme d'aimer. /* There is a shiver in the air, of things which pass; / And man is tired of writing, and woman of loving. ['Le Crépuscule du Matin']

22 *Là, tout n'est qu'ordre et beauté, / Luxe, calme et volupté.* For all things there are ordered, lovely, profuse, serene and pleasurable. ['L'Invitation au Voyage']

23 *J'ai plus de souvenirs que si j'avais mille ans.* I have more memories than if I were a thousand. ['Spleen']

24 *O Mort, vieux capitaine, il est temps! levons l'ancre!* Death, old captain, it is time, let us raise the anchor. ['Le Voyage']

25 *Il faut épater le bourgeois.* One must shock the bourgeois. [Attr.]

Baxter, Richard (1615–1691)

1 I preached as never sure to preach again, / And as a dying man to dying men. [*Love Breathing Thanks and Praise*]

Bayly, Thomas Haynes (1797–1839)

2 Absence makes the heart grow fonder, / Isle of Beauty, Fare thee well! ['Isle of Beauty']

3 I'm saddest when I sing. [Title of poem]

Beatty, David, Earl (1871–1936)

4 There's something wrong with our bloody ships to-day, Chatfield. Steer two points nearer the enemy. [Attr. remark during Battle of Jutland, 1916]

Beaumarchais, Pierre-Augustin de (1732–1799)

5 *Aujourd'hui ce qui ne vaut pas la peine d'être dit, on le chante.* Today if something is not worth saying, people sing it. [*Le Barbier de Seville*, I]

6 *Je me presse de rire de tout, de peur d'être obligé d'en pleurer.* I make myself laugh at everything, in case I should have to weep. [Ib.]

7 *Boire sans soif et faire l'amour en tout temps, madame, il n'y a que ça qui nous distingue des autres bêtes.* Drinking when we are not thirsty and making love all year round, madam; that is all there is to distinguish us from the other animals. [Ib. II]

8 *Parce que vous êtes un grand seigneur, vous vous croyez un grand génie!...Vous vous êtes donné la peine de naître, et rien de plus.* Because you are a great lord, you think you are a great genius. You have taken the trouble to be born, but no more. [*Mariage de Figaro*, V]

9 *Tout finit par des chansons.* Everything ends in songs. [Ib., last line]

Beaumont, Francis (1584–1616) and John Fletcher (1579–1625)

10 You are no better than you should be. [*The Coxcomb*, IV]

11 This is a pretty flim-flam. [*The Knight of the Burning Pestle*, II]

12 Deeds, not words shall speak me. [*The Lover's Progress*, III]

13 Faith Sir, he went away with a flea in's ear. [Ib. IV]

14 I'll put a spoke among your wheels. [*The Mad Lover*, III]

15 All your better deeds / Shall be in water writ, but this in marble. [*The Nice Valour*, V]

16 Kiss till the cow comes home. [*The Scornful Lady*, II]

17 There is no other purgatory but a woman. [Ib. III]

18 It would talk. / Lord, how it talk't! [Ib. IV]

Beauvoir, Simone de (1908–1986)

19 One is not born a woman, one becomes one. [*The Second Sex*]

Beckett, Samuel (1906–)

20 Nothing happens, nobody comes, nobody goes, it's awful. [*Waiting for Godot*]

21 Nothing to be done. [Ib. *passim*]

Beckford, William (1759–1844)

22 He did not think with the Caliph Omar Ben Adalaziz, that it was necessary to make a hell of this world to enjoy paradise in the next. [*Vathek*]

23 I am not over-fond of resisting temptation. [Ib.]

Bede, The Venerable (673–735)

24 When we compare the present life of man with that time of which we have no knowledge, it seems to me like the swift flight of a lone sparrow through the banqueting-hall where you sit in the winter months...This sparrow flies swiftly in through one door of the hall, and out through another...Similarly, man appears on earth for a little while, but we know nothing of what went on before this life, and what follows. [*Ecclesiastical History*, II; trans. Sherley-Price]

Bee, Bernard Elliot (1823–1861)

1 Let us determine to die here, and we will conquer. There is Jackson standing like a stone wall. Rally behind the Virginians. [Remark at Battle of Bull Run, 1861)

Beecham, Sir Thomas (1879–1961)

2 A musicologist is a man who can read music but can't hear it. [Attr.]

3 [Of a rival conductor] A sort of musical Malcolm Sargent. [Attr.]

Beer, Thomas (1889–1940)

4 I agree with one of your reputable critics that a taste for drawing-rooms has spoiled more poets than ever did a taste for gutters. [*The Mauve Decade*]

Beerbohm, Sir Max (1872–1956)

5 Most women are not so young as they are painted. [*A Defence of Cosmetics*]

6 To give an accurate and exhaustive account of that period would need a far less brilliant pen than mine. [*1880*]

7 [At school] I was a modest, good-humoured boy. It is Oxford that has made me insufferable. ['Going back to school']

8 Undergraduates owe their happiness chiefly to the fact that they are no longer at school...The nonsense which was knocked out of them at school is all gently put back at Oxford or Cambridge. [Ib.]

9 Mankind is divisible into two great classes: hosts and guests. [*Hosts and Guests*]

10 'After all,' as a pretty girl once said to me, 'women are a sex by themselves, so to speak.' [*The Pervasion of Rouge*]

11 The dullard's envy of brilliant men is always assuaged by the suspicion that they will come to a bad end. [*Zuleika Dobson*, 4]

12 'I don't,' she added, 'know anything about music, really. But I know what I like.' [Ib. 16]

Beers, Ethel Lynn (1827–1879)

13 All quiet along the Potomac to-night, / No sound save the rush of the river, / While soft falls the dew on the face of the dead — / The picket's off duty forever. ['All Quiet Along the Potomac']

Beethoven, Ludwig Van (1770–1827)

14 *Muss es sein? Es muss sein.* Must it be? It must be. [Epigraph to String Quartet in F Major, Op. 135]

Behan, Brendan (1923–1964)

15 Pound notes is the best religion in the world. [*The Hostage*]

16 Never throw stones at your mother, / You'll be sorry for it when she's dead, / Never throw stones at your mother, / Throw bricks at your father instead. [Ib.]

Behn, Aphra (1640–1689)

17 Of all that writ, he was the wisest bard, who spoke this mighty truth — / He that knew all that ever learning writ, / Knew only this — that he knew nothing yet. [*The Emperor of the Moon*, I]

18 Love ceases to be a pleasure, when it ceases to be a secret. [*The Lover's Watch, Four o'clock*]

19 Faith, Sir, we are here to-day and gone tomorrow. [*The Lucky Chance*, IV]

20 Variety is the soul of pleasure. [*The Rover*, Part II, I]

21 Money speaks sense in a language all nations understand. [Ib. III]

Bell, Alexander Graham (1847–1922)

22 Mr. Watson, come here: I want you. [First words spoken on his telephone, 1876]

Belloc, Hilaire (1870–1953)

23 Child! Do not throw this book about; / Refrain from the unholy pleasure / Of cutting all the pictures out! / Preserve it as your chiefest treasure. [*Bad Child's Book of Beasts*, Dedication]

1 A manner rude and wild / Is common at your age. [Ib. Introduction]

2 I shoot the Hippopotamus / With bullets made of platinum, / Because if I use leaden ones / His hide is sure to flatten 'em. [Ib. 'The Hippopotamus']

3 The chief defect of Henry King / Was chewing little bits of string. [*Cautionary Tales*, 'Henry King']

4 'Oh, my friends, be warned by me, / That breakfast, dinner, lunch, and tea / Are all the human frame requires...' / With that the wretched child expires. [Ib.]

5 And always keep a hold of Nurse / For fear of finding something worse. [Ib. 'Jim']

6 To see that Interesting Play / The Second Mrs. Tanqueray. [Ib. 'Matilda']

7 There's nothing worth the wear of winning, / But laughter and the love of friends. ['Dedicatory Ode']

8 But I will sit beside my fire, / And put my hand before my eyes, / And trace, to fill my heart's desire, / The last of all our Odysseys. [Ib.]

9 It is the business of the wealthy man / To give employment to the artisan. [*More Peers*, 'Lord Finchley']

10 Whatever happens, we have got / The Maxim Gun, and they have not. ['The Modern Traveller']

11 Like many of the upper class / He liked the sound of broken glass. [*New Cautionary Tales*, 'About John']

12 A line I stole with subtle daring / From Wing-Commander Maurice Baring. [Ib.]

13 It is the best of all trades, to make songs, and the second best to sing them. [*On Everything*]

14 When I am dead, I hope it may be said / 'His sins were scarlet, but his books were read.' ['On His Books']

15 The fleas that tease in the high Pyrenees. ['Tarantella']

16 But when you have lost your Inns drown your empty selves, for you will have lost the last of England. [*This and That*, 'On Inns']

17 I will hold my house in the high wood / Within a walk of the sea, / And the men that were boys when I was a boy / Shall sit and drink with me. ['The South Country']

Bellow, Saul (1915-)

18 But literary intellectuals who began with an avant-garde bias against the great public seem to have changed their minds about it. They have returned to the majority, to the masses, but as demagogues and not as writers. ['Culture Now: Some Animadversions, Some Laughs']

19 The great enemy of progressive ideals is not the Establishment but the limitless dullness of those who take them up. [*To Jerusalem and Back*]

20 It is not inconceivable that a man might find freedom and identity by killing his oppressor. But as a Chicagoan, I am rather skeptical about this. Murderers are not improved by murdering. ['A World Too Much with Us']

Benda, Julien (1867-1956)

21 *La Trahison des Clercs.* The treachery of the intellectuals. [Title of book]

Beneš, Eduard (1884-1948)

22 To make peace in Europe possible, the last representative of the pre-war generation must die and take his pre-war mentality into the grave with him. [Interview, 1929]

Benét, Stephen (1898-1943)

23 Bury my heart at Wounded Knee. ['American Names']

24 ...the lounging mirth of cracker-barrel men, / Snowed in by winter, spitting at the fire, / And telling the disreputable truth / With the sad eye that marks the perfect liar. ['Poem']

Bennett, Arnold (1867-1931)

25 'Ye can call it influenza if ye like,' said Mrs. Machin. 'There was no influenza in my young days. We called a cold a cold.' [*The Card*, 8]

1 'And yet,' demanded Councillor Barlow...'what great cause is he identified with?' — 'He is identified,' said the speaker, 'with the great cause of cheering us all up.' [Ib. 12]

2 My general impression is that Englishmen act better than Frenchmen, and French women better than English women. [*The Crisis in the Theatre*]

3 Pessimism, when you get used to it, is just as agreeable as optimism. [*Things That Have Interested Me*]

4 The price of justice is eternal publicity. [Ib.]

5 The test of a first-rate work, and a test of your sincerity in calling it a first-rate work, is that you finish it. [Ib.]

6 Journalists say a thing that they know isn't true, in the hope that if they keep on saying it long enough it *will* be true. [*The Title*]

7 Being a husband is a whole-time job. That is why so many husbands fail. They cannot give their entire attention to it. [Ib.]

Bentham, Jeremy (1748–1832)

8 Stretching his hand out to catch the stars, he forgets the flowers at his feet. [*Deontology*]

9 It is with government as with medicine, its only business is the choice of evils. Every law is an evil, for every law is an infraction of liberty. [*Principles of Morals and Legislation*]

10 All punishment is mischief: all punishment in itself is evil. [Ib.]

11 ...this sacred truth — that the greatest happiness of the greatest number is the foundation of morals and legislation. [*Works*, X; (quoting Francis Hutcheson)]

Bentley, Edmund Clerihew (1875–1956)

12 The art of Biography / Is different from Geography. / Geography is about Maps, / But Biography is about chaps. [*Biography for Beginners*]

13 John Stuart Mill, / By a mighty effort of will, / Overcame his natural bonhomie / And wrote 'Principles of Political Economy.' [Ib.]

14 Sir Humphrey Davy / Abominated gravy. / He lived in the odium / Of having discovered Sodium. [Ib.]

15 Sir Christopher Wren / Said, 'I am going to dine with some men. / If anybody calls / Say I am designing St. Paul's.' [Ib.]

Bentley, Richard (1662–1742)

16 It is a pretty poem, Mr. Pope, but you must not call it Homer. [Johnson, *Life of Pope*]

17 [Of claret] It would be port if it could. [Attr.]

Berkeley, Bishop George (1685–1753)

18 Westward the course of empire takes its way; / The first four acts already past, / A fifth shall close the drama with the day: / Time's noblest offspring is the last. ['On the Prospect of Planting Arts and Learning in America']

Bernard of Cluny (fl. 12th century)

19 Jerusalem the golden, / With milk and honey blest. [Hymn; trans. J.M. Neale]

Bernard, William Bayle (1807–1875)

20 A Storm in a Teacup. [Title of farce, 1854]

Berryman, John (1914–1972)

21 Life, friends, is boring. We must not say so. [*Dream Songs*, 14]

22 — I seldom *go* to *films*. They are too exciting, / Said the Honourable Possum. [Ib. 53]

Bethell, Richard, Baron Westbury (1800–1873)

23 His Lordship says he will turn it over in what he is pleased to call his mind. [Nash, *Life of Westbury*]

Bethman Hollweg, Theobald von (1856–1921)

1 Just for a word — 'neutrality', a word which in wartime has so often been discarded, just for a scrap of paper — Great Britain is going to make war. [Letter, 1914]

Betjeman, Sir John (1906–1984)

2 Phone for the fish-knives, Norman, / As Cook is a little unnerved. ['How to Get on in Society']

3 It's awf'lly bad luck on Diana, / Her ponies have swallowed their bits; / She fished down their throats with a spanner / And frightened them all into fits. ['Hunter Trials']

4 Come, friendly bombs, and fall on Slough / To get it ready for the plough. ['Slough']

5 Miss Joan Hunter Dunn, Miss Joan Hunter Dunn, / I can hear from the car-park the dance has begun. ['A Subaltern's Love Song']

6 Broad of Church and broad of mind, / Broad before and broad behind, / A keen ecclesiologist, / A rather dirty Wykehamist. ['The Wykehamist']

Betterton, Thomas (1635–1710)

7 Actors speak of things imaginary as if they were real, while you preachers too often speak of things real as if they were imaginary. [Reply to Archbishop of Canterbury]

Bevan, Aneurin (1897–1960)

8 If you carry this resolution and follow out all its implications and do not run away from it you will send a Foreign Secretary, whoever he may be, naked into the conference chamber. [Speech opposing unilateral nuclear disarmament, 1957]

9 A desiccated calculating machine. [Attr. remark, sometimes said to refer to Hugh Gaitskell]

Bhagavadgita

10 I am become death, the destroyer of worlds. [Quoted by J. Robert Oppenheimer on seeing the first nuclear explosion]

The Bible (King James Version)

N.B. for quotations from Vulgate, see under **Vulgate**

GENESIS

11 In the beginning God created the heaven and the earth.
And the earth was without form, and void; and darkness was upon the face of the deep. And the Spirit of God moved upon the face of the waters.
And God said, Let there be light: and there was light. [1:1–3]

12 And the evening and the morning were the first day. [1:5]

13 And God saw that it was good. [1:10]

14 And God said, Let us make man in our image, after our likeness. [1:26]

15 Be fruitful, and multiply, and replenish the earth, and subdue it. [1:28]

16 It is not good that the man should be alone; I will make him an help meet for him. [2:18]

17 And the rib, which the Lord God had taken from man, made he a woman, [2:22]

18 Now the serpent was more subtil than any beast of the field. [3:1]

19 The woman whom thou gavest to be with me, she gave me of the tree, and I did eat. [3:12]

20 What is this that thou hast done? [3:13]

21 The serpent beguiled me, and I did eat. [Ib.]

22 For dust thou art, and unto dust thou shalt return. [3:19]

23 Am I my brother's keeper? [4:9]

24 And Enoch walked with God: and he was not; for God took him. [5:24]

25 There were giants in the earth in those days. [6:4]

26 And God remembered Noah. [8:1]

27 While the earth remaineth, seedtime and harvest, and cold and heat, and summer and winter, and day and night shall not cease. [8:22]

28 Let there be no strife, I pray thee, between thee and me...for we be brethren. [13:8]

1 But his wife looked back from behind him, and she became a pillar of salt. [19:26]

2 And he sold his birthright unto Jacob. [25:33]

3 Behold, Esau my brother is a hairy man, and I am a smooth man. [27:11]

4 The voice is Jacob's voice, but the hands are the hands of Esau. [27:22]

5 And he dreamed, and behold a ladder set upon the earth and the top of it reached to heaven: and behold the angels of God ascending and descending on it. [28:12]

6 Surely the Lord is in this place; and I knew it not. [28:16]

7 I will not let thee go, except thou bless me. [32:26]

8 Now Israel loved Joseph more than all his children, because he was the son of his old age; and he made him a coat of many colours. [37:3]

9 Behold, this dreamer cometh. [37:19]

10 Ye are spies; to see the nakedness of the land ye are come. [42:9]

11 Then shall ye bring down my gray hairs with sorrow to the grave. [42:38]

12 Ye shall eat the fat of the land. [45:18]

EXODUS

13 Who made thee a prince and a judge over us? [2:14]

14 I have been a stranger in a strange land. [2:22]

15 Behold, the bush burned with fire, and the bush was not consumed. [3:2]

16 Put off thy shoes from off thy feet, for the place whereon thou standest is holy ground. [3:5]

17 A land flowing with milk and honey. [3:8]

18 The Lord God of your fathers, the God of Abraham, the God of Isaac, and the God of Jacob. [3:15]

19 Let my people go. [7:16]

20 And the Lord went before them by day in a pillar of a cloud, to lead them the way; and by night in a pillar of fire, to give them light. [13:21]

21 Thou shalt not kill. [20:13]

22 Thou shalt not commit adultery. [20:14]

23 Thou shalt not steal. [20:15]

24 Thou shalt not bear false witness against thy neighbour. [20:16]

25 Thou shalt not covet thy neighbour's house, thou shalt not covet thy neighbour's wife, nor his manservant, nor his maidservant, nor his ox, nor his ass, nor anything that is thy neighbour's. [20:17]

26 Life for life,
Eye for eye, tooth for tooth, hand for hand, foot for foot,
Burning for burning, wound for wound, stripe for stripe. [21:23–25]

27 Thou shalt not suffer a witch to live. [22:18]

28 Thou shalt have no other gods before me. [20:3]

29 Thou shalt not make unto thee any graven image, or any likeness of anything that is in heaven above, or that is in the earth beneath, or that is in the water under the earth:
Thou shalt not bow down thyself to them, nor serve them: for I the Lord thy God am a jealous God, visiting the iniquity of the fathers upon the children unto the third and fourth generation of them that hate me. [20:4–5]

30 Thou shalt not take the name of the Lord thy God in vain. [20:7]

31 Remember the sabbath day, to keep it holy. [20:8]

32 Six days shalt thou labour, and do all thy work,
But the seventh day is the sabbath of the Lord thy God: in it thou shalt not do any work. [20:9–10]

33 For in six days the Lord made heaven and earth, the sea and all that in them is, and rested the seventh day: wherefore the Lord blessed the sabbath day, and hallowed it. [20:11]

34 Honour thy father and thy mother: that thy days may be long upon the land which the Lord thy God giveth thee. [20:12]

LEVITICUS

1 Let him go for a scapegoat into the wilderness. [16:10]

2 Thou shalt love thy neighbour as thyself. [19:18]

NUMBERS

3 The Lord bless thee, and keep thee: The Lord make his face shine upon thee, and be gracious unto thee. The Lord lift up his countenance upon thee, and give thee peace. [6:24–26]

4 Be sure your sin will find you out. [32:23]

DEUTERONOMY

5 For the Lord thy God is a jealous God. [6:15]

6 Man doth not live by bread only, but by every word that proceedeth out of the mouth of the Lord doth man live. [8:3]

7 A dreamer of dreams. [13:1]

8 Thou shalt not muzzle the ox when he treadeth out the corn. [25:4]

9 As thy days, so shall thy strength be. [33:5]

10 The eternal God is thy refuge, and underneath are the everlasting arms. [33:27]

JOSHUA

11 Be strong and of good courage; be not afraid, neither be thou dismayed: for the Lord thy God is with thee, whithersoever thou goest. [1:9]

12 Hewers of wood and drawers of water. [9:21]

13 I am going the way of all the earth. [13:14]

JUDGES

14 The stars in their courses fought against Sisera. [5:20]

15 He asked water, and she gave him milk; she brought forth butter in a lordly dish. [5:25]

16 Why is his chariot so long in coming? why tarry the wheels of his chariots? [5:28]

17 Faint, yet pursuing. [8:4]

18 Out of the eater came forth meat, and out of the strong came forth sweetness. [14:14]

19 With the jawbone of an ass, heaps upon heaps, with the jaw of an ass have I slain a thousand men. [15:16]

20 The Philistines be upon thee, Samson. [16:9]

21 He wist not that the Lord was departed from him. [16:20]

22 In those days there was no king in Israel, but every man did that which was right in his own eyes. [17:16]

23 From Dan even to Beer-sheba. [20:1]

RUTH

24 Intreat me not to leave thee, or to return from following after thee: for whither thou goest, I will go; and where thou lodgest I will lodge: thy people shall be my people, and thy God my God:
Where thou diest, will I die, and there will I be buried: the Lord do so to me, and more also, if ought but death part thee and me. [1:16–17]

I SAMUEL

25 Speak, Lord; for thy servant heareth. [3:9]

26 And she named the child I-chabod, saying, The glory is departed from Israel. [4:21]

27 Is Saul also among the prophets? [10:11]

28 God save the king. [10:24]

29 The Lord hath sought him a man after his own heart. [13:14]

30 Come up to us and we will shew you a thing. [14:12]

31 To obey is better than sacrifice, and to hearken than the fat of rams. [15:22]

32 For the Lord seeth not as man seeth: for man looketh on the outward appearance, but the Lord looketh on the heart. [16:7]

33 Go, and the Lord be with thee. [17:37]

34 Am I a dog, that thou comest to me with staves? [17:43]

35 Saul hath slain his thousands, and David his ten thousands. [18:7]

1 Behold, I have played the fool, and have erred exceedingly. [26:21]

II SAMUEL

2 Tell it not in Gath, publish it not in the streets of Askelon; lest the daughters of the Philistines rejoice, lest the daughters of the uncircumcised triumph. [1:20]

3 Saul and Jonathan were lovely and pleasant in their lives, and in their death they were not divided. [1:23]

4 Thy love to me was wonderful, passing the love of women. [1:26]

5 How are the mighty fallen, and the weapons of war perished. [1:27]

6 And David danced before the Lord with all his might. [6:14]

7 Thou art the man. [12:7]

8 I shall go to him, but he shall not return to me. [12:22]

9 Would God I had died for thee, O Absalom, my son, my son! [18:33]

10 The sweet psalmist of Israel. [23:1]

I KINGS

11 Behold, the half was not told me. [10:7]

12 My father hath chastised you with whips, but I will chastise you with scorpions. [12:11]

13 An handful of meal in a barrel, and a little oil in a cruse. [17:12]

14 How long halt ye between two opinions? [18:21]

15 He is talking, or he is pursuing, or he is in a journey, or peradventure he sleepeth, and must be awaked. [18:27]

16 But the Lord was not in the wind: and after the wind an earthquake: but the Lord was not in the earthquake; And after the earthquake a fire: but the Lord was not in the fire: and after the fire a still small voice. [19:11–12]

17 Hast thou found me, O mine enemy? [21:20]

18 And a certain man drew a bow at a venture, and smote the king of Israel between the joints of the harness. [22:34]

II KINGS

19 Go up, thou bald head. [2:23]

20 There is death in the pot. [4:40]

21 He shall know that there is a prophet in Israel. [5:8]

22 Are not Abana and Pharpar, rivers of Damascus, better than all the waters of Israel? [5:12]

23 The driving is like the driving of Jehu, the son of Nimshi; for he driveth furiously. [9:20]

I CHRONICLES

24 Let the heavens be glad, and let the earth rejoice: and let men say among the nations, The Lord reigneth. [16:31]

25 And he died in a good old age, full of days, riches and honour: and Solomon his son reigned in his stead. [29:28]

II CHRONICLES

26 And behold, the one half of the greatness of thy wisdom was not told me: for thou exceedest the fame that I heard. [9:6]

27 Be ye strong therefore, and let not your hands be weak: for your work shall be rewarded. [15:7]

ESTHER

28 Let it be written among the laws of the Persians and the Medes, that it be not altered. [1:19]

29 Thus shall it be done to the man whom the king delighteth to honour. [6:6]

JOB

30 And the Lord said unto Satan, Whence comest thou? Then Satan answered the Lord, and said, From going to and fro in the earth, and from walking up and down in it. [1:7]

31 Doth Job fear God for naught? [1:9]

32 The Lord gave, and the Lord hath taken away; blessed be the name of the Lord. [1:21]

33 All that a man hath will he give for his life. [2:4]

34 Curse God, and die. [2:9]

1 Man is born unto trouble, as the sparks fly upward. [5:7]

2 He shall return no more to his house, neither shall his place know him any more. [7:10]

3 Canst thou by searching find out God? [11:7]

4 No doubt but ye are the people, and wisdom shall perish with you. [12:2]

5 Man that is born of a woman is of few days, and full of trouble. [14:1]

6 I know that my redeemer liveth. [19:25]

7 I was eyes to the blind, and feet was I to the lame. [29:15]

8 Who is this that darkeneth counsel by words without knowledge? [38:2]

9 Where wast thou when I laid the foundations of the earth? [38:4]

10 When the morning stars sang together, and all the sons of God shouted for joy. [38:7]

11 Canst thou draw out leviathan with an hook? [41:1]

12 So the Lord blessed the latter end of Job more than his beginning. [42:12]

PSALMS

13 Why do the heathen rage, and the people imagine a vain thing? [2:1]

14 Out of the mouth of babes and sucklings hast thou ordained strength. [8:2]

15 When I consider thy heavens, the work of thy fingers, the moon and the stars, which thou hast ordained; What is man, that thou art mindful of him? and the son of man, that thou visitest him? [8:3–4]

16 Thou hast made him a little lower than the angels. [8:5]

17 The fool hath said in his heart, There is no God. [14:1]

18 The lines are fallen unto me in pleasant places; yea, I have a goodly heritage. [16:6]

19 The Lord is my rock, and my fortress, and my deliverer; my God, my strength, in whom I will trust. [18:2]

20 The Lord is my shepherd; I shall not want.
He maketh me to lie down in green pastures: he leadeth me beside the still waters.
He restoreth my soul: he leadeth me in the paths of righteousness for his name's sake.
Yea, though I walk through the valley of the shadow of death, I will fear no evil: for thou art with me; thy rod and thy staff they comfort me.
Thou preparest a table before me in the presence of mine enemies: thou anointest my head with oil: my cup runneth over.
Surely goodness and mercy shall follow me all the days of my life: and I will dwell in the house of the Lord for ever. [23:1–6]

21 The earth is the Lord's, and the fulness thereof; the world, and they that dwell therein. [24:1]

22 The heavens declare the glory of God; and the firmament sheweth his handiwork. [19:1]

23 More to be desired are they than gold, yea, than much fine gold: sweeter also than honey and the honeycomb. [19:10]

24 Strong bulls of Bashan have beset me round. [22:12]

25 Lift up your heads, O ye gates; and be ye lift up, ye everlasting doors; and the King of glory shall come in. Who is this King of glory? The Lord strong and mighty, the Lord mighty in battle. [24:7–8]

26 I have seen the wicked in great power, and spreading himself like a green bay tree. [37:35]

27 I waited patiently for the Lord; and he inclined unto me, and heard my cry. [40:1]

28 Yea, mine own familiar friend, in whom I trusted, which did eat of my bread, hath lifted up his heel against me. [41:9]

29 As the hart panteth after the water brooks, so panteth my soul after thee, O God. [42:1]

30 Deep calleth unto deep at the noise of thy waterspouts. [42:7]

31 My heart is inditing a great matter...my tongue is the pen of a ready writer. [45:1]

1 God is our refuge and strength, a very present help in trouble.
Therefore will not we fear, though the earth be removed, and though the mountains be carried into the midst of the sea. [46:1-2]

2 O that I had wings like a dove! [55:6]

3 They have digged a pit before me, into the midst whereof they are fallen themselves. [57:6]

4 O God, thou art my God; early will I seek thee: my soul thirsteth for thee, my flesh longeth for thee in a dry and thirsty land, where no water is. [63:1]

5 When I remember thee upon my bed, and meditate on thee in the night watches. [63:6]

6 Then the Lord awaked as one out of sleep, and like a mighty man that shouteth by reason of wine.
And he smote his enemies in the hinder parts. [78:65-6]

7 How amiable are thy tabernacles, O Lord of hosts!
My soul longeth, yea, even fainteth for the courts of the Lord: my heart and my flesh crieth out for the living God.
Yea, the sparrow hath found an house, and the swallow a nest for herself, where she may lay her young, even thine altars, O Lord of hosts, my King, and my God.
Blessed are they that dwell in thy house: they will be still praising thee. [84:1-4]

8 For a day in thy courts is better than a thousand. I had rather be a doorkeeper in the house of my God, than to dwell in the tents of wickedness. [84:10]

9 Mercy and truth are met together; righteousness and peace have kissed each other. [85:10]

10 For a thousand years in thy sight are but as yesterday when it is past, and as a watch in the night. [90:4]

11 The days of our years are threescore and ten; and if by reason of strength they be fourscore years, yet is their strength labour and sorrow. [90:10]

12 For he shall give his angels charge over thee, to keep thee in all thy ways. [91:11]

13 It is a good thing to give thanks unto the Lord, and to sing praises unto thy name, O most High;
To shew forth thy loving kindness in the morning, and thy faithfulness every night,
Upon an instrument of ten strings, and upon the psaltery; upon the harp with a solemn sound. [92:1-3]

14 The righteous shall flourish like the palm-tree: he shall grow like a cedar in Lebanon. [92:12]

15 O come, let us sing unto the Lord; let us make a joyful noise to the rock of our salvation.
Let us come before his presence with thanksgiving, and make a joyful noise unto him with psalms.
For the Lord is a great God, and a great King above all gods.
In his hand are the deep places of the earth: the strength of the hills is his also.
The sea is his, and he made it: and his hands formed the dry land.
O come, let us worship and bow down: let us kneel before the Lord our maker. [95:1-6]

16 O sing unto the Lord a new song: sing unto the Lord, all the earth.
Sing unto the Lord, bless his name; shew forth his salvation from day to day.
Declare his glory among the heathen, his wonders among all people.
For the Lord is great, and greatly to be praised: he is to be feared above all gods. [96:1-4]

17 Bless the Lord, O my soul: and all that is within me, bless his holy name. [103:1]

18 As for man, his days are as grass: as a flower of the field, so he flourisheth. [103:15]

19 And wine that maketh glad the heart of man, and oil to make his face to shine. [104:15]

20 They that go down to the sea in ships, that do business in great waters.
These see the works of the Lord, and his wonders in the deep. [107:23-4]

21 The fear of the Lord is the beginning of wisdom. [111:10]

1 Precious in the sight of the Lord is the death of his saints. [116:15]

2 The stone which the builders refused is become the head stone of the corner. [118:22]

3 Thy word is a lamp unto my feet, and a light unto my path. [119:105]

4 I will lift up mine eyes unto the hills, from whence cometh my help.
My help cometh from the Lord, which made heaven and earth.
He will not suffer thy foot to be moved: he that keepeth thee will not slumber. [121:1-3]

5 The Lord shall preserve thee from all evil: he shall preserve thy soul.
The Lord shall preserve thy going out and thy coming in from this time forth, and even for evermore. [121:7-8]

6 I was glad when they said unto me, Let us go into the house of the Lord. [122:1]

7 They that sow in tears, shall reap in joy. [126:5]

8 Except the Lord build the house, they labour in vain that build it: except the Lord keep the city, the watchman waketh but in vain. [127:1]

9 By the rivers of Babylon, there we sat down, yea, we wept when we remembered Zion. [137:1]

10 We hanged our harps upon the willows in the midst thereof. [137:2]

11 How shall we sing the Lord's song in a strange land? [137:4]

12 Lord, I cry unto thee: make haste unto me; give ear unto my voice, when I cry unto thee. [141:1]

13 Put not your trust in princes, nor in the son of man, in whom there is no help. [146:3]

14 He delighteth not in the strength of the horse: he taketh not pleasure in the legs of a man. [147:10]

PROVERBS

15 Her ways are ways of pleasantness, and all her paths are peace. [3:17]

16 Wisdom is the principal thing; therefore get wisdom: and with all thy getting get understanding. [4:7]

17 The path of the just is as the shining light that shineth more and more unto the perfect day. [4:18]

18 Go to the ant thou sluggard; consider her ways, and be wise. [6:6]

19 As an ox goeth to the slaughter. [7:22]

20 Wisdom hath builded her house, she hath hewn out her seven pillars. [9:1]

21 Stolen waters are sweet. [9:17]

22 A wise son maketh a glad father. [10:1]

23 A righteous man regardeth the life of his beast. [12:10]

24 Hope deferred maketh the heart sick. [13:12]

25 He that spareth his rod hateth his son. [13:24]

26 A soft answer turneth away wrath. [15:1]

27 Better is a dinner of herbs where love is, than a stalled ox and hatred therewith. [15:17]

28 Pride goeth before destruction, and an haughty spirit before a fall. [16:18]

29 A merry heart doeth good like a medicine. [17:22]

30 Wine is a mocker, strong drink is raging. [20:1]

31 It is naught, it is naught, saith the buyer: but when he is gone his way, then he boasteth. [20:14]

32 Train up a child in the way he should go: and when he is old he will not depart from it. [22:6]

33 Look not thou upon the wine when it is red. [23:31]

34 Heap coals of fire upon his head. [25:22]

35 Answer a fool according to his folly. [26:5]

36 As a dog returneth to his vomit, so a fool returneth to his folly. [26:11]

37 Boast not thyself of to morrow; for thou knowest not what a day may bring forth. [27:1]

38 Faithful are the wounds of a friend. [27:6]

39 The wicked flee when no man pursueth: but the righteous are as bold as a lion. [28:1]

1 Where there is no vision, the people perish. [28:18]

2 Who can find a virtuous woman? for her price is far above rubies. [31:10]

3 Her children arise up and call her blessed. [31:28]

ECCLESIASTES

4 Vanity of vanities, saith the Preacher, vanity of vanities; all is vanity. [1:2]

5 All is vanity and vexation of spirit. [1:14]

6 He that increaseth knowledge increaseth sorrow. [1:18]

7 To everything there is a season, and a time to every purpose under the heaven:
A time to be born and a time to die; a time to plant and a time to pluck that which is planted;
A time to kill, and a time to heal; a time to break down, and a time to build up;
A time to weep, and a time to laugh; a time to mourn, and a time to dance;
A time to cast away stones, and a time to gather stones together; a time to embrace and a time to refrain from embracing;
A time to get, and a time to lose; a time to keep, and a time to cast away;
A time to rend, and a time to sew; a time to keep silence, and a time to speak;
A time to love, and a time to hate; a time of war and a time of peace. [3:1–8]

8 God is in heaven, and thou upon earth: therefore let thy words be few. [5:2]

9 As the crackling of thorns under a pot, so is the laughter of a fool. [7:6]

10 Be not righteous over much. [7:16]

11 A living dog is better than a dead lion. [9:4]

12 Whatsoever thy hand findeth to do, do it with thy might. [9:10]

13 The race is not to the swift, nor the battle to the strong. [9:11]

14 Cast thy bread upon the waters: for thou shalt find it after many days. [11:1]

15 Remember now thy Creator in the days of thy youth. [12:1]

16 Of making many books there is no end; and much study is the weariness of the flesh. [12:12]

17 Fear God, and keep his commandments: for this is the whole duty of man. [12:13]

SONG OF SOLOMON

18 Let him kiss me with the kisses of his mouth: for thy love is better than wine. [1:2]

19 I am black, but comely, O ye daughters of Jerusalem. [1:15]

20 Stay me with flagons, comfort me with apples: for I am sick of love. [2:5]

21 For, lo, the winter is past, the rain is over and gone;
The flowers appear on the earth: the time of the singing of birds is come, and the voice of the turtle is heard in the land. [2:11–12]

22 Take us the foxes, the little foxes, that spoil the vines. [2:15]

23 I sleep, but my heart waketh. [5:2]

24 What is thy beloved more than another beloved, O thou fairest among women? [5:7]

25 We have a little sister, and she hath no breasts. [8:8]

ISAIAH

26 Though your sins be as scarlet, they shall be as white as snow. [1:18]

27 They shall beat their swords into plowshares, and their spears into pruninghooks: nation shall not lift up sword against nation, neither shall they learn war any more. [2:4]

28 What mean ye that ye beat my people to pieces and grind the faces of the poor? saith the Lord God of hosts. [3:15]

29 Woe unto them that join house to house, that lay field to field, till there be no place, that they may be placed alone in the midst of the earth. [5:8]

30 Woe unto them that call evil good, and good evil. [5:20]

1 Woe is me! for I am undone; because I am a man of unclean lips, and I dwell in the midst of a people of unclean lips. [6:5]

2 Whom shall I send, and who will go for us? Then said I, Here am I; send me. [6:8]

3 The people that walked in darkness have seen a great light. [9:2]

4 For unto us a child is born, unto us a son is given: and the government shall be upon his shoulder; and his name shall be called Wonderful, Counsellor, The mighty God, The everlasting Father, The Prince of Peace. [9:6]

5 And there shall come forth a rod out of the stem of Jesse, and a Branch shall grow out of his roots. [11:1]

6 The wolf also shall dwell with the lamb, and the leopard shall lie down with the kid. [11:6]

7 And the lion shall eat straw like the ox. [11:7]

8 How art thou fallen from heaven, O Lucifer, son of the morning! [14:12]

9 Watchman, what of the night? [21:11]

10 Let us eat and drink; for to-morrow we shall die. [22:13]

11 He will swallow up death in victory; and the Lord God will wipe away tears from off all faces. [25:8]

12 The bread of adversity, and the waters of affliction. [30:20]

13 The desert shall rejoice, and blossom as the rose. [35:1]

14 Sorrow and sighing shall flee away. [35;10]

15 Set thine house in order. [38:1]

16 The voice of him that crieth in the wilderness, Prepare ye the way of the Lord, make straight in the desert a highway for our God.
Every valley shall be exalted, and every mountain and hill shall be made low: and the crooked shall be made straight, and the rough places plain:
And the glory of the Lord shall be revealed and all flesh shall see it together: for the mouth of the Lord hath spoken it. [40:3–5]

17 All flesh is grass, and all the goodliness thereof is as the flower of the field. [40:6]

18 He shall feed his flock like a shepherd: he shall gather the lambs with his arm, and carry them in his bosom, and shall gently lead those that are with young. [40:11]

19 Have ye not known? Have ye not heard? Hath it not been told you from the beginning? [40:21]

20 They that wait upon the Lord shall renew their strength: they shall mount up with wings as eagles; they shall run, and not be weary; and they shall walk, and not faint. [40:31]

21 There is no peace, saith the Lord, unto the wicked. [48:22]

22 How beautiful upon the mountains are the feet of him that bringeth good tidings. [52:7]

23 Who hath believed our report? and to whom is the arm of the Lord revealed? [53:1]

24 He hath no form nor comeliness; and when we shall see him, there is no beauty that we should desire him.
He is despised and rejected of men; a man of sorrows and acquainted with grief; and we hid as it were our faces from him; he was despised, and we esteemed him not.
Surely he hath borne our griefs and carried our sorrows. [53:2–4]

25 All we like sheep have gone astray; we have turned every one to his own way; and the Lord hath laid on him the iniquity of us all. [53:6]

26 Seek ye the Lord while he may be found, call ye upon him while he is near. [55:6]

27 For my thoughts are not your thoughts, nor are your ways my ways, saith the Lord. [55:8]

28 Their feet run to evil, and they make haste to shed innocent blood. [59:7]

29 He hath sent me to bind up the broken-hearted, to proclaim liberty to the captives, and the opening of the prison to them that are bound. [61:1]

30 I have trodden the winepress alone. [63:3]

JEREMIAH

1 And they shall fight against thee; but they shall not prevail against thee; for I am with thee, saith the Lord, to deliver thee. [1:19]

2 They were as fed horses in the morning: every one neighed after his neighbour's wife. [5:8]

3 The harvest is past, the summer is ended, and we are not saved. [8:20]

4 Is there no balm in Gilead? [8:22]

5 Can the Ethiopian change his skin, or the leopard his spots? [13:23]

6 The heart is deceitful above all things, and desperately wicked. [17:9]

7 As the partridge sitteth on eggs, and hatcheth them not; so he that getteth riches, and not by right. [17:11]

8 And seekest thou great things for thyself? seek them not. [45:5]

LAMENTATIONS OF JEREMIAH

9 Is it nothing to you, all ye that pass by? behold, and see if there be any sorrow like unto my sorrow. [1:12]

10 The wormwood and the gall. [3:19]

EZEKIEL

11 The fathers have eaten sour grapes, and the children's teeth are set on edge. [18:2]

12 Son of man, can these bones live? [37:3]

13 O ye dry bones, hear the word of the Lord. [37:4]

DANIEL

14 But if ye worship not, ye shall be cast the same hour into the midst of a burning fiery furnace. [3:15]

15 And this is the writing that was written, MENE, MENE, TEKEL, UPHARSIN. [5:25]

16 Thou art weighed in the balances and art found wanting. [5:27]

17 Thy kingdom is divided, and given to the Medes and the Persians. [5:28]

HOSEA

18 They have sown the wind, and they shall reap the whirlwind. [8:7]

JOEL

19 I will restore to you the years that the locust hath eaten. [2:25]

20 I will pour out my spirit upon all flesh; and your sons and your daughters shall prophesy, your old men shall dream dreams, and your young men shall see visions. [2:28]

AMOS

21 Can two walk together, except they be agreed? [3:3]

22 Ye were as a firebrand plucked out of the burning. [4:11]

JONAH

23 So they cast lots, and the lot fell upon Jonah. [1:7]

24 Jonah was in the belly of the fish three days and three nights. [1:17]

MICAH

25 But thou, Bethlehem Ephratah, though thou be little among the thousands of Judah, yet out of thee shall he come forth unto me that is to be ruler in Israel. [5:2]

HABAKKUK

26 Write the vision, and make it plain upon tables, that he may run that readeth it. [2:2]

ZECHARIAH

27 I was wounded in the house of my friends. [13:6]

MALACHI

28 Unto you that fear my name shall the Sun of righteousness arise with healing in his wings. [4:2]

APOCRYPHA

29 *Magna est veritas et praevalet.* Great is Truth, and mighty above all things. [I *Esdras*, 4:41]

30 Through envy of the devil came death into the world. [*Wisdom of Solomon*, 2:24]

31 He that toucheth pitch shall be defiled therewith. [Ib. 13:1]

32 How agree the kettle and the earthen pot together? [Ib. 13:2]

1 All wickedness is but little to the wickedness of a woman. [Ib. 25:19]

2 Leave off first for manners' sake. [Ib. 31:17]

3 Let us now praise famous men, and our fathers that begat us. [Ib. 44:1]

4 And some there be, which have no memorial. [Ib. 44:9]

5 Their bodies are buried in peace; but their name liveth for evermore. [Ib. 44:14]

6 It was an holy and good thought. [II *Maccabees*, 12:45]

MATTHEW

7 And she shall bring forth a son, and thou shalt call his name JESUS: for he shall save his people from their sins. [1:21]

8 There came wise men from the east to Jerusalem,
Saying, Where is he that is born King of the Jews? for we have seen his star in the east, and are come to worship him. [2:1–2]

9 They presented unto him gifts; gold, and frankincense, and myrrh. [2:11]

10 The voice of one crying in the wilderness, Prepare ye the way of the Lord, make his paths straight. [3:3]

11 O generation of vipers, who hath warned you to flee from the wrath to come? [3:7]

12 This is my beloved Son, in whom I am well pleased. [3:17]

13 Man shall not live by bread alone, but by every word that proceedeth out of the mouth of God. [4:4]

14 Thou shalt not tempt the Lord thy God. [4:7]

15 Angels came and ministered unto him. [4:11]

16 Fishers of men. [4:19]

17 Blessed are the poor in spirit: for theirs is the kingdom of heaven.
Blessed are they that mourn: for they shall be comforted.
Blessed are the meek: for they shall inherit the earth.
Blessed are they which do hunger and thirst after righteousness: for they shall be filled.
Blessed are the merciful: for they shall obtain mercy.
Blessed are the pure in heart: for they shall see God.
Blessed are the peacemakers: for they shall be called the children of God. [5:3–9]

18 Ye are the salt of the earth: but if the salt have lost his savour, wherewith shall it be salted? [5:13]

19 Whosoever shall compel thee to go a mile, go with him twain. [5:41]

20 Love your enemies, bless them that curse you, do good to them that hate you, and pray for them which spitefully use you, and persecute you. [5:44]

21 He maketh his sun to rise on the evil and on the good, and sendeth rain on the just and on the unjust. [5:45]

22 Be ye therefore perfect, even as your Father which is in heaven is perfect. [5:48]

23 Let not thy left hand know what thy right hand doeth. [6:3]

24 After this manner therefore pray ye:
Our Father which art in heaven,
Hallowed be thy name,
Thy kingdom come. Thy will be done in earth, as it is in heaven.
Give us this day our daily bread.
And forgive us our debts, as we forgive our debtors.
And lead us not into temptation, but deliver us from evil: For thine is the kingdom, and the power, and the glory, for ever. Amen. [6:9–13]

25 Lay not up for yourselves treasures upon earth, where moth and rust doth corrupt, and where thieves break through and steal:
But lay up for yourselves treasures in heaven. [6:19–20]

26 Where your treasure is, there will your heart be also. [6:21]

27 No man can serve two masters:...Ye cannot serve God and mammon. [6:24]

28 Consider the lilies of the field, how they grow; they toil not, neither do they spin. [6:28]

29 Seek ye first the kingdom of God, and his righteousness; and all these things shall be added unto you. [6:33]

1 Take therefore no thought for the morrow; for the morrow shall take thought for the things of itself. Sufficient unto the day is the evil thereof. [6:34]

2 Judge not, that ye be not judged. [7:1]

3 Neither cast ye your pearls before swine. [7:6]

4 Ask, and it shall be given you; seek, and ye shall find; knock, and it shall be opened unto you. [7:7]

5 Beware of false prophets, which come to you in sheep's clothing, but inwardly they are ravening wolves. [7:15]

6 By their fruits ye shall know them. [7:20]

7 I have not found so great faith, no, not in Israel. [8:10]

8 Let the dead bury their dead. [8:22]

9 They that be whole need not a physician, but they that are sick. [9:12]

10 I am not come to call the righteous, but sinners to repentance. [9:13]

11 Be ye therefore wise as serpents, and harmless as doves. [10:16]

12 Are not two sparrows sold for a farthing? and one of them shall not fall on the ground without your Father. [10:29]

13 He that findeth his life shall lose it: and he that loseth his life for my sake shall find it. [10:39]

14 Come unto me, all ye that labour and are heavy laden, and I will give you rest. [11:28]

15 He that is not with me is against me. [12:30]

16 The kingdom of heaven is like to a grain of mustard seed. [13:31]

17 A prophet is not without honour, save in his own country, and in his own house. [13:57]

18 Be of good cheer; it is I; be not afraid. [14:27]

19 O thou of little faith, wherefore didst thou doubt? [14:31]

20 If the blind lead the blind, both shall fall into the ditch. [15:14]

21 Thou art Peter, and upon this rock I will build my church; and the gates of hell shall not prevail against it. [16:18]

22 Get thee behind me, Satan. [16:23]

23 What is a man profited, if he shall gain the whole world, and lose his own soul? [16:26]

24 If thine eye offend thee, pluck it out. [18:9]

25 For where two or three are gathered together in my name, there am I in the midst of them. [18:20]

26 Thou shalt love thy neighbour as thyself. [19:19]

27 With men this is impossible; but with God all things are possible. [19:26]

28 But many that are first shall be last; and the last shall be first. [19:30]

29 For many are called, but few are chosen. [22:14]

30 Ye blind guides, which strain at a gnat, and swallow a camel. [23:24]

31 Render therefore unto Caesar the things which are Caesar's; and unto God the things which are God's. [22:21]

32 Ye shall hear of wars and rumours of wars. [24:6]

33 Heaven and earth shall pass away, but my words shall not pass away. [24:35]

34 Well done, thou good and faithful servant. [25:21]

35 I was a stranger and ye took me in: Naked and ye clothed me: I was sick, and ye visited me: I was in prison, and ye came unto me. [25:35–36]

36 If it be possible, let this cup pass from me. [26:39]

37 The spirit indeed is willing, but the flesh is weak. [26:41]

38 All they that take the sword shall perish with the sword. [26:52]

39 He took water, and washed his hands before the multitude, saying, I am innocent of the blood of this just person: see ye to it. [27:24]

40 He saved others; himself he cannot save. [27:42]

1 My God, my God, why hast thou forsaken me? [27:46]

MARK

2 The sabbath was made for man, and not man for the sabbath. [2:27]

3 If a house be divided against itself, that house cannot stand. [3:25]

4 My name is Legion: for we are many. [5:9]

5 Clothed, and in his right mind. [5:15]

6 And they that did eat of the loaves were about five thousand men. [6:44]

7 Lord, I believe; help thou mine unbelief. [9:24]

8 Suffer the little children to come unto me, and forbid them not: for such is the kingdom of God. [10:14]

9 It is easier for a camel to go through the eye of a needle than for a rich man to enter into the kingdom of God. [10:25 (cf. Matthew, 19:24)]

10 Go ye into all the world, and preach the gospel to every creature. [16:15]

LUKE

11 Because there was no room for them in the inn. [2:7]

12 And, lo, the angel of the Lord came upon them, and the glory of the Lord shone round about them: and they were sore afraid. [2:9]

13 Behold, I bring you good tidings of great joy. [2:10]

14 Glory to God in the highest, and on earth peace, good will toward men. [2:14]

15 Lord, now lettest thou thy servant depart in peace, according to thy word. [2:29]

16 Wist ye not that I must be about my Father's business? [2:49]

17 Physician, heal thyself. [4:23]

18 Love your enemies, do good to them which hate you. [6:27]

19 No man, having put his hand to the plough, and looking back, is fit for the kingdom of God. [9:62]

20 The labourer is worthy of his hire. [10:7]

21 A certain man went down from Jerusalem to Jericho, and fell among thieves. [10:30]

22 He passed by on the other side. [10:31]

23 Go, and do thou likewise. [10:37]

24 Thou fool, this night thy soul shall be required of thee. [12:20]

25 I have married a wife, and therefore I cannot come. [14:20]

26 The poor, and the maimed, and the halt, and the blind. [14:21]

27 Joy shall be in heaven over one sinner that repenteth, more than over ninety and nine just persons, which need no repentance. [15:7]

28 He would fain have filled his belly with the husks that the swine did eat. [15:16]

29 Bring hither the fatted calf, and kill it. [15:23]

30 God, I thank thee, that I am not as other men are. [18:11]

31 If these should hold their peace, the stones would immediately cry out. [19:40]

32 Nevertheless not my will, but thine, be done. [22:42]

33 Father, forgive them; for they know not what they do. [23:34]

34 Father, into thy hands I commend my spirit. [23:46]

35 He was known of them in breaking of bread. [24:35]

JOHN

36 In the beginning was the Word, and the Word was with God, and the Word was God. [1:1]

37 The light shineth in darkness; and the darkness comprehended it not. [1:5]

38 And the Word was made flesh, and dwelt among us. [1:14]

39 Can there any good thing come out of Nazareth? [1:46]

40 Thou hast kept the good wine until now. [2:10]

41 The wind bloweth where it listeth. [3:8]

1 God so loved the world, that he gave his only begotten Son, that whosoever believeth in him should not perish, but have everlasting life. [3:16]

2 God is a Spirit: and they that worship him must worship him in spirit and in truth. [4:24]

3 Rise, take up thy bed, and walk. [5:8]

4 He that is without sin among you, let him first cast a stone at her. [8:7]

5 And ye shall know the truth, and the truth shall make thee free. [8:32]

6 The night cometh, when no man can work. [9:4]

7 He is of age; ask him. [9:21]

8 The good shepherd giveth his life for the sheep. [10:11]

9 Jesus wept. [11:35]

10 The poor always ye have with you. [12:8]

11 Let not your heart be troubled: ye believe in God, believe also in me. [14:1]

12 In my Father's house are many mansions. [14:2]

13 I am the way, the truth, and the life; no man cometh unto the Father, but by me. [14:6]

14 Greater love hath no man than this, that a man lay down his life for his friends. [15:13]

15 Pilate saith unto him, What is truth? [18:38]

16 What I have written, I have written. [19:22]

17 Except I shall see in his hands the print of the nails, and put my finger into the print of the nails, and thrust my hand into his side, I will not believe. [20:25]

18 Blessed are they that have not seen, and yet have believed. [20:29]

19 And there are also many other things which Jesus did, the which, if they should be written every one, I suppose that even the world itself could not contain the books that should be written. [21:25]

ACTS OF THE APOSTLES

20 Ye men of Galilee, why stand ye gazing up into heaven? [1:11]

21 Silver and gold have I none; but such as I have give I thee. [3:6]

22 Saul, Saul, why persecutest thou me? [9:4]

23 It is hard for thee to kick against the pricks. [9:5]

24 God is no respecter of persons. [10:34]

25 Come over into Macedonia, and help us. [16:9]

26 What must I do to be saved? [16:30]

27 For in him we live, and move, and have our being. [17:28]

28 It is more blessed to give than to receive. [20:35]

29 A citizen of no mean city. [21:39]

30 Paul, thou art beside thyself; much learning doth make thee mad. [26:24]

31 Almost thou persuadest me to be a Christian. [26:28]

ROMANS

32 The just shall live by faith. [1:17]

33 Let us do evil, that good may come. [3:8]

34 For all have sinned, and come short of the glory of God. [3:23]

35 The wages of sin is death. [6:23]

36 All things work together for good to them that love God. [8:28]

37 If God be for us, who can be against us? [8:31]

38 For I am persuaded, that neither death, nor life, nor angels, nor principalities, nor powers, nor things present, nor things to come,
Nor height, nor depth, nor any other creature, shall be able to separate us from the love of God, which is in Jesus Christ our Lord. [8:38–39]

39 Rejoice with them that do rejoice, and weep with them that weep. [12:15]

40 Vengeance is mine; I will repay, saith the Lord. [12:19]

1 The powers that be are ordained of God. [13:1]

2 The night is far spent, the day is at hand. [13:12]

I CORINTHIANS

3 I have planted, Apollos watered; but God gave the increase. [3:6]

4 Absent in body, but present in spirit. [5:3]

5 It is better to marry than to burn. [7:9]

6 I am made all things to all men. [9:22]

7 Though I speak with the tongues of men and of angels, and have not charity, I am become as sounding brass, or a tinkling cymbal.
...and though I have all faith, so that I could remove mountains, and have not charity, I am nothing.
And though I bestow all my goods to feed the poor, and though I give my body to be burned, and have not charity, it profiteth me nothing.
Charity suffereth long and is kind; charity envieth not; charity vaunteth not itself, is not puffed up,
Doth not behave itself unseemly, seeketh not her own, is not easily provoked, thinketh no evil;
Rejoiceth not in iniquity, but rejoiceth in the truth;
Beareth all things, believeth all things, hopeth all things, endureth all things.
Charity never faileth: but whether there be prophecies, they shall fail; whether they be tongues, they shall cease; whether there be knowledge, it shall vanish away. [13:2–8]

8 And now abideth faith, hope, charity, these three; but the greatest of these is charity. [13:13]

9 Let all things be done decently and in order. [14:40]

10 The last enemy that shall be destroyed is death. [15:26]

11 Behold, I shew you a mystery; We shall not all sleep, but we shall all be changed. [15:51]

12 O death, where is thy sting? O grave, where is thy victory? [15:55]

II CORINTHIANS

13 The letter killeth, but the spirit giveth life. [3:5]

14 God loveth a cheerful giver. [9:7]

15 There was given to me a thorn in the flesh, the messenger of Satan to buffet me. [12:7]

GALATIANS

16 Be not deceived; God is not mocked: for whatsoever a man soweth, that shall he also reap. [6:7]

EPHESIANS

17 ...children, tossed to and fro, and carried about with every wind of doctrine, by the sleight of men, and cunning craftiness. [4:14]

18 We are members one of another. [4:25]

19 Be ye angry, and sin not; let not the sun go down upon your wrath. [4:26]

20 Be not drunk with wine, wherein is excess; but be filled with the Spirit. [5:18]

21 Ye fathers, provoke not your children to wrath. [6:4]

22 Put on the whole armour of God. [6:11]

23 For we wrestle not against flesh and blood, but against principalities, against powers, against the rulers of the darkness of this world, against spiritual wickedness in high places. [6:12]

PHILIPPIANS

24 Work out your own salvation with fear and trembling. [2:12]

25 Whose God is their belly, and whose glory is their shame. [3:19]

26 The peace of God which passeth all understanding. [4:7]

27 Whatsoever things are true, whatsoever things are honest, whatsoever things are just, whatsoever things are pure, whatsoever things are lovely, whatsoever things are of good report; if there be any virtue, and if there be any praise, think on these things. [4:8]

1 I can do all things through Christ which strengtheneth me. [4:13]

COLOSSIANS

2 Luke, the beloved physician. [4:14]

I THESSALONIANS

3 Pray without ceasing. [5:17]

II THESSALONIANS

4 If any would not work, neither should he eat. [3:10]

I TIMOTHY

5 Old wives' fables. [4:7]

6 Drink no longer water, but use a little wine for thy stomach's sake and thine often infirmities. [5:23]

7 The love of money is the root of all evil. [6:10]

8 Fight the good fight of faith. [6:12]

9 Science falsely so called. [6:20]

II TIMOTHY

10 The husbandman that laboureth must be first partaker of the fruits. [2:6]

11 I have fought a good fight, I have finished my course, I have kept the faith. [4:7]

TITUS

12 Unto the pure all things are pure. [1:15]

HEBREWS

13 It is a fearful thing to fall into the hands of the living God. [10:31]

14 Faith is the substance of things hoped for, the evidence of things not seen. [11:1]

15 Seeing we also are compassed about with so great a cloud of witnesses. [12:1]

16 Whom the Lord loveth he chasteneth. [12:6]

17 Let brotherly love continue. [13:1]

18 Be not forgetful to entertain strangers: for thereby some have entertained angels unawares. [13:2]

19 For here we have no continuing city. [13:14]

JAMES

20 But be ye doers of the word, and not hearers only. [1:22]

21 Faith without works is dead. [2:20]

22 Resist the devil, and he will fly from you. [4:7]

23 Let your yea be yea; and your nay, nay. [5:12]

PETER

24 As newborn babes, desire the sincere milk of the word. [2:2]

25 Honour all men. Love the brotherhood. Fear God. Honour the king. [2:17]

26 Charity shall cover the multitude of sins. [4:8]

27 Your adversary the devil, as a roaring lion, walketh about, seeking whom he may devour. [5:8]

I JOHN

28 He that loveth not knoweth not God; for God is love. [4:8]

29 Perfect love casteth out fear. [4:18]

REVELATION

30 I am Alpha and Omega, the beginning and the ending, saith the Lord. [1:8]

31 I was in the Spirit on the Lord's day. [1:10]

32 I am he that liveth, and was dead; and behold, I am alive for evermore, Amen. [1:18]

33 I will not blot out his name out of the book of life. [3:5]

34 Because thou art lukewarm, and neither cold nor hot, I will spue thee out of my mouth. [3:15]

35 Behold, I stand at the door, and knock. [3:20]

36 Who is worthy to open the book, and to loose the seals thereof? [5:2]

37 And I looked, and behold a pale horse: and his name that sat on him was Death. [6:8]

38 God shall wipe away all tears from their eyes. [7:17]

1 When he had opened the seventh seal, there was silence in heaven about the space of half an hour. [8:1]

2 Babylon is fallen, is fallen, that great city. [14:8]

3 And the sea gave up the dead which were in it. [20:13]

4 And I saw a new heaven and a new earth: for the first heaven and the first earth were passed away; and there was no more sea. [21:1]

5 I will give unto him that is athirst of the fountain of the water of life freely. [21:6]

6 Behold, I come quickly. [22:12]

7 The grace of our Lord Jesus Christ be with you all. Amen. [22:21]

Bickerstaff, Isaac (c. 1735–1812)

8 Perhaps it was right to dissemble your love, / But — why did you kick me downstairs? ['An Expostulation']

9 There was a jolly miller once, / Lived on the river Dee; / He worked and sang from morn to night; / No lark more blithe than he. [*Love in a Village*, I]

10 And this the burthen of his song, / For ever us'd to be, / I care for nobody, not I, / If no one cares for me. [Ib.]

11 We all love a pretty girl — under the rose. [Ib. II]

Bierce, Ambrose (1842–c. 1914)

12 *Advice:* The smallest current coin. [*The Devil's Dictionary*]

13 *Bore:* A person who talks when you wish him to listen. [Ib.]

14 *Education:* That which discloses to the wise and disguises from the foolish their lack of understanding. [Ib.]

15 *Lawsuit:* A machine which you go into as a pig and come out as a sausage. [Ib.]

Bigod, Roger (1245–1306)

16 (Edward I: 'By God, earl, you shall either go or hang!') 'O King, I will neither go nor hang!' [*Hemingburgh's Chronicle*]

Bion (fl. 280 B.C.)

17 Though boys throw stones at frogs in sport, the frogs do not die in sport, but in earnest. [Quoted by Plutarch]

Binyon, Laurence (1869–1943)

18 They shall grow not old, as we that are left grow old: / Age shall not weary them, nor the years condemn. / At the going down of the sun and in the morning / We will remember them. [*Poems for the Fallen*]

Bismarck, Otto Von (1815–1898)

19 To youth I have but three words of counsel — work, work, work. [*Sayings of Bismarck*]

20 *Lieber Spitzkugeln als Spitzreden.* Better pointed bullets than pointed speeches. [Speech, 1850]

21 *Die Politik ist keine exakte Wissenschaft.* Politics is not an exact science. [Speech, 1863]

22 *Die Politik ist die Lehre von Möglichen.* Politics is the art of the possible. [Remark, 1867]

23 *Sie macht sich nur durch Blut und Eisen.* It can only be done by blood and iron. [Speech, 1886]

Blackstone, William (1723–1780)

24 The king never dies. [*Commentaries*, I]

25 That the king can do no wrong, is a necessary and fundamental principle of the English constitution. [Ib. III]

26 It is better that ten guilty persons escape than one innocent suffer. [Ib. IV]

Blake, William (1757–1827)

27 Tell me the acts, O historian, and leave me to reason upon them as I please; away with your reasoning and your rubbish! [*The Ancient Britons*]

28 To see a World in a Grain of Sand, / And a Heaven in a Wild Flower, / Hold Infinity in the palm of your hand, / And Eternity in an hour. [*Auguries of Innocence*]

29 A truth that's told with bad intent / Beats all the lies you can invent. [Ib.]

1 The soldier armed with sword and gun / Palsied strikes the summer sun. [Ib.]

2 Nought can deform the human race / Like to the armourer's iron brace. [Ib.]

3 A Robin Redbreast in a Cage / Puts all Heaven in a Rage. [Ib.]

4 A dog starv'd at his master's gate / Predicts the ruin of the State. [Ib.]

5 The whore and gambler, by the state / Licensed, build that nation's fate. / The harlot's cry from street to street / Shall weave old England's winding sheet. [Ib.]

6 As, long agone, / When men were first a nation grown, / Lawless they lived, till wantonness / And liberty began to increase, / And one man lay in another's way; / Then laws were made to keep fair play. ['Blind-Man's Buff']

7 Can Wisdom be put in a silver rod, / Or Love in a golden bowl? [*Book of Thel*]

8 I am sure this Jesus will not do, / Either for Englishman or Jew. [*The Everlasting Gospel*]

9 Great things are done when men and mountains meet; / This is not done by jostling in the street. ['Gnomic Verses']

10 But vain the sword, and vain the bow — / They never can work war's overthrow. ['The Grey Monk']

11 The hand of vengeance found the bed / To which the purple tyrant fled; / The iron hand crushed the tyrant's head, / And became a tyrant in his stead. [Ib.]

12 The god of war is drunk with blood, / The earth doth faint and fail; / The stench of blood makes sick the heavens; / Ghosts glut the throat of hell! ['Gwin, King of Norway']

13 I must Create a System, or be enslaved by another Man's; / I will not Reason and Compare: my business is to Create. [*Jerusalem*]

14 I care not whether a man is Good or Evil; all that I care / Is whether he is a Wise man or a Fool. Go! put off Holiness, / And put on Intellect. [Ib.]

15 For a tear is an intellectual thing, / And a sigh is the sword of an Angel King. [Ib.]

16 He who would do good to another must do it in Minute Particulars. / General Good is the plea of the scoundrel, hypocrite, and flatterer. [Ib.]

17 Sweet Prince, the arts of peace are great, / And no less glorious than those of war. [*King Edward the Third*]

18 Ambition is the growth of every clime. [Ib.]

19 Justice hath heaved a sword to plunge in Albion's breast; for Albion's sins are crimson-dyed. [*King John*, Prologue]

20 Without contraries is no progression. [*Marriage of Heaven and Hell*, 'The Argument']

21 Energy is Eternal Delight. [*Marriage of Heaven and Hell*]

22 The reason Milton wrote in fetters when he wrote of Angels and God, and at liberty when of Devils and Hell, is because he was a true Poet, and of the Devil's party without knowing it. [Ib. Note]

23 For everything that lives is holy. [Ib.]

24 One law for the lion and ox is oppression. [Ib.]

25 And did those feet in ancient time / Walk upon England's mountains green? / And was the holy Lamb of God / On England's pleasant pastures seen? [*Milton*, Preface]

26 And was Jerusalem builded here / Among these dark Satanic mills? [Ib.]

27 Bring me my bow of burning gold! / Bring me my arrows of desire! / Bring me my spear! O clouds, unfold! / Bring me my chariot of fire! [Ib.]

28 I will not cease from Mental Strife / Nor shall my Sword sleep in my hand / Till we have built Jerusalem, / In England's green and pleasant Land. [Ib.]

29 Mock on, mock on, Voltaire, Rousseau; / Mock on, mock on; 'tis all in vain! / You throw the sand against the wind, / And the wind blows it back again. ['Mock On']

1 The Atoms of Democritus / And Newton's Particles of Light / Are sands upon the Red sea shore / Where Israel's tents do shine so bright. [Ib.]

2 Never seek to tell thy love, Love that never told can be. [*Note-book*]

3 What is it men in women do require? / The lineaments of gratified desire. / What is it women do in men require? / The lineaments of gratified desire. [Ib.]

4 Drive your cart and your plough over the bones of the dead. [*Proverbs of Hell*]

5 No bird soars too high if he soars with his own wings. [Ib.]

6 Prisons are built with stones of Law, brothels with bricks of Religion. [Ib.]

7 Prudence is a rich, ugly, old maid courted by incapacity. [Ib.]

8 Truth can never be told so as to be understood, and not be believed. [Ib.]

9 You never know what is enough, unless you know what is more than enough. [Ib.]

10 The road of excess leads to the palace of wisdom. [Ib.]

11 Eternity is in love with the productions of time. [Ib.]

12 The tigers of wrath are wiser than the horses of instruction. [Ib.]

13 Damn braces. Bless relaxes. [Ib.]

14 Sooner murder an infant in its cradle than nurse unacted desires. [Ib.]

15 If the doors of perception were cleansed everything would appear as it is, infinite. ['A Memorable Fancy']

16 Samson, the strongest of the children of men, I sing; how he was foiled by woman's arts. [*Samson*]

17 Ten thousand spears are like the summer grass. [Ib.]

18 Manoa left his fields to sit in the house, and take his evening's rest from labour — the sweetest time that God hath allotted mortal man. [Ib.]

19 Oppression stretches his rod over our land, our country is ploughed with swords, and reaped in blood. [Ib.]

20 How sweet I roamed from field to field, / And tasted all the summer's pride, / Till I the Prince of Love beheld / Who in the sunny beams did glide. ['Song']

21 Love seeketh not itself to please, / Nor for itself hath any care, / But for another gives its ease, / And builds a heaven in hell's despair. [*Songs of Experience*, 'The Clod and the Pebble']

22 Is this a holy thing to see / In a rich and fruitful land, / Babes reduced to misery, / Fed with cold and usurous hand? [Ib. 'Holy Thursday']

23 I was angry with my friend, / I told my wrath, my wrath did end. / I was angry with my foe, / I told it not, my wrath did grow. [Ib. 'A Poison Tree']

24 Tiger! Tiger! burning bright / In the forests of the night, / What immortal hand or eye, / Could frâme thy fearful symmetry? [Ib. 'The Tiger']

25 In every cry of every man, / In every infant's cry of fear, / In every voice, in every ban, / The mind-forged manacles I hear. [Ib. 'London']

26 Ah, Sun-flower! weary of time. [Ib. 'Ah, Sun-flower']

27 My mother groan'd, my father wept, / Into the dangerous world I leapt; / Helpless, naked, piping loud, / Like a fiend hid in a cloud. [Ib. 'Infant Sorrow']

28 For Mercy has a human heart, / Pity a human face, / And Love, the human form divine, / And Peace, the human dress. [*Songs of Innocence*, 'The Divine Image']

29 Then cherish pity, lest you drive an angel from your door. [Ib. 'Holy Thursday']

30 Little Lamb, who made thee? / Dost thou know who made thee? [Ib. 'The Lamb']

31 My mother bore me in the southern wild, / And I am black, but O! my soul is white; / White as an angel is the English child, / But I am black, as if bereaved of light. [Ib. 'The Little Black Boy']

1 'When the sun rises, do you not see a round disc of fire somewhat like a guinea?' 'O no, no, I see an innumerable company of the heavenly host crying, "Holy, Holy, Holy is the Lord God Almighty."' [*A Vision of the Last Judgment*]

2 Such Artists as Reynolds are at all times Hired by the Satans for the Depression of Art — A Pretence of Art, to destroy Art. [Annotations to Reynolds' *Discourses*]

Blind Harry the Minstrel (fl. 1470)

3 Now leiff thi myrth, now leiff thi haill plesance; / Now leiff thi bliss, now leiff thi childis age; / Now leiff thi youth, now folow thi hard chance; / Now leiff thi lust, now leiff thi mariage; / Now leiff thi luff, for thou sall loss a gage / Quhilk never in erd sall be redemyt agayne. [*Wallace* (Attr. Blind Harry)]

4 In thee was wyt, fredom, and hardines; / In thee was truth, manheid, and nobilnes; / In thee was rewll, in thee was governans; / In thee was wertu withoutys warians. [Ib.]

Boccaccio, Giovanni (c. 1313–1375)

5 Do as we say, and not as we do. [*Decameron*, 3]

Boethius, Anicius Manlius Severinus (A.D. c. 480–525)

6 *In omni adversitate fortunae, infelicissimum est genus infortunii, fuisse felicem.* At every blow of fate, the cruellest kind of misfortune is to have been happy. [*De Consolatione Philosophiae*, II]

7 *Nihil est miserum nisi cum putes; contraque beata sors omnis est aequanimatate tolerantis.* Nothing is miserable unless you think it so; conversely, every lot is happy if you are content with it. [Ib.]

8 *Quis legem dat amantibus? Major lex amor est sibi.* Who can give a law to lovers? Love is a greater law unto itself. [Ib. III]

Bogart, Humphrey (1899–1957)

9 Here's looking at you, kid. [*Casablanca*]

Bohr, Niels Henrik David (1885–1962)

10 An expert is a man who has made all the mistakes which can be made in a very narrow field. [Attr.]

Boileau-Despréaux, Nicolas (1636–1711)

11 *Enfin Malherbe vint, et, le premier en France, / Fit sentir dans les vers une juste cadence.* At last came Malherbe, and, the first in France to do so, made verse flow smoothly. [*L'Art Poétique*]

12 *La pénible fardeau de n'avoir rien à faire.* The terrible burden of having nothing to do. [*Épitres*, XI]

Bolingbroke, Henry St. John, Viscount (1678–1751)

13 I have read somewhere or other — in Dionysius of Halicarnassus, I think — that History is Philosophy teaching by examples. [*On the Study of History*]

14 Nations, like men, have their infancy. [Ib.]

15 [Of Thucydides and Xenophon] They maintained the dignity of history. [Ib.]

16 Truth lies within a little and certain compass, but error is immense. [*Reflections upon Exile*]

17 The Idea of a Patriot King. [Title of book]

18 Plain truth will influence half a score of men at most in a nation, or an age, while mystery will lead millions by the nose. [Letter, 1721]

Boorstin, Daniel (1914–)

19 The celebrity is a person who is known for his well-knownness. [*The Image*]

Booth, General William (1829–1912)

1 This Submerged Tenth — is it, then, beyond the reach of the nine-tenths in the midst of whom they live? [*In Darkest England*]

Borgia, Cesare (1476–1507)

2 *Aut Caesar aut nihil.* Emperor or nothing. [Motto]

Borrow, George (1803–1881)

3 'Life is sweet, brother.' 'Do you think so?' 'Think so! — There's night and day, brother, both sweet things; sun, moon and stars, brother, all sweet things; there's likewise a wind on the heath. Life is very sweet, brother; who would wish to die?' [*Lavengro*, 25]

4 A losing trade, I assure you, sir: literature is a drug. [Ib. 30]

5 Good ale, the true and proper drink of Englishmen. He is not deserving of the name of Englishman who speaketh against ale, that is good ale. [Ib. 48]

6 Youth will be served, every dog has his day, and mine has been a fine one. [Ib. 92]

Bosquet, Pierre François Joseph (1810–1861)

7 *C'est magnifique mais ce n'est pas la guerre.* It is magnificent, but it is not war. [Remark on witnessing the Charge of the Light Brigade, 1854]

Bossidy, John Collins (1860–1928)

8 And this is good old Boston, / The home of the bean and the cod, / Where the Lowells talk only to Cabots, / And the Cabots talk only to God. [Toast at Harvard dinner, 1910]

Bossuet, Jacques-Bénigne (1627–1704)

9 *L'Angleterre, ah, la perfide Angleterre.* England, perfidious England. [*Sermon sur la Circoncision*]

Boulay de la Meurthe, Antoine (1761–1840)

10 *C'est pire qu'un crime, c'est une faute.* It is worse than a crime; it is a blunder. [Remark on execution of the Duc d'Enghien, 1804]

Boulton, Matthew (1711–1780)

11 [Of his steam engine] I am selling what the whole world wants: power. [Letter]

Bourdillon, F.W. (1852–1921)

12 The night has a thousand eyes, / And the day but one; / Yet the light of the bright world dies, / With the dying sun. ['Light']

Bowen, Lord (1835–1894)

13 The rain it raineth on the just / And also on the unjust fella: / But chiefly on the just, because / The unjust steals the just's umbrella. [Quoted in Sichel, *Sands of Time*]

Boyd, Mark Alexander (1563–1601)

14 Twa gods guides me; the ane of tham is blin', / Yea and a bairn brocht up in vanitie; / The next a wife ingenrit of the sea, / And lichter nor a dauphin with her fin. [Sonnet]

Bradford, John (?1510–1555)

15 But for the grace of God there goes John Bradford. [Remark on criminals going to the gallows]

Bradley, F.H. (1846–1924)

16 Metaphysics is the finding of bad reasons for what we believe upon instinct; but to find these reasons is no less an instinct. [*Appearance and Reality*, Preface]

17 Unearthly ballet of bloodless categories. [*Principles of Logic*, III]

Bradley, Omar Nelson (1893–1981)

18 The wrong war, at the wrong place, at the wrong time, and with the wrong enemy. [On proposal to carry the Korean War into China, 1951]

Braham, John (c. 1774-1856)

1 England, home and beauty. [*The Americans*]

Brando, Marlon (1924-)

2 We'll make him an offer he can't refuse. [*The Godfather*]

3 An actor's a guy who, if you ain't talking about him, ain't listening. [*Observer*, 'Sayings of the Week', 1956]

Braxfield, Lord (1722-1799)

4 [To an eloquent culprit at the bar] Ye're a vera clever chiel, man, but ye wad be nane the waur o' a hanging. [Lockhart, *Life of Scott*]

5 [The butler gave up his place because Lady Braxfield was always scolding him] Lord! Ye've little to complain o': ye may be thankfu' ye're no married to her. [Cockburn, *Memorials*]

6 [To a juryman] Come awa, Maister Horner, come awa, and help us to hang ane o' thae daamned scoondrels. [Ib.]

7 [Gerald, a political prisoner, remarked that Christ had been a reformer] Muckle he made o' that; he was hanget. [Ib.]

8 Let them bring me prisoners, and I'll find them law. [Attr. by Cockburn]

Brecht, Bertolt (1898-1956)

9 Unhappy the land that is in need of heroes. [*Galileo*, sc.13]

10 *Erst Kommt das Fressen, dann Kommt die Moral.* Fodder comes first, then morality. [*Threepenny Opera*, II]

Bridges, Matthew (1800-1894) and Thring, Godfrey (1823-1903)

11 Crown Him with many crowns, / The Lamb upon His throne: / Hark how the heavenly anthem drowns / All music but its own. [Hymn]

Bridges, Robert (1844-1930)

12 I never shall love the snow again / Since Maurice died. ['I Never Shall Love the Snow Again']

13 When men were all asleep the snow came flying, / In large white flakes falling on the city brown, / Stealthily and perpetually settling and loosely lying, / Hushing the latest traffic of the drowsy town. ['London Snow']

14 'O look at the trees!' they cried, 'O look at the trees!' [Ib.]

Bridie, James (1888-1951)

15 'London! Pompous Ignorance sits enthroned there and welcomes Pretentious Mediocrity with flattery and gifts. Oh, dull and witless city! Very hell for the restless, inquiring, sensitive soul. Paradise for the snob, the parasite and the prig; the pimp, the placeman and the cheapjack.' [*The Anatomist*, III]

16 'The Heart of Man, we are told, is deceitful and desperately wicked. However that may be, it consists of four chambers, the right ventricle, the left ventricle, the left auricle, the right auricle...' [Ib.]

17 Boredom is a sign of satisfied ignorance, blunted apprehension, crass sympathies, dull understanding, feeble powers of attention and irreclaimable weakness of character. [*Mr. Bolfry*]

Bright, John (1811-1889)

18 The angel of death has been abroad throughout the land; you may almost hear the beating of his wings. [Speech, 1855]

19 England is the mother of Parliaments. [Speech, 1865]

20 [Of Disraeli] He is a self-made man, and worships his creator. [Remark, c. 1868]

21 Force is not a remedy. [Speech, 1880]

Brillat-Savarin, Anthelme (1755-1826)

22 *Dis-moi ce que tu manges, je te dirai ce que tu es.* Tell me what you eat and I will tell you what you are. [*Physiologie du Gout*]

23 *La découverte d'un mets nouveau fait plus pour le bonheur du genre humain que la découverte d'une étoile.* The discovery of a new dish does more for the happiness of man than the discovery of a star. [Ib.]

Bronowski, Jacob (1908–1974)

1 Science has nothing to be ashamed of, even in the ruins of Nagasaki. [*Science and Human Values*]

Brontë, Anne (1820–1849)

2 The human heart is like Indian rubber: a little swells it, but a great deal will not burst it. [*Agnes Grey*, 13]

3 There is always a 'but' in this imperfect world. [*The Tenant of Wildfell Hall*, 22]

4 All our talents increase in the using, and every faculty, both good and bad, strengthens by exercise. [Ib. 23]

Brontë, Charlotte (1816–1855)

5 Conventionality is not morality. Self-righteousness is not religion. To attack the first is not to assail the last. To pluck the mask from the face of the Pharisee, is not to lift an impious hand to the Crown of Thorns. [*Jane Eyre*, Preface]

6 Reader, I married him. [Mr. Rochester] [Ib. 38]

7 Had I been in anything inferior to him, he would not have hated me so thoroughly, but I knew all that he knew, and, what was worse, he suspected that I kept the padlock of silence on mental wealth in which he was no sharer. [*The Professor*, 4]

8 Novelists should never allow themselves to weary of the study of real life. [Ib. 19]

9 If there is one notion I hate more than another, it is that of marriage — I mean marriage in the vulgar, weak sense, as a mere matter of sentiment. [*Shirley*, 2]

10 Alfred and I intended to be married in this way almost from the first; we never meant to be spliced in the humdrum way of other people. [*Villette*, 42]

11 Life, believe, is not a dream, / So dark as sages say; / Oft a little morning rain / Foretells a pleasant day! ['Life']

Brontë, Emily (1818–1848)

12 Oh, for the time when I shall sleep / Without identity. ['Oh, For the Time When I Shall Sleep']

13 No coward soul is mine, / No trembler in the world's storm-troubled sphere: / I see Heaven's glories shine, / And faith shines equal, arming me from fear. ['Last Lines']

14 Vain are the thousand creeds / That move men's hearts: unutterably vain; / Worthless as withered weeds. [Ib.]

15 Oh dreadful is the check — intense the agony — / When the ear begins to hear and the eye begins to see; / When the pulse begins to throb, the brain to think again; / The soul to feel the flesh and the flesh to feel the chain! ['The Prisoner']

16 Sweet Love of youth, forgive if I forget thee / While the World's tide is bearing me along: / Sterner desires and darker hopes beset me, / Hopes which obscure but cannot do thee wrong. ['Remembrance']

17 He was, and is yet, most likely, the wearisomest, self-righteous pharisee that ever ransacked a Bible to rake the promises to himself and fling the curses on his neighbours. [*Wuthering Heights*, 5]

18 My love for Heathcliff resembles the eternal rocks beneath: — a source of little visible delight, but necessary. [Ib. 9]

19 I lingered round them, under that benign sky: watched the moths fluttering among the heath and hare-bells; listened to the soft wind breathing through the grass; and wondered how anyone could ever imagine unquiet slumbers for the sleepers in that quiet earth. [Ib. last lines]

Brooke, Rupert (1887–1915)

20 And I shall find some girl perhaps, / And a better one than you, / With eyes as wise, but kindlier, / And lips as soft, but true / And I dare say she will do. ['The Chilterns']

21 Blow out, you bugles, over the rich Dead! ['The Dead']

1 These laid the world away; poured out the red / Sweet wine of youth. [Ib.]

2 Because God put His adamantine fate / Between my sullen heart and its desire, / I swore that I would burst the Iron Gate, / Rise up, and curse Him on His throne of fire. ['Failure']

3 For Cambridge people rarely smile, / Being urban, squat, and packed with guile. ['Grantchester']

4 Here tulips bloom as they are told; / Unkempt about those hedges blows / An English unofficial rose. [Ib.]

5 Stands the Church clock at ten to three? / And is there honey still for tea? [Ib.]

6 The cool kindliness of sheets, that soon / Smooth away trouble; and the rough male kiss of blankets. ['The Great Lover']

7 And in that Heaven of all their wish, / There shall be no more land, say fish. ['Heaven']

8 I thought when love for you died, I should die. / It's dead. Alone, mostly strangely, I live on. ['The Life Beyond']

9 Now, God be thanked Who has matched us with His hour, / And caught our youth, and wakened us from sleeping. ['Peace']

10 Nothing to shake the laughing heart's long peace there / But only agony and that has ending; / And the worst friend and enemy is but Death. [Ib.]

11 Leave the sick hearts that honour could not move, / And half-men, and their dirty songs and dreary, / And all the little emptiness of love. [Ib.]

12 If I should die, think only this of me: / That there's some corner of a foreign field / That is for ever England. ['The Soldier']

13 A dust whom England bore, shaped, made aware, / Gave once, her flowers to love, her ways to roam, / A body of England's breathing English air, / Washed by the rivers, blest by the suns of home. [Ib.]

14 And laughter, learnt of friends; and gentleness, / In hearts at peace, under an English heaven. [Ib.]

Brougham, Lord Henry (1778–1868)

15 Education makes a people easy to lead, but difficult to drive; easy to govern, but impossible to enslave. [Attr.]

16 The great Unwashed. [Attr.]

Brown, Thomas (1663–1704)

17 A leap into the dark. [*Letters from the Dead*]

18 I do not love you, Dr. Fell, / But why I cannot tell; / But this I know full well, / I do not love you, Dr. Fell. [Trans. of an Epigram of Martial]

Brown, Thomas Edward (1830–1897)

19 A garden is a lovesome thing, God wot! ['My Garden']

Browne, Sir Thomas (1605–1682)

20 He who discommendeth others obliquely commendeth himself. [*Christian Morals*]

21 The created world is but a small parenthesis in eternity. [Ib.]

22 Life itself is but the shadow of death, and souls but the shadows of the living. All things fall under this name. The sun itself is but the dark *simulacrum*, and light but the shadow of God. [*The Garden of Cyrus*]

23 Were the happiness of the next world as closely apprehended as the felicities of this, it were a martyrdom to live. [*Hydrotaphia* (*Urn Burial*)]

24 What song the Sirens sang, or what name Achilles assumed when he hid himself among the women, though puzzling questions, are not beyond all conjecture. [Ib.]

25 But the iniquity of oblivion blindly scattereth her poppy, and deals with the memory of men without distinction to merit of perpetuity. [Ib.]

26 Herostratus lives that burnt the Temple of Diana — he is almost lost that built it. [Ib.]

27 Diuturnity is a dream and a folly of expectation. [Ib.]

1 A man may be in as just possession of truth as of a city, and yet be forced to surrender. [Ib.]

2 I love to lose myself in a mystery; to pursue my reason to an *O altitudo!* [*Religio Medici*]

3 Obstinacy in a bad cause, is but constancy in a good. [Ib.]

4 To believe only possibilities, is not faith, but mere Philosophy. [Ib.]

5 God is like a skilful Geometrician. [Ib.]

6 I am not so much afraid of death, as ashamed thereof; 'tis the very disgrace and ignominy of our natures. [Ib.]

7 No man can justly censure or condemn another, because indeed no man truly knows another. [Ib.]

8 There is surely a piece of divinity in us, something that was before the elements, and owes no homage unto the sun. [Ib.]

9 We all labour against our own cure, for death is the cure of all diseases. [Ib.]

Browne, Sir William (1692-1774)

10 The King to Oxford sent a troop of horse, / For Tories own no argument but force: / With equal skill to Cambridge books he sent, / For Whigs admit no force but argument. [Reply to Trapp's Epigram]

Browning, Elizabeth Barrett (1806-1861)

11 Of writing many books there is no end. [*Aurora Leigh*, 1]

12 Let no one till his death / Be called unhappy. Measure not the work, / Until the day's out and the labour done. [Ib. 5]

13 Since when was genius found respectable? [Ib. 6]

14 The devil's most devilish when respectable. [Ib. 7]

15 Earth's crammed with heaven, / And every common bush afire with God. [Ib.]

16 'Yes,' I answered you last night; / 'No,' this morning, sir, I say. / Colours seen by candle-light / Will not look the same by day. ['The Lady's Yes']

17 What was he doing, the great god Pan, / Down in the reeds by the river? / Spreading ruin and scattering ban, / Splashing and paddling with hoofs of a goat, / And breaking the golden lilies afloat / With the dragon-fly on the river. ['A Musical Instrument']

18 If thou must love me, let it be for naught / Except for love's sake only. [*Sonnets from the Portuguese*, 14]

19 How do I love thee? Let me count the ways. [Ib. 43]

20 I shall but love thee better after death. [Ib.]

21 There, Shakespeare, on whose forehead climb / The crowns o' the world. Oh, eyes sublime, / With tears and laughters for all time! [*A Vision of Poets*, 100]

Browning, Robert (1812-1889)

22 I have dared and done, for my resting-place is found, / The C major of this life: so, now I will try to sleep. ['Abt Vogler']

23 Ah, but a man's reach should exceed his grasp, / Or what's a heaven for? ['Andrea del Sarto']

24 I am grown peaceful as old age tonight. / I regret a little, I would change still less. [Ib.]

25 There up and spoke a brisk little somebody, / Critic and whippersnapper, in a rage / To set things right. ['Balaustion's Adventure']

26 Truth that peeps / Over the edge when dinner's done, / And body gets its sop and holds its noise / And leaves soul free a little. ['Bishop Blougram's Apology']

27 The grand Perhaps. [Ib.]

28 The common problem, yours, mine, everyone's, / Is not to fancy what were fair in life / Provided it could be, — but, finding first / What may be, then find how to make it fair. [Ib.]

1 Just when we are safest, there's a sunset-touch, / A fancy from a flower-bell, some one's death, / A chorus-ending from Euripides, — / And that's enough for fifty hopes and fears / As old and new at once as Nature's self, / To rap and knock and enter in our soul. [Ib.]

2 All we have gained then by our unbelief / Is a life of doubt diversified by faith, / For one of faith diversified by doubt: / We called the chess-board white, — we call it black. [Ib.]

3 If once we choose belief, on all accounts / We can't be too decisive in our faith. [Ib.]

4 Brave with the needlework of Noodledom. [Ib.]

5 I show you doubt, to prove that faith exists. [Ib.]

6 Gigadibs the literary man, / Who played with spoons. [Ib.]

7 Blue as a vein o'er the Madonna's breast. ['The Bishop Orders his Tomb in St. Praxed's Church']

8 And brown Greek manuscripts, / And mistresses with great smooth marbly limbs. [Ib.]

9 Letting the rank tongue blossom into speech. ['Caliban upon Setebos']

10 He must be wicked to deserve such pain. ['Childe Roland to the Dark Tower Came']

11 Toads in a poisoned tank, / Or wild cats in a red-hot iron cage. [Ib.]

12 He took such cognisance of men and things. [Ib.]

13 In youth I looked to these very skies, / And probing their immensities, / I found God there. ['Christmas Eve']

14 For the loving worm within its clod, / Were diviner than a loveless god. [Ib.]

15 And I have written three books on the soul, / Proving absurd all written hitherto, / And putting us to ignorance again. ['Cleon']

16 There's a world of capability / For joy, spread round about us, meant for us, / Inviting us. [Ib.]

17 She should never have looked at me, / If she meant I should not love her! ['Cristina']

18 Progress, man's distinctive mark alone, / Not God's, and not the beasts': God is, they are, / Man partly is and wholly hopes to be. ['A Death in the Desert']

19 Stung by the splendour of a sudden thought. [Ib.]

20 Open my heart and you will see / Graved inside of it, 'Italy.' ['De Gustibus']

21 Karshish, the picker up of learning's crumbs, / The not-incurious in God's handiwork. ['An Epistle']

22 That puff of vapour from his mouth, man's soul. [Ib.]

23 The man's fantastic will is the man's law. [Ib.]

24 Truth never hurts the teller. ['Fifine at the Fair']

25 Where the haters meet / In the crowded city's horrible street. ['The Flight of the Duchess']

26 When the liquor's out, why clink the cannikin? [Ib.]

27 Your business is to paint the souls of men. ['Fra Lippo Lippi']

28 If you get simple beauty and nought else, / You get about the best thing God invents. [Ib.]

29 You should not take a fellow eight years old, / And make him swear to never kiss the girls. [Ib.]

30 Oh, if we draw a circle premature, / Heedless of far gain, / Greedy for quick returns of profit, sure, / Bad is our bargain. ['A Grammarian's Funeral']

31 The low man goes on adding one to one, / His hundred's soon hit: / This high man, aiming at a million / Misses a unit. [Ib.]

32 God help all poor souls lost in the dark! ['The Heretic's Tragedy']

33 Oh, to be in England, / Now that April's there. ['Home-Thoughts from Abroad']

34 That's the wise thrush; he sings each song twice over, / Lest you should think he never could recapture / The first fine careless rapture! [Ib.]

1 Nobly, nobly Cape St. Vincent to the North-west died away. ['Home-Thoughts from the Sea']

2 I sprang to the stirrup, and Joris, and he; / I galloped, Dirck galloped, we galloped all three. ['How they brought the Good News from Ghent to Aix.']

3 Women hate a debt as men a gift. ['In a Balcony']

4 I count life just a stuff / To try the soul's strength on, educe the man. [Ib.]

5 'You're wounded!' 'Nay,' the soldier's pride / Touched to the quick, he said: / 'I'm killed, Sire!' And his chief beside / Smiling the boy fell dead. ['Incident of the French Camp']

6 Who knows but the world may end to-night? ['The Last Ride Together']

7 Just for a handful of silver he left us, / Just for a riband to stick in his coat. ['The Lost Leader']

8 One more devils'-triumph, and sorrow for angels, / One wrong more to man, one more insult to God! [Ib.]

9 Never glad confident morning again! [Ib.]

10 Ah, did you once see Shelley plain, / And did he stop and speak to you / And did you speak to him again? / How strange it seems, and new! ['Memorabilia']

11 That's my last Duchess painted on the wall, / Looking as if she were alive. ['My Last Duchess', first lines]

12 She liked whate'er / She looked on, and her looks went everywhere. [Ib.]

13 I gave commands / Then all smiles stopped together. [Ib.]

14 Never the time and the place / And the loved one all together! ['Never the Time and the Place']

15 Works done least rapidly, Art most cherishes. ['Old Pictures in Florence']

16 God be thanked, the meanest of his creatures / Boasts two soul-sides, one to face the world with, / One to show a woman when he loves her. ['One Word More']

17 Truth is within ourselves. [*Paracelsus*]

18 God is the perfect poet, / Who in his person acts his own creations. [Ib.]

19 I give the fight up: let there be an end, / A privacy, an obscure nook for me. / I want to be forgotten even by God. [Ib.]

20 Like plants in mines which never saw the sun, / But dream of him, and guess where he may be, / And do their best to climb and get to him. [Ib.]

21 It was roses, roses, all the way, / With myrtle mixed in my path like mad. ['The Patriot']

22 [To Shelley] Sun-treader, life and light be thine for ever! ['Pauline']

23 Ah, thought which saddens while it soothes! ['Pictor Ignotus']

24 Rats! / They fought the dogs and killed the cats, / And bit the babies in the cradles. ['The Pied Piper of Hamelin']

25 And the muttering grew to a grumbling / And the grumbling grew to a mighty rumbling / And out of the houses rats came tumbling. [Ib.]

26 So munch on, crunch on, take your nuncheon, / Breakfast, supper, dinner, luncheon! [Ib.]

27 The lark's on the wing / The snail's on the thorn / God's in his heaven — / All's right with the world. ['Pippa Passes']

28 In the morning of the world, / When earth was nigher heaven than now. [Ib.]

29 Fear death? — to feel the fog in my throat, / The mist in my face. ['Prospice']

30 Whoso mounts the throne / For beauty, knowledge, strength, should stand alone, / And mortals love the letters of his name. ['Protus']

31 Grow old along with me! / The best is yet to be, / The last of life for which the first was made: / Our times are in His hand / Who saith, 'A whole I planned, / Youth shows but half; trust God: see all, nor be afraid!' ['Rabbi Ben Ezra']

32 Irks care the crop-full bird? Frets doubt the maw-crammed beast? [Ib.]

1 Now, who shall arbitrate? / Ten men love what I hate, / Shun what I follow, slight what I receive. [Ib.]

2 My times be in Thy hand! / Perfect the cup as planned! / Let age approve of youth, and death complete the same! [Ib.]

3 Well, British Public, ye who like me not. [*The Ring and the Book*, I]

4 Youth means love, / Vows can't change nature, priests are only men. [Ib. I]

5 The story always old and always new. [Ib. II]

6 Everyone soon or late comes round by Rome. [Ib. V]

7 Faultless to a fault. [Ib. IX]

8 White shall not neutralize the black, nor good / Compensate bad in man, absolve him so: / Life's business being just the terrible choice. [Ib. X]

9 It is the glory and good of Art, / That Art remains the one way possible / Of speaking truth, to mouths like mine at least. [Ib. XII]

10 'Tis not what man does which exalts him, but what a man would do! ['Saul']

11 Plague take all your pedants, say I! ['Sibrandus Schafraburgensis']

12 If hate killed men, Brother Lawrence, / God's blood, would not mine kill you! ['Soliloquy of the Spanish Cloister']

13 One who never turned his back but marched breast forward, / Never doubted clouds would break, / Never dreamed, though right were worsted, wrong would triumph / Held we fall to rise, are baffled to fight better, / Sleep to wake. ['Summum Bonum', epilogue]

14 What of soul was left, I wonder, when the kissing had to stop? ['A Toccata of Galuppi's']

15 *Bang, whang, whang*, goes the drum, *tootle-te- tootle*, the fife / Oh a day in the city square, there is no such pleasure in life. ['Up at a Villa — Down in the City']

16 What's become of Waring / Since he gave us all the slip? [*Waring*, first lines]

17 Ichabod, Ichabod, / The glory is departed! [Ib.]

Brummel, Beau (1778–1840)

18 Who's your fat friend? [Said of the Prince of Wales, 1813]

Bryan, William Jennings (1860–1925)

19 I shall not help crucify mankind upon a cross of gold. I shall not aid in pressing down upon the bleeding brow of labour this crown of thorns. [Speech, 1894]

20 The humblest citizen of all the land, when clad in the armour of a righteous cause is stronger than all the hosts of error. [Speech, 1896]

21 An orator is a man who says what he thinks and feels what he says. [Hibben, *The Peerless Leader*]

Buchan, John (1875–1940)

22 To live for a time close to great minds is the best kind of education. [*Memory Hold the Door*]

23 An atheist is a man who has no invisible means of support. [Variously attr.]

Buchanan, Robert Williams (1841–1901)

24 All that is beautiful shall abide, / All that is base shall die. ['Balder the Beautiful']

25 The buying and the selling, and the strife / Of little natures. ['De Berney']

26 But his eddication to his ruination had not been over nice, / And his stupid skull was choking full of vulgar prejudice. ['Phil Blood's Leap']

27 A race that binds / Its body in chains and calls them Liberty, / And calls each fresh link Progress. ['Titan and Avatar']

28 Beauty and Truth, though never found, are worthy to be sought. ['To David in Heaven']

Buckingham, George Villiers, 2nd Duke of (1628-1687)

1 What the devil does the plot signify, except to bring in fine things? [*The Rehearsal*, III]

2 Ay, now the plot thickens very much upon us. [Ib.]

3 The world is made up for the most part of fools and knaves. ['To Mr. Clifford, on his Humane Reason']

Buckoll, H. J. (1803-1871)

4 Lord, dismiss us with thy blessing, / Thanks for mercies past received. [Hymn for Rugby School Chapel]

Buffon, Comte de (1707-1788)

5 *Le style est l'homme même.* Style is the man. ['Discours sur le Style']

6 *Le génie n'est qu'une plus grande aptitude à la patience.* Genius is naught but a greater aptitude for patience. [Attr.]

Bullet, Gerald (1893-1958)

7 So, when a new book comes his way, / By someone still alive to-day, / Our Honest John, with right good will, / Sharpens his pencil for the kill. ['A Reviewer']

Bülow, Count von (1849-1929)

8 We wish to throw no one into the shade, but we demand our own place in the sun. [Speech, 1897]

Bulwer-Lytton, Edward (1803-1873)

9 In science, read, by preference, the newest works; in literature, the oldest. [*Caxtoniana*]

10 Beneath the rule of men entirely great / The pen is mightier than the sword. [*Richelieu*, II]

Bunn, Alfred (1796-1860)

11 Alice, where art thou? [Title of song]

12 I dreamt that I dwelt in marble halls, / With vassals and serfs at my side. [*The Bohemian Girl*, II]

Buñuel, Luis (1900-1983)

13 I am still an atheist, thank God. [Attr.]

Bunyan, John (1628-1688)

14 As I walk'd through the wilderness of this world. [*The Pilgrim's Progress*, I]

15 The name of the slough was Despond. [Ib.]

16 It beareth the name of Vanity-Fair, because the town where 'tis kept, is lighter than vanity. [Ib.]

17 Hanging is too good for him, said Mr. Cruelty. [Ib.]

18 A castle, called Doubting-Castle, the owner whereof was Giant Despair. [Ib.]

19 Now Giant Despair had a wife, and her name was Diffidence. [Ib.]

20 Then I saw there was a way to hell, even from the gates of heaven. [Ib.]

21 So I awoke, and behold it was a dream. [Ib.]

22 ...a man that could look no way but downwards, with a muck-rake in his hand...The man did neither look up nor regard, but raked to himself the straws, the small sticks, and dust of the floor. [Ib. II]

23 One leak will sink a ship, and one sin will destroy a sinner. [Ib.]

24 He that is down need fear no fall, / He that is low no pride. [Ib.]

25 Who would true valour see, / Let him come hither. [Ib.]

26 Who so beset him round / With dismal stories, / Do but themselves confound — / His strength the more is. [Ib.]

27 Then fancies flee away! / I'll fear not what men say. / I'll labour night and day / To be a pilgrim. [Ib.]

28 My sword, I give to him that shall succeed me in my pilgrimage, and my courage and skill to him that can get it. [Ib.]

29 So he passed over, and all the trumpets sounded for him on the other side. [Ib.]

Burgess, Gelett (1866-1951)

30 I never saw a Purple Cow, / I never hope to see one; / But I can tell you, anyhow, / I'd rather see than be one! [Rhyme]

1 Ah, yes! I wrote the 'Purple Cow' — / I'm sorry, now, I wrote it! / But I can tell you, anyhow, / I'll kill you if you quote it! [*Burgess Nonsense Book*]

2 Love is only chatter, / Friends are all that matter. ['Willy and the Lady']

3 Bromides and sulphites. [Remark on conversation of the mass and the élite respectively]

Burgon, John William (1813–1888)

4 Match me such marvel save in Eastern clime, / A rose-red city 'half as old as Time'! ['Petra']

Burke, Edmund (1729–1797)

5 Well is it known that ambition can creep as well as soar. [*Letters on a Regicide Peace*, 3]

6 There is, however, a limit at which forbearance ceases to be a virtue. [*Observations on 'The present state of the nation'*]

7 The age of chivalry is gone. That of sophisters, economists and calculators has succeeded: and the glory of Europe is extinguished for ever. [*Reflections on the Revolution in France*]

8 A state without the means of some change is without the means of its conservation. [Ib.]

9 Government is a contrivance of human wisdom to provide for human *wants*. Men have a right that these wants should be provided for by this wisdom. [Ib.]

10 Kings will be tyrants from policy, when subjects are rebels from principle. [Ib.]

11 Who now reads Bolingbroke? Who ever read him through? [Ib.]

12 I am convinced that we have a degree of delight, and that no small one, in the real misfortunes and pains of others. [*On the Sublime and Beautiful*]

13 To complain of the age we live in, to murmur at the present possessors of power, to lament the past, to conceive extravagant hopes of the future, are the common dispositions of the greatest part of mankind. [*Thoughts on the Cause of the Present Discontents*]

14 The circumstances are in a great measure new. We have hardly any landmarks from the wisdom of our ancestors to guide us. [Ib.]

15 When bad men combine, the good must associate; else they will fall, one by one, an unpitied sacrifice in a contemptible struggle. [Ib.]

16 You choose a member indeed; but when you have chosen him, he is not member of Bristol, but he is a member of *parliament*. [Speech at Bristol, 1774]

17 It is the nature of all greatness not to be exact. [Speech (on American taxation), 1774]

18 Passion for fame; a passion which is the instinct of all great souls. [Ib.]

19 To tax and to please, no more than to love and to be wise, is not given to men. [Ib.]

20 The march of the human mind is slow. [Speech (on conciliation with America), 1775]

21 Young man, there is America — which at this day serves for little more than to amuse you with stories of savage men, and uncouth manners; yet shall, before you taste of death, show itself equal to the whole of that commerce which now attracts the envy of the world. [Ib.]

22 The use of force alone is but *temporary*. It may subdue for a moment; but it does not remove the necessity of subduing again: and a nation is not governed, which is perpetually to be conquered. [Ib.]

23 The mysterious virtue of wax and parchment. [Ib.]

24 I do not know the method of drawing up an indictment against a whole people. [Ib.]

25 All protestantism, even the most cold and passive, is a sort of dissent. But the religion most prevalent in our northern colonies is a refinement on the principle of resistance; it is the dissidence of dissent, and the protestantism of the Protestant religion. [Ib.]

26 The people are the masters. [Speech, 1780]

1 The people never give up their liberties / but under some delusion. [Speech, 1784]

2 An event...upon which it is difficult to speak, and impossible to be silent. [Speech (on impeachment of Warren Hastings), 1789]

3 Those who have been once intoxicated with power, and have derived any kind of emolument from it, even though but for one year, can never willingly abandon it. [Letter, 1791]

4 The only infallible criterion of wisdom to vulgar judgements — success. [Letter, 1791]

5 Tyrants seldom want pretexts. [Ib.]

6 The only thing necessary for the triumph of evil is for good men to do nothing. [Attr.]

Burne-Jones, Sir Edward (1833–1898)

7 I mean by a picture a beautiful, romantic dream of something that never was, never will be — in a light better than any lights that ever shone — in a land no one can define or remember, only desire — and the forms divinely beautiful—and then I wake up, with the waking of Brynhild. [Letter]

Burney, Fanny (1752–1840)

8 Dancing? Oh, dreadful! How it was ever adopted in a civilized country I cannot find out; 'tis certainly a Barbarian exercise, and of savage origin. [*Cecilia*, 3]

9 Travelling is the ruin of all happiness! There's no looking at a building here after seeing Italy. [Ib. 4]

10 One really lives nowhere; one does but vegetate, and wish it all at an end. [Ib. 7]

11 'Do you come to the play without knowing what it is?' 'Oh, yes, sir, yes, very frequently. I have no time to read play-bills. One merely comes to meet one's friends, and show that one's alive.' [*Evelina*, 20]

12 Nothing is so delicate as the reputation of a woman; it is at once the most beautiful and most brittle of all human things. [Ib. 39]

13 Indeed, the freedom with which Dr. Johnson condemns whatever he disapproves is astonishing. [*Diary*, 1778]

Burns, Robert (1759–1796)

14 O Thou! Whatever title suit thee — / Auld Hornie, Satan, Nick, or Clootie. ['Address to the Deil']

15 Then gently scan your brother man, / Still gentler sister woman; / Tho' they may gang a kennin wrang, / To step aside is human. ['Address to the Unco Guid']

16 Ae fond kiss, and then we sever; / Ae fare-weel, and then for ever! ['Ae Fond Kiss']

17 Had we never lov'd sae kindly, / Had we never lov'd sae blindly, / Never met — or never parted, / We had ne'er been broken-hearted. [Ib.]

18 Should auld acquaintance be forgot, / And never brought to mind? ['Auld Lang Syne']

19 Freedom and whisky gang thegither, / Tak aff your dram! ['Author's Earnest Cry and Prayer']

20 To see her is to love her, / And love but her for ever, / For Nature made her what she is, / And ne'er made anither! ['Bonnie Lesley']

21 An' Charlie he's my darling, my darling, my darling, / Charlie he's my darling, the young Chevalier. ['Charlie he's my darling'; *see* Hogg]

22 Gin a body meet a body / Coming through the rye; / Gin a body kiss a body, / Need a body cry? ['Coming Through the Rye']

23 Contented wi' little and cantie wi' mair, / Whene'er I foregather wi' Sorrow and Care, / I gie them a skelp, as they're creepin' alang, / Wi' a cog o' guid swats and an auld Scottish sang. ['Contented wi' Little']

1 From scenes like these old Scotia's grandeur springs, / That makes her loved at home, revered abroad: / Princes and lords are but the breath of kings, / 'An honest man's the noblest work of God.' ['The Cotter's Saturday Night']

2 I wasna fou, but just had plenty. ['Death and Dr. Hornbook']

3 On ev'ry hand it will allow'd be, / He's just — nae better than he should be. ['Dedication to Gavin Hamilton']

4 But ae the best dance e'er cam to the Land / Was, the de'il's awa wi' th'Exciseman. ['The De'il's awa wi' th'Exciseman']

5 Who will not sing *God Save the King* / Shall hang as high's the steeple; / But while we sing *God Save the King*, / We'll ne'er forget the People! ['Does Haughty Gaul Invasion Threat?']

6 But Facts are chiels that winna ding, / An' downa be disputed. ['A Dream']

7 A Gentleman who held the patent for his honours immediately from Almighty God. ['Elegy on Capt. Matthew Henderson']

8 The heart ay's the part ay / That makes us right or wrang. ['Epistle to Davie']

9 What's a' your jargon o' your schools, / Your Latin names for horns and stools; / If honest Nature made you fools, / What sairs your grammars? ['First Epistle to Lapraik']

10 Gie me ae spark o' Nature's fire, / That's a' the learning I desire. [Ib.]

11 Just now I've taen the fit o' rhyme, / My barmie noddle's working prime. ['Epistle to James Smith']

12 Some rhyme a neebor's name to lash; / Some rhyme (vain thought!) for needfu' cash; / Some rhyme to court the countra clash, / An' raise a din; / For me, an aim I never fash: / I rhyme for fun. [Ib.]

13 An' fareweel deer, deluding Woman, / The joy of joys. [Ib.]

14 Green grow the rashes O, / Green grow the rashes O; / The sweetest hours that e'er I spend, / Are spent among the lasses O! ['Green Grow the Rashes']

15 O, gie me the lass that has acres o' charms, / O, gie me the lass wi' the weel-stockit farms. ['Hey for a Lass wi' a Tocher']

16 Leeze me on drink! it gies us mair / Than either school or college; / It ken'les wit, it waukens lear, / It pangs us fou o' knowledge. ['The Holy Fair']

17 There's some are fou o' love divine, / There's some are fou o' brandy; / An monie jobs that day begin, / May end in houghmagandie / Some ither day. [Ib.]

18 O Thou that in the heavens does dwell, / Wha, as it pleases best Thysel, / Sends ane to heaven, and ten to hell, / A' for Thy glory, / And no' for ony guid or ill, / They've done afore Thee! ['Holy Willie's Prayer']

19 Yet I am here, a chosen sample, / To show Thy grace is great and ample: / I'm here a pillar o' Thy temple, / Strong as a rock, / A guide, a buckler, and example / To a' Thy flock! [Ib.]

20 But yet, O Lord! confess I must, / At times I'm fashed wi' fleshly lust; / And sometimes, too, wi' warldly trust, / Vile self gets in; / But Thou remembers we are dust, / Defil'd wi' sin. [Ib.]

21 The rank is but the guinea's stamp, / The man's the gowd for a' that. ['Is there for Honest Poverty?']

22 A man's a man for a' that. [Ib.]

23 For a' that, an' a' that, / It's comin yet for a' that, / That man to man the world o'er / Shall brithers be for a' that. [Ib.]

24 John Anderson my jo, John, / When we were first acquent, / Your locks were like the raven, / Your bonny brow was brent. ['John Anderson My Jo']

25 Some have meat and cannot eat, / Some cannot eat that want it: / But we have meat and we can eat, / Sae let the Lord be thankit. ['The Kirkcudbright Grace']

26 Wae worth thy power, thou cursed leaf! / Fell source of a' my woe and grief, / For lack o' thee I've lost my lass, / For lack o' thee I scrimp my glass. ['Lines written on a Bank Note']

1 Poor Andrew that tumbles for sport / Let naebody name wi' a jeer: / There's even, I'm tauld, i' the Court / A tumbler ca'd the Premier. [*Love and Liberty* (or *The Jolly Beggars*)]

2 But och! they catch'd him at the last, / And bound him in a dungeon fast. / My curse upon them every one — / They've hang'd my braw John Highlandman! [Ib.]

3 Whistle owre the lave o't. [Ib.]

4 [Of women] Their tricks an' craft hae put me daft, / They've taen me in, an a' that; / But clear your decks, an' here's the Sex! / I like the jads for a' that. [Ib.]

5 A fig for those by law protected! / Liberty's a glorious feast! / Courts for cowards were erected, / Churches built to please the priest! [Ib.]

6 May coward shame distain his name, / The wretch that dares not die! ['Macpherson's Farewell']

7 Man's inhumanity to man / Makes countless thousands mourn! ['Man was made to Mourn']

8 If I'm design'd yon lordling's slave — / By Nature's law design'd — / Why was an independent wish / E'er planted in my mind? [Ib.]

9 My heart's in the Highlands, my heart is not here; / My heart's in the Highlands a-chasing the deer. ['My Heart's in the Highlands']

10 O, my Luve's like a red red rose / That's newly sprung in June: / O my Luve's like the melodie / That's sweetly play'd in tune. ['My Love is like a Red Red Rose']

11 Hear, Land o' Cakes, and brither Scots. ['On Captain Grose's Peregrinations']

12 A chield's amang you taking notes, / And, faith, he'll prent it. [Ib.]

13 An idiot race, to honour lost — / Who know them best, despise them most. ['On Seeing the Royal Palace at Stirling in Ruins']

14 Scots, wha hae wi' Wallace bled, / Scots, wham Bruce has aften led, / Welcome to your gory bed, / Or to victorie. ['Scots, Wha Hae']

15 By Oppression's woes and pains! / By your sons in servile chains! / We will drain our dearest veins, / But they shall be free! [Ib.]

16 Hail, Poesie! thou nymph reserv'd! / In chase o' thee, what crowds hae swerv'd / Frae Common Sense, or sunk ennerv'd / 'Mang heaps o' clavers; / And Och! o'er aft thy joes hae starv'd / 'Mid a' thy favors! ['Sketch']

17 But pleasures are like poppies spread — / You seize the flow'r, its bloom is shed; / Or like the snow falls in the river — / A moment white — then melts for ever; / Or like the Borealis race, / That flit ere you can point their place; / Or like the rainbow's lovely form / Evanishing amid the storm. ['Tam o' Shanter']

18 As Tammie glowr'd, amaz'd, and curious, / The mirth and fun grew fast and furious; / The piper loud and louder blew, / The dancers quick and quicker flew, / They reel'd, they set, they cross'd, they cleekit, / Till ilka carlin swat and reekit, / And cost her duddies to the wark, / And linket at it in her sark! [Ib.]

19 Even Satan glowr'd, and fidg'd fu' fain, / And hotch'd and blew wi' might and main: / Till first ae caper, syne anither, / Tam tint his reason a' thegither, / And roars out, 'Weel done, Cutty-sark!' [Ib.]

20 He'll hae misfortunes great and sma', / But aye a heart aboon them a'. ['There was a Lad']

21 That I for poor auld Scotland's sake, / Some usefu' plan or beuk could make, / Or sing a sang at least. ['To the Guidwife of Wauchope House']

22 Fair fa' your honest sonsie face, / Great chieftain o' the puddin'-race! ['To a Haggis']

23 O wad some Power the giftie gie us / To see oursels as others see us! / It wad frae monie a blunder free us, / An' foolish notion: / What airs in dress an' gait wad lea'e us / An' ev'n devotion! ['To a Louse']

24 Wee, sleekit, cow'rin', tim'rous beastie, / O what a panic's in thy breastie! ['To a Mouse']

1 I'm truly sorry man's dominion / Has broken Nature's social union, / An' justifies that ill opinion / Which makes thee startle / At me, thy poor, earth-born companion / An' fellow mortal. [Ib.]

2 The best laid schemes o' mice an' men / Gang aft a-gley. [Ib.]

3 Their sighin', cantin', grace-proud faces, /Their three mile prayers, and half mile graces. ['To the Rev. John McMath']

4 We labour soon, we labour late, / To feed the titled knave, man, / And a' the comfort we're to get, / Is that ayont the grave, man. ['The Tree of Liberty']

5 I see how folk live that hae riches; / But surely poor-folk maun be wretches! ['The Twa Dogs']

6 But human bodies are sic fools, / For a' their colleges and schools, / That when nae real ills perplex them, / They mak enow themsels to vex them. [Ib.]

7 O whistle, and I'll come to you, my lad. ['Whistle, and I'll come to you, my Lad']

8 We are na fou, we're nae that fou, / But just a drappie in our e'e! / The cock may craw, the day may daw, / And ay we'll taste the barley-bree! ['Willie Brew'd a Peck o' Maut']

9 Her nose and chin they threaten ither. ['Willie's Wife']

10 Ye banks and braes o' bonny Doon, / How can ye bloom sae fresh and fair? / How can ye chant, ye little birds, / And I sae weary fu' o' care? ['Ye Banks and Braes o' Bonny Doon']

11 To be overtopped in anything else I can bear: but in the tests of generous love I defy all mankind. [Letter to Clarinda]

12 I am quite transported at the thought that ere long, perhaps very soon, I shall bid an eternal adieu to all the pains, and uneasiness and disquietudes of this weary life; for I assure you I am heartily tired of it, and, if I do not very much deceive myself I could contentedly and gladly resign it. [Letter to his Father]

13 As for this world I despair of ever making a figure in it — I am not formed for the bustle of the busy nor the flutter of the gay. I shall never again be capable of it. [Ib.]

14 ...the story of Wallace poured a Scottish prejudice in my veins, which will boil along there till the floodgates of life shut in eternal rest. [Letter to Dr. John Moore]

15 Whatever mitigates the woes or increases the happiness of others, this is my criterion of goodness; and whatever injures society at large, or any individual in it, this is my measure of iniquity. [Ib.]

16 What a rocky-hearted, perfidious Succubus was that Queen Elizabeth! Judas Iscariot was a sad dog to be sure, but still his demerits sink to insignificance, compared with the doings of the infernal Bess Tudor. [Ib.]

17 I am a strict economist; not, indeed, for the sake of the money; but one of the principal parts in my composition is a kind of pride of stomach; and I scorn to fear the face of any man living. [Letter to John Murdoch]

18 After all my boasted independence, curst necessity compels me to implore you for five pounds...Do, for God's Sake, send me that sum, and that by return of post...Forgive, forgive me! [Letter to George Thomson]

19 Don't let the awkward squad fire over me. [Cunningham, *Life*]

Burroughs, Edgar Rice (1875–1950)

20 Me Tarzan, you Jane. [*Tarzan of the Apes*]

Burton, Robert (1577–1640)

21 All my joys to this are folly, / Naught so sweet as Melancholy. [*Anatomy of Melancholy*, 'Author's Abstract of Melancholy']

22 They lard their lean books with the fat of others' works. [Ib. 'Democritus to the Reader']

23 Like watermen, that row one way and look another. [Ib.]

1 All poets are mad. [Ib.]

2 *Hinc quam sit calamus saevior ense patet.* Hence it is clear how much more cruel the pen is than the sword. [Ib.]

3 One was never married, and that's his hell; another is, and that's his plague. [Ib.]

4 What is a ship but a prison [Ib. II]

5 Tobacco, divine, rare, superexcellent tobacco, which goes far beyond all their panaceas, potable gold, and philosopher's stones, a sovereign remedy to all diseases. [Ib.]

6 Let me not live, saith Aretine's Antonia, if I had not rather hear thy discourse than see a play! [Ib. III]

7 To enlarge or illustrate this — is to set a candle in the sun. [Ib.]

8 Diogenes struck the father when the son swore. [Ib.]

9 England is a paradise for women, and hell for horses: Italy a paradise for horses, hell for women. [Ib.]

10 One religion is as true as another. [Ib.]

Bussy-Rabutin, Comte de (1618-1693)

11 *L'absence est à l'amour ce qu'est au feu le vent; it éteint le petit, il allume le grand.* Absence is to love what wind is to fire; it extinguishes the small, it inflames the great. [*Histoire amoureuse des Gaules*]

Butler, Bishop Joseph (1692-1752)

12 But to *us*, probability is the very guide of life. [*The Analogy of Religion*]

13 Things and actions are what they are, and the consequences of them will be what they will be: why then should we desire to be deceived? [*Fifteen Sermons*, 7]

Butler, Nicholas Murray (1862-1947)

14 An expert is one who knows more and more about less and less. [Attr.]

Butler, R.A. (1902-1982)

15 Politics is the art of the possible. [Epigraph to *The Art of the Possible*]

Butler, Samuel (1612-1680)

16 For rhetoric he could not ope / His mouth, but out there flew a trope. [*Hudibras*, I]

17 For all a rhetorician's rules / Teach nothing but to name his tools. [Ib.]

18 For he, by geometric scale, / Could take the size of pots of ale;... / And wisely tell what hour o' th' day / The clock doth strike, by algebra. [Ib.]

19 And prove their doctrine orthodox / By apostolic blows and knocks. [Ib.]

20 What ever sceptic could inquire for; / For every why he had a wherefore. [Ib.]

21 For rhyme the rudder is of verses, / With which like ships they steer their courses. [Ib.]

22 Cleric before, and Lay behind; / A lawless linsy-woolsy brother, / Half of one order, half another. [Ib.]

23 Some have been beaten till they know / What wood a cudgel's of by th' blow; / Some kick'd, until they can feel whether / A shoe be Spanish or neats-leather. [Ib. II]

24 She that with poetry is won / Is but a desk to write upon. [Ib.]

25 Oaths are but words, and words but wind. [Ib.]

26 As the ancients / Say wisely, Have a care o' th' main chance, / And look before you ere you leap; / For, as you sow, you are like to reap. [Ib.]

27 What makes all doctrines plain and clear? / About two hundred pounds a year. / And that which was prov'd true before, / Prove false again? Two hundred more. [Ib. III]

28 He that complies against his will, / Is of his own opinion still. [Ib. III]

29 For, those that fly, may fight again, / Which he can never do that's slain. [Ib.]

Butler, Samuel (1835-1902)

30 It has been said that the love of money is the root of all evil. The want of money is so quite as truly. [*Erewhon*, 20]

31 Though God cannot alter the past, historians can. [*Erewhon Revisited*, 14]

1 'Man wants but little here below' but likes that little good — and not too long in coming. [*Further Extracts from the Notebooks*]

2 An honest God's the noblest work of man. [Ib; *see* Pope, *Essay on Man*, IV]

3 A hen is only an egg's way of making another egg. [*Lie and Habit*]

4 How thankful we ought to feel that Wordsworth was only a poet and not a musician. Fancy a symphony by Wordsworth! Fancy having to sit it out! [*Notebooks*]

5 An apology for the devil: it must be remembered that we have heard only one side of the case; God has written all the books. [Ib.]

6 The phrase 'unconscious humour' is the one contribution I have made to the current literature of the day. [Ib.]

7 God is Love, I dare say. But what a mischievous devil Love is. [Ib.]

8 To live is like love, all reason is against it, and all healthy instinct for it. [Ib.]

9 Parents are the last people on earth who ought to have children. [Ib.]

10 The public buys its opinions as it buys its meat, or takes in its milk, on the principle that it is cheaper to do this than keep a cow. So it is, but the milk is more likely to be watered. [Ib.]

11 I do not mind lying, but I hate inaccuracy. [Ib.]

12 The world will, in the end, follow only those who have despised as well as served it. [Ib.]

13 Life is one long process of getting tired. [Ib.]

14 Life is the art of drawing sufficient conclusions from insufficient premises. [Ib.]

15 All progress is based upon a universal innate desire on the part of every organism to live beyond its income. [Ib.]

16 When the righteous man turneth away from his righteousness that he hath committed and doeth that which is neither quite lawful nor quite right, he will generally be found to have gained in amiability what he has lost in holiness. [Ib.]

17 To himself every one is an immortal; he may know that he is going to die, but he can never know that he is dead. [Ib.]

18 We think as we do, mainly because other people think so. [Ib.]

19 The history of art is the history of revivals. [Ib.]

20 O God! O Montreal! ['Psalm of Montreal']

21 The advantage of doing one's praising for oneself is that one can lay it on so thick and exactly in the right places. [*The Way of All Flesh*, 61]

22 'Tis better to have loved and lost than never to have lost at all. [Ib. 77; *see* Tennyson, *In Memoriam*]

Bygraves, Max (1922-)

23 I've arrived, and to prove it, I'm here. [Quoted in Halliwell, *Filmgoers' Book of Quotes*]

Byrom, John (1692-1763)

24 Where you find / Bright passages that strike your mind, / And which perhaps you may have reason / To think on at another season, — / — Take them down in black and white. ['Hint to a Young Person']

25 God bless the King! — I mean the Faith's Defender; / God bless (no harm in blessing) the Pretender! / But who Pretender is, or who is King, / God bless us all! — that's quite another thing. ['To an Officer in the Army']

Byron, George Gordon, Lord (1788-1824)

26 For what were all these country patriots born? / To hunt, and vote, and raise the price of corn? ['The Age of Bronze']

27 In short, he was a perfect cavaliero, / And to his very valet seem'd a hero. [*Beppo*]

1 His heart was one of those which most enamour us, / Wax to receive, and marble to retain. [Ib.]

2 Mark! where his carnage and his conquests cease! / He makes a solitude, and calls it — peace! ['The Bride of Abydos']

3 Adieu, adieu! my native shore / Fades o'er the waters blue. [*Childe Harold*, I]

4 Convention is the dwarfish demon styled / That foiled the knights in Marialva's dome. [Ib.]

5 Ambition's honoured fools. [Ib.]

6 And must they fall? the young, the proud, the brave, / To swell one bloated Chief's unwholesome reign? [Ib.]

7 Here all were noble, save Nobility; / None hugged a Conqueror's chain, save fallen Chivalry! [Ib.]

8 War, war is still the cry, 'War even to the knife!' [Ib.]

9 Well didst thou speak, Athena's wisest son! / 'All that we know, is, nothing can be known.' [Ib. II]

10 Fair Greece! Sad relic of departed worth! / Immortal, though no more; though fallen, great! [Ib.]

11 A schoolboy's tale, the wonder of an hour. [Ib.]

12 The last, the worst, dull spoiler, who was he? [Ib.]

13 The Ocean Queen, the free Britannia, bears / The last poor plunder from a bleeding land. [Ib.]

14 But midst the crowd, the hum, the shock of men, / To hear, to see, to feel, and to possess. [Ib.]

15 Hereditary Bondsmen! know ye not / Who would be free themselves must strike the blow? [Ib.]

16 Death in the front, Destruction in the rear! [Ib.]

17 What is the worst of woes that wait on Age? / What stamps the wrinkle deeper on the brow? / To view each loved one blotted from Life's page, / And be alone on earth, as I am now. [Ib.]

18 Since my young days of passion — joy or pain — / Perchance my heart and harp have lost a string — / And both may jar. [Ib. III]

19 Years steal / Fire from the mind as vigour from the limb; / And Life's enchanted cup but sparkles near the brim. [Ib.]

20 On with the dance! let joy be unconfined; / No sleep till morn, when Youth and Pleasure meet / To chase the glowing Hours with flying feet. [Ib.]

21 There is a very life in our despair, / Vitality of poison. [Ib.]

22 That untaught innate philosophy, / Which, be it Wisdom, Coldness, or deep Pride, / Is gall and wormwood to an enemy. [Ib.]

23 ...the madmen who have made men mad / By their contagion; Conquerors and Kings, / Founders of sects and systems. [Ib.]

24 He who ascends to mountain tops, shall find / The loftiest peaks most wrapt in clouds and snow; / He who surpasses or subdues mankind, / Must look down on the hate of those below. [Ib.]

25 To fly from, need not be to hate, mankind. [Ib.]

26 I live not in myself, but I become / Portion of that around me; and to me / High mountains are a feeling, but the hum / Of human cities torture. [Ib.]

27 For 'tis nature to advance or die. [Ib.]

28 I have not loved the World, nor the World me; / I have not flattered its rank breath, nor bowed / To its idolatries a patient knee, / Nor coined my cheek to smiles. [Ib.]

29 There was a sound of revelry by night [Ib.]

30 Like to the apples on the Dead Sea's shore, / All ashes to the taste. [Ib.]

31 I stood in Venice, on the Bridge of Sighs; / A palace and a prison on each hand. [Ib. IV]

32 Where Venice sate in state, throned on her hundred isles! [Ib.]

1 There is a pleasure in the pathless woods, / There is a rapture on the lonely shore, / There is society, where none intrudes, / By the deep sea and music in its roar; / I love not man the less, but Nature more. [Ib.]

2 Then farewell, Horace; whom I hated so, / Not for thy faults but mine. [Ib.]

3 His manly brow / Consents to death, but conquers agony. [Ib.]

4 He heard it, but he heeded not — his eyes / Were with his heart, and that was far away. [Ib.]

5 He, their sire, / Butcher'd to make a Roman holiday. [Ib.]

6 While stands the Coliseum, Rome shall stand: / When falls the Coliseum, Rome shall fall; / And when Rome falls — the World. [Ib.]

7 The fatal facility of the octo-syllabic verse. [*The Corsair*, Preface]

8 Such hath it been — shall be — beneath the sun / The many still must labour for the one. [Ib. I]

9 The weak alone repent. [Ib. II]

10 The fountain moves without a wind: but shall / The ripple of a spring change my resolve? [*The Deformed Transformed*]

11 The flower of Adam's bastards. [Ib.]

12 Your old philosophers / Beheld mankind as mere spectators of / The Olympic games. When I behold a prize / Worth wrestling for I may be found a Milo. [Ib.]

13 The Assyrian came down like the wolf on the fold. ['Destruction of Sennacherib']

14 I wish he would explain his explanation. [*Don Juan*, Dedication]

15 My way is to begin with the beginning. [Ib. I]

16 What men call gallantry, and gods adultery, / Is much more common where the climate's sultry. [Ib.]

17 Even innocence itself has many a wile, / And will not dare to trust itself with truth, / And love is taught hypocrisy from youth. [Ib.]

18 Christians have burnt each other, quite persuaded / That all the Apostles would have done as they did. [Ib.]

19 Whether it was she did not see, or would not, / Or, like all very clever people, could not. [Ib.]

20 A little still she strove, and much repented, / And whispering 'I will ne'er consent' — consented. [Ib.]

21 Thou shalt believe in Milton, Dryden, Pope; / Thou shalt not set up Wordsworth, Coleridge, Southey. [Ib.]

22 Man's love is of man's life a thing apart, / 'Tis woman's whole existence. [Ib.]

23 A solitary shriek, the bubbling cry / Of some strong swimmer in his agony. [Ib. II]

24 Let us have wine and women, mirth and laughter, / Sermons and soda water the day after. [Ib.]

25 Man, being reasonable, must get drunk; / The best of life is but intoxication: / Glory, the grape, love, gold, in these are sunk / The hopes of all men, and of every nation. [Ib.]

26 There's nought, no doubt, so much the spirit calms / As rum and true religion. [Ib.]

27 Alas! the love of women! it is known / To be a lovely and a fearful thing! [Ib.]

28 Each kiss a heart-quake, — for a kiss's strength, / I think it must be reckon'd by its length. [Ib.]

29 In her first passion woman loves her lover, / In all the others all she loves is love. [Ib. III]

30 All tragedies are finish'd by a death, / All comedies are ended by a marriage. [Ib.]

31 The isles of Greece, the isles of Greece! / Where burning Sappho loved and sung, / Where grew the arts of war and peace, / Where Delos rose, and Phoebus sprung! [Ib.]

32 Think you, if Laura had been Petrarch's wife, / He would have written sonnets all his life? [Ib. III]

33 He was the mildest manner'd man / That ever scuttled ship or cut a throat. [Ib.]

34 The mountains look on Marathon — / And Marathon looks on the sea; / And musing there an hour alone, / I dream'd that Greece might still be free. [Ib.]

1 We learn from Horace, 'Homer sometimes sleeps'; / We feel without him, Wordsworth sometimes wakes. [Ib.]

2 Nothing so difficult as a beginning / In poesy, unless perhaps the end. [Ib. IV]

3 I've stood upon Achilles' tomb, / And heard Troy doubted; time will doubt of Rome. [Ib.]

4 And if I laugh at any mortal thing, / 'Tis that I may not weep. [Ib.]

5 That all-softening, overpowering knell, / The tocsin of the soul — the dinner-bell. [Ib. V]

6 There is a tide in the affairs of women, / Which, taken at the flood, leads — God knows where. [Ib. VI; *see* Shakespeare, *Julius Caesar*, IV.3]

7 A lady of a 'certain age,' which means / Certainly aged. [Ib.]

8 Must I restrain me through the fear of strife / From holding up the nothingness of life? [Ib. VII]

9 'Let there be light!' said God, 'and there was light!' / 'Let there be blood!' says man, and there's a sea! [Ib.]

10 And, after all, what is a lie? 'Tis but / The truth in masquerade. [Ib. XI]

11 'Tis strange the mind, that very fiery particle, / Should let itself be snuff'd out by an article. [Ib.]

12 Nought's permanent among the human race, / Except the Whigs *not* getting into place. [Ib.]

13 And hold up to the sun my little taper. [Ib. XII]

14 Merely innocent flirtation. / Not quite adultery, but adulteration. [Ib.]

15 Now hatred is by far the longest pleasure; / Men love in haste, but they detest at leisure. [Ib. XIII]

16 The English winter — ending in July, / To recommence in August. [Ib.]

17 Society is now one polish'd horde, / Form'd of two mighty tribes, the *Bores* and *Bored*. [Ib.]

18 Of all the horrid, hideous notes of woe, / Sadder than owl-songs or the midnight blast, / Is that portentous phrase, 'I told you so'. [Ib. XIV]

19 'Tis strange — but true; for truth is always strange; / Stranger than fiction. [Ib.]

20 Between two worlds life hovers like a star, / 'Twixt night and morn, upon the horizon's verge. / How little do we know that which we are! / How less what we may be! [Ib. XV]

21 I'll publish, right or wrong: / Fools are my theme, let satire be my song. [*English Bards and Scotch Reviewers*]

22 'Tis pleasant, sure, to see one's name in print; / A Book's a Book, altho' there is nothing in't. [Ib.]

23 With just enough of learning to misquote. [Ib.]

24 Better to err with Pope than shine with Pye. [Ib.]

25 Oh, Amos Cottle! — Phoebus! what a name / To fill the speaking trump of future fame! [Ib.]

26 Let simple Wordsworth chime his childish verse, / And brother Coleridge lull the babe at nurse. [Ib.]

27 [Of Wordsworth] Who, both by precept and example, shows / That prose is verse, and verse is merely prose. [Ib.]

28 Be warm but pure: be amorous but chaste. [Ib.]

29 Who killed John Keats? / 'I,' says the Quarterly, / So savage and Tartarly; / ''Twas one of my feats.' ['John Keats']

30 Maid of Athens, ere we part, / Give, oh give me back my heart! / Or, since that has left my breast, / Keep it now, and take the rest! ['Maid of Athens']

31 I know thee for a man of many thoughts. [*Manfred*, I]

32 I passed / The nights of years in sciences untaught. [Ib.]

33 We are the fools of time and terror: Days / Steal on us, and steal from us; yet we live, / Loathing our life, and dreading still to die. [Ib.]

34 Knowledge is not happiness, and science / But an exchange of ignorance for that / Which is another kind of ignorance. [Ib. II]

1 There is an order / Of mortals on the earth, who do become / Old in their youth, and die ere middle age. [Ib. III]

2 Old man! 'tis not so difficult to die. [Ib.]

3 My days are in the yellow leaf; / The flowers and fruits of love are gone; / The worm, the canker, and the grief / Are mine alone! ['On This Day I Complete my Thirty-Sixth Year']

4 My hair is grey, but not with years, / Nor grew it white / In a single night, / As men's have grown from sudden fears. ['The Prisoner of Chillon']

5 I am the very slave of circumstance / And impulse — borne away with every breath! [*Sardanapalus*, IV]

6 She walks in beauty, like the night. ['She Walks in Beauty']

7 So we'll go no more a-roving / So late into the night / Though the heart be still as loving, / And the moon be still as bright. ['So We'll Go No More A-Roving']

8 'Tis vain to struggle — let me perish young — / Live as I lived, and love as I have loved; / To dust if I return, from dust I sprung. ['Stanzas to the Po']

9 Oh, talk not to me of a name great in story; / The days of our youth are the days of our glory; / And the myrtle and ivy of sweet two-and-twenty / Are worth all your laurels, though ever so plenty. ['Stanzas Written on the Road between Florence and Pisa']

10 I knew it was love, and I felt it was glory. [Ib.]

11 Saint Peter sat by the celestial gate: / His keys were rusty, and the lock was dull, / So little trouble had been given of late. [*The Vision of Judgement*]

12 That household virtue, most uncommon, / Of constancy to a bad, ugly woman. [Ib.]

13 For by many stories, / And true, we learn the angels all are Tories. [Ib.]

14 If I should meet thee / After long years, / How should I greet thee? — / With silence and tears. ['When We Two Parted']

15 But I never see any one much improved by matrimony. All my coupled contemporaries are bald and discontented. [Journal, 1813]

16 Cleopatra strikes me as the epitome of her sex — fond, lively, sad, tender, teasing, humble, haughty, beautiful, the devil! — coquettish to the last, as well with the 'asp' as with Antony. [Ib.]

17 The more I see of men, the less I like them. If I could but say so of women too, all would be well. [Ib. 1814]

18 If I could always read, I should never feel the want of society. [Ib.]

19 There is something to me very softening in the presence of a woman, — some strange influence, even if one is not in love with them — which I cannot at all account for, having no very high opinion of the sex. [Ib.]

20 The only pleasure of fame is that it paves the way to pleasure, and the more intellectual our pleasure, the better for the pleasure and for us too. It was, however, agreeable to have heard our fame before dinner, and a girl's harp after. [Ib. 1821]

21 What is poetry? The feeling of a Former world and Future. [Ib.]

22 The Impression of Parliament upon me was that its members are not formidable as *speakers*, but very much so as an audience. [*Detached Thoughts*, 11]

23 Cicero himself, and probably the Messiah, could never have alter'd the vote of a single Lord of the Bedchamber or Bishop. [Ib. 2]

24 But I am convinced of the advantages of looking at mankind instead of reading about them, and the bitter effects of staying at home with all the narrow prejudices of an islander, that I think there should be a law amongst us, to set our young men abroad for a term, among the few allies our wars have left us. [Letter]

25 You should have a softer pillow than my heart. [Letter to Lady Byron]

26 I am sure my bones would not rest in an English grave, or my clay mix with the earth of that country. [Letter, 1817]

1 When a proposal is made to emancipate or relieve, you hesitate, you deliberate for years, you temporize and tamper with the minds of men; but a death-bill must be passed off-hand, without a thought of the consequences. [Maiden speech in House of Lords, 1812]

2 I awoke one morning and found myself famous. [Remark on instantaneous success of *Childe Harold*]

Cabell, James Branch (1879–1958)

3 The optimist proclaims that we live in the best of all possible worlds; and the pessimist fears this is true. [*The Silver Stallion*]

Caesar, Augustus (63 B.C.–A.D. 14)

4 *Urbem ... excoluit adeo, uti iure sit gloriatus marmoream se relinquere, quam latericiam accepisset.* He so improved the city that he justly boasted that he found it brick and left it marble. [Suetonius, *Divus Augustus*]

5 *Ad Graecas Kalendas.* At the Greek Kalends (i.e. never). [Ib.]

Caesar, Caius Julius (c. 102–44 B.C.)

6 *Gallia est omnis divisa in partas tres.* All Gaul is divided into three parts. [*De Bello Gallico*, I]

7 *Fere libenter homines id quod volunt credunt.* Men willingly believe what they wish. [Ib.]

8 Caesar's wife must be above suspicion. [Attr. by Plutarch, *Life*]

9 I had rather be first in a village than second at Rome. [Ib.]

10 *Iacta alea est.* The die is cast. [Remark on crossing the Rubicon]

11 *Veni, vidi, vici.* I came, I saw, I conquered. [Letter, 47 B.C.]

12 *Et tu Brute?* You too, Brutus? [Last words]

Cagney, James (1904–1986)

13 Look, Ma! Top of the world! [*White Heat*]

Calderón de la Barca, Pedro (1600–1681)

14 Fame, like water, bears up the lighter things, and lets the weighty sink. [*Adventures of Five Hours*]

Caligula (A.D. 12–41)

15 *Utinam populus Romanus unam cervicem haberet!* Would that the Roman people had only one neck! [Suetonius, *Life*]

Callimachus (c. 305–240 B.C.)

16 A great book is like a great evil. [Fragment]

Calverley, C.S. (1831–1884)

17 The heart which grief hath cankered / Hath one unfailing remedy — the Tankard. ['Beer']

18 For I've read in many a novel that, unless they've souls that grovel, / Folks *prefer* in fact a hovel to your dreary marble halls. ['In the Gloaming']

19 Meaning, however, is no great matter. ['Lovers, and a Reflection']

20 How Eugene Aram, though a thief, a liar, and a murderer, / Yet, being intellectual, was amongst the noblest of mankind. ['Of Reading']

Camden, William (1551–1623)

21 Betwixt the stirrup and the ground / Mercy I asked, mercy I found. ['Epitaph for a Man Killed by Falling from His Horse']

Cameron, Simon (1789–1889)

22 An honest politician is one who, when he is bought, will stay bought. [Remark]

Campbell, Joseph (1881–1944)

23 As a white candle / In a holy place, / So is the beauty / Of an aged face. ['The Old Woman']

Campbell, Mrs. Patrick (1865–1940)

24 Marriage: the deep, deep peace of the double bed after the hurly-burly of the chaise-longue. [Quoted in Cooper and Hartman, *Violets and Vinegar*]

Campbell, Roy (1901–1957)

1 You praise the firm restraint with which they write — / I'm with you there, of course: / They use the snaffle and the curb all right, / But where's the bloody horse? ['Adamastor: On Some South African Novelists']

Campbell, Thomas (1777–1844)

2 O leave this barren spot to me! / Spare, woodman, spare the beechen tree. ['The Beech-Tree's Petition']

3 Tomorrow let us do or die! [*Gertrude of Wyoming*]

4 On Linden, when the sun was low, / All bloodless lay the untrodden snow, / And dark as winter was the flow / Of Iser, rolling rapidly. ['Hohenlinden']

5 The combat deepens. On, ye brave, / Who rush to glory, or the grave! [Ib.]

6 Better be courted and jilted / Than never be courted at all. ['The Jilted Nymph']

7 The waters wild went o'er his child, / And he was left lamenting. ['Lord Ullin's Daughter']

8 'Tis distance lends enchantment to the view, / And robes the mountain in its azure hue. [*Pleasures of Hopes*, I]

9 And muse on Nature with a poet's eye. [Ib. II]

10 What millions died — that Caesar might be great! [Ib.]

11 One moment may with bliss repay / Unnumbered hours of pain. ['The Ritter Bann']

12 The sentinel stars set their watch in the sky. ['The Soldier's Dream']

13 Ye Mariners of England / That guard our native seas, / Whose flag has braved, a thousand years, / The battle and the breeze. ['Ye Mariners of England']

14 With thunders from her native oak / She quells the floods below. [Ib.]

15 Now Barabbas was a publisher. [Also attr. to Byron]

Campion, Thomas (1567–1620)

16 Never weather-beaten sail more willing bent to shore, / Never tired pilgrim's limbs affected slumber more. [*Book of Airs*]

17 There is garden in her face, / Where roses and white lilies grow. [Ib.]

18 There cherries grow, which none may buy / Till 'Cherry ripe' themselves do cry. [Ib.]

19 Those cherrries fairly do enclose / Of orient pearl a double row; / Which when her lovely laughter shows, / They look like rosebuds fill'd with snow. [Ib.]

Camus, Albert (1913–1960)

20 *Il semblait être l'ami de tous les plaisirs normaux, sans en être l'esclave.* He seemed to indulge in all the usual pleasures without being enslaved by any of them. [*La Peste*]

21 *Là était la certitude, dans le travail de tous les jours...L'essentiel était de bien faire son métier.* There, in day-to-day work, was certainty... Doing one's job well was what mattered. [Ib.]

22 *...la peste avait enlevé à tous le pouvoir de l'amour et même de l'amitié. Car l'amour demande un peu d'avenir, et il n'y avait plus pour nous que des instants.* The plague had deprived us all of the capacity for love and even for friendship. For love must have some future, and for us there were only moments. [Ib.]

23 *Ils savaient maintenant que s'il est une chose qu'on puisse désirer toujours et obtenir quelquefois, c'est la tendresse humaine.* They now knew that if there is one thing which can always be desired and sometimes obtained, it is human kindness. [Ib.]

Canning, George (1770–1827)

24 [Of a Jacobin] A steady patriot of the world alone, / The friend of every country but his own. ['New Morality']

25 And finds, with keen discriminating sight, / Black's not so black; / nor white so very white. [Ib.]

26 But of all plagues, good Heaven, thy wrath can send, / Save me, oh, save me, from the candid friend. [Ib.]

1 I called the New World into existence, to redress the balance of the Old. [Speech, 1826]

Carew, Thomas (c. 1595–c. 1639)

2 Thou didst pay / The debts of our penurious bankrupt age. ['An Elegy upon the Death of Dr. John Donne']

3 Here lies a King that rul'd, as he thought fit / The universal Monarchy of wit; / Here lie two Flamens, and both those, the best, / Apollo's first, at last, the true God's Priest. [Ib.]

4 I was foretold, your rebel sex, / Nor love, nor pity knew. ['A Deposition from Love']

5 Give me more love or more disdain; / The torrid or the frozen zone. ['Mediocrity in Love Rejected']

6 Ask me no more where Jove bestows, / When June is past, the fading rose; / For in your beauty's orient deep / These flowers, as in their causes, sleep. ['Song']

Carey, Henry (c. 1693–1743)

7 God save our gracious king! / Long live our noble king! ['God Save the King' (also attr. to others)]

8 Confound their politics, / Frustrate their knavish tricks. [Ib.]

9 Namby-Pamby, pilly-piss, / Rhimy-pim'd on Missy Miss / Tartaretta Tartaree, / That her father's gracy grace / Might give him a placy place. ['Namby-Pamby']

10 Of all the girls that are so smart / There's none like pretty Sally, / She is the darling of my heart, / And she lives in our alley. ['Sally in our Alley']

11 Of all the days that's in the week / I dearly love but one day — / And that's the day that comes betwixt / A Saturday and Monday. [Ib.]

Carlyle, Thomas (1795–1881)

12 The barrenest of all mortals is the sentimentalist. [*Characteristics*]

13 A well-written Life is almost as rare as a well-spent one. [*Critical and Miscellaneous Essays*, 'Richter']

14 It is the Age of Machinery, in every outward and inward sense of that word. [Ib. 'Signs of the Times']

15 The life of man, says our friend Herr Sauerteig, the life of even the meanest man, it were good to remember, is a poem. [Ib. 'Count Cagliostro, Flight First']

16 The foul sluggard's comfort: 'It will last my time.' [Ib. 'Count Cagliostro, Flight Last']

17 There is no life of a man, faithfully recorded, but is a heroic poem of its sort, rhymed or unrhymed. [Ib. 'Sir Walter Scott']

18 Under all speech that is good for anything there lies a silence that is better. Silence is deep as Eternity; speech is shallow as Time. [Ib.]

19 A witty statesman said, you might prove anything by figures. [Ib. 'Chartism']

20 The three great elements of modern civilization, Gunpowder, Printing, and the Protestant Religion. [Ib. 'State of German Literature']

21 What is all knowledge too but recorded experience, and a product of history; of which, therefore, reasoning and belief, no less than action and passion, are essential materials? [Ib. 'On History']

22 'Genius' (which means transcendent capacity of taking trouble, first of all). [*Frederick the Great*, IV]

23 Happy the people whose annals are blank in history-books! [Ib. XVI]

24 For, as I take it, Universal History, the history of what man has accomplished in this world, is at bottom the History of the Great Men who have worked here. [*Heroes and Hero Worship*, I]

1 It is well said, in every sense, that a man's religion is the chief fact with regard to him. A man's or a nation of men's. By religion I do not mean here the church creed which he professes, the articles of faith which he will sign and, in words or otherwise, assert; not this wholly, in many cases not this at all. We see men of all kinds of professed creeds attain to almost all degrees of worth or worthlessness under each or any of them. This is not what I call religion, this profession and assertion, which is often only a profession and assertion from the outworks of man, from the mere argumentative region of him, if even so deep as that. But the thing a man does practically believe (and this is often enough *without* asserting it even to himself, much less to others). [Ib.]

2 The illimitable, silent, never-resting thing called Time, rolling, rushing on, swift, silent, like an all embracing ocean-tide, on which we and all the Universe swim like exhalations. [Ib.]

3 Worship is transcendent wonder. [Ib.]

4 No sadder proof can be given by a man of his own littleness than disbelief in great men. [Ib.]

5 No great man lives in vain. The history of the world is but the biography of great men. [Ib.]

6 France was long a despotism tempered by epigrams. [*History of the French Revolution*, I]

7 A whiff of grapeshot. [Ib.]

8 [Robespierre] The sea-green Incorruptible. [Ib. II]

9 Aristocracy of the Money bag. [Ib.]

10 [Economics] The Dismal Science. [*Latter-Day Pamphlets*]

11 Transcendental moonshine. [*Life of John Sterling*]

12 Cash payment is not the sole nexus of man with man. [*Past and Present*, III]

13 Blessed is he who has found his work; let him ask no other blessedness. [Ib.]

14 Captains of industry. [Ib. IV]

15 No man who has once heartily and wholly laughed can be altogether irreclaimably bad. [*Sartor Resartus*, I]

16 Man is a tool-using animal. [Ib.]

17 An unmetaphorical style you shall in vain seek for: is not your very *Attention* a *Stretching-to*? [Ib.]

18 The everlasting No. [Ib. II (chapter title)]

19 Close thy Byron; open thy Goethe. [Ib. II]

20 Any road, this simple Entepfuhl road, will lead you to the end of the world! [Ib.]

21 But the world is an old woman, and mistakes any gilt farthing for a gold coin; whereby being often cheated, she will thenceforth trust nothing but the common copper. [Ib.]

22 O thou who art able to write a Book, which once in the two centuries or oftener there is a man gifted to do, envy not him whom they name the City-builder, and inexpressibly pity him whom they name Conqueror or City-burner! [Ib.]

23 Man's unhappiness, as I construe, comes of his greatness; it is because there is an Infinite in him, which with all his cunning he cannot quite bury under the Finite. [Ib.]

24 It is a mathematical fact that the casting of this pebble from my hand alters the centre of gravity of the universe. [Ib. III]

25 That tough faculty of reading. [Ib.]

26 If Jesus Christ were to come to-day, people would not even crucify him. They would ask him to dinner, and hear what he had to say, and make fun of it. [Remark]

27 Macaulay is well for a while, but one wouldn't *live* under Niagara. [Quoted in Wintle and Kenin, *Dictionary of Biographical Quotations*]

Carnegie, Andrew (1835–1919)

28 Surplus wealth is a sacred trust which its possessor is bound to administer in his lifetime for the good of the community. [*The Gospel of Wealth*]

1 Pioneering does not pay. [Hendrick, *Life*]

Carnegie, Dale (1888–1955)

2 How to Win Friends and Influence People. [Title of book]

Carroll, Lewis (1832–1898)

3 'What is the use of a book,' thought Alice, 'without pictures or conversations?' [*Alice in Wonderland*, 1]

4 'Curiouser and curiouser!' cried Alice. [Ib. 2]

5 How cheerfully he seems to grin, / How neatly spreads his claws, / And welcomes little fishes in / With gently smiling jaws! [Ib.]

6 'Why,' said the Dodo, 'the best way to explain it is to do it.' [Ib. 3]

7 The Duchess! The Duchess! Oh my dear paws! / Oh my fur and whiskers! [Ib. 4]

8 'You are old, Father William,' the young man said, / 'And your hair has become very white; / And yet you incessantly stand on your head — / Do you think, at your age, it is right?' [Ib. 5]

9 'Would you tell me, please, which way I ought to go from here?' 'That depends a good deal on where you want to get to,' said the Cat. [Ib. 6]

10 Speak roughly to your little boy, / And beat him when he sneezes; / He only does it to annoy, / Because he knows it teases. [Ib. 6]

11 Twinkle, twinkle, little bat! / How I wonder what you're at! / Up above the world you fly! / Like a teatray in the sky. [Ib. 7]

12 'Have some wine,' the March Hare said in an encouraging tone. Alice looked all round the table, but there was nothing on it but tea. 'I don't see any wine,' she remarked. 'There isn't any,' said the March Hare. [Ib.]

13 'Tis the voice of the Lobster; I heard him declare, / 'You have baked me too brown, I must sugar my hair.' [Ib. 8]

14 Beautiful Soup, so rich and green, / Waiting in a hot tureen! [Ib.]

15 The Queen was in a furious passion, and went stamping about, and shouting, 'Off with his head!' or 'Off with her head!' about once in a minute. [Ib.]

16 'A cat may look at a king,' said Alice. [Ib.]

17 'It was the *best* butter,' the March Hare meekly replied. [Ib.]

18 'Just about as much right,' said the Duchess, 'as pigs have to fly.' [Ib. 9]

19 We called him Tortoise because he taught us. [Ib.]

20 And the moral of that is — 'Oh, 'tis love, 'tis love that makes the world go round!' [Ib.]

21 Take care of the sense, and the sounds will take care of themselves. [Ib.]

22 'Will you walk a little faster?' said a whiting to a snail, / 'There's a porpoise close behind us, and he's treading on my tail.' [Ib. 10]

23 Will you, won't you, will you, won't you, will you join the dance? [Ib.]

24 The Queen of Hearts, she made some tarts, / All on a summer day: / The Knave of Hearts, he stole those tarts, / And took them quite away! [Ib. 11]

25 'Begin at the beginning,' the King said, gravely, 'and go on till you come to the end: then stop.' [Ib. 12]

26 'That's not a regular rule: you invented it just now.' 'It's the oldest rule in the book,' said the King. 'Then it ought to be Number One,' said Alice. [Ib. 12]

27 No! No! — Sentence first — verdict afterwards. [Ib.]

28 'Twas brillig, and the slithy toves / Did gyre and gimble in the wabe; / All mimsy were the borogoves, / And the mome raths outgrabe. [*Alice Through the Looking-Glass*, 1]

29 'And hast thou slain the Jabberwock? / Come to my arms, my beamish boy! / O frabjous day! Callooh! Callay!' / He chortled in his joy. [Ib.]

30 'Now, *here*, you see, it takes all the running *you* can do, to keep in the same place. If you want to get somewhere else, you must run at least twice as fast as that!' [Ib. 2]

1 'Contrariwise,' continued Tweedledee, 'if it was so, it might be; and if it were so, it would be: but as it isn't, it ain't. That's logic.' [Ib. 4]

2 'The time has come,' the Walrus said, / 'To talk of many things: / Of shoes — and ships — and sealing wax — / Of cabbages — and kings — / And why the sea is boiling hot / And whether pigs have wings.' [Ib.]

3 'I'm very brave generally,' he went on in a low voice: 'only to-day I happen to have a headache.' [Ib.]

4 'It's a poor sort of memory that only works backwards,' the Queen remarked. [Ib. 5]

5 The rule is, jam tomorrow and jam yesterday — but never jam to-day. [Ib.]

6 'There's no use trying,' she said: 'one *can't* believe impossible things.' 'I dare say you haven't had much practice,' said the Queen. 'When I was your age, I always did it for half an hour a day. Why, sometimes I've believed as many as six impossible things before breakfast.' [Ib.]

7 'When *I* use a word,' Humpty Dumpty said in a rather scornful tone, 'it means just what I choose it to mean, — neither more nor less.' [Ib. 6]

8 It's as large as life and twice as natural. [Ib. 7]

9 He's an Anglo-Saxon Messenger — and those are Anglo-Saxon attitudes. [Ib.]

10 'There's nothing like eating hay when you're faint'...'I didn't say there was nothing *better*,' the King replied, 'I said there was nothing *like* it.' [Ib.]

11 But I was thinking of a plan / To dye one's whiskers green. [Ib.]

12 'Speak when you're spoken to!' the Red Queen sharply interrupted her. [Ib. 9]

13 What I tell you three times is true. ['Hunting of the Snark, 1']

14 He thought he saw a Rattlesnake / That questioned him in Greek, / He looked again and found it was / The Middle of Next Week. [*Sylvie and Bruno*]

Cary, Phoebe (1824–1871)

15 And though hard be the task, / 'Keep a stiff upper lip'. ['Keep a Stiff Upper Lip']

Catechism [Shorter]

16 Man's chief end is to glorify God, and to enjoy him forever.

17 The Scriptures principally teach what man is to believe concerning God, and what duty God requires of man.

18 I should renounce the devil and all his works, the pomps and vanity of this wicked world, and all the sinful lusts of the flesh.

19 All mankind by their fall lost communion with God, are under his wrath and curse, and so made liable to all the miseries in this life, to death itself, and to the pains of hell for ever.

20 No mere man since the fall is able in this life perfectly to keep the commandments of God, but doth daily break them in thought, word, and deed.

21 *Q.* What meanest thou by this word *Sacrament*?
A. I mean an outward and visible sign of an inward and spiritual grace given unto us.

Cato the Elder (234–149 B.C.)

22 *Delenda est Carthago.* Carthage must be destroyed. [Pliny, *Natural History*]

23 I would rather see a young man blush than turn pale. [Ib.]

24 I would much rather have men ask why I have no statue than why I have one. [Ib.]

25 In all my life, I have never repented but of three things: that I trusted a woman with a secret, that I went by sea when I might have gone by land, and that I passed a day in idleness. [Ib.]

26 Do not buy what you want, but what you need; what you do not need is dear at a farthing. [*Reliquae*]

Catullus, Caius Valerius (87–c. 54 B.C.)

1 *Passer mortuus est meae puellae, / Passer, deliciae meae puellae.* My lady's sparrow is dead, the sparrow which was my lady's delight. [*Carmina*, 3]

2 *Sed haec prius fuere.* But this is over now. [Ib. 4]

3 *Vivamus, mea Lesbia, atque amemus, / Rumoresque senum severiorum / Omnes unius aestimemus assis.* Lesbia, let us live and love, and pay no heed to all the tales of grim old men. [Ib. 5]

4 *Da mi basia mille.* Give me a thousand kisses. [Ib.]

5 *O quid solutis est beatius curis?* What is more blessed than to cast cares aside? [Ib. 31]

6 *Nam risu inepto res ineptior nulla est.* For there is nothing sillier than a silly laugh. [Ib. 39]

7 *Sed mulier cupido quod dicit amanti, / In vento et rapida scribere oportet aqua.* But what a woman says to her ardent lover should be written in wind and running water. [Ib. 70]

8 *Odi et amo: quare id factum, fortasse requiris. / Nescio, sed fieri sentio et excrucior.* I hate and I love: why I do so you may indeed ask. I do not know, but I feel it happen and am in agony. [Ib. 85]

9 *Atque in perpetuum, frater, ave atque vale.* And forever, brother, hail and farewell! [Ib. 101]

10 *At non effugies meos iambos.* But you shall not escape my iambics. [Fragment]

Cavell, Edith (1865–1915)

11 I realize that patriotism is not enough. I must have no hatred or bitterness towards anyone. [Last words]

Cavour, Camillo (1810–1861)

12 Throughout Italy we are ready to proclaim this great principle: a free Church in a free State. [Speech, 1861]

Centlivre, Susannah (c. 1667–1723)

13 The real Simon Pure. [*A Bold Stroke for a Wife*, V]

Cervantes, Miguel de (1547–1616)

14 *El Caballero de la Triste Figura.* The Knight of the Sorrowful Countenance. [*Don Quixote*, I, 19]

15 *La mejor salsa del mundo es el hambre.* The best sauce in the world is hunger. [Ib. II, 5]

16 *Muchos pocos hacen un mucho.* Mony a mickle maks a muckle. [Ib.]

17 *Religión* es *la caballería.* Religion *is* knight-errantry. [Ib. II, 8]

18 *Es un entreverado loco, lleno de lúcidos intervalos.* He's a muddled fool, full of lucid intervals. [Ib. II, 18]

19 *Dos linages solos hay en el mundo, como decía una abuela mía, que son el tener y el no tener.* There are but two families in the world as my grandmother used to say, the Haves and the Have-nots. [Ib. II, 20]

20 *Digo, pacienca y barajar.* I say patience, and shuffle the cards. [Ib. II, 23]

21 *Los buenos pintores imitan la naturaleza, pero los malos la vomitan.* Good painters imitate nature, bad ones vomit it. [*El Licenciado Vidriera*]

Chalmers, Patrick Reginald (1872–1942)

22 What's lost upon the roundabouts we pulls up on the swings! ['Green Days and Blue Days: Roundabouts and Swings']

Chamberlain, Joseph (1836–1914)

23 Learn to think Imperially. [Speech, 1904]

24 We are not downhearted. The only trouble is, we cannot understand what is happening to our neighbours. [Speech, 1906]

Chamberlain, Neville (1869–1940)

25 In war, whichever side may call itself the victor, there are no winners, but all are losers. [Speech, 1938]

1 How horrible, fantastic, incredible it is that we should be digging trenches and trying on gas-masks here because of a quarrel in a far-away country between people of whom we know nothing [Czechoslovakia]. [Speech, 1938]

2 I believe it is peace for our time...peace with honour. [Speech after Munich Agreement, 1938]

3 Hitler has missed the bus. [Speech, 1940]

Chamfort, Nicolas (1741–1794)

4 *L'amour, tel qu'il existe dans la société, n'est que l'échange de deux fantaisies et le contact de deux épidermes.* Love, as it exists in society, is nothing but the exchange of two fantasies and the contact of two skins. [*Maximes et Pensées*, 6]

5 *Les pauvres sont les nègres de l'Europe.* The poor are the blacks of Europe. [Ib. 8]

6 *Sois mon frère, ou je te tue.* Be my brother, or I kill you. [Carlyle, *History of the French Revolution*, II]

Chandler, Raymond (1888–1959)

7 Down these mean streets a man must go who is not himself mean. [*The Simple Art of Murder*]

8 When in doubt have a man come through a door with a gun in his hand. [Ib.]

Chaplin, Charles (1889–1977)

9 All I need to make a comedy is a park, a policeman and a pretty girl. [*My Autobiography*]

Chapman, George (c. 1559–c. 1634)

10 O incredulity! the wit of fools. [*De Guiana*]

11 We have watered our horses in Helicon. [*May-Day*, III]

12 And let a scholar all Earth's volumes carry, / He will be but a walking dictionary. [*Tears of Peace*]

Charles I (1600–1649)

13 I see all the birds are flown. [Said of the five Members of Parliament, 1642]

14 Therefore I tell you (and I pray God it be not laid to your Charge) — that I am the Martyr of the People. [Speech on scaffold, 1649]

Charles II (1630–1685)

15 It is upon the navy under the Providence of God that the safety, honour and welfare of this realm do chiefly attend. [Preamble to Articles of War]

16 This is very true: for my words are my own and my actions are my ministers'. [Comment on Rochester's epitaph on him]

17 [Charles II] said once to myself that he was no atheist but he could not think God would make a man miserable only for taking a little pleasure out of the way. [Burnet, *History of My Own Times*]

18 [Of Presbyterianism] Not a religion for gentlemen. [Ib.]

19 His nonsense suits their nonsense. [Ib.]

20 [Of Nell Gwynn] Let not poor Nelly starve. [Attr.]

21 Brother, I am too old to go again to my travels. [Attr.]

22 He had been, he said, an unconscionable time dying; but he hoped that they would excuse it. [Macaulay, *History of England*]

Charles V, Emperor (1500–1558)

23 An iron hand in a velvet glove. [Carlyle, *Latter-Day Pamphlets*]

24 I speak Spanish to God, Italian to women, French to men, and German to my horse. [Attr.]

Chaucer, Geoffrey (c. 1340–1400)

25 She was so ferforth yeven hym to plese, / That al that lyked him hit dyde her ese. [*Anelida and Arcite*]

26 So thirleth with the poynt of remembraunce / The swerde of sorowe, ywhet with fals plesaunce. [Ib.]

1 Whan that Aprill with his shoures soote / The droghte of March hath perced to the roote, / And bathed every veyne in swich licour / Of which vertu engendred is the flour. [*Canterbury Tales*, Prologue]

2 Thanne longen folk to goon on pilgrimages. [Ib.]

3 He loved chivalrie, / Trouthe and honour, fredom and curteisie. [Ib. The Knight]

4 He nevere yet no vileynye ne sayde / In al his lyf unto no maner wight. / He was a verray, parfit gentil knyght. [Ib.]

5 And Frenssh she spak ful faire and fetisly, / After the scole of Stratford atte Bowe, / For Frenssh of Parys was to hire unknowe. [Ib. The Prioresse]

6 His heed was balled, that shoon as any glas, / And eek his face, as he hadde been enoynt. [Ib. The Monk]

7 He yaf nat of that text a pulled hen, / That seith that hunters ben nat hooly men. [Ib.]

8 He knew the tavernes wel in every toun. [Ib. The Frere]

9 A Clerk ther was of Oxenford also, / That unto logyk hadde long ygo. [Ib. The Clerk]

10 Sownynge in mortal vertu was his speche, / And gladly wolde he lerne and gladly teche. [Ib.]

11 Nowher so bisy a man as he ther nas, / And yet he seemed bisier than he was. [Ib. The Sergeant of the Lawe]

12 It snewed in his hous of mete and drynke. [Ib. The Franklin]

13 She was a worthy womman al hir lyve: / Housbondes at chirche dore she hadde fyve, / Withouten oother coompaignye in youthe, — / But thereof nedeth nat to speke as nowthe. [Ib. The Wife of Bath]

14 This noble ensample to his sheep he yaf, / That first he wroghte, and afterward he taughte. [Ib. The Parson]

15 But Cristes loore and his apostles twelve / He taughte, but first he folwed it hymselve. [Ib.]

16 With scalled browes blake and piled berd, / Of his visage children were aferd. [Ib. The Somnour]

17 Well koude he rede a lessoun or a storie, / But alderbest he song an offertorie. [Ib. The Pardoner]

18 And therefore, at the kynges court, my brother, / Ech man for hymself, ther is noon oother. ['Knight's Tale']

19 Thanked be Fortune and hir false wheel, / That noon estaat assureth to be weel. [Ib.]

20 Wostow nat wel the olde clerkes sawe, / That 'who shal yeve a lovere any lawe?' / Love is a gretter lawe, by my pan, / Than may be yeve to an erthely man. [Ib.]

21 A man mot nedes love, maugree his heed. [Ib.]

22 The bisy larke, messeger of day. [Ib.]

23 The smylere with the knyf under the cloke. [Ib.]

24 To maken vertu of necessitee. [Ib.]

25 For pitee renneth soon in gentil herte. [Ib.]

26 The grettest clerkes been noght the wysest man. ['Reve's Tale']

27 I hate hym that my vices telleth me, / And so doo mo, God woot, of us than I. ['Wife of Bath's Tale', Prologue]

28 Wommen desiren to have sovereynetee / As wel over hir housbond as hir love, / And for to been in maistrie hym above. [Ib.]

29 Experience though noon auctoritee / Were in this world, is right ynough for me / To speke of wo that is in marriage. [Ib.]

30 But, Lord Crist! whan that it remembreth me / Upon my yowthe, and on my jolitee, / It tikleth me aboute my herte roote. / Unto this day it dooth myn herte boote / That I have had my world as in my time. [Ib.]

31 But yet I hadde alwey a coltes tooth. / Gat-tothed I was, and that bicam me wel. [Ib.]

32 Wel ofter of the welle than of the tonne / She drank. ['Clerkes Tale']

1 Though clerkes preise wommen but a lite, / Ther kan no man in humblesse hym acquite / As womman kan. [Ib.]

2 A wyf wol laste, and in thyn hous endure, / Wel lenger than thee list, paraventure. ['Merchant's Tale']

3 My theme is alwey oon, and evere was — / *Radix malorum est cupiditas.* ['Pardoner's Tale', Prologue]

4 Nay, I wol drynke licour of the vyne, / And have a joly wenche in every toun. [Ib.]

5 O wombe! O bely! O stynking cod / Fulfilled of dong and of corrupcion! [Ib.]

6 What is bettre than wisdom? Womman. And what is bettre than a good womman? No-thing. ['Tale of Melibee']

7 No deyntee morsel passed thurgh hir throte; / Hir diete was accordant to hir cote. ['Nun's Priest's Tale']

8 This gentil cok hadde in his governaunce / Sevene hennes for to doon al his pleasaunce, / Whiche were his sustres and his paramours. [Ib.]

9 And on a Friday fil al this meschaunce. [Ib.]

10 'By God,' quod he, 'for pleynly, at a word, / Thy drasty rymyng is nat worth a toord!' ['Sir Thopas']

11 Of al the floures in the mede, / Thanne love I most thise floures white and rede, / Swiche as men callen daysyes in our toun. [*The Legend of Good Women*, Prologue]

12 Welcome, somer, oure governour and lord! [Ib.]

13 Wel by reson, men it calle may / The 'dayesye', or elles the 'ye of day'. [Ib.]

14 The lyf so short, the craft so long to lerne, / Th'assay so hard, so sharp the conquerynge. [*The Parliament of Fowls*]

15 For out of olde feldes, as men seith, / Cometh al this newe corn from yere to yere; / And out of olde bokes, in good feith, / Cometh al this newe science that men lere. [Ib.]

16 Know thyself first immortal, / And loke ay besyly thow werche and wysse / To commune profit, and thow shalt not mysse / To comen swiftly to that place deere / That full of blysse is and of soules cleere. [Ib.]

17 The tyme, that may not sojourne, / But goth, and may never retourne, / As watir that doun renneth ay, / But never drope retourne may. [*Romaunt of the Rose*]

18 Povert al aloon, / That not a penny had in wolde, / All though she hir clothis solde, / And though she shulde anhonged be; / For nakid as a worm was she. [Ib.]

19 O blynde world, O blynde entencioun! / How often falleth all the effect contraire / Of surquidrie and foul presumpcion; / For kaught is proud, and kaught is debonaire. [*Troilus and Criseyde*, I]

20 For it is seyd 'man maketh ofte a yerde / With which the maker is hymself ybeten.' [Ib.]

21 It is nought good a sleping hound to wake. [Ib. III]

22 The worst kinde of infortune is this, / A man to have ben in prosperitee, / And it remembren, when it passed is. [Ib.]

23 Oon ere it herde, at other out it wente. [Ib. IV]

24 O moral Gower. [Ib. V]

25 Go litel bok, go, litel myn tragedye, / Ther God thi makere yet, er that he dye, / So sende myght to make in som comedye! [Ib.]

26 And down from thennes faste he gan avyse / This litel spot of erthe, that with the se / Embraced is, and fully gan despise / This wrecched world, and held al vanite / To respect of the pleyn felicite / That is in hevene above. [Ib.]

27 O yonge, fresshe folkes. [Ib.]

Chekhov, Anton (1860-1904)

28 I'm in mourning for my life. [*The Seagull*, I]

29 When a woman isn't beautiful, people always say, 'You have lovely eyes, you have lovely hair.' [*Uncle Vanya*, III]

1 Medicine is my lawful wife and literature my mistress. [Letter, 1888]

2 He was a rationalist, but he had to confess that he liked the ringing of church bells. [Note Book]

Cherry-Garrard, Apsley (1886–1959)

3 Polar exploration is at once the cleanest and most isolated way of having a bad time which has been devised. [*The Worst Journey in the World*]

Chesterfield, Philip Dormer Stanhope, Earl of (1694–1773)

4 In scandal as in robbery, the receiver is always thought as bad as the thief. [*Advice to his Son*, 'Rules for Conversation']

5 In my mind, there is nothing so illiberal and so ill-bred, as audible laughter. [Ib. 'Graces']

6 In my opinion, parsons are very like other men, and neither the better nor the worse, for wearing a black gown. [*Letters to his Son*, 1746]

7 The knowledge of the world is only to be acquired in the world, and not in a closet. [Ib.]

8 An injury is much sooner forgotten than an insult. [Ib.]

9 Take the tone of the company you are in. [Ib. 1747]

10 There is a Spanish proverb, which says very justly, / Tell me whom you live with, and I will tell you who you are. [Ib.]

11 Do as you would be done by is the surest method that I know of pleasing. [Ib.]

12 I recommend you to take care of the minutes; for hours will take care of themselves. [Ib.]

13 [Of women] A man of sense only trifles with them, plays with them, humours and flatters them, as he does with a sprightly and forward child; but he neither consults them about, nor trusts them with, serious matters. [Ib. 1748]

14 Advice is seldom welcome; and those who want it the most always like it the least. [Ib.]

15 Speak of the moderns without contempt, and of the ancients without idolatry. [Ib.]

16 Wear your learning, like your watch, in a private pocket: and do not merely pull it out and strike it; merely to show that you have one. [Ib.]

17 If Shakespeare's genius had been cultivated, those beauties, which we so justly admire in him, would have been undisgraced by those extravagancies, and that nonsense, with which they are so frequently accompanied. [Ib.]

18 Women, then, are only children of a larger growth: they have an entertaining tattle, and sometimes wit; but for solid, reasoning good-sense, I never knew in my life one that had it, or who reasoned or acted consequentially for four and twenty hours together. [Ib.]

19 It must be owned, that the Graces do not seem to be natives of Great Britain; and I doubt, the best of us here have more of rough than of polished diamond. [Ib.]

20 Due attention to the inside of books, and due contempt for the outside, is the proper relation between a man of sense and his books. [Ib. 1749]

21 Idleness is only the refuge of weak minds. [Ib.]

22 Women are much more like each other than men: they have, in truth, but two passions, vanity and love; these are their universal characteristics. [Ib.]

23 Swallow all your learning in the morning, but digest it in company in the evenings. [Ib. 1751]

24 A chapter of accidents. [Ib. 1753]

25 Religion is by no means a proper subject of conversation in a mixed company. [Letter]

26 It is an undoubted truth, that the less one has to do, the less time one finds to do it in. One yawns, one procrastinates, one can do it when one will, and therefore one seldom does it at all. [Letter]

1 The fame of a conqueror; a cruel fame, that arises from the destruction of the human species. [Ib.]

2 I assisted at the birth of that most significant word, flirtation, which dropped from the most beautiful mouth in the world. [*The World*]

3 The pleasure is momentary, the position ridiculous and the expense damnable. [Attr.]

Chesterton, Gilbert Keith (1874–1936)

4 Chuck it, Smith! ['Antichrist']

5 The strangest whim has seized me ... After all / I think I will not hang myself today. ['A Ballad of Suicide']

6 I tell you naught for your comfort, / Yea, naught for your desire, / Save that the sky grows darker yet / And the sea rises higher. [*Ballad of the White Horse*, I]

7 For the great Gaels of Ireland / Are the men that God made mad, / For all their wars are merry, / And all their songs are sad. [Ib. II]

8 Fools! For I also had my hour; / One far fierce hour and sweet: / There was a shout about my ears, / And palms before my feet. ['The Donkey']

9 They died to save their country and they only saved the world. ['The English Graves']

10 The folk that live in Liverpool, their heart is in their boots; / They go to hell like lambs, they do, because the hooter hoots. ['Me Heart']

11 John Grubby, who was short and stout / And troubled with religious doubt, / Refused about the age of three / To sit upon the curate's knee. ['The New Freethinker']

12 All the easy speeches / That comfort cruel men. ['O God of Earth and Altar']

13 Before the Roman came to Rye or out to Severn strode, / The rolling English drunkard made the rolling English road. ['The Rolling English Road']

14 The night we went to Birmingham by way of Beachy Head. [Ib.]

15 We only know the last sad squires ride slowly towards the sea, / And a new people takes the land: and still it is not we. ['The Secret People']

16 Smile at us, pay us, pass us; but do not quite forget. / For we are the people of England, that never have spoken yet. [Ib.]

17 The souls most fed with Shakespeare's flame / Still sat unconquered in a ring, / Remembering him like anything. ['The Shakespeare Memorial']

18 God made the wicked Grocer / For a mystery and a sign, / That men might shun the awful shops / And go to inns to dine. ['Song against Grocers']

19 And the faith of the poor is faint and partial, / And the pride of the rich is all for sale, / And the chosen heralds of England's Marshal / Are the sandwich-men of the *Daily Mail*. ['A Song of Defeat']

20 Where Life was slain and Truth was slandered / On that one holier hill than Rome. ['To F. C. in Memoriam Palestine']

21 And Noah he often said to his wife when he sat down to dine, / 'I don't care where the water goes if it doesn't get into the wine.' ['Wine and Water']

22 'My country, right or wrong,' is a thing that no patriot would think of saying except in a desperate case. It is like saying, 'My mother, drunk or sober.' [*The Defendant*]

23 It is the supreme proof of a man being prosaic that he always insists on poetry being poetical. [*The Everlasting Man*]

24 To be the weakest camp is to be in the strongest school. [*Heretics*]

25 The artistic temperament is a disease that afflicts amateurs. [Ib.]

26 The human race, to which so many of my readers belong... [*The Napoleon of Notting Hill*]

27 You can never have a revolution in order to establish a democracy. You must have a democracy in order to have a revolution. [*Tremendous Trifles*]

1 Hardy became a sort of village atheist brooding and blaspheming over the village idiot. [*The Victorian Age in Literature*]

2 The Christian ideal has not been tried and found wanting. It has been found difficult; and left untried. [*What's Wrong with the World*]

3 If a thing is worth doing, it is worth doing badly. [Ib.]

4 Democracy means government by the uneducated, while aristocracy means government by the badly educated. [*New York Times*, 1931]

5 A man must love a thing very much if he not only practises it without any hope of fame and money, but even practises it without any hope of doing it well. [Quoted in Mackay, *The Harvest of a Quiet Eye*]

6 AM IN WOLVERHAMPTON STOP WHERE OUGHT I TO BE [Telegram to wife]

Chomsky, Noam (1928-)

7 Colourless green ideas sleep furiously. [Sentence illustrating independence of meaning and grammatical structure]

Churchill, Charles (1731-1764)

8 Though by whim, envy, or resentment led, / They damn those authors whom they never read. [*The Candidate*]

9 Thy danger chiefly lies in acting well; / No crime's so great as daring to excel. ['Epistle to William Hogarth']

10 By different methods different men excel; / But where is he who can do all things well? [Ib.]

11 It can't be Nature, for it is not sense. ['The Farewell']

12 Just to the windward of the law. [*The Ghost*, III]

13 Wise fear, you know, / Forbids the robbing of a foe; / But what, to serve our private ends, / Forbids the cheating of our friends? [Ib.]

14 He sicken'd at all triumphs but his own. [*Rosciad*]

15 So much they talk'd, so very little said. [Ib.]

16 The two extremes appear like man and wife, / Coupled together for the sake of strife. [Ib.]

Churchill, Lord Randolph (1849-1894)

17 Ulster will fight; Ulster will be right. [Letter, 1886]

18 [Of Gladstone] An old man in a hurry. [Speech, 1886]

19 [Of decimal points] I never could make out what those damned dots meant. [Quoted by Winston Churchill]

Churchill, Sir Winston (1874-1965)

20 It cannot in the opinion of His Majesty's Government be classified as slavery in the extreme acceptance of the word without some risk of terminological inexactitude. [Speech, House of Commons, 1906]

21 The maxim of the British people is 'Business as usual'. [Speech, 1914]

22 I cannot forecast to you the action of Russia. It is a riddle wrapped in a mystery inside an enigma. [Broadcast, 1939]

23 I have nothing to offer but blood, toil, tears, and sweat. [Speech, May, 1940]

24 We shall not flag or fail. We shall fight in France, we shall fight on the seas and oceans, we shall fight with growing confidence and growing strength in the air, we shall defend our island, whatever the cost may be, we shall fight on the beaches, we shall fight on the landing grounds, we shall fight in the fields and in the streets, we shall fight in the hills; we shall never surrender. [Ib. June, 1940]

25 Let us therefore brace ourselves to our duties, and so bear ourselves that, if the British Empire and its Commonwealth last for a thousand years, men will still say, 'This was their finest hour.' [Ib. June, 1940]

26 The battle of Britain is about to begin. [Ib. July, 1940]

27 Never in the field of human conflict was so much owed by so many to so few. [Ib. Aug., 1940]

1 We do not covet anything from any nation except their respect. [Broadcast to the French people, Oct., 1940]

2 Give us the tools, and we will finish the job. [Broadcast, 1941]

3 The people of London with one voice would say to Hitler, 'You do your worst, and we will do our best.' [Speech, June, 1941]

4 Do not let us speak of darker days; let us rather speak of sterner days. These are not dark days; these are great days — the greatest days our country has ever lived; and we must all thank God that we have been allowed, each of us according to our stations, to play a part in making these days memorable in the history of our race. [Speech, 1941]

5 When I warned them [the French Government] that Britain would fight on alone whatever they did, their Generals told their Prime Minister and his divided Cabinet, 'In three weeks England will have her neck wrung like a chicken.' Some chicken! Some neck! [Speech, 1941]

6 The soft underbelly of the Axis. [Speech, 1942]

7 This is not the end. It is not even the beginning of the end. But it is, perhaps, the end of the beginning. [Speech after El Alamein, 1942]

8 I have not become the King's First Minister in order to preside over the liquidation of the British Empire. [Speech, 1942]

9 The empires of the future are empires of the mind. [Speech, 1943]

10 Beware, for the time may be short. A shadow has fallen across the scenes so lately lighted by the Allied victory. Nobody knows what Soviet Russia and its Communist international organization intend to do in the immediate future. From Stettin in the Baltic to Trieste in the Adriatic an Iron Curtain has descended across the Continent. [Speech, 1946]

11 It is a good thing for an uneducated man to read books of quotations. [*My Early Life*, 9]

12 No one can guarantee success in war, but only deserve it. [*The Second World War*, II]

Cibber, Colley (1671–1757)

13 Off with his head — so much for Buckingham. [*Richard III* (adapted from Shakespeare), IV]

14 Perish the thought! [Ib. V]

15 Stolen sweets are best. [*The Rival Fools*]

Cicero, Marcus Tullius (106–43 B.C.)

16 There is nothing so absurd but some philosopher has said it. [*De Divinatione*]

17 *Salus populi suprema est lex.* The welfare of the people is the ultimate law. [*De Legibus*]

18 *Summum bonum.* The greatest good. [*De Officiis*]

19 *Cedant arma togae, concedat laurea laudi.* Let arms yield to the toga, the laurel crown to praise. [Ib.]

20 *Numquam se minus otiosum esse quam cum otiosus, nec minus solum quam solus esset.* Never less idle than when free from work, nor less alone than when completely alone. [Ib.]

21 *Otium cum dignitate.* Leisure with dignity. [*De Oratore*]

22 *Poetarum licentiae liberiora.* The freedom of poetic licence. [Ib.]

23 *Mens cuiusque is est quisque.* Each man's mind is the man himself. [*De Republica*]

24 *Quo usque, Catilina, abutere patientia nostra?* How long, O Catiline, will you abuse our patience? [*In Catilinam*]

25 *O tempora! O mores!* What an age! What customs! [Ib.]

26 *Civis Romanus sum.* I am a Roman citizen. [*In Verrem*]

27 *Silent enim leges inter arma.* Laws are inoperative in war. [*Pro Milone*]

28 *Cui bono?* Who stands to gain? [Ib.]

29 *Neminem saltare sobrius, nisi forte insanit.* No sober man dances, unless he happens to be mad. [*Pro Murena*]

1 I would rather be wrong with Plato than right with such men as these. [*Tusculan Disputations*]

Clare, John (1793–1864)

2 He could not die when the trees were green, / For he loved the time too well. ['The Dying Child']

3 I am — yet what I am, none cares or knows. ['I Am']

4 Untroubling and untroubled where I lie / The grass below, / Above, the vaulted sky. [Ib.]

5 Language has not the power to speak what love indites: / The soul lies buried in the ink that writes. [Attr.]

Clarendon, Edward Hyde, Earl of (1609–1674)

6 [Of Cromwell] He will be looked upon by posterity as a brave bad man. [*History of the Rebellion*, final words]

Clarke, Arthur Charles (1917–)

7 When a distinguished but elderly scientist states that something is possible, he is almost certainly right. When he states that something is impossible, he is very probably wrong. (Clarke's First Law.) [*Profile of the Future*]

Claudius, Matthias (1740–1815)

8 We plough the fields, and scatter / The good seed on the land, / But it is fed and watered / By God's almighty hand; / He sends the snow in winter, / The warmth to swell the grain, / The breezes and the sunshine / And soft refreshing rain. [Hymn; trans. J.M. Campbell]

Clausewitz, Karl von (1780–1831)

9 War is nothing but the continuation of politics by other means. [*On War*]

Clay, Henry (1777–1852)

10 I had rather be right than be President. [Remark, 1839]

Clemenceau, Georges (1841–1929)

11 It is far easier to make war than to make peace. [Speech, 1919]

12 America is the only nation in history which miraculously has gone directly from barbarism to degeneration without the usual interval of civilization. [Quoted in Peter, *Quotations for Our Time*]

13 Mr. Wilson bores me with his Fourteen Points; why, God Almighty has only ten. [Quoted in Wintle and Kenin, *Dictionary of Biographical Quotations*]

Cleveland, John (1613–1658)

14 Had Cain been Scot, God would have changed his doom, / Nor forced him wander, but confined him home. ['The Rebel Scot']

Clive, Lord Robert (1725–1774)

15 By God, Mr. Chairman, at this moment I stand astonished at my own moderation! [Reply during Parliamentary cross-examination, 1773]

Clough, Arthur Hugh (1819–1861)

16 I am in love, you say; I do not think so, exactly. [*Amours de Voyage*, II]

17 Whither depart the souls of the brave that die in the battle, / Die in the lost, lost fight, for the cause that perishes with them? [Ib. V]

18 They are married and gone to New Zealand. [*The Bothie of Tober-na-Vuolich*, IX]

19 My pleasure of thought is the pleasure of thinking / How pleasant it is to have money, heigh ho! / How pleasant it is to have money. [*Dipsychus*]

20 And almost everyone when age, / Disease, or sorrows strike him, / Inclines to think there is a God, / Or something very like Him. [Ib.]

21 Do not adultery commit; / Advantage rarely comes of it. ['The Latest Decalogue']

22 Thou shalt not kill; but need'st not strive / Officiously to keep alive. [Ib.]

23 Thou shalt not covet; but tradition / Approves all forms of competition. [Ib.]

1 Say not, the struggle naught availeth, / The labour and the wounds are vain, / The enemy faints not, nor faileth, / And as things have been they remain. ['Say Not, the Struggle Naught Availeth']

2 If hopes were dupes, fears may be liars. [Ib.]

3 That out of sight is out of mind / Is true of most we leave behind. [*Songs in Absence*, 'That Out of Sight']

4 Where lies the land to which the ship would go? ['Where lies the Land']

Cobbett, William (1762–1835)

5 To be poor and independent is very nearly an impossibility. [*Advice to Young Men*]

6 Nouns of number, or multitude, such as *Mob*, Parliament, Rabble, House of Commons, Regiment, Court of King's Bench, Den of Thieves and the like. [*English Grammar*, 'Syntax as Relating to Pronouns']

7 Machines are the produce of the mind of man; and their existence distinguishes the civilized man from the savage. [*Letter to the Luddites of Nottingham*]

8 From a very early age, I had imbibed the opinion, that it was every man's duty to do all that lay in his power to leave his country as good as he had found it. [*Political Register*, 1832]

9 [Of London] But what is to be the fate of the great wen of all? The monster, called...'the metropolis of the empire'? [*Rural Rides*]

Cobden, Richard (1804–1865)

10 I believe it has been said that one copy of *The Times* contains more useful information than the whole of the historical works of Thucydides. [Speech, 1850]

Cochran, Charles B. (1872–1951)

11 I still prefer a good juggler to a bad Hamlet. [*Observer*, 'Sayings of the Week', 1943]

Cockburn, Lord Henry (1779–1854)

12 [Of Robert Dundas] It was impossible not to like the owner of the look. [*Memorials*, 3]

13 It used to be said that if Hermand had made the heavens, he would have permitted us fixed stars. His constitutional animation never failed to carry him a flight beyond ordinary mortals. [Ib.]

Cocteau, Jean (1891–1963)

14 The essential in daring is to know how far one can go too far. [*Le Coq et l'Arlequin*]

15 *Victor Hugo...un fou qui se croyait Victor Hugo.* Victor Hugo...a madman who thought he was Victor Hugo. [*Opium*]

16 The worst tragedy for a poet is to be admired through being misunderstood. [*Le Rappel à L'Ordre*]

17 One does not blame an epoch; one congratulates oneself on not having belonged to it. [Ib.]

18 If it has to choose who will be crucified, the crowd will always save Barabbas. [Ib.]

19 Art is science in the flesh. [Ib.]

Coghill, Anna Louisa (1836–1907)

20 Work, for the night is coming, / When man works no more. [Hymn]

Coke, Sir Edward (1552–1634)

21 Reason is the life of the law, nay the common law itself is nothing else but reason. [*Institutes*, 'Commentary upon Littleton']

22 Syllables govern the world. [Ib.]

23 Six hours in sleep, in law's grave study six, / Four spend in prayer, the rest on Nature fix. [*Pandects*]

24 The house of everyone is to him as his castle and fortress, as well for his defence against injury and violence, as for his repose. [*Semayne's Case*]

25 We have a maxim in the House of Commons...that old ways are the safest and surest ways. [Speech, 1628]

Coleridge, Samuel Taylor (1772–1834)

1 It is an ancient Mariner, / And he stoppeth one of three. / 'By thy long grey beard and glittering eye, / Now wherefore stopp'st thou me?' [*The Ancient Mariner*, 1]

2 He holds him with his glittering eye — / The Wedding-Guest stood still, / And listens like a three-years' child: / The Mariner hath his will. [Ib.]

3 The Wedding-Guest here beat his breast, / For he heard the loud bassoon. [Ib.]

4 With my cross-bow / I shot the Albatross. [Ib.]

5 The fair breeze blew, the white foam flew, / The furrow followed free; / We were the first that ever burst / Into that silent sea. [Ib. 2]

6 As idle as a painted ship / Upon a painted ocean. [Ib.]

7 Water, water, everywhere, / And all the boards did shrink; / Water, water, everywhere, / Nor any drop to drink. [Ib.]

8 Yea, slimy things did crawl with legs / Upon the slimy sea. [Ib.]

9 The Sun's rim dips; the stars rush out: / At one stride comes the dark. [Ib. 3]

10 'I fear thee, ancient Mariner! / I fear thy skinny hand! / And thou art long, and lank, and brown, / As is the ribbed sea-sand.' [Ib. 4]

11 Alone, alone, all, all alone, / Alone on a wide, wide sea! / And never a soul took pity on / My soul in agony. [Ib.]

12 A spring of love gushed from my heart, / And I blessed them unawares. [Ib.]

13 Oh! Sleep it is a gentle thing / Beloved from pole to pole, / To Mary Queen the praise be given! / She sent the gentle sleep from Heaven, / That slid into my soul. [Ib. 5]

14 Then like a pawing horse let go, / She made a sudden bound. [Ib.]

15 Like one, that on a lonesome road / Doth walk in fear and dread, / And having once turned round walks on, / And turns no more his head; Because he knows, a frightful fiend / Doth close behind him tread. [Ib. 6]

16 He prayeth best, who loveth best / All things both great and small; / For the dear God who loveth us, / He made and loveth all. [Ib. 7]

17 A sadder and a wiser man, / He rose the morrow morn. [Ib.]

18 Alas! they had been friends in youth; / But whispering tongues can poison truth. [*Christabel*]

19 Often do the spirits / Of great events stride on before the events, / And in to-day already walks to-morrow. ['Death of Wallenstein']

20 Well! If the Bard was weatherwise, who made / The grand old ballad of Sir Patrick Spence. ['Dejection']

21 I may not hope from outward forms to win / The passion and the life, whose fountains are within. [Ib.]

22 For what is freedom, but the unfettered use / Of all the powers which God for use had given? ['The Destiny of Nations']

23 From his brimstone bed at break of day / A walking the Devil is gone, / To visit his snug little farm the Earth, / And see how his stock goes on. ['The Devil's Thoughts']

24 And the Devil did grin, for his darling sin / Is pride that apes humility. [Ib.]

25 What is an Epigram? a dwarfish whole, / Its body brevity, and wit its soul. ['Epigram']

26 Swans sing before they die — 'twere no bad thing / Should certain persons die before they sing. ['Epigram on a Volunteer Singer']

27 [Of Britain, 1798] A vain, speech-mouthing, speech-reporting guild, / One benefit-club for mutual flattery. ['Fears in Solitude']

28 All adoration of the God in nature, / All lovely and all honourable things, / Whatever makes this mortal spirit feel / The joy and greatness of its future being? / There lives nor form nor feeling in my soul / Unborrowed from my country. [Ib.]

29 The frost performs its secret ministry, / Unhelped by any wind. ['Frost at Midnight']

1 The secret ministry of frost / Shall hand them up in silent icicles, / Quietly shining to the quiet moon. [Ib.]

2 He was unfortunately called out by a person on business from Porlock. ['Kubla Khan', Preliminary note]

3 In Xanadu did Kubla Khan / A stately pleasure-dome decree: / Where Alph, the sacred river, ran / Through caverns measureless to man / Down to a sunless sea. ['Kubla Khan']

4 Woman wailing for her demon-lover. [Ib.]

5 And 'mid this tumult Kubla heard from far / Ancestral voices prophesying war! [Ib.]

6 A damsel with a dulcimer / In a vision once I saw. [Ib.]

7 And close your eyes with holy dread, / For he on honey-dew hath fed, / And drunk the milk of Paradise. [Ib.]

8 Trochee trips from long to short; / From long to long in solemn sort / Slow Spondee stalks; strong foot! yet ill able / Ever to come up with Dactyl trisyllable. / Iambics march from short to long; — / With a leap and a bound the swift Anapaests throng. ['Metrical Feet']

9 With Donne, whose muse on dromedary trots, / Wreathe iron pokers into true-love knots; / Rhyme's sturdy cripple, fancy's maze and clue, / Wit's forge and fire-blast, meaning's press and screw. ['On Donne's Poetry']

10 Ah! far removed from all that glads the sense, / From all that softens or ennobles Man, The wretched Many! ['Religious Musings']

11 The innumerable multitude of Wrongs / By man on man inflicted. [Ib.]

12 He who begins by loving Christianity better than Truth will proceed by loving his own sect or church better than Christianity, and end by loving himself better than all. [*Aids to Reflection: Moral and Religious Aphorisms*]

13 The primary imagination I hold to be the living power and prime agent of all human perception, and as a repetition in the finite mind of the eternal act of creation in the infinite I AM. The secondary imagination ...dissolves, diffuses, dissipates, in order to recreate; or where this process is rendered impossible, yet still at all events it struggles to idealize and to unify. [*Biographia Literaria*]

14 Fancy, on the contrary, has no other counters to play with, but fixities and definites. The fancy is indeed no other than a mode of memory emancipated from the order of time and space. [Ib.]

15 That willing suspension of disbelief for the moment, which constitutes poetic faith. [Ib.]

16 Our myriad-minded Shakespeare. [Ib.]

17 No man was ever yet a great poet, without being at the same time a profound philosopher. [Ib.]

18 The dwarf sees farther than the giant, when he has the giant's shoulder to mount on. [*The Friend*]

19 Reviewers are usually people who would have been poets, historians, biographers, etc., if they could; they have tried their talents at one or at the other, and have failed; therefore they turn critics. [Lecture on Shakespeare and Milton]

20 [Of Iago] The motive-hunting of motiveless malignity. [*Notes on the Tragedies of Shakespeare*, 'Othello']

21 A Fall of some sort or other — the creation as it were, of the non-absolute — is the fundamental postulate of the moral history of man. Without this hypothesis, man is unintelligible; with it, every phenomenon is explicable. [*Table-Talk*]

22 [Of Edmund Kean] To see him act is like reading Shakespeare by flashes of lightning. [Ib.]

23 [Of Swift] The soul of Rabelais dwelling in a dry place. [Ib.]

1 I wish our clever young poets would remember my homely definitions of prose and poetry; that is prose = words in their best order; poetry = the best words in their best order. [Ib.]

2 Talk not with scorn of Authors — it was the chattering of the Geese that saved the Capitol. [*Notebooks*]

3 Men, I think, have to be weighed, not counted. [Quoted in Mackay, *The Harvest of a Quiet Eye*]

Collingbourne, William (d. 1484)

4 The Cat, the Rat, and Lovell our dog, / Rulen all England under an Hog. [Comment on Richard III]

Collingwood, Robin George (1889–1943)

5 Perfect freedom is reserved for the man who lives by his own work and in that work does what he wants to do. [*Speculum Mentis*]

Collins, John Churton (1848–1908)

6 To ask advice is in nine cases out of ten to tout for flattery. [*Maxims and Reflections*]

Collins, Mortimer (1827–1876)

7 A man is as old as he's feeling, / A woman as old as she looks. ['The Unknown Quantity']

Collins, William (1721–1759)

8 If aught of oaten stop, or pastoral song, / May hope, O pensive Eve, to soothe thine ear. ['Ode to Evening']

9 How sleep the brave, who sink to rest, / By all their country's wishes blest! ['Ode Written in the Year 1746']

10 By fairy hands their knell is rung, / By forms unseen their dirge is sung. [Ib.]

11 Too nicely Jonson knew the critic's part, / Nature in him was almost lost in Art. ['Verses to Sir Thomas Hanmer']

Colman, George, the Younger (1762–1836)

12 Not to be sneezed at. [*The Heir at Law*, II]

13 Says he, 'I am a handsome man, but I'm a gay deceiver.' [*Love Laughs at Locksmiths*, II]

Colson, Charles (1931–)

14 I would walk over my grandmother if necessary to get Nixon re-elected. [Attr.]

Colton, Charles Caleb (c. 1780–1832)

15 When you have nothing to say, say nothing. [*Lacon*]

16 Imitation is the sincerest form of flattery. [Ib.]

17 Examinations are formidable even to the best prepared, for the greatest fool may ask more than the wisest man can answer. [Ib.]

18 Man is an embodied paradox, a bundle of contradictions. [Ib.]

19 Friendship often ends in love; but love in friendship — never. [Ib.]

20 Subtract from many modern poets all that may be found in Shakespeare, and trash will remain. [Ib.]

21 Some read to think, — these are rare; some to unite, — these are common; and some to talk, — and these form the great majority. [Ib.]

22 Of the professions it may be said that soldiers are becoming too popular, parsons too lazy, physicians too mercenary, and lawyers too powerful. [Ib.]

23 True contentment depends not on what we have; a tub was large enough for Diogenes, but a world was too little for Alexander. [Ib.]

Confucius (c. 550–c. 478 B.C.)

24 True goodness springs from a man's own heart. All men are born good. [*Analects*]

25 An oppressive government is more to be feared than a tiger. [Ib.]

26 Things that are done, it is needless to speak about...Things that are past, it is needless to blame. [Ib.]

27 The cautious seldom err. [Ib.]

1 Virtue is not left to stand alone. He who practises it will have neighbours. [Ib.]

2 What you do not want done to yourself, do not do to others. [Ib.]

3 Gravity is only the bark of wisdom's tree, but it preserves it. [Ib.]

4 Men's natures are alike; it is their habits that carry them far apart. [Ib.]

5 The mirror reflects all objects, without being sullied. [Ib.]

6 Study the past, if you would divine the future. [Ib.]

7 The scholar who cherishes the love of comfort, is not fit to be deemed a scholar. [Ib.]

8 The heart of the wise, like a mirror, should reflect all objects without being sullied by any. [Ib.]

9 Learning without thought is labour lost; thought without learning is perilous. [Ib.]

10 What the superior man seeks is in himself: what the small man seeks is in others. [Ib.]

11 In all things, success depends upon previous preparation, and without such preparation there is sure to be failure. [Ib.]

12 For one word a man is often deemed to be wise, and for one word he is often deemed to be foolish. We should be careful indeed what we say. [Ib.]

13 Everything has its beauty but not everyone sees it. [Ib.]

14 They must often change who would be constant in happiness or wisdom. [Ib.]

15 Without knowing the force of words, it is impossible to know men. [Ib.]

16 To see what is right and not to do it is want of courage. [Ib.]

17 Better a diamond with a flaw than a pebble without. [Ib.]

Congreve, William (1670–1729)

18 Retired to their tea and scandal, according to their ancient custom. [*The Double Dealer*, I.1]

19 She lays it on with a trowel. [Ib. III.10]

20 See how love and murder will out. [Ib. IV.6]

21 No mask like open truth to cover lies, / As to go naked is the best disguise. [Ib. V]

22 Music alone with sudden charms can bind / The wandering sense, and calm the troubled mind. ['Hymn to Harmony']

23 I am always of the opinion with the learned, if they speak first. [*Incognita*]

24 I know that's a secret, for it's whispered everywhere. [*Love for Love*, III.3]

25 Music has charms to soothe a savage breast. [*The Mourning Bride*, I.1]

26 Heav'n has no rage, like love to hatred turn'd, Nor Hell a fury, like a woman scorn'd. [Ib. III.8]

27 Even silence may be eloquent in love. [*The Old Bachelor*, II.2]

28 Thus grief still treads upon the heels of pleasure: / Married in haste, we may repent at leisure. [Ib. V.8]

29 Courtship to marriage, as a very witty prologue to a very dull Play. [Ib. V.10]

30 Alack, he's gone the way of all flesh. ['*Squire Bickerstaff Detected* (Attr.)]

31 Beauty is the lover's gift. [*The Way of the World*, II.4]

32 A little disdain is not amiss; a little scorn is alluring. [Ib. III.5]

33 I nauseate walking; 'tis a country diversion, I loathe the country. [Ib. IV.4]

34 Let us be as strange as if we had been married a great while, and as well-bred as if we were not married at all. [Ib. IV.5]

35 I hate your odious provisoes. [Ib. V.5]

36 These articles subscrib'd, if I continue to endure you a little longer, I may by degrees dwindle into a wife. [Ib.]

Connolly, Cyril (1903–1974)

37 Whom the gods wish to destroy they first call promising. [*Enemies of Promise*]

1 There is no more sombre enemy of good art than the pram in the hall. [Ib.]

2 Imprisoned in every fat man a thin one is wildly signalling to be let out. [*The Unquiet Grave*]

Conrad, Joseph (1857-1924)

3 Proverbs are art — cheap art. As a general rule they are not true; unless indeed they happen to be mere platitudes. [*Gaspar Ruiz*]

4 Mistah Kurtz — he dead. [*The Heart of Darkness*]

5 The horror! The horror! [Ib.]

6 In the destructive element immerse. [*Lord Jim*]

7 Don't talk to me of your Archimedes' lever...Give me the right word and the right accent and I will move the world. [*A Personal Record*, Preface]

8 All ambitions are lawful except those which climb upward on the miseries or credulities of mankind. [Ib.]

9 The terrorist and the policeman both come from the same basket. [*The Secret Agent*]

10 The fatal imperfection of all the gifts of life, which makes of them a delusion and a snare. [*Victory*]

Constantine, Emperor (c. A.D. 288-337)

11 *In hoc signo vinces.* In this sign thou shalt conquer. [Attr. words of Constantine's vision, A.D. 312]

Cook, A.J. (1885-1931)

12 Not a minute on the day, not a penny off the pay. [Slogan used during General Strike, 1926]

Cook, Eliza (1818-1889)

13 I love it, I love it; and who shall dare / To chide me for loving that old armchair? ['The Old Armchair']

Cook, James (1728-1778)

14 Altho' the discoveries made in this Voyage are not great, yet I flatter myself that they are such as may merit the attention of their Lordships, and altho' I have failed in discovering the so much talk'd of southern Continent (which perhaps do not exist) and which I myself had so much at heart, yet I am confident that no part of the failure of such discovery can be laid at my Charge. [Letter reporting on *Endeavour* expedition, 1770]

15 I presume this Voyage will be found as Compleat as any before made to the South Seas, on the same account. [Ib.]

Coolidge, Calvin (1872-1933)

16 The governments of the past could fairly be characterized as devices for maintaining in perpetuity the place and position of certain privileged classes...The Government of the United States is a device for maintaining in perpetuity the rights of the people, with the ultimate extinction of all privileged classes. [Speech, 1924]

17 The business of America is business. [Speech, 1925]

18 They hired the money, didn't they? [Remark on Allied war debts, 1925]

Corneille, Pierre (1606-1684)

19 We triumph without glory when we conquer without danger. [*Le Cid*]

20 *Et enfin la clémence est la plus belle marque / Qui fasse à l'univers connaître un vrai monarque.* Ultimately, mercy is the surest sign by which the world may distinguish a true king. [*Cinna*]

21 He who allows himself to be insulted, deserves to be. [*Héraclius*]

22 *Faites votre devoir et laissez faire aux dieux.* Do your duty, and leave the rest to the Gods. [*Horace*]

Cornfeld, Bernard (1927-)

23 Do You Sincerely Want to be Rich? [Title of book]

Cornford, Frances Crofts (1886–1960)

1 O fat white woman whom nobody loves, / Why do you walk through the fields in gloves? ['To a Fat Lady Seen from a Train']

2 Magnificently unprepared / For the long littleness of life. ['Rupert Brooke']

Cornuel, Madame Anne Bigot de (1605–1694)

3 *Il n'y a point de grand homme pour son valet de chambre.* No man is a hero to his valet. [Attr. (Similar sentiments attr. to Antigonus Gonatas, King of Thessaly, Madame de Sévigné, Nicolas Catinat, Goethe, and Montaigne.)]

Cory, William (1823–1892)

4 Jolly boating weather, / And a hay harvest breeze / ...Swing, swing together / With your body between your knees. ['Eton Boating Song']

Coué, Emile (1857–1926)

5 *Tous les jours, à tous points de vue, je vais de mieux en mieux.* Every day, in every way, I am getting better and better. [Motto]

Cousin, Victor (1792–1867)

6 *Il faut de la religion pour la religion, de la morale pour la morale, comme de l'art pour l'art.* We must have religion for religion's sake, morality for morality's sake, as with art for art's sake. [Lecture, 1818]

Coventry, Thomas, Baron (1578–1640)

7 Our wooden walls are the strength and safety of our kingdom. [Speech in Star Chamber, 1635]

Coward, Sir Noël (1899–1973)

8 Life without faith is an arid business. [*Blithe Spirit*, I]

9 Time is the reef upon which all our frail mystic ships are wrecked. [Ib.]

10 I don't give a hoot about posterity. Why should I worry about what people think of me when I'm dead as a doornail anyway? [*Present Laughter*, I]

11 Everybody worships me, it's nauseating. [Ib.]

12 Very flat, Norfolk. [*Private Lives*, I]

13 Extraordinary how potent cheap music is. [Ib.]

14 Certain women should be struck regularly, like gongs. [Ib. III]

15 Comedies of manners swiftly become obsolete when there are no longer any manners. [*Relative Values*, I]

16 Don't let's be beastly to the Germans. ['Don't Let's Be Beastly to the Germans']

17 Mad about the boy, / It's pretty funny but I'm mad about the boy. ['Mad about the Boy']

18 Mad dogs and Englishmen go out in the mid-day sun. ['Mad Dogs and Englishmen']

19 Don't put your daughter on the stage, Mrs. Worthington. ['Mrs. Worthington']

Cowley, Abraham (1618–1667)

20 Love in her sunny Eyes does basking play; / Love walks the pleasant Mazes of her Hair. ['The Change']

21 Fill all the glasses there, for why / Should every creature drink but I, / Why man of morals, tell me why? ['Drinking']

22 God the first garden made, and the first city Cain. ['The Garden']

23 His faith perhaps, in some nice Tenets might / Be wrong; his Life I'm sure, was in the right. ['On the Death of Mr. Crashaw']

24 Life is an incurable disease. ['To Dr. Scarborough']

25 Well then; I now do plainly see / The busy world and I shall ne'er agree. ['The Wish']

1 Ah, yet, e'er I descend to th' grave / May I a small house, and a large garden have! / And a few friends, and many books, both true, / Both wise, and both delightful too! / And since Love ne'er will from me flee, / A Mistress moderately fair, / And good as guardian angels are, / Only belov'd, and loving me! [Ib.]

Cowley, Hannah (1743-1809)

2 Five minutes! Zounds! I have been five minutes too late all my life-time. [*The Belle's Stratagem*, I]

3 But what is woman? — only one of Nature's agreeable blunders. [*Who's the Dupe?*, II]

Cowper, William (1731-1800)

4 But misery still delights to trace / Its semblance in another's case. ['The Castaway']

5 We perished, each alone: / But I beneath a rougher sea, / And whelmed in deeper gulfs than he. [Ib.]

6 Grief is itself a med'cine. [*Charity*]

7 He found it inconvenient to be poor. [Ib.]

8 Pelting each other for the public good. [Ib.]

9 A fool must now and then be right, by chance. ['Conversation']

10 A noisy man is always in the right. [Ib.]

11 Pernicious weed! whose scent the fair annoys, / Unfriendly to society's chief joys, / Thy worst effect is banishing for hours / The sex whose presence civilizes ours. [Ib.]

12 War lays a burden on the reeling state, / And peace does nothing to relieve the weight. [*Expostulation*]

13 Thousands... / Kiss the book's outside who ne'er look within. [Ib.]

14 And diff'ring judgments serve but to declare / That truth lies somewhere, if we knew but where. [*Hope*]

15 For loss of time, / Although it griev'd him sore, / Yet loss of pence, full well he knew, / Would trouble him much more. ['John Gilpin']

16 O'erjoyed was he to find / That, though on pleasure she was bent, / She had a frugal mind. [Ib.]

17 Oh! for a closer walk with God. [*Olney Hymns*, 1]

18 What peaceful hours I once enjoyed! / How sweet their memory still! / But they have left an aching void, / The world can never fill. [Ib.]

19 Can a woman's tender care / Cease towards the child she bare? [Ib. 18]

20 And Satan trembles when he sees / The weakest saint upon his knees. [Ib. 29]

21 God moves in a mysterious way / His wonders to perform. [Ib. 35]

22 Judge not the Lord by feeble sense, / But trust him for his grace; / Behind a frowning providence / He hides a smiling face. [Ib.]

23 God is his own interpreter, / And he will make it plain. [Ib.]

24 Sometimes a light surprises / The Christian while he sings; / It is the Lord who rises / With healing in His wings. [Ib. 49]

25 Toll for the brave — / The brave! that are no more: / All sunk beneath the wave, / Fast by their native shore. ['On the Loss of the Royal George']

26 How much a dunce that has been sent to roam / Excels a dunce that has been kept at home. [*The Progress of Error*]

27 The poplars are felled, farewell to the shade, / And the whispering sound of the cool colonnade! ['The Poplar Field']

28 I am monarch of all I survey, / My right there is none to dispute. ['The Solitude of Alexander Selkirk']

29 O solitude! where are the charms / That sages have seen in thy face? [Ib.]

30 [Pope] Made poetry a mere mechanic art; / And ev'ry warbler has his tune by heart. [*Table Talk*]

31 Freedom has a thousand charms to show, / That slaves, howe'er contented, never know. [Ib.]

1 Stamps God's own name upon a lie just made / To turn a penny in the way of trade. [Ib.]

2 God made the country, and man made the town. [*The Task*, I, 'The Sofa']

3 Variety's the very spice of life, / That gives all its flavour. [Ib. II, 'The Timepiece']

4 Slaves cannot breathe in England, if their lungs / Receive our air, that moment they are free; / They touch our country, and their shackles fall. [Ib.]

5 England, with all thy faults, I love thee still. [Ib.]

6 Domestic happiness, thou only bliss / Of Paradise that has surviv'd the fall! [Ib. III, 'The Garden']

7 I was a stricken deer, that left the herd / Long since. [Ib.]

8 Detested sport, / That owes its pleasures to another's pain. [Ib.]

9 Who loves a garden loves a greenhouse too. [Ib.]

10 The cups, / That cheer but not inebriate. [Ib. IV]

11 Knowledge is proud that he has learn'd so much; / Wisdom is humble that he knows no more. [Ib.]

12 Nature is but a name for an effect, / Whose cause is God. [Ib.]

13 A cheap but wholesome salad from the brook. [Ib.]

Crabbe, George (1754–1832)

14 Habit with him was all the test of truth, / 'It must be right: I've done it from my youth.' [*The Borough*, 'The Vicar']

15 This books can do — nor this alone: they give / New views to life, and teach us how to live; / They soothe the grieved, the stubborn they chastise; / Fools they admonish, and confirm the wise, / Their aid they yield to all: they never shun / The man of sorrow, nor the wretch undone; / Unlike the hard, the selfish, and the proud, / They fly not from the suppliant crowd; / Nor tell to various people various things, / But show to subjects, what they show to kings. [*The Library*]

16 A master-passion is the love of news. [*The Newspaper*]

17 Secrets with girls, like loaded guns with boys, / Are never valued till they make a noise. [*Tales of the Hall*, 'The Maid's Story']

18 'The game,' he said, 'is never lost till won.' [Ib. 'Gretna Green']

Cranmer, Thomas (1489–1556)

19 This is the hand that wrote it and therefore it shall suffer first punishment. [At the stake, 1556]

Crashaw, Richard (c. 1612–1649)

20 Love, thou art absolute sole Lord / Of life and death. ['Hymn to St. Teresa']

21 I would be married, but I'd have no wife, / I would be married to a single life. ['On Marriage']

22 ...two faithful fountains; / Two walking baths; two weeping motions; / Portable, and compendious oceans. ['The Weeper']

23 Two went to pray? O rather say / One went to brag, th'other to pray. [*Steps to the Temple*, 'Two went up into the Temple to Pray']

24 All is Caesar's; and what odds / So long as Caesar's self is God's? [Ib. 'Mark 12']

25 And when life's sweet fable ends, / Soul and body part like friends; / No quarrels, murmurs, no delay; / A kiss, a sigh, and so away. ['Temperance']

26 Whoe'er she be, / That not impossible she / That shall command my heart and me. ['Wishes to His Supposed Mistress']

27 A face made up, / Out of no other shop / Than what nature's white hand sets ope. [Ib.]

28 A Cheek where grows / More than a Morning Rose: / Which to no Box his being owes. [Ib.]

29 Lips, where all Day / A lover's kiss may play, / Yet carry nothing thence away. [Ib.]

Creighton, Mandell (1843–1901)

30 No people do so much harm as those who go about doing good. [*Life*, 1904]

Croker, John Wilson (1780–1857)

1 A game which a sharper once played with a dupe, entitled, 'Heads I win, tails you lose.' [*Croker Papers*]

2 We now are, as we always have been, decidedly and conscientiously attached to what is called the Tory, and which might with more propriety be called the Conservative, party. [*Quarterly Review*, 1830]

Cromwell, Oliver (1599–1658)

3 I beseech you, in the bowels of Christ think it possible you may be mistaken. [Letter to the General Assembly of the Church of Scotland, 1650]

4 The dimensions of this mercy are above my thoughts. It is, for aught I know, a crowning mercy. [Letter, 1651]

5 [Referring to the mace] What shall we do with the bauble? Take it away! [Remark on dissolving Parliament, 1653]

6 You have sat too long here for any good you have been doing. Depart, I say, and let us have done with you. In the name of God, go! [Ib.]

7 Necessity hath no law. [Speech, 1654]

8 You have accounted yourselves happy on being environed with a great ditch from all the world beside. [Ib. 1658]

9 Mr. Lely, I desire you would use all your skill to paint my picture freely like me, and not flatter me at all; but remark all these roughnesses, pimples, warts, and everything as you see me, otherwise I will never pay a farthing for it. [Remark]

10 Not what they want but what is good for them. [Attr. remark]

Cummings, E.E. (1894–1962)

11 anyone lived in a pretty how town / (with up so floating many bells down) / spring summer autumn winter / he sang his didn't he danced his did. ['anyone lived in a pretty how town']

12 'next to of course god america i / love you land of the pilgrims' and so forth oh. ['next to of course god']

13 listen: there's a hell / of a good universe next door; let's go. ['pity this busy monster, manunkind']

14 who pays any attention / to the syntax of things / will never wholly kiss you. ['since feeling is first']

Cunningham, Allan (1784–1842)

15 The lark shall sing me hame in my ain countree. ['It's Hame and It's Hame']

16 Wha the deil hae we got for a King, / But a wee, wee German lairdie! ['The Wee, Wee German Lairdie']

17 A wet sheet and a flowing sea, / A wind that follows fast / And fills the white and rustling sail / And bends the gallant mast. ['A Wet Sheet and a Flowing Sea']

18 ...the hollow oak our palace is, / Our heritage the sea. [Ib.]

Curran, John Philpot (1750–1817)

19 The condition upon which God hath given liberty to man is eternal vigilance; which condition if he break, servitude is at once the consequence of his crime, and the punishment of his guilt. [Speech, 1790]

Cyprian, St. (d. 258)

20 *Habere non potest Deum patrem qui ecclesiam non habet matrem.* He cannot have God as his father who has not the Church as his mother. [*De Unitate Ecclesiae*]

21 *Salus extra ecclesiam non est.* There is no salvation outside the Church. [Letter]

Dali, Salvador (1904–)

22 There is only one difference between a madman and me. I am not mad. [Remark, 1956]

Dana, Charles Anderson (1819–1897)

23 All the goodness of a good egg cannot make up for the badness of a bad one. [*The Making of a Newspaper Man*]

24 When a dog bites a man that is not news, but when a man bites a dog that is news. [*New York Sun*, 1882]

Dante Alighieri (1265–1321)

1 *Nel mezzo del cammin di nostra vita.* In the middle of the road of our life. [*Inferno*, 1]

2 *Lasciate ogni speranza voi ch'entrate.* Abandon hope, all ye who enter here. [Ib. 3]

3 *Questi non hanno speranza di morte.* These have not hope of death. [Ib.]

4 *Il gran rifiuto.* The great refusal. [Ib.]

5 *L'arte vostra quella, quanto puote, / Segue, come il maestro fa il discente, / Si che vostr'arte a Dio quasi è nipote.* Art, as far as it can, follows nature, as a pupil imitates his master; thus your art must be, as it were, God's grandchild. [Ib. 11]

6 *Onorate l'altissimo poeta.* Honour the greatest poet. [Ib.]

7 *Ahi fiera compagnia! ma nella chiesa / Coi santi ed in taverna coi ghiottoni.* Ah, proud company! In church with saints and in taverns with gluttons. [Ib. 22]

8 *Chè, seggendo in piuma, / In fama non si vien, nè sotto coltre.* For fame is not won by lying on a feather bed nor under a canopy. [Ib. 24]

9 *E cortesia fu in lui esser villano.* To be rude to him was courtesy. [Ib. 33]

10 *E'n la sua volontade e nostra pace.* In His will is our peace. [*Paradiso*, 3]

11 *Tu proverai si come sa di sale / Lo pane altrui, e com' è duro calle / Lo scendere e il salir per l'altrui scale.* You will find how salt is the taste of another's bread, and how hard is the way up and down another's stairs. [Ib. 17]

12 *Vien, retro a me, e lascia dir le genti.* Come, follow me and leave the world to chatter. [*Purgatorio*, 5]

13 *Sta come torre ferma, che non crolla / Giammai la cima per soffiar de' venti.* Be as a strong tower, that never bows its head to the force of the wind. [Ib.]

Danton, Georges (1759–1794)

14 *De l'audace, et encore de l'audace, et toujours de l'audace!* Boldness and more boldness, and always boldness! [Speech, 1792]

15 My address will soon be Annihilation. As for my name you will find it in the Pantheon of History. [Response at his trial, 1794]

Darwin, Charles (1809–1882)

16 We must, however, acknowledge, as it seems to me, that man with all his noble qualities...still bears in his bodily frame the indelible stamp of his lowly origin. [*Descent of Man*, conclusion]

17 Believing as I do that man in the distant future will be a far more perfect creature than he now is, it is an intolerable thought that he and all other sentient beings are doomed to complete annihilation after such long-continued slow progress. To those who fully admit the immortality of the human soul, the destruction of our world will not appear so dreadful. [*Life and Letters*]

18 I have called this principle, by which each slight variation, if useful, is preserved, by the term of Natural Selection. [*The Origin of Species*, 3]

19 The struggle for existence. [Ib.]

20 The expression often used by Mr. Herbert Spencer of the Survival of the Fittest is more accurate, and is sometimes equally convenient. [Ib.]

Daudet, Alphonse (1840–1897)

21 *Des coups d'épée, messieurs, des coups d'épée! Mais pas de coups d'épingle!* Strokes of the sword, gentlemen, strokes of the sword! Not pin pricks! [*Tartarin de Tarascon*, 1]

Davenant, Charles (1656–1714)

22 Custom, that unwritten law, / By which the people keep even kings in awe. [*Circe*, II]

Davenant, William (1606–1668)

23 Frail Life! in which, through Mists of human breath, / We grope for Truth, and make our Progress slow. ['The Christians Reply to the Philosopher']

24 I shall sleep like a top. [*The Rivals*, III]

1 For I must go where lazy Peace / Will hide her drowsy head; / And, for the sport of kings, increase / The number of the dead. ['The Soldier Going to the Field']

Davidson, John (1857–1909)

2 'In shuttered rooms let others grieve, / And coffin thought in speech of lead; / I'll tie my heart upon my sleeve: / It is the Badge of Men,' he said. ['The Badge of Men']

3 He wrought at one great work for years; / The world passed by with lofty look: / Sometimes his eyes were dashed with tears; / Sometimes his lips with laughter shook. ['A Ballad of Heaven']

4 He doubted; but God said 'Even so; / Nothing is lost that's wrought with tears: / The music that you made below / Is now the music of the spheres.' [Ib.]

5 Seraphs and saints with one great voice / Welcomed the soul that knew not fear; / Amazed to find it could rejoice, / Hell raised a hoarse, half-human cheer. ['A Ballad of Hell']

6 He cursed the canting moralist, / Who measures right and wrong. ['A Ballad of a Poet Born']

7 'My time is filched by toil and sleep; / My heart,' he thought, 'is clogged with dust; / My soul that flashed from out the deep, / A magic blade, begins to rust.' ['A Ballad of a Workman']

8 For this was in the North, where Time stands still / And Change holds holiday, where Old and New / Welter upon the Borders of the world, / And savage faith works woe. ['A Ballad in Blank Verse on the Making of a Poet']

Davies, Sir John (1569–1626)

9 Skill comes so slow, and life so fast doth fly, / We learn so little and forget so much. [*Nosce Teipsum*, Introduction]

10 Judge not the play before the play be done. ['Respice Finem']

Davies, William Henry (1870–1940)

11 A rainbow and a cuckoo's song / May never come together again; / May never come / This side the tomb. ['A Great Time']

12 What is this life if, full of care, / We have no time to stand and stare? ['Leisure']

Davis, Bette (1908–)

13 Fasten your seat belts, it's going to be a bumpy night. [*All About Eve*]

14 [Of a starlet] I see — she's the original good time that was had by all. [Quoted in Halliwell, *Filmgoers' Book of Quotes*]

Davis, Jefferson (1808–1889)

15 All we ask is to be let alone. [Attr. remark in Inaugural Address as President of Confederate States of America, 1861]

Davis, Sammy, Junior (1925–)

16 Being a star has made it possible for me to get insulted in places where the average Negro could never hope to get insulted. [*Yes I can*]

Debs, Eugene Victor (1855–1926)

17 While there is a lower class, I am in it. While there is a criminal class I am of it. While there is a soul in prison, I am not free. [*Labor and Freedom*]

Decatur, Stephen (1779–1820)

18 Our country! In her intercourse with foreign nations, may she always be in the right; but our country, right or wrong. [Mackenzie, *Life of Decatur*]

Defoe, Daniel (c. 1661–1731)

19 The best of men cannot suspend their fate: / The good die early, and the bad die late. ['Character of the late Dr. S. Annesley']

20 Nature has left this tincture in the blood, / That all men would be tyrants if they could. ['The Kentish Petition']

1 Wherever God erects a house of prayer, / The Devil always builds a chapel there; / And 'twill be found, upon examination, / The latter has the largest congregation. [*The True-Born Englishman*, I]

2 Your Roman-Saxon-Danish-Norman English. [Ib.]

3 From this amphibious, ill-born mob began / That vain, ill-natur'd thing, an Englishman. [Ib.]

4 And of all plagues with which mankind are curst, / Ecclesiastic tyranny's the worst. [Ib. II]

5 When kings the sword of justice first lay down, / They are no kings, though they possess the crown. / Titles are shadows, crowns are empty things, / The good of subjects is the end of kings. [Ib.]

6 Robin, Robin, Robin Crusoe, poor Robin Crusoe! Where are you, Robin Crusoe? Where are you? Where have you been? [*The Life and Adventures of Robinson Crusoe*, I]

7 It happened one day, about noon, going towards my boat, I was exceedingly surprised with the print of a man's naked foot on the shore, which was very plain to be seen in the sand. I stood like one thunderstruck, or as if I had seen an apparition. [Ib.]

8 Necessity makes an honest man a knave. [*Serious Reflections of Robinson Crusoe*]

De Gaulle, Charles (1890–1970)

9 *Vive le Québec! Vive le Québec libre!* Long live Quebec! Long live free Quebec! [Speech, Quebec, 1967]

Dekker, Thomas (c. 1570–c. 1641)

10 The best of men / That e'er wore earth about him, was a sufferer / A soft, meek, patient, humble, tranquil spirit, / The first true gentleman that ever breath'd. [*The Honest Whore*, I]

11 Golden slumbers kiss your eyes, / Smiles awake you when you rise. [*Patient Grissill*, I]

12 Art thou poor, yet hast thou golden slumbers? / Oh sweet content! / Art thou rich, yet is thy mind perplexed? / Oh, punishment! [Ib.]

De La Mare, Walter (1873–1956)

13 Ann, Ann! / Come! quick as you can! / There's a fish that *talks* / In the frying-pan. ['Alas, Alack']

14 He is crazed with the spell of far Arabia, / They have stolen his wits away. ['Arabia']

15 Nought but vast sorrow was there — / The sweet cheat gone. ['The Ghost']

16 I met at eve the Prince of Sleep, / His was a still and lovely face, / He wandered through a valley steep, / Lovely in a lonely place. ['I Met at Eve']

17 'Is there anybody there?' said the traveller, / Knocking on the moonlit door. ['The Listeners']

18 'Tell them that I came, and no one answered, / That I kept my word,' he said. [Ib.]

19 It's a very odd thing — / As odd as can be — / That whatever Miss T eats / Turns into Miss T. ['Miss T']

20 Slowly, silently, now the moon / Walks the night in her silver shoon. ['Silver']

De Mille, Cecil B. (1881–1959)

21 The public is always right. [Quoted in Colombo, *Wit and Wisdom of the Moviemakers*]

Demosthenes (385–322 B.C.)

22 I decline to buy repentance at the cost of ten thousand drachmas. [Aulus Gellius, *Noctes Atticae*]

23 The easiest thing of all is to deceive one's self; for what a man wishes he generally believes to be true. [*Olynthiaca*, 3]

24 There is one safeguard known generally to the wise, which is an advantage and security to all, but especially to democracies against despots — suspicion. [*Philippics*, 2]

Denham, John (1615–1669)

25 Oh, could I flow like thee, and make thy stream / My great example, as it is my theme! / Though deep yet clear, though gentle yet not dull; / Strong without rage, without o'erflowing full. [*Cooper's Hill*]

Dennis, John (1657–1734)

1 A man who could make so vile a pun, would not scruple to pick a pocket. [*Gentleman's Magazine*, 1781]

2 See how the rascals use me! They will not let my play run and yet they steal my thunder! [Remark at a production of *Macbeth*]

De Quincey, Thomas (1785–1859)

3 It is most absurdly said, in popular language, of any man, that he is *disguised* in liquor; for, on the contrary, most men are disguised by sobriety. [*Confessions of an English Opium Eater*]

4 Better to stand ten thousand sneers than one abiding pang, such as time could not abolish, of bitter self-reproach. [Ib.]

5 Thou hast the keys of Paradise, oh just, subtle, and mighty opium! [Ib. 2, 'The Pleasures of Opium']

6 If a man once indulges himself in murder, very soon he comes to think little of robbing; and from robbing he comes next to drinking and sabbath-breaking, and from that to incivility and procrastination. [Ib.]

7 All that is literature seeks to communicate power; all that is not literature, to communicate knowledge. [*Letters to a Young Man*, 3]

8 Murder Considered as One of the Fine Arts. [Title of Essay]

Descartes, René (1596–1650)

9 *Cogito, ergo sum.* I think, therefore I am. [*Le Discours de la Méthode*]

10 *La lecture de tous les bons livres est comme une conversation avec les plus honnêtes gens des siècles passés.* The reading of all good books is like a conversation with the finest men of past centuries. [Ib.]

Deschamps, Eustache (c. 1345–1406)

11 *Qui pendre la sonnette au chat?* Who will bell the cat? [Ballade]

Desmoulins, Camille (1760–1794)

12 Clemency is also a revolutionary measure. [Speech, 1793]

Deutsch, Babette (1895–1982)

13 You also, laughing one, / Tosser of balls in the sun, / Will pillow your bright head / By the incurious dead. ['A Girl']

14 Old women sit, stiffly, mosaics of pain... / Their memories: a heap of tumbling stones, / Once builded stronger than a city wall. ['Old Women']

Dewar, Lord Thomas Robert (1864–1930)

15 The road to success is filled with women pushing their husbands along. [Epigram]

Dewey, John (1859–1952)

16 It is strange that the one thing that every person looks forward to, namely old age, is the one thing for which no preparation is made. [Attr.]

Dibdins, Thomas (1771–1841)

17 Oh! what a snug little Island, / A right little, tight little Island! ['The Snug Little Island']

Dickens, Charles (1812–1870)

18 There are strings...in the human heart that had better not be wibrated. [*Barnaby Rudge*, 22]

19 Jarndyce and Jarndyce still drags its dreary length before the Court, perennially hopeless. [*Bleak House*, 1]

20 This is a London particular... A fog, miss. [Ib. 3]

21 'Not to put too fine a point upon it' — a favourite apology for plain-speaking with Mr. Snagsby. [Ib. II]

22 In came Mrs. Fezziwig, one vast substantial smile. [*A Christmas Carol*, 2]

23 'God bless us every one!' said Tiny Tim. [Ib. 3]

24 Barkis is willin'. [*David Copperfield*, 5]

25 'When a man says he's willin',' said Mr. Barkis... 'it's as much as to say, that a man's waitin' for a answer.' [Ib.8]

1 'In case anything turned up,' which was his [Mr. Micawber's] favourite expression. [Ib. II]

2 Annual income twenty pounds, annual expenditure nineteen nineteen six, result happiness. Annual income twenty pounds, annual expenditure twenty pounds ought and six, result misery. [Ib. 12]

3 We are so very 'umble. [Ib. 17]

4 I only ask for information. [Ib. 20]

5 'It was as true,' said Mr. Barkis, '...as taxes is. And nothing's truer than them.' [Ib. 21]

6 Accidents will occur in the best-regulated families. [Ib. 28]

7 'People can't die, along the coast,' said Mr. Peggoty, 'except when the tide's pretty nigh out. They can't be born, unless it's pretty nigh in — not properly born, till flood. He's a going out with the tide.' [Ib. 30]

8 Mrs. Crupp had indignantly assured him that there wasn't room to swing a cat there; but, as Mr. Dick justly observed to me, sitting down on the foot of the bed, nursing his leg, 'You know, Trotwood, I don't want to swing a cat. I never do swing a cat. Therefore, what does that signify to *me*!' [Ib. 35]

9 Circumstances beyond my individual control. [Ib. 49]

10 I'm Gormed — and I can't say no fairer than that! [Ib. 63]

11 He's tough, ma'am, tough is J.B. Tough, and devilish sly! [*Dombey and Son*, 7]

12 What the Waves were always saying. [Ib. 16, chapter heading]

13 Train up a fig-tree in the way it should go, and when you are old sit under the shade of it. [Ib. 19]

14 If you could see my legs when I take my boots off, you'd form some idea of what unrequited affection is. [Ib. 48]

15 Your sister is given to government. [*Great Expectations*]

16 I had cherished a profound conviction that her bringing me up by hand, gave her no right to bring me up by jerks. [Ib. 8]

17 He calls the knaves, Jacks, this boy! ... and what coarse hands he has! And what thick boots! [Ib. 8]

18 On the Rampage, Pip, and off the Rampage, Pip; such is Life! [Ib. 15]

19 Get hold of portable property. [Ib. 24]

20 You don't object to an aged parent, I hope? [Ib. 25]

21 'Now, what I want is, Facts. Teach these boys and girls nothing but Facts. Facts alone are wanted in life. Plant nothing else, and root out everything else... Stick to Facts, sir!' [*Hard Times*, I, 1]

22 'I canna tell what will better aw this — but I can tell what I know will never do't. The strong hand will never do't. Vict'ry and triumph will never do't. Agreeing fur to mak' one side unnat'rally and fur ever wrong, will never do't... Most of aw, rating 'em as so much power, and reg'latin' 'em as if they was figures in a soom, or machines, wi'out souls to weary and souls to hope — this will never do't, sir, till God's work is unmade.' [Ib. II, 21]

23 Whatever was required to be done, the Circumlocution Office was beforehand with all the public departments in the art of perceiving — HOW NOT TO DO IT. [*Little Dorrit*, I, 10]

24 In company with several other old ladies of both sexes. [Ib. I, 17]

25 It was not a bosom to repose upon, but it was a capital bosom to hang jewels upon. [Ib. I, 21]

26 He won't go out, even in the back-yard, when there's no linen; but when there's linen to keep the neighbours' eyes off, he'll sit there, hours. Hours he will. Says he feels as if it was groves! [Ib. I, 22]

27 You can't make a head and brains out of a brass knob with nothing in it. You couldn't when your Uncle George was living; much less when he's dead. [Ib. I, 23]

28 Papa, potatoes, poultry, prunes and prism, are all very good words for the lips; especially prunes and prism. [Ib. II, 5]

29 Once a gentleman, and always a gentleman. [Ib. II, 28]

1 Any man may be in good spirits and good temper when he's well dressed. There an't much credit in that. [*Martin Chuzzlewit*, 5]

2 There might be some credit in being jolly. [Ib.]

3 With affection beaming in one eye, and calculation shining out the other. [Ib. 8]

4 Let us be moral. Let us contemplate existence. [Ib. 9]

5 Here's the rule, for bargains: 'Do other men, for they would do you.' That's the true business precept. [Ib. 11]

6 'She's the sort of woman now,' said Mould... 'one would almost feel disposed to bury for nothing: and do it neatly, too!' [Ib. 25]

7 He'd make a lovely corpse. [Ib.]

8 'Sairey,' says Mrs. Harris, 'sech is life. Vich likeways is the hend of all things!' [Ib. 29]

9 'Bother Mrs. Harris!' said Betsey Prig... 'I don't believe there's no sich a person!' [Ib. 49]

10 But the words she spoke of Mrs. Harris lambs could not forgive. No, nor worms forget. [Ib.]

11 He had but one eye, and the popular prejudice runs in favour of two. [*Nicholas Nickleby*, 4]

12 As she frequently remarked when she made any such mistake, it would all be the same a hundred years hence. [Ib. 9]

13 There are only two styles of portrait painting; the serious and the smirk. [Ib. 10]

14 I pity his ignorance and despise him. [Ib. 15]

15 This is all very well, Mr. Nickleby, and very proper, so far as it goes — so far as it goes, but it doesn't go far enough. [Ib. 16]

16 Language was not powerful enough to describe the infant phenomenon. [Ib. 23]

17 All is gas and gaiters. [Ib. 49]

18 My life is one demd horrid grind! [Ib. 64]

19 Fan the sinking flame of hilarity with the wing of friendship; and pass the rosy wine. [*The Old Curiosity Shop*, 7]

20 It's calm and — what's that word again — critical! — no — classical, that's it — it is calm and classical. [Ib. 27]

21 It was a maxim with Foxey — our revered father, gentlemen — 'Always suspect everybody.' [Ib. 66]

22 Oliver Twist has asked for more! [*Oliver Twist*, 2]

23 Known by the *sobriquet* of 'The artful Dodger'. [Ib.]

24 There's light enough for what I've got to do. [Ib. 47]

25 'If the law supposes that,' said Mr. Bumble... 'the law is a ass — a idiot.' [Ib. 51]

26 The question about everything was, would it bring a blush to the cheek of a young person? [*Our Mutual Friend*, I, 11]

27 He do the Police in different voices. [Ib. I, 16]

28 I think... that it is the best club in London. [The House of Commons] [Ib. II, 3]

29 Queer Street is full of lodgers just at present. [Ib. III, 1]

30 A slap-up gal in a bang-up chariot. [Ib. II, 8]

31 [Nicodemus Boffin] The Golden Dustman. [Ib. III, 5]

32 'An observer of human nature, sir,' said Mr. Pickwick. [*Pickwick Papers*, 2]

33 'It wasn't the wine,' murmured Mr. Snodgrass, in a broken voice, 'It was the salmon.' [Ib. 8]

34 I wants to make your flesh creep. [Ib.]

35 'Suppose there are two mobs?' suggested Mr. Snodgrass. 'Shout with the largest,' replied Mr. Pickwick. [Ib. 13]

36 Tongue; well that's a wery good thing when it an't a woman's. [Ib. 19]

37 Mr. Weller's knowledge of London was extensive and peculiar. [Ib. 20]

38 Poverty and oysters always seem to go together. [Ib. 22]

1 It's over, and can't be helped, and that's one consolation, as they always says in Turkey, ven they cuts the wrong man's head off. [Ib. 23]

2 Wery glad to see you, indeed, and hope our acquaintance may be a long 'un, as the gen'l'm'n said to the fi' pun' note. [Ib. 25]

3 Our noble society for providing the infant negroes in the West Indies with flannel waistcoats and moral pocket handkerchiefs. [Ib.]

4 When you're a married man, Samivel, you'll understand a good many things as you don't understand now; but vether it's worth while goin' through so much to learn so little, as the charityboy said when he got to the end of the alphabet, is a matter o' taste. [Ib. 27]

5 'Eccentricities of genius, Sam,' said Mr. Pickwick. [Ib. 30]

6 Never sign a walentine with your own name. [Ib. 33]

7 It's my opinion, sir, that this meeting is drunk, sir! [Ib.]

8 'Do you spell it with a "V" or a "W"?' inquired the judge. 'That depends upon the taste and fancy of the speller, my Lord,' replied Sam. [Ib. 34]

9 Mr. Phunky, blushing to the very whites of his eyes, tried to look as if he didn't know that everybody was gazing at him, a thing which no man ever succeeded in doing yet, or, in all reasonable probability, ever will. [Ib.]

10 We know, Mr. Weller — we, who are men of the world — that a good uniform must work its way with the women, sooner or later. [Ib. 37]

11 As it is, I don't think I can do with anythin' under a female markis. I might keep up with a young 'ooman o' large property as hadn't a title, if she made wery fierce love to me. Not else. [Ib.]

12 A friendly swarry, consisting of a boiled leg of mutton with the usual trimmings. [Ib.]

13 Anythin' for a quiet life, as the man said wen he took the sitivation at the lighthouse. [Ib. 43]

14 Wich is your partickler wanity? Vich wanity do you like the flavour on best, sir? [Ib. 45]

15 Vell, gov'ner, ve must all come to it, one day or another. [Ib. 52]

16 A smattering of everything, and a knowledge of nothing. [*Sketches by Boz*, 'Sentiment']

17 Grief never mended no broken bones, and as good people's wery scarce, what I says is, make the most on 'em. [Ib. 'Gin Shops']

18 It was the best of times, it was the worst of times, it was the age of wisdom, it was the age of foolishness, it was the epoch of belief, it was the epoch of incredulity, it was the season of Light, it was the season of Darkness, it was the spring of hope, it was the winter of despair, we had everything before us, we had nothing before us, we were all going direct to Heaven, we were all going direct the other way. [*A Tale of Two Cities*, I, 1]

19 It is a far, far better thing that I do, than I have ever done; it is a far, far better rest that I go to, than I have ever known. [Ib. III, 15]

Dickinson, Emily (1830–1886)

20 After great pain, a formal feeling comes — / The Nerves sit ceremonious, like Tombs. ['After great pain']

21 Because I could not stop for Death — / He kindly stopped for me — / The Carriage held but just Ourselves — / And Immortality. ['Because I could not stop']

22 I heard a Fly buzz — when I died. ['I heard a Fly buzz']

23 These are the days when skies put on / The old, old sophistries of June, — / A blue and gold mistake. ['Indian Summer']

24 My life closed twice before its close. ['My life closed twice']

25 Parting is all we know of heaven / And all we need of hell. [Ib.]

26 There came a wind like a bugle; / It quivered through the grass. ['There came a wind']

1 How dreary to be somebody! / How public, like a frog / To tell your name the livelong day / To an admiring bog! [*Poems*]

Dickinson, John (1732-1808)

2 Our cause is just. Our union is complete. ['Declaration on Taking up Arms', 1775]

3 Then join hand in hand, brave Americans all, — / By uniting we stand, by dividing we fall. ['The Liberty Song']

Diderot, Denis (1713-1784)

4 Men will never be free until the last king is strangled with the entrails of the last priest. [*Dithyrambe sur la fête des rois*]

5 *L'esprit de l'escalier*. Staircase wit [i.e. a retort conceived too late]. [*Paradoxe sur le Comédien*]

Diodorus Siculus (c. 1st century B.C.)

6 Medicine for the soul. [Inscription over library door in Alexandria] [*History*, I]

Diogenes (the Cynic) (c. 412-323 B.C.)

7 I do not know whether there are gods, but there ought to be. [Tertullian, *Ad Nationes*]

8 [Asked by Alexander if he wanted anything] Yes, stand a little out of my sun. [Plutarch, *Life of Alexander*]

9 I am looking for an honest man. [Diogenes Laertius, *Diogenes*]

10 I am a citizen of the world [*Kosmopolites*: origin of the word 'cosmopolitan']. [Ib.]

11 I am called a dog because I fawn on those who give me anything, I yelp at those who refuse, and I set my teeth in rascals. [Ib.]

12 If I were running in the stadium, ought I to slacken my pace when approaching the goal? Ought I not rather to put on speed? [Ib.]

13 The foundation of every state is the education of its youth. [Stobaeus, *Florilegium*]

Disraeli, Benjamin (1804-1881)

14 No Government can be long secure without a formidable opposition. [*Coningsby*, II, 1]

15 Conservatism discards Prescription, shrinks from Principle, disavows Progress: having reflected all respect for antiquity, it offers no redress for the present, and makes no preparation for the future. [Ib. II, 5]

16 A sound Conservative government ...Tory men and Whig measures. [Ib. II, 6]

17 Almost everything that is great has been done by youth. [Ib. III, 1]

18 Youth is a blunder; Manhood a struggle; Old Age a regret. [Ib.]

19 Time is the great physician. [*Endymion*, VI, 9]

20 When a man fell into his anecdotage it was a sign for him to retire from the world. [*Lothair*, 28]

21 I have always thought that every woman should marry — and no man. [Ib. 30]

22 You know who the critics are? The men who have failed in literature and art. [Ib. 35]

23 I was told that the Privileged and the People formed Two Nations. [*Sybil*, IV, 8]

24 The Youth of a Nation are the Trustees of Posterity. [Ib. VI, 13]

25 There is moderation even in excess. [*Vivian Grey*, II, 6]

26 All Paradise opens! Let me die eating ortolans to the sound of soft music! [*The Young Duke*, I, 10]

27 Experience is the child of Thought, and Thought is the child of Action. We cannot learn men from books. [Ib. V, 1]

28 Marriage is the greatest earthly happiness when founded on complete sympathy. [Letter to Gladstone]

29 Though I sit down now, the time will come when you will hear me. [Maiden Speech, 1837]

30 The Continent will not suffer England to be the workshop of the world. [Speech, 1838]

1 A starving population, an absentee aristocracy, and an alien Church, and in addition the weakest executive in the world. That is the Irish question. [Speech, 1844]

2 A Conservative government is an organized hypocrisy. [Speech, 1845]

3 The right honourable gentleman [Sir Robert Peel] caught the Whigs bathing, and walked away with their clothes. [Speech, 1845]

4 Finality is not the language of politics. [Speech, 1859]

5 Is man an ape or an angel? Now I am on the side of the angels. [Speech, 1864]

6 Upon the education of the people of this country the fate of this country depends. [Speech, 1874]

7 Lord Salisbury and myself have brought you back peace — but peace, I hope, with honour. [Speech, 1878]

8 [Of Gladstone] A sophistical rhetorician, inebriated with the exuberance of his own verbosity. [Speech, 1878]

9 Never complain, never explain. [Attr.]

10 Damn your principles! Stick to your party. [Attr.]

11 [To Queen Victoria] We authors, Ma'am. [Attr.]

12 When I want to read a novel I write one. [Attr.]

13 Next to knowing when to seize an opportunity, the most important thing in life is to know when to forego an advantage. [Attr.]

14 She did not know which came first, the Greeks or the Romans, but she was a wonderful woman. [Remark to Sir William Harcourt]

15 [Asked if Queen Victoria should visit him during his last illness] No, it is better not. She would only ask me to take a message to Albert. [Quoted in Wintle and Kenin, *Dictionary of Biographical Quotations*]

Dobson, Austin (1840-1921)

16 Fame is a food that dead men eat, — / I have no stomach for such meat. ['Fame is a Food']

17 Time goes, you say? Ah no! / Alas, Time stays, *we* go. ['The Paradox of Time']

Doddridge, Philip (1702-1751)

18 O happy day, that fixed my choice / On Thee, my Saviour and my God! [Hymn]

19 'Tis done! the great transaction's done! / I am my Lord's and He is mine. [Ib.]

Donatus, Aelius (fl. 4th century A.D.)

20 *Pereant, inquit, qui ante nos nostra dixerunt.* Confound those who have said our remarks before us. [St. Jerome, *Commentaries on Ecclesiastes*]

Donne, John (c. 1571-1631)

21 Twice or thrice had I loved thee, / Before I knew thy face or name; / So in a voice, so in a shapeless flame, / Angels affect us oft, and worship'd be. ['Air and Angels']

22 Just such disparity / As is 'twixt Air and Angels' purity, / 'Twixt women's love and men's will ever be. [Ib.]

23 All other things, to their destruction draw, / Only our love hath no decay; / This, no tomorrow hath, nor yesterday, / Running it never runs from us away, / But truly keeps his first, last, everlasting day. ['The Anniversary']

24 Come live with me, and be my love, / And we will some new pleasures prove / Of golden sands, and crystal brooks, / With silken lines, and silver hooks. ['The Bait']

25 For Godsake hold your tongue, and let me love. ['The Canonization']

26 Chang'd loves are but chang'd sorts of meat, / And when he hath the kernel eat, / Who doth not fling away the shell? ['Community']

27 No man is an *Island*, entire of it self. [*Devotions*]

28 Any man's *death* diminishes *me*, because I am involved in *Mankind*; And therefore never send to know for whom the *bell* tolls; It tolls for *thee*. [Ib.]

1 Love built on beauty, soon as beauty dies. [*Elegies*, 2, 'The Anagram']

2 Women are like the Arts, forc'd unto none, / Open to all searchers, unpriz'd if unknown. [Ib. 3, 'Change']

3 O, let me not serve so, as those men serve / Whom honours smokes at once fatten and starve. [Ib. 6]

4 No Spring, nor Summer Beauty hath such grace, / As I have seen in one Autumnal face. [Ib. 9, 'The Autumnal']

5 So, if I dream I have you, I have you, / For, all our joys are but fantastical. [Ib. 10, 'The Dream']

6 And must she needs be false because she's fair? [Ib. 15, 'The Expostulation']

7 May Wolves tear out his heart, Vultures his eyes, / Swine eat his bowels, and his falser tongue, / That utter'd all, be to some Raven flung. [Ib.]

8 By our first strange and fatal interview / By all desires which thereof did ensue. [Ib. 16, 'On His Mistress']

9 Nurse, O! my love is slain; I saw him go / O'er the white Alps alone. [Ib.]

10 How happy were our Sires in ancient times, / Who held plurality of loves no crime! [Ib. 17]

11 O my America! my new-found-land. [Ib. 19, 'Going to Bed']

12 So, so, break off this last lamenting kiss, / Which sucks two souls, and vapours both away. ['The Expiration']

13 Love's mysteries in souls do grow, / But yet the body is his book. ['The Ecstasy']

14 So must pure lovers' souls descend / T'affections, and to faculties, / Which sense may reach and apprehend, / Else a great Prince in prison lies. [Ib.]

15 And new philosophy calls all in doubt, / The element of fire is quite put out. ['The First Anniversary']

16 'Tis all in pieces, all coherence gone; / All just supply and all relation. [Ib.]

17 Yet, because outward storms the strongest break, / And strength itself by confidence grows weak, / This new world may be safer, being told / The dangers and diseases of the old. [Ib.]

18 I wonder by my troth what thou, and I / Did, till we lov'd? ['The Good-Morrow']

19 Or snorted we in the Seven Sleepers den? [Ib.]

20 And now good morrow to our waking souls, / Which watch not one another out of fear. [Ib.]

21 I am a little world made cunningly / Of Elements, and an Angelic spright. [*Holy Sonnets*, 5]

22 At the round earth's imagined corners, blow / Your trumpets, Angels. [Ib. 7]

23 All whom war, dearth, age, agues, tyrannies, / Despair, law, chance, hath slain. [Ib. 7]

24 Death be not proud, though some have called thee / Mighty and dreadful, for thou art not so. [Ib. 10]

25 One short sleep past, we wake eternally, / And death shall be no more; Death, thou shalt die. [Ib.]

26 What if this present were the world's last night? [Ib. 13]

27 Batter my heart, three person'd God; for, you / As yet but knock. [Ib. 14]

28 Take me to you, imprison me, for I / Except you enthrall me, never shall be free, / Nor ever chaste, except you ravish me. [Ib. 14]

29 Since I am coming to that Holy room, / Where, with thy Quire of Saints for evermore, / I shall be made thy Music; As I come / I tune the Instrument here at the door, / And what I must do then, think now before. ['Hymn to God my God, in my Sickness']

30 Wilt thou forgive that sin where I begun, / Which was my sin, though it were done before? / Wilt thou forgive that sin through which I run, / And do them still: though still I do deplore? / When thou hast done, thou hast not done, / For, I have more. ['Hymn to God the Father']

1 When I died last, and, Dear I die / As often as from thee I go, / Though it be but an hour ago, / And Lovers' hours be full eternity, / I can remember yet. ['The Legacy']

2 I long to talk with some old lover's ghost, / Who died before the god of Love was born. ['Love's Deity']

3 Love's not so pure, and abstract, as they use / To say, which have no Mistress but their Muse, / But as all else, being elemented too, / Love sometimes would contemplate, sometimes do. ['Love's Growth']

4 I never stoop'd so low, as they / Which on an eye, cheek, lip can prey, / Seldom to them, which soar no higher / Then virtue or the mind to admire. ['Negative Love']

5 'Tis the year's midnight, and it is the day's. ['Nocturnal upon St. Lucy's Day']

6 The world's whole sap is sunk: / The general balm th'hydroptic earth hath drunk. [Ib.]

7 I sing the progress of a deathless soul, / Whom Fate, which God made, but doth not control, / Plac'd in most shapes. [*The Progress of the Soul*, 1]

8 A bracelet of bright hair about the bone. ['The Relic']

9 Giddy fantastic Poets of each land. [*Satyres*, 1]

10 On a huge hill, / Cragged, and steep, Truth stands, and he that will / Reach her, about must, and about must go; / And what the hill's suddenness resists, win so. [Ib. 3]

11 But 'twere little to have chang'd our room, / If, as we were in this our living Tomb / Oppress'd with ignorance, we still were so. / Poor soul, in this thy flesh what dost thou know? ['The Second Anniversary']

12 And yet one watches, starves, freezes, and sweats, / To know but Catechisms and Alphabets / Of unconcerning things, matters of fact; / How others on our stage their parts did Act; / What Caesar did, yea, and what Cicero said. [Ib.]

13 Her pure and eloquent blood / Spoke in her cheeks, and so distinctly wrought, / That one might almost say, her body thought. [Ib.]

14 Go, and catch a falling star, / Get with child a mandrake root, / Tell me, where all past years are, / Or who cleft the Devil's foot. ['Song']

15 And swear / No where / Lives a woman true, and fair. [Ib.]

16 Busy old fool, unruly Sun, / Why dost thou thus, / Through windows, and through curtains call on us? ['The Sun-Rising']

17 Love, all alike, no season knows, nor clime, / Nor hours, days, months, which are the rags of time. [Ib.]

18 I am two fools, I know, / For loving, and for saying so / In whining Poetry. ['The Triple Fool']

19 Grief brought to numbers cannot be so fierce, / For, he tames it, that fetters it in verse. [Ib.]

20 But he who loveliness within / Hath found, all outward loathes, / For he who colour loves, and skin, /Loves but their oldest clothes. ['The Undertaking']

21 Man is a lump, where all beasts kneaded be, / Wisdom makes him an Ark where all agree; / The fool, in whom these beasts do live at jar, / Is sport to others, and a Theatre. ['To Sir Edward Herbert']

22 Dull sublunary lovers love / (Whose soul is sense) cannot admit / Absence, because it doth remove / Those things which elemented it. ['A Valediction Forbidding Mourning']

23 But we by a love, so much refin'd, / That our selves know not what it is, / Inter-assured of the mind, / Care less, eyes, lips, and hands to miss. [Ib.]

24 Thy firmness makes my circle just, / And makes me end, where I begun. [Ib.]

25 John Donne, Anne Donne, Un-done. [Letter to his wife]

Dostoevsky, Fyodor (1821–1881)

26 We are familiar merely with the everyday, apparent and current, and this only in so far as it appears to us, whereas the ends and the beginnings still constitute to man a realm of the fantastic. [*Diary of a Writer*]

Douglas, Lord Alfred (1870–1945)

1 I am the Love that dare not speak its name. ['Two Loves']

Douglas, Archibald, Fifth Earl of Angus (c. 1449–1514)

2 I shall bell the cat. [Attr.]

Douglas, Keith (1920–1944)

3 Remember me when I am dead / And simplify me when I'm dead. ['Simplify me when I'm dead']

Dowson, Ernest (1867–1900)

4 I have forgot much, Cynara! gone with the wind. ['*Non Sum Qualis Eram*']

5 I cried for madder music and stronger wine, / But when the feast is finish'd and the lamps expire, / Then falls thy shadow, Cynara!... / I have been faithful to thee, Cynara! in my fashion. [Ib.]

6 They are not long, the days of wine and roses. ['*Vitae Summa Brevis*']

Doyle, Sir Arthur Conan (1859–1930)

7 The more featureless and commonplace a crime is, the more difficult is it to bring it home. ['The Boscombe Valley Mystery']

8 All other men are specialists, but his specialism is omniscience. ['Bruce-Partington Plans']

9 It has long been an axiom of mine that the little things are infinitely the most important. ['A Case of Identity']

10 It is my belief, Watson, founded upon my experience, that the lowest and vilest alleys of London do not present a more dreadful record of sin than does the smiling and beautiful countryside. ['Copper Beeches']

11 'Excellent!' I [Dr. Watson] cried. 'Elementary,' said he [Holmes]. ['The Crooked Man']

12 [Of Moriarty] The Napoleon of crime. ['The Final Problem']

13 A man should keep his little brain attic stocked with all the furniture that he is likely to use, and the rest he can put away in the lumber-room of his library, where he can get it if he wants it. ['Five Orange Pips']

14 It is quite a three-pipe problem. ['The Red-Headed League']

15 It is a capital mistake to theorize before one has data. ['Scandal in Bohemia']

16 You see, but you do not observe. ['Scandal in Bohemia']

17 An experience of women which extends over many nations and three separate continents. [*The Sign of Four*]

18 The Baker Street irregulars. [Ib.]

19 How often have I said to you that when you have eliminated the impossible, whatever remains, *however improbable*, must be the truth. [Ib.]

20 You know my methods. Apply them. [Ib. (Also, with slight variations, in other stories)]

21 'Is there any other point to which you would wish to draw my attention?' 'To the curious incident of the dog in the night-time.' 'The dog did nothing in the night-time.' 'That was the curious incident,' remarked Sherlock Holmes. ['Silver Blaze']

22 London, that great cesspool into which all the loungers of the Empire are irresistibly drained. [*A Study in Scarlet*]

23 The giant rat of Sumatra, a story for which the world is not yet prepared. ['Sussex Vampire']

24 The vocabulary of Bradshaw is nervous and terse, but limited. [*The Valley of Fear*]

25 Mediocrity knows nothing higher than itself, but talent instantly recognizes genius. [Ib.]

Drake, Sir Francis (c. 1540–1596)

26 I remember Drake, in the vaunting style of a soldier, would call the Enterprise [of Cadiz, 1587] the singeing of the King of Spain's Beard. [Bacon, *Considerations touching a War with Spain*]

1 There is plenty of time to win this game, and to thrash the Spaniards too. [Attr. in *Dictionary of National Biography*]

Drayton, Michael (1563-1631)

2 Ill news hath wings, and with the wind doth go, / Comfort's a cripple and comes ever slow. [*The Barrons' Wars*, II]

3 The mind is free, whate'er afflict the man, / A King's a King, do Fortune what she can. [Ib. V]

4 Thus when we fondly flatter our desires, / Our best conceits do prove the greatest liars. [Ib. VI]

5 Fair stood the wind for France / When we our sails advance, / Nor now to prove our chance / Longer will tarry. [*To the Cambro-Britons*, 'Agincourt']

6 Next these, learn'd Jonson, in this list I bring, / Who had drunk deep of the Pierian spring. ['Of Poets and Poesy']

7 Neat Marlowe, bathed in the Thespian springs, / Had in him those brave translunary things / That the first poets had; his raptures were / All air and fire, which made his verse clear, / For that fine madness still he did retain / Which rightly should possess a poet's brain. [Ib.]

8 Since there's no help, come let us kiss and part. [*Sonnets*, 'Idea']

Dressler, Marie (1869-1934)

9 If ants are such busy workers, how come they find time to go to all the picnics? [Quoted in Cowan, *The Wit of Women*]

Drummond, Thomas (1797-1840)

10 Property has its duties as well as its rights. [Letter, 1838]

Dryden, John (1631-1700)

11 In pious times, ere priestcraft did begin, / Before polygamy was made a sin. [*Absalom and Achitophel*, Part I]

12 Then Israel's monarch, after Heaven's own heart, / His vigorous warmth did, variously, impart / To wives and slaves: and, wide as his command, / Scatter'd his Maker's image through the land. [Ib.]

13 Whate'er he did was done with so much ease, / In him alone 'twas natural to please. [Ib.]

14 Gods they had tried of every shape and size / That godsmiths could produce or priests devise. [Ib.]

15 Pleased with the danger, when the waves went high / He sought the storms; but for a calm unfit, / Would steer too nigh the sands to boast his wit. / Great wits are sure to madness near alli'd, / And thin partitions do their bounds divide. [Ib.]

16 In friendship false, implacable in hate, / Resolved to ruin or to rule the state. [Ib.]

17 So easy still it proves in factious times / With public zeal to cancel private crimes. [Ib.]

18 All empire is no more than power in trust, / Which, when resumed, can be no longer just. [Ib.]

19 Better one suffer than a nation grieve. [Ib.]

20 A man so various that he seem'd to be / Not one, but all mankind's epitome. [Ib.]

21 During his office treason was no crime, / The sons of Belial had a glorious time. [Ib.]

22 Youth, beauty, graceful action seldom fail; / But common interest always will prevail. / And pity never ceases to be shown / To him who makes the people's wrongs his own. [Ib.]

23 Not is the people's judgement always true: / The most may err as grossly as the few. [Ib.]

24 None but the brave deserves the fair. ['Alexander's Feast']

25 Drinking is the soldier's pleasure... / Sweet is pleasure after pain. [Ib.]

26 At length, with love and wine at once oppressed, / The vanquished victor sunk upon her breast. [Ib.]

1 See the Furies arise! / See the snakes that they rear, / How they hiss in their hair, / And the sparkles that flash from their eyes. [Ib.]

2 And, like another Helen, fired another Troy. [Ib.]

3 Men are but children of a larger growth. [*All for Love*, IV]

4 Our author by experience finds it true, / 'Tis much more hard to please himself than you. [*Aureng-Zebe*, Prologue]

5 When I consider life, 'tis all a cheat; / Yet, fooled with hope, men favour the deceit. [Ib. IV]

6 Yet dull religion teaches us content; / But when we ask it where that blessing dwells, / It points to pedant colleges and cells. [*The Conquest of Granada*, II]

7 Fair though you are / As summer mornings, and your eyes more bright / Than stars that twinkle in a winter's night. [Ib. III]

8 Treaties are but the combat of the brain, / Where still the strongest lose, the weaker gain. [Ib.]

9 Theirs was the giant race before the flood. ['Epistle to Mr. Congreve']

10 Here lies my wife: here let her lie! / Now she's at rest, and so am I. ['Epitaph intended for his wife']

11 His grandeur he derived from Heaven alone, / For he was great, ere fortune made him so. ['Heroic Stanzas after Cromwell's Funeral']

12 By education most have been misled; / So they believe, because they so were bred. / The priest continues what the nurse began, / And thus the child imposes on the man. [*The Hind and the Panther*]

13 Either be wholly slaves or wholly free. [Ib.]

14 And love's the noblest frailty of the mind. [*The Indian Emperor*, II]

15 Fairest Isle, all isles excelling, / Seat of pleasure, and of loves; / Venus here will choose her dwelling, / And forsake her Cyprian groves. [*King Arthur*, V (Song of Venus)]

16 All human things are subject to decay, / And, when fate summons, monarchs must obey. [*Mac Flecknoe*]

17 Thou last great Prophet of Tautology. [Ib.]

18 The rest to some faint meaning make pretence, / But Shadwell never deviates into sense. [Ib.]

19 But now the world's o'er stocked with prudent men. [*The Medal*]

20 Dim, as the borrowed beams of moon and stars / To lonely, weary, wandering travellers / Is reason to the soul. [*Religio Laici*]

21 How can the less the greater comprehend? / Or finite reason reach Infinity? [Ib.]

22 But since men will believe more than they need; / And every man will make himself a creed, / In doubtful questions 'tis the safest way / To learn what unsuspected ancients say. [Ib.]

23 And this unpolished rugged verse I chose / As fittest for discourse and nearest prose. [Ib.]

24 A very merry, dancing, drinking, / Laughing, quaffing, and unthinking time. ['Secular Masque']

25 All, all of a piece throughout; / Thy chase had a beast in view; / Thy wars brought nothing about; / Thy lovers were all untrue. / 'Tis well an old age is out, / And time to begin a new. [Ib.]

26 From harmony, from heavenly harmony / This universal frame began. ['Song for St. Cecilia's Day']

27 The trumpet's loud clangour / Excites us to arms. [Ib.]

28 And Music shall untune the sky. [Ib.]

29 Wit will shine / Through the harsh cadence of a rugged line. ['To the Memory of Mr. Oldham']

30 Happy the man, and happy he alone, / He, who can call to-day his own: / He who, secure within, can say, / To-morrow do thy worst, for I have lived to-day. [Translation of Horace, Odes, III, 29]

1 [Of Shakespeare] He was the man who of all modern, and perhaps ancient poets, had the largest and most comprehensive soul. [*Essay of Dramatic Poesy*]

2 [Of Ben Jonson] He was not only a professed imitator of Horace, but a learned plagiary of all the others; you track him everywhere in their snow. [Ib.]

3 [Of Chaucer] Here is God's plenty. [*Fables*, Preface]

4 [Of Chaucer] He is a perpetual fountain of good sense. [Ib.]

5 Cousin Swift, you will never be a poet. [Johnson, *Lives of the Poets*]

Dubček, Alexander (1921-)

6 Socialism with a human face. [Attr.]

Dudley, Sir Henry Bate (1745-1824)

7 Wonders will never cease. [Letter to Garrick, 1776]

Duffield, George (1818-1888)

8 Stand up! stand up for Jesus, / Ye soldiers of the Cross! [Hymn]

Dukes, Ashley (1885-1959)

9 Adventure must be held in delicate fingers. It should be handled, not embraced. It should be sipped, not swallowed at a gulp. [*The Man with a Load of Mischief*, 1]

10 The woman who runs will never lack followers. [Ib.]

11 Men reason to strengthen their own prejudices, and not to disturb their adversary's convictions. [Ib. 2]

12 The tender passion is much overrated by the poets. They have their living to earn, poor fellows. [Ib. 3]

Dumas, Alexandre (1803-1870)

13 *Cherchez la femme*. Look for the woman. [*Les Mohicans de Paris*; also attr. Joseph Fouché (1763-1820)]

14 *Tous pour un, un pour tous*. All for one, one for all. [*Les Trois Mousquetiers*]

Du Maurier, George (1834-1896)

15 She had all the virtues but one. [*Trilby*]

16 [Of a husband] Feed the brute. [*Punch*, 1886]

Dunbar, William (c. 1465-c. 1530)

17 The Devil sa deavit was with their yell, / That in the deepest pot of hell / He smoorit them with smoke. ['The Dance of the Seven Deidly Sinnis']

18 The bank was green, the brook was full of breamis, / The stanneris clear as stern in frosty nicht. ['The Golden Targe']

19 Be merry, man! and tak nocht far in mind / The wavering of this wrechit world of sorrow; / To God be hummill, and to the friend be kind, / And with thy neebouris glaidly len' and borrow. ['Hermes the Philosopher']

20 Na gude in thine save only that thou spendis. [Ib.]

21 Without gladness availis no tresour. [Ib.]

22 Flattery wearis ane furrit gown, / And fabet with the lord does roun, / And truth stands barrit at the dune. ['Into this World May None Assure']

23 Our plesance here is all vain glory, / This fals world is but transitory, / The flesh is bruckle, the Feynd is slee: / *Timor Mortis conturbat me*. ['Lament for the Makaris']

24 Unto the deid gois all Estatis, / Princis, Prelatis, and Potestatis, / Baith rich and poor of all degree: / *Timor Mortis conturbat me*. [Ib.]

25 London, thou art the flour of cities all! ['London']

26 I wauk, I turn, sleep may I nocht, / I vexit am with heavy thocht; / This warld all owre I cast about, / And aye the mair I am in doubt; / The mair that I remead have socht. ['Meditation in Winter']

27 God give to thee ane blissed chance, / And of all virtue abundance, / And grace ay for to persevere, / In hansel of this guid new year. ['New Year's Gift']

1 Gif thou has micht, be gentle and free; / And gif thou stands in povertie, / Of thine awn will to it consent; / And riches sall return to thee: / He has eneuch that is content. ['Of Content']

2 Great men for taking and oppressioun, / Are set full famous at the Sessioun, / And poor tokaris are hangit hie, / Shamit for ever and their succession: / In taking suld discretioun be. ['Of Discretion in Taking']

Dundy, Elaine (1927-)

3 The question actors most often get asked is how they can bear saying the same things over and over again night after night, but God knows the answer to *that* is, don't we all *anyway*; might as well get paid for it. [*The Dud Avocado*, 9]

Dyer, John (fl. 18th century)

4 And he that will his health deny, / Down among the dead men let him lie. [Toast: 'Here's a Health to the King']

Dyer, John (c. 1700-1758)

5 A little rule, a little sway, / A sunbeam in a winter's day, / Is all the proud and mighty have / Between the cradle and the grave. [*Grongar Hill*]

Dylan, Bob (1941-)

6 How many roads must a man walk down / Before you call him a man? / ... The answer, my friend, is blowin' in the wind, / The answer is blowin' in the wind. ['Blowin' in the Wind']

7 A Hard Rain's A-Gonna Fall. [Title of song]

8 Money doesn't talk, it swears. ['It's Alright, Ma (I'm Only Bleeding)']

9 She takes just like a woman, yes, she does / She makes love just like a woman, yes, she does / And she aches just like a woman / But she breaks just like a little girl. ['Just Like a Woman']

10 She knows there's no success like failure / And that failure's no success at all. ['Love Minus Zero/No Limit']

11 Come mothers and fathers / Throughout the land/ And don't criticize / What you can't understand. ['The Times They Are A-Changin'']

Eban, Abba (1915-)

12 History teaches us that men and nations behave wisely once they have exhausted all other alternatives. [*Observer*, 'Sayings of the Week', 1970]

Eden, Anthony (1897-1977)

13 We are not at war with Egypt. We are in armed conflict. [*Observer*, 'Sayings of the Week', 1956]

Edgeworth, Maria (1767-1849)

14 Well! some people talk of morality, and some of religion, but give me a little snug property. [*The Absentee*, 2]

15 And all the young ladies...said...that to be sure a love match was the only thing for happiness, where the parties could any way afford it. [*Castle Rackrent*]

16 Business was his aversion; pleasure was his business. [*The Contrast*, 2]

17 There is one distinguishing peculiarity of the Irish bull — its horns are tipped with brass. [*Irish Bulls*, 9]

Edison, Thomas Alva (1847-1931)

18 Genius is one per cent inspiration and ninety-nine per cent perspiration. [Newspaper interview]

Edmeston, James (1791-1867)

19 Lead us, heavenly Father, lead us / O'er the world's tempestuous sea. [Hymn]

Edward III (1312-1377)

20 [Of the Black Prince at Crécy] Let the boy win his spurs. [Froissart's *Chronicle*]

Edward VII (1841-1910)

21 We are all socialists now. [Attr.]

Edward VIII [later Duke of Windsor] (1894–1972)

1 I have found it impossible to carry the heavy burden of responsibility and to discharge my duties as King as I would wish to do without the help and support of the woman I love. [Broadcast, 1936]

Edwards, Oliver (1711–1791)

2 I have tried too in my time to be a philosopher; but, I don't know how, cheerfulness was always breaking in. [Boswell, *Life of Johnson*]

Einstein, Albert (1879–1955)

3 An empty stomach is not a good political adviser. [*Cosmic Religion*]

4 Only a life lived for others is a life worthwhile. ['Defining Success']

5 Peace cannot be kept by force. It can only be achieved by understanding. [*Notes on Pacifism*]

6 Imagination is more important than knowledge. [*On Science*]

7 I never think of the future. It comes soon enough. [Interview, 1930]

8 Why does this magnificent applied science which saves work and makes life easier bring us so little happiness? The simple answer runs: Because we have not yet learned to make sensible use of it. [Address, California Institute of Technology, 1931]

9 If my theory of relativity is proven successful, Germany will claim me as a German and France will declare that I am a citizen of the world. Should my theory prove untrue, France will say that I am a German and Germany will declare that I am a Jew. [Address, Sorbonne, Paris]

10 Before God we are all equally wise — equally foolish. [Ib.]

11 I shall never believe that God plays dice with the world. [Attr.]

12 Common sense is the collection of prejudices acquired by age eighteen. [Attr.]

Eliot, George (1819–1880)

13 A prophetess? Yea, I say unto you, and more than a prophetess — a uncommon pretty young woman. [*Adam Bede*, 1]

14 It's them that takes advantage that get advantage i' this world. [Ib. 32]

15 He was like a cock who thought the sun had risen to hear him crow. [Ib. 33]

16 I'm not denyin' the women are foolish: God Almighty made 'em to match the men. [Ib. 53]

17 A blush is no language: only a dubious flag-signal which may mean either of two contradictories. [*Daniel Deronda*, 35]

18 A woman can hardly ever choose...she is dependent on what happens to her. She must take meaner things, because only meaner things are within her reach. [*Felix Holt*, 27]

19 'Abroad', that large home of ruined reputations. [Ib. Epilogue]

20 Man's life was spacious in the early world: / It paused, like some slow ship with sail unfurled / Waiting in seas by scarce a wavelet curled; / Beheld the slow star-paces of the skies, / And grew from strength to strength through centuries; / Saw infant trees fill out their giant limbs, / And heard a thousand times the sweet bird's marriage hymns. [*The Legend of Jubal*]

21 This is a puzzling world, and Old Harry's got a finger in it. [*The Mill on the Floss*, III, 9]

22 I've never any pity for conceited people, because I think they carry their comfort about with them. [Ib. V, 4]

23 The happiest women, like the happiest nations, have no history. [Ib. VI, 3]

24 I should like to know what is the proper function of women, if it is not to make reasons for husbands to stay at home, and still stronger reasons for bachelors to go out. [Ib. VI, 6]

25 In every parting there is an image of death. [*Scenes of Clerical Life*, 'Amos Barton']

1 There's nothing like a dairy if folks want a bit o' worrit to make the days pass. [*Silas Marner*, 17]

2 'Tis God gives skill, / But not without men's hands: He could not make / Antonio Stradivari's violins / Without Antonio. Get thee to thy easel. ['Stradivarius']

3 Debasing the moral currency. [*Theophrastus Such*, title of essay]

Eliot, T.S. (1888–1965)

4 Pray for us now and at the hour of our birth. ['Animula']

5 Because I do not hope to turn again / Because I do not hope / Because I do not hope to turn. ['Ash Wednesday']

6 Teach us to care and not to care / Teach us to sit still. [Ib.]

7 Lady, three white leopards sat under a juniper tree / In the cool of the day. [Ib.]

8 You shouldn't interrupt my interruptions: / That's really worse than interrupting. [*The Cocktail Party*]

9 Miss Nancy Ellicot smoked / And danced all the modern dances; / And her aunts were not quite sure how they felt about it, / But they knew that it was modern. ['Cousin Nancy']

10 Those to whom nothing has ever happened / Cannot understand the unimportance of events. [*The Family Reunion*]

11 Time present and time past / Are both perhaps present in time future, / And time future contained in time past. [*Four Quartets*, 'Burnt Norton']

12 Human kind / Cannot bear very much reality. [Ib.]

13 At the still point of a turning world. [Ib.]

14 Only through time time is conquered. [Ib.]

15 In my beginning is my end. [Ib. 'East Coker']

16 The wounded surgeon plies the steel / That questions the distempered part. [Ib.]

17 Each venture / Is a new beginning, a raid on the inarticulate / With shabby equipment always deteriorating / In the general mess of imprecision of feeling. [Ib.]

18 Our concern was speech, and speech impelled us / To purify the dialect of the tribe. [Ib. 'Little Gidding']

19 We shall not cease from exploration / And the end of all our exploring / Will be to arrive where we started / And know the place for the first time. [Ib.]

20 In the juvescence of the year / Came Christ the tiger. ['Gerontion']

21 After such knowledge, what forgiveness? Think now / History has many cunning passages, contrived corridors / And issues: deceives with whispering ambitions, / Guides us by vanities. [Ib.]

22 Thoughts of a dry brain in a dry season. [Ib.]

23 We are the hollow men / We are the stuffed men / Leaning together / Headpiece filled with straw. ['The Hollow Men']

24 Between the idea / And the reality / Between the motion / And the act / Falls the Shadow. [Ib.]

25 This is the way the world ends / Not with a bang but a whimper. [Ib.]

26 A cold coming we had of it, / Just the worst time of the year / For a journey. ['Journey of the Magi']

27 But no longer at ease here, in the old dispensation, / With an alien people clutching their gods. / I should be glad of another death. [Ib.]

28 Let us go then, you and I, / When the evening is spread out against the sky / Like a patient etherized upon a table. ['Love Song of J. Alfred Prufrock']

29 In the room the women come and go / Talking of Michelangelo. [Ib.]

30 The yellow fog that rubs its back upon the window-panes. [Ib.]

31 Have known the evenings, mornings, afternoons, / I have measured out my life with coffee spoons. [Ib.]

32 I should have been a pair of ragged claws / Scuttling across the floors of silent seas. [Ib.]

1 I grow old...I grow old.../ I shall wear the bottoms of my trousers rolled.../ Do I dare to eat a peach? [Ib.]

2 They are rattling breakfast plates in the basement kitchens, / And along the trampled edges of the street / I am aware of the damp souls of housemaids / Sprouting despondently at area gates. ['Morning at the Window']

3 Men will not hate you / Enough to defame or to execrate you, / But pondering the qualities that you lacked / Will only try to find the historical fact. [*Murder in the Cathedral*]

4 However certain our expectation / The moment foreseen may be unexpected / When it arrives. [Ib.]

5 The last temptation is the greatest treason: / To do the right deed for the wrong reason. [Ib.]

6 The winter evening settles down / With smells of steaks in passageways. / Six o'clock. / The burnt-out ends of smoky days. ['Preludes']

7 Let us take air, in a tobacco trance, / Admire the monuments, / Discuss the late events, / Correct our watches by the public clocks. / Then sit for half an hour and drink our bocks. ['Portrait of a Lady']

8 Every son would have his motor-cycle, / And daughters ride away on casual pillions. ['The Rock']

9 In the land of lobelias and tennis flannels, / The rabbit shall burrow and the thorn revisit, / The nettle shall flourish on the gravel court, / And the wind shall say 'Here were decent, godless people; / Their only monument the asphalt road / And a thousand lost golf balls.' [Ib.]

10 Many are engaged in writing books and printing them, / Many desire to see their names in print, / Many read nothing but the race reports. [Ib.]

11 That's all the facts when you come to brass tacks: / Birth, and copulation and death. [*Sweeney Agonistes*]

12 April is the cruellest month, breeding / Lilacs out of the dead land. [*The Waste Land*, 'The Burial of the Dead']

13 And I will show you something different from either / Your shadow at morning striding behind you, / Or your shadow at evening rising to meet you / I will show you fear in a handful of dust. [Ib.]

14 Unreal City, / Under the brown fog of a winter dawn, / A crowd flowed over London Bridge, so many, / I had not thought death had undone so many. [Ib.]

15 'Jug Jug' to dirty ears. [Ib. 'A Game of Chess']

16 O O O O that Shakespeherian Rag — / It's so elegant / So intelligent. [Ib.]

17 When lovely woman stoops to folly and / Paces about her room again, alone, / She smoothes her hair with automatic hand, / And puts a record on the gramophone. [Ib. 'The Fire Sermon']

18 Musing upon the king my brother's wreck / And on the king my father's death before him. [Ib.]

19 These fragments have I shored against my ruins. [Ib. 'What the Thunder Said']

20 Webster was much possessed by death / And saw the skull beneath the skin / ... Daffodil bulbs instead of balls / Stared from the sockets of the eyes! ['Whispers of Immortality']

21 No artist produces great art by a deliberate attempt to express his own personality. ['Four Elizabethan Dramatists']

22 In the seventeenth century a dissociation of sensibility set in from which we have never recovered. ['The Metaphysical Poets']

23 Poetry is not a turning loose of emotion, but an escape from emotion; it is not the expression of personality, but an escape from personality. ['Tradition and the Individual Talent']

Elizabeth I (1533–1603)

24 I am your anointed Queen. I will never be by violence constrained to do anything. I thank God I am endued with such qualities that if I were turned out of the Realm in my petticoat I were able to live in any place in Christome. [Attr. speech, 1566]

1 I know I have the body of a weak and feeble woman, but I have the heart and stomach of a king, and of a king of England too; and think foul scorn that Parma or Spain, or any prince of Europe, should dare to invade the borders of my realm. [Speech on the approach of the Armada, 1588]

2 Though God hath raised me high, yet this I count the glory of my crown: that I have reigned with your loves. [The Golden Speech, 1601]

3 God may pardon you, but I never can. [Remark to Countess of Nottingham]

4 [To Sir Walter Raleigh] I have known many persons who turned their gold into smoke, but you are the first to turn smoke into gold. [Quoted in Wintle and Kenin, *Dictionary of Biographical Quotations*]

5 Must! Is must a word to be addressed to princes? [Attr.]

Ellerton, John (1826–93)

6 The day Thou gavest, Lord, is ended; / The darkness falls at Thy behest; / To Thee our morning hymns ascended, / Thy praise shall sanctify our rest. [Hymn]

7 Thy throne shall never, / Like earth's proud empires, pass away. [Ib.]

Elliot, Jane (1727–1805)

8 I've heard them lilting, at the ewe milking. / Lasses a' lilting, before dawn of day; / But now they are moaning, on ilka green loaning; / The flowers of the forest are a' wede awae. ['The Flowers of the Forest']

Elliott, Ebenezer (1781–1849)

9 What is a communist? One who hath yearnings / For equal division of unequal earnings. [Epigram]

Ellis, George (1753–1815)

10 Snowy, Flowy, Blowy, / Showery, Flowery, Bowery, / Hoppy, Croppy, Droppy, / Breezy, Sneezy, Freezy. ['The Twelve Months']

Ellis, Henry Havelock (1859–1939)

11 What we call 'Progress' is the exchange of one nuisance for another nuisance. [*Impressions and Comments*]

12 God is an unutterable Sigh in the Human Heart, said the old German mystic. And therewith said the last word. [Ib.]

13 The absence of flaw in beauty is itself a flaw. [Ib.]

14 The whole religious complexion of the modern world is due to the absence from Jerusalem of a lunatic asylum. [Ib.]

15 Every artist writes his own autobiography. [*The New Spirit*]

16 Beauty is the child of love. [Ib.]

17 In many a war it has been the vanquished, not the victor, who has carried off the finest spoils. [*The Soul of Spain*]

Ellwood, Thomas (1639–1713)

18 Thou hast said much here of 'Paradise Lost'; but what hast thou to say of 'Paradise found'? [Remark to Milton, 1665]

Eluard, Paul (1895–1952)

19 *Adieu tristesse / Bonjour tristesse / Tu es inscrite dans les lignes du plafond.* Farewell sadness, hello sadness, you are written in the lines of the ceiling. ['A peine défigurée']

Emerson, Ralph Waldo (1803–1882)

20 Novels are as useful as Bibles if they teach you the secret that the best of life is conversation, and the greatest success is confidence. [*Conduct of Life*, 'Behaviour']

21 As there is use in medicine for poison, so the world cannot move without rogues. [Ib. 'Power']

22 Art is a jealous mistress, and if a man have a genius for painting, poetry, music, architecture, or philosophy, he makes a bad husband and an ill provider. [Ib. 'Wealth']

23 The manly part is to do with might and main what you can do. [Ib.]

1 The Frenchman invented the ruffle, the Englishman added the shirt. [*English Traits*]

2 They [the English] think him the best dressed man, whose dress is so fit for his use that you cannot notice or remember to describe it. [Ib.]

3 Adhere to your own act, and congratulate yourself if you have done something strange and extravagant, and broken the monotony of a decorous age. [*Essays*]

4 Nothing astonishes men so much as common-sense and plain dealing. [Ib. 'Art']

5 Fear is an instructor of great sagacity and the herald of all revolutions. [Ib. 'Compensation']

6 A friend may well be reckoned the masterpiece of Nature. [Ib. 'Friendship']

7 Let the soul be assured that somewhere in the universe it should rejoin its friend, and it would be content and cheerful alone for a thousand years. [Ib.]

8 It was a high counsel that I once heard given to a young person, 'Always do what you are afraid to do.' [Ib. 'Heroism']

9 There is properly no history; only biography. [Ib. 'History']

10 Living blood and a passion of kindness does at last distinguish God's gentlemen from Fashion's. [Ib. 'Manners']

11 To believe your own thought, to believe that what is true for you in your private heart is true for all men — that is genius. [Ib. 'Self-Reliance']

12 Society everywhere is in conspiracy against the manhood of every one of its members. [Ib.]

13 Whoso would be a man, must be a nonconformist. [Ib.]

14 A foolish consistency is the hobgoblin of little minds, adored by little statesmen and philosophers and divines. With consistency a great soul has simply nothing to do. [Ib.]

15 Shove Jesus and Judas equally aside. [Ib.]

16 I like the silent church before the service begins, better than any preaching. [Ib.]

17 No law can be sacred to me but that of my nature. Good and bad are but names very readily transferable to that or this; the only right is what is after my own constitution; the only wrong what is against it. [Ib.]

18 It is easy in the world to live after the world's opinion; it is easy in solitude after our own; but the great man is he who in the midst of the crowd keeps with perfect sweetness the independence of solitude. [Ib.]

19 What is a weed? A plant whose virtues have not yet been discovered. [*Fortune of the Republic*]

20 Earth laughs in flowers. [*Hamatreya*]

21 Here once the embattled farmers stood, / And fired the shot heard round the world. ['Hymn Sung at the Completion of the Concord Monument']

22 In your sane hour, you shall see that not a line has yet been written; that for all the poetry that is in the world your first sensation on entering a wood or standing on the shore of a lake has not been chanted yet...And yet for all this it must be owned that literature has truly told us that the cock crows in the mornings. [*Journals*]

23 A day is a miniature eternity. [Ib.]

24 When divine souls appear men are compelled by their own self-respect to distinguish them. [Ib.]

25 I trust a good deal to common fame, as we all must. If a man has good corn, or wood, or boards, or pigs, to sell, or can make better chairs or knives, crucibles, or church organs, than anybody else, you will find a broad, hard-beaten road to his house, though it be in the woods. [Ib. 'Common Fame']

26 Artists must be sacrificed to their art. Like bees, they must put their lives into the sting they give. [*Letters and Social Aims*, 'Inspiration']

27 Next to the originator of a good sentence is the first quoter of it. [Ib. 'Quotation and Originality']

1 When Shakespeare is charged with debts to his authors, Landor replies: 'Yet he was more original than his originals. He breathed upon dead bodies and brought them into life.' [Ib.]

2 Good manners are made up of petty sacrifices. [Ib. 'Social Aims']

3 It is only when the mind and character slumber that the dress can be seen. [Ib.]

4 It is a lesson which all history teaches wise men, to put trust in ideas, and not in circumstances. [*Miscellanies*, 'War']

5 Light is the first of painters. There is no object so foul that intense light will not make it beautiful. [*Nature*]

6 The Americans have little faith. They rely on the power of the dollar. [*Nature, Addresses and Lectures*, 'Man the Reformer']

7 We are taught by great actions that the universe is the property of every individual in it. [Ib. 'Beauty']

8 There is a little formula, couched in pure Saxon, which you may hear in the corners of the streets and in the yard of the dame's school, from very little republicans: 'I'm as good as you be,' which contains the essence of the Massachusetts Bill of Rights and of the American Declaration of Independence. [*Natural History of Intellect*, 'Boston']

9 The bitterest tragic element in life is the belief in a brute Fate or Destiny. [Ib. 'The Tragic']

10 We are wiser than we know. [*New England Reformers*]

11 Every hero becomes a bore at last. [*Representative Men*]

12 Never read any book that is not a year old. [*Society and Solitude*, 'Books']

13 'Well,' said Red Jacket (to one who complained he had not enough time), 'I suppose you have all there is.' [Ib. 'Works and Days']

14 The machine unmakes the man. Now that the machine is so perfect, the engineer is nobody. [Ib.]

15 Life is good only when it is magical and musical, a perfect timing and consent, and when we do not anatomize it...You must hear the bird's song without attempting to render it into nouns and verbs. [Ib.]

16 A man builds a fine house; and now he has a master, and a task for life; he is to furnish, watch, show it, and keep it in repair, the rest of his days. [Ib.]

17 Write it on your heart that every day is the best day in the year. No man has learned anything rightly until he knows that every day is Doomsday. [Ib.]

18 Now that is the wisdom of a man, in every instance of his labour, to hitch his wagon to a star, and see his chore done by the gods themselves. [Ib. 'Civilization']

19 Nature is full of freaks, and now puts an old head on young shoulders, and then a young heart beating under fourscore winters. [Ib. 'Old Age']

20 There is no knowledge that is not power. [Ib.]

21 As soon as there is life there is danger. [Ib. 'Public and Private']

22 Other world! There is no other world! Here or nowhere is the whole fact. [*Uncollected Lectures*, 'Natural Religion']

23 Spring still makes spring in the mind / When sixty years are told. ['The World Soul']

Empson, William (1906-1984)

24 Waiting for the end, boys, waiting for the end. / What is there to be or do? ['Just a Smack at Auden']

25 Slowly the poison the whole blood stream fills. / It is not the effort nor the failure tires. / The waste remains, the waste remains and kills. ['Missing Dates']

Engels, Friedrich (1820-1895)

26 The state is not abolished, it withers away. [*Anti-Dühring*]

27 Freedom is the recognition of necessity. [Quoted in Mackay, *The Harvest of a Quiet Eye*]

Ennius (239–169 B.C.)

1 *Simia, quam similis turpissima bestia, nobis.* How like us is the ape, most horrible of beasts. [Cicero, *De Natura Deorum*]

2 [Of Q. Fabius Maximus] *Unus homo nobis cunctando restituit rem.* One man by delaying saved the situation for us. [Cicero, *De Senectute*]

3 *Quem metuunt, oderunt.* They hate whom they fear. [*Thyestes*]

Erasmus, Gerard Didier (c. 1465–1536)

4 *Scitum est inter caecos luscum regnare posse.* It is well known, that among the blind the one-eyed man is king. [*Adagia*]

5 *A fronte praecipitium, a tergo lupi.* A precipice in front, wolves behind. [Ib.]

6 *Dulce bellum inexpertis.* War is sweet to those who do not fight. [Ib.]

7 Is not the Turk a man and a brother? [*Querela Pacis*]

Estienne, Henri (1531–1598)

8 *Si jeunesse savoit; si vieillesse pouvoit.* If youth only knew; if age only could. [*Les Prémices*]

Etherege, Sir George (1635–1691)

9 Writing, Madam, 's a mechanic part of wit! A gentleman should never go beyond a song or a billet. [*The Man of Mode*, IV]

10 Whate'er you say, I know all beyond High-Park's a desert to you. [Ib. V]

Euclid (fl. c. 300 B.C.)

11 [To Ptolemy I] There is no royal road to geometry. [Proclus, *Commentaria in Euclidem*]

12 *Quod erat demonstrandum.* Which was to be proved. [*Elements* (Latin version)]

13 *Pons asinorum.* The bridge of asses. [Ib.]

Euripides (c. 485–406 B.C.)

14 My tongue swore, but my mind was still unpledged. [*Hippolytus*]

15 The day is for honest men, the night for thieves. [*Iphigenia in Tauris*]

16 Those whom God wishes to destroy, he first makes mad. [Fragment]

Evans, Abel (1697–1737)

17 Lie heavy on him, Earth! for he / Laid many a heavy load on thee! ['Epitaph on Sir John Vanbrugh, Architect of Blenheim Palace']

Evelyn, John (1620–1706)

18 I saw Hamlet Prince of Denmark played, but now the old plays begin to disgust this refined age. [*Diary*, 1661]

Ewer, William Norman (1885–1976)

19 I gave my life for freedom — This I know: / For those who bade me fight had told me so. ['The Souls']

20 How odd / Of God / To choose / The Jews. ['How Odd']

Fabyan, Robert (d. 1513)

21 Finally he paid the debt of nature. [*New Chronicles*, II]

Fanon, Frantz (1925–1961)

22 For the black man there is only one destiny. And it is white. [*Black Skin, White Masks*]

Faraday, Michael (1791–1867)

23 It may be a weed instead of a fish that, after all my labour, I may at last pull up. [Letter, 1831]

Farmer, Edward (c. 1809–1876)

24 I have no pain, dear mother, now; / But oh! I am so dry: / Just moisten poor Jim's lips once more; / And, mother, do not cry! ['The Collier's Dying Child']

Farquhar, George (1678–1707)

25 My Lady Bountiful. [*The Beaux Stratagem*, I.1]

26 'Tis still my maxim, that there is no scandal like rags, nor any crime so shameful as poverty. [Ib.]

27 No woman can be a beauty without a fortune. [Ib. II.2]

1 There are secrets in all families. [Ib. III.3]

2 How a little love and good company improves a woman. [Ib. IV.1]

3 Spare all I have, and take my life. [Ib. V.2]

4 Charming women can true converts make, / We love the precepts for the teacher's sake. [*The Constant Couple*, V.3]

5 Crimes, like virtues, are their own rewards. [*The Inconstant*, IV.2]

6 Money is the sinews of love, as of war. [*Love and a Bottle*, II.1]

7 Poetry's a mere drug, Sir. [Ib. III.2]

Faulkner, William (1897–1962)

8 The writer's only responsibility is to his art...If a writer has to rob his mother, he will not hesitate; the 'Ode on a Grecian Urn' is worth any number of old ladies. [Attr.]

Fawcett, John (1740–1817)

9 Blest be the tie that binds / Our hearts in Jesus's love. [Hymn]

Fawkes, Guy (1570–1606)

10 Desperate diseases require desperate remedies. [Quoted in *Dictionary of National Biography*]

Ferdinand I, Emperor (1503–1564)

11 *Fiat justitia, et pereat mundus.* Let justice be done though the world perish. [Attr.] or *Fiat justitia ruat caelum.* Let justice be done though the heavens fall.

Fergusson, Sir James (1832–1907)

12 I have heard many arguments which influenced my opinion, but never one which influenced my vote. [Attr.]

Fergusson, Robert (1750–1774)

13 [Sunday] And wad maist trow some people chose / To change their faces wi' their clo'es, / And fain was gar ilk neibour think / They thirst for goodness as for drink. ['Auld Reekie']

14 And thou, great god of *Aquavitae*! / Wha sway'st the empire o' this city; — / Whan fou, we're sometimes capernoity; — / Be thou prepar'd / To hedge us frae that black banditti, / The City Guard. ['The Daft Days']

15 So, Delia, when her beauty's flown, / Trades on a bottom not her own, / And labours to escape detection / By putting on a false complexion. ['On Seeing a Lady Paint Herself']

Feuerbach, Ludwig (1804–1872)

16 *Der Mensch ist, was er isst.* Man is what he eats. [*Blätter für Literarische Unterhaltung*, 1850]

Fielding, Henry (1707–1754)

17 The devil take me, if I think anything but love to be the object of love. [*Amelia*, V]

18 One fool at least in every married couple. [Ib. IX, 4]

19 I am as sober as a judge. [*Don Quixote in England*, III]

20 Oh! The roast beef of England, / And old England's roast beef. [*The Grub Street Opera*, III]

21 He in a few minutes ravished this fair creature, or at least would have ravished her, if she had not, by a timely compliance, prevented him. [*Jonathan Wild*]

22 There were particularly two parties...the former were called *cavaliers* and *tory rory ranter boys.* [Ib.]

23 Greatness consists in bringing all manner of mischief on mankind, and goodness in removing it from them. [Ib.]

24 Now a comic romance is a comic epic-poem in prose. [*Joseph Andrews*, Preface]

25 It hath been thought a vast commendation of a painter to say his figures seem to breathe; but surely it is much greater and nobler applause, that they appear to think. [Ib.]

26 To whom nothing is given, of him can nothing be required. [Ib. II, 8]

27 What a silly fellow must he be who would do the devil's work for nothing. [Ib.]

1 I describe not men, but manners; not an individual, but a species. [Ib. III, 1]

2 Public schools are the nurseries of all vice and immorality. [Ib. III, 5]

3 Some folks rail against other folks because other folks have what some folks would be glad of. [Ib. IV, 6]

4 Love and scandal are the best sweeteners of tea. [*Love in Several Masques*, IV]

5 A newspaper, which consists of just the same number of words, whether there be news in it or not...may, likewise, be compared to a stagecoach, which performs constantly the same course, empty as well as full. [*Tom Jones*, II]

6 Thwackum was for doing justice, and leaving mercy to Heaven. [Ib. III, 10]

7 O! more than Gothic ignorance. [Ib. VII, 3]

8 An amiable weakness. [Ib. X, 8]

9 His designs were strictly honourable, as the phrase is; that is, to rob a lady of her fortune by way of marriage. [Ib. XI, 4]

10 He the best player!...Why, I could act as well as he myself. I am sure, if I had seen a ghost, I should have looked in the very same manner, and done just as he did...The king for my money! He speaks all his words distinctly, half as loud again as the other. Anybody may see he is an actor. [Ib. XVI, 5]

11 All Nature wears one universal grin. [*Tom Thumb*, I.1]

Fields, W.C. (1878–1946)

12 On the whole, I'd rather be in Philadelphia. [His own epitaph]

FitzGerald, Edward (1809–1883)

13 Awake! for Morning in the Bowl of Night / Has flung the Stone that puts the Stars to Flight: / And Lo! the Hunter of the East has caught / The Sultan's Turret in a Noose of Light. [*Rubáiyát of Omar Khayyám*, 1st Ed.]

14 Come, fill the Cup, and in the Fire of Spring / The Winter Garment of Repentance fling: / The Bird of Time has but a little way / To fly — and Lo! the Bird is on the Wing. [Ib.]

15 Here with a Loaf of Bread beneath the Bough, / A Flask of Wine, a Book of Verse — and Thou / Beside me singing in the Wilderness — / And Wilderness is Paradise enow! [Ib.]

16 Ah, take the Cash in hand and waive the Rest; / Oh, the brave Music of a *distant* Drum! [Ib.]

17 I sometimes think that never blows so red / The Rose as where some buried Caesar bled. [Ib.]

18 Lo! some we loved, the loveliest and best / That Time and Fate of all their Vintage prest, / Have drunk their Cup a Round or two before, / And one by one crept silently to Rest. [Ib.]

19 Myself when young did eagerly frequent / Doctor and Saint, and heard great argument / About it and about: but evermore / Came out by the same Door wherein I went. [Ib.]

20 Ah, fill the Cup: — what boots it to repeat / How Time is slipping underneath our Feet: / Unborn TO-MORROW and dead YESTERDAY, / Why fret about them if TO-DAY be sweet! [Ib.]

21 The Grape that can with Logic absolute / The Two-and-Seventy jarring Sects confute. [Ib.]

22 Strange, is it not? that of the myriads who / Before us pass'd the door of Darkness through, / Not one returns to tell us of the Road, / Which to discover we must travel too. [Ib.]

23 'Tis all a Chequer-board of Nights and Days / Where Destiny with Men for Pieces plays: / Hither and thither moves, and mates, and slays, / And one by one back in the Closet lays. [Ib.]

24 The Ball no question makes of Ayes and Noes, / But Right or Left, as strikes the Player goes. [Ib.]

25 The Moving Finger writes; and, having writ, / Moves on: nor all thy Piety nor Wit / Shall lure it back to cancel half a Line, / Nor all thy Tears wash out a Word of it. [Ib.]

26 ...that inverted Bowl they call the Sky. [Ib.]

27 Who *is* the Potter, pray, and who the Pot? [Ib.]

1 I often wonder what the Vintners buy / One half so precious as the Goods they sell. [Ib.]

2 Ah Love! Could you and I with Fate conspire / To grasp this sorry Scheme of Things entire, / Would we not shatter it to bits — and then / Re-mould it nearer to the Heart's Desire. [Ib.]

Fitzgerald, F. Scott (1896–1940)

3 In the real dark night of the soul it is always three o'clock in the morning. [*The Crack-Up*]

4 'What'll we do with ourselves this afternoon?' cried Daisy, 'and the day after that, and the next thirty years?' [*The Great Gatsby*]

Fitzsimmons, Robert (1862–1917)

5 The bigger they come, the harder they fall. [Remark before boxing match, 1902]

Flecker, James Elroy (1884–1915)

6 Half to forget the wandering and the pain, / Half to remember days that have gone by, / And dream and dream that I am home again! ['Brumana']

7 When even lovers find their peace at last, / And Earth is but a star, that once had shone. [*The Golden Journey to Samarkand*]

8 For lust of knowing what should not be known, / We take the Golden Road to Samarkand. [*Hassan*]

9 And with great lies about his wooden horse / Set the crew laughing, and forgot his course. ['The Old Ships']

10 O friend unseen, unborn, unknown, / Student of our sweet English tongue, / Read out my words at night, alone: / I was a poet, I was young. ['To a Poet a Thousand Years Hence']

Fletcher, Andrew, of Saltoun (1655–1716)

11 Like him that lights a candle to the sun. [Letter]

12 I knew a very wise man who believed that...if a man were permitted to make all the ballads, he need not care who should make the laws of a nation. And we find that most of the ancient legislators thought they could not well reform the manners of any city without the help of a lyric, and sometimes of a dramatic poet. [Letter, 1704].

Fletcher, John (1579–1625)

13 And he that will go to bed sober, / Falls with the leaf still in October. [*The Bloody Brother*, II.2]

14 It's impossible to ravish me / I'm so willing. [*The Faithful Shepherdess*, III.1]

15 Of all the paths lead to a woman's love / Pity's the straightest. [*The Knight of Malta*, I.1]

Florio, John (1553–1625)

16 England is the paradise of women, the purgatory of men, and the hell of horses. [*Second Frutes*]

Foch, Ferdinand (1851–1929)

17 *Mon centre cède, ma droite recule, situation excellente. J'attaque!* My centre gives way, my right retreats; situation excellent. I shall attack. [Attr. dispatch during Battle of Marne]

18 Hostilities will cease along the whole front at the 11th hour, French o'clock, on Nov. 11. Allied troops will not cross, until further orders, the line reached on that date and that hour. [Command announcing the armistice, 1918]

Fontaine, Jean de la (1621–1695)

19 *Je plie et ne romps pas.* I bend and do not break. [*Fables*, 'Le Chêne et le Roseau']

20 *C'est double plaisir de tromper le trompeur.* It is double pleasing to trick the trickster. [Ib. 'Le Coq et le Renard']

21 *La raison du plus fort est toujous la meilleure.* The argument of the stronger man is always the best. [Ib. 'Le Loup et l'Agneau']

1 *La mort ne surprend point le sage, / Il est toujours prêt à partir.* Death does not surprise a wise man, he is always ready to leave. [Ib. 'La Mort et le Mourant']

2 *Aucun chemin de fleurs ne conduit à la gloire.* No road of flowers leads to glory. [Ib. 'Les Deux Aventuriers et le Talisman']

3 *De la peau de lion l'âne s'étant vêtu / Etoit craint partout à la ronde.* Dressed in the lion's skin, the ass spread terror far and wide. [Ib. 'L'Ane vêtu de la peau du Lion']

4 *Hélas! on voit que de tout temps, / Les Petits ont pâti des sottises des Grands.* Alas, it seems that for all time the Small have suffered from the folly of the Great. [Ib. 'Les Deux Taureaux et la Grenouille']

5 *En tout chose il faut considérer la fin.* In all matters one must consider the end. [Ib. 'Le Renard et le Bouc']

Fontenelle, Bernard (1657-1757)

6 I detest war: it ruins conversation. [Quoted in Auden, *A Certain World*]

Foote, Samuel (1720-1777)

7 Born in a cellar...and living in a garret. [*The Author*]

8 He is not only dull in himself but the cause of dullness in others. [Boswell, *Life of Johnson*]

9 For as the old saying is, / When house and land are gone and spent / Then learning is most excellent. [*Taste*]

Ford, Ford Madox (1873-1939)

10 This is the saddest story I have ever heard. [*The Good Soldier*, first sentence]

Ford, Henry (1863-1947)

11 History is bunk. [Remark, 1919]

12 [Of Model-T Fords] You can have any colour, so long as it's black. [Attr.]

Ford, John (c. 1586-1639)

13 Green indiscretion, flattery of greatness, / Rawness of judgement, wilfulness in folly, / Thoughts vagrant as the wind, and as uncertain. [*The Broken Heart*]

14 Revenge proves its own executioner. [Ib. IV.1]

15 He hath shook hands with time. [Ib. V.2]

16 Parthenophil is lost, and I would see him; / For he is like to something I remember, / A great while since, a long, long time ago. ['The Lover's Melancholy']

Forgy, Howell (1908-)

17 Praise the Lord and pass the ammunition. [Attr. remark at Pearl Harbour, 1941]

Forster, E.M. (1879-1970)

18 Beethoven's Fifth Symphony is the most sublime noise that ever penetrated into the ear of man. [*Howard's End*, 5]

19 Personal relations are the important thing for ever and ever, and not this outer life of telegrams and anger. [Ib. 19]

20 Only connect! [Ib. 22]

21 Yes — oh dear, yes — the novel tells a story. [*Aspects of the Novel*]

22 If I had to choose between betraying my country and betraying my friend, I hope I should have the guts to betray my country. [*Two Cheers for Democracy*, 'What I Believe']

Fouché, Joseph (1763-1820)

23 *C'est pire qu'un crime; c'est une faute.* It is worse than a crime; it is a mistake. [Remark on execution of Duc d'Enghien, 1804; also attr. Antoine Boulay de la Meurthe (1761-1840)]

Fourier, François Charles Marie (1772-1837)

24 Instead of by battles and Ecumenical Councils, the rival portions of humanity will one day dispute each other's excellence in the manufacture of little cakes. [Emerson, *Lectures and Biographical Sketches*]

Fox, Charles James (1749–1806)

1 [Of the Fall of the Bastille] How much the greatest event it is that ever happened in the world! and how much the best! [Letter, 1789]

France, Anatole (1844–1924)

2 *Le hasard c'est peut-être le pseudonyme de Dieu, quand il ne veut pas signer.* Chance is perhaps God's pseudonym when he does not want to sign. [*Le Jardin d'Epicure*]

3 The law, in its majestic equality, forbids the rich as well as the poor to sleep under bridges, to beg in the streets, and to steal bread. [Cournos, *Modern Plutarch*]

4 It is better to understand little than to misunderstand a lot. [*Revolt of the Angels*]

5 *Le bon critique est celui qui raconte les aventures de son âme au milieu des chefs-d'oeuvre.* The good critic is one who recounts the adventures of his soul among masterpieces. [*La Vie Littéraire*]

Francis I of France (1494–1547)

6 *Tout est perdu fors l'honneur.* All is lost save honour. [Attr. remark after losing Battle of Pavia, 1525]

Franklin, Benjamin (1706–1790)

7 Remember that time is money. [*Advice to Young Tradesman*]

8 Be in general virtuous, and you will be happy. ['On Early Marriages']

9 He's the best physician that knows the worthlessness of the most medicines. [*Poor Richard's Almanac*, 1733]

10 To lengthen thy life, lessen thy meals. [Ib.]

11 Where there's marriage without love, there will be love without marriage. [Ib. 1734]

12 Necessity never made a good bargain. [Ib. 1735]

13 Three may keep a secret, if two of them are dead. [Ib.]

14 At twenty years of age, the will reigns; at thirty, the wit; and at forty, the judgement. [Ib. 1741]

15 Experience keeps a dear school, but fools will learn in no other. [Ib. 1743]

16 Many have been ruined by buying good pennyworths. [Ib. 1747]

17 Many foxes grow grey, but few grow good. [Ib. 1749]

18 The golden age never was the present age. [Ib. 1750]

19 Little strokes fell great oaks. [Ib.]

20 Old boys have their playthings as well as young ones; the difference is only in price. [Ib. 1752]

21 If you would know the value of money, go and try to borrow some; for he that goes a borrowing goes a sorrowing. [Ib. 1754]

22 He that lives upon hope will die fasting. [Ib. 1758, Preface]

23 A little neglect may breed mischief... for want of a nail, the shoe was lost; for want of a shoe, the horse was lost; and for want of a horse the rider was lost. [Ib.]

24 Early to bed and early to rise, / Makes a man healthy, wealthy and wise. [Ib. 1758]

25 Creditors have better memories than debtors. [Ib.]

26 No nation was ever ruined by trade. [*Thoughts on Commercial Subjects*]

27 Here Skugg lies snug / As a bug in a rug. [Letter to Miss Shipley, 1772]

28 There never was a good war, or a bad peace. [Letter, 1783]

29 In this world nothing can be said to be certain, except death and taxes. [Letter, 1789]

30 We must all hang together, or, most assuredly, we shall all hang separately. [Remark, Independence Day, 1776]

31 Man is a tool-making animal. [Boswell, *Life of Johnson*]

32 What is the use of a new-born child? [Attr. on being asked the use of a new invention]

33 There are more old drunkards than old doctors. [Attr.]

Frederick the Great (1712–1786)

1 My people and I have come to an agreement which satisfies us both. They are to say what they please, and I am to do what I please. [Attr.]

2 A crown is merely a hat that lets the rain in. [Remark on declining a formal coronation, 1740]

3 Rogues, would you live for ever? [Command to hesitant troops]

Frere, John Hookham (1769–1846)

4 The feather'd race with pinions skim the air — / Not so the mackerel, and still less the bear! ['Progress of Man']

Frost, Robert (1875–1963)

5 I have been one acquainted with the night. ['Acquainted with the Night']

6 Earth's the right place for love: / I don't know where it's likely to go better. ['Birches']

7 One could do worse than be a swinger of birches. [Ib.]

8 Home is the place where, when you have to go there, / They have to take you in. ['The Death of the Hired Man']

9 I would have written of me on my stone: / I had a lover's quarrel with the world. ['Epitaph']

10 Some say the world will end in fire, / Some say in ice. / From what I've tasted of desire / I hold with those who favour fire. ['Fire and Ice']

11 The land was ours before we were the land's. ['The Gift Outright']

12 Something there is that doesn't love a wall. ['Mending Wall']

13 He only says, 'Good fences make good neighbours.' [Ib.]

14 I never dared be radical when young / For fear it would make me conservative when old. ['Precaution']

15 We dance round in a ring and suppose, / But the Secret sits in the middle and knows. ['The Secret Sits']

16 The woods are lovely, dark, and deep, / But I have promises to keep, / And miles to go before I sleep, / And miles to go before I sleep. ['Stopping by Woods on a Snowy Evening']

17 Scholars get theirs [knowledge] with conscientious thoroughness along projected lines of logic; poets theirs cavalierly and as it happens in and out of books. They stick to nothing deliberately, but let what will stick to them like burrs where they walk in the fields. ['The Figure a Poem Makes']

18 A poem may be worked over once it is in being, but may not be worried into being. [Ib.]

19 Writing free verse is like playing tennis with the net down. [Address, 1935]

20 Poetry is a way of taking life by the throat. [*Vogue*, 1963]

Froude, James Anthony (1818–1894)

21 Wild animals never kill for sport. Man is the only one to whom the torture and death of his fellow creatures is amusing in itself. [*Oceana*, 5]

22 Fear is the parent of cruelty. ['Party Politics']

Fry, Christopher (1907–)

23 Who should question then / Why we lean our bicycle against a hedge / And go into the house of God? / Who shall question / That coming out from our doorsteps / We have discerned a little, we have known / More than the gossip that comes to us over our gates? ['The Boy with a Cart']

24 I've begun to believe that the reasonable / Is an invention of man, altogether in opposition / To the facts of creation. [*The Firstborn*, III]

25 What, after all, / Is a halo? It's only one more thing to keep clean. [*The Lady's Not For Burning*, I]

26 What is official / Is incontestable. It undercuts / the problematical world and sells us life / At a discount. [Ib.]

27 I know I am not / A practical person; legal matters and so forth / Are Greek to me, except, of course, / That I understand Greek. [Ib. II]

1 The Great Bear is looking so geometrical / One would think that something or other could be proved. [Ib. III]

2 Where in this small-talking world can I find / A longitude with no platitude? [Ib.]

3 Oh, the unholy mantrap of love! [Ib.]

4 Life and death / Is cat and dog in this double-bed of a world. [*A Phoenix Too Frequent*]

5 It doesn't do a man any good, daylight. / It means up and doing, and that means up to no good. / The best life is led horizontal. [*Thor, With Angels*]

6 I know an undesirable character / When I see one; I've been one myself for years. [*Venus Observed*, II]

Fuller, Thomas (1608–1661)

7 He was a very valiant man who first ventured on eating of oysters. [*History of the Worthies of England*]

8 Light (God's eldest daughter) is a principal beauty in building. [*Holy and Profane State*, 'Of Building']

9 Anger is one of the sinews of the soul; he that wants it hath a maimed mind. [Ib. 'Of Anger']

10 Learning hath gained most by those books by which the printers have lost. [Ib. 'Of Books']

11 It is always darkest just before the day dawneth. [*Pisgah Sight*]

Fyleman, Rose (1877–1957)

12 There are fairies at the bottom of our garden. ['Fairies']

Gable, Clark (1901–1960)

13 Frankly, my dear, I don't give a damn. [*Gone With the Wind*]

Gabor, Zsa-Zsa (?1921–)

14 Never despise what it says in the women's magazines: it may not be subtle but neither are men. [*Observer*, 'Sayings of the Week', 1976]

Gaisford, Rev. Thomas (1779–1855)

15 The study of Greek literature...not only elevates above the vulgar herd, but leads not infrequently to positions of considerable emolument. [Sermon, Oxford Cathedral]

Gaitskell, Hugh (1906–1963)

16 [Referring to Labour Party] There are some of us who will fight, fight, and fight again to save the Party we love. [Speech, 1960]

Galbraith, J. K. (1908–)

17 The Affluent Society [Title of book]

Galileo Galilei (1564–1642)

18 *Eppur si muove.* But it does move. [Attr. (probably apocryphal)]

Gallagher, William (1881–1965)

19 We are for our own people. We want to see them happy, healthy and wise, drawing strength from cooperation with the peoples of other lands, but also contributing their full share to the general well-being. Not a broken-down pauper and mendicant, but a strong, living partner in the progressive advancement of civilization. [*The Case for Communism*]

Gandhi, Mahatma (1869–1948)

20 [When asked what he thought of Western civilization] I think it would be an excellent idea. [Attr.]

Garbo, Greta (1905–)

21 I never said, 'I want to be alone.' I only said, 'I want to be *let* alone.' There is all the difference. [Quoted in Colombo, *Wit and Wisdom of the Moviemakers*]

García Lorca, Federico (1899–1936)

1 *A las cinco de la tarde. / Eran las cinco en punto de la tarde. / Un niño trajo la blanca sábana / a las cinco de la tarde.* At five in the afternoon. It was precisely five in the afternoon. A boy brought the white sheet at five in the afternoon. [*Llanto por Ignacio Sánchez Mejías*]

2 *Ni un solo momento, viejo hermoso Walt Whitman, / he dejado de ver tu barba llena de mariposas.* Not for a moment, beautiful aged Walt Whitman, have I ceased seeing your beard full of butterflies. ['Oda a Walt Whitman']

3 *Verde que te quiero verde, / Verde viento. Verdes ramas.* Green I love you green. Green wind. Green branches. ['Romance sonámbulo']

Garrick, David (1717–1779)

4 Here lies Nolly Goldsmith, for shortness call'd Noll, / Who wrote like an angel, but talk'd like poor Poll. [Impromptu epitaph on Goldsmith]

Garrison, William Lloyd (1805–1879)

5 I am in earnest — I will not equivocate — I will not excuse — I will not retreat a single inch — and I will be heard! [Salutatory address of *The Liberator*, 1831]

Gaskell, Elizabeth (1810–1865)

6 A man is *so* in the way in the house! [*Cranford*, 1]

7 We were none of us musical, though Miss Jenkyns beat time, out of time, by way of appearing to be so. [Ib.]

8 Bombazine would have shown a deeper sense of her loss. [Ib. 7]

Gauguin, Paul (1848–1903)

9 Many excellent cooks are spoiled by going into the arts. [Cournos, *Modern Plutarch*]

10 Civilization is paralysis. [Ib.]

11 Art is either a plagiarist or a revolutionist. [Huneker, *Pathos of Distance*]

Gautier, Théophile (1811–1872)

12 *Plutôt la barbarie que l'ennui.* Sooner barbarity than boredom. [Attr.]

Gavarni (1801–1866)

13 *Les enfants terribles. Lit.* the terrible children [i.e. people given to unconventional conduct or indiscreet remarks] [Title of a series of prints]

Gay, John (1685–1732)

14 I rage, I melt, I burn, / The feeble God has stabb'd me to the heart. [*Acis and Galatea*, II]

15 O ruddier than the cherry, / O sweeter than the berry, / O nymph more bright / Than moonshine night, / Like kidlings blithe and merry. [Ib.]

16 Do you think your mother and I should have liv'd comfortably so long together, if ever we had been married? [*The Beggar's Opera*, I]

17 Well, Polly; as far as one woman can forgive another, I forgive thee. [Ib.]

18 If with me you'd fondly stray, / Over the hills and far away. [Ib.]

19 I think you must ev'n do as other widows — buy yourself weeds, and be cheerful. [Ib. II]

20 How happy could I be with either, / Were t'other dear charmer away! [Ib.]

21 She who has never lov'd, has never liv'd. [The Captives, II]

22 Then nature rul'd, and love, devoid of art, / Spoke the consenting language of the heart. [*Dione*, Prologue]

23 Whence is thy learning? Hath thy toil / O'er books consum'd the midnight oil? [*Fables*, Introduction]

24 Where yet was ever found a mother, / Who'd give her booby for another? [Ib. 3]

25 Those who in quarrels interpose, / Must often wipe a bloody nose. [Ib. 34]

26 Life is a jest; and all things show it. / I thought so once; but now I know it. ['My Own Epitaph']

1 No, sir, tho' I was born and bred in England, I can dare to be poor, which is the only thing nowadays men are ashamed of. [*Polly*, I]

Geddes, Sir Eric (1875–1937)

2 We will get out of her [Germany] all you can squeeze out of a lemon and a bit more...I will squeeze her until you can hear the pips squeak. [Speech, 1918]

George I (1660–1727)

3 I hate all Boets and Bainters. [Campbell, *Lives of the Chief Justices*]

George II (1683–1760)

4 [Of General Wolfe] Mad, is he? Then I hope he will *bite* some of my other generals. [Attr.]

George III (1738–1820)

5 'Was there ever,' cried he, 'such stuff as great part of Shakespeare? Only one must not say so... Is there not sad stuff?' [Fanny Burney, *Diary*]

George IV (1762–1830)

6 Harris, I am not well; pray get me a glass of brandy. [On first meeting his fiancée, Caroline of Brunswick, 1795]

George V (1865–1936)

7 How is the Empire? [Attr. last words]

8 Bugger Bognor. [Attr. last words, when told he would soon be convalescing in Bognor Regis.]

George, Henry (1839–1897)

9 The man who gives me employment, which I must have or suffer, that man is my master, let me call him what I will. [*Social Problems*]

Gibbon, Edward (1737–1794)

10 I spent fourteen months at Magdalen College; they proved the fourteen months the most idle and unprofitable of my whole life. [*Autobiography*]

11 I sighed as a lover, I obeyed as a son. [Ib.]

12 [Of London] Crowds without company, dissipation without pleasure. [Ib.]

13 It was at Rome, on the 15th October, 1764, as I sat musing amidst the ruins of the Capitol, while the barefooted friars were singing vespers in the Temple of Jupiter, that the idea of writing the decline and fall of the city first started to my mind. [Ib.]

14 The first of earthly blessings, independence. [Ib.]

15 My English text is chaste, and all licentious passages are left in the decent obscurity of a learned language. [Ib.]

16 The various modes of worship, which prevailed in the Roman world, were all considered by the people as equally true; by the philosopher as equally false; and by the magistrate as equally useful. [*Decline and Fall of the Roman Empire*, 2]

17 The principles of a free constitution are irrecoverably lost, when the legislative power is nominated by the executive. [Ib. 3]

18 History...is, indeed, little more than the register of the crimes, follies, and misfortunes of mankind. [Ib.]

19 [Of Emperor Gordian the Younger] Twenty-two acknowledged concubines, and a library of sixty-two thousand volumes attested the variety of his inclinations; and from the productions which he left behind him, it appears that both the one and the other were designed for use rather than for ostentation. [Ib. 7]

20 Corruption, the most infallible symptom of constitutional liberty. [Ib. 21]

21 In every deed of mischief he had a heart to resolve, a head to contrive, and a hand to execute. [Ib. 48]

22 The winds and waves are always on the side of the ablest navigators. [Ib. 68]

23 All that is human must retrograde if it does not advance. [Ib. 71]

24 My early and invincible love of reading...I would not exchange for the treasures of India. [*Memoirs*]

25 I was never less alone than when by myself. [Ib.]

Gibbons, Stella (1902-)

1 Something nasty in the woodshed. [*Cold Comfort Farm, passim*]

Gibbs, Wolcott (1902-1958)

2 Where it all will end, knows God! ['Time ... Fortune...Life...Luce', parody of *Time* magazine]

Gide, André (1869-1951)

3 *L'acte gratuit.* The gratuitous action. [*Les Caves du Vatican, passim*]

Gilbert, William Schwenck (1836-1911)

4 In all the woes that curse our race / There is a lady in the case. [*Fallen Fairies*, 2]

5 The padre said, 'Whatever have you been and gone and done?' ['Gentle Alice Brown']

6 [Of the Duke of Plaza Toro] He led his regiment from behind — / He found it less exciting. [*The Gondoliers*, I]

7 Of that there is no manner of doubt — / No probable, possible shadow of doubt — / No possible doubt whatever. [Ib.]

8 Oh, 'tis a glorious thing, I ween, / To be a regular Royal Queen! / No half-and-half affair, I mean, / But a right-down regular Royal Queen! [Ib.]

9 Take a pair of sparkling eyes. [Ib. II]

10 Take my counsel, happy man; / Act upon it, if you can! [Ib.]

11 Now, that's the kind of king for me — / He wished all men as rich as he, / So to the top of every tree / Promoted everybody. [Ib.]

12 When everyone is somebodee / Then no one's anybody! [Ib.]

13 'And I'm never, never sick at sea!' / 'What, never? / 'No, never!' / 'What, *never*?' / 'Hardly ever!' [*H.M.S. Pinafore*, I]

14 I always voted at my party's call, / And I never thought of thinking for myself at all. [Ib.]

15 When I was a lad I served a term / As office boy to an Attorney's firm. / I cleaned the windows and I swept the floor, / And I polished up the handle of the big front door. / I polished up that handle so carefullee / That now I am the Ruler of the Queen's Navee! [Ib.]

16 I never use a big, big D. [Ib.]

17 But in spite of all temptations / To belong to other nations, / He remains an Englishman. [Ib. II]

18 Bow, bow, ye lower middle classes! / Bow, bow, ye tradesmen, bow, ye masses. [*Iolanthe*, I]

19 Hearts just as pure and fair / May beat in Belgrave Square / As in the lowly air / Of Seven Dials. [Ib.]

20 I often think it's comical / How Nature always does contrive / That every boy and every gal, / That's born into this the world alive, / Is either a little Liberal, / Or else a little Conservative! [Ib.]

21 The House of Peers, throughout the war, / Did nothing in particular, / And did it very well. [Ib. II]

22 A wandering minstrel I — / A thing of shreds and patches, / Of ballads, songs and snatches, / And dreamy lullaby! [*The Mikado*, I]

23 I can trace my ancestry back to a protoplasmal primordial atomic globule. Consequently, my family pride is something inconceivable. [Ib.]

24 It revolts me, but I do it! [Ib.]

25 I accept refreshment at any hands, however lowly. [Ib.]

26 I've got a little list / Of society offenders who might well be underground / And who never would be missed. [Ib.]

27 Three little maids from school are we, / Pert as a schoolgirl well can be. [Ib.]

28 Awaiting the sensation of a short, sharp shock, / From a cheap and chippy chopper on a big black block. [Ib.]

29 My object all sublime / I shall achieve in time — / To let the punishment fit the crime — / The punishment fit the crime. [Ib. II]

1 On a cloth untrue, / With a twisted cue / And elliptical billiard balls. [Ib.]

2 Something lingering, with boiling oil in it, I fancy. [Ib.]

3 Merely corroborative detail, intended to give artistic verisimilitude to an otherwise bald and unconvincing narrative. [Ib.]

4 The flowers that bloom in the spring, / Tra la, have nothing to do with the case. [Ib.]

5 On a tree by a river a little tom-tit / Sang 'Willow, titwillow, titwillow!' / And I said to him, 'Dicky-bird, why do you sit? / Singing Willow, titwillow, titwillow?' [Ib.]

6 'Is it weakness of intellect, birdie?' I cried, / 'Or a rather tough worm in your little inside?' [Ib.]

7 But the peripatetics / Of long-haired aesthetics / Are very much more to their taste. [*Patience*, I]

8 You must lie upon the daisies and discourse in novel phrases of your complicated state of mind, / The meaning doesn't matter if it's only idle chatter of a transcendental kind. / And everyone will say, / As you walk your mystic way, / 'If this young man expresses himself in terms too deep for *me*, / Why, what a very singularly deep young man this deep young man must be!' [Ib.]

9 Though the Philistines may jostle, you will rank as an apostle in the high aesthetic band, / If you walk down Piccadilly with a poppy or a lily in your medieval hand. [Ib.]

10 A greenery-yallery, Grosvenor Gallery, / Foot-in-the-grave young man! [Ib. II]

11 It is, it is a glorious thing / To be a Pirate King. [*The Pirates of Penzance*, I]

12 In short, in matters vegetable, animal, and mineral, / I am the very model of a modern Major-General. [Ib.]

13 When a felon's not engaged in his employment — / Or maturing his felonious little plans — / His capacity for innocent enjoyment — / Is just as great as any honest man's. [Ib. II]

14 A policeman's lot is not a happy one. [Ib.]

15 He combines the manners of a Marquis with the morals of a Methodist. [*Ruddigore*, I]

16 All baronets are bad. [Ib.]

17 If you wish in this world to advance / Your merits you're bound to enhance, / You must stir it and stump it, / And blow your own trumpet, / Or, trust me, you haven't a chance! [Ib.]

18 For duty, duty must be done; / The rule applies to everyone. [Ib.]

19 I can't say fairer than that, can I? [Ib.]

20 Oh! a Baronet's rank is exceedingly nice, But the title's uncommonly dear at the price! [Ib. II]

21 Oh! my name is John Wellington Wells, / I'm a dealer in magic and spells. [*The Sorcerer*, I]

22 She may very well pass for forty-three / In the dusk with a light behind her. [*Trial by Jury*]

23 For now I am a Judge, / And a good Judge too. [Ib.]

24 Whatever valour true is found, / True modesty will there abound. [*Yeomen of the Guard*, I]

25 It's a song of a merryman, moping mum, / Whose soul was sad, and whose glance was glum, / Who, sipped no sup, and who craved no crumb, / As he sighed for the love of a ladye. [Ib.]

Ginsberg, Alan (1926–)

26 I saw the best minds of my generation destroyed by madness, starving hysterical naked. [*Howl*, first line]

Gladstone, William Ewart (1809–1898)

27 [On Naples] This is the negation of God erected into a system of government. [*Letter to Lord Aberdeen*, 1851]

28 The resources of civilization are not yet exhausted. [Speech, 1881]

1 All the world over, I will back the masses against the classes. [Speech, 1886]

2 I would tell them of my own intention to keep my own counsel...and I will venture to recommend them, as an old Parliamentary hand, to do the same. [Speech, 1886]

3 You cannot fight against the future. Time is on our side. [Speech on Reform Bill, 1886]

Gloucester, William, Duke of (1776–1805)

4 Another damned, thick, square book. Always scribble, scribble, scribble! Eh! Mr. Gibbon? [Boswell, *Life of Johnson*]

Godard, Jean-Luc (1930–)

5 Cinema is truth twenty-four times a second. [*Le Petit Soldat*]

6 Of course a film should have a beginning, a middle and an end. But not necessarily in that order. [Quoted in Halliwell, *Filmgoers' Book of Quotes*]

Godwin, William (1756–1836)

7 The log was burning brightly, / 'Twas a night that should banish all sin, / For the bells were ringing the Old Year out, / And the New Year in. ['The Miner's Dream of Home']

Goering, Hermann (1893–1946)

8 Guns will make us powerful; butter will only make us fat. [Broadcast, 1936]

9 When I hear anyone talk of Culture, I reach for my revolver. [Attr. Probably derived from Hanns Johst, *Schlageter* (1934)]

Goethe, Johann Wolfgang von (1749–1832)

10 *Wer reitet so spät durch Nacht und Wind? / Es ist der Vater mit seinem Kind.* Who rides so late through the night and storm? It is the father with his child. ['Erlkönig']

11 *Es irrt der Mensch, so lang er strebt.* While man aspires, he errs. [*Faust*, I]

12 *Ich bin der Geist der stets verneint.* I am the spirit that forever denies. [Ib.]

13 *Entbehren sollst Du! sollst entbehren! / Das ist der ewige Gesang.* Deny yourself! You must deny yourself! That is the never-ending song. [Ib.]

14 *Grau, teuer Freund, ist alle Theorie / Und grün des Lebens goldner Baum.* All theory, dear friend, is grey; but the precious tree of life is green. [Ib.]

15 *Die Tat ist alles, nicht der Ruhm.* The act is all, the reputation nothing. [Ib. II]

16 *Sah ein Knab' ein Röslein stehn, / Röslein auf der Heiden.* In the woods a boy one day, saw a wild rose growing. ['Heidenröslein']

17 *In der Kunst ist das Beste gut genug.* In art the best is good enough. [*Italienische Reise*]

18 *Entzwei' und gebiete! Tüchtig Wort; / Verein' und leite! Bess'rer Hort.* Divide and rule, a sound motto. Unite and lead a better one. [*Sprüche in Reimen*]

19 *Es bildet ein Talent sich in der Stille, / Sich ein Charakter in dem Strom der Welt.* Talent grows in peace, character in the current of affairs. [*Tasso*, I]

20 *Mein Vermächtniss, wie herrlich weit und breit! / Die Zeit ist mein Vermächtniss mein Acker ist die Zeit.* How great is my inheritance, how wide and spacious. / Time is my inheritance, my estate is time. [*Wilhelm Meisters Wanderjahre*]

21 *Du kannst, denn du sollst.* You can, for you must. [*Xenien*]

22 Classicism is health, romanticism is sickness. [*Conversations with Eckermann*]

23 Architecture is frozen music. [Ib.]

24 *Mehr Licht!* More light! [Last words]

Goldoni, Carlo (1707–1793)

25 *Bello è il rossore, ma è incommodo qualche volta.* The blush is beautiful, but it is sometimes inconvenient. [*Pamela*]

Goldsmith, Oliver (1728–1774)

1 As writers become more numerous, it is natural for readers to become more indolent. [*The Bee*]

2 On whatever side we regard the history of Europe, we shall perceive it to be a tissue of crimes, follies and misfortunes. [*The Citizen of the World*]

3 Ill fares the land, to hast'ning ills a prey, / Where wealth accumulates, and men decay. [*The Deserted Village*]

4 But a bold peasantry, their country's pride, / When once destroyed, can never be supplied. [Ib.]

5 Trade's unfeeling train / Usurp the land and dispossess the swain. [Ib.]

6 And the loud laugh that spoke the vacant mind. [Ib.]

7 Truth from his lips prevail'd with double sway, / And fools, who came to scoff, remain'd to pray. [Ib.]

8 Full well they laugh'd with counterfeited glee, / At all his jokes, for many a joke had he. [Ib.]

9 And still they gazed, and still the wonder grew, / That one small head could carry all he knew. [Ib.]

10 And, e'en while fashion's brightest arts decoy, / The heart distrusting asks, if this be joy. [Ib.]

11 Ye friends to truth, ye statesmen, who survey / The rich man's joys increase, the poor's decay, / 'Tis yours to judge, how wide the limits stand / Between a splendid and a happy land. [Ib.]

12 The man of wealth and pride / Takes up a space that many poor supplied. [Ib.]

13 Ten thousand baneful arts combined / To pamper luxury, and thin mankind. [Ib.]

14 And in that town a dog was found, / As many dogs there be, / Both mongrel, puppy, whelp, and hound, / And curs of low degree. ['Elegy on the Death of a Mad Dog']

15 The man recover'd of the bite, / The dog it was that died. [Ib.]

16 All his faults are such that one loves him still the better for them. [*The Good-Natured Man*, I]

17 Don't let us make imaginary evils, when you know we have so many real ones to encounter. [Ib.]

18 This same philosophy is a good horse in the stable, but an arrant jade on a journey. [Ib.]

19 I love everything that's old; old friends, old times, old manners, old books, old wine. [*She Stoops to Conquer*, I]

20 As for disappointing them I should not so much mind; but I can't abide to disappoint myself. [Ib.]

21 This is Liberty-Hall, gentlemen. [Ib. II]

22 Such is the patriot's boast, where'er we roam, / His first, best country ever is, at home. [*The Traveller*]

23 How small, of all that human hearts endure, / That part which laws or kings can cause or cure. [Ib.]

24 And honour sinks where commerce long prevails. [Ib.]

25 I was ever of opinion, that the honest man who married and brought up a large family, did more service than he who continued single and only talked of population. [*The Vicar of Wakefield*, 1]

26 I chose my wife, as she did her wedding gown, not for a fine glossy surface, but such qualities as would wear well. [Ib. 1]

27 I...showed her that books were sweet, unreproaching companions to the miserable, and that if they could not bring us to enjoy life, they could at least teach us to endure it. [Ib. 22]

28 As ten millions of circles can never make a square, so the united voice of myriads cannot lend the smallest foundation to falsehood. [Ib. 26]

29 There is no arguing with Johnson; for if his pistol misses fire, he knocks you down with the butt end of it. [Boswell, *Life of Johnson*]

30 As I take my shoes from the shoemaker, and my coat from the tailor, so I take my religion from the priest. [Ib.]

Goldwater, Barry (1909-)

1 Extremism in the defence of liberty is no vice. [Speech, 1964]

Goldwyn, Samuel (1884-1974)

2 You can include me out. [Quoted in Colombo, *Wit and Wisdom of the Moviemakers*]

3 I read part of it all the way through. [Ib.]

4 I'll give you a definite maybe. [Ib.]

5 A verbal contract isn't worth the paper it's written on. [Ib.]

6 Why should people go out and pay money to see bad films when they can stay at home and see bad television for nothing? [*Observer*, 'Sayings of the Week', 1956]

7 Anyone who goes to see a psychiatrist ought to have his head examined. [Attr.]

8 Messages are for Western Union. [Quoted in Halliwell, *Filmgoers' Book of Quotes*]

Gordon, Adam Lindsay (1833-1870)

9 Life is mostly froth and bubble, / Two things stand like stone, / Kindness in another's trouble, / Courage in your own. [*Ye Wearie Wayfarer*]

Goschen, George, Lord (1831-1907)

10 We have stood alone in that which is called isolation — our splendid isolation, as one of our colonial friends was good enough to call it. [Speech, 1896]

Grade, Lew (1906-)

11 All my shows are great, Some of them are bad. But they are all great. [*Observer*, 'Sayings of the Week', 1975]

Grafton, Richard (d. 1572?)

12 Thirty days hath November, / April, June, and September, / February hath twenty-eight alone, / And all the rest have thirty-one. [*Abridgement of the Chronicles of England*, Introduction]

Graham, Billy (1918-)

13 May the Lord bless you real good. [Benediction]

Graham, Harry (1874-1936)

14 Billy, in one of his nice new sashes, / Fell in the fire and was burnt to ashes; / Now, although the room grows chilly, / I haven't the heart to poke poor Billy. [*Ruthless Rhymes for Heartless Homes*, 'Tender-Heartedness']

Grahame, Kenneth (1859-1932)

15 Believe me, my young friend, there is *nothing* — absolutely nothing — half so much worth doing as simply messing about in boats. [*The Wind in the Willows*, 1]

16 The clever men at Oxford / Know all that there is to be knowed. / But they none of them know one half as much / As intelligent Mr. Toad. [Ib.]

Grainger, James (c. 1721-1766)

17 Now, Muse, let's sing of *rats*. [*The Sugar-Cane*, MS version; quoted in Boswell, *Life of Johnson*]

Grant, Ulysses S. (1822-1885)

18 I know no method to secure the repeal of bad or obnoxious laws so effective as their stringent execution. [Inaugural Address, 1869]

19 Let no guilty man escape, if it can be avoided...No personal considerations should stand in the way of performing a public duty. [Note on letter, 1875]

Granville, George, Baron Lansdowne (1666-1735)

20 Of all the plagues with which the world is curst, / Of every ill, a woman is the worst. [*The British Enchanters*, II]

21 Bright as the day, and like the morning, fair, / Such Cloe is ... and common as the air. ['Cloe']

Grass, Günter (1927-)

22 The trend is towards the bourgeois-smug. [*The Tin Drum*]

Graves, John Woodcock (1795–1886)

1 D'ye ken John Peel with his coat so gay? / D'ye ken John Peel at the break of day? / D'ye ken John Peel when he's far away / With his hounds and his horn in the morning? ['John Peel']

Graves, Robert (1895–1985)

2 Children are dumb to say how hot the day is, / How hot the scent is of the summer rose. ['The Cool Web']

3 He grips the tankard of brown ale / That spills a generous foam: / Oft-times he drinks, they say, and winks / At drunk men lurching home. ['The General Elliott']

4 'What did the Mayor do?' / 'I was coming to that.' ['Welsh Incident']

5 The moral of the Scilly Islanders who earned a precarious livelihood by taking in one another's washing is that they never upset their carefully balanced island economy by trying to horn into the laundry trade of the mainland; and that nowhere in the Western Hemisphere was washing so well done. [*Collected Poems*, 1938–1945, Preface]

Gray, Thomas (1716–1771)

6 Ruin seize thee, ruthless King! / Confusion on thy banners wait. ['The Bard']

7 In gallant trim the gilded vessel goes, / Youth on the prow, and Pleasure at the helm. [Ib.]

8 Weave the warp, and weave the woof, / The winding-sheet of Edward's race. [Ib.]

9 The curfew tolls the knell of parting day, / The lowing herd wind slowly o'er the lea, / The ploughman homeward plods his weary way, / And leaves the world to darkness and to me. ['Elegy Written in a Country Churchyard']

10 Let not ambition mock their useful toil. [Ib.]

11 Each in his narrow cell for ever laid, / The rude forefathers of the hamlet sleep. [Ib.]

12 The short and simple annals of the poor. [Ib.]

13 Some village-Hampden, that with dauntless breast / The little tyrant of his fields withstood; / Some mute inglorious Milton here may rest, / Some Cromwell guiltless of his country's blood. [Ib.]

14 Forbad to wade through slaughter to a throne. [Ib.]

15 The paths of glory lead but to the grave. [Ib.]

16 Full many a gem of purest ray serene. [Ib.]

17 Full many a flower is born to blush unseen, / And waste its sweetness on the desert air. [Ib.]

18 Far from the madding crowd's ignoble strife. [Ib.]

19 Owls would have hooted in St. Peter's choir, / And foxes stunk and littered in St. Paul's. ['Impromptu on Lord Holland's Seat']

20 What female heart can gold despise? / What cat's averse to fish? ['Ode on the Death of a Favourite Cat']

21 A fav'rite has no friend! [Ib.]

22 Alas, regardless of their doom, / The little victims play! ['Ode on a Distant Prospect of Eton College']

23 Where ignorance is bliss, / 'Tis folly to be wise. [Ib.]

24 The meanest flowret of the vale, / The simplest note that swells the gale, / The common sun, the air, and skies, / To him are opening paradise. ['Ode on the Pleasure Arising from Vicissitude']

25 The language of the age is never the language of poetry. [Letter, 1742]

Greeley, Horace (1811–1872)

26 Go West, young man, and grow up with the country. [*Hints toward Reform*]

Green, Matthew (1696–1737)

27 They politics like ours profess, / The greater prey upon the less. ['The Grotto']

28 Fling but a stone, the giant dies. / Laugh and be well. [*The Spleen*]

Greene, Robert (1560–1592)

1 [Shakespeare] is an upstart crow, beautified with our feathers, that with his tiger's heart wrapped in a player's hide, supposes he is as well able to bumbast out a blank verse as the best of you; and...is in his own conceit the only Shake-scene in a country. [*Groatsworth of Wit*]

Gregory I (540–604)

2 *Responsum est, quod Angli vocarentur. At ille: 'Bene,' inquit, 'nam et angelicam habent faciem, et tales angelorum in caelis decet esse coheredes.'* They replied that they were called Angles. But he said, 'It is good; for they have the countenance of angels, and such should be the co-heirs of the angels in heaven.' [Bede, *Historia Ecclesiastica*]

Gregory VII (c. 1020–1085)

3 *Dilexi justitiam et odivi iniquitatem: propterea morior in exilio.* I have loved justice and hated iniquity: therefore I die in exile. [Last words]

Grellet, Stephen (1773–1855)

4 I expect to pass through this world but once; any good thing therefore that I can do, or any kindness that I can show to any fellow-creature, let me do it now; let me not defer or neglect it, for I shall not pass this way again. [Attr.]

Greville, Fulke, First Baron Brooke (1554–1628)

5 Fire and people do in this agree, / They both good servants, both ill masters be. ['Inquisition upon Fame']

6 Oh wearisome condition of humanity! / Born under one law, to another bound: / Vainly begot, and yet forbidden vanity; / Created sick, commanded to be sound. [*Mustapha*, V]

Grey, Edward, Viscount of Falloden (1862–1933)

7 The lamps are going out all over Europe; we shall not see them lit again in our lifetime. [August, 1914]

Griffiths, Trevor (1935–)

8 Comedy is medicine. [*Comedians*, I]

Guedalla, Philip (1889–1944)

9 The work of Henry James has always seemed divisible by a simple dynastic arrangement into three reigns: James I, James II, and the Old Pretender. [*Collected Essays*, IV]

10 People who jump to conclusions rarely alight on them. [*Observer*, 'Sayings of the Week', 1924]

Guinan, Texas (1884–1933)

11 Fifty million Frenchmen can't be wrong. [Attr.]

Gunn, Thom (1929–)

12 You know I know you know I know you know. ['Carnal Knowledge']

13 One is always nearer by not keeping still. ['On The Move']

Gurney, Dorothy (1858–1932)

14 One is nearer God's Heart in a garden / Than anywhere else on earth. ['God's Garden']

Gwyn, Nell (c. 1650–1687)

15 Good people, let me pass. I am the *Protestant* whore. [Said during the Popish Terror, 1681]

Hadrian (A.D. 76–138)

16 *Animula vagula blandula, / Hospes comesque corporis, / Quae nunc abibis in loca / Pallidula rigida nudula, / Nec ut soles dabis iocos!* Ah fleeting Spirit! wand'ring Fire, / That long hast warm'd my tender Breast, / Must thou no more this Frame inspire? / No more a pleasing, cheerful Guest? / Whither, ah whither art thou flying! / To what dark, undiscover'd Shore? / Thou seem'st all trembling, shivr'ing, dying, / And Wit and Humour are no more! ['Ad Animam Suam'; trans. Pope]

Haig, Douglas, First Earl (1861–1928)

1 Every position must be held to the last man: there must be no retirement. With our backs to the wall, and believing in the justice of our cause, each one of us must fight on to the end. [Order, 12 April 1918)

Hale, Sir Matthew (1609–1676)

2 Christianity is part of the Common Law of England. [Blackstone, *Commentaries*]

Halifax, George Savile, Marquis of (1633–1695)

3 Love is a passion that hath friends in the garrison. [*Advice to a Daughter*]

4 This innocent word 'Trimmer' signifies no more than this, that if men are together in a boat, and one part of the company would weigh it down on one side, another would make it lean as much to the contrary. [*Character of a Trimmer*, Preface]

5 Men are not hanged for stealing horses, but that horses may not be stolen. [*Political...Thoughts and Reflections*]

6 When the people contend for their Liberty, they seldom get anything by their Victory but new masters. [Ib.]

7 Halifax said he had known many kicked down stairs, but never knew any kicked up stairs before. [Burnet, *History of My Own Times*]

Hall, Joseph (1574–1656)

8 I first adventure, follow me who list / And be the second English satirist. [*Virgidemiae*, Preface]

Hamilton, Sir William (1788–1856)

9 On earth there is nothing great but man; in man there is nothing great but mind. [*Lectures on Metaphysics*]

Hammond, Percy (1873–1936)

10 The human knee is a joint and not an entertainment. [Mark Sullivan, *Our Times*]

Hancock, John (1737–1793)

11 There, I guess King George will be able to read that. [Remark on signing American Declaration of Independence]

Hankey, Kate (1834–1911)

12 Tell me the old, old story / Of unseen things above, / Of Jesus and His glory, / Of Jesus and His love. / Tell me the story simply, / As to a little child; / For I am weak and weary, / And helpless, and defiled. [Hymn]

Haraucourt, Edmond (1856–1941)

13 *Partir c'est mourir un peu.* To depart is to die a little. [*Seul*]

Hardy, Oliver (1892–1957)

14 Here's another fine mess you've gotten me into. [Quoted in Colombo, *Wit and Wisdom of the Moviemakers*]

Hardy, Thomas (1840–1928)

15 When the Present has latched its postern behind my tremulous stay, / And the May month flaps its glad green leaves like wings, / Delicate-filmed as new-spun silk, will the neighbours say, / 'He was a man who used to notice such things'? ['Afterwards']

16 Yet saw he something in the lives / Of those who ceased to live / That rounded them with majesty, / Which living failed to give. ['The Casterbridge Captains']

17 The Immanent Will that stirs and urges everything. ['The Convergence of the Twain' (on the sinking of the *Titanic*)]

18 Till the Spinner of the Years / Said 'Now!' And each one hears, / And consummation comes, and jars two hemispheres. [Ib.]

19 So little cause for carolings / Of such ecstatic sound / Was written on terrestrial things / Afar or nigh around, / That I could think there trembled through / His happy good-night air / Some blessed Hope, whereof he knew / And I was unaware. ['The Darkling Thrush']

1 When shall the softer, saner politics, / Whereof we dream, have play in each proud land? ['Departures']

2 Yet portion of that unknown plain / Will Hodge for ever be. ['Drummer Hodge']

3 A local cult called Christianity. [*The Dynasts*, I]

4 My argument is that War makes rattling good history; but Peace is poor reading. [Ib. II]

5 But what's one woman's fortune more or less / Beside the schemes of kings. [Ib.]

6 Well, World, you have kept faith with me, / Kept faith with me; / Upon the whole you have proved to be / Much as you said you were. ['He Never Expected Much']

7 Yonder a maid and her wight / Come whispering by: / War's annals will cloud into night / Ere their story die. ['In Time of "The Breaking of Nations"']

8 If someone said on Christmas Eve, / 'Come; see the oxen kneel, / In the lonely barton by yonder coomb / Our childhood used to know', / I should go with him in the gloom, / Hoping it might be so. ['The Oxen']

9 Of course poets have morals and manners of their own, and custom is no argument with them. [*Hand of Ethelberta*, 2]

10 Ethelberta breathed a sort of exclamation, not right out, but stealthily, like a parson's damn. [Ib. 26]

11 Done because we are too menny. [*Jude the Obscure*, VI, 2]

12 'Justice' was done, and the President of the Immortals (in Aeschylean phrase) had ended his sport with Tess. [*Tess of the D'Urbervilles*, 59]

13 Good, but not religious good. [*Under the Greenwood Tree*, 2]

14 That man's silence is wonderful to listen to. [Ib. 14]

Hare, Maurice Evan (1886–1967)

15 There once was a man who said, 'Damn! / It is borne in upon me I am / An engine that moves / In predestinate grooves, / I'm not even a bus, I'm a tram.' [Limerick]

Harington, Sir John (1561–1612)

16 Treason doth never prosper, what's the reason? / For if it prosper, none dare call it treason. [*Epigrams*, IV]

Harlow, Jean (1911–1937)

17 Excuse me while I slip into something more comfortable. [*Hell's Angels*, quoted in Colombo, *Wit and Wisdom of the Moviemakers*]

Harrington, James (1611–1677)

18 No man can be a Politician, except he be first an Historian or a Traveller; (for except he can see what Must be, or what May be, he is no Politician). [*The Commonwealth of Oceana*]

Harris, Joel Chandler (1848–1908)

19 De wimmin, dey does de talkin' en de flyin', en de mens, dey does de walkin' en de pryin', en betwixt en betweenst um, dey ain't much dat don't come out. [*Brother Rabbit and His Famous Foot*]

20 Bred en bawn in a brier-patch! [*Legends of the Old Plantation*]

21 Tar-baby ain't sayin' nuthin', en Brer Fox, he lay low. [Ib.]

22 Hit look lak sparrer-grass, hit feel lak sparrer-grass, hit tas'e lak sparrer-grass, en I bless ef 'taint sparrer-grass. [*Nights with Uncle Remus*]

23 Licker talks mighty loud w'en it git loose from de jug. [*Uncle Remus*, Plantation Proverbs]

24 Hongry rooster don't cackle w'en he fine a wum. [Ib.]

25 Lazy fokes' stummucks don't git tired. [Ib.]

26 Youk'n hide de fier, but w'at you gwine do wid de smoke? [Ib.]

Harte, Bret (1836–1902)

27 Thar ain't no sense / In gittin' riled! ['Jim']

1 And he smiled a kind of sickly smile, and curled up on the floor, / And the subsequent proceedings interested him no more. ['The Society upon the Stanislaus']

Hartley, L.P. (1895–1972)

2 The past is a foreign country: they do things differently there. [*The Go-Between*, first sentence]

Harvey, William (1578–1657)

3 *Ex ovo omnia*. Everything from an egg. [*De Generatione Animalium*]

Haskins, Minnie Louise (1875–1957)

4 I said to a man who stood at the gate of the year: 'Give me a light that I may tread safely into the unknown.' And he replied: 'Go out into the darkness and put your hand into the hand of God. That shall be to you better than a light, and safer than a known way.' [*God Knows*]

Hawker, Robert Stephen (1803–1875)

5 And have they fixed the where and when? / And shall Trelawney die? / Here's twenty thousand Cornishmen / Will know the reason why! ['Song of the Western Men']

Hay, Ian (1876–1952)

6 Funny-peculiar or funny-ha-ha? [*The Housemaster*, III]

Hayes, J. Milton (fl. 1911)

7 There's a one-eyed yellow idol to the north of Khatmandu, / There's a little marble cross below the town, / There's a broken-hearted woman tends the grave of Mad Carew, / And the Yellow God forever gazes down. ['The Green Eye of the Yellow God']

Hazlitt, William (1778–1830)

8 Wrong dressed out in pride, pomp and circumstance, has more attraction than abstract right. ['Coriolanus']

9 [Of Scott] His worst is better than any other person's best. [*English Literature*, 14]

10 You will hear more good things on the outside of a stagecoach from London to Oxford than if you were to pass a twelvemonth with the undergraduates, or heads of colleges, of that famous city. ['The Ignorance of the Learned']

11 [Of Wordsworth] He is totally deficient in all the machinery of poetry. [*Lectures on the English Poets*]

12 [Of Coleridge] He talked on for ever; and you wished him to talk on for ever. [Ib.]

13 Sir Walter Scott (when all's said and done) is an inspired butler. ['Mrs. Siddons']

14 So have I loitered my life away, reading books, looking at pictures, going to plays, hearing, thinking, writing on what pleased me best. I have wanted only one thing to keep me happy, but wanting that have wanted everything. ['My First Acquaintance with Poets']

15 There is nothing good to be had in the country, or if there is, they will not let you have it. ['Observations on Mr. Wordsworth's *Excursion*']

16 No young man believes he shall ever die. ['On the Feeling of Immortality in Youth']

17 Without the aid of prejudice and custom, I should not be able to find my way across the room. ['On Prejudice']

18 The art of pleasing consists in being pleased. [*Round Table*, 'On Manner']

19 Rules and models destroy genius and art. [*Sketches and Essays*, 'On Taste']

20 [Scott] would make a bad hand of a description of the *Millennium*, unless he could lay the scene in Scotland five hundred years ago, and then he would want facts and worm-eaten parchments to support his drooping style. [*The Spirit of the Age*]

21 Violent antipathies are always suspicious, and betray a secret affinity. [*Table Talk*]

22 The English (it must be owned) are rather a foul-mouthed nation. [Ib. 'On Criticism']

1 One of the pleasantest things in the world is going on a journey; but I like to go by myself. [Ib. 'On Going a Journey']

2 The love of liberty is the love of others; the love of power is the love of ourselves. ['The Times Newspaper']

3 Well, I've had a happy life. [Last words]

Hearst, William Randolph (1863–1951)

4 You furnish the pictures and I'll furnish the war. [Attr. instruction to news photographer reporting from peaceful foreign country]

Heath, Edward (1916–)

5 This would, at a stroke, reduce the rise of prices. [Press release of campaign speech, 1970]

6 The unacceptable face of capitalism. [Speech, 1973]

Heber, Reginald (1783–1826)

7 By cool Siloam's shady rill / How sweet the lily grows! [Hymn]

8 From Greenland's icy mountains, / From India's coral strand, / Where Afric's sunny fountains / Roll down their golden sand. / From many an ancient river, / From many a palmy plain, / They call us to deliver / Their land from error's chain. [Hymn]

9 Though every prospect pleases, / And only man is vile. [Ib.]

Hegel, Georg Wilhelm (1770–1831)

10 *Was die Erfahrung aber und die Geschichte lehren, ist dieses das Völker und Regierungen niemals etwas aus der Geschichte gelernt.* But what experience and history teach is this, that peoples and governments have never learned anything from history. [*Philosophy of History*]

11 *Was vernünftig ist, das ist wirklich: und was wirklich ist, das ist vernünftig.* What is reasonable is true, and what is true is reasonable. [*Rechtsphilosophie*]

Heine, Heinrich (1797–1856)

12 *Ich weiss nicht, was soll es bedeuten / Das ich so traurig bin, / Ein Märchen aus alten Zeiten, / Dass kommt mir nicht aus dem Sinn.* I do not know why I am so sad; there is an old fairy tale that I cannot get out of my mind. ['Die Lorelei']

13 *Est ist eine alte Geschichte, / Doch bleibt sie immer neu.* It is an ancient story, yet it is ever new. ['Lyrisches Intermezzo']

14 Wherever books are burned, men too are eventually burned. [Attr.]

15 When people talk about a wealthy man of my creed, they call him an Israelite; but if he is poor they call him a Jew. [MS. Papers]

16 *Dieu me pardonnera. C'est son métier.* God will pardon me. It is his profession. [Last words]

Heller, Joseph (1923–)

17 There was only one catch and that was Catch-22, which specified that a concern for one's own safety in the face of dangers that were real and immediate was the process of a rational mind. [*Catch-22*, 5]

Helpman, Robert (1909–1986)

18 The trouble with nude dancing is that not everything stops when the music stops. [Comment on *Oh! Calcutta!*]

Helps, Sir Arthur (1813–1875)

19 Reading is sometimes an ingenious device for avoiding thought. [*Friends in Council*]

20 What a blessing this smoking is! perhaps the greatest that we owe to the discovery of America. [Ib.]

21 There is one statesman of the present day, of whom I always say that he would have escaped making the blunders that he has made if he had only ridden more in omnibuses. [Ib.]

Hemans, Felicia Dorothea (1793–1835)

1 The boy stood on the burning deck / Whence all but he had fled; / The flame that lit the battle's wreck / Shone round him o'er the dead. ['Casabianca']

2 The stately homes of England, / How beautiful they stand! ['The Homes of England']

Hemingway, Ernest (1898–1961)

3 The world is a fine place and worth fighting for. [*For Whom the Bell Tolls*]

4 [Courage] Grace under pressure. [Attr.]

Henley, William Ernest (1849–1903)

5 I thank whatever gods may be / For my unconquerable soul. [*Echoes*, 'Invictus']

6 In the fell clutch of circumstance, / I have not winced nor cried aloud: / Under the bludgeonings of chance / My head is bloody, but unbowed. [Ib.]

7 I am the master of my fate: / I am the captain of my soul. [Ib.]

8 Madam Life's a piece in bloom / Death goes dogging everywhere; / She's the tenant of the room, / He's the ruffian on the stair. [Ib. 'To W.R.']

Henri IV of France (1553–1610)

9 One catches more flies with a spoonful of honey than with twenty casks of vinegar. [Attr.]

10 *Les grands mangeurs et les grands dormeurs sont incapables de rien faire de grand.* Great eaters and great sleepers are incapable of doing anything great. [Attr.]

11 [Of James VI and I] The wisest fool in Christendom. [Attr. Also attr. to Sully]

12 *Paris vaut bien une messe.* Paris is well worth a mass. [Attr.]

13 In my kingdom I want there to be no peasant so poor that he cannot have a chicken in his pot every Sunday. [Attr.]

Henry II (1133–1189)

14 [Of Becket] Will no one free me of this turbulent priest? [Attr.]

Henry VIII (1491–1547)

15 I perceive that that man [Cranmer] hath the right sow by the ear. [Letter, 1529]

Henry, Matthew (1662–1714)

16 The better day, the worse deed. [*Commentaries*, Genesis 3:6]

17 To their own second and sober thoughts. [Ib. Job 6:29]

18 All this and heaven too. [Attr.]

Henry, O. (1862–1910)

19 It was beautiful and simple as all truly great swindles are. ['The Octopus Marooned']

20 Take it from me — he's got the goods. ['The Unprofitable Servant']

21 Turn up the lights, I don't want to go home in the dark. [Last words]

Henry, Patrick (1736–1799)

22 Caesar had his Brutus — Charles the First, his Cromwell and George the Third — ['Treason,' cried the Speaker]...*may profit by their example.* If *this* be treason, make the most of it. [Speech in the Virginia Convention, 1765]

23 Give me liberty, or give me death! [Speech, 1775]

Henryson, Robert (c. 1425–1506)

24 There was no solace mycht his sobbing cease, / Bot cryit aye, with cairis cauld and keen: / 'Where art thou gane, my luve Eurydices?' [*Orpheus and Eurydice*]

25 The man that will nocht when he may / Sall have nocht when he wald. [*Robene and Makyne*]

26 Yit efter joy ofttimes cumis care, / And trouble efter great prosperitie. [*The Taill of the Uponlandis Mous and the Burges Mous*]

1 Nocht is your fairness bot ane fading flour, / Nocht is your famous laud and high honour / Bot wind inflate in other mennis earis; / Your rosing reid to rotting sall retour. [*The Testament of Cresseid*]

2 I lat you wit, thair is richt few thairout / Quhome ye may traist to have trew lufe againe. / Preif quhen ye will, your labour is in vaine. / Thairfoir, I reid, ye tak theme as ye find; / For they ar sad as widdercock in wind. [Ib.]

Henshaw, Bishop Joseph (1603-1679)

3 One doth but breakfast here, another dines, he that liveth longest doth but sup; we must all go to bed in another world. [*Horae Succisivae*]

Hepburn, Katharine (1909-)

4 I don't care what is written about me as long as it isn't true. [Quoted in Cooper and Hartman, *Violets and Vinegar*]

Heraclitus (fl. 6th century B.C.)

5 All things flow; nothing abides. [Quoted by Plato]

6 It is impossible to step twice into the same river. [Ib.]

Herbert, Sir A.P. (1890-1971)

7 Don't let's go to the dogs to-night / For mother will be there. ['Don't Let's Go to the Dogs']

8 Don't tell my mother I'm living in sin, / Don't let the old folks know. ['Don't Tell My Mother']

9 A highbrow is the kind of person who looks at a sausage and thinks of Picasso. ['The Highbrow']

10 I'm not a jealous woman, but I can't see what he sees in her. ['I Can't Think What He Sees in Her']

11 I wouldn't be too ladylike in love if I were you. ['I Wouldn't be Too Ladylike']

12 Let's find out what everyone is doing, / And then stop everyone from doing it. ['Let's Stop Somebody']

13 Once people start on all this Art / Goodbye, moralitee! ['Lines for a Worthy Person']

14 This high official, all allow, / Is grossly overpaid. / There wasn't any Board; and now / There isn't any trade. ['On the President of the Board of Trade']

15 The Common Law of England has been laboriously built about a mythical figure — the figure of 'The Reasonable Man'. [*Uncommon Law*]

16 People must not do things for fun. We are not here for fun. There is no reference to fun in any Act of Parliament. [Ib.]

17 The Englishman never enjoys himself except for a noble purpose. [Ib.]

18 An Act of God was defined as *something which no reasonable man could have expected.* [Ib.]

Herbert, Edward, Baron Herbert of Cherbury (1583-1648)

19 O that our love might take no end / Or never had beginning took! ['An Ode upon a Question moved, Whether Love should continue for ever?']

20 For where God doth admit the fair, / Think you that he excludeth Love? [Ib.]

Herbert, George (1593-1633)

21 Ah, my dear God, though I am clean forgot, / Let me not love Thee, if I love Thee not. [*The Temple*, 'Affliction']

22 Let all the world in ev'ry corner sing / My God and King. [Ib. 'Antiphon']

23 A verse may find him who a sermon flies, / And turn delight into a sacrifice. [Ib. 'The Church Porch']

24 Drink not the third glass, — which thou can'st not tame / When once it is within thee. [Ib.]

25 Wit's an unruly engine, wildly striking / Sometimes a friend, sometimes the engineer. [Ib.]

26 The stormy working soul spits lies and froth. [Ib.]

27 Kneeling ne'er spoil'd silk stocking. [Ib.]

1 I struck the board, and cry'd, 'No more; / I will abroad.' / What, shall I ever sigh and pine? / My lines and life are free; free as the road, / Loose as the wind. [Ib. 'The Collar']

2 Thy rope of sands / Which petty thoughts have made. [Ib.]

3 Throw away thy rod, / Throw away thy wrath: / O my god, / Take the gentle path. [Ib. 'Discipline']

4 Death is still working like a mole, / And digs my grave at each remove. [Ib. 'Grace']

5 Who says that fictions only and false hair / Become a verse? Is there in truth no beauty? / Is all good structure in a winding stair? [Ib. 'Jordan']

6 Love bade me welcome; yet my soul drew back, / Guilty of dust and sin. [Ib. 'Love']

7 Man is all symmetry, / Full of proportions, one limb to another, / And all to all the world besides. [Ib. 'Man']

8 Let the world's riches, which dispersed lie, / Contract into a span. [Ib. 'The Pulley']

9 If goodness lead him not, yet weariness / May toss him to My breast. [Ib.]

10 My God, my verse is not a crown, / No point of honour, or gay suit, / No hawk, or banquet, or renown, / Nor a good sword, nor yet a lute. [Ib. 'The Quiddity']

11 At length I heard a ragged noise and mirth / Of thieves and murderers: there I him espied, / Who straight, 'Your suit is granted,' said, and died. [Ib. 'Redemption']

12 Was ever grief like mine? [Ib. 'The Sacrifice']

13 Only a sweet and virtuous soul, / Like season'd timber, never gives; / But though the whole world turn to coal, / Then chiefly lives. [Ib. 'Virtue']

14 The God of Love my Shepherd is, / And He that doth me feed, / While He is mine, and I am His, / What can I want or need? [Ib. '23rd Psalm']

15 Take heed of a young wench, a prophetess, and a Latin-bred woman. [*Jacula Prudentum*]

16 A cheerful look makes a dish a feast. [Ib.]

17 Music helps not the toothache. [Ib.]

Herford, Oliver (1863–1935)

18 The bubble winked at me and said, / 'You'll miss me brother, when you're dead.' [Toast: 'The Bubble Winked']

Herrick, Robert (1591–1674)

19 I sing of brooks, of blossoms, birds, and bowers: / Of April, May, of June and July-flowers. / I sing of May-poles, Hock-carts, wassails, wakes, / Of bride-grooms, brides, and of their bridal-cakes. [*Hesperides*, 'The Argument of his Book']

20 I write of youth, of love, and have access / By these, to sing of cleanly-wantonness. [Ib.]

21 Cherry-ripe, ripe, ripe I cry, / Full and fair ones; come and buy. [Ib. 'Cherry-Ripe']

22 Then while time serves, and we are but decaying; / Come, my Corinna, come, let's go a-Maying. [Ib. 'Corinna's Going a-Maying']

23 Fair daffodils, we weep to see / You haste away so soon. [Ib. 'Daffodils']

24 A sweet disorder in the dress / Kindles in clothes a wantonness. [Ib. 'Delight in Disorder']

25 Fain would I kiss my Julia's dainty leg, / Which is as white and hairless as an egg. [Ib. 'On Julia's Legs']

26 Sweet, be not proud of those two eyes, / Which star-like sparkle in their skies. [Ib. 'To Dianeme']

27 Gather ye rose-buds while ye may, / Old Time is still a-flying: / And this same flower that smiles to-day, / To-morrow will be dying. [Ib. 'To the Virgins, to Make Much of Time']

28 Whenas in silks my Julia goes, / Then, then (methinks) how sweetly flows / The liquefaction of her clothes. [Ib. 'Upon Julia's Clothes']

Hervey, Lord (1696–1743)

1 Whoever would lie usefully should lie seldom. [*Memoirs of the Reign of George II*]

Heywood, John (c. 1497–c. 1580)

2 All a green willow, willow; / All a green willow is my garland. ['The Green Willow']

Hickson, William Edward (1803–1870)

3 If at first you don't succeed, / Try, try, again. ['Try and Try Again']

Hill, Aaron (1685–1750)

4 Tender-hearted stroke a nettle, / And it stings you for your pains; / Grasp it like a man of mettle, / And it soft as silk remains. ['Verses Written on a Window in Scotland']

Hill, Joe (1879–1914)

5 You'll get pie in the sky when you die. ['The Preacher and the Slave']

Hill, Rowland (1744–1833)

6 He did not see any reason why the devil should have all the good tunes. [E.W. Broome, *Rev. Rowland Hill*]

Hillary, Sir Edmund (1919–)

7 Well, we knocked the bastard off. [Attr. remark after first ascent of Mt. Everest, 1953]

Hindenburg, Paul von (1847–1934)

8 As an English General has very truly said, 'The German army was stabbed in the back.' [Statement in Reichstag, 1919]

Hippocrates (c. 460–357 B.C.)

9 [Of medicine] The life so short, the art so long to learn, opportunity fleeting, experience treacherous, judgement difficult. [*Aphorisms*, 1] The opening phrases are often quoted in Latin as *Ars longa, vita brevis.*

10 For extreme illnesses extreme remedies are most fitting. [Ib. 6]

Hitchcock, Alfred (1899–1980)

11 Drama is life with the dull bits cut out. [*Observer*, 'Sayings of the Week', 1960]

12 Television has brought murder back into the home — where it belongs. [Quoted in Colombo, *Wit and Wisdom of the Moviemakers*]

13 I deny that I ever said that actors are cattle. What I said was 'actors should be treated like cattle'. [Attr.]

Hitler, Adolf (1889–1945)

14 The great mass of the people...will more easily fall victim to a big lie than to a small one. [*Mein Kampf*]

15 My patience is now at an end. [Speech, 1938]

16 It is the last territorial claim which I have to make in Europe [Sudetenland]. [Speech, 1938]

Hobbes, Thomas (1588–1679)

17 Words are wise men's counters, they do but reckon with them: but they are the money of fools. [*Leviathan*, I, 4]

18 Sudden glory is the passion which maketh those grimaces called laughter. [Ib. I, 6]

19 During the time men live without a common power to keep them all in awe, they are in that condition which is called war; and such a war as is of every man against every man. [Ib. I, 13]

20 No arts; no letters; no society; and which is worst of all, continual fear and danger of violent death; and the life of man, solitary, poor, nasty, brutish, and short. [Ib.]

21 Force, and fraud, are in war the two cardinal virtues. [Ib.]

22 Covenants without the sword are but words and of no strength to secure a man at all. [Ib.]

23 The praise of ancient authors proceeds not from the reverence of the dead, but from the competition and mutual envy of the living. [Ib.]

24 I am about to take my last voyage, a great leap in the dark. [Last words]

Hodgson, Ralph (1871–1962)

1 'Twould ring the bells of Heaven / The wildest peal for years, / If Parson lost his senses / And people came to theirs, / And he and they together / Knelt down with angry prayers / For tamed and shabby tigers / And dancing dogs and bears, / And wretched, blind, pit ponies, / And little hunted hares. ['The Bells of Heaven']

Hoffmann, Heinrich (1809–1874)

2 Take the soup away! / O take the nasty soup away! / I won't have any soup today. [*Struwwelpeter*, 'Augustus']

3 Boys, leave the black-a-moor alone! / For if he tries with all his might, / He cannot change from black to white. [Ib. 'The Inky Boys']

4 Look at little Johnny there, / Little Johnny Head-In-Air! [Ib. 'Johnny Head-in-Air']

5 'Ah!' said Mamma. 'I knew he'd come / To naughty little Suck-a-Thumb.' [Ib. 'The Little Suck-a-Thumb']

Hogg, James (1770–1835)

6 Where the pools are bright and deep, / Where the grey trout lies asleep, / Up the river and o'er the lea / That's the way for Billy and me. ['A Boy's Song']

7 And Charlie is my darling, / The young Chevalier. [*Jacobite Relics of Scotland*; *see* Burns]

8 Better lo'ed ye canna be, / Will ye no come back again? [Ib.]

9 O, love, love, love; Love is like a dizziness; / It winna let a poor body gang about his business! ['Love is Like a Dizziness']

10 For Kilmeny had been she knew not where, / And Kilmeny has seen what she could not declare. ['The Queen's Wake']

Holmes, Rev. John H. (1879–1964)

11 The universe is not hostile, nor yet is it friendly. It is indifferent. [*A Sensible Man's View of Religion*]

Holmes, Oliver Wendell (1809–1894)

12 A country clergyman with a one-storey intellect and a one-horse vocabulary. [*The Autocrat of the Breakfast Table*]

13 The axis of the earth sticks out visibly through the centre of each and every town and city. [Ib.]

14 Man has his will, — but woman has her way. [Ib.]

15 The wonderful one-hoss shay. ['The Deacon's Masterpiece']

16 A general flavour of mild decay. [Ib.]

17 Lean, hungry, savage anti-everythings. ['A Modest Request']

18 A moment's insight is sometimes worth a life's experience. [*The Professor at the Breakfast Table*]

19 To be seventy years young is sometimes far more cheerful and hopeful than to be forty years old. ['On the Seventieth Birthday of Julia Ward Howe']

Home, John (1722–1808)

20 In the first days / Of my distracting grief, I found myself — / As women wish to be, who love their lords. [*Douglas*, I]

21 He seldom errs / Who thinks the worst he can of womankind. [Ib. III]

22 Like Douglas conquer, or like Douglas die. [Ib.]

23 Bold and erect the Caledonian stood, / Old was his mutton, and his claret good; / Let him drink port, the English statesmen cried — / He drank the poison and his spirit died. [Lockhart, *Life of Scott*]

Homer (fl. c. 8th century B.C.)

24 Achilles' wrath, to Greece the direful spring / Of woes unnumber'd, heavenly goddess, sing. [*Iliad*, I, opening lines, in Pope's translation]

25 Rosy-fingered dawn. [Ib. and *passim*]

26 Winged words. [Ib. and *passim*]

27 The wine-dark sea. [Ib. and *passim*]

28 As the generation of leaves, so is that of men. [Ib. VI]

1 Always to be best and distinguished above others. [Ib.]

2 He saw the cities of many men, and knew their minds. [*Odyssey*, III]

Hood, Thomas (1799–1845)

3 Take her up tenderly / Lift her with care; / Fashioned so slenderly, / Young, and so fair! ['The Bridge of Sighs']

4 Ben Battle was a soldier bold, / And used to war's alarms: / But a cannon-ball took off his legs, / So he laid down his arms! ['Faithless Nellie Gray']

5 They went and told the sexton, and / The sexton toll'd the bell. ['Faithless Sally Brown']

6 I remember, I remember, / The house where I was born, / The little window where the sun / Came peeping in at morn. ['I Remember']

7 But now 'tis little joy / To know I'm farther off from heav'n / Than when I was a boy. [Ib.]

8 For that old enemy the gout / Had taken him in toe! ['Lieutenant Luff']

9 For one of the pleasures of having a rout, / Is the pleasure of having it over. [*Miss Kilmansegg*, 'Her Dream']

10 When Eve upon the first of Men / The apple press'd with specious cant, / Oh! what a thousand pities then / That Adam was not Adamant! ['A Reflection']

11 Oh! God! that bread should be so dear, / And flesh and blood so cheap! ['The Song of the Shirt']

12 There is a silence where hath been no sound, / There is a silence where no sound may be, / In the cold grave — under the deep, deep sea, / Or in the wide desert where no life is found. ['Silence']

13 Holland...lies so low they're only saved by being dammed. [*Up the Rhine*]

Hooker, Richard (c. 1554–1600)

14 He that goeth about to persuade a multitude, that they are not so well governed as they ought to be, shall never want attentive and favourable hearers. [*Ecclesiastical Polity*]

15 Change is not made without inconvenience, even from worse to better. [Quoted by Dr. Johnson, Preface to his *Dictionary*]

Hooper, Ellen Sturgis (1816–1841)

16 I slept, and dreamed that life was Beauty; / I woke, and found that life was Duty. ['Beauty and Duty']

Hoover, Herbert Clark (1874–1964)

17 Rugged individualism. [Speech, 1928]

Hope, Anthony (1863–1933)

18 Economy is going without something you do want in case you should, some day, want something you probably won't want. [*The Dolly Dialogues*, 12]

19 'You oughtn't to yield to temptation.' 'Well, somebody must, or the thing becomes absurd.' [Ib. 14]

20 'Boys will be boys—'
'And even that...wouldn't matter if we could only prevent girls from being girls.' [Ib. 16]

21 '*Bourgeois*,' I observed, 'is an epithet which the riff-raff apply to what is respectable, and the aristocracy to what is decent.' [Ib. 17]

22 I wish you would read a little poetry sometimes. Your ignorance cramps my conversation. [Ib. 22]

Hope, Laurence (1865–1904)

23 Pale hands I loved beside the Shalimar, / Where are you now? Who lies beneath your spell? ['Pale Hands I Loved']

Hopkins, Gerald Manley (1844–1889)

24 The world is charged with the grandeur of God. ['God's Grandeur']

25 I wake and feel the fell of dark, not day. ['I wake and feel the fell']

26 O the mind, mind has mountains; cliffs of fall / Frightful, sheer, no-man-fathomed. ['No Worst, there is None']

27 Glory be to God for dappled things. ['Pied Beauty']

28 Margaret, are you grieving / Over Golden-grove unleaving? ['Spring and Fall']

1 Look at the stars! look, look up at the skies! / Oh look at all the fire-folk sitting in the air! / The bright boroughs, the circle-citadels there! ['The Starlight Night']

2 I caught this morning morning's minion, kingdom of daylight's dauphin, dapple-dawn-drawn Falcon. ['The Windhover']

3 My heart in hiding / Stirred for a bird, — the achieve of, the mastery of the thing! [Ib.]

Hopkins, Jane Ellice (1836–1904)

4 Gift, like genius, I often think, only means an infinite capacity for taking pains. [*Work amongst Working Men*; *see* Carlyle, *Frederick the Great*]

Horace (65–8 B.C.)

5 *Brevis esse laboro, / Obscurus fio.* I struggle to be brief, and I become obscure. [*Ars Poetica*]

6 *Grammatici certant et adhuc sub iudice lis est.* Scholars dispute, and the case is still before the courts. [Ib.]

7 *Difficile est proprie communia dicere.* It is hard to say common things in an original way. [Ib.]

8 *In medias res.* To the heart of the matter. [Ib.]

9 *Parturient montes, nascetur ridiculus mus.* The mountains will be in labour, and a ridiculous mouse will be born. [Ib.]

10 *Laudator temporis acti.* A praiser of times past. [Ib.]

11 *Omne tulit punctum qui miscuit utile dulci, / Lectorem delectando pariter monendo.* He has won every point who has mixed profit with pleasure, by delighting the reader while instructing him. [Ib.]

12 *Indignor quandoque bonus dormitat Homerus.* When worthy Homer nods, I am offended. [Ib.]

13 *Ut pictura poesis.* Poetry is like painting. [Ib.]

14 *Nonumque prematur in annum.* It should not be published for nine years. [Ib.]

15 *Si possis recte, si non, quocumque modo rem.* If possible, make money honestly; if not, make it by any means. [*Epistles*, I, 1]

16 *Ira furor brevis est.* Anger is a brief madness. [Ib. I, 2]

17 *Naturam expellas furca, tamen usque recurret.* Though you drive away Nature with a pitchfork she always returns. [Ib. I, 10]

18 *Caelum non animum mutant qui trans mare currunt.* They change their clime, but not their minds, who rush across the sea. [Ib. I, 12]

19 *Concordia discors.* Harmony in discord. [Ib.]

20 *Volat irrevocabile verbum.* The word flies and cannot be recalled. [Ib. I, 18]

21 *Graecia capta ferum victorem cepit et artes, / Intulit agresti Latio.* Occupied Greece subdued her fierce conqueror, and introduced the arts to rustic Latium. [Ib. II, 1]

22 *Si foret in terris, rideret Democritus.* If he were on earth, Democritus would laugh. [Ib.]

23 *Atque inter silvas Academi quaerere verum.* And seek after truth in the groves of Academe. [Ib. II, 2]

24 *Quodsi me lyricis vatibus inseres, / Sublimi feriam sidera vertice.* But if you include me among the lyric poets, I shall touch the stars with my exalted head. [*Odes*, I, 1]

25 *Pallida Mors, aequo pulsat pede pauperum tabernas / Regumque turris.* Pale Death, with impartial foot, strikes at poor men's hovels and the towers of kings. [Ib. I, 4]

26 *Vitae summa brevis spem nos vetat incohare longam.* Life's short span forbids us to set out after far-reaching hopes. [Ib.]

27 *Nil desperandum Teucro duce et auspice Teucro.* No need to despair under Teucer's leadership and protection. [Ib. I, 7]

28 *Carpe diem, quam minimum credula postero.* Snatch at today and trust as little as you can in tomorrow. [Ib. I, 11]

29 *O matre pulchra filia pulchrior.* O fairer daughter of a fair mother. [Ib. I, 16]

1 *Integer vitae scelerisque purus.* A man of upright life and free from guilt. [Ib. I, 22]

2 *Persicos odi, puer, apparatus.* I hate that Persian luxury, boy. [Ib. I, 38]

3 *Eheu fugaces, Posthume, Posthume, / Labuntar anni.* Alas, Posthumus, Posthumus, the fleeting years are slipping by. [Ib. II, 14]

4 *Nihil est ab omni / Parte beatum.* Nothing brings complete happiness. [Ib. II, 16]

5 *Odi profanum vulgus et arceo.* I hate the common crowd and avoid them. [Ib. III, 1]

6 *Virginibus puerisque canto.* I sing for girls and boys. [Ib.]

7 *Cur valle permutem Sabina / Divitias operosiores?* Why should I exchange my Sabine valley for wealth that brings more troubles? [Ib. III, 1]

8 *Dulce et decorum est pro patria mori.* It is a fine and seemly thing to die for one's country. [Ib. III, 2]

9 *Si fractus illabatur orbis, / Impavidum ferient ruinae.* If the world should crack and fall on him, the ruins would strike him unafraid. [Ib. III, 3]

10 *O fons Bandusiae splendidior vitro.* O spring of Bandusia, clearer than glass. [Ib. III, 13]

11 *Magnas inter opes inops.* A poor man surrounded by riches. [Ib. III, 16]

12 *Exegi monumentum aere perennius.* I have raised a monument more lasting than bronze. [Ib. III, 30]

13 *Non omnis moriar.* I shall not altogether die. [Ib.]

14 *Non sum qualis eram bonae / Sub regno Cinarae.* I am not what I was when dear Cinara was my queen. [Ib. IV, 1]

15 *Diffugere nives, redeunt iam gramina campis / Arboribusque comae.* The snows have scattered and fled; already the grass comes again in the fields and the leaves on the trees. [Ib. IV, 7]

16 *Dignum laude virum Musa vetat mori.* He who deserves praise the Muse forbids to die. [Ib. IV, 8]

17 *Disiecti membra poetae.* The broken limbs of a poet. [*Satires*, I, 3]

18 *Solventur risu tabulae.* The case will be closed with a laugh. [Ib. II, 1]

Horsley, Bishop Samuel (1733–1806)

19 The mass of the people have nothing to do with the laws but to obey them. [Speech, 1795]

Housman, Alfred Edward (1859–1936)

20 The chestnut casts his flambeaux. [*Last Poems*, 9]

21 O often have I washed and dressed / And what's to show for all my pain? / Let me lie abed and rest: / Ten thousand times I've done my best / And all's to do again. [Ib.]

22 What God abandoned, these defended, / And saved the sum of things for pay. [Ib. 'Epitaph on an Army of Mercenaries']

23 Tell me not here, it needs not saying, / What tune the enchantress plays. [Ib. 40]

24 The cuckoo shouts all day at nothing / In leafy dells alone. [Ib.]

25 For nature, heartless, witless nature, / Will neither care nor know / What stranger's feet may find the meadow / And trespass there and go. [Ib.]

26 Life, to be sure, is nothing much to lose; / But young men think it is, and we were young. [*More Poems*, 36]

27 O, God will save her, fear you not: / Be you the men you've been, / Get you the sons your fathers got, / And God will save the Queen. [*A Shropshire Lad*, 1]

28 When I was one-and-twenty / I heard a wise man say, / 'Give crowns and pounds and guineas / But not your heart away.' [Ib. 13]

29 Is my team ploughing, / That I was used to drive? [Ib. 27]

30 On Wenlock Edge the wood's in trouble. [Ib. 31]

31 Today the Roman and his trouble / Are ashes under Uricon. [Ib.]

1 Clunton and Clunbury, / Clungunford and Clun, / Are the quietest places / Under the sun. [Ib. 50]

2 The man that runs away / Lives to die another day. [Ib. 'The Day of Battle']

3 O many a peer of England brews / Livelier liquor than the Muse, / And malt does more than Milton can / To justify God's ways to man. [Ib. 62]

4 Experience has taught me, when I am shaving of a morning, to keep watch over my thoughts, because, if a line of poetry strays into my memory, my skin bristles so that the razor ceases to act. ['The Name and Nature of Poetry']

Howe, Julia Ward (1819-1910)

5 Mine eyes have seen the glory of the coming of the Lord: / He is trampling out the vintage where the grapes of wrath are stored. ['Battle Hymn of the Republic']

Howell, James (c. 1594-1666)

6 One hair of a woman can draw more than a hundred pair of oxen. [*Familiar Letters*, II, 4]

7 This life at best is but an inn, / And we the passengers. [Ib. II, 73]

Howitt, Mary (1799-1888)

8 'Will you walk into my parlour?' said a spider to a fly. ['The Spider and the Fly']

Hoyle, Edmond (1672-1769)

9 When in doubt, win the trick. [*Hoyle's Games*, 'Whist, Twenty-four Short Rules for Learners']

Hubbard, Elbert (1859-1915)

10 Life is just one damned thing after another. [*A Thousand and One Epigrams*]

11 Men are not punished for their sins, but by them. [Ib.]

12 Editor: a person employed by a newspaper whose business it is to separate the wheat from the chaff and to see that the chaff is printed. [Ib.]

Hughes, Thomas (1822-1896)

13 Life isn't all beer and skittles. [*Tom Brown's Schooldays*, I]

14 He never wants anything but what's right and fair; only when you come to settle what's right and fair, it's everything that he wants and nothing that you want. And that's his idea of a compromise. Give me the Brown compromise when I'm on his side. [Ib. II, 2]

15 [Of cricket] It's more than a game. It's an institution. [Ib. II, 7]

Hugo, Victor (1802-1885)

16 *Le mot, c'est le Verbe, et le Verbe, c'est Dieu.* The word is the Verb, and the Verb is God. [*Contemplations*]

17 In the twentieth century, war will be dead, the scaffold will be dead, hatred will be dead, frontier boundaries will be dead, dogmas will be dead; man will live. He will possess something higher than all these — a great country, the whole earth, and a great hope, the whole heaven. [*The Future of Man*]

18 *On résiste à l'invasion des armées; on ne résiste pas à l'invasion des idées.* The invasion of armies is resisted; the invasion of ideas is not. [*Histoire d'un Crime*]

19 *Le beau est aussi utile que l'utile. Plus peut-être.* The beautiful is as useful as the useful. Perhaps more so. [*Les Misérables*]

20 Art has its fanatics and even its monomaniacs. [*Ninety-three*]

21 Jesus wept; Voltaire smiled. [Oration on Voltaire, 1878]

22 England has two books: the Bible and Shakespeare. England made Shakespeare but the Bible made England. [Quoted in Simcox, *Treasury of Quotations on Christian Themes*]

Hull, Josephine (1886-1957)

23 Playing Shakespeare is very tiring. You never get to sit down, unless you're a King. [Quoted in Cowan, *The Wit of Women*]

Hume, David (1711-1776)

1 Custom, then, is the great guide of human life. [*Enquiry Concerning Human Understanding*]

2 Nothing appears more surprising to those who consider human affairs with a philosophical eye, than the ease with which the many are governed by the few. [*First Principles of Government*]

3 Never literary attempt was more unfortunate than my Treatise of Human Nature. It fell *deadborn from the press.* [*My Own Life*]

4 Avarice, the spur of industry. ['Of Civil Liberty']

5 Beauty in things exists in the mind which contemplates them. ['Of Tragedy']

6 No testimony is sufficient to establish a miracle, unless the testimony be of such a kind that its falsehood would be more miraculous than the fact which it endeavours to establish. ['Of Miracles']

Hunt, G.W. (1829-1904)

7 We don't want to fight, but, by jingo if we do, / We've got the ships, we've got the men, we've got the money too. [Music hall song, 1878]

Hunt, Leigh (1784-1859)

8 Abou Ben Adhem (may his tribe increase!) / Awoke one night from a deep dream of peace. ['Abou Ben Adhem and the Angel']

9 Write me as one that loves his fellow-men. [Ib.]

10 And lo! Ben Adhem's name led all the rest. [Ib.]

11 You strange, astonished-looking, angle-faced, / Dreary-mouthed, gaping wretches of the sea. ['The Fish, the Man, and the Spirit']

12 Jenny kissed me when we met...Say I'm growing old, but add, / Jenny kissed me. ['Rondeau']

13 The two divinest things a man has got; / A lovely woman in a rural spot. [*The Story of Rimini*]

Huss, Jan (c. 1370-1415)

14 *O sancta simplicitas!* O holy simplicity! [Attr. On seeing a peasant bringing a faggot to Huss's own stake]

Hutcheson, Francis (1694-1746)

15 Wisdom denotes the pursuing of the best ends by the best means. [*Inquiry into the Original of our Ideas of Beauty and Virtue*, I]

16 That action is best which procures the greatest happiness of the greatest number. [Ib. II]

Huxley, Aldous (1894-1963)

17 The proper study of mankind is books. [*Chrome Yellow*]

18 A poor degenerate from the ape, / Whose hands are four, whose tail's a limb, / I contemplate my flaccid shape / And know I may not rival him / Save with my mind. ['First Philosopher's Song']

19 But when the wearied Band / Swoons to a waltz, I take her hand, / And there we sit in peaceful calm, / Quietly sweating palm to palm. ['Frascati's']

20 It is far easier to write ten passably effective sonnets, good enough to take in the not too inquiring critic, than one effective advertisement that will take in a few thousand of the uncritical buying public. [*On the Margin*]

21 The solemn foolery of scholarship for scholarship's sake. [*The Perennial Philosophy*]

22 Parody and caricature are the most penetrating of criticisms. [*Point Counter Point*]

23 There is no substitute for talent. Industry and all the virtues are of no avail. [Ib.]

24 Silence is as full of potential wisdom and wit as the unhewn marble of great sculpture. [Ib.]

25 That all men are equal is a proposition to which, at ordinary times, no sane individual has ever given his assent. [*Proper Studies*]

26 Those who believe that they are exclusively in the right are generally those who achieve something. [Ib.]

1 Facts do not cease to exist because they are ignored. [Ib.]

2 Defined in psychological terms, a fanatic is a man who consciously overcompensates a secret doubt. [Ib.]

3 Success — 'The bitch-goddess, Success,' in William James's phrase — demands strange sacrifices from those who worship her. [Ib.]

4 Living is an art; and to practise it well, men need, not only acquired skill, but also a native tact and taste. [*Texts and Pretexts*]

5 In the upper and lower churches of St. Francis, Giotto and Cimabue showed that art had once worshipped something other than itself. [*Those Barren Leaves*]

6 There's only one corner of the universe you can be certain of improving, and that's your own self. [*Time Must Have a Stop*]

7 To his dog, every man is Napoleon; hence the constant popularity of dogs. [Attr.]

Huxley, Sir Julian Sorell (1887–1975)

8 The ant herself cannot philosophize — / While man does that, and sees, and keeps a wife, / And flies, and talks, and is extremely wise. ['For a Book of Essays']

Huxley, Thomas Henry (1825–1895)

9 I took thought and invented what I conceived to be the appropriate title of 'agnostic.' ...To my great satisfaction, the term took: and when the *Spectator* had stood godfather to it, any suspicion in the minds of respectable people... was, of course, completely lulled. [*Agnosticism*]

10 The great tragedy of Science — the slaying of a beautiful hypothesis by an ugly fact. ['Biogenesis and Abiogenesis']

11 Science is nothing but trained and organized common sense. ['The Method of Zadig']

12 If a little knowledge is dangerous, where is the man who has so much as to be out of danger? [*Science and Culture*]

13 History warns us that it is the customary fate of new truths to begin as heresies and to end as superstitions. [Ib.]

14 The great end of life is not Knowledge but Action. [*Technical Education*]

15 I am too much of a sceptic to deny the possibility of anything. [Letter, 1886]

16 Try to learn something about everything and everything about something. [Memorial stone]

Ibárruri, Dolores ['La Pasionaria'] (1895–)

17 *No pasarán!* They shall not pass. [Spanish Republican slogan]

18 It is better to die on your feet than to live on your knees. [Speech, 1936]

Ibsen, Henrik (1828–1906)

19 The minority is always right. [*An Enemy of the People*, IV]

20 The most dangerous foe to truth and freedom in our midst is the compact majority. Yes, the damned, compact liberal majority. [Ib.]

21 One should never put on one's best trousers to go out to battle for freedom and truth. [Ib. V]

22 What's a man's first duty? / The answer's brief: To be himself. [*Peer Gynt*, II]

23 Take the saving lie from the average man and you take his happiness away, too. [*The Wild Duck*, III]

Illich, Ivan (1926–)

24 Man must choose whether to be rich in things or in the freedom to use them. [*Deschooling Society*]

Inge, William Ralph (1860–1954)

25 Literature flourishes best when it is half a trade and half an art. [*The Victorian Age*]

1 A man may build himself a throne of bayonets, but he cannot sit upon it. [Marchant, *Wit and Wisdom of Dean Inge*]

Ingersoll, Robert Greene (1833–1899)

2 In nature there are neither rewards nor punishments — there are consequences. [*Lectures and Essays*]

Irving, Washington (1783–1859)

3 A woman's whole life is a history of the affections. [*The Sketch Book*, 'The Broken Heart']

4 A sharp tongue is the only edged tool that grows keener with constant use. [Ib. 'Rip Van Winkle']

5 They who drink beer will think beer. [Ib. 'Stratford']

6 The almighty dollar, that great object of universal devotion throughout our land... [*Wolfert's Roost*, 'The Creole Village']

Isherwood, Christopher (1904–1986)

7 I am a camera with its shutter open, quite passive, recording, not thinking. [*Goodbye to Berlin*]

James I of Scotland (1394–1437)

8 The bird, the beast, the fish eke in the sea, / They live in freedom everich in his kind; / And I a man, and lackith liberty. [*The Kingis Quair*]

9 Worshippe, ye that loveris been, this May, / For of your blisse the Kalendis are begun, / And sing with us, away, Winter, away! / Come, Summer, come the sweet seasoun and sun. [Ib.]

10 So far I fallen was in loves dance, / That suddenly my wit, my countenance, / My heart, my will, my nature, and my mind / Was changit right clean in another kind. [Ib.]

James V of Scotland (1512–1542)

11 It cam' wi' a lass, and it'll gang wi' a lass. [Remark on rule of Stuart dynasty in Scotland, 1542]

James VI of Scotland and I of England (1566–1625)

12 A branch of the sin of drunkenness, which is the root of all sins. [*A Counterblast to Tobacco*]

13 A custom loathesome to the eye, hateful to the nose, harmful to the brain, dangerous to the lungs, and in the black, stinking fume thereof, nearest resembling the horrible Stygian smoke of the pit that is bottomless. [Ib.]

14 I will govern according to the common weal, but not according to the common will. [Remark, 1621]

15 No bishop, no king. [Attr. remark, Hampton Court Conference]

16 Dr. Donne's verses are like the peace of God; they pass all understanding. [Attr.]

James, Henry (1843–1916)

17 The deep well of unconscious cerebration. [*The American*]

18 Huge American rattle of gold. [*The American Scene*]

19 The only obligation to which in advance we may hold a novel, without incurring the accusation of being arbitrary, is that it be interesting. [*The Art of Fiction*]

20 What is character but the determination of incident? what is incident but the illustration of character? [Ib.]

21 We must grant the artist his subject, his idea, his *donnée*: our criticism is applied only to what he makes of it. [Ib.]

22 The historian, essentially, wants more documents than he can really use; the dramatist only wants more liberties than he can really take. [*The Aspern Papers*]

23 Her grace of ease was perfect, but it was all grace of ease, not a single shred of it grace of uncertainty or difficulty. [*Crapy Cornelia*]

24 Vereker's secret, my dear man — the general intention of his books: the string the pearls were strung on, the buried treasure, the figure in the carpet. [*The Figure in the Carpet*]

1 It takes a great deal of history to produce a little literature. [*Life of Nathaniel Hawthorne*]

2 Dramatize, dramatize! [*Prefaces*]

3 [Of his own death] So here it is at last, the distinguished thing. [Attr.]

James, William (1842–1910)

4 There is no more miserable human being than one in whom nothing is habitual but indecision. [*Principles of Psychology*]

5 The bitch-goddess, Success. [Quoted by Aldous Huxley, *Proper Studies*]

6 A great many people think they are thinking when they are merely rearranging their prejudices. [Attr.]

Jefferson, Thomas (1743–1826)

7 Indeed I tremble for my country when I reflect that God is just. [*Notes on Virginia*]

8 A little rebellion now and then is a good thing. [Letter, 1787]

9 The tree of liberty must be refreshed from time to time with the blood of patriots and tyrants. It is its natural manure. [Letter, 1787]

10 [On public offices] Whenever a man has cast a longing eye on them, a rottenness begins in his conduct. [Letter, 1799]

11 If a due participation of office is a matter of right, how are vacancies to be obtained? Those by death are few; by resignation none. [Letter, 1801]

12 Advertisements contain the only truths to be relied on in a newspaper. [Letter, 1819]

13 When a man assumes a public trust, he should consider himself as public property. [Remark, 1807]

Jeffrey, Francis, Lord (1773–1850)

14 [On Wordsworth's *Excursion*] This will never do. [*Edinburgh Review*, 1814]

Jensen, Oliver (1914–   )

15 I haven't checked these figures but 87 years ago, I think it was, a number of individuals organized a governmental set-up here in this country, I believe it covered certain Eastern areas, with this idea they were following up based on a sort of national independence arrangement and the program that every individual is just as good as every other individual. [Parody of Lincoln's Gettysburg Address, as delivered by Eisenhower]

Jerome, Jerome K. (1859–1927)

16 It is impossible to enjoy idling thoroughly unless one has plenty of work to do. [*Idle Thoughts of an Idle Fellow*]

17 Love is like the measles; we all have to go through it. [Ib.]

18 The world must be getting old, I think; it dresses so very soberly now. [Ib.]

19 I like work; it fascinates me. I can sit and look at it for hours. I love to keep it by me: the idea of getting rid of it nearly breaks my heart. [Three Men in a Boat, 3]

20 But there, everything has its drawbacks, as the man said when his mother-in-law died, and they came down on him for the funeral expenses. [Ib.]

Jerome, St. (c. 342–420)

21 *Cur ergo haec ipse non facis?* Why do you not practise what you preach? [*Letters*, 48]

22 *Venerationi mihi semper fuit non verbosa rusticas, sed sancta simplicitas.* My reverence has always been for holy simplicity rather than wordy vulgarity. [Ib. 57]

23 *Noli equi dentes inspicere donati.* Never look a gift horse in the mouth. [*On the Epistle to the Ephesians*]

Jerrold, Douglas William (1803–1857)

24 Religion's in the heart, not in the knees. [*The Devil's Ducat*, I]

1 The ugliest of trades have their moments of pleasure. Now, if I were a grave-digger, or even a hangman, there are some people I could work for with a great deal of enjoyment. [*Wit and Opinions of Douglas Jerrold*]

2 Love's like the measles — all the worse when it comes late in life. [Ib.]

3 That fellow would vulgarize the day of judgment. [Ib.]

4 We love peace, as we abhor pusillanimity; but not peace at any price. [Ib.]

Joad, C.E.M. (1891–1953)

5 It all depends on what you mean by... [Response to BBC Brains Trust questions]

Joan of Arc (?1412–1431)

6 You think when you have slain me you will conquer France, but that you will never do. Though there were a hundred thousand God-dammees more in France than there are, they will never conquer that kingdom. [Attr.]

Johnson, Hiram (1866–1945)

7 The first casualty when war comes is truth. [Speech, 1917]

Johnson, Lionel (1867–1902)

8 The saddest of all Kings / Crown'd, and again discrown'd. ['By the Statue of King Charles I at Charing Cross']

Johnson, Lyndon Baines (1908–1973)

9 [Of J. Edgar Hoover, chief of the FBI] I'd much rather have that fellow inside the tent pissing out, than outside pissing in. [Attr.]

Johnson, Samuel (1709–1784)

10 I have protracted my work till most of those whom I wished to please have sunk into the grave, and success and miscarriage are empty sounds; I therefore dismiss it with frigid tranquillity, having little to fear or hope from censure or praise. [*Dictionary*, Preface]

11 *Excise.* A hateful tax levied upon commodities. [*Dictionary*]

12 *Net.* Anything reticulated or decussated at equal distances, with interstices between the intersections. [Ib.]

13 *Oats.* A grain, which in England is generally given to horses, but in Scotland supports the people. [Ib.]

14 The soul completes the triumph of thy face: / I thought, forgive my fair, the greatest force, / The strongest triumph of the female soul / Was but to choose the graces of a day; / To tune the tongue, to teach the eyes to roll, / Dispose the colours of the flowing robe, / And add new roses to the faded cheek. [*Irene*]

15 I know not whether it be not peculiar to the Scots to have attained the liberal without the manual arts, to have excelled in ornamental knowledge, and to have wanted not only the elegancies, but the conveniences of common life. [*Journey to the Western Isles*]

16 A Scotchman must be a very sturdy moralist who does not love Scotland better than truth. [Ib.]

17 That man is little to be envied whose patriotism would not gain force upon the plain of Marathon, or whose piety would not grow warmer among the ruins of Iona. [Ib.]

18 Whatever withdraws us from the power of our senses; whatever makes the past, the distant, or the future, predominate over the present, advances us in the dignity of thinking beings. [Ib.]

19 Nor will any wise man presume to say, 'Had I been in Savage's condition, I should have lived or written better than Savage.' [*Life of Savage*]

20 [Of metaphysical conceits] The most heterogeneous ideas are yoked by violence together. [*Lives of the English Poets*, Cowley]

21 Language is the dress of thought. [Ib.]

22 The father of English criticism. [Ib. Dryden]

1 The *Churchyard* abounds with images which find a mirror in every mind, and with sentiments to which every bosom returns an echo. [Ib. Gray]

2 If Pope be not a poet, where is poetry to be found? [Ib. Pope]

3 An acrimonious and surly republican. [Ib. Milton]

4 [Of Garrick's death] That stroke of death, which has eclipsed the gaiety of nations and impoverished the public stock of harmless pleasure. [Ib. Edmund Smith]

5 Fate never wounds more deep the gen'rous heart, / Than when a blockhead's insult points the dart. [*London*]

6 This mournful truth is ev'rywhere confess'd, / Slow rises worth by poverty depress'd. [Ib.]

7 The stage but echoes back the public voice. / The drama's laws the drama's patrons give, / For we that live to please must please to live. ['Prologue at the Opening of Drury Lane']

8 Men more frequently require to be reminded than informed. [*Rambler*, 2]

9 The business of a poet, said Imlac, is to examine, not the individual but the species;...he does not number the streaks of the tulip, or describe the different shades in the verdure of the forest. [*Rasselas*, 10]

10 Human life is everywhere a state in which much is to be endured, and little to be enjoyed. [Ib. 11]

11 Marriage has many pains, but celibacy has no pleasures. [Ib. 26]

12 I am sometimes disposed to think with the severer casuists of most nations that marriage is rather permitted than approved, and that none, but by the instigation of a passion too much indulged, entangle themselves with indissoluble compacts. [Ib.]

13 Of these wishes that they had formed they well knew that none could be obtained. [Ib. 49, last paragraph]

14 Nothing can please many, and please long, but just representations of general nature. [Preface to Shakespeare]

15 A quibble is to Shakespeare what luminous vapours are to the traveller: he follows it at all adventures; it is sure to lead him out of his way and sure to engulf him in the mire. [Ib.]

16 How is it that we hear the loudest yelps for liberty among the drivers of negroes? [*Taxation No Tyranny*]

17 Let observation with extensive view, / Survey mankind, from China to Peru; / Remark each anxious toil, each eager strife, / And watch the busy scenes of crowded life. [*The Vanity of Human Wishes*]

18 There mark what ills the scholar's life assail, / Toil, envy, want, the patron, and the jail. [Ib.]

19 His fall was destined to a barren strand, / A petty fortress, and a dubious hand; / He left the name, at which the world grew pale, / To point a moral, or adorn a tale. [Ib.]

20 From Marlb'rough's eyes the streams of dotage flow, / And Swift expires a driv'ler and a show. [Ib.]

21 With these celestial Wisdom calms the mind, / And makes the happiness she does not find. [Ib.]

22 The only end of writing is to enable the readers better to enjoy life, or better to endure it. [*Works*, X]

23 I put my hat upon my head, / I walked into the Strand, / And there I met another man / Whose hat was in his hand. [Parody of ballad]

24 In my early years I read very hard. It is a sad reflection, but a true one, that I knew almost as much at eighteen as I do now. [Boswell, *Life*, I]

25 I'll come no more behind your scenes, David: for the silk stockings and white bosoms of your actresses excite my amorous propensities. [Ib.]

26 A man may write at any time, if he will set himself doggedly to it. [Ib.]

1 Is not a Patron, my Lord, one who looks with unconcern on a man struggling for life in the water, and, when he has reached ground, encumbers him with help? [Ib.]

2 [Of Chesterfield's *Letters*] They teach the morals of a whore, and the manners of a dancing master. [Ib.]

3 Sir, we are a nest of singing birds. [Ib.]

4 A man, Sir, should keep his friendship in constant repair. [Ib.]

5 [Of literary criticism] You may scold a carpenter who has made you a bad table, though you cannot make a table. It is not your trade to make tables. [Ib.]

6 But, Sir, let me tell you, the noblest prospect which a Scotchman ever sees, is the high road that leads him to England! [Ib.]

7 Sir, a woman's preaching is like a dog's walking on his hinder legs. It is not done well; but you are surprised to find it done at all. [Ib.]

8 This was a good dinner enough, to be sure; but it was not a dinner to *ask* a man to. [Ib.]

9 [Asked the reason for a mistake in his Dictionary] Ignorance, madam, sheer ignorance. [Ib.]

10 Lexicographer: a writer of dictionaries, a harmless drudge. [Ib.]

11 He insisted on people praying with him; and I'd as lief pray with Kit Smart as anyone else. [Ib.]

12 He never passes a church without pulling off his hat. This shews that he has good principles. [Ib.]

13 A man ought to read just as inclination leads him; for what he reads as a task will do him little good. [Ib.]

14 Truth, Sir, is a cow which will yield such people no more milk, and so they are gone to milk the bull. [Ib.]

15 Your levellers wish to level *down* as far as themselves; but they cannot bear levelling *up* to themselves. [Ib.]

16 I love the University of Salamanca; for when the Spaniards were in doubt as to the lawfulness of their conquering America, the University of Salamanca gave it as their opinion that it was not lawful. [Ib.]

17 [Kicking a stone in order to disprove Berkeley's theory of the non-existence of matter] I refute it *thus*. [Ib.]

18 [Of Sir John Hawkins] A very unclubbable man. [Ib.]

19 We *know* our will is free, and *there's* an end on't. [Ib. II]

20 [Of *Gulliver's Travels*] When once you have thought of big men and little men, it is very easy to do all the rest. [Ib.]

21 Why, Sir, most schemes of political improvement are very laughable things. [Ib.]

22 Want of tenderness is want of parts, and is no less a proof of stupidity than of depravity. [Ib.]

23 A gentleman who had been very unhappy in marriage married immediately after his wife died. Dr. Johnson said, it was the triumph of hope over experience. [Ib.]

24 Nobody can write the life of a man, but those who have eat and drunk and lived in social intercourse with him. [Ib.]

25 There is more knowledge of the heart in one letter of Richardson's than in all Tom Jones. [Ib.]

26 Why, Sir, if you were to read Richardson for the story, your impatience would be so much fretted, that you would hang yourself. But you must read him for the sentiment, and consider the story as only giving occasion to the sentiment. [Ib.]

27 Much may be made of a Scotchman, if he be *caught* young. [Ib.]

28 Read over your compositions, and where ever you meet with a passage which you think is particularly fine, strike it out. [Ib.]

29 I hope I shall never be deterred from detecting what I think a cheat, by the menaces of a ruffian. [Ib. Letter to Macpherson]

1 There are few ways in which a man can be more innocently employed than in getting money. [Ib.]

2 Patriotism is the last refuge of a scoundrel. [Ib.]

3 In lapidary inscriptions a man is not upon oath. [Ib.]

4 Nothing odd will do long. *Tristram Shandy* did not last. [Ib.]

5 [Of Thomas Gray] He was dull in a new way, and that made many people think him *great.* [Ib.]

6 [Of the Scots] Their learning is like bread in a besieged town: every man gets a little, but no man gets a full meal. [Ib.]

7 Knowledge is of two kinds. We know a subject ourselves, or we know where we can find information upon it. [Ib.]

8 There is now less flogging in our great schools than formerly, but then less is learned there; so that what the boys get at one end they lose at the other. [Ib.]

9 There is nothing which has yet been contrived by man, by which so much happiness is produced as by a good tavern or inn. [Ib.]

10 A man who has not been in Italy, is always conscious of an inferiority, from his not having seen what it is expected a man should see. The grand object of travelling is to see the shores of the Mediterranean. [Ib. III]

11 If I had no duties, and no reference to futurity, I would spend my life in driving briskly in a post-chaise with a pretty woman. [Ib.]

12 Here's to the next insurrection of the negroes in the West Indies. [Ib.]

13 Every man thinks meanly of himself for not having been a soldier, or not having been at sea. [Ib.]

14 No man but a blockhead ever wrote, except for money. [Ib.]

15 Depend upon it, Sir, when a man knows he is to be hanged in a fortnight, it concentrates his mind wonderfully. [Ib.]

16 When a man is tired of London, he is tired of life; for there is in London all that life can afford. [Ib.]

17 [Of ghosts] All argument is against it; but all belief is for it. [Ib.]

18 Were it not for imagination, Sir, a man would be as happy in the arms of a chambermaid as of a Duchess. [Ib.]

19 Though we cannot out-vote them we will out-argue them. [Ib.]

20 Seeing Scotland, Madam, is only seeing a worse England. It is seeing the flower fade away to the naked stalk. [Ib.]

21 Claret is the liquor for boys; port for men; but he who aspires to be a hero must drink brandy. [Ib.]

22 [To an abusive Thames waterman] Sir, your wife, under pretence of keeping a bawdy-house, is a receiver of stolen goods. [Ib. IV]

23 [Of *Ossian*] A man might write such stuff for ever, if he would *abandon* his mind to it. [Ib.]

24 Sir, I look upon every day to be lost in which I do not make a new acquaintance. [Ib.]

25 The man who is asked by an author what he thinks of his work, is put to the torture, and is not obliged to speak the truth. [Ib.]

26 There are people whom one should like very well to drop, but would not wish to be dropt by. [Ib.]

27 Clear your *mind* of cant...You may *talk* in this manner; it is a mode of talking in Society: but don't *think* foolishly. [Ib.]

28 No man is a hypocrite in his pleasures. [Ib.]

29 [On his deathbed] I will be conquered; I will not capitulate. [Ib.]

30 [Of Bathurst] a man to my very heart's content: he hated a fool, and he hated a rogue, and he hated a whig; he was a very good hater. [*Johnsonian Miscellanies*, I]

31 I would advise no man to marry...who is not likely to propagate understanding. [Ib.]

32 He [Charles James Fox] talked to me at club one day concerning Catiline's conspiracy — so I withdrew my attention and thought about Tom Thumb. [Ib.]

1 It is very strange, and very melancholy, that the paucity of human pleasures should persuade us ever to call hunting one of them. [Ib.]

2 [On a celebrated violinist's performance] Difficult do you call it, Sir? I wish it were impossible. [Ib. II]

3 A man is in general better pleased when he has a good dinner upon his table, than when his wife talks Greek. [Ib.]

4 I dogmatize and am contradicted, and in this conflict of opinions and sentiments I find delight. [Ib.]

5 Abstinence is as easy to me as temperance would be difficult. [Ib.]

6 What is written without effort is in general read without pleasure. [Ib.]

7 Love is the wisdom of the fool and the folly of the wise. [Ib.]

8 [To Boswell] You have but two topics, yourself and me, and I'm sick of both. [Boswell, *London Journal*]

9 I am always sorry when any language is lost, because languages are the pedigree of nations. [Boswell, *Tour to the Hebrides*]

Johnstone, John Benn (1803–1891)

10 I want you to assist me in forcing her on board the lugger; once there, I'll frighten her into marriage. [*The Gipsy Farmer*; usually quoted as 'Once aboard the lugger and the maid is mine']

Jolson, Al (1886–1950)

11 You ain't heard nothin' yet, folks! [*The Jazz Singer*]

Jones, John Paul (1747–1792)

12 I have not yet begun to fight. [Response from a sinking ship, 1779]

Jonson, Ben (1572–1637)

13 Fortune, that favours fools. [*The Alchemist*, Prologue]

14 Yea, I will eat exceedingly, and prophesy. [*Bartholomew Fair*, I.6]

15 Where it concerns himself, / Who's angry at a slander makes it true. [*Catiline his Conspiracy*, III.1]

16 So they be ill men, / If they spake worse, 'twere better: for of such / To be dispraised, is the most perfect praise. [*Cynthia's Revels*, III.2]

17 True happiness / Consists not in the multitude of friends, / But in the worth and choice. [Ib.]

18 Queen and huntress, chaste and fair. [Ib. V.3]

19 If he were / To be made honest by an act of parliament, / I should not alter in my faith of him. [*The Devil is an Ass*, IV.1]

20 Alas, all the castles I have, are built with air, thou know'st. [*Eastward Ho*, II.2]

21 Still to be neat, still to be drest, / As you were going to a feast. [*Epicoene*, I.1]

22 And did act, what now we moan, / Old men so duly, / As sooth the Parcae thought him one, / He play'd so truly. ['Epitaph on Solomon Pavy']

23 But being so much too good for earth, / Heaven vows to keep him. [Ib.]

24 I do honour the very flea of his dog. [*Every Man in His Humour*, IV.2]

25 Come, leave the loathèd stage, / And the more loathsome age, / Where pride and impudence, in faction knit, / Usurp the chair of wit! ['Ode to Himself']

26 Rest in soft peace, and, ask'd say here doth lie / Ben Jonson his best piece of poetry. ['On My First Son']

27 Drink to me only with thine eyes, / And I will pledge with mine; / Or leave a kiss but in the cup, / And I'll not look for wine. ['To Celia']

28 Though thou hadst small Latin, and less Greek. ['To the Memory of... Shakespeare']

29 He was not of an age, but for all time! [Ib.]

30 For a good poet's made as well as born. [Ib.]

31 Sweet Swan of Avon. [Ib.]

32 She is Venus when she smiles / But she's Juno when she walks, / And Minerva when she talks. [*Underwoods*, 'Celebration of Charis']

1 Good morning to the day: and next, my gold! / Open the shrine that I may see my saint. [*Volpone*, I.1]

2 Come, my Celia, let us prove, / While we can, the sports of love. [Ib. III.5]

3 I remember the players have often mentioned it as an honour to Shakespeare that in his writing (whatsoever he penned) he never blotted out a line. My answer hath been, 'Would that he had blotted a thousand.' Which they thought a malevolent speech. I had not told posterity this, but for their ignorance, who chose that circumstance to commend their friend by wherein he most faulted; and to justify mine own candour; for I loved the man, and do honour his memory, on this side idolatry, as much as any. [*Discoveries*]

4 He hath consumed a whole night in lying looking to his great toe, about which he hath seen Tartars and Turks, Romans and Carthaginians, fight in his imagination. [*Conversations with Drummond*]

Jordan, Thomas (c. 1612-1685)

5 Our God and soldier we alike adore, / Just at the brink of ruin, not before: / The danger past, both are alike requited; / God is forgotten, and our soldier slighted. [Epigram]

Jowett, Benjamin (1817-1893)

6 One man is as good as another until he has written a book. [*Letters*, I]

7 My dear child, you must believe in God in spite of what the clergy tell you. [Attr.]

Joyce, James (1882-1941)

8 riverrun, past Eve and Adam's, from swerve of shore to bend of bay, brings us by a commodius vicus of recirculation back to Howth Castle and Environs. [*Finnegans Wake*, first words]

9 That ideal reader suffering from an ideal insomnia. [Ib.]

10 The flushpots of Euston and the hanging garments of Marylebone. [Ib.]

11 Ireland is the old sow that eats her farrow. [*A Portrait of the Artist as a Young Man*]

12 The artist, like the God of creation, remains within or behind or beyond or above his handiwork, invisible, refined out of existence, indifferent, paring his fingernails. [Ib.]

13 Welcome, O life! I go to encounter for the millionth time the reality of experience and to forge in the smithy of my soul the uncreated conscience of my race. [Ib.]

14 Stately, plump Buck Mulligan came from the stairhead, bearing a bowl of lather on which a mirror and a razor lay crossed. [*Ulysses*, I, first sentence]

15 The snotgreen sea. The scrotumtightening sea. [Ib.]

16 When I makes tea I makes tea, as old mother Grogan said. And when I makes water I makes water...Begob, ma'am, says Mrs. Cahill, God send you don't make them in the one pot. [Ib.]

17 Agenbite of inwit. [Ib. *passim*]

18 We feel in England that we have treated you [Irish] rather unfairly. It seems history is to blame. [Ib.]

19 Ineluctable modality of the visible. [Ib.]

20 History is a nightmare from which I am trying to awake. [Ib. II]

21 Come forth, Lazarus! And he came fifth and lost the job. [Ib.]

22 I put my arms around him yes and drew him down to me so he could feel my breasts all perfume yes and his heart was going like mad and yes I said yes I will Yes. [Ib. III, final words]

Julian the Apostate (A.D. 332-363)

23 *Vicisti, Galilaee*. You have conquered, Galilaean. [Last words]

Juliana of Norwich (1343-1443)

24 Sin is behovely, but all shall be well and all shall be well and all manner of things shall be well. [*Revelations of Divine Love*, 27]

Junius (fl. 1769)

1 The liberty of the press is the *Palladium* of all the civil, political, and religious rights of an Englishman. [*Letters*, Dedication]

2 To be acquainted with the merit of a ministry, we need only observe the condition of the people. [Ib. 1]

3 The right of election is the very essence of the constitution. [Ib. 2]

4 Is this the wisdom of a great minister? or is it the ominous vibration of a pendulum? [Ib. 12]

5 There is a holy mistaken zeal in politics as well as in religion. By persuading others, we convince ourselves. [Ib. 35]

6 There is something about him, which even treachery cannot trust. [Ib. 49]

Juvenal (c. A.D. 60–130)

7 *Difficile est saturam non scribere.* It is difficult not to write satire. [*Satires*, I]

8 *Probitas laudatur et alget.* Honesty is praised and is neglected. [Ib.]

9 *Si natura negat, facit indignatio versum.* If nature refuses, indignation makes verses. [Ib.]

10 *Nil habet infelix paupertas durius in se / Quam quod ridiculos homines facit.* The hardest thing about the miseries of poverty is that it makes men ridiculous. [Ib. III]

11 *Omnia Romae / Cum pretio.* Everything in Rome is at a price. [Ib.]

12 *Rara avis in terris nigroque simillima cycno.* A rare bird upon the earth, and very like a black swan. [Ib. VI]

13 *Sed quis custodiet ipsos / Custodes?* But who is to guard the guards themselves? [Ib.]

14 *Scribendi cacoethes.* The itch to write. [Ib. VII]

15 *Nobilitas sola est atque unica virtus.* Virtue alone is true nobility. [Ib. VIII]

16 *Cantabit vacuus coram latrone viator.* The empty-handed traveller will sing openly at the robber. [Ib. X]

17 *Duas tantum res anxius optat, / Panem et circenses.* The troubled [Roman people] long for two things only: bread and circuses. [Ib.]

18 *Orandum est ut sit mens sana in corpore sano.* You should pray for a healthy mind in a healthy body. [Ib.]

Kafka, Franz (1883–1924)

19 As Gregor Samsa awoke one morning from uneasy dreams he found himself transformed in his bed into a gigantic insect. ['Metamorphosis', first sentence]

20 But the hands of one of the partners were already at K.'s throat, while the other thrust the knife into his heart and turned it there twice. With failing eyes K. could still see the two of them, cheek leaning against cheek, immediately before his face, watching the final act. 'Like a dog!' he said: it was as if he meant the shame of it to outlive him. [*The Trial*, last words; trans. Willa and Edwin Muir]

21 In the fight between you and the world, back the world. [Attr.]

Kant, Immanuel (1724–1804)

22 Two things fill the mind with ever-increasing wonder and awe, the more often and the more intensely the mind is drawn to them: the starry heavens above me and the moral law within me. [*Critique of Pure Reason*, conclusion]

23 I am never to act without willing that the maxim by which I act should become a universal law. [*Critique of Practical Reason*]

Karr, Alphonse (1808–1890)

24 *Plus ça change, plus c'est la même chose.* The more things change the more they are the same. [*Les Guêpes*, 1849]

25 *Si l'on veut abolir la peine de mort en ce cas, que MM les assassins commencent.* If we want to abolish the death penalty, let our friends the murderers make the first move. [Ib.]

26 Every man has three characters: that which he exhibits, that which he has, and that which he thinks he has. [Attr.]

Kaufmann, Christoph (1753–1795)

1 *Sturm und Drang*. Storm and stress [Name invented in connection with Maximilien Klinger's play *Die Wirrwarr* (1775)]

Kavanagh, Ted (1892–1958)

2 Can I do you now, sir? [Quoted in Halliwell, *Filmgoer's Book of Quotes*]

3 Don't forget the diver. [Ib.]

4 After you, Claude...no, after you, Cecil... [Ib.]

5 I go, I come back. [Ib.]

6 I don't mind if I do. [Ib.]

Kearney, Denis (1847–1907)

7 Horny-handed sons of toil. [Speech, c. 1878)

Keats, John (1795–1821)

8 Season of mists and mellow fruitfulness. ['To Autumn']

9 Who hath not seen thee oft amid thy store? [Ib.]

10 Where are the songs of Spring? Ay, where are they? [Ib.]

11 O what can ail thee, Knight-at-arms / Alone and palely loitering; / The sedge has wither'd from the lake, / And no birds sing. ['La Belle Dame Sans Merci']

12 And there I shut her wild, wild eyes / With kisses four. [Ib.]

13 La belle Dame sans Merci / Hath thee in thrall! [Ib.]

14 ...the fam'd memoirs of a thousand years, / Written by Crafticant, and published / By Parpaglion and Co. ['The Cap and Bells']

15 A thing of beauty is a joy for ever: / Its loveliness increases; it will never / Pass into nothingness. [*Endymion*, I]

16 ...the inhuman dearth / Of noble natures. [Ib.]

17 Wherein lies happiness? In that which becks / Our ready minds to fellowship divine, / A fellowship with essence. [Ib.]

18 A hope beyond the shadow of a dream. [Ib.]

19 But this is human life: the war, the deeds, / The disappointment, the anxiety, / Imagination's struggles, far and nigh, / All human. [Ib. II]

20 He ne'er is crown'd / With immortality, who fears to follow / Where airy voices lead. [Ib.]

21 Since Ariadne was a vintager. [Ib.]

22 It is a flaw / In happiness, to see beyond our bourn, — / It forces us in summer skies to mourn, / It spoils the singing of the nightingale. ['Epistle to J.H. Reynolds']

23 St. Agnes' Eve — Ah, bitter chill it was! / The owl, for all his feathers, was a-cold. [*The Eve of St. Agnes*]

24 The joys of all his life were said and sung. [Ib.]

25 The silver, snarling trumpets 'gan to chide. [Ib.]

26 The music, yearning like a God in pain. [Ib.]

27 By degrees / Her rich attire creeps rustling to her knees. [Ib.]

28 Sudden a thought came like a full-blown rose, / Flushing his brow. [Ib.]

29 Full on this casement shone the wintry moon, / And threw warm gules on Madeline's fair breast. [Ib.]

30 And the long carpets rose along the gusty floor. [Ib.]

31 The Beadsman, after thousand aves told, / For aye unsought-for slept among his ashes cold. [Ib.]

32 Fanatics have their dreams, wherewith they weave / A paradise for a sect; the savage too / From forth the loftiest fashion of his sleep / Guesses at Heaven. [*The Fall of Hyperion*, I]

33 Every man whose soul is not a clod / Hath visions. [Ib.]

34 The poet and the dreamer are distinct, / Diverse, sheer opposite, antipodes. / The one pours out a balm upon the world, / The other vexes it. [Ib.]

35 Ever let the fancy roam, / Pleasure never is at home. ['Fancy']

36 Where's the cheek that doth not fade, / Too much gaz'd at? Where's the maid / Whose lip mature is ever new? [Ib.]

1 Deep in the shady sadness of a vale / Far sunken from the healthy breath of morn, / Far from the fiery noon, and eve's one star, / Sat gray-hair'd Saturn, quiet as a stone. [*Hyperion. A Fragment*, I]

2 No stir of air was there, / Not so much life as on a summer's day / Robs not one light seed from the feather'd grass. [Ib.]

3 O aching time! O moments big as years. [Ib.]

4 Those green-rob'd senators of mighty woods, / Tall oaks. [Ib.]

5 And still they were the same bright, patient stars. [Ib.]

6 Unseen before by Gods or wondering men. [Ib.]

7 And only blind from sheer supremacy. [Ib. II]

8 To bear all naked truths, / And to envisage circumstance, all calm, / That is the top of sovereignty. [Ib.]

9 For 'tis the eternal law / That first in beauty should be first in might. [Ib.]

10 I stood tip-toe upon a little hill. ['I Stood Tip-toe upon a Little Hill']

11 A little noiseless noise among the leaves. [Ib.]

12 Here are sweet peas, on tip-toe for a flight. [Ib.]

13 Why were they proud? again we ask aloud. / Why in the name of Glory were they proud? [*Isabella*]

14 'For cruel 'tis,' said she, / 'To steal my Basil-pot away from me.' [Ib.]

15 Real are the dreams of Gods, and smoothly pass / Their pleasures in a long immortal dream. [*Lamia*, I]

16 Love in a hut, with water and a crust, / Is — Love forgive us! — cinders, ashes, dust. [Ib. II]

17 Do not all charms fly / At the mere touch of cold philosophy? [Ib.]

18 But vain is now the burning and the strife, / Pangs are in vain, until I grow high-rife / With old Philosophy. ['Lines on Seeing a Lock of Milton's Hair']

19 Bards of Passion and of Mirth, / Ye have left your souls on earth! / Have ye souls in heaven too? ['Ode']

20 Thou still unravish'd bride of quietness, / Thou foster-child of silence and slow time. ['Ode on a Grecian Urn']

21 Heard melodies are sweet, but those unheard / Are sweeter. [Ib.]

22 For ever wilt thou love, and she be fair! [Ib.]

23 For ever warm and still to be enjoy'd, / For ever panting and for ever young. [Ib.]

24 O Attic shape! Fair attitude! [Ib.]

25 Thou, silent form, dost tease us out of thought / As doth eternity: Cold Pastoral! [Ib.]

26 'Beauty is truth, truth beauty,' — that is all / Ye know on earth, and all ye need to know. [Ib.]

27 And evenings steep'd in honied indolence. ['Ode on Indolence']

28 For I would not be dieted with praise, / A pet-lamb in a sentimental farce. [Ib.]

29 No, no, go not to Lethe, neither twist / Wolf's-bane, tight-rooted, for its poisonous wine. ['Ode on Melancholy']

30 But when the melancholy fit shall fall / Sudden from heaven like a weeping cloud, / ...Then glut thy sorrow on a morning rose, / ...Or on the wealth of globèd peonies; / Or if thy mistress some rich anger shows, / Emprison her soft hand, and let her rave, / And feed deep, deep upon her peerless eyes. [Ib.]

31 She dwells with Beauty —Beauty that must die; / And Joy, whose hand is ever at his lips / Bidding adieu. [Ib.]

32 Ay, in the very temple of Delight / Veil'd Melancholy has her sovran shrine. [Ib.]

33 My heart aches, and a drowsy numbness pains / My sense, as though of hemlock I had drunk. ['Ode to a Nightingale']

34 O for a draught of vintage! that hath been / Cool'd a long age in the deep-delved earth. [Ib.]

35 Full of the true, the blushful Hippocrene, / With beaded bubbles winking at the brim. [Ib.]

1 Fade far away, dissolve, and quite forget / What thou among the leaves hast never known, / The weariness, the fever and the fret / Here, where men sit and hear each other groan. [Ib.]

2 Where youth grows pale, and spectre-thin, and dies. [Ib.]

3 Away! away! for I will fly to thee, / Not charioted by Bacchus and his pards, / But on the viewless wings of Poesy. [Ib.]

4 Already with thee! tender is the night. [Ib.]

5 Darkling I listen; and, for many a time / I have been half in love with easeful Death. [Ib.]

6 Thou wast not born for death, immortal Bird! / No hungry generations tread thee down; / The voice I hear this passing night was heard / In ancient days by emperor and clown: / Perhaps the self-same song that found a path / Through the sad heart of Ruth, when, sick for home, / She stood in tears amid the alien corn; / The same that oft-times hath / Charm'd magic casements, opening on the foam / Of perilous seas, in faery lands forlorn. [Ib.]

7 Was it a vision, or a waking dream? / Fled is that music:— / Do I wake or sleep? [Ib.]

8 O latest born and loveliest vision far / Of all Olympus' faded hierarchy. ['Ode to Psyche']

9 A bright torch, and a casement ope at night, / To let the warm Love in! [Ib.]

10 Stop and consider! life is but a day; / A fragile dewdrop on its perilous way / From a tree's summit. ['Sleep and Poetry']

11 O for ten years, that I may overwhelm / Myself in poesy; so I may do the deed / That my own soul has to itself decreed. [Ib.]

12 They sway'd about upon a rocking horse, / And thought it Pegasus. [Ib.]

13 A thousand handicraftsmen wore the mask / Of Poesy. Ill-fated, impious race! [Ib.]

14 A drainless shower / Of light is poesy; 'tis the supreme of power; / 'Tis might half slumb'ring on its own right arm. [Ib.]

15 And they shall be accounted poet kings / Who simply tell the most heart-easing things. [Ib.]

16 Bright star, would I were steadfast as thou art — / Not in lone splendour hung aloft the night / And watching, with eternal lids apart, / Like nature's patient, sleepless Eremite, / The moving waters at their priestlike task / Of pure ablution round earth's human shores. [*Sonnets*, 'Bright Star']

17 Still, still to hear her tender-taken breath, / And so live ever — or else swoon to death. [Ib.]

18 To sit upon an Alp as on a throne, / And half forget what world or worldling meant. [Ib. 'Happy is England']

19 There is a budding morrow in midnight. [Ib. 'To Homer']

20 Fame, like a wayward girl, will still be coy / To those who woo her with too slavish knees. [Ib. 'On Fame']

21 Much have I travell'd in the realms of gold, / And many goodly states and kingdoms seen. [Ib. 'On First Looking into Chapman's Homer']

22 Then felt I like some watcher of the skies / When a new planet swims into his ken; / Or like stout Cortez when with eagle eyes / He star'd at the Pacific — and all his men / Look'd at each other with a wild surmise — / Silent, upon a peak in Darien. [Ib.]

23 The poetry of earth is never dead. [Ib. 'On the Grasshopper and Cricket']

24 To one who has been long in city pent, / 'Tis very sweet to look into the fair / And open face of heaven. [Ib. 'To One Who Has Been Long']

25 When I have fears that I may cease to be / Before my pen has glean'd my teeming brain. [Ib. 'When I have Fears']

26 Then on the shore / Of the wide world I stand alone, and think / Till love and fame to nothingness do sink. [Ib.]

1 What can I do to drive away / Remembrance from my eyes? ['What can I Do?']

2 Woman! when I behold thee flippant, vain, / Inconstant, childish, proud, and full of fancies. ['Woman! When I Behold Thee']

3 The excellence of every art is its intensity, capable of making all disagreeables evaporate, from their being in close relationship with beauty and truth. [Letter to George and Tom Keats, 1817]

4 Negative Capability, that is, when a man is capable of being in uncertainties, mysteries, doubts, without any irritable reaching after fact and reason. [Ib.]

5 A long poem is a test of invention which I take to be the Polar star of poetry, as fancy is the sails, and imagination the rudder. [Letter to Benjamin Bailey, 1817]

6 I am certain of nothing but the holiness of the heart's affections and the truth of imagination — what the imagination seizes as beauty must be truth — whether it existed before or not. [Letter to Benjamin Bailey, 1817]

7 I have never yet been able to perceive how anything can be known for truth by consecutive reasoning — and yet it must be. [Ib.]

8 O for a life of sensations rather than of thoughts! [Ib.]

9 The imagination may be compared to Adam's dream — he awoke and found it truth. [Ib.]

10 I do think better of womankind than to suppose they care whether Mister John Keats five feet high likes them or not. [Letter to Benjamin Bailey, 1818]

11 So I do believe...that works of genius are the first things in this world. [Letter to George and Tom Keats, 1818]

12 There is nothing stable in the world; uproar's your only music. [Letter to George and Tom Keats, 1818]

13 Scenery is fine — but human nature is finer. [Letter to Benjamin Bailey, 1818]

14 Axioms in philosophy are not axioms until they are proved upon our pulses. [Letter to J.H. Reynolds, 1818]

15 Were it in my choice I would reject a petrarchal coronation — on account of my dying day, and because women have cancers. [Letter to Benjamin Bailey, 1818]

16 A poet is the most unpoetical of anything in existence, because he has no identity; he is continually informing and filling some other body. [Letter to Richard Woodhouse, 1818]

17 I am ambitious of doing the world some good. If I should be spared, that may be the work of maturer years — in the interval I will assay to reach to as high a summit in Poetry as the nerve bestowed upon me will suffer. [Ib.]

18 I think I shall be among the English Poets after my death. [Letter to George and Georgiana Keats, 1818]

19 The roaring of the wind is my wife and the stars through the window pane are my children. The mighty abstract idea I have of beauty in all things stifles the more divided and minute domestic happiness...The opinion I have of the generality of women — who appear to me as children to whom I would rather give a sugar plum than my time, forms a barrier against matrimony which I rejoice in. [Letter to George and Georgiana Keats, 1818]

20 We hate poetry that has a palpable design upon us — and if we do not agree, seems to put its hand in its breeches pocket. [Letter to J.H. Reynolds, 1818]

21 Poetry should surprise by a fine excess, and not by singularity; it should strike the reader as a wording of his own highest thoughts, and appear almost a remembrance. [Letter to John Taylor, 1818]

22 If poetry comes not naturally as leaves to a tree it had better not come at all. [Ib.]

23 Shakespeare led a life of allegory: his works are the comments on it. [Letter to George and Georgiana Keats, 1819]

1 Call the world if you please 'the vale of Soul-making'. [Letter to George and Georgiana Keats, 1819]

2 I am convinced more and more day by day that fine writing is next to fine doing, the top thing in the world. [Letter to J.H. Reynolds, 1819]

3 I have met with women whom I really think would like to be married to a poem, and to be given away by a novel. [Letter to Fanny Brawne, 1819]

4 Load every rift of your subject with ore. [Letter to Shelley, 1820]

5 Here lies one whose name was writ in water. [Epitaph for himself]

Keble, John (1792–1866)

6 The trivial round, the common task, / Would furnish all we ought to ask; / Room to deny ourselves; a road / To bring us, daily, nearer God. [*The Christian Year*, 'Morning']

7 Be ev'ry mourner's sleep tonight / Like infant's slumbers, pure and light. [Ib. 'Evening']

8 There is a book, who runs may read, / Which heavenly truth imparts, / And all the lore its scholars need, / Pure eyes and Christian hearts. [Hymn]

Kempis, Thomas à (c. 1380–1471)

9 Verily, when the day of judgement comes, we shall not be asked what we have read, but what we have done. [*De Imitatione Christi*, 1]

10 The humble knowledge of thyself is a surer way to God than the deepest search after science. [Ib.]

11 Man proposes, but God disposes. [Ib.]

12 *Sic transit gloria mundi.* Thus the glory of the world passes away. [Ib. 3]

13 Would that we had spent one whole day well in this whole world! [Ib. 23]

Ken, Bishop Thomas (1637–1711)

14 Teach me to live, that I may dread / The grave as little as my bed. ['Evening Hymn']

15 Praise God from whom all blessings flow, / Praise him all creatures here below. ['Midnight Hymn']

Kennedy, John F. (1917–1963)

16 We stand today on the edge of a new frontier. [Speech, 1960]

17 As a free man, I take pride in the words *Ich bin ein Berliner*. [Speech to West Berliners, 1963]

Kennedy, Robert F. (1925–1968)

18 One fifth of the people are against everything all the time. [*Observer*, 'Sayings of the Week', 1964]

Kepler, Johannes (1571–1630)

19 O God, I am thinking Thy thoughts after Thee. [Remark (while studying astronomy)]

Kethe, William (fl. 1593)

20 All people that on earth do dwell, / Sing to the Lord with cheerful voice. / Him serve with mirth, His praise forth tell; / Come ye before him and rejoice. [Hymn]

21 His truth at all times firmly stood, / And shall from age to age endure. [Ib.]

Key, Francis Scott (1779–1843)

22 'Tis the star-spangled banner; O long may it wave / O'er the land of the free, and the home of the brave! ['The Star-Spangled Banner']

Keynes, J.M. (1883–1946)

23 Whenever you save five shillings you put a man out of work for a day. [*Observer*, 'Sayings of the Week', 1931]

24 In the long run...we are all dead. [Attr.]

Khruschev, Nikita (1894–1971)

25 Whether you like it or not, history is on our side. We will bury you! [Speech to Western ambassadors, 1956]

Kierkegaard, Sören (1813–1855)

26 Life can only be understood backwards; but it must be lived forwards. [*Life*]

Kilmer, Joyce (1886–1918)

1 I think that I shall never see / A poem lovely as a tree. ['Trees']

King, Benjamin (1857–1894)

2 Nothing to do but work, / Nothing to eat but food, / Nothing to wear but clothes / To keep one from going nude. ['The Pessimist']

King, Bishop Henry (1592–1669)

3 But hark! My pulse like a soft drum / Beats my approach, tells thee I come. ['The Exequy']

4 We that did nothing study but the way / To love each other, with which thoughts the day / Rose with delight to us, and with them set, / Must learn the hateful art, how to forget. ['The Surrender']

King, Martin Luther (1929–1968)

5 I have a dream. [Various Speeches, 1963]

6 Riots are the language of the unheard. [Attr.]

7 I want to be the white man's brother, not his brother-in-law. [Attr.]

Kingsley, Charles (1819–1875)

8 Be good, sweet maid, and let who will be clever; / Do noble things, not dream them, all day long. ['A Farewell, to C.E.G.']

9 What we can we will be, / Honest Englishmen. / Do the work that's nearest, / Though it's dull at whiles, / Helping, when we meet them, / Lame dogs over stiles. ['Letter to Thomas Hughes']

10 To be discontented with the divine discontent, and to be ashamed with the noble shame, is the very germ and first upgrowth of all virtue. [*Health and Education*]

11 When all the world is young, lad, / And all the trees are green; / And every goose a swan, lad / And every lass a queen. [Song from *The Water Babies*: 'Young and Old']

12 For men must work, and women must weep, / And there's little to earn, and many to keep. ['The Three Fishers']

13 He did not know that a keeper is only a poacher turned outside in, and a poacher a keeper turned inside out. [*The Water Babies*, 1]

14 As thorough an Englishman as ever coveted his neighbour's goods. [Ib. 4]

15 The loveliest fairy in the world; and her name is Mrs. Doasyouwouldbedoneby. [Ib.]

16 More ways of killing a cat than choking her with cream. [*Westward Ho!*, 20]

Kingsmill, Hugh (1889–1949)

17 What, still alive at twenty-two, / A clean upstanding lad like you? / Sure, if your throat 'tis hard to slit, / Slit your girl's, and swing for it. ['Poem after A.E. Housman']

Kipling, Rudyard (1865–1936)

18 England's on the anvil — hear the hammers ring — Clanging from the Severn to the Tyne. ['The Anvil']

19 Oh, East is East, and West is West, and never the twain shall meet. ['The Ballad of East and West']

20 Four things greater than all things are, — / Women and Horses and Power and War. ['Ballad of the King's Jest']

21 And a woman is only a woman but a good cigar is a Smoke. ['The Betrothed']

22 O where are you going to, all you Big Steamers, / With England's own coal, up and down the salt seas.? ['Big Steamers']

23 (Boots — boots — boots — boots — movin' up an' down again!) / There's no discharge in the war! ['Boots']

24 Teach us delight in simple things, / And mirth that has no bitter springs. [Ib.]

25 But Iron — Cold Iron — is master of them all. ['Cold Iron']

26 But the Devil whoops, as he whooped of old: / 'It's clever, but is it Art?' ['The Conundrum of the Workshops']

27 An' they're hangin' Danny Deever in the mornin'. ['Danny Deever']

1 The 'eathen in 'is blindness must end where 'e began, / But the backbone of the Army is the Non-commissioned man! ['The 'Eathen']

2 And what should they know of England who only England know? ['The English Flag']

3 For the female of the species is more deadly than the male. ['The Female of the Species']

4 There is but one task for all — / One life for each to give. / What stands if Freedom fall? / Who dies if England live? ['For All We Have and Are']

5 We're poor little lambs who've lost our way, / Baa! Baa! Baa! / We're little black sheep who've gone astray, / Baa-aa-aa! / Gentleman-Rankers out on the spree, / Damned from here to Eternity, / God ha' mercy on such as we, / Baa! Yah! Bah! ['Gentleman-Rankers']

6 And the measure of our torment is the measure of our youth. [Ib.]

7 And the Glory of the Garden it shall never pass away! ['The Glory of the Garden']

8 You're a better man than I am, Gunga Din! ['Gunga Din']

9 There are nine and sixty ways of constructing tribal lays, / And — every — single — one — of — them — is — right! ['In the Neolithic Age']

10 If you can keep your head when all about you / Are losing theirs and blaming it on you. ['If']

11 If you can fill the unforgiving minute / With sixty seconds' worth of distance run, / Yours is the Earth and everything that's in it, / And — which is more — you'll be a Man, my son! [Ib.]

12 If you can dream — and not make dreams your master. [Ib.]

13 With the flannelled fools at the wicket or the muddied oafs at the goal. ['The Islanders']

14 He walked by himself, and all places were alike to him. [*Just So Stories*, 'The Cat That Walked by Himself']

15 The great, grey-green, greasy Limpopo River, all set about with fever-trees. [Ib. 'The Elephant's Child']

16 There lived a Parsee from whose hat the rays of the sun were reflected in more-than-oriental-splendour. [Ib. 'How the Rhinoceros Got His Skin']

17 'Nice,' said the small 'stute Fish. 'Nice but nubbly,' [Ib. 'How the Whale Got his Throat']

18 A man of infinite-resource-and-sagacity. [Ib.]

19 I've taken my fun where I found it, / An' now I must pay for my fun. ['The Ladies']

20 We have had a jolly good lesson, and it serves us jolly well right. ['The Lesson']

21 Pull out, pull out, on the Long Trail — the trail that is always new! ['The Long Trail']

22 On the road to Mandalay, / Where the flyin'-fishes play, / An' the dawn comes up like thunder outer China 'crost the Bay! ['Mandalay']

23 The toad beneath the harrow knows / Exactly where each tooth-point goes. ['Pagett M.P.']

24 The tumult and the shouting dies; / The Captains and the Kings depart. ['Recessional']

25 Lest we forget — lest we forget! [Ib.]

26 Such boastings as the Gentiles use, / Or lesser breeds without the Law. [Ib.]

27 Them that asks no questions isn't told a lie. / Watch the wall, my darling, while the Gentlemen go by! ['A Smuggler's Song']

28 Being kissed by a man who didn't wax his moustache was — like eating an egg without salt. [*Soldiers Three*, 'The Gadsbys, Poor Dear Mamma']

29 God gives all men all earth to love, / But, since man's heart is small, / Ordains for each one spot shall prove / Beloved over all. ['Sussex']

30 Take my word for it, the silliest woman can manage a clever man; but it needs a very clever woman to manage a fool. ['Three and — an Extra']

31 It's Tommy this, an' Tommy that, an' 'Chuck him out, the brute!' / But it's 'Saviour of 'is country' when the guns begin to shoot. ['Tommy']

1 When 'Omer smote 'is bloomin' lyre, / 'E'd 'eard men sing by land an' sea; / An' what 'e thought 'e might require, / 'E went an' took — the same as me! ['When 'Omer Smote 'is Bloomin' Lyre']

2 The White Man's Burden [Title of poem]

3 He travels the fastest who travels alone. ['The Winners']

4 [Of newspaper barons] Power without responsibility — the prerogative of the harlot throughout the ages. [Quoted by Baldwin in speech, 1931]

Kissinger, Henry (1923-)

5 Power is the ultimate aphrodisiac. [Attr.]

Klee, Paul (1879–1940)

6 Art does not reproduce what we see; rather, it makes us see. ['Creative Credo']

Klopstock, Friedrich (1724–1803)

7 [Of one of his poems] God and I both knew what it meant once; now God alone knows. [Attr. Also attr. to Browning]

Knopf, Edwin H. (1899-)

8 The son-in-law also rises. [Quoted in Colombo, *Wit and Wisdom of the Moviemakers*]

Knox, John (?1505–1572)

9 The First Blast of the Trumpet Against the Monstrous Regiment of Women [Title of pamphlet]

10 To promote a Woman to bear rule, superiority, dominion or empire, above any Realm, Nation, or City, is repugnant to Nature; contumely to God, a thing most contrarious to his revealed will and approved ordinance, and finally it is the subversion of good Order, of all equity and justice. [*The First Blast of the Trumpet Against the Monstrous Regiment of Women*, first sentence]

Knox, Ronald (1888–1957)

11 There was once a man who said 'God / Must think it exceedingly odd / If he finds that this tree / Continues to be / When there's no one about in the Quad.' [Attr.; for reply *see* Anon., 'Dear Sir, your astonishment's odd']

Knox, Vicesimus (1752–1821)

12 Can anything be more absurd than keeping women in a state of ignorance, and yet so vehemently to insist on their resisting temptation? [*Liberal Education*, I]

Kyd, Thomas (1558-1594)

13 Oh eyes, no eyes, but fountains fraught with tears; / Oh life, no life, but lively form of death; / Oh world, no world, but mass of public wrongs. [*The Spanish Tragedy*, III.2]

14 My son — and what's a son? A thing begot / Within a pair of minutes, thereabout, / A lump bred up in darkness. [Ib. III.11]

15 Why then I'll fit you. [Ib. IV.1]

16 Hieronymo's mad againe. [Ib. Quoted by T.S. Eliot, *The Waste Land*]

La Bruyère, Jean de (1645–1696)

17 *Les médecins laissent mourir, les charlatans tuent.* The doctors allow one to die, the charlatans kill. [*Les Caractères*]

18 *Le commencement et le déclin de l'amour se font sentir par l'embarras où l'on est de se trouver seuls.* The beginning and the decline of love make themselves felt in the embarrassment on being left alone together. [Ib. 'Du Coeur']

19 Everything has been said, and we come too late after more than seven thousand years in which Man has lived and thought. [Ib. 'Des ouvrages de l'esprit']

20 The pleasure of criticizing takes away from us the pleasure of being moved by some very fine things. [Ib.]

Laforgue, Jules (1860–1887)

21 *Ah! que la vie est quotidienne.* Oh, what an everyday affair life is. ['Complainte sur certains ennuis']

Lamb, Lady Caroline (1785–1828)

1 [Of Byron] Mad, bad, and dangerous to know. [Journal, 1812]

Lamb, Charles (1775–1834)

2 'Presents,' I often say 'endear Absents.' [*Essays of Elia*, 'A Dissertation upon Roast Pig']

3 We are nothing; less than nothing, and dreams. We are only what might have been, and must wait upon the tedious shores of Lethe millions of ages before we have existence, and a name. [Ib. 'Dream Children']

4 Coleridge holds that a man cannot have a pure mind who refuses apple-dumplings. I am not certain but he is right. [Ib. 'Grace Before Meat']

5 I am, in plainer words, a bundle of prejudices — made up of likings and dislikings. [Ib. 'Imperfect Sympathies']

6 I have been trying all my life to like Scotchmen, and am obliged to desist from the experiment in despair. [Ib.]

7 There is an order of imperfect intellects (under which mine must be content to rank) which...is essentially anti-Caledonian. [Ib.]

8 In everything that relates to science, I am a whole Encyclopaedia behind the rest of the world. [Ib. 'The Old and New Schoolmaster']

9 The human species, according to the best theory I can form of it, is composed of two distinct races, *the men who borrow*, and *the men who lend*. [Ib. 'The Two Races of Men']

10 Not many sounds in life, and I include all urban and all rural sounds, exceed in interest a knock at the door. [Ib. 'Valentine's Day']

11 [Of tobacco] Stinking'st of the stinking kind, / Filth of the mouth and fog of the mind, / Africa, that brags her foison / Breeds no such prodigious poison. ['A Farewell to Tobacco']

12 For thy sake, Tobacco, I / Would do any thing but die. [Ib.]

13 I love to lose myself in other men's minds. When I am not walking, I am reading; I cannot sit and think. Books think for me. [*Last Essays of Elia*, 'Detached Thoughts on Books and Reading']

14 I can read anything which I call a *book*. There are things in that shape which I cannot allow for such. In this catalogue of *books which are no books — biblia a-biblia* — I reckon Court Calendars, Directories, ...Almanacs, Statutes at Large, the works of Hume, Gibbon...
and, generally, all those volumes which 'no gentleman's library should be without.' [Ib.]

15 All, all are gone, the old familiar faces. ['The Old Familiar Faces']

16 The greatest pleasure I know, is to do a good action by stealth, and to have it found out by accident. ['Table Talk by the Late Elia']

17 Cultivate simplicity, Coleridge. [Letter, 1796]

18 I came home...hungry as a hunter. [Letter, 1800]

19 Nothing puzzles me more than time and space; and yet nothing troubles me less, as I never think about them. [Letter, 1810]

20 Anything awful makes me laugh. I misbehaved once at a funeral. [Letter, 1815]

21 [Of Coleridge] His face when he repeats his verses hath its ancient glory, an Archangel a little damaged. [Letter, 1816]

22 How I like to be liked, and what I do to be liked! [Letter, 1821]

23 May my last breath be drawn through a pipe and exhaled in a pun. [Quoted in Wintle and Kenin, *Dictionary of Biographical Quotations*]

Lambton, John, Earl of Durham (1792–1840)

24 He said he considered £40,000 a year a moderate income — such a one as a man *might jog on with*. [Quoted in *The Creevey Papers*]

Landor, Walter Savage (1775–1864)

1 George the First was always reckoned / Vile, but viler George the Second; / And what mortal ever heard / Any good of George the Third? / When from earth the Fourth descended / God be praised, the Georges ended! [Epigram]

2 I strove with none; for none was worth my strife; / Nature I loved, and next to Nature, Art; / I warmed both hands before the fire of life; / It sinks, and I am ready to depart. ['Finis']

3 Ah, what avails the sceptred race! / Ah, what the form divine! ['Rose Aylmer']

4 There are no fields of amaranth on this side of the grave: there are no voices, O Rhodope! that are not soon mute, however tuneful: there is no name, with whatever emphasis of passionate love repeated, of which the echo is not faint at last. [*Imaginary Conversations*, 'Aesop and Rhodope']

5 Prose on certain occasions can bear a great deal of poetry: on the other hand, poetry sinks and swoons under a moderate weight of prose. [Ib. 'Archdeacon Hare and Walter Landor']

6 I shall dine late; but the dining-room will be well lighted, the guests few and select. [Ib.]

Lang, Andrew (1844–1912)

7 St. Andrews by the Northern Sea, / That is a haunted town to me! ['Almae Matres']

8 There's a joy without canker or cark, / There's a pleasure eternally new, / 'Tis to gloat on the glaze and the mark / Of China that's ancient and blue. ['Ballade of Blue China']

9 Our hearts are young 'neath wrinkled rind: / Life's more amusing than we thought. ['Ballade of Middle Age']

10 A house full of books, and a garden full of flowers. ['Ballade of True Wisdom']

11 They hear like Ocean on a western beach / The surge and thunder of the Odyssey. ['The Odyssey']

Langbridge, Frederick (1849–1923)

12 Two men look out through the same bars: / One sees the mud, and one the stars. ['A Cluster of Quiet Thoughts']

Langland, William (c. 1330–c. 1400)

13 In a somer seson whan soft was the sonne. [*Piers Plowman*, Prologue (B Text)]

14 A faire felde ful of folke fonde I there bytwene / Of all manner of men, the mene and riche, / Worchyng and wandrying as the world asketh. [Ib.]

15 A glotoun of wordes. [Ib.]

16 Grammere, that grounde is of alle. [Ib. (C Text)]

Lao-tze (fl. c. 550 B.C.)

17 Acting without design, occupying oneself without making a business of it, finding the great in what is small and the many in the few, repaying injury with kindness, effecting difficult things while they are easy, and managing great things in their beginnings: this is the method of Tao. [*Tao Te Ching*]

18 To joy in conquest is to joy in the loss of human life. [Ib.]

19 The further one goes, the less one knows. [Ib.]

20 Heaven and Earth have no pity; they regard all things as straw dogs. [Ib.]

21 A journey of a thousand miles must begin with a single step. [Ib.]

La Rochefoucauld, François, Duc de (1613–1680)

22 *On n'est jamais si heureux ni si malheureux qu'on s'imagine.* One is never so happy or so unhappy as one thinks. [*Maximes*, 49]

23 *On peut trouver des femmes qui n'ont jamais eu de galanterie, mais il est rare d'en trouver qui n'en aient jamais eu qu'une.* One can find women who have never had a love affair, but it is rare to find a woman who has had only one. [Ib. 73]

1 *La gloire des grands hommes se doit toujours mesurer aux moyens dont ils se sont servis pour l'acquérir.* The glory of great men must always be measured by the means they have used to obtain it. [Ib. 157]

2 *L'hypocrisie est un hommage que le vice rend à la vertu.* Hypocrisy is the homage that vice pays to virtue. [Ib. 218]

3 *On s'ennuie presque toujours avec les gens qui il n'est pas permis de s'ennuyer.* We are almost always bored by the very people whom we must not find boring. [Ib. 352]

4 *On peut être plus fin qu'un autre, mais non pas plus fin que tous les autres.* One can be astuter than another, but not astuter than all the others. [Ib. 394]

5 Everyone complains of his memory; nobody of his judgment. [Attr.]

La Rochefoucauld-Liancourt, Duc de (1747–1827)

6 *Non, Sire, c'est une révolution.* No, Sire, it is a revolution. [In reply to Louis XVI's question '*C'est une révolte?*' on hearing of the fall of the Bastille]

Larkin, Philip (1922–1985)

7 What will survive of us is love. ['An Arundel Tomb']

8 Hatless, I take off / My cycle-clips in awkward reverence. ['Church-going']

9 Nothing, like something, happens anywhere. ['I Remember, I Remember']

10 Why should I let the toad *work* / Squat on my life? ['Toads']

Latimer, Bishop Hugh (c. 1485–1555)

11 Be of good comfort, Master Ridley, and play the man. We shall this day light such a candle by God's grace in England, as (I trust) shall never be put out. [Foxe, *Actes and Monuments*]

Lawrence, D. H. (1885–1930)

12 Love is the great Asker. ['End of Another Home Holiday']

13 Once God was all negroid, as now he is fair. ['Grapes']

14 How beastly the bourgeois is / especially the male of the species. ['How Beastly the Bourgeois Is']

15 Have you built your ship of death, O have you? / O build your ship of death, for you will need it. ['The Ship of Death']

16 And so, I missed my chance with one of the lords / Of life. / And I have something to expiate; / A pettiness. ['Snake']

17 Money is our madness, our vast collective madness. ['Money Madness']

18 Loud peace propaganda makes war seem imminent. ['Peace and War']

19 To the Puritan all things are impure, as somebody says. [*Etruscan Places*, 'Cerveteri']

20 Pornography is the attempt to insult sex, to do dirt on it. ['Pornography and Obscenity']

21 Never trust the artist. Trust the tale. [*Studies in Classic American Literature*, 'The Spirit of Place']

22 The novel is the one bright book of life. ['Why the Novel Matters']

Lawrence, James (1781–1813)

23 Don't give up the ship. [Last words, during naval battle]

Lazarus, Emma (1849–1887)

24 Give me your tired, your poor, / Your huddled masses yearning to breathe free. [Verse inscribed on Statue of Liberty]

Leacock, Stephen Butler (1869–1944)

25 Lord Ronald said nothing; he flung himself from the room, flung himself upon his horse and rode madly off in all directions. ['Gertrude the Governess']

26 I detest life-insurance agents; they always argue that I shall someday die, which is not so. [*Literary Lapses*, 'Insurance Up to Date']

1 The parent who could see his boy as he really is, would shake his head and say: 'Willie, is no good: I'll sell him.' ['The Lot of a Schoolmaster']

2 Advertising may be described as the science of arresting the human intelligence long enough to get money from it. [Quoted in Prochow, *The Public Speaker's Treasure Chest*]

3 A half truth in argument, like a half brick, carries better. [Quoted in Flesch, *The Book of Unusual Quotations*]

Lear, Edward (1812–1888)

4 There was an Old Man with a beard, / Who said, 'It is just as I feared! — / Two Owls and a Hen, / Four Larks and a Wren, / Have all built their nests in my beard! [*Book of Nonsense*]

5 'How pleasant to know Mr. Lear!' / Who has written such volumes of stuff! / Some think him ill-tempered and queer, / But a few think him pleasant enough. [*Nonsense Songs*, Preface]

6 On the coast of Coromandel / Where the early pumpkins blow, / In the middle of the woods, / Lived the Yonghy-Bonghy-Bó. [Ib. 'The Courtship of the Yonghy-Bonghy-Bó']

7 The Dong! — the Dong! / The Dong with the Luminous Nose! [Ib. 'The Dong with the Luminous Nose']

8 Far and few, far and few, / Are the lands where the Jumblies live; / Their heads are green, and their hands are blue, / And they went to sea in a Sieve. [Ib. 'The Jumblies']

9 They called aloud 'Our Sieve ain't big, / But we don't care a button! We don't care a fig!' [Ib.]

10 The Owl and the Pussy-Cat went to sea / In a beautiful pea-green boat. / They took some honey, and plenty of money, / Wrapped up in a five-pound note. / The Owl looked up to the Stars above / And sang to a small guitar, / 'Oh lovely Pussy! — O Pussy, my love, / What a beautiful Pussy you are.' [Ib. 'The Owl and the Pussy-Cat']

11 'Dear Pig, are you willing to sell for one shilling / Your ring?' Said the Piggy, 'I will.' [Ib.]

12 They dined on mince, and slices of quince, / Which they ate with a runcible spoon; / And hand in hand, on the edge of the sand, / They danced by the light of the moon. [Ib.]

Leary, Timothy (1920–)

13 Turn on, tune in, and drop out. [*The Politics of Ecstasy*]

Leavis, F.R. (1895–1978)

14 The Sitwells belong to the history of publicity rather than of poetry. [*New Bearings in English Poetry*]

Le Corbusier (1887–1965)

15 *Une maison est une machine-à-habiter.* A house is a machine for living in. [*Vers une architecture*]

Lee, Henry (1756–1818)

16 [Of Washington] First in war, first in peace, and first in the hearts of his countrymen. [Resolution in Congress, 1799]

Lee, Nathaniel (1653–1692)

17 When Greeks joined Greeks, then was the tug of war! [*The Rival Queens*, IV.2]

Lee, Robert E. (1807–1870)

18 Duty then is the sublimest word in our language. Do your duty in all things. You cannot do more. You should never wish to do less. [Inscription in the Hall of Fame]

19 It is well that war is so terrible — we would grow too fond of it. [Remark, 1862]

Leland, Charles Godfrey (1824–1903)

20 Hans Breitmann gife a barty — / Vhere ish dat barty now? / Vhere ish de lofely golden cloud / Dat float on de moundain's prow? [*Breitmann Ballads*, 'Hans Breitmann's Barty']

Lenin, V.I. (1870–1924)

21 We shall now proceed to construct the socialist order. [Speech, 1917]

Lennon, John (1940–1980)

1 We're more popular than Jesus Christ now. [Remark in interview]

Lenthall, William (1591–1662)

2 May it please Your Majesty, I have neither eye to see nor tongue to speak in this place but as this House is pleased to direct me, whose servant I am. [Reply as Speaker of House of Commons to Charles I, 1642, when asked whether he had seen the five M.P.s whose arrest Charles had ordered]

Léon, Fray Luis de (c. 1527–1591)

3 As we were saying the other day. [Attr. Resuming a lecture after five years' imprisonment]

Leoncavallo, Ruggiero (1857–1919)

4 *La commedia é finita.* The comedy is over. [*I Pagliacci*, last words]

Lessing, Gotthold Ephraim (1729–1781)

5 A single thankful thought raised to heaven is the most perfect prayer. [*Minna von Barnhelm*, II]

6 Absolute truth belongs to Thee alone. [*Wolfenbüttler Fragmente*]

L'Estrange, Sir Roger (1616–1704)

7 It is with our passions as it is with fire and water, they are good servants, but bad masters. [*Aesop's Fables*, 38]

Levant, Oscar (1906–1972)

8 Strip the phony tinsel off Hollywood and you'll find the real tinsel underneath. [Quoted in Halliwell, *Filmgoer's Book of Quotes*]

Leverhulme, Viscount (1851–1925)

9 Half the money I spend on advertising is wasted, and the trouble is I don't know which half. [Ogilvy, *Confessions of an Advertising Man*]

Lévis, Duc de (1764–1830)

10 *Noblesse oblige.* Nobility has obligations. [*Maximes et réflexions*]

Lévi-Strauss, Claude (1908–)

11 *La langue est une raison humaine qui a ses raisons, et que l'homme ne connaît pas.* Language is a kind of human reason, which has its internal logic of which man knows nothing. [*La Pensée Sauvage*; *see* Pascal, *Pensées*, IV, 277]

Lewes, G. H. (1817–1878)

12 Murder, like talent, seems occasionally to run in families. [*Physiology of Common Life*, 12]

Lewis, C.S. (1898–1963)

13 She's the sort of woman who lives for others — you can tell the others by their hunted expression. [*The Screwtape Letters*, 26]

Lewis, Sinclair (1885–1951)

14 Our American professors like their literature clear, cold, pure, and very dead. [Address to Swedish Academy, 1930]

15 It Can't Happen Here [Title of novel]

Lewis, Wyndham (1884–1957)

16 In its essence the purpose of satire — whether verse or prose — is aggression...Satire has a great big blaring target. If successful, it blasts a great big hole in the centre. ['Note on Verse-Satire']

Leybourne, George (?–1884)

17 He flies through the air with the greatest of ease, / This daring young man on the flying trapeze. ['The Man on the Flying Trapeze']

Liberace, Wlaziu Valentino (1920–1987)

18 I cried all the way to the bank. [*Autobiography*]

Lichtenberg, Georg Cristoph (1742–1799)

1 There can hardly be a stranger commodity in the world than books. Printed by people who don't understand them; sold by people who don't understand them; bound, criticized and read by people who don't understand them, and now even written by people who don't understand them. [*A Doctrine of Scattered Occasions*]

2 Doubt everything at least once — even the proposition that two and two are four. [*Reflections*]

Ligne, Charles-Joseph, Prince de (1735–1814)

3 *Le Congrès ne marche pas, il danse.* The Congress is getting nowhere; it dances. [Remark on Congress of Vienna]

Lincoln, Abraham (1809–1865)

4 You can fool some of the people all of the time, and all of the people some of the time, but you cannot fool all of the people all the time. [Attr. Speech, 1856]

5 The ballot is stronger than the bullet. [Speech, 1856]

6 I believe this government cannot endure permanently half-slave and half-free. I do not expect the Union to be dissolved...but I do expect it will cease to be divided. [Speech, 1858]

7 I leave you, hoping that the lamp of liberty will burn in your bosoms, until there shall no longer be a doubt that all men are created free and equal. [Speech, 1858]

8 The probability that we may fail in the struggle ought not to deter us from the support of a cause we believe to be just. [Speech, 1859]

9 In giving freedom to the slave, we assure freedom to the free — honourable alike in what we give and what we preserve. [Speech, 1862]

10 Fourscore and seven years ago, our fathers brought forth upon this continent a new nation conceived in liberty, and dedicated to the proposition that all men are created equal. [Address, Gettysburg, 1863]

11 The world will little note nor long remember what we say here, but it can never forget what they did here...It is rather for us to be here dedicated to the great task remaining before us — that from these honoured dead we take increased devotion to that cause for which they gave the last full measure of devotion; that we here highly resolve that these dead shall not have died in vain; that this nation, under God, shall have a new birth of freedom; and that government of the people, by the people, for the people, shall not perish from the earth. [Ib.]

12 It is not best to swap horses while crossing a river. [Speech, 1864]

13 With malice toward none, with charity for all, with firmness in the right, as God gives us to see the right. [Second Inaugural Address, 1865]

14 When you have got an elephant by the hind leg, and he is trying to run away, it's best to let him run. [Remark, 1865]

15 I don't know who my grandfather was; I am much more concerned to know what his grandson will be. [Gross, *Lincoln's Own Stories*]

16 Character is like a tree and reputation like its shadow. The shadow is what we think of it; the tree is the real thing. [Ib.]

17 He reminds me of the man who murdered both his parents, and then, when sentence was about to be pronounced, pleaded for mercy on the grounds that he was an orphan. [Ib.]

18 Better to remain silent and be thought a fool than to speak out and remove all doubt. [Attr.]

19 [On losing an election] Like a little boy who has stubbed his toe in the dark...too old to cry, but it hurt too much to laugh. [Attr. by Adlai Stevenson]

Lindsay, Sir David (c. 1490–1555)

20 Let everie man keip weil ane toung, / And everie woman tway. [*Satyre of the Thrie Estaitis*]

1 What vails your kingdome, and your rent, / And all your great treasure; / Without ye haif ane mirrie lyfe, / And cast aside all sturt, and stryfe. [Ib.]

2 We think them verray naturall fules, / That lernis ouir mekle at the sculis. ['Complaynt to the King']

Linklater, Eric (1899–1974)

3 While swordless Scotland, sadder than its psalms, / Fosters its sober youth on national alms / To breed a dull provincial discipline, / Commerce its god and golf its anodyne. ['Preamble to a Satire']

4 For the scientific acquisition of knowledge is almost as tedious as a routine acquisition of wealth. [*White Man's Saga*]

Linnaeus, Carl (1707–1778)

5 *Natura non facit saltus.* Nature does not make jumps. [*Philosophia Botanica*]

Litvinoff, Maxim (1876–1951)

6 Peace is indivisible. [Speech to League of Nations, 1936]

Livy (59 B.C.-A.D. 17)

7 *Vae victis.* Woe to the vanquished. [*History*, V]

8 *Pugna magna victi sumus.* In a battle, a great battle, *we* were defeated! [Ib. XXII]

9 *In rebus asperis et tenui spe fortissima quaeque consilia tutissima sunt.* In grave difficulties and with little hope, the boldest measures are the safest. [Ib. XXV]

Lloyd, Marie (1870–1922)

10 I'm one of the ruins Cromwell knocked about a bit. [Music hall song]

11 A little of what you fancy does you good. [Music hall song]

Lloyd, Robert (1733–1764)

12 Who teach the mind its proper face to scan, / And hold the faithful mirror up to man. ['The Actor']

13 Slow and steady wins the race. ['The Hare and the Tortoise']

Lloyd George, David (1863–1945)

14 The House of Lords is not the watchdog of the constitution: it is Mr. Balfour's poodle. [Speech, 1908]

15 A fully equipped duke costs as much to keep up as two Dreadnoughts; and dukes are just as great a terror and they last longer. [Speech, 1909]

16 What is our task? To make Britain a fit country for heroes to live in. [Speech, 1918]

17 The finest eloquence is that which gets things done; the worst is that which delays them. [Speech at Paris Peace Conference, 1919]

18 Love your neighbour is not merely sound Christianity; it is good business. [*Observer*, 'Sayings of the Week', 1921]

19 The Right Honourable gentleman has sat so long on the fence that the iron has entered his soul. [Attr. speech in Parliament]

Locke, John (1632–1704)

20 New opinions are always suspected, and usually opposed, without any reason but because they are not already common. [*Essay concerning Human Understanding*]

21 No man's knowledge here can go beyond his experience. [Ib. II]

22 Wherever Law ends, Tyranny begins. [*Second Treatise of Government*]

Locker-Lampson, Frederick (1821–1895)

23 The world's as ugly, ay, as sin, / And almost as delightful. ['The Jester's Plea']

24 And many are afraid of God — / And more of Mrs. Grundy. [Ib.]

Lodge, David (1935–)

25 Literature is mostly about having sex and not much about having children; life is the other way round. [*The British Museum is Falling Down*, 4]

Lodge, Thomas (1558–1625)

26 Love, in my bosom, like a bee, / Doth suck his sweet. ['Love, In My Bosom']

Logau, Friedrich von (1605–1655)

1 *Gottesmühlen mahlen langsam, mahlen aber trefflich klein.* The mills of God grind slow, but they grind exceeding small. [*Sinngedichte*, III]

London, Jack (1876–1916)

2 The Call of the Wild [Book title]

Longfellow, Henry Wadsworth (1807–1882)

3 I shot an arrow into the air, / It fell to earth, I knew not where. ['The Arrow and the Song']

4 You are better than all the ballads / That ever were sung or said; / For ye are living poems, / And all the rest are dead. ['Children']

5 The cares that infest the day / Shall fold their tents, like the Arabs, / And as silently steal away. ['The Day is Done']

6 The shades of night were falling fast, / As through an Alpine village passed / A youth, who bore, 'mid snow and ice, / A banner with the strange device, / Excelsior! ['Excelsior']

7 'Try not the Pass!' the old man said; / 'Dark lowers the tempest overhead.' [Ib.]

8 When she was good / She was very, very good, / But when she was bad she was horrid. ['Home Life of Longfellow']

9 You would attain to the divine perfection, / And yet not turn your back upon the world. [*Michael Angelo*, I]

10 The men that women marry, / And why they marry them, will always be / A marvel and a mystery to the world. [Ib.]

11 A boy's will is the wind's will, / And the thoughts of youth are long, long thoughts. ['My Lost Youth']

12 Not in the clamour of the crowded street, / Not in the shouts and plaudits of the throng, / But in ourselves, are triumph and defeat. ['The Poets']

13 Tell me not, in mournful numbers, / Life is but an empty dream! ['A Psalm of Life']

14 Life is real! Life is earnest! / And the grave is not its goal. [Ib.]

15 Lives of great men all remind us / We can make our lives sublime, / And, departing, leave behind us / Footprints on the sands of time. [Ib.]

16 A Lady with a Lamp shall stand / In the great history of the land. ['Santa Filomena']

17 By the shores of Gitche Gumee, / By the shining Big-Sea-Water, / Stood the wigwam of Nokomis, / Daughter of the Moon, Nokomis. [*The Song of Hiawatha*, 'Hiawatha's Childhood']

18 From the waterfall he named her, / Minnehaha, Laughing Water. [Ib. 'Hiawatha and Mudjekeewis']

19 As unto the bow the cord is, / So unto the man is woman; / Though she bends him, she obeys him, / Though she draws him, yet she follows; / Useless each without the other! [Ib. 'Hiawatha's Wooing']

20 Ships that pass in the night, and speak each other in passing. [*Tales of a Wayside Inn*, 'The Theologian's Tale']

21 Under the spreading chestnut tree / The village smithy stands. ['The Village Blacksmith']

22 Something attempted, something done. [Ib.]

23 It was the schooner Hesperus, / That sailed the wintry sea; / And the skipper had taken his little daughter, / To bear him company. ['The Wreck of the Hesperus']

24 But the father answered never a word, / A frozen corpse was he. [Ib.]

Loos, Anita (1893–1981)

25 Gentlemen Prefer Blondes [Title of book]

26 Kissing your hand may make you feel very very good but a diamond and safire bracelet lasts forever. [*Gentlemen Prefer Blondes*]

27 A girl with brains ought to do something with them besides think. [Ib.]

Louis XIV of France (1638-1715)

1 *L'État c'est moi.* I am the State. [Attr.]

2 *Toutes les fois que je donne une place vacante, je fais cent mécontents et un ingrat.* Every time I make an appointment, I make a hundred men discontented and one ungrateful. [Attr.]

3 *J'ai failli attendre.* I was almost made to wait. [Attr.]

4 *Dieu, a-t-il donc oublié ce que j'ai fait pour lui?* Has God then forgotten what I have done for him? [Attr., on hearing of the French defeat at Malplaquet]

Louis XVIII of France (1755-1824)

5 *L'exactitude est la politesse des rois.* Punctuality is the politeness of kings. [Attr.]

Lovelace, Richard (1618-1658)

6 When thirsty grief in wine we steep, / When healths and draughts go free, / Fishes, that tipple in the deep, / Know no such liberty. ['To Althea, from Prison']

7 Stone Walls do not a Prison make / Nor Iron bars a Cage; / Minds innocent and quiet take / That for an hermitage. [Ib.]

8 Tell me not (Sweet) I am unkind, / That from the nunnery / Of thy chaste breast, and quiet mind, / To war and arms I fly. ['To Lucasta, Going to the Wars']

9 I could not love thee (Dear) so much, / Lov'd I not Honour more. [Ib.]

10 Lady, it is already Morn, / And 'twas last night I swore to thee / That fond impossibility. ['The Scrutiny']

11 With spoils of meaner Beauties crown'd, / I laden will return to thee. [Ib.]

Lovell, Maria (1803-1877)

12 Two souls with but a single thought, / Two hearts that beat as one. [*Ingomar the Barbarian*, II]

Lover, Samuel (1797-1868)

13 When once the itch of literature comes over a man, nothing can cure it but the scratching of a pen. [*Handy Andy*]

14 'Now women are mostly troublesome cattle to deal with mostly,' said Goggins. [Ib.]

Lowe, Robert (1811-1892)

15 I believe it will be absolutely necessary that you should prevail on our future masters to learn their letters. [Speech on Reform Bill, 1867]

Lowell, James Russell (1819-1891)

16 You've a darned long row to hoe. [*The Biglow Papers*]

17 There comes Poe with his raven like Barnaby Rudge, / Three-fifths of him genius, and two-fifths sheer fudge. [*A Fable for Critics*]

18 It's wal enough agin a king / To dror resolves an' triggers, — / But libbaty's a kind o' thing / Thet don't agree with niggers. ['The Pious Editor's Creed']

19 I mean in preyin' till one bursts / On wut the party chooses, / An' in convartin' public trusts, / To very privit uses. [Ib.]

20 I don't care how hard money is / Ez long ez mine's paid punctooal. [Ib.]

21 I *don't* believe in princerple, / But O, I *du* in interest. [Ib.]

22 A wise scepticism is the first attribute of a good critic. ['Shakespeare Once More']

23 And what is so rare as a day in June? / Then, if ever, come perfect days. [*Vision of Sir Launfal*, I]

Lowell, Robert (1917-1977)

24 Everywhere, / giant finned cars nose forward like fish; / a savage servility / slides by on grease. ['For the Union Dead']

25 This is death, / To die and know it. This is the Black Widow, death. ['Mr. Edwards and the Spider']

1 Sailor, can you hear / The Pequod's sea wings, beating landward, fall / Headlong and break on our Atlantic wall / Off 'Sconset. ['The Quaker Graveyard in Nantucket', II]

2 The Lord survives the rainbow of His will. [Ib. VII]

Loyola, St. Ignatius (1491–1556)

3 Teach us, good Lord, to serve Thee as Thou deservest: / To give and not to count the cost; / To fight and not to heed the wounds; / To toil and not to seek for rest; / To labour and not to ask for any reward / Save that of knowing that we do Thy will. ['Prayer for Generosity']

Lucan (A.D. 39–65)

4 *Nil actum credens, dum quid superesset agendum.* Thinking nothing done while there were still things to do. [*Civil War*, II]

5 *Plus est quam vita salusque / Quod perit.* More was lost than mere life and safety. [Ib. VII]

6 *Etiam periere ruinae.* The very ruins have been destroyed. [Ib. IX]

Lucretius (c. 95–55 B.C.)

7 *Tantum religio potuit suadere malorum.* Religion could lead to so much evil. [*De Rerum Natura*, I]

8 *Nil posse creari / De nilo.* Nothing can be created from nothing. [Ib.]

9 *Stillicidi casus lapidem cavat.* Continual drips hollow out a stone. [Ib.]

10 *Inque brevi spatio mutantur saecla animantum / Et quasi cursores vitai lampada tradunt.* In a short while the generations of the living are changed and like runners pass on the torch of life. [Ib. II]

11 *Nil igitur mors est ad nos neque pertinet hilum, / Quandoquidem natura animi mortalis habetur.* Death therefore is nothing to us nor does it matter a jot, since the nature of the soul we have is mortal. [Ib.]

12 *Mortalem vitam mors cum immortalis ademit.* Immortal death will visit mortal life. [Ib.]

13 *Ut quod ali cibus est aliis fuat acre venenum.* What is food to one is to others bitter poison. [Ib. IV]

Lunt, Alfred (1893–1977)

14 [On acting] Speak in a loud clear voice and try not to bump into the furniture. [Quoted in Halliwell, *Filmgoer's Book of Quotes.* Also attr. to Noël Coward]

Luther, Martin (1483–1546)

15 *Ein feste Burg ist unser Gott, / Ein gute Wehr und Waffen.* A safe stronghold our God is still, / A trusty shield and weapon. [Hymn; trans. Carlyle]

16 The ancient prince of hell / Hath risen with purpose fell; / Strong mail of craft and power / He weareth in this hour; / On earth is not his fellow. [Ib.]

17 *Hier stehe ich. Ich kann nicht anders.* Here I stand. I can do no other. [Speech at Diet of Worms]

18 *Esto peccator et pecca fortiter, sed fortius fide et gaude in Christo.* Be a sinner and sin strongly, but believe and rejoice in Christ even more strongly. [Letter to Melanchthon]

19 *Wer nicht liebt Wein, Weib und Gesang, / Der bleibt ein Narr sein Leben lang.* He who does not love wine, woman and song remains a fool for the rest of his life. [Attr.]

Lyly, John (1554–1606)

20 Cupid and my Campaspe play'd / At cards for kisses, Cupid paid. [*Campaspe*, III.5]

21 What bird so sings, yet does so wail? / O 'tis the ravish'd nightingale. / Jug, jug, jug, jug, tereu, she cries, / And still her woes at midnight rise. [Ib. V.1]

Lyte, Henry Francis (1793–1847)

22 Abide with me: fast falls the eventide; / The darkness deepens; Lord, with me abide. [Hymn]

23 Change and decay in all around I see: / O Thou who changest not, abide with me. [Ib.]

McArthur, Douglas (1880–1964)

1 I shall return. [Message on leaving the Philippines, 1942]

Macaulay, Thomas Babington, Lord (1800–1859)

2 Obadiah Bind-their-kings-in-chains-and their-nobles-with-links-of-iron. ['The Battle of Naseby']

3 By those white cliffs I never more must see, / By that dear language which I spake like thee, / Forget all feuds, and shed one English tear / O'er English dust. A broken heart lies here. ['A Jacobite's Epitaph']

4 Lars Porsena of Clusium / By the nine gods he swore / That the great house of Tarquin / Should suffer wrong no more. [*Lays of Ancient Rome*, 'Horatius', 1]

5 To every man upon this earth / Death cometh soon or late. / And how can man die better / Than facing fearful odds, / For the ashes of his fathers, / And the temples of his Gods? [Ib. 27]

6 Now who will stand on either hand, / And keep the bridge with me? [Ib. 29]

7 But those behind cried 'Forward!' / And those before cried 'Back!' [Ib. 50]

8 O Tiber! father Tiber! / To whom the Romans pray, / A Roman's life, a Roman's arms, / Take thou in charge this day! [Ib. 59]

9 And even the ranks of Tuscany / Could scarce forbear to cheer. [Ib. 60]

10 The English Bible, a book which, if everything else in our language should perish, would alone suffice to show the whole extent of its beauty and power. [*Essays*, 'John Dryden']

11 His imagination resembled the wings of an ostrich. It enabled him to run, though not to soar. [Ib.]

12 The gallery in which the reporters sit has become a fourth estate of the realm. [*Historical Essays* (*Edinburgh Review*, 1828)]

13 Every schoolboy knows who imprisoned Montezuma, and who strangled Atahualpa. [Ib. 1840]

14 Some traveller from New Zealand shall, in the midst of a vast solitude, take his stand on a broken arch of London Bridge to sketch the ruins of St. Paul's. [Ib. 1840]

15 Thus our democracy was, from an early period, the most aristocratic, and our aristocracy the most democratic in the world. [*History of England*, I]

16 The Puritan hated bear-baiting, not because it gave pain to the bear, but because it gave pleasure to the spectators. [Ib.]

17 There were gentlemen and there were seamen in the navy of Charles the Second. But the seamen were not gentlemen; and the gentlemen were not seamen. [Ib.]

18 Perhaps no person can be a poet, or can even enjoy poetry, without a certain unsoundness of mind. [*Literary Essays*, 'Milton']

19 Nothing is so useless as a general maxim. [Ib. 'Machiavelli']

20 We know of no spectacle so ridiculous as the British public in one of its periodical fits of morality. [Ib. 'Moore's Life of Byron']

21 We prefer a gipsy by Reynolds to his Majesty's head on a sign-post. [Ib.]

22 From the poetry of Lord Byron they drew a system of ethics, compounded of misanthropy and voluptuousness, a system in which the two great commandments were, to hate your neighbour, and to love your neighbour's wife. [Ib.]

23 Boswell is the first of biographers. [Ib. 'Samuel Johnson']

24 [Of Richard Steele] He was a rake among scholars, and a scholar among rakes. [Ib. 'Addison']

McClellan, George (1826–1885)

25 All quiet along the Potomac. [Attr. in American Civil War; *see* E.L. Beers, 'The Picket Guard']

McCrae, John (1872–1918)

26 In Flanders fields the poppies blow / Between the crosses, row on row, / That mark our place. ['In Flanders Fields']

1 Take up our quarrel with the foe: / To you from failing hands we throw / The torch; be yours to hold it high. / If ye break faith with us who die / We shall not sleep, though poppies grow / In Flanders fields. [Ib.]

MacDiarmid, Hugh (1892–1978)

2 Oot o' the way, my senses five, / I ken a' you can tell, / Oot o' the way, my thochts, for noo' / I maun face God mysel'. ['Ballad of the Five Senses']

3 Earth, thou bonnie broukit bairn! / — But greet, an' in your tears ye'll droun / The haill clanjamfrie! ['The Bonnie Broukit Bairn']

4 It's easier to lo'e Prince Charlie / Than Scotland — mair's the shame! ['Bonnie Prince Charlie']

5 Fegs, God's no blate gin he stirs up / The men o' Crowdieknowe! ['Crowdieknowe']

6 I amna' fou' sae muckle as tired — deid dune. [*A Drunk Man Looks at the Thistle*, first line]

7 You canna gang to a Burns supper even / Wi'oot some wizened scrunt o' a knock-knee / Chinee turns roon to say, 'Him Haggis — velly goot!' / And ten to wan the piper is a Cockney. [Ib.]

8 I'll ha'e nae hauf-way hoose, but aye be whaur / Extremes meet — it's the only way I ken / To dodge the curst conceit o' bein' richt / That damns the vast majority o' men. [Ib.]

9 And this deid thing, whale-white obscenity, / This horror that I writhe in — is my soul! [Ib.]

10 Nae doot they're sober, as a Scot ne'er was, / Each tethered to a punctual snorin' missus, / Whilst I, pure fule, owre continents unkent / And wine-dark oceans waunder like Ulysses. [Ib.]

11 And on my lips ye'll heed nae mair, / And in my hair forget, / The seed o' a' the men that in / My virgin womb ha'e met. [Ib.]

12 He's no' a man ava', / And lacks a proper pride, / Gin less than a' the warld / Can ser' him for a bride! [Ib.]

13 And as at sicna times am I, / I wad ha'e Scotland to my eye / Until I saw a timeless flame / Tak' Auchtermuchty for a name, / And kent that Ecclefechan stood / As pairt o' an eternal mood. [Ib.]

14 I tae ha'e heard Eternity drip water / (Aye water, water!), drap by drap / On the a'e nerve. [Ib.]

15 The wee reliefs we ha'e in booze, / Or wun at times in carnal states, / May hide frae us but canna cheenge / The silly horrors o' oor fates. [Ib.]

16 Hauf his soul a Scot maun use / Indulgin' in illusions, / And hauf in gettin' rid o' them / And comin' to conclusions. [Ib.]

17 And Jesus and a nameless ape / Collide and share the selfsame shape / That nocht terrestrial can escape. [Ib.]

18 A Scottish poet maun assume / The burden o' his people's doom, / And dee to brak' their livin' tomb. [Ib.]

19 O I ha'e Silence left, / — 'And weel ye micht,' / Sae Jean'll say, 'efter sic a nicht!' [Ib., closing lines]

20 Aulder than mammoth or than mastodon / Deep i' the herts o' a' men lurk scaut-heid / Skrymmorie monsters few daur look upon. ['Gairmscoile']

21 Other masters may conceivably write / Even yet in C major, / But we — we take the perhaps 'primrose path' / To the dodecaphonic bonfire. [*In Memoriam James Joyce*]

22 God through the wrong end of a telescope. ['Of John Davidson']

23 There are plenty of ruined buildings in the world but no ruined stones. ['On a Raised Beach']

24 What happens to us / Is irrelevant to the world's geology / But what happens to the world's geology / Is not irrelevant to us. [Ib.]

25 And I lo'e love / Wi' a scunner in't. ['Scunner']

26 Poetry like politics maun cut / The cackle and pursue real ends, / Unerringly as Lenin, and to that / Its nature better tends. ['Second Hymn to Lenin']

1 This Bolshevik bog! Suits me doon to the grun'! ['Tarras']

MacDonald, George (1824-1905)

2 Where did you come from, baby dear? / Out of the everywhere into here. [*At the Back of the North Wind*, 33]

3 Here lie I, Martin Elginbrodde: / Hae mercy o' my soul, Lord God; / As I wad do, were I Lord God, / And you were Martin Elginbrodde. [*David Elginbrod*, I]

MacDonald, Ramsay (1866-1937)

4 We hear war called murder. It is not: it is suicide. [*Observer*, 'Sayings of the Week', 1930]

McGonagall, William (1825-1902)

5 Beautiful city of Glasgow, I now conclude my muse, / And to write in praise of thee my pen does not refuse; / And, without fear of contradiction, I will venture to say / You are the second grandest city in Scotland at the present day. ['Glasgow']

6 Beautiful Railway Bridge of the Silv'ry Tay! / Alas, I am very sorry to say / That ninety lives have been taken away / On the last Sabbath day of 1879, / Which will be remember'd for a very long time. ['The Tay Bridge Disaster']

Machiavelli, Niccolo di Bernardo dei (1469-1527)

7 For titles do not reflect honour on men, but rather men on their titles. [*Dei Discorsi*, 3]

8 So it happened that all the armed prophets were victorious, and all the unarmed perished. [*Il Principe*, 6]

9 Fortune is a woman, and therefore friendly to the young, who command her with audacity. [Ib. 25]

McIver, Charles D. (1860-1906)

10 When you educate a man you educate an individual; when you educate a woman you educate a whole family. [Address at women's college]

MacKay, Charles (1814-1889)

11 There's a good time coming, boys, / A good time coming. ['The Good Time Coming']

Mackenzie, Sir Compton (1883-1972)

12 The slavery of being waited upon that is more deadening than the slavery of waiting upon other people. [*The Adventures of Sylvia Scarlett*]

13 I don't believe in principles. Principles are only excuses for what we want to think or what we want to do. [Ib.]

14 Prostitution. Selling one's body to keep one's soul: this is the meaning of the sins that were forgiven to the woman because she loved much: one might say of most marriages that they were selling one's soul to keep one's body. [Ib.]

Mackintosh, Sir James (1765-1832)

15 The Commons, faithful to their system, remained in a wise and masterly inactivity. [*Vindiciae Gallicae*]

MacLeish, Archibald (1892-1982)

16 A poem should not mean / But be. ['Ars poetica']

MacLeod, Norman (1812-1872)

17 Courage, brother! do not stumble, / Though thy path be dark as night. [Hymn]

McLuhan, Marshall (1911-1980)

18 The new electronic interdependence recreates the world in the image of a global village. [*The Gutenberg Galaxy*]

19 The medium is the message. [*Understanding Media*]

Macmillan, Harold (1894-1986)

20 Most of our people have never had it so good. [Speech, 1957]

21 The wind of change is blowing through this continent [Africa]. [Speech, 1960]

1 As usual the Liberals offer a mixture of sound and original ideas. Unfortunately none of the sound ideas is original and none of the original ideas is sound. [*Observer*, 'Sayings of the Week', 1961]

2 Little local difficulties. [Comment on Cabinet crisis, 1958]

MacNeice, Louis (1907–1963)

3 It's no go the merrygoround, it's no go the rickshaw, / All we want is a limousine and a ticket for the peep show. ['Bagpipe Music']

4 World is crazier and more of it than we think, / Incorrigibly plural. ['Snow']

5 The Drunkenness of things being various. [Ib.]

Madariaga, Salvador de (1886–1979)

6 First, the sweetheart of the nation, then her aunt, woman governs America because America is a land where boys refuse to grow up. ['Americans are Boys']

Maeterlinck, Maurice (1862–1949)

7 *Il n'y a pas de morts.* There are no dead. [*L'Oiseau bleu*, IV.2]

Magna Carta (1215)

8 Except by the lawful judgment of his peers and by the law of the land. [39]

9 To no one will we sell, or deny, or delay, right or justice. [40]

Maistre, Joseph de (1753–1821)

10 Every country has the government it deserves. [Letter, 1811]

11 Scratch a Russian and you will find a Tartar. [Attr.]

Mallarmé, Stéphane (1842–1898)

12 *La chair est triste, hélas! et j'ai lu tous les livres.* The flesh is sad, alas, and I have read all the books. ['Brise Marin']

13 *Donner un sens plus pur aux mots de la tribu.* To give a purer meaning to the language of the tribe. ['Le Tombeau d'Edgar Poe']

Mallory, George Leigh (1886–1924)

14 [Asked why he wished to climb Mt. Everest] Because it is there.

Malory, Sir Thomas (d. 1471)

15 Whoso pulleth out this sword of this stone and anvil is rightwise King born of all England. [*Le Morte D'Arthur*, I, 4]

16 In the midst of the lake Arthur was ware of an arm clothed in white samite, that held a fair sword in that hand. [Ib. I, 25]

Malthus, Thomas Robert (1766–1834)

17 Population, when unchecked, increases in a geometrical ratio. Subsistence only increases in an arithmetical ratio. [*Essay on Population*]

Mann, Horace (1796–1859)

18 Lost, yesterday, somewhere between Sunrise and Sunset, two golden hours, each set with sixty diamond minutes. No reward is offered, for they are gone for ever. ['Lost, Two Golden Hours']

Mansfield, Katherine (1888–1923)

19 England is merely an island of beef flesh swimming in a warm gulf stream of gravy. ['The Modern Soul']

Mao Tse-Tung (1893–1976)

20 Letting a hundred flowers blossom and a hundred schools of thought contend is the policy for promoting the progress of the arts and the sciences. [Speech, 'On the Correct Handling of Contradictions', 1957]

21 Political power grows out of the barrel of a gun. [*Quotations from Chairman Mao*]

22 Imperialism is a paper tiger. [Ib.]

Marcy, William (1786–1857)

23 To the victor belong the spoils of the enemy. [Speech, 1832]

Marie-Antoinette (1755–1793)

1 *Qu'ils mangent de la brioche.* Let them eat cake. [Attr. (but much older)]

Marlowe, Christopher (1564–1593)

2 Sweet Analytics, 'tis thou has ravished me. [*Doctor Faustus*, I.1]

3 What doctrine call you this, *Che sera, sera*, What will be, shall be? [Ib.]

4 Why this is hell, nor am I out of it: / Thinkst thou that I who saw the face of God, / And tasted the eternal joys of heaven, / Am not tormented with ten thousand hells / In being deprived of everlasting bliss? [Ib. I.3]

5 Hell hath no limits nor is circumscrib'd / In one self place, where we are is Hell, / And where Hell is, there must we ever be. [Ib. II.1]

6 Christ cannot save thy soul, for he is just. [Ib. II.2]

7 Was this the face that launch'd a thousand ships / And burnt the topless towers of Ilium? / Sweet Helen, make me immortal with a kiss! / Her lips suck forth my soul: see, where it flies! [Ib. V.1]

8 O, thou art fairer than the evening's air / Clad in the beauty of a thousand stars. [Ib.]

9 Now thou hast but one bare hour to live, / And then thou must be damned perpetually. / Stand still you ever-moving spheres of heaven, / That time may cease, and midnight never come. [Ib. V.2]

10 *O lente, lente currite, noctis equi:* The stars move still, time runs, the clock will strike, / The devil will come, and Faustus must be damn'd. [Ib.]

11 See see where Christ's blood streams in the firmament. / One drop would save my soul, half a drop, ah my Christ. [Ib.]

12 O soul, be changed into little water drops, / And fall into the ocean, ne'er be found. [Ib.]

13 Ugly hell, gape not! come not, Lucifer! / I'll burn my books! [Ib.]

14 Cut is the branch that might have grown full straight, / And burnèd is Apollo's laurel bough, / That some time grew within this learnèd man. [Ib. Epilogue]

15 My heart is an anvil unto sorrow, / Which beats upon it like the Cyclops' hammers, / And with the noise turns up my giddy brain, / And makes me frantic for my Gaveston. [*Edward II*, I]

16 Fair blows the wind for France. [Ib.]

17 My men, like satyrs grazing on the lawns, / Shall with their goat feet dance the antic hay. [Ib.]

18 It lies not in our power to love, or hate, / For will in us is over-rul'd by fate. [*Hero and Leander*, I]

19 Where both deliberate, the love is slight; / Whoever loved that loved not at first sight? [Ib.]

20 Like untun'd golden strings all women are / Which long time lie untouch'd, will harshly jar. [Ib.]

21 Albeit the world think Machiavel is dead, / Yet was his soul but flown beyond the Alps. [*The Jew of Malta*, Prologue]

22 I count religion but a childish toy, / And hold there is no sin but ignorance. [Ib.]

23 Infinite riches in a little room. [Ib. I.1]

24 Thus trails our fortune in by land and sea, / And thus are we on every side enrich'd. [Ib.]

25 And better one want for a common good, / Than many perish for a private man. [Ib.]

26 As for myself, I walk abroad o' nights / And kill sick people groaning under walls: / Sometimes I go about and poison wells. [Ib. II.3]

27 Here come two religious caterpillars. [Ib. IV.1]

28 *Barnadine:* Thou hast committed —
Barabas: Fornication: but that was in another country; / And besides, the wench is dead. [Ib.]

1 Come live with me, and be my love, / And we will all the pleasures prove, / That hills and valleys, dales and fields, / Woods or steepy mountain yields. ['The Passionate Shepherd to his Love']

2 From jigging veins of rhyming mother-wits, / And such conceits as clownage keeps in pay, / We'll lead you to the stately tent of war. [*Tamburlaine the Great*, I, Prologue]

3 Zenocrate, lovelier than the love of Jove, / Brighter than is the silver Rhodope, / Fairer than whitest snow on Scythian Hills. [Ib.]

4 Accurs'd be he that first invented war! [Ib.]

5 Is it not passing brave to be a King, / And ride in triumph through Persepolis? [Ib.]

6 Nature that framed us of four elements, / Warring within our breasts for regiment, / Doth teach us all to have aspiring minds. [Ib.]

7 Until we reach the ripest fruit of all, / That perfect bliss and sole felicity, / The sweet fruition of an earthly crown. [Ib.]

8 Ah fair Zenocrate, divine Zenocrate, / Fair is too foul an epithet for thee. [Ib.]

9 Not all the curses which the Furies breathe / Shall make me leave so rich a prize as this. [Ib.]

10 That with thy looks canst clear the darken'd sky, / And calm the rage of thundering Jupiter. [Ib.]

11 Now walk the angels on the walls of heaven, / As sentinels to warn th'immortal souls, / To entertain divine Zenocrate. [Ib.]

12 Holla, ye pampered jades of Asia! / What, can ye draw but twenty miles a-day? [Ib. II]

13 Tamburlaine, the Scourge of God, must die. [Ib.]

Marquis, Don (1878–1937)

14 but wotthehell wotthehell / oh I should worry and fret / death and I will coquette / there s a dance in the old dame yet / toujours gai toujours gai. [*archy and mehitabel*, 'the song of mehitabel']

15 now and then / there is a person born / who is so unlucky / that he runs into accidents / which started out to happen / to somebody else [*archys life of mehitabel*, 'archy says']

Marryat, Frederick (1792–1848)

16 We always took care of number one. [*Frank Mildmay*, 19]

17 As you are not prepared, as the Americans say, *to go the whole hog*, we will part good friends. [*Japhet*, 54]

18 She call me a damned nigger, and say like massa like man. [*King's Own*, 19]

19 As savage as a bear with a sore head. [Ib. 26]

20 [Of an illegitimate baby] If you please, ma'am, it was a very little one. [*Mr. Midshipman Easy*, 3]

21 As melancholy as a sick monkey. [Ib. 21]

22 It's just six of one and half-a-dozen of the other. [*The Pirate*, 4]

23 Every man paddle his own canoe. [*Settlers in Canada*, 8]

Marshall, Thomas (1854–1925)

24 What this country needs is a good five-cent cigar. [Remark to Chief Clerk of U.S. Senate]

Martial (c. A.D. 43–c. 104)

25 *Lasciva est nobis pagina, vita proba.* My poems are licentious, but my life is pure. [*Epigrams*, I]

26 *Laudant illa sed ista legunt.* They praise those verses but they read something else. [Ib. IV]

27 *Non est vivere, sed valere vita est.* Life is not living, but being healthy. [Ib. VI]

28 *Quod tam grande sophos clamat tibi turba togata, / Non tu, Pomponi, cena diserta tua est.* When your crowd of followers applaud you so loudly, Pompónius, it is not you but your banquet that is eloquent. [Ib.]

29 *Rus in urbe.* The country in town. [Ib. XII]

Marvell, Andrew (1621–1678)

1 Where the remote Bermudas ride / In th'ocean's bosom unespied. ['Bermudas']

2 He hangs in shades the orange bright, / Like golden lamps in a green light. [Ib.]

3 He cast (of which we rather boast) / The Gospel's pearls upon our coast. [Ib.]

4 My Love is of a birth as rare / As 'tis for object strange and high: / It was begotten by despair / Upon Impossibility. ['The Definition of Love']

5 As Lines so Loves *oblique* may well / Themselves in every Angle greet: / But ours so truly *Parallel*, / Though infinite can never meet. [Ib.]

6 Earth cannot shew so brave a Sight / As when a single Soul does fence / The Batteries of alluring Sense, / And Heaven views it with delight. ['A Dialogue between the Resolved Soul and Created Pleasure']

7 But all resistance against her is vain, / Who has the advantage both of Eyes and Voice. / And all my Forces needs must be undone, / She having gained both the Wind and Sun. ['The Fair Singer']

8 Engines more keen than ever yet / Adorned Tyrants Cabinet; / Of which the most tormenting are / Black Eyes, red Lips, and curled Hair. ['The Gallery']

9 How vainly men themselves amaze / To win the Palm, the Oak, or Bays. ['The Garden']

10 No white nor red was ever seen / So am'rous as this lovely green. [Ib.]

11 Society is all but rude, / To this delicious solitude. [Ib.]

12 What wond'rous life is this I lead! [Ib.]

13 Meanwhile the Mind, from pleasure less, / Withdraws into its happiness: / The Mind, that Ocean where each kind / Does straight its own resemblance find. [Ib.]

14 Annihilating all that's made / To a green Thought in a green Shade. [Ib.]

15 He nothing common did or mean / Upon that memorable scene: / But with his keener eye / The axe's edge did try. ['An Horatian Ode']

16 When I beheld the Poet blind, yet bold, / In slender Book his vast Design unfold. ['On Mr. Milton's Paradise Lost']

17 Ye country comets, that portend / No war, nor prince's funeral, / Shining to no higher end / Than to presage the grasses' fall. ['The Mower to the Glow-worms']

18 Who can foretell for what high cause / This Darling of the Gods was born! ['The Picture of Little T.C. in a Prospect of Flowers']

19 Had we but world enough, and time, / This coyness, Lady, were no crime. ['To His Coy Mistress']

20 My vegetable love should grow / Vaster than empires, and more slow. [Ib.]

21 But at my back I always hear / Times wingèd Chariot hurrying near. [Ib.]

22 The Grave's a fine and private place / But none I think do there embrace. [Ib.]

23 Let us roll all our strength and all / Our sweetness up into one ball, / And tear our pleasures with rough strife / Thorough the iron gates of life. [Ib.]

24 But now the salmon-fishers moist / Their leathern boats begin to hoist; / And, like Antipodes in shoes, / Have shod their heads in their canoes. ['Upon Appleton House']

Marx, Groucho (1895–1977)

25 Either he's dead or my watch has stopped. [*A Day at the Races*]

26 Remember, men, we're fighting for this woman's honour; which is probably more than she ever did. [*Duck Soup*]

27 I resign. I wouldn't want to belong to any club that would have me as a member. [Attr.]

Marx, Karl (1818–1883)

28 A spectre is haunting Europe — the spectre of Communism. [*Communist Manifesto*]

1 The workers have nothing to lose but their chains in this. They have a world to win. Workers of the world, unite! [Ib.]

2 From each according to his abilities, to each according to his needs. [*Critique of the Gotha Programme*]

3 Religion...is the opium of the people. [*Critique of Hegel's Philosophy of Right*]

4 Without doubt machinery has greatly increased the number of well-to-do idlers. [*Das Kapital*]

5 The philosophers have only interpreted the world in various ways; the point, however, is to change it. [*Theses on Feuerbach*, 11]

6 The class struggle necessarily leads to the dictatorship of the proletariat. [Letter, 1852]

Mary Queen of Scots (1542–1587)

7 England is not all the world. [Said at her trial, 1586]

Mary Tudor (1516–1558)

8 When I am dead and opened, you shall find 'Calais' lying in my heart. [Attr.]

Masefield, John (1878–1966)

9 Oh some are fond of Spanish wine, and some are fond of French. ['Captain Stratton's Fancy']

10 Quinquireme of Nineveh from distant Ophir / Rowing home to haven in sunny Palestine, / With a cargo of ivory, / And apes and peacocks, / Sandalwood, cedarwood and sweet white wine. ['Cargoes']

11 I must down to the seas again, to the lonely sea and the sky, / And all I ask is a tall ship and a star to steer her by. ['Sea Fever']

12 I must down to the seas again, to the vagrant gypsy life, / To the gull's way and the whale's way where the wind's like a whetted knife; / And all I ask is a merry yarn from a laughing fellow rover, / And a quiet sleep and a sweet dream when the long trick's over. [Ib.]

13 It's good to be out on the road and going one knows not where. ['Tewkesbury Road']

14 I never hear the west wind but tears are in my eyes, / For it comes from the west lands, the old brown hills, / And April's in the west wind, and daffodils. ['The West Wind']

Mass

15 *Dominus vobiscum. / Et cum spiritu tuo.* The Lord be with you. / And with thy spirit.

16 *Mea culpa, mea culpa, mea maxima culpa.* Through my fault, my fault, my most grievous fault.

17 *Requiem aeternam dona eis, Domine: et lux perpetua luceat eis.* Grant them eternal rest, O Lord; and let perpetual light shine on them. [At Requiem Masses]

18 *Sursum corda.* Lift up your hearts.

19 *Agnus Dei, qui tollis peccata mundi, miserere nobis.* Lamb of God, who takest away the sins of the world, have mercy upon us.

20 *Requiescant in pace.* May they rest in peace. [At Requiem Masses]

Massinger, Philip (1583–1640)

21 He that would govern others, first should be / The master of himself. [*The Bondman*, I.3]

22 The devil turned precisian! [*A New Way to Pay Old Debts*, I.1]

23 Patience, the beggar's virtue. [Ib. V.1]

24 Death has a thousand doors to let out life: / I shall find one. [*A Very Woman*, V.4]

Maugham, William Somerset (1874–1965)

25 People ask you for criticism, but they only want praise. [*Of Human Bondage*]

26 Like all weak men he laid an exaggerated stress on not changing one's mind. [Ib.]

27 It's no use crying over spilt milk, because all the forces of the universe were bent on spilling it. [Ib.]

28 Impropriety is the soul of wit. [*The Moon and Sixpence*]

Mearns, Hughes (1875–1965)

1 As I was going up the stair / I met a man who wasn't there. / He wasn't there again to-day. / I wish, I wish he'd stay away. ['The Psychoed']

Melbourne, William Lamb, Viscount (1779–1848)

2 Things have come to a pretty pass when religion is allowed to invade the sphere of private life. [Remark]

3 I wish I was as cocksure of anything as Tom Macaulay is of everything. [Cowper, *Preface to Lord Melbourne's Papers*]

4 It is not much matter which we say, but mind, we must all say *the same.* [Attr.]

5 Damn it all, another Bishop dead — I verily believe they die to vex me. [Attr.]

6 Nobody ever did anything very foolish except from some strong principle. [Attr.]

7 While I cannot be regarded as a pillar, I must be regarded as a buttress of the church, because I support it from the outside. [Attr.]

Melville, Herman (1819–1891)

8 God bless Captain Vere! [*Billy Budd*]

9 'With mankind,' he would say 'forms, measured forms, are everything.' [Ib.]

10 Call me Ishmael. [*Moby Dick*, 1, first words]

11 In youth we are, but in age we seem. [*Pierre*]

Menander (c. 342–292 B.C.)

12 Whom the gods love dies young. [*The Double Deceiver*]

Mencken, H. L. (1880–1956)

13 Every normal man must be tempted, at times, to spit on his hands, hoist the black flag, and begin slitting throats. [*Prejudices*]

14 Women hate revolutions and revolutionists. They like men who are docile, and well-regarded at the bank, and never late at meals. [Ib.]

15 Poetry is a comforting piece of fiction set to more or less lascivious music. [Ib.]

16 Faith may be defined briefly as an illogical belief in the occurrence of the improbable. [Ib.]

17 If, after I depart this vale, you ever remember me and have thought to please my ghost, forgive some sinner and wink your eye at some homely girl. [Epitaph for himself]

Meredith, George (1828–1909)

18 They need their pious exercises less / Than schooling in the Pleasures. ['A Certain People']

19 Around the ancient track marched, rank on rank, / The army of unalterable law. ['Lucifer in Starlight']

20 Not till the fire is dying in the grate, / Look we for any kinship with the stars. [*Modern Love*]

21 We'll sit contentedly / And eat our pot of honey on the grave. [Ib.]

22 More brain, O Lord, more brain! [Ib.]

23 Ah, what a dusty answer gets the soul / When hot for certainties in this our life! [Ib.]

24 I expect that Woman will be the last thing civilized by Man. [*The Ordeal of Richard Feverel*, 1]

25 The sun is coming down to earth, and the fields and the waters shout to him golden shouts. [Ib. 19]

26 Kissing don't last: cookery do! [Ib. 28]

27 Speech is the small change of silence. [Ib. 34]

28 Cynicism is intellectual dandyism. [*The Egoist*, 7]

29 To plod on and still keep the passion fresh. [Ib. 12]

Meredith, Owen [Lord Lytton] (1831–1891)

30 Genius does what it must, and Talent does what it can. ['Last Words of a Sensitive Second-Rate Poet']

Merritt, Dixon Lanier (1879–1954)

1 A wonderful bird is the pelican, / His bill will hold more than his belican. / He can take in his beak / Food enough for a week, / But I'm damned if I see how the helican. ['The Pelican']

Metternich, Prince Clement (1773–1859)

2 When Paris sneezes, Europe catches cold. [Remark, 1830]

3 Italy is a geographical expression. [Letter, 1849]

Meynell, Alice (1847–1922)

4 With the first dream that comes with the first sleep / I run, I run, I am gathered to thy heart. ['Renouncement']

5 She walks — the lady of my delight — / A shepherdess of sheep. ['The Shepherdess']

Mies van der Rohe, Ludwig (1886–1969)

6 Less is more. [Quoted in *New York Herald Tribune*, 1959]

Mill, John Stuart (1806–1873)

7 Ask yourself whether you are happy, and you cease to be so. [*Autobiography*, 5]

8 No great improvements in the lot of mankind are possible, until a great change takes place in the fundamental constitution of their modes of thought. [Ib. 7]

9 The Conservatives...being by the law of their existence the stupidest party. [*Considerations on Representative Government*, 7 (footnote)]

10 Protection, therefore, against the tyranny of the magistrate is not enough: there needs protection also against the tyranny of the prevailing opinion and feeling. [*On Liberty*, Introduction]

11 Another grand determining principle of the rules of conduct...has been the servility of mankind towards the supposed preferences or aversions of their temporal masters, or of their gods. [Ib.]

12 The sole end for which mankind are warranted, individually or collectively, in interfering with the liberty of action of any of their number, is self-protection. [Ib.]

13 If all mankind minus one, were of one opinion, and only one person were of the contrary opinion, mankind would be no more justified in silencing that one person, than he, if he had the power, would be justified in silencing mankind. [Ib. 2]

14 History teems with instances of truth put down by persecution...It is a piece of idle sentimentality that truth, merely as truth, has any inherent power denied to error, of prevailing against the dungeon and the stake. [Ib.]

15 A people, it appears, may be progressive for a certain length of time, and then stop. When does it stop? When it ceases to possess individuality. [Ib. 3]

16 Whatever crushes individuality is despotism, by whatever name it may be called. [Ib.]

17 ...mere conformers to commonplace, or time-servers for truth, whose arguments on all great subjects are meant for their hearers, and are not those which have convinced themselves. [Ib.]

18 Persons require to possess a title, or some other badge of rank, or of the consideration of people of rank, to be able to indulge somewhat in the luxury of doing as they like without detriment to their estimation. [Ib.]

19 I am not aware that any community has a right to force another to be civilized. [Ib. 4]

20 Liberty consists in doing what one desires. [Ib. 5]

21 The worth of a State, in the long run, is the worth of the individuals composing it. [Ib.]

22 When the land is cultivated entirely by the spade and no horses are kept, a cow is kept for every three acres of land. [*Principles of Political Economy*, II, 6]

23 Unearned increment. [Ib. V, 2]

1 The principle which regulates the existing social relations between the two sexes — the legal subordination of one sex to the other — is wrong in itself, and now one of the chief hindrances to human improvement. [*The Subjection of Women*, 1]

Millay, Edna St. Vincent (1892–1950)

2 Childhood is the kingdom where nobody dies. / Nobody that matters, that is. ['Childhood is the Kingdom where Nobody dies']

3 My candle burns at both ends; / It will not last the night; / But ah, my foes, and oh my friends — / It gives a lovely light! [*Figs from Thistles*, 'First Fig']

4 Presently / Every bed is narrow. ['Passer Mortuus Est']

Miller, Arthur (1915–)

5 Nobody dast blame this man. A salesman is got to dream, boy. It comes with the territory. [*Death of a Salesman*]

6 Attention, attention must finally be paid to such a person. [Ib.]

Miller, William (1810–1872)

7 Wee Willie Winkie / Rins through the toon; / Upstairs an' doonstairs / In his nicht goon. ['Wee Willie Winkie']

Milman, H.H. (1791–1868)

8 Ride on! ride on in majesty! / In lowly pomp ride on to die. [Hymn]

Milne, A.A. (1882–1956)

9 And nobody knows / (Tiddely pom), / How cold my toes / (Tiddely pom), / How cold my toes / (Tiddely pom), / Are growing. [*The House at Pooh Corner*, 1]

10 Isn't it funny / How a bear likes honey? / Buzz! Buzz! Buzz! / I wonder why he does? [*Winnie-the-Pooh*, 1]

11 Silly old Bear! [Ib. 2]

12 I am a Bear of Very Little Brain, and long words Bother me. [Ib. 4]

13 Time for a little something. [Ib. 6]

14 'Pathetic,' he said. 'That's what it is. Pathetic.' [Ib.]

15 It's a Useful Pot...And it's for putting things in. [Ib. 6]

16 King John was not a good man — / He had his little ways, / And sometimes no one spoke to him / For days and days and days. [*Now We Are Six*, 'King John's Christmas']

17 They're changing guard at Buckingham Palace — / Christopher Robin went down with Alice. [*When We Were Very Young*, 'Buckingham Palace']

18 You must never go down to the end of the town if you don't go down with me. [Ib. 'Disobedience']

19 I do like a little bit of butter to my bread! [Ib. 'The King's Breakfast']

20 Little Boy kneels at the foot of the bed, / Droops on the little hands, little gold head; / Hush! Hush! Whisper who dares! / Christopher Robin is saying his prayers. [Ib. 'Vespers']

Milner, Alfred, Viscount (1854–1925)

21 If we believe a thing to be bad, and if we have a right to prevent it, it is our duty to try to prevent it and to damn the consequences. [Speech, 1909]

Milton, John (1608–1674)

22 Blest pair of Sirens, pledges of Heaven's joy, / Sphere-born harmonious sisters, Voice and Verse. ['At a Solemn Music']

23 Come, knit hands, and beat the ground, / In a light fantastic round. [*Comus*]

24 ...it was the sound / Of Riot, and ill-manag'd Merriment. [Ib.]

25 Virtue could see to do what virtue would / By her own radiant light, though sun and moon / Were in the flat sea sunk. [Ib.]

26 ...courtesy, / Which oft is sooner found in lowly sheds / With smoky rafters, than in tap'stry Halls / And Courts of Princes, where it first was nam'd, / And yet is most pretended. [Ib.]

27 Himself is his own dungeon. [Ib.]

1 Beauty is nature's coin, must not be hoarded, / But must be current, and the good thereof / Consists in mutual and partak'n bliss. [Ib.]

2 Hence vain, deluding joys, / The brood of folly without father bred. ['Il Penseroso']

3 Hail divinest Melancholy. [Ib.]

4 Sweet bird, that shunn'st the noise of folly, / Most musical, most melancholy! [Ib.]

5 Far from all resort of mirth, / Save the cricket on the hearth. [Ib.]

6 With even step, and musing gait, / And looks commercing with the skies. [Ib.]

7 And add to these retired Leisure, / That in trim Gardens takes his pleasure. [Ib.]

8 Or let my Lamp at midnight hour, / Be seen in some high lonely Tower, / Where I may oft outwatch the Bear, / With thrice great Hermes. [Ib.]

9 ...th'unseen Genius of the Wood. [Ib.]

10 And storied Windows richly dight, / Casting a dim religious light. [Ib.]

11 Hence, loathed Melancholy, / Of Cerberus, the blackest midnight born. ['L'Allegro']

12 Sport that wrinkled Care derides, / And Laughter holding both his sides. / Come, and trip it as ye go / On the light fantastic toe. [Ib.]

13 And if I give thee honour due, / Mirth, admit me of thy crew / To live with her, and live with thee, / In unreproved pleasures free. [Ib.]

14 While the Cock with lively din, / Scatters the rear of darkness thin. [Ib.]

15 Of herbs, and other country messes, / Which the neat-handed Phyllis dresses. [Ib.]

16 ...many a youth, and many a maid, / Dancing in the Chequer'd shade; / And young and old come forth to play / On a Sunshine Holyday, / Till the live-long daylight fail, / Then to the Spicy Nut-brown Ale. [Ib.]

17 Or sweetest Shakespeare, fancy's child, / Warble his native Wood-notes wild. [Ib.]

18 The melting voice through mazes running. [Ib.]

19 Yet once more, O ye Laurels, and once more / Ye Myrtles brown, with Ivy never-sear, / I come to pluck your Berries, harsh and crude. ['Lycidas']

20 For Lycidas is dead, dead ere his prime / Young Lycidas, and hath not left his peer. [Ib.]

21 But O the heavy change, now thou art gone, / Now thou art gone, and never must return! [Ib.]

22 For we were nursed upon the self-same hill, / Fed the same flock, by fountain, shade, and rill. [Ib.]

23 Were it not better done as others use, / To sport with Amaryllis in the shade, / Or with the tangles of Neaera's hair? [Ib.]

24 Fame is the spur that the clear spirit doth raise / (That last infirmity of Noble mind) / To scorn delights, and live laborious days. [Ib.]

25 Comes the blind Fury with th' abhorred shears, / And slits the thin-spun life. [Ib.]

26 Fame is no plant that grows on mortal soil, / Nor in the glistering foil / Set off to th' world, nor in broad rumour lies. [Ib.]

27 The Pilot of the Galilean lake, / Two massey Keys he bore of metals twain; / (The Golden opes, the Iron shuts amain). [Ib.]

28 Blind mouths! that scarce themselves know how to hold / A Sheep-hook. [Ib.]

29 ...their lean and flashy songs / Grate on their scrannel Pipes of wretched straw, / The hungry Sheep look up, and are not fed. [Ib.]

30 But that two-handed engine at the door, / Stands ready to smite once, and smite no more. [Ib.]

31 Return, Alpheus, the dread voice is past, / That shrunk thy streams. [Ib.]

32 Look homeward, Angel, now, and melt with ruth. [Ib.]

33 At last he rose, and twitch'd his Mantle blue: / Tomorrow to fresh Woods, and Pastures new. [Ib.]

1 It was the Winter wild, / While the Heav'n-borne child, / All meanly wrapt in the rude manger lies. ['On the Morning of Christ's Nativity']

2 Ring out ye Crystal spheres, / Once bless our human ears. [Ib.]

3 Time will run back, and fetch the age of gold, / And speckl'd vanity / Will sicken soon and die. [Ib.]

4 What needs my Shakespeare for his honour'd bones, / The labour of an age in piled stones. ['On Shakespeare']

5 If any ask for him, it shall be said, / 'Hobson has supped, and's newly gone to bed.' ['On the University Carrier']

6 Rhyme being no necessary Adjunct or true Ornament of Poem or good Verse, in longer Works especially, but the Invention of a barbarous Age, to set off wretched matter and lame Metre. [*Paradise Lost*, Introduction]

7 Of Man's First Disobedience, and the Fruit / Of that Forbidden Tree, whose mortal taste / Brought Death into the World, and all our woe. [Ib. I]

8 Things unattempted yet in Prose or Rhyme. [Ib.]

9 I may assert Eternal Providence, / And justify the ways of God to men. [Ib.]

10 ...aspiring / To set himself in Glory above his Peers, / He trusted to have equal'd the most High. [Ib.]

11 Him the Almighty Power / Hurl'd headlong flaming from th'Ethereal Sky / With hideous ruin and combustion down / To bottomless perdition. [Ib.]

12 No light, but rather darkness visible. [Ib.]

13 But O how fall'n! how chang'd / From him who in the happy Realms of Light / Cloth'd with transcendent brightness didst outshine / Myriads though bright. [Ib.]

14 What though the field be lost? / All is not lost; the unconquerable Will, / And study of revenge, immortal hate, / And courage never to submit or yield. [Ib.]

15 The mind is its own place, and in itself / Can make a Heav'n of Hell, a Hell of Heav'n. [Ib.]

16 To reign is worth ambition though in Hell: / Better to reign in Hell, than serve in Heav'n. [Ib.]

17 Thick as Autumnal Leaves that strow the Brooks / In Vallambrosa, where th'Etrurian shades / High overarch'd imbower. [Ib.]

18 For Spirits when they please / Can either Sex assume, or both. [Ib.]

19 ...the Sons / Of Belial, flown with insolence and wine. [Ib.]

20 The reign of Chaos and old Night. [Ib.]

21 ...and instead of rage / Deliberate valour breath'd, firm and unmov'd. [Ib.]

22 Tears such as Angels weep, burst forth. [Ib.]

23 For who can yet believe, though after loss, / That all these puissant Legions, whose exile / Hath emptied Heav'n, shall fail to re-ascend / Self-rais'd, and repossess their native seat? [Ib.]

24 ...who overcomes / By force, hath overcome but half his foe. [Ib.]

25 Space may produce new Worlds. [Ib.]

26 To Noon he fell, from Noon to dewy Eve, / A Summer's day; and with the setting Sun / Dropt from the Zenith like a falling Star. [Ib.]

27 High on a Throne of Royal State, which far / Outshone the wealth of Ormus and of Ind, / Or where the gorgeous East with richest hand / Showers on her Kings Barbaric Pearl and Gold, / Satan exalted sat. [Ib. II]

28 Where there is then no good / For which to strive, no strife can grow up there / From Faction. [Ib.]

29 His trust was with th'Eternal to be deem'd / Equal in strength, and rather than be less / Car'd not to be at all. [Ib.]

30 [Belial]...his Tongue / Dropt Manna, and could make the worse appear / The better reason. [Ib.]

31 I should be much for open War, O Peers, / As not behind in hate. [Ib.]

1 For who would lose, / Though full of pain, this intellectual being, / Those thoughts that wander through Eternity? [Ib.]

2 Thus Belial with words cloth'd in reason's garb / Counsel'd ignoble ease, and peaceful sloth. [Ib.]

3 ...preferring / Hard liberty before the easy yoke / Of servile Pomp. [Ib.]

4 Advise if this be worth / Attempting, or to sit in darkness here / Hatching vain Empires. [Ib.]

5 But first whom shall we send / In search of this new World, whom shall we find / Sufficient? who shall tempt with wandering feet / The dark unbottom'd infinite Abyss? [Ib.]

6 O shame to men! Devil with Devil damn'd / Firm concord holds: men only disagree / Of Creatures rational, though under hope / Of heavenly Grace; and God proclaiming peace, / Yet live in hatred, enmity, and strife / Among themselves, and levy cruel wars, / Wasting the Earth, each other to destroy. [Ib.]

7 Long is the way / And hard, that out of Hell leads up to Light. [Ib.]

8 Rocks, Caves, Lakes, Fens, Bogs, Dens, and shades of Death. [Ib.]

9 I fled, and cry'd out Death; / Hell trembl'd at the hideous Name, and sigh'd / From all her Caves, and back resounded Death. [Ib.]

10 Confusion worse confounded. [Ib.]

11 At whose sight all the Stars / Hide their diminished heads. [Ib. IV]

12 Warring in Heav'n against Heav'n's matchless King. [Ib.]

13 Which way I fly is Hell; myself am Hell. [Ib.]

14 Imparadis'd in one another's arms. [Ib.]

15 Evil be thou my Good. [Ib.]

16 Yielded with coy submission, modest pride, / And sweet reluctant amorous delay. [Ib.]

17 Th'unwieldy Elephant / To make them mirth us'd all his might, and wreath'd / His Lithe Proboscis. [Ib.]

18 Hail wedded Love, mysterious Law, true source / Of human offspring, sole propriety / In Paradise of all things common else. [Ib.]

19 With thee conversing I forget all time. [Ib.]

20 Him there they found / Squat like a Toad, close at the ear of Eve. [Ib.]

21 Best Image of my self and dearer half. [Ib. V]

22 Hear all ye Angels, Progeny of Light, / Thrones, Dominations, Princedoms, Virtues, Powers. [Ib.]

23 But what if better counsels might erect / Our minds and teach us to cast off this Yoke? / Will ye submit your necks, and choose to bend / The supple knee? [Ib.]

24 Headlong themselves they threw / Down from the verge of Heav'n, eternal wrath / Burnt after them to the bottomless pit. [Ib. VI]

25 That Man may know he dwells not in his own; / An Edifice too large for him to fill, / Lodg'd in a small partition, and the rest / Ordain'd for uses to his Lord best known. [Ib. VIII]

26 ...the sum of earthly bliss. [Ib.]

27 The serpent subtlest beast of all the field. [Ib. IX]

28 As one who long in populous City pent, / Where Houses thick and Sewers annoy the Air. [Ib.]

29 ...nothing lovelier can be found / In woman, than to study household good, / And good works in her Husband to promote. [Ib.]

30 Earth felt the wound, and Nature from her seat / Sighing through all her Works gave signs of woe, / That all was lost. [Ib.]

31 Yet I shall temper so / Justice with Mercy. [Ib. X]

32 On all sides, from innumerable tongues / A dismal universal hiss, the sound / Of public scorn. [Ib.]

33 Destruction with destruction to destroy. [Ib.]

1 The World was all before them, where to choose / Their place of rest, and Providence their guide: / They hand in hand with wand'ring steps and slow, / Through Eden took their solitary way. [Ib. XII]

2 I who ere while the happy Garden sung, / By one man's disobedience lost, now sing / Recover'd Paradise to all mankind. [*Paradise Regained*, I]

3 Women, when nothing else, beguil'd the heart / Of wisest Solomon, and made him build, / And made him bow to the Gods of his Wives. [Ib. II]

4 Riches are needless then, both for themselves, / And for thy reason why they should be sought, / To gain a Sceptre, oftest better miss'd. [Ib.]

5 They err who count it glorious to subdue / By Conquest far and wide, to over-run / Large Countries, and in field great Battles win. [Ib. III]

6 The childhood shews the man, / As morning shews the day. [Ib. IV]

7 The first and wisest of them all profess'd / To know this only, that he nothing knew. [Ib.]

8 But headlong joy is ever on the wing, / In Wintry solstice like the shortn'd light / Soon swallow'd up in dark and long out-living night. ['The Passion']

9 Ask for this great Deliverer now, and find him / Eyeless in Gaza, at the Mill with slaves. [*Samson Agonistes*]

10 O impotence of mind, in body strong! / But what is strength without a double share / Of wisdom. [Ib.]

11 O dark, dark, dark, amid the blaze of noon, / Irrecoverably dark, total Eclipse / Without all hope of day! [Ib.]

12 For him I reckon not in high estate / Whom long descent of birth / Or the sphere of fortune raises. [Ib.]

13 What boots it at one gate to make defence, / And at another to let in the foe? [Ib.]

14 Samson hath quit himself / Like Samson, and heroically hath finish'd / A life heroic. [Ib.]

15 ...that grounded maxim / So rife and celebrated in the mouths / Of wisest men; that to the public good / Private respects must yield. [Ib.]

16 Oh how comely it is and how reviving / To the Spirits of just men long oppres'd! / When God into the hands of their deliverer / Puts invincible might / To quell the mighty of the Earth. [Ib.]

17 And calm of mind all passion spent. [Ib.]

18 Now the bright morning Star, Day's harbinger, / Comes dancing from the East, and leads with her / The Flow'ry May ['Song on May Morning']

19 Time, the subtle thief of youth. [*Sonnets*, 7]

20 Licence they mean when they cry liberty. [Ib. 12]

21 Avenge, O Lord, thy slaughtered Saints, whose bones / Lie scattered on the Alpine mountains cold; / Ev'n them who kept thy truth so pure of old, / When all our Fathers worshipped Stocks and Stones. [Ib. 15, 'On the late Massacre at Piedmont']

22 When I consider how my light is spent, / Ere half my days, in this dark world and wide, / And that one Talent which is death to hide, / Lodg'd with me useless. [Ib. 16, 'On His Blindness']

23 Thousands at his bidding speed / And post o'er Land and Ocean without rest: / They also serve who only stand and wait. [Ib.]

24 New Presbyter is but Old Priest writ Large. [Ib. 'On the New Forcers of Conscience under the Long Parliament']

25 For what can War, but endless war still breed? [Ib. 'On Fairfax']

26 In vain doth Valour bleed / While Avarice, and Rapine share the land. [Ib.]

27 Peace hath her victories / No less renowned than war. ['To the Lord General Cromwell']

28 Help us to save free Conscience from the paw / Of hireling wolves whose Gospel is their maw. [Ib.]

1 He who would not be frustrate of his hope to write well hereafter in laudable things ought himself to be a true poem. [*Apology for Smectymnuus*]

2 As good almost kill a man as kill a good book: who kills a man kills a reasonable creature, God's image; but he who destroys a good book, kills reason itself, kills the image of God, as it were in the eye. [*Areopagitica*]

3 A good book is the precious life-blood of a master spirit, embalmed and treasured up on purpose to a life beyond life. [Ib.]

4 Methinks I see in my mind a noble and puissant nation rousing herself like a strong man after sleep, and shaking her invincible locks. Methinks I see her as an eagle mewing her mighty youth, and kindling her undazzled eyes at the full midday beam. [Ib.]

5 I cannot praise a fugitive and cloistered virtue, unexercised and unbreathed, that never sallies out and sees her adversary, but slinks out of the race where that immortal garland is to be run for, not without dust and heat. [Ib.]

6 Though all the winds of doctrine were let loose to play upon the earth, so Truth be in the field, we do injuriously, by licensing and prohibiting to misdoubt her strength. [Ib.]

7 ...the right path of a virtuous and noble Education, laborious indeed at the first ascent, but else so smooth, so green, so full of goodly prospect, and melodious sounds on every side, that the harp of Orpheus was not more charming. [*On Education*]

Mirabeau, Comte de (1749–1791)

8 War is the national industry of Prussia. [Attr.]

Missal

9 *O felix culpa, quae talem ac tantum meruit habere Redemptorum.* O happy fault, which has earned such and so great a Redeemer. ['Exsultet' on Holy Saturday]

Mitford, Mary Russell (1787–1855)

10 I have discovered that our great favourite, Miss Austen, is my country-woman...with whom mamma before her marriage was acquainted. Mamma says that she was then the prettiest, silliest, most affected, husband-hunting butterfly she ever remembers. [Letter to Sir William Elford, 1815]

Mola, Emilio (1887–1937)

11 *La quinta columna.* The fifth column. [Comment on hopes of civilian uprising in Madrid, 1937]

Molière (1622–1673)

12 *Il faut manger pour vivre et non pas vivre pour manger.* One should eat to live, not live to eat. [*L'Avare*, III.5]

13 *Par ma foi! il y a plus de quarante ans que je dis de la prose sans que j'en susse rien.* Good Heavens! For more than forty years I have been speaking prose without knowing it. [*Le Bourgeois Gentilhomme*, II.4]

14 *Tout ce qui n'est point prose est vers; et tout ce qui n'est point vers est prose.* All that is not prose is verse; and all that is not verse is prose. [Ib.]

15 *On ne meurt qu'une fois, et c'est pour si longtemps!* One dies but once, and that's for such a long time! [*Le Dépit Amoureux*, V.3]

16 *Mais qui rit d'autrui / Doit craindre qu'en revanche on rie aussi de lui.* But the man who laughs at anyone must be afraid that in return the other also laughs at him. [*L'Ecole des Femmes*, I]

17 *Le mariage, Agnès, n'est pas un badinage.* Marriage, Agnès, is not a joke. [Ib. III]

18 *Je vis de bonne soupe et non de beau langage.* I live on good food, not fine words. [*Les Femmes Savantes*, II.7]

19 *La beauté du visage est un frêle ornement, / Une fleur passagère, un éclat d'un moment, / Et qui n'est attaché qu'à la simple épiderme.* Beauty of face is a frail ornament, a passing flower, a momentary brightness belonging to the skin. [Ib. III]

1 *Que diable allait-il faire dans cette galère?* How the devil would he be involved in this business? [*Les Fourberies de Scapin*, II.7]

2 *Oui, cela était autrefois ainsi, mais nous avons changé tout cela.* Yes, it used to be so, but we have changed all that. [*Le Médecin Malgré Lui*, II.4]

3 *C'est une folie à nulle autre seconde, / De vouloir se mêler à corriger le monde.* It is folly second to none wanting to busy oneself putting the world to rights. [*Le Misanthrope*, I.1]

4 *Ils commencent ici par faire pendre un homme et puis ils lui font son procès.* Here they hang a man first, and try him afterwards. [*Monsieur de Pourceaugnac*, III.2]

5 *On est aisément dupé par ce qu'on aime.* One is easily deceived by what one loves. [*Tartuffe*, IV]

6 *Le ciel défend, de vrai, certains contentements / Mais on trouve avec lui des accommodements.* It is true that Heaven forbids certain pleasures, but one finds certain compromises. [Ib. IV.5]

7 *L'homme est, je vous l'avoue, un méchant animal.* Man, I can assure you, is a wicked creature. [Ib. V]

Monroe, Marilyn (1926–1962)

8 [To the question 'Did you have anything on?'] I had the radio on. [Attr.]

Monsell, J.S.B. (1811–1875)

9 Fight the good fight / With all thy might. [Hymn]

Montagu, Lady Mary Wortley (1689–1762)

10 Satire should, like a polished razor keen, / Wound with a touch that's scarcely felt or seen. ['To the Imitator of...Horace']

11 This world consists of men, women, and Herveys. [Letter]

Montaigne, Michel de (1533–1592)

12 *Il faut être toujours botté et prêt à partir.* One should always have one's boots on and be ready to go. [*Essai*, I, 20]

13 *L'utilité de vivre n'est pas en l'espace, elle est en l'usage.* The value of life is not the length of it, but the use we make of it. [Ib.]

14 *Il se faut réserver une arrière boutique...en laquelle nous établissions notre vraie liberté.* We must keep a little back shop...where we may establish our own true liberty. [Ib. I, 39]

15 *Pour juger des choses grandes et hautes, il faut une âme de même.* To judge great and lofty matters, a man must have such a soul. [Ib. I, 42]

16 *Mon métier et mon art, c'est vivre.* To know how to live is all my calling and all my art. [Ib. II, 6]

17 *Que sais-je?* What do I know? [Ib. II, 12]

18 When I play with my cat, who knows whether she gets more amusement out of me than I get from her? [Ib.]

19 *Ceux qui ont apparié notre vie à un songe, ont eu de la raison, à l'aventure plus qu'ils ne pensaient...Nous veillons dormants, et veillants dormons.* Those who have compared our life to a dream were, by chance, more right than they thought...We are awake while sleeping, and sleeping while awake. [Ib.]

20 [Of marriage] It happens as with cages: the birds without are desperate to get in, and those within despair of getting out. [Ib. III, 5]

21 Women are not altogether in the wrong when they refuse the rules of life prescribed in the world, forsomuch as only men have established them without their consent. [Ib.]

22 Science without conscience is but death of the soul. [Quoted in Simcox, *Treasury of Quotations on Christian Themes*]

Montesquieu, Charles, Baron de (1689–1755)

23 Liberty is the right of doing whatever the laws permit. [*De l'Esprit des Lois*, XI, 3]

24 If triangles invented a god, he would be three-sided. [*Lettres persanes*, 59]

1 *Les Anglais sont occupés; ils n'ont pas le temps d'être polis.* The English are busy; they do not have time to be polite. [*Pensées diverses*]

Montgomery, Bernard Law, Viscount of El Alamein (1887-1976)

2 Anyone who votes Labour ought to be locked up. [Speech, 1959]

Montgomery, James (1771-1854)

3 Hail to the Lord's Anointed, / Great David's greater Son! / Hail, in the time appointed, / His reign on earth begun! [Hymn]

Montrose, James Graham, Marquis of (1612-1650)

4 He either fears his fate too much, / Or his deserts are small, / That dare not put it to the touch, / To win or lose it all. ['My Dear and Only Love']

Moore, Clement C. (1779-1863)

5 'Twas the night before Christmas, when all through the house / Not a creature was stirring, not even a mouse. ['A Visit from St. Nicholas']

6 'Happy Christmas to all, and to all a goodnight!' [Ib.]

Moore, Edward (1712-1757)

7 This is adding insult to injuries. [*The Foundling*, V]

Moore, George (1852-1933)

8 All reformers are bachelors. [*The Bending of the Bough*, I]

9 A man travels the world over in search of what he needs and returns home to find it. [*The Brook Kerith*, 11]

10 Art must be parochial in the beginning to be cosmopolitan in the end. [*Hail and Farewell*]

11 The lot of critics is to be remembered by what they failed to understand. [*Impressions and Opinions*]

Moore, Marianne (1887-1972)

12 I, too dislike it: there are things that are important beyond all this fiddle. ['Poetry']

13 Not till the poets among us can be / 'literalists of / the imagination' — above / insolence and triviality and can present / for inspection, imaginary gardens with real toads in them, shall we have / it. ['Poetry', first version]

14 My father used to say, / 'Superior people never make long visits.' ['Silence']

15 Nor was he insincere in saying, 'Make my house / your inn.' / Inns are not residences. [Ib.]

Moore, Thomas (1779-1852)

16 Yet, who can help loving the land that has taught us / Six hundred and eighty-five ways to dress eggs? [*The Fudge Family in Paris*]

17 Believe me, if all those endearing young charms, / Which I gaze on so fondly today. [*Irish Melodies*, 'Believe Me']

18 You may break, you may shatter the vase, if you will, / But the scent of the roses will hang round it still. [Ib. 'Farewell! But Whenever']

19 The harp that once through Tara's halls / The soul of music shed, / Now hangs as mute on Tara's walls / As if that soul were fled. [Ib. 'The Harp that Once']

20 No, there's nothing half so sweet in life / As love's young dream. [Ib. 'Love's Young Dream']

21 The Minstrel Boy to the war is gone, / In the ranks of death you'll find him; / His father's sword he has girded on, / And his wild harp slung behind him. [Ib. 'The Minstrel Boy']

22 'Tis the last rose of summer / Left blooming alone; / All her lovely companions / Are faded and gone. [Ib. ''Tis the Last Rose']

23 Like Dead Sea fruits, that tempt the eye, / But turn to ashes on the lips! [*Lalla Rookh*, 'The Fire-Worshippers']

24 That prophet ill sustains his holy call / Who finds not heav'ns to suit the tastes of all. [Ib. 'The Veiled Prophet']

25 Oft, in the stilly night. [*National Airs*, 'Oft in the Stilly Night']

Mordaunt, Thomas Osbert (1730–1809)

1 Sound, sound the clarion, fill the fife, / Throughout the sensual world proclaim, / One crowded hour of glorious life / Is worth an age without a name. ['Verses written during the War, 1756–63']

More, Hannah (1745–1833)

2 For you'll ne'er mend your fortunes, nor help the just cause, / By breaking of windows, or breaking of laws. ['Address to the Meeting in Spa Fields']

3 He lik'd those literary cooks / Who skim the cream of others' books; / And ruin half an author's graces / By plucking bon-mots from their places. [*Daniel*]

More, Sir Thomas (1478–1535)

4 Your sheep, that were wont to be so meek and tame, and so small eaters, now, as I hear say, be become so great devourers, and so wild, that they eat up and swallow down the very men themselves. [*Utopia*, I]

5 I pray you, Master Lieutenant, see me safe up, and for my coming down let me shift for myself. [On ascending the scaffold]

6 [Pushing aside his beard on the block] This hath not offended the king. [Bacon, *Apophthegms*]

Morell, Thomas (1703–1784)

7 See, the conquering hero comes! / Sound the trumpets, beat the drums! [*Joshua*]

Morgan, Charles (1894–1958)

8 One cannot shut one's eyes to things not seen with eyes. [*The River Line*, 3]

Morris, Desmond (1928–)

9 The Naked Ape [i.e. *Homo sapiens*] [Title of book]

Morris, George Pope (1745–1838)

10 Woodman, spare that tree! / Touch not a single bough! / In youth it sheltered me, / And I'll protect it now. ['Woodman, Spare That Tree']

Morris, William (1834–1896)

11 If you want a golden rule that will fit everybody, this is it: Have nothing in your houses that you do not know to be useful, or believe to be beautiful. ['The Beauty of Life']

12 Dreamer of dreams, born out of my due time, / Why should I strive to set the crooked straight? [*The Earthly Paradise*, 'An Apology']

13 Forget six counties overhung with smoke, / Forget the snorting steam and piston stroke, / Forget the spreading of the hideous town; / Think rather of the pack-horse on the down, / And dream of London, small and white and clean, / The clear Thames bordered by its gardens green. [Ib. 'The Wanderers']

14 The majesty / That from man's soul looks through his eager eyes. [*Life and Death of Jason*]

15 All their devices for cheapening labour simply resulted in increasing the burden of labour. [*News from Nowhere*]

Morse, Samuel (1791–1872)

16 What God hath wrought. [First message sent on his telegraph, 1844]

Morton, J.B. ['Beachcomber'] (1893–1979)

17 Dr. Strabismus (Whom God Preserve). [*The Best of Beachcomber*]

18 SIXTY HORSES WEDGED IN A CHIMNEY The story to fit this sensational headline has not turned up yet. [Ib.]

Morton, Thomas (1764–1838)

19 Always ding, dinging Dame Grundy into my ears — what will Mrs. Grundy zay? What will Mrs. Grundy think? [*Speed the Plough*, I.1]

Motley, John Lothrop (1814–1877)

20 [Of William of Orange] As long as he lived, he was the guiding-star of a whole brave nation, and when he died the little children cried in the streets. [*Rise of the Dutch Republic*, VI, 7]

1 Give us the luxuries of life, and we will dispense with its necessities. [Attr.]

Motteux, Peter Anthony (1660–1718)

2 The devil was sick, the devil a monk would be; / The devil was well, and the devil a monk he'd be. [*Gargantua and Pantagruel* (Translation of Rabelais)]

Mourie, Graham (1952–)

3 Nobody ever beats Wales at rugby, they just score more points. [Quoted in Keating, *Caught by Keating*]

Mumford, Ethel (1878–1940)

4 Don't take the will for the deed; get the deed. [Quoted in Cowan, *The Wit of Women*]

5 In the midst of life we are in debt. [Ib.]

6 Knowledge is power if you know it about the right person. [Ib.]

Murdoch, Iris (1919–)

7 He lives in a sort of rosy haze with Jesus and Mary and Buddha and Shiva and the Fisher King all chasing round and round dressed up as people in Chelsea. [*The Black Prince*, Part One]

Musset, Alfred de (1810–1857)

8 *Malgré moi l'infini me tourmente.* In spite of myself, infinity still torments me. ['L'Espoir en Dieu']

Napier, Charles James (1782–1853)

9 *Peccavi!* I have sinned. [Despatch after occupation of Sind, 1843]

Napoleon I (1769–1821)

10 *Soldats, songez que, du haut de ces pyramides quarante siècles vous contemplent.* Think of it, soldiers, from the summit of these pyramids, forty centuries look down upon you. [Speech, Battle of the Pyramids, 1798]

11 France has more need of me than I have need of France. [Speech, 1813]

12 *Tout soldat français porte dans sa giberne le bâton de maréchal de France.* Every French soldier carries a French marshal's baton in his knapsack. [E. Blaze, *La Vie Militaire sous l'Empire*]

13 *Quant au courage moral, il avait trouvé fort rare, disait-il, celui de deux heures après minuit; c'est-à-dire le courage de l'improviste.* As for moral courage, he had, he said, very rarely encountered two o'clock in the morning courage; that is, the courage of the unprepared. [*Mémorial de Ste. Hélène*]

14 *La carrière ouverte aux talentes.* The career open to talents. [Attr.]

15 Has he luck? [Attr. question of potential officers]

16 *L'Angleterre est une nation de boutiquiers.* England is a nation of shopkeepers. [Attr.]

17 *Du sublime au ridicule il n'y a qu'un pas.* It is but a step from the sublime to the ridiculous. [Attr.]

Nash, Ogden (1902–1971)

18 If I could but spot a conclusion, I should race to it. ['All, All Are Gone']

19 To be an Englishman is to belong to the most exclusive club there is. ['England Expects']

20 I am a conscientious man, when I throw rocks at seabirds I leave no tern unstoned. ['Everybody's Mind to Me a Kingdom Is']

21 You two can be what you like, but since I am the big fromage in this family, I prefer to think of myself as the Gorgon Zola. ['Medusa and the Mot Juste']

22 Any kiddie in school can love like a fool, / But hating, my boy, is an art. ['Plea for Less Malice Toward None']

23 Candy / Is dandy / But liquor / Is quicker. ['Reflection on Ice-Breaking']

24 When Ah itchez, Ah scratchez. ['Requiem']

25 I think that I shall never see / A billboard lovely as a tree. / Indeed, unless the billboards fall / I'll never see a tree at all. ['Song of the Open Road']

1 Sure, deck your lower limbs in pants; / Yours are the limbs, my sweeting. / You look divine as you advance — / Have you seen yourself retreating? ['What's the Use?']

Nashe, Thomas (1567-1601)

2 Brightness falls from the air; / Queens have died young and fair; / Dust hath closed Helen's eye. / I am sick, I must die. / Lord, have mercy on us. ['In Time of Pestilence']

3 Spring, the sweet spring, is the year's pleasant king; / Then blooms each thing, then maids dance in a ring, / Cold doth not sting, the pretty birds do sing; / Cuckoo, jug-jug, pu-we, to-witta-woo. [*Summer's Last Will and Testament*, 'Spring']

4 From winter, plague and pestilence, good Lord, deliver us! [Ib. 'Autumn']

Neale, John Mason (1818-1866)

5 Art thou weary, art thou languid, / Art thou sore distressed? [Hymn]

6 If I ask Him to receive me, / Will he say me nay? [Ib.]

Nelson, Horatio, Viscount Nelson (1758-1805)

7 Westminster Abbey or victory. [Remark at Battle of Cape St. Vincent, 1797]

8 Before this time tomorrow I shall have gained a peerage, or Westminster Abbey. [Remark at Battle of the Nile, 1798]

9 I have only one eye — I have a right to be blind sometimes...I really do not see the signal. [Remark at Battle of Copenhagen, 1801]

10 This is too warm work, Hardy, to last long. [Remark at Battle of Trafalgar, 1805]

11 England expects every man will do his duty. [Ib.]

12 Thank God, I have done my duty. [Ib.]

13 Kiss me, Hardy. [Ib.]

14 You must hate a Frenchman as you hate the devil. [Southey, *Life of Nelson*]

Nero (A.D. 37-68)

15 *Qualis artifex pereo!* What an artist dies with me! [Attr.]

Nerval, Gérard de (1808-1855)

16 *Dieu est mort! le ciel est vide — / Pleurez! enfants, vous n'avez plus de père.* God is dead! Heaven is empty — Weep, children, you no longer have a father. [Epigraph to 'Le Christ aux Oliviers']

17 *Je suis le ténébreux, — le veuf, — l'inconsolé, / Le prince d'Aquitaine à la tour abolie.* I am the shadowy one — the bereaved — the disconsolate — the prince of Aquitaine with the ruined tower. ['El Desdichado']

Nevins, Allan (1890-1971)

18 Offering Germany too little, and offering even that too late. [*Current History*, 1935]

Newbolt, Sir Henry (1862-1938)

19 Drake he's in his hammock an' a thousand mile away / (Capten, art tha' sleepin' there below?). ['Drake's Drum']

20 There's a breathless hush in the Close tonight — / Ten to make and the match to win. ['Vitai Lampada']

21 'Play up! play up! and play the game!' [Ib.]

22 'Ye have robb'd,' said he, 'ye have slaughter'd and made an end, / Take your ill-got plunder, and bury the dead.' ['He Fell Among Thieves']

Newman, John Henry, Cardinal (1801-1890)

23 He has attempted (as I call it) to *poison the wells*. [*Apologia pro Vita Sua*]

24 It would be a gain to the country were it vastly more superstitious, more bigoted, more gloomy, more fierce in its religion than at present it shows itself to be. [Ib.]

25 From the age of fifteen, dogma has been the fundamental principle of my religion: I know no other religion; I cannot enter into the idea of any other sort of religion; religion, as a mere sentiment, is to me a dream and a mockery. [Ib.]

1 I recollect an acquaintance saying to me that 'the Oriel Common Room stank of Logic'. [Ib.]

2 Ten thousand difficulties do not make one doubt. [Ib.]

3 It is almost a definition of a gentleman to say that he is one who never inflicts pain. [*The Idea of a University*]

4 It is as absurd to argue men, as to torture them, into believing. [Sermon, 1831]

5 When men understand what each other mean, they see, for the most part, that controversy is either superfluous or hopeless. [Sermon, 1839]

6 Lead, kindly Light, amid the encircling gloom, / Lead Thou me on. [Hymn]

7 Keep Thou my feet; I do not ask to see / The distant scene, — one step enough for me. [Ib.]

8 Though you can believe what you choose, you must believe what you ought. [Letter, 1848]

News of the World

9 All human life is there. [Slogan]

Newton, Isaac (1642–1727)

10 Whence is it that nature does nothing in vain; and whence arises all that order and beauty which we see in the world? [*Opticks*]

11 I do not know what I may appear to the world, but to myself I seem to have been only a boy playing on the seashore, and diverting myself in now and then finding a smoother pebble or a prettier shell than ordinary, whilst the great ocean of truth lay all undiscovered before me. [Brewster, *Memoirs of Newton*]

12 If I have done the public any service, it is due to patient thought. [Letter to Dr. Bentley]

13 If I have seen further it is by standing on the shoulders of giants. [Letter, 1676]

14 O Diamond! Diamond! thou little knowest the mischief done! [Attr. remark to dog that knocked over a candle which burned 'the almost finished labours of some years']

Newton, John (1725–1807)

15 How sweet the Name of Jesus sounds / In a believer's ear! / It soothes his sorrows, heals his wounds, / And drives away his fear. [Hymn]

16 It makes the wounded spirit whole, / And calms the troubled breast; / 'Tis manna to the hungry soul, / And to the weary rest. [Ib.]

Nicholas I, Emperor of Russia (1796–1855)

17 Russia has two generals in whom she can confide — Generals Janvier and Février. [*Punch*, 1853]

18 [Of Turkey] We have on our hands a sick man — a seriously sick man. [Attr.]

Niebuhr, Reinhold (1892–1971)

19 God grant me the serenity to accept the things I cannot change, the courage to change the things I can, and the wisdom to distinguish the one from the other. [Prayer adopted by Alcoholics Anonymous]

Nietzsche, Friedrich Wilhelm (1844–1900)

20 The thought of suicide is a great consolation; it has helped me through many a weary night. [*Beyond Good and Evil*, IV]

21 If you gaze for long into an abyss, the abyss gazes also into you. [Ib.]

22 *Herren-Moral und Sklaven-Moral.* Master morality and slave morality. [Ib.]

23 My time has not yet come either; some are born posthumously. [*Ecce Homo*]

24 *Gott ist tot; aber so wie die Art der Menschen ist, wird es vielleicht noch jahrtausendlang Höhlen geben, in denen man seinen Schatten zeigt.* God is dead; but looking at the way Man is, there will probably be caves for thousands of years to come in which his shadow will be seen. [*The Gay Science*, III]

25 *Moralität ist Herden-Instinkt in Einzelnen.* Morality is the herd-instinct in individuals. [Ib.]

26 *Gefährlich leben!* Live dangerously! [Ib. IV]

1 Underlying all these noble races the predator is unmistakable, that magnificent blond beast ravening after plunder and victory. [*The Genealogy of Morals*, I]

2 What really raises one's indignation against suffering is not suffering intrinsically, but the senselessness of suffering. [Ib. II]

3 *Ich lehre euch den Übermenschen. Der Mensch ist etwas, das überwunden werden soll.* I teach you the superman. Man is something to be surpassed. [*Thus Spake Zarathustra*]

4 Sleeping is no mean art; for its sake one must stay awake all day. [Ib.]

5 Is man only a blunder of God, or God only a blunder of man? [*The Twilight of the Idols*]

Nightingale, Florence (1820–1910)

6 Too kind — too kind. [Remark when handed insignia of the Order of Merit on her deathbed]

Nivelle, General Robert (1856–1924)

7 *Ils ne passeront pas.* They shall not pass. [Statement at Battle of Verdun, 1916; often attr. Pétain]

Nixon, Richard (1913–)

8 You won't have Nixon to kick around any more. [Remark to Press after losing election, 1962]

9 This has to be the greatest week in the history of the world since the creation. [Speech on first moon-landing, 1969]

10 It is time for the great silent majority of Americans to stand up and be counted. [Speech, 1970]

11 There can be no whitewash at the White House. [*Observer*, 'Sayings of the Week', 1973]

Nock, Albert J. (1873–1945)

12 It is an economic axiom as old as the hills that goods and services can be paid for only with goods and services. [*Memoirs of a Superfluous Man*, III, 3]

North, Christopher (1785–1854)

13 Minds like ours, my dear James, must always be above national prejudices, and in all companies it gives me true pleasure to declare, that, as a people, the English are very little indeed inferior to the Scotch. [*Noctes Ambrosianae*, 9]

14 His Majesty's dominions, on which the sun never sets. [Ib. 20]

15 Laws were made to be broken. [Ib. 24]

Northcote, Sir Stafford (1818–1887)

16 [Of Gladstone] That grand old man. [Speech, 1882]

Norton, Caroline (1808–1877)

17 All our calm is in that balm — / Not lost but gone before. ['Not Lost but Gone Before']

Novalis (1772–1801)

18 Fate and character are the same thing. [*Heinrich von Ofterdingen*, II. Often quoted as 'Character is destiny']

19 *Ein Gottbetrunkener Mensch.* A God-intoxicated man. [Attr. remark on Spinoza]

Noyes, Alfred (1880–1958)

20 And you shall wander hand in hand with love in summer's wonderland; / Go down to Kew in lilac-time (it isn't far from London!) ['Barrel Organ']

21 The wind was a torrent of darkness among the gusty trees, / The moon was a ghostly galleon tossed upon cloudy seas. ['The Highwayman']

22 The landlord's black-eyed daughter, / Bess, the landlord's daughter, / Plaiting a dark red love-knot into her long black hair. [Ib.]

Nursery Rhymes

(For sources, the reader is referred to the authoritative Oxford Dictionary of Nursery Rhymes*)*

1 A frog he would a-wooing go, / Heigh ho! says Rowley, / A frog he would a-wooing go, / Whether his mother would let him or no. / With a rowley, powley, gammon and spinach, / Heigh ho! says Anthony Rowley.

2 As I was going to St. Ives, / I met a man with seven wives.

3 A wise old owl lived in an oak; / The more he saw the less he spoke; / The less he spoke the more he heard. / Why can't we all be like that wise old bird?

4 Baa, baa, black sheep, / Have you any wool? / Yes, sir, yes, sir, / Three bags full; / One for the master, / And one for the dame, / And one for the little boy who lives down the lane.

5 Boys and girls come out to play, / The moon doth shine as bright as day.

6 Bye, baby bunting, / Daddy's gone a-hunting, / Gone to get a rabbit skin / To wrap the baby bunting in.

7 Ding, dong, bell, / Pussy's in the well. / Who put her in? / Little Johnny Green. / Who pulled her out? / Little Timmy Stout.

8 Doctor Foster went to Gloucester / In a shower of rain; / He stepped in a puddle, / Right up to his middle, / And never went there again.

9 Georgie Porgie, pudding and pie, / Kissed the girls and made them cry; / When the boys came out to play, / Georgie Porgie ran away.

10 Goosey, goosey gander, / Whither shall I wander? / Upstairs and downstairs / And in my lady's chamber.

11 Hey diddle diddle, / The cat and the fiddle, / The cow jumped over the moon; / The little dog laughed / To see such sport, / And the dish ran away with the spoon.

12 Hickory, dickory, dock, / The mouse ran up the clock. / The clock struck one, / The mouse ran down, / Hickory, dickory, dock.

13 How many miles to Babylon? / Three score miles and ten. / Can I get there by candle-light? / Yes, and back again.

14 Humpty Dumpty sat on a wall, / Humpty Dumpty had a great fall. / All the king's horses, / And all the king's men, / Couldn't put Humpty together again.

15 Hush-a-bye, baby, on the tree top, / When the wind blows the cradle will rock; / When the bough breaks the cradle will fall, / Down will come baby, cradle, and all.

16 I had a little nut tree, / Nothing would it bear / But a silver nutmeg / And a golden pear; / The King of Spain's daughter / Came to visit me, / And all for the sake / Of my little nut tree.

17 I'm the king of the castle, / Get down, you dirty rascal.

18 Jack and Jill went up the hill / To fetch a pail of water; / Jack fell down and broke his crown, / And Jill came tumbling after.

19 Jack Sprat could eat no fat, / His wife could eat no lean, / And so between them both, you see, / They licked the platter clean.

20 King Charles the First walked and talked / Half an hour after his head was cut off.

21 Ladybird, ladybird, / Fly away home, / Your house is on fire / And your children are gone.

22 Lavender's blue, diddle, diddle, / Lavender's green; / When I am king, diddle, diddle, / You shall be queen.

23 Little Bo-peep has lost her sheep, / And can't tell where to find them; / Leave them alone, and they'll come home, / And bring their tails behind them.

24 Little Boy Blue, / Come blow your horn.

25 Little Jack Horner / Sat in the corner, / Eating a Christmas pie; / He put in his thumb, / And pulled out a plum, / And said, What a good boy am I!

26 Little Miss Muffet / Sat on a tuffet, / Eating her curds and whey; / There came a big spider, / Who sat down beside her / And frightened Miss Muffet away.

27 Little Polly Flinders / Sat among the cinders, / Warming her pretty little toes.

1 London Bridge is falling down, / My fair lady.

2 Mary had a little lamb, / Its fleece was white as snow; / And everywhere that Mary went / The lamb was sure to go.

It followed her to school one day, / That was against the rule; / It made the children laugh and play / To see a lamb at school.

3 Mary, Mary, quite contrary, / How does your garden grow? / With silver bells and cockle shells, / And pretty maids all in a row.

4 My mother said that I never should / Play with the gypsies in the wood; / If I did, she would say, / Naughty girl to disobey.

5 Old King Cole / Was a merry old soul, / And a merry old soul was he; / He called for his pipe, / And he called for his bowl, / And he called for his fiddlers three.

6 Old Mother Hubbard / Went to the cupboard, / To fetch her poor dog a bone; / But when she came there / The cupboard was bare / And so the poor dog had none.

7 Oranges and lemons, / Say the bells of St. Clement's. / You owe me five farthings, / Say the bells of St. Martin's.

8 Peter, Peter, pumpkin eater, / Had a wife and couldn't keep her; / He put her in a pumpkin shell / And there he kept her very well.

9 Peter Piper picked a peck of pickled pepper.

10 Pussy cat, pussy cat, where have you been? / I've been to London to look at the queen.

11 Ride a cock-horse to Banbury Cross, / To see a fine lady upon a white horse; / Rings on her fingers and bells on her toes, / And she shall have music wherever she goes.

12 Ring-a-ring o' roses, / A pocket full of posies, / A-tishoo! A-tishoo! / We all fall down.

13 Rub-a-dub-dub, / Three men in a tub, / And how do you think they got there? / The butcher, the baker, / The candlestick-maker.

14 Simple Simon met a pieman, / Going to the fair; / Says Simple Simon to the pieman, / Let me taste your ware.

15 Sing a song of sixpence, / A pocket full of rye; / Four and twenty blackbirds, / Baked in a pie.

When the pie was opened, / The birds began to sing; / Wasn't that a dainty dish, / To set before the king?

The king was in his counting-house, / Counting out his money; / The queen was in the parlour, / Eating bread and honey.

16 Solomon Grundy, / Born on a Monday.

17 Taffy was a Welshman, Taffy was a thief, / Taffy came to my house and stole a piece of beef.

18 The north wind doth blow, / And we shall have snow, / And what will poor robin do then? / Poor thing.

19 The queen of Hearts / She made some tarts, / All on a summer's day; / The Knave of Hearts / He stole the tarts, / And took them clean away.

20 There was a crooked man, and he walked a crooked mile, / He found a crooked sixpence against a crooked stile; / He bought a crooked cat, which caught a crooked mouse, / And they all lived together in a little crooked house.

21 There was a little girl, and she had a little curl / Right in the middle of her forehead; / When she was good, she was very, very good, / But when she was bad, she was horrid.

22 There was an old woman who lived in a shoe, / She had so many children she didn't know what to do.

23 This is the house that Jack built.

24 This little pig went to market, / This little pig stayed at home, / This little pig had roast beef, / This little pig had none, / And this little pig cried, Wee-wee-wee-wee-wee, / I can't find my way home.

25 Three blind mice, see how they run! / They all ran after the farmer's wife, / She cut off their tails with a carving knife, / Did ever you see such a thing in your life, / As three blind mice?

1 Three little kittens they lost their mittens, / And they began to cry.

2 Tom, Tom, the piper's son, / Stole a pig and away he run.

3 What is your fortune, my pretty maid? / My face is my fortune, sir, she said.

4 Who killed Cock Robin? / I, said the Sparrow, / With my bow and arrow, / I killed Cock Robin.
Who saw him die? / I, said the Fly, / With my little eye, / I saw him die.

Oates, Captain L.E.G. (1880–1912)

5 I am just going outside, and may be some time. [Last words, quoted in Captain Scott's diary]

O'Casey, Sean (1884–1964)

6 I am going where life is more like life than it is here. [*Cock-a-Doodle Dandy*, III]

7 Th' whole worl's...in a terr...ible state o'...chassis! [*Juno and the Paycock*, I]

8 The Polis as Polis, in this city, is Null an' Void! [Ib. III]

9 [Of P.G. Wodehouse] English literature's performing flea. [Wodehouse, *Performing Flea*]

Ochs, Adolph S. (1858–1935)

10 All the news that's fit to print. [Motto of the *New York Times*]

Ogden, C.K. (1889–1957) and Richards, I.A. (1893–1979)

11 The belief that words have a meaning of their own account is a relic of primitive word magic, and it is still a part of the air we breathe in nearly every discussion. [*The Meaning of Meaning*]

Ogilvy, James, Earl of Seafield (1664–1730)

12 Now there's an end of ane old song. [On signing the Act of Union, 1707]

O'Keeffe, John (1747–1847)

13 Amo, amas, I love a lass, / As a cedar tall and slender; / Sweet cowslip's grace / Is her nom'native case, / And she's of the feminine gender. [*The Agreeable Surprise*, II.2]

14 Fat, fair and forty. ['Irish Minnie']

15 You should always except the present company. [*London Hermit*, I.2]

Opie, John (1761–1807)

16 [Asked how he mixed his colours] I mix them with my brains, sir. [Quoted in Samuel Smiles, *Self-Help*]

Oppenheimer, J. Robert (1904–1967)

17 The physicists have known sin; and this is a knowledge which they cannot lose. [Lecture, 1947]

Orczy, Baroness (1864–1947)

18 We seek him here, we seek him there, / Those Frenchies seek him everywhere. / Is he in heaven? — Is he in hell? / That demmed, elusive Pimpernel? [*The Scarlet Pimpernel*, 12]

Orwell, George (1903–1950)

19 Four legs good, two legs bad. [*Animal Farm*, 3]

20 All animals are equal, but some animals are more equal than others. [Ib. 10]

21 England is not the jewelled isle of Shakespeare's much-quoted passage, nor is it the inferno depicted by Dr. Goebbels. More than either it resembles a family, a rather stuffy Victorian family, with not many black sheep in it but with all its cupboards bursting with skeletons. It has rich relations who have to be kow-towed to and poor relations who are horribly sat upon, and there is a deep conspiracy about the source of the family income. It is a family in which the young are generally thwarted and most of the power is in the hands of irresponsible uncles and bedridden aunts. Still, it is a family. [*England, Your England*]

22 ...a cult of cheeriness and manliness, beer and cricket, briar pipes and monogamy, and it was at all times possible to earn a few guineas by writing an article denouncing 'highbrows.' [*Inside the Whale*]

23 Big Brother is watching you. [*1984*]

1 *Doublethink* means the power of holding two contradictory beliefs in one's mind simultaneously, and accepting both of them. [Ib.]

2 Newspeak was the official language of Oceania. [Ib.]

3 The quickest way of ending a war is to lose it. [*Shooting an Elephant*]

Osborne, John (1929-)

4 I keep looking back, as far as I can remember, and I can't think what it was like to feel young, really young. [*Look Back in Anger*, I]

5 There aren't any good, brave causes left. If the big bang does come, and we all get killed off, it won't be in aid of the old-fashioned, grand design. It'll just be for the Brave New-nothing-very-much-thank-you. [Ib. III]

6 The injustice of it is almost perfect! The wrong people going hungry, the wrong people being loved, the wrong people dying. [Ib.]

O'Sullivan, John L. (1813-1895)

7 All government is evil, and the parent of evil...The best government is that which governs least. [*United States Magazine and Democratic Review*, 1837]

Otis, James (1725-1783)

8 Taxation without representation is tyranny. [Attr.]

Otway, Thomas (1652-1685)

9 What mighty ills have not been done by woman! / Who was't betrayed the Capitol? — A woman! / Who lost Mark Antony the world? — A woman! / Who was the cause of a long ten years' war, / And laid at last old Troy in ashes? — Woman! / Destructive, damnable, deceitful woman! [*The Orphan*, III.1]

10 No praying, it spoils business. [*Venice Preserv'd*, II]

Ovid (43 B.C.-A.D. 18)

11 *Procul hinc, procul este, severi!* Keep well away from here, you moralizers! [*Amores*, II, 1]

12 *Delectant etiam castas praeconia formae; / Virginibus curae grataque forma sua est.* Even honest girls like to hear their beauty praised; even the innocent are worried and pleased by their looks. [*Ars Amatoria*, I]

13 *Quae dant, quaeque negant, gaudent tamen esse rogatae.* Whether they give or refuse, women are glad to have been asked. [Ib.]

14 *Forsitan et nostrum nomen miscebitur istis.* Perhaps our name will be linked with these. [Ib. III]

15 *Virginibus cordi grataque forma suaest.* Dear to girls' hearts is their own beauty. [*De Medicamine Faciei*]

16 *Iam seges est ubi Troia fuit.* There is now a cornfield where Troy once was. [*Heroides*, I]

17 *Inopem me copia fecit.* Plenty has impoverished me. [*Metamorphoses*, III]

18 *Tempus edax rerum.* Time the devourer of all things. [Ib. XV]

19 *Tu quoque.* Thou also. [*Tristia*, II]

Owen, Robert (1771-1858)

20 All the world is queer save thee and me, and even thou art a little queer. [Attr. remark on dissolving business partnership]

Owen, Roderic (1921-)

21 The important thing is to know when to laugh, or since laughing is somewhat undignified, to smile. [*The Golden Bubble*]

Owen, Wilfred (1893-1918)

22 What passing-bells for these who die as cattle? / Only the monstrous anger of the guns. / Only the stuttering rifles' rapid rattle / Can patter out their hasty orisons. ['Anthem for Doomed Youth']

23 The old Lie: *Dulce et decorum est / Pro patria mori.* ['Dulce et decorum est']

24 It seemed that out of battle I escaped / Down some profound dull tunnel, long since scooped / Through granites which titanic wars had groined. ['Strange Meeting']

1 I am the enemy you killed, my friend. [Ib.]

2 My subject is War, and the pity of War. The Poetry is in the pity. [*Poems*, 'Preface']

Oxenstierna, Count Axel (1583–1654)

3 Do you not know, my son, with how little wisdom the world is ruled? [Letter, 1648]

Paine, Thomas (1737–1809)

4 The sublime and the ridiculous are often so nearly related, that it is difficult to class them separately. [*The Age of Reason*, II]

5 These are the times that try men's souls. [*The American Crisis*, 1776]

6 Government, even in its best state, is but a necessary evil; in its worst state, an intolerable one. [*Common Sense*, 1]

7 [Of Burke] As he rose like a rocket, he fell like the stick. [*Letter to His Addressers*, 1792]

8 [Of Burke's *Reflections on the Revolution in France*] He pities the plumage, but forgets the dying bird. [*Rights of Man*, I]

9 Man is not the enemy of Man, but through the medium of a false system of government. [Ib.]

10 My country is the world, and my religion is to do good. [Ib. II]

Palafox, José de (1780–1847)

11 War to the knife. [Attr. reply to demand for surrender at siege of Saragossa, 1808]

Palmer, H.R. (1834–1907)

12 Yield not to temptation, for yielding is sin; / Each victory will help you some other to win. [Hymn]

13 Shun evil companions; bad language disdain; / God's name hold in reverence, nor take it in vain. [Ib.]

Palmerston, Henry John Temple, Viscount (1784–1865)

14 As the Roman, in days of old, held himself free from indignity when he could say *Civis Romanus sum*; so also a British subject, in whatever land he may be, shall feel confident that the watchful eye and the strong arm of England will protect him against injustice and wrong. [Speech, 1850]

15 [Of the Schleswig-Holstein question] There are only three men who have ever understood it: one was Prince Albert, who is dead; the second was a German professor, who became mad. I am the third — and I have forgotten all about it. [Attr. Quoted in Palmer, *Quotations in History*]

16 Die, my dear Doctor, that's the last thing I shall do! [Attr. last words]

Pankhurst, Emmeline (1858–1928)

17 The argument of the broken pane of glass is the most valuable argument in modern politics. [*Votes for Women*]

Papprill, Ross F. (1908–1975)

18 There are two kinds of people in the world: those who believe there are two kinds of people in the world, and those who don't. [Attr.]

Parker, Dorothy (1893–1967)

19 Men seldom make passes / At girls who wear glasses. ['News Item']

20 Why is it no one ever sent me yet / One perfect limousine, do you suppose? / Ah no, it's always just my luck to get / One perfect rose. ['One Perfect Rose']

21 Razors pain you; / Rivers are damp; / Acids stain you; / And drugs cause cramp. ['Resumé']

22 She ran the whole gamut of the emotions from A to B. [Attr. remark on a performance by Katharine Hepburn]

23 How could they tell? [Attr. remark on hearing that President Coolidge had died]

Parker, Ross (1914-) and Charles, Hughie (1907-)

1 There'll always be an England / While there's a country lane. ['There'll Always Be an England']

Parkinson, Cyril Northcote (1909-)

2 Work expands so as to fill the time available for its completion. [*Parkinson's Law*]

Parkman, Francis (1823-1893)

3 The public demands elocution rather than reason of those who address it...On matters of the greatest interest it craves to be excited or amused. [*The Tale of the 'Ripe Scholar'*]

Parnell, Charles Stewart (1846-1891)

4 No man has a right to fix the boundary of the march of a nation: no man has a right to say to his country — thus far shalt thou go and no further. [Speech, 1885]

Pascal, Blaise (1623-1662)

5 *Je n'ai fait celle-ci plus longue que parce que je n'ai pas eu le loisir de la faire plus courte.* I have only made this letter longer because I have not had time to make it shorter. [*Lettres Provinciales*]

6 *Tout le malheur des hommes vient d'une seule chose, qui est de ne savoir pas demeurer en repos dans une chambre.* All the troubles of men are caused by one single thing, which is their inability to stay quietly in a room. [*Pensées*, II, 139]

7 *Le nez de Cléopâtre: s'il eût été plus court, toute la face de la terre aurait changé.* If Cleopatra's nose had been shorter the whole history of the world would have been different. [Ib. II, 162]

8 *Le silence éternel de ces espaces infinis m'effraie.* The eternal silence of these infinite spaces terrifies me. [Ib. III, 206]

9 *On mourra seul.* We shall die alone. [Ib. III, 211]

10 *Le coeur a ses raisons que la raison ne connaît point.* The heart has its reasons which the mind knows nothing of. [Ib. IV, 277]

11 *L'homme n'est qu'un roseau, le plus faible de la nature; mais c'est un roseau pensant.* Man is only a reed, the feeblest thing in nature; but he is a thinking reed. [Ib. VI, 347]

12 *Se moquer de la philosophie, c'est vraiment philosopher.* To ridicule philosophy is really to philosophize. [Ib. 430]

Pasteur, Louis (1822-1895)

13 *Dans les champs de l'observation, l'hasard ne favorise que les esprits préparés.* In the field of observation, chance favours only the prepared mind. [Lecture, 1854]

Pater, Walter (1839-1894)

14 [Of the *Mona Lisa*] She is older than the rocks among which she sits; like the vampire, she has been dead many times, and learned the secrets of the grave. [*Studies in the History of the Renaissance*, 'Leonardo da Vinci']

15 All art constantly aspires towards the condition of music. [Ib. 'Giorgione']

16 To burn always with this hard, gemlike flame, to maintain this ecstasy, is success in life. [Ib. 'Conclusion']

17 Not to discriminate every moment some passionate attitude in those about us, and in the brilliancy of their gifts some tragic dividing of forces on their ways, is, on this short day of frost and sun, to sleep before evening. [Ib.]

18 The love of art for art's sake. [Ib.]

Paterson, Andrew (1864-1941)

19 Once a jolly swagman camped by a billabong, / Under the shade of a kulibar tree, / And he sang as he sat and waited for his billy-boil, / You'll come a-waltzing, Matilda, with me.' ['Waltzing Matilda']

Patmore, Coventry (1823-1896)

1 'I saw you take his kiss!' ''Tis true.' / 'O modesty!' ''Twas strictly kept: / He thought me asleep; at least, I knew / He thought I thought he thought I slept.' [*The Angel in the House*, II, 'The Kiss']

2 For want of me the world's course will not fail: / When all its work is done, the lie shall rot; / The truth is great, and shall prevail, / When none cares whether it prevail or not. [*The Unknown Eros*, I, 12]

3 He that but once too nearly hears / The music of forfended spheres / Is thenceforth lonely, and for all / His days as one who treads the Wall / Of China, and, on this hand, sees / Cities and their civilities / And, on the other, lions. [*The Victories of Love*, I, 2]

Payn, James (1830-1898)

4 I have never a piece of toast / Particularly long and wide, / But fell upon the sanded floor, / And always on the buttered side. [*Chamber's Journal*, 1884]

Payne, J.H. (1792-1852)

5 Mid pleasures and palaces though we may roam, / Be it never so humble, there's no place like home. ['Home, Sweet Home']

Peacock, Thomas Love (1785-1866)

6 Respectable means rich, and decent means poor. I should die if I heard my family called decent. [*Crotchet Castle*, 3]

7 A book that furnishes no quotations is, *me judice*, no book — it is a plaything. [Ib. 9]

8 I almost think it is the ultimate destiny of science to exterminate the human race. [*Gryll Grange*]

9 'I distinguish the picturesque and the beautiful, and I add to them, in the laying out of grounds, a third and distinct character, which I call *unexpectedness*.' 'Pray, sir,' said Mr. Milestone, 'by what name do you distinguish this character, when a person walks round the grounds for the second time?' [*Headlong Hall*, 4]

10 If ifs and ands were pots and pans / There'd be no work for the tinkers. ['Manley']

11 The mountain sheep are sweeter, / But the valley sheep are fatter; / We therefore deemed it meeter / To carry off the latter. [*The Misfortunes of Elphin*, 'The War-Song of Dinas Vawr']

12 Seamen three! What men be ye? / Gotham's three Wise Men we be. [*Nightmare Abbey*, 11, 'Three Men of Gotham']

Peele, George (c. 1558-c. 1597)

13 Whenas the rye reach to the chin, / And chopcherry, chopcherry ripe within, / Strawberries swimming in the cream, / And schoolboys playing in the stream, / Then O, then O, then O, my true love said, / Till that time come again, / She could not live a maid. [*The Old Wives' Tale*]

Pemberton, Max (1863-1950)

14 A negro preacher having vainly attempted to collect money from a peripatetic flock, thanked God that he had got his hat back. [Attr.]

Pembroke, The 10th Earl (1734-1794)

15 Dr. Johnson's sayings would not appear so extraordinary, were it not for his *bow-wow way*. [Boswell, *Life*]

Penn, William (1644-1718)

16 It is a reproach to religion and government to suffer so much poverty and excess. [*Reflections and Maxims*]

17 Men are generally more careful of the breed of their horses and dogs than of their children. [Ib.]

Pepys, Samuel (1633-1703)

18 And so to bed. [*Diary*, 1660]

19 A silk suit, which cost me much money, and I pray God to make me able to pay for it. [Ib. 1660]

1 I went out to Charing Cross, to see Major-General Harrison hanged, drawn and quartered; which was done there, he looking as cheerful as any man could do in that condition. [Ib. 1660]

2 A good, honest and painful sermon. [Ib. 1661]

3 I see it is impossible for the King to have things done as cheap as other men. [Ib. 1662]

4 While we were talking came by several poor creatures carried by, by constables, for being at a conventicle...I would to God they would either conform, or be more wise, and not be catched! [Ib. 1664]

5 Strange to say how a good dinner and feasting reconciles everybody. [Ib. 1665]

6 Strange to say what delight we married people have to see these poor fools decoyed into our condition. [Ib.]

7 Music and women I cannot but give way to, whatever my business is. [Ib. 1666]

8 But it is pretty to see what money will do. [Ib. 1668]

Pericles (c. 495–429 B.C.)

9 Wait for that wisest of counsellors, Time. [Plutarch, *Life*]

Persius Flaccus, Aulus (A.D. 34–62)

10 *Nec te quaesiveris extra.* Ask no opinion but your own. [*Satires*, I]

11 *Venienti occurrite morbo.* Confront disease at its first stage. [Ib. III]

Petronius Arbiter (?–A.D. 66)

12 *Cave canem.* Beware of the dog. [*Satyricon*]

13 *Abiit ad plures.* He has joined the great majority. [Ib.]

14 *Scimus te prae litteras fatuum esse.* We know that you are mad with much learning. [Ib.]

15 *Curiosa felicitas.* A painstaking facility [of style]. [Ib.]

16 *Litteratum esse, quos odisse divites solent.* A man of letters, of the kind that rich men hate. [Ib.]

Phelps, E.J. (1822–1900)

17 The man who makes no mistakes does not usually make anything. [Speech, 1899]

Philip, Rear Admiral (1840–1900)

18 Don't cheer, men; those poor devils are dying. [Said at the Battle of Santiago, 1898]

Philips, John (1676–1709)

19 Happy the man, who void of cares and strife, / In silken, or in leathern purse retains / A splendid shilling. ['The Splendid Shilling', parody of Milton]

Phillips, Stephen (1864–1915)

20 A man not old, but mellow, like good wine. [*Ulysses*, III]

Phillips, Wendell (1811–1884)

21 Every man meets his Waterloo at last. [Lecture, 1859]

22 One, on God's side, is a majority. [Ib.]

Picasso, Pablo (1881–1973)

23 *Je ne cherche pas; je trouve.* I do not search; I find. [Attr.]

Pindar (518–438 B.C.)

24 Water is best. [*Olympian Odes*, I]

25 My soul, do not search for immortal life, but exhaust the boundaries of possibility. [*Pythian Odes*, III]

Pindar, Peter (1738–1819)

26 What rage for fame attends both great and small! / Better be damned than mentioned not at all! ['To the Royal Academicians']

Pinero, Sir Arthur Wing (1855–1934)

27 While there's tea there's hope. [*The Second Mrs. Tanqueray*, I]

28 What beautiful fruit! I love fruit when it's expensive. [Ib.]

29 From forty to fifty a man is at heart either a stoic or a satyr. [Ib.]

Pinter, Harold (1930-)

1 If only I could get down to Sidcup! I've been waiting for the weather to break. He's got my papers, this man I left them with. [*The Caretaker*, I]

2 [Asked what his plays are about] The weasel under the cocktail cabinet. [J. Russell Taylor, *Anger and After*]

Pitt, William, Earl of Chatham (1708-1778)

3 The atrocious crime of being a young man...I shall neither attempt to palliate nor deny. [Speech, House of Commons, 1741]

4 The poorest man may in his cottage bid defiance to all the forces of the Crown. It may be frail — its roof may shake — the wind may blow through it — the rain may enter — but the King of England cannot enter — all his force dares not cross the threshold of the ruined tenement! [Speech, 1763?]

5 Where law ends, there tyranny begins. [Speech, 1770]

6 You cannot conquer America. [Speech, 1777]

7 I invoke the genius of the Constitution. [Ib.]

Pitt, William (1759-1806)

8 Necessity is the plea for every infringement of human freedom. It is the argument of tyrants; it is the creed of slaves. [Speech, 1783]

9 England has saved herself by her exertions, and will, as I trust, save Europe by her example. [Speech, 1805]

10 Roll up that map; it will not be wanted these ten years. [Remark, on map of Europe, after hearing report of Battle of Austerlitz]

11 I think I could eat one of Bellamy's veal pies. [Attr. last words]

12 Oh, my country! how I leave my country! [Attr. last words]

Planché, James Robinson (1796-1880)

13 It would have made a cat laugh. [*The Queen of the Frogs*, I.4]

Plath, Sylvia (1932-1963)

14 Tomorrow I will be sweet God, I will set them free. / The box is only temporary. ['The Arrival of the Bee Box']

15 Every woman adores a Fascist, / The boot in the face, the brute / Brute heart of a brute like you. ['Daddy']

16 Daddy, daddy, you bastard, I'm through. [Ib.]

17 Dying / Is an art, like everything else. / I do it exceptionally well. ['Lady Lazarus']

Plato (c. 429-347 B.C.)

18 That man is wisest who, like Socrates, realizes that his wisdom is worthless. [*Apologia of Socrates*]

19 Man was not born for himself but for his country. [*Epistles*, 9]

20 Time brings everything. [*Greek Anthology*, 9]

21 Through obedience learn to command. [*Leges*]

22 The good is the beautiful. [*Lysis*]

23 Poets utter great and wise things which they do not themselves understand. [*Republic*, II]

24 The rulers of the State are the only ones who should have the privilege of lying, either at home or abroad; they may be allowed to lie for the good of the State. [Ib. III]

25 Our object in the construction of the state is the greatest happiness of the whole, and not that of any one class. [Ib. IV]

26 They see only their own shadows, or the shadows of one another, which the fire throws on the opposite wall of the cave. [Ib. VII]

27 Democracy passes into despotism. [Ib. VIII]

28 Nothing in the affairs of men is worthy of great anxiety. [Ib. X]

29 Every king springs from a race of slaves, and every slave has had kings among his ancestors. [*Theaetetus*]

Plautus, Titus Maccius (c. 254-184 B.C.)

1 *Lupus est homo homini.* Man is a wolf to man. [*Asinaria*]

2 To blow and swallow at the same time is not easy. [*Mostellaria*]

3 *Tetigisti acu.* You've hit the nail on the head. (*lit.* You have touched it with a needle.) [*Rudens*]

4 *Miles gloriosus.* The boastful soldier. [Title of play]

Pliny the Elder (A.D. 23-79)

5 *Ex Africa semper aliquid novi.* There is always something new out of Africa. [*Natural History*, VIII (altered)]

6 *In vino veritas.* Truth is in wine. [Ib. XIV]

7 *Ne supra crepidam sutor iudicaret.* The cobbler should not judge beyond his last. [Ib.]

8 *Cum grano salis.* With a grain of salt. [Ib. XXIII]

Plutarch (c. A.D. 46-120)

9 A traveller at Sparta, standing long upon one leg, said to a Lacedaemonian, 'I do not believe you can do as much.' 'True,' said he, 'but every goose can.' [*Laconic Apothegms*]

10 The great god Pan is dead. [*Morals*, 'Of Isis and Osiris']

11 Alexander wept when he heard from Anaxarchus that there was an infinite number of worlds...he said: 'Do you not think it lamentable that with such a vast multitude of worlds, we have not yet conquered one?' [*On the Tranquility of the Mind*]

12 It is indeed desirable to be well descended, but the glory belongs to our ancestors. [*On the Training of Children*]

Poe, Edgar Allan (1809-1849)

13 It was many and many a year ago, / In a kingdom by the sea, / That a maiden there lived whom you may know / By the name of Annabel Lee; / And this maiden she lived with no other thought / Than to love and be loved by me. ['Annabel Lee']

14 But we loved with a love which was more than love — / I and my Annabel Lee. [Ib.]

15 Keeping time, time, time, / In a sort of Runic rhyme, / To the tintinnabulation that so musically wells / From the bells, bells, bells, bells. ['The Bells']

16 The play is the tragedy, 'Man,' / And its hero the Conqueror Worm. ['The Conqueror Worm']

17 The fever call'd 'Living' / Is conquered at last. ['For Annie']

18 Take thy beak from out my heart, and take thy form from off my door! / Quoth the Raven, 'Nevermore'. ['The Raven']

19 The glory that was Greece / And the grandeur that was Rome. ['To Helen']

Polybius (c. 204-c. 122 B.C.)

20 On any occasion when one can discover the cause of events, one should not resort to the gods. [Attr.]

Pomfret, John (1667-1702)

21 Near some fair town, I'd have a private Seat, / Built uniform, not little, nor too great. [*The Choice*]

22 We live and learn, but not the wiser grow. [*Reason*]

Pompadour, Madame de (1721-1764)

23 *Après nous le déluge.* After us the flood. [Remark after Battle of Rossbach, 1757]

Poole, John (c. 1786-1872)

24 I hope I don't intrude? [*Paul Pry*, I.2]

Pope, Alexander (1688-1744)

25 Books and the Man I sing, the first who brings / The Smithfield Muses to the Ear of Kings. [*The Dunciad*, I, first lines]

26 Still Dunce the second reigns like Dunce the first. [Ib.]

27 Maggots half-form'd in rhyme exactly meet, / And learn to crawl upon poetic feet. [Ib.]

1 While pensive Poets painful vigils keep, / Sleepless themselves, to give their readers sleep. [Ib.]

2 Now Night descending, the proud scene was o'er, / But liv'd, in Settle's numbers, one day more. [Ib.]

3 Sinking from thought to thought, a vast profound! [Ib.]

4 For thee explain a thing till all men doubt it, / And write about it, and about it. [Ib.]

5 Some Daemon stole my pen (forgive th' offence) / And once betray'd me into common sense. [Ib.]

6 And cackling save the monarchy of Tories. [Ib.]

7 And gentle Dullness ever loves a joke. [Ib. II]

8 Thames, / The King of Dykes! than whom, no sluice of mud / With deeper sable blots than silver flood. [Ib.]

9 Smit with love of Poetry and Prate. [Ib.]

10 All crowd, who foremost shall be damn'd to fame. [Ib. III]

11 Flow, Welsted, flow! / like thine inspirer, Beer, / Tho' stale, not ripe; tho' thin, yet never clear; / So sweetly mawkish, and so smoothly dull; / Heady, not strong, and foaming tho' not full. [Ib.]

12 The Right Divine of Kings to govern wrong. [Ib. IV]

13 We bring to one dead level ev'ry mind. [Ib.]

14 Stretch'd on the rack of a too easy chair. [Ib.]

15 Turn what they will to Verse, their toil is vain, / Critics like me shall make it Prose again. [Ib.]

16 To happy Convents, bosom'd deep in vines, / Where slumber Abbots, purple as their wines. [Ib.]

17 All Classic learning lost on Classic ground. [Ib.]

18 The mind, in Metaphysics at a loss, / May wander in a wilderness of Moss. [Ib.]

19 Lo! thy dread Empire, Chaos! is restor'd; / Light dies before thy uncreating word: / Thy hand, great Anarch! lets the curtain fall; / And Universal Darkness buries All. [Ib. last lines]

20 Is it, in heav'n, a crime to love too well? ['Elegy to the Memory of an Unfortunate Lady']

21 A heap of dust alone remains of thee; / 'Tis all thou art, and all the proud shall be! [Ib.]

22 The world forgetting, by the world forgot. [*Eloisa to Abelard*]

23 Most women have no characters at all. [Epistle to a Lady]

24 A very heathen in the carnal part, / Yet still a sad, good Christian at her heart. [Ib.]

25 Chaste to her Husband, frank to all beside, / A teeming Mistress, but a barren Bride. [Ib.]

26 Virtue she finds too painful an endeavour, / Content to dwell in Decencies for ever. [Ib.]

27 In men, we various ruling passions find, / In women, two almost divide the kind; / Those, only fix'd, they first or last obey, / The love of pleasure, and the love of sway. [Ib.]

28 Men, some to Bus'ness, some to Pleasure take; / But every woman is at heart a Rake: / Men, some to Quiet, some to public Strife; / But ev'ry Lady would be Queen for life. [Ib.]

29 Still round and round the ghosts of beauty glide, / And haunt the places where their honour died. / See how the world its veterans rewards! / A youth of frolics, an old age of cards. [Ib.]

30 And mistress of herself, though China fall. [Ib.]

31 Shut, shut the door, good John! fatigu'd I said, / Tie up the knocker; say I'm sick, I'm dead. [*Epistle to Dr. Arbuthnot*]

32 Destroy his fib or sophistry — in vain! / The creature's at his dirty work again. [Ib.]

33 As yet a child, nor yet a fool to fame, / I lisp'd in numbers, for the numbers came. [Ib.]

1 The Muse but serv'd to ease some friend, not wife, / To help me thro' this long disease, my life. [Ib.]

2 Pretty! in amber to observe the forms / Of hairs, or straws, or dirt, or grubs, or worms! / The things, we know, are neither rich nor rare, / But wonder how the Devil they got there. [Ib.]

3 And he, whose fustian's so sublimely bad, / It is not poetry, but prose run mad. [Ib.]

4 Damn with faint praise, assent with civil leer, / And without sneering, teach the rest to sneer; / Willing to wound, and yet afraid to strike, / Just hint a fault, and hesitate dislike. [Ib.]

5 So obliging, that he ne'er oblig'd. [Ib.]

6 Curst be the verse, how well soe'er it flow, / That tends to make one worthy man my foe. [Ib.]

7 Let Sporus tremble — 'What? that thing of silk, / Sporus, that mere white curd of ass's milk? / Satire or sense, alas! can Sporus feel? / Who breaks a butterfly upon a wheel?' [Ib.]

8 Yet let me flap this bug with gilded wings — / This painted child of dirt, that stinks and stings. [Ib.]

9 Eternal smiles his emptiness betray, / As shallow streams run dimpling all the way. [Ib.]

10 Unlearn'd, he knew no schoolman's subtle art, / No language, but the language of the heart. [Ib.]

11 She went, to plain-work, and to purling brooks, / Old-fashion'd halls, dull aunts, and croaking rooks. ['Epistle to Miss Blount, on her leaving the Town']

12 To muse, and spill her solitary tea, / Or o'er cold coffee trifle with the spoon. [Ib.]

13 But thousands die, without or this or that, / Die, and endow a College, or a Cat. [*Epistle to Lord Bathurst*]

14 The ruling Passion, be it what it will, / The ruling Passion conquers Reason still. [Ib.]

15 Where London's column, pointing at the skies, / Like a tall bully, lifts the head, and lies. [Ib.]

16 Consult the genius of the place in all. [*Epistle to Lord Burlington*]

17 To rest, the cushion and soft Dean invite, / Who never mentions Hell to ears polite. [Ib.]

18 Another age shall see the golden ear / Imbrown the slope, and nod on the parterre, / Deep harvest bury all his pride had plann'd, / And laughing Ceres reassume the land. [Ib.]

19 'Tis from high life high characters are drawn; / A saint in crape is twice a saint in lawn. [*Epistle to Lord Cobham*]

20 'Odious! in woollen! 'twould a saint provoke!' [Ib.]

21 All Manners take a tincture from our own; / Or come discolour'd thro' our Passions shown. [Ib.]

22 'One would not, sure, be frightful when one's dead: / And — Betty — give this cheek a little red.' [Ib.]

23 I am his Highness' dog at Kew; / Pray, tell me sir, whose dog are you? [Epigram for a royal dog collar]

24 Nature, and Nature's laws lay hid in night: / God said, *Let Newton be!* and all was light. [Epitaph for Sir Isaac Newton]

25 'Tis with our judgements as our watches, none / Go just alike, yet each believes his own. [*Essay on Criticism*]

26 Let such teach others who themselves excel, / And censure freely who have written well. [Ib.]

27 Some have at first for Wits then Poets past, / Turn'd Critics next, and prov'd plain fools at last. [Ib.]

28 A *little learning* is a dang'rous thing; / Drink deep, or taste not the Pierian spring: / There shallow draughts intoxicate the brain, / And drinking largely sobers us again. [Ib.]

29 True Wit is Nature to advantage dress'd, / What oft was thought, but ne'er so well express'd. [Ib.]

30 Words are like leaves; and where they most abound, / Much fruit of sense beneath is rarely found. [Ib.]

31 Be not the first by whom the new are tried, / Nor yet the last to lay the old aside. [Ib.]

1 As some to church repair, / Not for the doctrine but the music there. [Ib.]

2 True ease in writing comes from art, not chance, / As those move easiest who have learn'd to dance. / 'Tis not enough no harshness gives offence, / The sound must seem an echo to the sense. [Ib.]

3 Fondly we think we honour merit then, / When we but praise ourselves in other men. [Ib.]

4 Good-nature and good-sense must ever join; / To err is human, to forgive, divine. [Ib.]

5 The bookful blockhead, ignorantly read, / With loads of learned lumber in his head. [Ib.]

6 For Fools rush in where Angels fear to tread. [Ib.]

7 And the same age saw Learning fall, and Rome. [Ib.]

8 Let us (since Life can little more supply / Than just to look about us and to die) / Expatiate free o'er all this scene of man; / A mighty maze! but not without a plan. [*Essay on Man*, I]

9 Laugh where we must, be candid where we can; / But vindicate the ways of God to man. [Ib.]

10 Then say not Man's imperfect, Heav'n in fault; / Say rather, Man's as perfect as he ought. [Ib.]

11 Who sees with equal eye as God of all, / A hero perish or a sparrow fall, / Atoms or systems into ruin hurl'd, / And now a bubble burst, and now a world. [Ib.]

12 Hope springs eternal in the human breast: / Man never is, but always to be blest. [Ib.]

13 Men would be Angels, Angels would be Gods, / Aspiring to be Gods, if Angels fell, / Aspiring to be Angels, Men rebel. [Ib.]

14 Say what the use, were finer optics giv'n, / T'inspect a mite, not comprehend the heav'n? [Ib.]

15 Why has not man a microscopic eye? / For this plain reason, man is not a fly. [Ib.]

16 The spider's touch, how exquisitely fine! / Feels at each thread, and lives along the line. [Ib.]

17 All nature is but art unknown to thee; / All chance, direction which thou canst not see; / All discord, harmony not understood; / All partial evil, universal good; / And, spite of pride, in erring reason's spite, / One truth is clear, 'Whatever IS, is RIGHT.' [Ib.]

18 Know then thyself, presume not God to scan; / The proper study of Mankind is Man. [Ib. II]

19 Sole judge of truth, in endless error hurl'd; / The glory, jest, and riddle of the world! [Ib.]

20 Nor God alone in the still calm we find, / He mounts the storm, and walks upon the wind. [Ib.]

21 Pleasures are ever in our hands or eyes. [Ib.]

22 For Forms of Government let fools contest; / Whate'er is best administer'd is best: / For Modes of Faith let graceless zealots fight; / His can't be wrong whose life is in the right. [Ib. III]

23 Thus God and Nature link'd the gen'ral frame, / And bade Self-love and Social be the same. [Ib.]

24 O Happiness! our being's end and aim! [Ib. IV]

25 Go, like the Indian, in another life / Expect thy dog, thy bottle, and thy wife. [Ib.]

26 A Wit's a feather, and a Chief a rod; / An honest Man's the noblest work of God. [Ib.]

27 See Cromwell, damn'd to everlasting fame! [Ib.]

28 Slave to no sect, who takes no private road, / But looks through Nature, up to Nature's God. [Ib.]

29 Thou wert my guide, philosopher, and friend. [Ib.]

30 That virtue only makes our bliss below; / And all our knowledge is ourselves to know. [Ib. last lines]

31 Get place and wealth, if possible, with grace; / If not, by any means get wealth and place. [*Imitations of Horace*, *Epistle* I, 1]

32 Not to admire, is all the art I know, / To make men happy, and to keep them so. [Ib. *Epistle* I, 6]

1 Who now reads Cowley? if he pleases yet, / His moral pleases, not his pointed wit. [Ib. *Epistle* II, 1]

2 The people's voice is odd, / It is, and it is not, the voice of God. [Ib.]

3 Waller was smooth; but Dryden taught to join / The varying verse, the full-resounding line, / The long majestic march, and energy divine. [Ib.]

4 The last and greatest art, the art to blot. [Ib.]

5 There still remains, to mortify a wit, / The many-headed monster of the pit. [Ib.]

6 Let humble Allen, with an awkward shame, / Do good by stealth, and blush to find it fame. [Ib. *Epilogue to the Satires*, I]

7 Ask you what provocation I have had? / The strong antipathy of good to bad. [Ib. II]

8 Yes, I am proud; I must be proud to see / Men not afraid of God, afraid of me. [Ib.]

9 True friendship's laws are by this rule express'd, / Welcome the coming, speed the parting guest. [*Odyssey*, XV]

10 Happy the man, whose wish and care / A few paternal acres bound, / Content to breathe his native air, / In his own ground. ['Ode on Solitude']

11 Where'er you walk, cool gales shall fan the glade, / Trees, where you sit, shall crowd into a shade. [*Pastorals*, 'Summer']

12 Fame is at best an unperforming cheat; / But 'tis substantial happiness, *to eat*. ['Prologue for Mr. D'Urfey's Last Play']

13 What dire offence from am'rous causes springs, / What mighty contests rise from trivial things, / I sing. [*The Rape of the Lock*, I]

14 Puffs, powders, patches, / bibles, billet-doux. [Ib.]

15 Favours to none, to all she smiles extends; / Oft she rejects, but never once offends. [Ib. II]

16 If to her share some female errors fall, / Look on her face, and you'll forget 'em all. [Ib.]

17 Or stain her honour or her new brocade; / Forget her pray'rs, or miss a masquerade; / Or lose her heart, or necklace, at a ball. [Ib.]

18 Here thou, great Anna! whom three realms obey, / Dost sometimes counsel take — and sometimes Tea. [Ib. III]

19 The hungry judges soon the sentence sign, / And wretches hang that jury-men may dine. [Ib.]

20 Coffee, (which makes the politician wise, / And see through all things with his half-shut eyes). [Ib.]

21 Not louder shrieks to pitying heav'n are cast, / When husbands, or when lap-dogs breathe their last. [Ib.]

22 Oh hadst thou, Cruel! been content to seize / Hairs less in sight, or any Hairs but these! [Ib. IV]

23 Good Humour can prevail, / When airs, and flights, and screams, and scolding fail. [Ib. V]

24 Beauties in vain their pretty eyes may roll; / Charms strike the sight, but merit wins the soul. [Ib.]

25 Then teach me Heav'n! to scorn the guilty bays; / Drive from my breast that wretched lust of praise; / Unblemish'd let me live, or die unknown: / Oh, grant an honest Fame, or grant me none! [*The Temple of Fame*]

26 Not Chaos-like together crush'd and bruis'd, / But as the world, harmoniously confus'd: / Where order in variety we see, / And where tho' all things differ, all agree. [*Windsor Forest*]

27 The fox obscene to gaping tombs retires, / And savage howlings fill the sacred quires. [Ib.]

28 Oft as the mounting larks their notes prepare, / They fall, and leave their little lives in air. [Ib.]

29 And seas but join the regions they divide. [Ib.]

30 'Blessed is the man who expects nothing, for he shall never be disappointed,' was the ninth beatitude which a man of wit (who like a man of wit was a long time in gaol) added to the eighth. [Letter, 1725]

1 Here am I, dying of a hundred good symptoms. [Spence, *Anecdotes*]

Potter, Beatrix (1866–1943)

2 'No teeth, no teeth, no teeth!' said Mr. Jackson. [*The Tale of Mrs. Tittlemouse*]

3 You may go into the field or down the lane, but don't go into Mr. McGregor's garden. [*The Tale of Peter Rabbit*]

Potter, Stephen (1900–1971)

4 Gamesmanship or, The Art of Winning Games without actually Cheating [Title of book]

5 *How to be one up* — how to make the other man feel that something has gone wrong, however slightly. [*Lifemanship*]

Pound, Ezra (1885–1972)

6 Winter is icummen in, / Lhude sing Goddamn, / Raineth drop and staineth slop / And how the wind doth ramm! / Sing: Goddamn. ['Ancient Music'; *see* Anon., 'Summer is icummen in']

7 As a bathtub lined with white porcelain, / When the hot water gives out or goes tepid, / So is the slow cooling of our chivalrous passion, / O my much praised but-not-altogether-satisfactory lady. ['The Bath Tub']

8 Pull down thy vanity / Thou art a beaten dog beneath the hail, / A swollen magpie in a fitful sun, / Half black half white / Not knowst'ou wing from tail / Pull down thy vanity. [*Cantos*, LXXXI]

9 Bah! I have sung women in three cities, / But it is all the same; / And I will sing of the sun. ['Cino']

10 O how hideous it is / To see three generations of one house gathered together! / It is like an old tree with shoots, / And with some branches rotted and falling. ['Commission']

11 Nay, whatever comes / One hour was sunlit and the most high gods / May not make boast of any better thing / Than to have watched that hour as it passed. ['Erat Hora']

12 Free us for we perish / In this ever-flowing monotony / Of ugly print marks, black / Upon white parchment. ['The Eyes']

13 Come, let us pity those who are better off than we are. / Come, my friend, and remember that the rich have butlers and no friends, / And we have friends and no butlers. / Come, let us pity the married and unmarried. ['The Garret']

14 I'd seen a lot of his lot... / ever since Rhodez, / Coming down from the fair / of St. John, / With caravans, but never an ape or a bear. ['The Gypsy']

15 For three years, out of key with his time, / He strove to resuscitate the dead art / Of poetry. [*Hugh Selwyn Mauberley*]

16 His true Penelope was Flaubert, / He fished by obstinate isles; / Observed the elegance of Circe's hair / Rather than the mottoes on sun-dials. [Ib.]

17 Caliban casts out Ariel. [Ib.]

18 For an old bitch gone in the teeth, / For a botched civilization. [Ib.]

19 And give up verse, my boy, / there's nothing in it. [Ib.]

20 The apparition of these faces in the crowd; / Petals on a wet, black bough. ['In a Station of the Metro']

21 When I carefully consider the curious habits of dogs / I am compelled to conclude / That man is the superior animal. / When I consider the curious habits of man / I confess, my friend, I am puzzled. ['Meditatio']

22 So many thousand fair are gone down to Avernus, / Ye might let one remain above with us. ['Prayer for his Lady's Life']

23 O generation of the thoroughly smug and thoroughly uncomfortable. ['Salutation']

24 Come, my songs, let us speak of perfection — / We shall get ourselves rather disliked. ['Salvationists']

25 Will people accept them? / (i.e. these songs). / As a timorous wench from a centaur / (or a centurion), / Already they flee, howling in terror. ['Tenzone']

1 Wining the ghosts of yester-year. ['Villonaud for this Yule']

2 Literature is news that STAYS news. [*ABC of Reading*]

3 Great Literature is simply language charged with meaning to the utmost possible degree. [*How to Read*]

Powell, Enoch (1912-)

4 As I look ahead I am filled with foreboding. Like the Roman I seem to see 'The River Tiber foaming with much blood.' [Speech, 1968]

Praed, W.M. (1802-1839)

5 My own Araminta, say 'No!' ['A Letter of Advice']

6 For all who understood admired, / And some who did not understand them. ['The Vicar']

Prayer, Book of Common

7 Dearly beloved brethren, the Scripture moveth us in sundry places to acknowledge and confess our manifold sins and wickedness. [Morning Prayer, first words]

8 We have erred and strayed from thy ways like lost sheep...We have left undone those things which we ought to have done; And we have done those things which we ought not to have done; And there is no health in us...A godly, righteous and sober life. [Ib. General Confession]

9 And forgive us our trespasses, As we forgive them that trespass against us. [Ib. The Lord's Prayer]

10 As it was in the beginning, is now, and ever shall be; world without end. Amen. [Gloria]

11 An infinite Majesty. [Te Deum Laudamus]

12 The noble army of martyrs. [Ib.]

13 O let the Earth bless the Lord: yea, let it praise him, and magnify him for ever. [Benedicite]

14 I believe in God the Father Almighty, Maker of heaven and earth: And in Jesus Christ his only Son our Lord, Who was conceived by the Holy Ghost, Born of the Virgin Mary, Suffered under Pontius Pilate, Was crucified, dead and buried, He descended into hell; The third day he rose again from the dead, He ascended into heaven, And sitteth on the right hand of God the Father Almighty; From thence he shall come to judge the quick and the dead. [The Apostles' Creed]

15 Give peace in our time, O Lord. / Because there is none other that fighteth for us, but only thou, O God. [Versicles]

16 The author of peace and lover of concord, in knowledge of whom standeth our eternal life, whose service is perfect freedom. [Second Collect, for Peace]

17 In Quires and Places where they sing. [Rubric after Third Collect]

18 That peace which the world cannot give. [Evening Prayer, Second Collect]

19 Lighten our darkness, we beseech thee, O Lord; and by thy great mercy defend us from all perils and dangers of this night. [Third Collect]

20 Have mercy upon us miserable sinners. [The Litany]

21 Deceits of the world, the flesh and the devil. [Ib.]

22 The fruits of the Spirit. [Ib.]

23 All sorts and conditions of men...all who profess and call themselves Christians. [Prayers and Thanksgivings upon Several Occasions]

24 Give us grace that we may cast away the works of darkness, and put upon us the armour of light. [Collects, 1st Sunday in Advent]

25 Hear them, read, mark, learn and inwardly digest them. [Ib. 2nd Sunday in Advent]

26 The glory that shall be revealed. [Ib. St. Stephen's Day]

27 The author and giver of all good things. [Ib. 7th Sunday after Trinity]

1 Serve thee with a quiet mind. [Ib. 21st Sunday after Trinity]

2 Stir up, we beseech, O Lord, the wills of thy faithful people; that they, plenteously bringing forth the fruit of good works, may of thee be plenteously rewarded. [Ib. 25th Sunday after Trinity]

3 Whom truly to know is everlasting life. [Ib. St. Philip and St. James's Day]

4 An open and notorious evil liver. [Holy Communion. Introductory Rubric]

5 Truly repented and amended his former naughty life. [Ib.]

6 Almighty God, unto whom all hearts be open, and from whom no secrets are hid; Cleanse the thoughts of our hearts by the inspiration of thy Holy Spirit. [Ib. Collect]

7 The peace of God, which passeth all understanding. [Nicene Creed, The Blessing]

8 Ye that do truly and earnestly repent you of your sins, and are in love and charity with your neighbours, and intend to lead a new life...Draw near with faith. [Ib. The Invitation]

9 It is very meet, right, and our bounden duty, that we should at all times, and in all places, give thanks unto thee, O Lord. [Ib. Hymn of Praise]

10 If any of you know cause, or just impediment, why these two persons should not be joined together in holy Matrimony, ye are to declare it. This is the first time of asking. [Solemnization of Matrimony, The Banns]

11 Dearly beloved, we are gathered together here in the sight of God, and in the face of this congregation, to join together this Man and this Woman in holy Matrimony. [Ib. Exhortation]

12 Let him now speak, or else hereafter forever hold his peace. [Ib.]

13 Wilt thou love her, comfort her, honour, and keep her in sickness and in health; and, forsaking all other, keep thee only unto her, so long as ye both shall live? [Ib. Betrothal]

14 To have and to hold from this day forward, for better for worse, for richer for poorer, in sickness and in health, to love and to cherish, till death us do part, according to God's holy ordinance; and thereto I plight thee my troth. [Ib.]

15 To love, cherish and to obey. [Ib.]

16 With this Ring I thee wed, with my body I thee worship, and with all my worldly goods I thee endow. [Ib. Wedding]

17 Those whom God hath joined together let no man put asunder. [Ib. The Prayer]

18 Consented together in holy wedlock. [Ib. Priest's Declaration]

19 Peace be to this house, and to all that dwell in it. [Visitation of the Sick]

20 In the midst of life we are in death. [Burial of the Dead, First Anthem]

21 We therefore commit his body to the ground; earth to earth, ashes to ashes, dust to dust; in sure and certain hope of the Resurrection to eternal life. [Ib. Interment]

22 We therefore commit his body to the deep, to be turned into corruption, looking for the resurrection of the body (when the sea shall give up her dead). [Forms of Prayer to be Used at Sea. At the Burial of their Dead at Sea]

23 Of Works of Supererogation. [Articles of Religion, 14]

Preston, Keith (1884–1927)

24 [Of democracy] An institution in which the whole is equal to the scum of all the parts. [*Pot Shots from Pegasus*]

Prior, Matthew (1664–1721)

25 Dear Cloe, how blubber'd is that pretty face! ['A Better Answer']

26 I court others in verse: but I love thee in prose: / And they have my whimsies, but thou hast my heart. [Ib.]

27 The merchant, to secure his treasure, / Conveys it in a borrowed name: / Euphelia serves to grace my measure; / But Chloe is my real flame. ['An Ode']

1 No, no, for my virginity, / When I lose that, says Rose, I'll die; / Behind the elms last night, cry'd Dick, / Rose, were you not extremely sick? ['A True Mind']

Procter, Adelaide (1825–1864)

2 Seated one day at the organ, / I was weary and ill at ease, / And my fingers wandered idly / Over the noisy keys. ['A Lost Chord']

3 But I struck one chord of music, / Like the sound of a great Amen. [Ib.]

Propertius, Sextus Aurelius (fl. 50 B.C.)

4 *Cedite Romani scriptores, cedite Grai! / Nescioquid maius nascitur Iliade.* Give way, Roman writers, give way, Greeks! Something greater than the Iliad is born. [*Elegies*, II]

5 *Magnum iter ascendo, sed dat mihi gloria vires.* The road is hard to climb, but glory gives me strength. [Ib. IV]

Protagoras (c. 485–c. 410 B.C.)

6 Man is the measure of all things. [Fragment]

Proudhon, Pierre-Joseph (1809–1865)

7 If I were asked to answer the following question: 'What is slavery?' and I should answer in one word, 'Murder!' my meaning would be understood at once. No further argument would be required to show that the power to take from a man his thought, his will, his personality, is a power of life and death, and that to enslave a man is to kill him. Why, then, to this other question: 'What is property?' may I not likewise answer 'Theft'? [*Qu'est-ce que la Propriété?*]

Proust, Marcel (1871–1922)

8 For a long time I used to go to bed early. [*A la Recherche du Temps Perdu, Du côté de chez Swann*, I, 1, first sentence; trans. Scott-Moncrieff]

9 The true paradises are paradises we have lost. [Ib. *Le Temps Retrouvé*, I, 1]

10 *Impossible venir, mensonge suit.* Cannot come, lie follows. [Ib.]

Pudney, John (1909–1977)

11 Do not despair / For Johnny head-in-air; / He sleeps as sound / As Johnny underground. ['For Johnny']

Pulteney, William, Earl of Bath (1684–1764)

12 Since twelve honest men have decided the cause, / And were judges of fact, tho' not judges of laws. ['The Honest Jury']

Punch

13 Advice to persons about to marry — 'Don't!' [1845]

14 What is better than presence of mind in a railway accident? Absence of body. [1849]

15 Never do to-day what you can put off till tomorrow. [1849]

16 'Who's 'im, Bill?' 'A stranger!' ''Eave 'arf a brick at 'im.' [1854]

17 Mun, a had na' been the-erre abune two hours when — *bang* — went saxpence!!! [1868]

18 Cats is 'dogs' and rabbits is 'dogs' and so's Parrats, but this 'ere 'Tortis' is an insect, and there ain't no charge for it. [1869]

19 Go directly — see what she's doing, and tell her she mustn't. [1872]

20 It's worse than wicked, my dear, it's vulgar. [1876]

21 I used your soap two years ago; since then I have used no other. [1884]

22 'I'm afraid you've got a bad egg, Mr. Jones.' 'Oh no, my Lord, I assure you!' Parts of it are excellent! [1895]

23 Look here, Steward, if this is coffee, I want tea; but if this is tea, then I wish for coffee. [1902]

Putnam, Israel (1718–1790)

24 Men, you are all marksmen — don't one of you fire until you see the whites of their eyes. [At the Battle of Bunker Hill, 1775]

Pyrrhus (319–272 B.C.)

25 [After a hard-won battle] Another such victory and we are lost. [Plutarch, *Life*]

Quarles, Francis (1592–1644)

1 Be wisely worldly, not worldly wise. [*Emblems*, II, 2]

2 The road to resolution lies by doubt: / The next way home's the farthest way about. [Ib. IV, 2]

3 My soul, sit thou a patient looker-on; / Judge not the play before the play is done: / Her plot has many changes; every day / Speaks a new scene; the last act crowns the play. ['Respice Finem']

4 Physicians of all men are most happy; what success soever they have, the world proclaimeth, and what faults they commit, the earth covereth. [*Hieroglyphics of the Life of Man*]

Quesnay, François (1694–1774)

5 [Of government interference] *Laissez faire, laissez passer*. Leave it alone, and let it happen. [Attr.]

Quiller-Couch, Sir Arthur (1863–1944)

6 He that loves but half of Earth / Loves but half enough for me. ['The Comrade']

7 The lion is the beast to fight: / He leaps along the plain, / And if you run with all your might, / He runs with all his mane. ['Sage Counsel']

8 The best is the best, though a hundred judges have declared it so. [*Oxford Book of English Verse*, Preface]

Quincy, Josiah (1772–1864)

9 As it will be the right of all, so it will be the duty of some, definitely to prepare for a separation, amicably if they can, violently if they must. [Speech on states' rights, 1811]

Quintilian (A.D. 42–118)

10 A liar should have a good memory. [*De Institutio Oratoria*]

Rabelais, François (c. 1494–1553)

11 *L'appétit vient en mangeant*. The appetite comes with eating. [*Gargantua*]

12 *Natura vacuum abhorret*. Nature abhors a vacuum. [Ib.]

13 *Fais ce que voudras*. Do what you will. [Ib.]

14 *Tirez le rideau, la farce est jouée*. Draw the curtain, the farce is over. [Attr. last words]

15 *Je m'en vais chercher un grand peut-être*. I go to seek a great perhaps. [Attr. last words]

Racine, Jean (1639–1699)

16 *Elle s'endormit du sommeil des justes*. She slept the sleep of the just. [*Abrégé de l'Histoire de Port Royal*]

17 *C'était pendant l'horreur d'une profonde nuit*. It was during the horror of a profoundly dark night. [*Athalie*, II]

18 *Elle flotte, elle hésite; en un mot, elle est femme*. She wavers, she hesitates, in a word, she is a woman. [Ib. III]

19 *C'est toi qui l'a nommé*. You have named him, not I. [*Phèdre*, I]

20 *Tel qui rit vendredi, dimanche pleurera*. He who laughs on Friday will weep on Sunday. [*Les Plaideurs*, I]

Rainborowe, Thomas (d. 1648)

21 The poorest he that is in England hath a life to live as the greatest he. [Speech in Army debates, 1647]

Raleigh, Sir Walter (c. 1552–1618)

22 If all the world and love were young, / And truth in every shepherd's tongue, / These pretty pleasures might me move / To live with thee, and be thy love. ['The Nymph's Reply to the Shepherd']

23 Only we die in earnest, that's no jest. ['On the Life of Man']

24 Give me my scallop-shell of quiet, / My staff of faith to walk upon, / My scrip of joy, immortal diet, / My bottle of salvation, / My gown of glory, hope's true gage, / And thus I'll make my pilgrimage. ['The Passionate Man's Pilgrimage']

25 Fain would I climb, yet fear I to fall. [Written on a window-pane]

1 O eloquent, just and mighty Death!...thou hast drawn together all the far-stretched greatness, all the pride, cruelty, and ambition of man, and covered it all over with these two narrow words, *Hic jacet*. [*History of the World*, V]

Raleigh, Sir Walter A. (1861-1922)

2 I wish I loved the Human Race; / I wish I loved its silly face; / I wish I liked the way it walks; / I wish I liked the way it talks; / And when I'm introduced to one, / I wish I thought *What Jolly Fun!* ['Wishes of an Elderly Man']

Ramsay, Allan (1686-1758)

3 Ane canna wive an' thrive baith in ae year. [*Scots Proverbs*]

4 A Scots mist will weet an Englishman to the skin. [Ib.]

5 Better a finger aff than aye wagging. [Ib.]

Rankin, J.E. (1828-1904)

6 God be with you till we meet again. [Hymn]

Ransome, Arthur (1884-1967)

7 BETTER DROWNED THAN DUFFERS IF NOT DUFFERS WONT DROWN. [*Swallows and Amazons*, 1]

Rattigan, Terence (1911-1977)

8 You can be in the Horse Guards and still be common, dear. [*Separate Tables*]

9 A nice, respectable, middle-class, middle-aged maiden lady, with time on her hands and the money to help her pass it...Let us call her Aunt Edna...Aunt Edna is universal, and to those who might feel that all the problems of the modern theatre might be solved by her liquidation, let me add that...she is also immortal. [*Collected Plays*, II, 'Preface']

Reade, Charles (1814-1884)

10 *Courage, mon ami, le diable est mort.* Courage, my friend, the devil is dead. [*The Cloister and the Hearth*, 24]

11 Make 'em laugh; make 'em cry; make 'em wait. [Attr. programme for serial novel]

Reed, Henry (1914-1986)

12 As we get older we do not get any younger. / Seasons return, and today I am fifty-five, / And this time last year I was fifty-four, / And this time next year I shall be sixty-two. ['Chard Whitlow', parody of T.S. Eliot]

13 It is, we believe, / Idle to hope that the simple stirrup-pump / Will extinguish hell. [Ib.]

14 To-day we have naming of parts. Yesterday / We had daily cleaning. And tomorrow morning, / We shall have what to do after firing. But to-day, / To-day we have naming of parts. ['Naming of Parts']

Reed, John (1887-1920)

15 Ten Days that Shook the World [Title of book on October Revolution in Russia]

Remarque, Erich Maria (1898-1970)

16 *Im Westen nichts Neues.* All Quiet on the Western Front [Title of book]

Renan, J. Ernest (1823-1892)

17 O Lord, if there is a Lord, save my soul, if I have a soul. ['A Sceptic's Prayer']

Rendall, Montague John (1862-1950)

18 Nation shall speak peace unto nation. [Motto of BBC]

Reuben, David (1933-)

19 Everything You've Always Wanted to Know About Sex, But Were Afraid to Ask. [Title of book and film]

Reynolds, Frederic (1765-1841)

20 How goes the enemy? [Said by Mr. Ennui, 'the time-killer'] [*The Dramatist*, I]

Reynolds, Sir Joshua (1723–1792)

1 If you have great talents, industry will improve them: if you have but moderate abilities, industry will supply their deficiency. [*Discourses*, 2]

2 A mere copier of nature can never produce anything great. [Ib. 3]

Rhodes, Cecil John (1853–1902)

3 The unctuous rectitude of my countrymen. [Speech, 1896]

4 So little done, so much to do! [Attr. last words]

Rhondda, Viscountess (1883–1958)

5 Women must come off the pedestal. Men put us up there to get us out of the way. [*Observer*, 'Sayings of the Week', 1920]

Rice, Sir Stephen (1637–1715)

6 I will drive a coach and six horses through the Act of Settlement. [Attr.]

Rice-Davies, Mandy (1944–)

7 He would, wouldn't he? [Remark during Profumo Affair, 1963, when told that her allegations of sexual intimacy had been denied]

Richard I (1157-1199)

8 *Dieu et mon droit.* God and my right. [Attr. 1198]

9 Lord, I pray Thee to suffer me not to see Thy Holy City, since I cannot deliver it from the hands of Thy enemies. [Attr. remark on sight of Jerusalem]

Richardson, Samuel (1689–1761)

10 She [my mother] says, I am too witty; Anglicè too pert; I, that she is too wise; that is to say, being likewise put into English, not so young as she has been. [*Clarissa*, II]

11 Desert and reward, I can assure her, seldom keep company. [Ib. IV]

12 Pity is but one remove from love. [*Sir Charles Grandison*, I]

13 That's the beauty of it; to offend and make up at pleasure. [Ib. III]

Rilke, Rainer Maria (1875–1926)

14 *So leben wir und nehmen immer Abschied.* Thus we live, forever saying farewell. [*Duino Elegies*, 8]

Ripley, R.L. (1893–1949)

15 Believe it or not. [Title of newspaper feature]

Roche, Sir Boyle (1743–1807)

16 What has posterity done for us? [Speech, 1780]

17 Mr. Speaker, I smell a rat; I see him forming in the air and darkening the sky; but I'll nip him in the bud. [Attr.]

Rochester, John Wilmot, Earl of (1647–1680)

18 The best good man, with the worst-natur'd muse. ['An Allusion to Horace']

19 Here lies our sovereign lord the King / Whose word no man relies on, / Who never said a foolish thing, / Nor ever did a wise one. [Epitaph written for Charles II; *see* Charles II, 'This is very true...']

20 Reason, an *ignus fatuus* of the mind. [Satire against Mankind]

21 Huddled in dirt the reasoning engine lies, / Who was so proud, so witty and so wise. [Ib.]

22 A merry monarch, scandalous and poor. ['Satire on King Charles II']

23 Love a woman? You're an ass. ['Song']

24 Ancient person, for whom I / All the flattering youth defy, / Long be it ere thou grow old, / Aching, shaking, crazy, cold; / But still continue as thou art, / Ancient person of my heart. ['Song of a Young Lady to her Ancient Lover']

Rogers, Samuel (1763–1855)

25 Think nothing done while aught remains to do. [*Human Life*]

26 Never less alone than when alone, / Those whom he loved so long and sees no more, / Loved and still loves — not dead — but gone before, / He gathers round him. [Ib.]

27 Many a temple half as old as time. [*Italy. A Farewell*]

1 When a new book is published, read an old one. [Attr.]

Rogers, Will (1879–1935)

2 You can't say civilization don't advance, however, for in every war they kill you a new way. [*Autobiography*]

3 Half our life is spent trying to find something to do with the time we have rushed through life trying to save. [Ib.]

4 I never met a man I didn't like. [Address, 1930]

5 Everything is funny as long as it is happening to someone else. [*The Illiterate Digest*]

6 The movies are the only business where you can go out front and applaud yourself. [Quoted in Halliwell, *Filmgoer's Book of Quotes*]

7 So live that you wouldn't be ashamed to sell the family parrot to the town gossip. [Attr.]

8 I don't make jokes — I just watch the government and report the facts. [Attr.]

Roland, Madame (1754–1793)

9 *O liberté! que de crimes on commet en ton nom!* O liberty! what crimes are committed in thy name! [Remark on mounting the scaffold]

10 The more I see of men, the better I like dogs. [Attr.]

Ronsard, Pierre (1524–1585)

11 *Quand vous serez bien vieille, au soir à la chandelle, / Assise auprès du feu, dévidant et filant, / Direz, chantant mes vers, en vous émerveillant, / Ronsard me célébrait du temps que j'étais belle.* When you are very old, and sit in the candle-light at evening, spinning by the fire, you will say, as you murmur my verses, wonder in your eyes, 'Ronsard sang of me in the days when I was fair.' [*Sonnets pour Hélène*]

Roosevelt, Franklin Delano (1882–1945)

12 I confess to pride in this coming generation. You are working out your own salvation; you are more in love with life; you play with fire openly, where we did in secret, and few of you are burned! [Address, 1926]

13 To stand upon the ramparts and die for our principles is heroic, but to sally forth to battle and win for our principles is something more than heroic. [Speech, 1928]

14 I pledge you — I pledge myself — to a new deal for the American people. [Speech, 1932]

15 The only thing we have to fear is fear itself. [First Inaugural Address, 1933]

16 We have always known that heedless self-interest was bad morals; we know now that it is bad economics. [Ib.]

17 I would dedicate this nation to the policy of the good neighbour. [Ib.]

18 I see one-third of a nation ill-housed, ill-clad, ill-nourished. [Second Inaugural Address, 1937]

19 A radical is a man with both feet firmly planted in the air. [Radio broadcast, 1939]

20 We must be the great arsenal of democracy. [Radio broadcast, 1940]

21 I ask you to judge me by the enemies I have made. [*Observer*, 'Sayings of the Week', 1932]

Roosevelt, Theodore (1858–1919)

22 Men who form the lunatic fringe in all reform movements. [*Autobiography*]

23 Gospel of spilt milk. [*The Great Adventure*]

24 We have room in this country for but one flag, the Stars and Stripes...We have room for but one loyalty, loyalty to the United States...We have room for but one language, the English language. [Ib.]

25 Hyphenated Americans. [*Metropolitan Magazine*, 1915]

1 No man is justified in doing evil on the ground of expediency. [*The Strenuous Life*]

2 If I must choose between peace and righteousness, I choose righteousness. [*Unwise Peace Treaties*]

3 The poorest way to face life is to face it with a sneer. [Speech]

4 There can be no fifty-fifty Americanism in this country. There is room here for only hundred per cent Americanism, only for those who are Americans and nothing else. [Speech, Saratoga]

5 I wish to preach not the doctrine of ignoble ease, but the doctrine of the strenuous life. [Speech, 1899]

6 The first requisite of a good citizen in this republic of ours is that he shall be able and willing to pull his weight. [Speech, 1902]

7 A man who is good enough to shed his blood for the country is good enough to be given a square deal afterwards. More than that no man is entitled to, and less than that no man shall have. [Speech, 1903]

8 No man needs sympathy because he has to work...Far and away the best prize that life offers is the chance to work hard at work worth doing. [Address, 1903]

9 If I have erred, I err in company with Abraham Lincoln. [Speech, 1912]

10 Nine-tenths of wisdom is being wise in time. [Speech, 1917]

11 I want to see you shoot the way you shout. [Speech, 1917]

12 Don't hit at all if it is honourably possible to avoid hitting; but *never* hit soft! [J.B. Bishop, *Theodore Roosevelt*]

13 It is better to be faithful than famous. [Riis, *Theodore Roosevelt, the Citizen*]

14 The most successful politician is he who says what everybody is thinking most often and in the loudest voice. [Quoted in Andrews, *Treasury of Humorous Quotations*]

15 Speak softly and carry a big stick. [Attr.]

Roscommon, Earl of (1633–1685)

16 Choose an author as you choose a friend. [*Essay on Translated Verse*]

17 Immodest words admit of no defence, / For want of decency is want of sense. [Ib.]

Rosebery, Earl of (1847–1929)

18 It is beginning to be hinted that we are a nation of amateurs. [Speech, 1900]

19 I must plough my furrow alone. [Speech, 1901]

Ross, Alan C. (1907–1980)

20 U and Non-U. [Title of essay]

Ross, Sir Ronald (1857–1932)

21 [Malaria] O million-murdering Death. [*In Exile*]

Rossetti, Christina Georgina (1830–1894)

22 This downhill path is easy, but there's no turning back. ['Amor Mundi']

23 'Come cheer up, my lads, 'tis to glory we steer' — / As the soldier remarked whose post lay in the rear. ['Couplet']

24 In the bleak mid-winter / Frosty wind made moan / ... In the bleak mid-winter, / Long ago. ['Mid-Winter']

25 Remember me when I am gone away, / Gone far away into the silent land. ['Remember']

26 Better by far you should forget and smile / Than you should remember and be sad. [Ib.]

27 Silence more musical than any song. ['Rest']

28 When I am dead, my dearest, / Sing no sad songs for me. ['When I am Dead']

29 And if thou wilt, remember, / And if thou wilt, forget. [Ib.]

30 Does the road wind up-hill all the way? / Yes, to the very end. / Will the day's journey take the whole long day? / From morn to night, my friend. ['Up-Hill']

Rossetti, Dante Gabriel (1828–1882)

1 Was it a friend or foe that spread these lies? / Nay, who but infants question in such wise? / 'Twas one of my most intimate enemies. ['Fragment']

2 A sonnet is a moment's monument, — / Memorial from the Soul's eternity / To one dead deathless hour. [*The House of Life,* I, Introduction]

3 I do not see them here; but after death / God knows I know the faces I shall see, / Each one a murdered self. [Ib. II, 'Lost Days']

4 Sleepless with cold commemorative eyes. [Ib. 'A Superscription']

5 When vain desire at last and vain regret / Go hand in hand to death. [Ib. 'The One Hope']

6 Teach the unforgetful to forget. [Ib.]

7 I have been here before, / But when or how I cannot tell: / I know the grass beyond the door, / The sweet keen smell, / The sighing sound, the lights around the shore. ['Sudden Light']

8 The sea hath no king but God alone. ['The White Ship']

9 Conception, my boy, *fundamental brainwork,* is what makes the difference in all art. [Letter]

10 The worst moment for the atheist is when he is really thankful and has nobody to thank. [Attr. Also attr. to Wendy Ward]

Rossini, Gioacchino (1792–1868)

11 Wagner has lovely moments but awful quarters of an hour. [Remark, 1867]

12 Give me a laundry-list and I will set it to music. [Attr.]

Roth, Philip (1933–)

13 So (said the doctor). Now vee may perhaps to begin. Yes? [*Portnoy's Complaint,* last words]

Rouget de Lisle, Claude-Joseph (1760–1836)

14 *Allons, enfants de la patrie, / Le jour de gloire est arrivé.* Come, children of this country, the day of glory is here. ['La Marseillaise']

15 *Aux armes, citoyens!* To arms, citizens! [Ib.]

Rousseau, Jean-Jacques (1712–1778)

16 *L'homme est né libre, et partout il est dans les fers.* Man is born free, and everywhere is in chains. [*Du Contrat Social*]

17 The English people imagine themselves to be free, but they are wrong: it is only during the election of members of parliament that they are so. [Ib.]

Roux, Joseph (1834–1886)

18 Science is for those who learn; poetry, for those who know. [*Meditations of a Parish Priest,* 1]

19 We love justice greatly, and just men but little. [Ib. 4]

20 The egoist does not tolerate egoism. [Ib. 9]

Rowe, Nicholas (1674–1718)

21 At length the morn and cold indifference came. [*The Fair Penitent,* I.1]

22 Is this that haughty, gallant, gay Lothario? [Ib. V.1]

23 Like Helen, in the night when Troy was sack'd, / Spectatress of the mischief which she made. [Ib.]

24 Death is the privilege of human nature, / And life without it were not worth our taking. [Ib.]

Rowland, Helen (1875–1950)

25 Before marriage, a man will lie awake thinking about something you said; after marriage, he'll fall asleep before you finish saying it. [Quoted in Cowan, *The Wit of Women*]

Runyon, Damon (1884–1946)

26 Her stomach thinks her throat is cut. ['Little Miss Marker']

1 Nicely-Nicely is known far and wide as a character who dearly loves to commit eating. ['Lonely Heart']

2 Always try to rub up against money, for if you rub up against money long enough, some of it may rub off on you. ['A Very Honourable Guy']

Rusk, Dean (1909-)

3 We're eye-ball to eye-ball and the other fellow just blinked. [Remark on Cuban crisis, 1962]

Ruskin, John (1819-1900)

4 [Of a painting by Whistler] I have seen, and heard, much of Cockney impudence before now; but never expected to hear a coxcomb ask two hundred guineas for flinging a pot of paint in the public's face. [*Fors Clavigera*, 79]

5 All violent feelings...produce in us a falseness in all our impressions of external things, which I would generally characterize as the 'Pathetic Fallacy'. [*Modern Painters*, III]

6 Mountains are the beginning and the end of all natural scenery. [Ib. IV]

7 If a book is worth reading, it is worth buying. [*Sesame and Lilies*]

8 How long most people would look at the best book before they would give the price of a large turbot for it! [Ib.]

9 I believe the right question to ask, respecting all ornament, is simply this: Was it done with enjoyment — was the carver happy while he was about it? [*The Seven Lamps of Architecture*, 5]

10 When we build, let us think that we build for ever. [Ib. 6]

11 Not only is there but one way of *doing* things rightly, but there is only one way of *seeing* them, and that is, seeing the whole of them. [*The Two Paths*, 2]

12 It ought to be quite as natural and straightforward a matter for a labourer to take his pension from his parish, because he has deserved well of his parish, as for a man in higher rank to take his pension from his country, because he has deserved well of his country. [*Unto this Last*, Preface]

13 Government and cooperation are in all things the laws of life; anarchy and competition, the laws of death. [Ib. 3]

14 Whereas it has long been known and declared that the poor have no right to the property of the rich, I wish it also to be known and declared that the rich have no right to the property of the poor. [Ib.]

15 There is no wealth but life. [Ib. 4]

16 There is really no such thing as bad weather, only different kinds of good weather. [Attr.]

Russell, Bertrand (1872-1970)

17 Aristotle maintained that women have fewer teeth than men; although he was twice married, it never occurred to him to verify this statement by examining his wives' mouths. [*The Impact of Science on Society*]

18 America...where law and custom alike are based upon the dreams of spinsters. [*Marriage and Morals*]

19 It is undesirable to believe a proposition when there is no ground whatever for supposing it true. [*Sceptical Essays*]

20 Every man, wherever he goes, is encompassed by a cloud of comforting convictions, which move with him like flies on a summer day. [Ib.]

21 Machines are worshipped because they are beautiful, and valued because they confer power; they are hated because they are hideous, and loathed because they impose slavery. [Ib.]

Russell, Lord John (1792-1878)

22 If peace cannot be maintained with honour, it is no longer peace. [Speech, 1853]

23 Among the defects of the Bill, which were numerous, one provision was conspicuous by its presence and another by its absence. [Speech, 1859]

Russell, Sir William Howard (1820–1907)

1 [Of the 93rd Highlanders at the Battle of Balaclava] That thin red line tipped with steel. [*The British Expedition to the Crimea*]

Ryle, Gilbert (1900–1976)

2 The dogma of the Ghost in the Machine. [*The Concept of Mind*]

Saikaku, Ihara (1642–1693)

3 Marrying off your daughter is a piece of business you may expect to do only once in a lifetime, and, bearing in mind that none of the losses are recoverable later, you should approach the matter with extreme caution. [*Nippon Eitai-gura*]

4 And why do people wilfully exhaust their strength in promiscuous living, when their wives are on hand from bridal night till old age — to be taken when required, like fish from a private pond. [Ib.]

Sainte-Beuve, Charles-Augustin (1804–1869)

5 *Le silence seul est le souverain mépris.* Silence is the supreme contempt. ['Mes Poisons']

6 *Et Vigny plus secret, / Comme en sa tour d'ivoire, avant midi rentrait.* And Vigny more secretive, as if in his ivory tower, returned before noon. ['Pensées d'Août']

Saki (1870–1916)

7 But, good gracious, you've got to educate him first. You can't expect a boy to be vicious till he's been to a good school. ['The Baker's Dozen']

8 I believe I once considerably scandalized her by declaring that clear soup was a more important factor in life than a clear conscience. ['The Blind Spot']

9 A little inaccuracy sometimes saves tons of explanation. ['The Comments of Maung Ka']

10 Waldo is one of those people who would be enormously improved by death. ['The Feast of Nemesis']

11 In baiting a mouse-trap with cheese, always leave room for the mouse. ['The Infernal Parliament']

12 He's simply got the instinct for being unhappy highly developed. ['The Match-Maker']

13 Oysters are more beautiful than any religion...There's nothing in Christianity or Buddhism that quite matches the sympathetic unselfishness of an oyster. [Ib.]

14 People may say what they like about the decay of Christianity; the religious system that produced green Chartreuse can never really die. ['Reginald on Christmas Presents']

15 The cook was a good cook, as cooks go; and as cooks go she went. ['Reginald on Besetting Sins']

16 Women and elephants never forget an injury. [Ib.]

17 The Western custom of one wife and hardly any mistresses. ['A Young Turkish Catastrophe']

Salisbury, Robert Cecil, Lord (1830–1903)

18 We are part of the community of Europe and we must do our duty as such. [Speech, 1888]

19 Our first duty is towards the people of this country, to maintain their interests and their rights; our second duty is to all humanity. [Speech, 1896]

20 By office boys for office boys. [Remark about the *Daily Mail*]

Sallust (86–34 B.C.)

21 *Alieni appetens, sui profusus.* Greedy for others' possessions, prodigal of his own. [*Catiline*, 5]

22 *Idem velle atque idem nolle, ea demum firma amicitia est.* To like and dislike the same things, that is indeed true friendship. [Ib. 20]

23 *Saltare elegantius, quam necesse est probae.* She could dance more skilfully than a virtuous woman need. [Ib. 25]

24 *Pro patria, pro liberis, pro aris atque focis suis.* For country, their children, their altars, and their hearths. [Ib. 59]

1 *Dux atque imperator vitae mortalium animus est.* The soul is the captain and ruler of the life of mortals. [*Jugurtha*, 1]

2 *Punica fide.* With Carthaginian faith [i.e. treachery]. [Ib. 35]

3 It is always easy to begin a war, but very difficult to stop one, since its beginning and end are not under the control of the same man. [Ib. 83]

Salvandy, Narcisse Achille (1795–1856)

4 *Nous dansons sur un volcan.* We are dancing on a volcano. [Remark before revolution of 1830]

Sandburg, Carl (1878–1967)

5 The fog comes / on little cat feet. ['Fog']

6 Sometime they'll give a war and nobody will come. ['The People, Yes']

Santayana, George (1863–1952)

7 Those who cannot remember the past are condemned to repeat it. [*The Life of Reason*, I]

8 Fanaticism consists in redoubling your effort when you have forgotten your aim. [Ib.]

9 Nothing is so poor and melancholy as art that is interested in itself and not in its subject. [Ib. IV]

10 Music is essentially useless, as life is. [*Little Essays*]

11 To be interested in the changing seasons is, in this middling zone, a happier state of mind than to be hopelessly in love with spring. [Ib.]

12 There is no cure for birth and death save to enjoy the interval. [*Soliloquies in England*]

13 It is a great advantage for a system of philosophy to be substantially true. [*The Unknowable*]

Sargent, John Singer (1856–1925)

14 Every time I paint a portrait I lose a friend. [Attr.]

Sartre, Jean-Paul (1905–1980)

15 *Mauvaise foi.* Bad faith. [*Sketch for a Theory of the Emotions*]

16 Man is condemned to be free. [*Existentialism and Humanism*]

17 Hell is other people. [*Huis clos*]

18 Three o'clock is always too late or too early for anything you want to do. [*Nausea*]

19 The writer, a free man addressing free men, has only one subjct — freedom. [*What Is Literature?*]

Sassoon, Siegfried (1886–1967)

20 If I were fierce and bald and short of breath, / I'd live with scarlet Majors at the Base, / And speed glum heroes up the line to death. ['Base Details']

21 And when the war is done and youth stone dead / I'd toddle safely home and die — in bed. [Ib.]

22 Does it matter? — losing your legs? / ...For people will always be kind. ['Does it Matter?']

23 You are too young to fall asleep for ever; / And when you sleep you remind me of the dead. ['The Dug-Out']

24 'He's a cheery old card,' grunted Harry to Jack / As they slogged up to Arras with rifle and pack.../ But he did for them both with his plan of attack. ['The General']

25 Everyone suddenly burst out singing. ['Everyone Sang']

Savage, Richard (1698–1743)

26 No tenth transmitter of a foolish face. [*The Bastard*]

Schiller, Friedrich von (1759–1805)

27 *Freude, schöner Götterfunken, / Tochter aus Elysium, / Wir betreten feuertrunken, / Himmlische, dein Heiligtum.* O Joy, lovely gift of the gods, daughter of Paradise, divinity, we are inspired as we approach your sanctuary. ['An die Freude' (set to music by Beethoven in the last movement of his Ninth Symphony)]

28 *Alle Menschen werden Brüder, / Wo dein sanfter Flügel weilt.* In the shade of your soft wings, all men will be brothers. [Ib.]

1 *Mit der Dummheit kämpfen Götter selbst vergebens.* With stupidity the very gods contend in vain. [*Die Jungfrau von Orleans,* III.6]

2 Time consecrates; / And what is grey with age becomes religion. [*Die Piccolomini,* IV]

3 *Die Weltgeschichte ist das Weltgericht.* The world's history is the world's judgement. [Lecture, 1789]

4 *Und siegt Natur, so muss die Kunst entweichen.* When Nature conquers, Art must then give way. [Remark to Goethe]

Schleiermacher, F.E.D. (1768–1834)

5 [Of a celebrated philologist] He could be silent in seven languages. [Attr.]

Schumacher, E.F. (1911–1977)

6 Small is Beautiful [Title of book]

Scott, Alexander (c. 1525–c. 1584)

7 Luve is ane fervent fire. ['Lo! What it is to Luve']

Scott, Charles Prestwich (1846–1932)

8 Comment is free but facts are sacred. [*Manchester Guardian,* 1926]

Scott, Robert Falcon (1868–1912)

9 Great God! this is an awful place [the South Pole]. [*Journal,* 17 Jan. 1912]

10 For God's sake look after our people. [Ib. 25 Mar. 1912]

11 Had we lived, I should have had a tale to tell of the hardihood, endurance, and courage of my companions which would have stirred the heart of every Englishman. These rough notes and our dead bodies must tell the tale. [Message to the Public]

Scott, Sir Walter (1771–1832)

12 To the Lords of Convention 'twas Claver'se who spoke, / 'Ere the King's crown shall fall there are crowns to be broke; / So let each cavalier who loves honour and me, / Come follow the bonnet of Bonny Dundee. / Come fill up my cup, come fill up my can, / Come saddle your horses, and call up your men; / Come open the West Port, and let me gang free, / And it's room for the bonnets of Bonny Dundee!' ['Bonny Dundee']

13 But answer came there none. [*The Bridal of Triermain*]

14 The stag at eve had drunk his fill, / Where danced the moon on Monan's rill, / And deep his midnight lair had made / In lone Glenartney's hazel shade. [*The Lady of the Lake,* I]

15 Yet seem'd that tone, and gesture bland, / Less used to sue than to command. [Ib.]

16 Soldier, rest! thy warfare o'er, / Sleep the sleep that knows not breaking, / Dream of battled fields no more, / Days of danger, nights of waking. [Ib.]

17 Hail to the Chief who in triumph advances. [Ib. II]

18 Like the dew on the mountain, / Like the foam on the river, / Like the bubble on the fountain, / Thou art gone, and for ever! [Ib. III]

19 These are Clan Alpine's warriors true; / And, Saxon, — I am Roderick Dhu! [Ib. V]

20 The stern joy which warriors feel / In foemen worthy of their steel. [Ib.]

21 The way was long, the wind was cold, / The Minstrel was infirm and old; / His wither'd cheek and tresses grey, / Seemed to have known a better day. [*The Lay of the Last Minstrel,* Introduction]

22 Love rules the court, the camp, the grove, / And men below, and saints above; / For love is heaven, and heaven is love. [Ib. III]

23 For ne'er / Was flattery lost on poet's ear: / A simple race! they waste their toil / For the vain tribute of a smile. [Ib. IV]

1 Breathes there the man, with soul so dead, / Who never to himself hath said, / This is my own, my native land! / Whose heart hath ne'er within him burned / As home his footsteps he hath turned / From wandering on a foreign strand! [Ib. VI]

2 The wretch, concentred all in self, / Living, shall forfeit fair renown, / And, doubly dying, shall go down / To the vile dust, from whence he sprung, / Unwept, unhonour'd, and unsung. [Ib.]

3 O Caledonia! stern and wild, / Meet nurse for a poetic child! / Land of brown heath and shaggy wood, / Land of the mountain and the flood. [Ib.]

4 Thus, then, my noble foe I greet: / Health and high fortune till we meet / And then — what pleases Heaven. [*Lord of the Isles*, III]

5 To that dark inn, the grave! [Ib. VI]

6 But search the land of living men, / Where wilt thou find their like agen? [*Marmion*, I]

7 And come he slow, or come he fast, / It is but Death who comes at last. [Ib. II]

8 O young Lochinvar is come out of the West / Through all the wide border his steed was the best; / And save his good broadsword, he weapons had none. / He rode all unarm'd, and he rode all alone. / So faithful in love, and so dauntless in war, / There never was knight like the young Lochinvar. [Ib. V]

9 England was merry England, when / Old Christmas brought his sports again. [Ib.]

10 O what a tangled web we weave, / When first we practise to deceive. [Ib. VI]

11 And such a yell was there, / Of sudden and portentous birth, / As if men fought upon the earth, / And fiends in upper air. [Ib.]

12 O Woman! in our hours of ease, / Uncertain, coy, and hard to please, / And variable as the shade. [Ib.]

13 The stubborn spearmen still made good / Their dark impenetrable wood, / Each stepping where his comrade stood, / The instant that he fell. [Ib.]

14 It's no fish ye're buying — it's men's lives. [*The Antiquary*, 2]

15 Look not thou on beauty's charming, — / Sit thou still when kings are arming, — / Taste not when the wine-cup glistens, — / Speak not when the people listens, — / Stop thine ear against the singer, — / From the red gold keep thy finger, — / Vacant heart and hand, and eye, — / Easy live and quiet die. [*The Bride of Lammermoor*, 3]

16 Touch not the cat but [i.e. without] a glove. [*The Fair Maid of Perth*, 34; the motto of Clan Chattan]

17 But no one shall find me rowing against the stream. I care not who knows it — I write for the general amusement. [*The Fortunes of Nigel*, Introductory Epistle]

18 The hour is come, but not the man. [*The Heart of Midlothian*, 4]

19 Jock, when ye hae naething else to do, ye may be ay sticking in a tree; it will be growing, Jock, when ye're sleeping. [Ib. 8]

20 Proud Maisie is in the wood, / Walking so early, / Sweet Robin sits in the bush, / Singing so rarely. [Ib. 40]

21 When we had a king, and a chancellor, and parliament men o' our ain, we could aye pebble them wi stanes when they werena guid bairns; but naebody's nails can reach the length o' Lunnon. [*Malachi Malagrowther*]

22 The ae half of the warld thinks the tither daft. [*Redgauntlet*, 7]

23 But with morning cool repentance came. [*Rob Roy*, 12]

24 There's a gude time coming. [Ib. 32]

25 Speak out, sir, and do not Maister or Campbell me — my foot is on my native heath, and my name is Macgregor! [Ib. 34]

1 A man may drink and not be drunk; / A man may fight and not be slain; / A man may kiss a bonny lass, / And yet be welcome home again. [*Woodstock*, 27]

2 The Big Bow-Wow strain I can do myself like any now going; but the exquisite touch, which renders ordinary commonplace things and characters interesting, from the truth of the description and the sentiment, is denied to me. [*Journal*, 1826]

3 I would like to be there, were it but to see how the cat jumps. [Ib.]

4 We shall never learn to feel and respect our real calling and destiny, unless we have taught ourselves to consider every thing as moonshine, compared with the education of the heart. [Letter, 1825]

Scriven, Joseph (1820–1886)

5 What a Friend we have in Jesus, / All our sins and griefs to bear! / What a privilege to carry / Everything to God in prayer! [Hymn]

Seaman, Sir Owen (1861–1936)

6 She must know all the needs of a rational being, / Be skilled to keep counsel, to comfort, to coax / And, above all things else, be accomplished at seeing / My jokes. ['A Plea for Trigamy']

Sedley, Sir Charles (c. 1639–1701)

7 Love still has something of the sea / From whence his mother rose. ['Love still has Something']

8 Phyllis is my only joy, / Faithless as the winds or seas; / Sometimes coming, sometimes coy, / Yet she never fails to please. ['Song']

Seeger, Alan (1888–1916)

9 I have a rendezvous with Death, / At some disputed barricade, / At midnight in some flaming town. ['I Have a Rendezvous with Death']

Seeley, Sir John Robert (1834–1895)

10 We [the English] seem as it were to have conquered and peopled half the world in a fit of absence of mind. [*The Expansion of England*]

11 History is past politics, and politics present history. [*Growth of British Policy*]

Segal, Erich (1937–)

12 Love means never having to say you're sorry. [*Love Story*]

Selden, John (1584–1654)

13 Old friends are best. King James used to call for his old shoes; for they were easiest for his feet. [*Table Talk*, 'Friends']

14 Ignorance of the law excuses no man; not that all men know the law, but because 'tis an excuse every man will plead, and no man can tell how to confute him. [Ib. 'Law']

15 There never was a merry world since the fairies left off dancing, and the Parson left conjuring. [Ib. 'Parson']

16 There is not anything in the world so much abused as this sentence, *Salus populi suprema lex esto.* [Let public safety be the supreme law] [Ib. 'People']

17 Philosophy is nothing but discretion. [Ib. 'Philosophy']

18 Preachers say, Do as I say, not as I do. [Ib. 'Preaching']

Selfridge, H. Gordon (1858–1947)

19 The customer is always right. [Shop slogan]

Sellar, Walter Carruthers (1898–1951) and Yeatman, Robert Julian (1897–1968)

20 1066, And All That. [Title of book]

21 The Roman Conquest was, however, a *Good Thing*. [*1066, And All That*]

22 The Venomous Bead (author of *The Rosary*). [Ib.]

23 The Cavaliers (Wrong but Wromantic) and the Roundheads (Right but Repulsive). [Ib.]

1 The National Debt is a very Good Thing and it would be dangerous to pay it off for fear of Political Economy. [Ib.]

2 Napoleon's armies always used to march on their stomachs, shouting: 'Vive l'Intérieur!' [Ib.]

3 A Bad Thing: America was thus clearly top nation, and History came to a   [Ib.]

Seneca (c. 4 B.C.–A.D. 65)

4 There can be slain / No sacrifice to God more acceptable / Than an unjust and wicked king. [*Hercules Furens*; trans. Milton]

5 *Illi mors gravis incubat / Qui notus nimis omnibus / Ignotus moritur sibi.* On him does death lie heavily who, but too well known to all, dies to himself unknown. [*Thyestes*, II, Chorus; trans. Miller]

Service, Robert W. (1874–1958)

6 Ah! the clock is always slow; / It is later than you think. [*Ballads of a Bohemian*, 'Spring']

7 This is the Law of the Yukon, that only the Strong shall thrive; / That surely the Weak shall perish, and only the Fit survive. ['The Law of the Yukon']

8 Back at the bar, in a solo game, sat Dangerous Dan McGrew. ['The Shooting of Dan McGrew']

Seward, William (1801–1872)

9 There is a higher law than the Constitution. [Speech against Fugitive Slave Law, 1850]

Sexby, Edward (d. 1658)

10 Killing no Murder Briefly Discourst in Three Questions [Title of pamphlet]

Shacklock, Richard (fl. 1575)

11 Proud as peacocks. [*Hatchet of Heresies*]

Shadwell, Thomas (c. 1642–1692)

12 Words may be false and full of art, / Sighs are the natural language of the heart. [*Psyche*, III]

13 'Tis the way of all flesh. [*The Sullen Lovers*, V]

14 And wit's the noblest frailty of the mind. [*A True Widow*, II]

15 I am, out of the ladies' company, like a fish out of the water. [Ib. III]

16 Every man loves what he is good at. [Ib. V]

Shakespeare, William (1564–1616)

ALL'S WELL THAT ENDS WELL

17 Mine eyes smell onions; I shall weep soon. [V.3]

ANTONY AND CLEOPATRA

18 The triple pillar of the world transformed / Into a strumpet's fool. [I.1]

19 There's beggary in the love that can be reckoned. [Ib.]

20 Let Rome in Tiber melt. [Ib.]

21 I love long life better than figs. [I.2]

22 Where's my serpent of old Nile? [I.5]

23 My salad days, / When I was green in judgement, cold in blood. [Ib.]

24 The barge she sat in, like a burnish'd throne, / Burn'd on the water. [II.2]

25 For her person, it beggar'd all description. [Ib.]

26 Age cannot wither her, nor custom stale / Her infinite variety; other women cloy / The appetites they feed, but she makes hungry / Where most she satisfies. [Ib.]

27 Let's have one other gaudy night; call to me / All my sad captains. [III.11]

28 I am dying, Egypt, dying. [IV.13]

29 Let's do it after the high Roman fashion, / And make death proud to take us. [Ib.]

30 He words me, girls, he words me. [V.2]

31 I shall see some squeaking Cleopatra boy my greatness. [Ib.]

32 His biting is immortal; those that do die of it do seldom or never recover. [Ib.]

33 I wish you joy o' the worm. [Ib.]

1 Give me my robe, put on my crown; I have / Immortal longings in me. [Ib.]

2 Peace! peace! / Dost thou not see my baby at my breast, / That sucks the nurse asleep. [Ib.]

3 A lass unparallel'd. [Ib.]

AS YOU LIKE IT

4 Fleet the time carelessly, as they did in the golden world. [I.1]

5 O, how full of briers is this working-day world! [I.3]

6 Sweet are the uses of adversity, / Which like the toad, ugly and venomous, / Wears yet a precious jewel in his head. [II.1]

7 Sweep on, you fat and greasy citizens! [Ib.]

8 Ay, now I am in Arden; the more fool I: when I was at home, I was in a better place: but travellers must be content. [II.4]

9 Under the greenwood tree / Who loves to lie with me / ...Here shall he see / No enemy / But winter and rough weather. [II.5]

10 I can suck melancholy out of a song, as a weasel sucks eggs. [Ib.]

11 A fool, a fool! I met a fool i' the forest. [II.7]

12 And so, from hour to hour we ripe and ripe, / And then from hour to hour we rot and rot, / And thereby hangs a tale. [Ib.]

13 All the world's a stage, / And all the men and women merely players: / They have their exits and their entrances; / And one man in his time plays many parts, / His acts being seven ages. At first the infant, / Mewling and puking in the nurse's arms. / And then the whining schoolboy, with his satchel, / And shining morning face, creeping like snail / Unwillingly to school. [Ib.]

14 Then a soldier / ...Seeking the bubble reputation / Even in the cannon's mouth. [Ib.]

15 The lean and slipper'd pantaloon. [Ib.]

16 Second childishness and mere oblivion, / Sans teeth, sans eyes, sans taste, sans everything. [Ib.]

17 Blow, blow, thou winter wind, / Thou art not so unkind / As man's ingratitude. [Ib.]

18 O wonderful, wonderful, and most wonderful! and yet again wonderful, and after that, out of all whooping! [III.2]

19 Men have died from time to time, and worms have eaten them, but not for love. [IV.1]

20 O coz, coz, coz, my pretty little coz, that thou didst know how many fathom deep I am in love! [Ib.]

21 'Tis like the howling of Irish wolves against the moon. [V.2]

22 It was a lover and his lass, With a hey, and a ho, and a hey nonino. [V.3]

23 An ill-favoured thing, sir, but mine own. [V.4]

24 Your 'if' is the only peace-maker; much virtue in 'if'. [Ib.]

CORIOLANUS

25 Rubbing the poor itch of your opinion, / Make yourself scabs. [I.1]

26 You common cry of curs! whose breath I hate / As reek o' the rotten fens, whose loves I prize / As the dead carcasses of unburied men / That do corrupt my air, — I banish you. [III.3]

27 There is a world elsewhere. [Ib.]

28 Alone I did it. [V.5]

CYMBELINE

29 Boldness be my friend! [I.6]

30 Hark! hark! the lark at heaven's gate sings, / And Phoebus 'gins arise. [II.3]

31 Fear no more the heat o' the sun. [IV.2]

32 Golden lads and girls all must, / As chimney-sweeps, come to dust. [Ib.]

33 He that sleeps feels not the toothache. [V.4]

HAMLET

34 For this relief much thanks. [I.1]

35 Then it started like a guilty thing. [Ib.]

1 But look, the morn, in russet mantle clad, / Walks o'er the dew of yon high eastward hill. [Ib.]

2 A little more than kin, and less than kind. [I.2]

3 Seems, madam! Nay, it is; I know not 'seems'. [Ib.]

4 O! that this too too solid flesh would melt, / Thaw, and resolve itself into a dew. [Ib.]

5 How weary, stale, flat, and unprofitable / Seem to me all the uses of this world. / Fie on't! O fie! 'tis an unweeded garden. [Ib.]

6 Frailty, thy name is woman! [Ib.]

7 Thrift, thrift, Horatio! the funeral baked meats / Did coldly furnish forth the marriage tables. [Ib.]

8 He was a man, take him for all in all, / I shall not look upon his like again. [Ib.]

9 All is not well; / I doubt some foul play. [Ib.]

10 Costly thy habit as thy purse can buy / ...For the apparel oft proclaims the man. [I.3]

11 Neither a borrower, nor a lender be. [Ib.]

12 This above all: to thine own self be true. [Ib.]

13 It is a custom / More honoured in the breach than the observance. [I.4]

14 Angels and ministers of grace defend us! [Ib.]

15 Something is rotten in the state of Denmark. [Ib.]

16 I could a tale unfold. [I.5]

17 Murder most foul. [Ib.]

18 Yea from the table of my memory / I'll wipe away all trivial fond records. [Ib.]

19 O villain, villain, smiling, damned villain / ...One may smile, and smile, and be a villain. [Ib.]

20 There are more things in heaven and earth, Horatio, / Than are dreamt of in your philosophy. [Ib.]

21 To put an antic disposition on. [Ib.]

22 The time is out of joint; O cursed spite, / That ever I was born to set it right. [Ib.]

23 By indirections find directions out. [II.1]

24 Brevity is the soul of wit. [II.2]

25 More matter with less art. [Ib.]

26 Words, words, words. [Ib.]

27 Though this be madness, yet there is method in it. [Ib.]

28 There is nothing either good or bad, but thinking makes it so. [Ib.]

29 What a piece of work is a man! [Ib.]

30 Man delights not me; no, nor woman neither, though, by your smiling, you seem to say so. [Ib.]

31 I know a hawk from a handsaw. [Ib.]

32 The play, I remember, pleased not the million; 'twas caviare to the general. [Ib.]

33 Use every man after his desert and who would 'scape whipping? [Ib.]

34 O! what a rogue and peasant slave am I. [Ib.]

35 What's Hecuba to him or he to Hecuba / That he should weep for her? [Ib.]

36 The play's the thing / Wherein I'll catch the conscience of the king. [Ib.]

37 To be, or not to be: that is the question: / Whether 'tis nobler in the mind to suffer / The slings and arrows of outrageous fortune, / Or to take arms against a sea of troubles, / And by opposing end them? To die: to sleep; / No more; and, by a sleep to say we end / The heart-ache and the thousand natural shocks / That flesh is heir to, 'tis a consummation / Devoutly to be wish'd. To die, to sleep; / To sleep: perchance to dream: ay, there's the rub; / For in that sleep of death what dreams may come / When we have shuffled off this mortal coil, / Must give us pause. [III.1]

38 He himself might his quietus make / With a bare bodkin. [Ib.]

39 The undiscover'd country from whose bourn / No traveller returns. [Ib.]

40 Thus conscience doth make cowards of us all; / And thus the native hue of resolution / Is sicklied o'er with the pale cast of thought. [Ib.]

1 Get thee to a nunnery. [Ib.]

2 O, what a noble mind is here o'erthrown. [Ib.]

3 Speak the speech, I pray you, as I pronounced it to you, trippingly on the tongue. [III.2]

4 O! it offends me to the soul to hear a robustious periwig-pated fellow tear a passion to tatters, to very rags, to split the ears of the groundlings, who for the most part are capable of nothing but inexplicable dumb-shows and noise. [Ib.]

5 It out-herods Herod. [Ib.]

6 The purpose of playing, whose end, both at the first and now, was and is, to hold, as 'twere, the mirror up to nature. [Ib.]

7 Give me that man / That is not passion's slave. [Ib.]

8 What! frighted with false fire? [Ib.]

9 The lady doth protest too much, methinks. [Ib.]

10 We shall obey, were she ten times our mother. [III.2]

11 Let me be cruel, not unnatural; / I will speak daggers to her but use none. [Ib.]

12 Now I might do it pat, now he is praying. [III.3]

13 How now! a rat? Dead for a ducat, dead! [III.4]

14 A king of shreds and patches. [Ib.]

15 Lay not that flattering unction to your soul. [Ib.]

16 I must be cruel, only to be kind. [Ib.]

17 For 'tis the sport to have the engineer / Hoist with his own petar. [Ib.]

18 I'll lug the guts into the neighbour room. [Ib.]

19 There's such divinity doth hedge a king, / That treason doth but peep to what it would. [IV.5]

20 There's rosemary, that's for remembrance. [Ib.]

21 Alas! poor Yorick. I knew him, Horatio; a fellow of infinite jest. [V.1]

22 Now get you to my lady's chamber, and tell her, let her paint an inch thick, to this favour she must come. [Ib.]

23 To what base uses we may return, Horatio. [Ib.]

24 A ministering angel shall my sister be. [Ib.]

25 There's a divinity that shapes our ends, / Rough-hew them how we will. [V.2]

26 Not a whit, we defy augury; there's a special providence in the fall of a sparrow...The readiness is all. [Ib.]

27 A hit, a very palpable hit. [Ib.]

28 This fell sergeant, death, / Is strict in his arrest. [Ib.]

29 Absent thee from felicity awhile. [Ib.]

30 The rest is silence. [Ib.]

31 Rosencrantz and Guildenstern are dead. [Ib.]

HENRY IV, Part 1

32 I would to God thou and I knew where a commodity of good names were to be bought. [I.2]

33 I know you all, and will awhile uphold / The unyoked humour of your idleness. [Ib.]

34 If all the year were playing holidays, / To sport would be as tedious as to work. [Ib.]

35 By heaven methinks it were an easy leap / To pluck bright honour from the pale-faced moon. [I.3]

36 [Falstaff] lards the lean earth as he walks along. [II.2]

37 Out of this nettle, danger, we pluck this flower, safety. [II.3]

38 He that kills me some six or seven dozen of Scots at a breakfast, washes his hands, and says to his wife, 'Fie upon this quiet life! I want work.' [II.4]

39 Instinct is a great matter, I was a coward on instinct. [Ib.]

40 A plague of sighing and grief! It blows a man up like a bladder. [Ib.]

41 Banish plump Jack and banish all the world. [Ib.]

1 O monstrous! but one half-pennyworth of bread to this intolerable deal of sack! [Ib.]

2 *Glendower:* I can call spirits from the vasty deep.
Hotspur: Why so can I, or so can any man; / But will they come when you do call for them? [III.1]

3 Company, villainous company, hath been the spoil of me. [III.3]

4 Shall I not take mine ease at mine inn? [Ib.]

5 I saw young Harry with his beaver on. [IV.1]

6 Food for powder; they'll fill a pit as well as better: tush, man, mortal men, mortal men. [IV.2]

7 Rebellion lay in his way, and he found it. [V.1]

8 I would it were bed-time, Hal, and all well. [Ib.]

9 Honour pricks me on. Yea, but how if honour prick me off when I come on? [Ib.]

10 I like not such grinning honour as Sir Walter hath. [V.3]

11 When that this body did contain a spirit, / A kingdom for it was too small a bound; / But now two paces of the vilest earth / Is room enough. [Ib.]

12 Lord, Lord, how this world is given to lying! [V.4]

HENRY IV, Part 2

13 I am not only witty in myself, but the cause that wit is in other men. [I.2]

14 I was born about three of the clock in the afternoon, with a white head, and something of a round belly. [Ib.]

15 The young Prince hath misled me. I am the fellow with the great belly, and he my dog. [Ib.]

16 I can get no remedy against this consumption of the purse: borrowing only lingers and lingers it out, but the disease is incurable. [Ib.]

17 Is it not strange that desire should so many years outlive performance? [II.4]

18 Uneasy lies the head that wears a crown. [III.1]

19 There is a history in all men's lives, / Figuring the nature of the times deceas'd. [Ib.]

20 Death, as the Psalmist saith, is certain to all; all shall die. How a good yoke of bullocks at Stamford Fair? [III.2]

21 We have heard the chimes at midnight. [Ib.]

22 Thy wish was father, Harry, to that thought. [IV.5]

23 Under which king, Bezonian? speak or die. [V.3]

24 Let us take any man's horses; the laws of England are at my commandment. [Ib.]

25 I know thee not, old man: fall to thy prayers; / How ill white hairs become a fool and jester! [V.5]

HENRY V

26 O! for a Muse of fire. [I, Chorus]

27 This wooden O. [Ib.]

28 Now all the youth of England are on fire, / And silken dalliance in the wardrobe lies. [II, Chorus]

29 His nose was as sharp as a pen, and a' babbled of green fields. [II.3]

30 Once more unto the breach, dear friends, once more; / Or close the wall up with our English dead. / In peace there's nothing so becomes a man / As modest stillness and humility; / But when the blast of war blows in our ears, / Then imitate the action of the tiger: / Stiffen the sinews, summon up the blood, / Disguise fair nature with hard-favour'd rage. [III.1]

31 I see you stand like greyhounds in the slips, / Straining upon the start. [Ib.]

32 Cry 'God for Harry! England and Saint George!' [Ib.]

33 O! that we now had here / But one ten thousand of those men in England / That do no work today. [IV.3]

34 The fewer men, the greater share of honour. [Ib.]

35 But if it be a sin to covet honour / I am the most offending soul alive. [Ib.]

1 This day is called the feast of Crispian. [Ib.]

2 Old men forget: yet all shall be forgot / But he'll remember with advantages / What feats he did that day. [Ib.]

3 We few, we happy few, we band of brothers. [Ib.]

4 And gentlemen in England now a-bed / Shall think themselves accursed they were not here, / And hold their manhoods cheap whiles any speaks / That fought with us upon Saint Crispin's Day. [Ib.]

5 The naked, poor, and mangled Peace, / Dear nurse of arts, plenties, and joyful births. [V.1]

HENRY VI, Part 1

6 Hung be the heavens with black, yield day to night! [I.1]

7 Saint Martin's summer, halcyon days. [Ib.]

8 She's beautiful and therefore to be woo'd; / She is a woman, therefore to be won. [V.3]

HENRY VI, Part 2

9 Thrice is he arm'd that hath his quarrel just. [III.2]

10 And Adam was a gardener. [IV.2]

11 Away with him! away with him! he speaks Latin. [IV.7]

HENRY VI, Part 3

12 O tiger's heart wrapped in a woman's hide! [I.4]

HENRY VIII

13 Farewell! a long farewell, to all my greatness! [III.2]

14 I have ventured, / Like little wanton boys that swim on bladders, / This many summers in a sea of glory, / But far beyond my depth. [Ib.]

15 And when he falls, he falls like Lucifer, / Never to hope again. [Ib.]

16 Had I but served my God with half the zeal / I served my king, he would not in mine age / Have left me naked to mine enemies. [Ib.]

JULIUS CAESAR

17 You blocks, you stones, you worse than senseless things! / O you hard hearts, you cruel men of Rome, / Knew you not Pompey? [I.1]

18 Beware the Ides of March. [Ib.]

19 And bear the palm alone. [I.2]

20 Why, man, he doth bestride the narrow world / Like a Colossus; and we petty men / Walk under his huge legs. [Ib.]

21 The fault, dear Brutus, is not in our stars, / But in ourselves, that we are underlings. [Ib.]

22 Let me have men about me that are fat; / Sleek-headed men and such as sleep o' nights; / Yond' Cassius has a lean and hungry look; / He thinks too much: such men are dangerous. [Ib.]

23 For mine own part, it was Greek to me. [Ib.]

24 But men may construe things after their own fashion, / Clean from the purpose of the things themselves. [I.3]

25 It is the bright day that brings forth the adder; / And that craves wary walking. [II.1]

26 Between the acting of a dreadful thing / And the first motion, all the interim is / Like a phantasma or a hideous dream. [Ib.]

27 Let's carve him as a dish fit for the gods. [Ib.]

28 Lowliness is young ambition's ladder, / Whereto the climber-upward turns his face; / But when he once attains the upmost round, / He then unto the ladder turns his back, / Looks in the clouds, scorning the base degrees / By which he did ascend. [Ib.]

29 Cowards die many times before their deaths, / The valiant never taste of death but once. [II.2]

30 But I am constant as the northern star, / Of whose true-fix'd and resting quality / There is no fellow in the firmament. [III.1]

31 Et tu, Brute? [Ib.]

32 Cry, 'Havoc!' and let slip the dogs of war. [Ib.]

33 Not that I loved Caesar less, but that I loved Rome more. [III.2]

1 Friends, Romans, countrymen, lend me your ears; / I come to bury Caesar, not to praise him. / The evil that men do lives after them / The good is oft interred with their bones. [Ib.]

2 For Brutus is an honourable man; / So are they all, all honourable men. [Ib.]

3 Ambition should be made of sterner stuff. [Ib.]

4 If you have tears, prepare to shed them now. [Ib.]

5 See what a rent the envious Casca made. [Ib.]

6 This was the most unkindest cut of all. [Ib.]

7 I am Cinna the poet, I am Cinna the poet. [III.3]

8 Tear him for his bad verses, tear him for his bad verses! [Ib.]

9 A friendly eye could never see such faults. [IV.3]

10 There is a tide in the affairs of men, / Which taken at the flood, leads on to fortune; / Omitted, all the voyage of their life / Is bound in shallows and in miseries. [Ib.]

11 This was the noblest Roman of them all. [V.5]

12 His life was gentle, and the elements / So mix'd in him that Nature might stand up, / And say to all the world, 'This was a man!' [Ib.]

KING JOHN

13 Mad world! mad kings! mad composition! [II.1]

14 Bell, book, and candle shall not drive me back, / When gold and silver becks me to come on. [III.3]

15 To gild refined gold, to paint the lily, / To throw a perfume on the violet. [IV.2]

16 The spirit of the time shall teach me speed. [Ib.]

17 I beg cold comfort. [V.7]

18 Nought shall make us rue, / If England to itself do rest but true. [Ib.]

KING LEAR

19 Nothing will come of nothing: speak again. [I.1]

20 Now, gods, stand up for bastards. [I.2]

21 We make guilty of our disasters the sun, the moon, and the stars; as if we were villains by necessity, fools by heavenly compulsion. [Ib.]

22 Pat he comes, like the catastrophe of the old comedy. [Ib.]

23 How sharper than a serpent's tooth it is / To have a thankless child. [I.4]

24 O! Let me not be mad, not mad, sweet heaven. [I.5]

25 Blow, winds, and crack your cheeks! [III.2]

26 Rumble thy bellyful! Spit, fire! spout, rain! [Ib.]

27 There was never yet fair woman but she made mouths in a glass. [Ib.]

28 I am a man / More sinned against than sinning. [Ib.]

29 O! that way madness lies. [III.4]

30 Take physic, pomp. [Ib.]

31 Defy the foul fiend. [Ib.]

32 Unaccommodated man is no more but such a poor, bare, forked animal as thou art. [Ib.]

33 'Tis a naughty night to swim in. [Ib.]

34 The prince of darkness is a gentleman. [Ib.]

35 Child Roland to the dark tower came, / His word was still, Fie, foh, and fum, / I smell the blood of a British man. [Ib.]

36 Out, vile jelly! [III.7]

37 The worst is not; / So long as we can say, 'This is the worst.' [IV.1]

38 As flies to wanton boys, are we to the gods; / They kill us for their sport. [Ib.]

39 Let copulation thrive. [IV.6]

40 Give me an ounce of civet, good apothecary, to sweeten my imagination. [Ib.]

41 *Gloucester:* O! Let me kiss that hand. *Lear:* Let me wipe it first, it smells of mortality. [Ib.]

1 Get thee glass eyes; / And, like a scurvy politician, seem / To see the things thou dost not. [Ib.]

2 We came crying hither. [Ib.]

3 When we are born, we cry that we are come / To this great stage of fools. [Ib.]

4 I am bound / Upon a wheel of fire. [IV.7]

5 Men must endure / Their going hence, even as their coming hither: / Ripeness is all. [V.2]

6 The gods are just, and of our pleasant vices / Make instruments to plague us. [V.3]

7 Her voice was ever soft, / Gentle and low, an excellent thing in woman. [Ib.]

8 Never, never, never, never, never! / Pray you, undo this button. [Ib.]

9 The weight of this sad time we must obey, / Speak what we feel; not what we ought to say. / The oldest hath borne most: we that are young / Shall never see so much, nor live so long. [Ib.]

LOVE'S LABOUR'S LOST

10 Spite of cormorant devouring Time. [I.1]

11 From women's eyes this doctrine I derive. [IV.3]

12 For where is any author in the world / Teaches such beauty as a woman's eye? / Learning is but an adjunct to ourself. [Ib.]

13 They have been at a great feast of learning, and stolen the scraps. [V.1]

14 He draweth out the thread of his verbosity finer than the staple of his argument. [Ib.]

15 A jest's prosperity lies in the ear / Of him that hears it, never in the tongue / Of him that makes it. [V.2]

16 Cuckoo, / Cuckoo, cuckoo: O word of fear, / Unpleasing to a married ear. [Ib.]

17 Then nightly sings the staring owl / Tu-who; / Tu-whit, tu-who — a merry note, / While greasy Joan doth keel the pot. [Ib.]

18 The words of Mercury are harsh after the songs of Apollo. [Ib.]

MACBETH

19 When shall we three meet again / In thunder, lightning, or in rain? [I.1]

20 Fair is foul, and foul is fair. [Ib.]

21 What bloody man is that? [I.2]

22 Two truths are told, / As happy prologues to the swelling act / Of the imperial theme. [I.3]

23 Nothing in his life / Became him like the leaving it. [Ib.]

24 There's no art / To find the mind's construction in the face. [Ib.]

25 Yet do I fear thy nature; / It is too full o' the milk of human kindness / To catch the nearest way. [Ib.]

26 Unsex me here, / And fill me from the crown to the toe top full / Of direst cruelty. [I.5]

27 This castle hath a pleasant seat. [I.6]

28 If it were done when 'tis done, then 'twere well / It were done quickly. [I.7]

29 That but this blow / Might be the be-all and the end-all here, / But here, upon this bank and shoal of time, / We'd jump the life to come. [Ib.]

30 Pity, like a naked new-born babe, / Striding the blast. [Ib.]

31 I have no spur / To prick the sides of my intent, but only / Vaulting ambition, which o'erleaps itself / And falls on the other. [Ib.]

32 Letting 'I dare not' wait upon 'I would', / Like the poor cat i' the adage. [Ib.]

33 I dare do all that may become a man; / Who dares do more is none. [Ib.]

34 But screw your courage to the sticking-place, / And we'll not fail. [Ib.]

35 Is this a dagger which I see before me / The handle toward my hand? [II.1]

36 A dagger of the mind, a false creation, / Proceeding from the heat-oppressèd brain. [Ib.]

37 As they had seen me with these hangman's hands. [II.2]

1 Methought I heard a voice cry, 'Sleep no more! / Macbeth does murder sleep,' the innocent sleep, / Sleep that knits up the ravelled sleave of care. [Ib.]

2 That which hath made them drunk hath made me bold. [Ib.]

3 Will all great Neptune's ocean wash this blood / Clean from my hand? No, this my hand will rather / The multitudinous seas incarnadine, / Making the green one red. [Ib.]

4 A little water clears us of this deed. [Ib.]

5 Wake Duncan with thy knocking! I would thou couldst! [Ib.]

6 The primrose way to the everlasting bonfire. [II.3]

7 Confusion now hath made his masterpiece! [Ib.]

8 There's nothing serious in mortality, / All is but toys. [Ib.]

9 To be thus is nothing; / But to be safely thus. [III.1]

10 We have scotch'd the snake, not killed it. [III.2]

11 After life's fitful fever he sleeps well. [Ib.]

12 But now I am cabin'd, cribb'd, confin'd, bound in / To saucy doubts and fears. [III.4]

13 Now, good digestion wait upon appetite, / And health on both! [Ib.]

14 Stand not upon the order of your going, / But go at once. [Ib.]

15 Double, double, toil and trouble; / Fire burn and cauldron bubble. [IV.1]

16 By the pricking of my thumbs, / Something wicked this way comes. [Ib.]

17 A deed without a name. [Ib.]

18 What! will the line stretch out to the crack of doom? [Ib.]

19 Stands Scotland where it did? [IV.3]

20 What! all my pretty chickens and their dam, / At one fell swoop? [Ib.]

21 Out, damned spot! out, I say! [V.1]

22 Yet who would have thought the old man had so much blood in him? [Ib.]

23 All the perfumes of Arabia will not sweeten this little hand. [Ib.]

24 The devil damn thee black, thou cream-fac'd loon! [V.3]

25 My way of life / Is fall'n into the sear, the yellow leaf. [Ib.]

26 Curses, not loud but deep. [Ib.]

27 Canst thou not minister to a mind diseased? [Ib.]

28 She should have died hereafter; / There would have been a time for such a word, / To-morrow, and to-morrow, and to-morrow, / Creeps in this petty pace from day to day, / To the last syllable of recorded time; / And all our yesterdays have lighted fools / The way to dusty death. Out, out, brief candle! / Life's but a walking shadow, a poor player, / That struts and frets his hour upon the stage, / And then is heard no more; it is a tale / Told by an idiot, full of sound and fury, / Signifying nothing. [V.5]

29 Fear not, till Birnam wood / Do come to Dunsinane. [V.7]

30 I bear a charmed life. [Ib.]

31 Macduff was from his mother's womb / Untimely ripp'd. [Ib.]

32 Lay on, Macduff; / And damn'd be him that first cries, 'Hold, / enough!' [Ib.]

MEASURE FOR MEASURE

33 'Tis one thing to be tempted, Escalus, / Another thing to fall. [II.1]

34 Condemn the fault and not the actor of it? [II.2]

35 Man, proud man, / Drest in a little brief authority. [Ib.]

36 Be absolute for death; either death or life / Shall thereby be the sweeter. [III.1]

37 If I must die, / I will encounter darkness as a bride, / And hug it in my arms. [Ib.]

38 Ay, but to die, and go we know not where; / To lie in cold obstruction and to rot. [Ib.]

39 There, at the moated grange, resides this dejected Mariana. [Ib.]

40 Take, O take those lips away, / That so sweetly were forsworn. [IV.1]

THE MERCHANT OF VENICE

1 Gratiano speaks an infinite deal of nothing, more than any man in all Venice. His reasons are as two grains of wheat, hid in two bushels of chaff: you shall seek all day ere you find them; and, when you have found them, they are not worth the search. [I.1]

2 Sometimes from her eyes / I did receive fair speechless messages. [Ib.]

3 They are as sick that surfeit with too much, as they that starve with nothing. [I.2]

4 If to do were as easy as to know what were good to do, chapels had been churches, and poor men's cottages princes' palaces. [Ib.]

5 God made him, and therefore let him pass for a man. [Ib.]

6 Ships are but boards, sailors but men; there be land-rats and water-rats, land-thieves and water-thieves. [I.3]

7 The devil can cite Scripture for his purpose. [Ib.]

8 A goodly apple rotten at the heart. [Ib.]

9 Mislike me not for my complexion, / The shadowed livery of the burnished sun. [II.1]

10 It is a wise father that knows his own child. [Ib.]

11 All that glisters is not gold, / Often have you heard that told. [II.6]

12 My daughter! O my ducats! O my daughter! [II.8]

13 Hath not a Jew eyes? hath not a Jew hands, organs, dimensions, senses, affections, passions? [III.1]

14 If you prick us, do we not bleed? if you tickle us, do we not laugh? if you poison us, do we not die? and if you wrong us, shall we not revenge? [Ib.]

15 Tell me where is fancy bred, / Or in the heart or in the head? [III.2]

16 So may the outward shows be least themselves: / The world is still deceived with ornament. [III.2]

17 The pound of flesh which I demand of him / Is dearly bought, 'tis mine, and I will have it. [IV.1]

18 I am a tainted wether of the flock. [Ib.]

19 The quality of mercy is not strained, / It droppeth as the gentle rain from heaven / Upon the place beneath: it is twice blessed; / It blesseth him that gives and him that takes. [Ib.]

20 And earthly power doth then show likest God's / When mercy seasons justice. [Ib.]

21 To do a great right, do a little wrong. [Ib.]

22 A Daniel come to judgement. [Ib.]

23 How sweet the moonlight sleeps upon this bank! / Here we will sit, and let the sounds of music / Creep in our ears. [V.1]

24 Such harmony is in immortal souls; / But whilst this muddy vesture of decay / Doth grossly close it in, we cannot hear it. [Ib.]

25 I am never merry when I hear sweet music. [Ib.]

26 How far that little candle throws his beams! / So shines a good deed in a naughty world. [Ib.]

THE MERRY WIVES OF WINDSOR

27 We burn daylight. [II.1]

28 Why, then the world's mine oyster. [Ib.]

29 Marry, this is the short and long of it. [Ib.]

30 I cannot tell what the dickens his name is. [III.2]

31 I have a kind of alacrity in sinking. [III.5]

32 A man of my kidney. [Ib.]

33 There is a divinity in odd numbers, either in nativity, chance or death. [V.1]

A MIDSUMMER NIGHT'S DREAM

34 The course of true love never did run smooth. [I.1]

35 Love looks not with the eyes, but with the mind, / And therefore is wing'd Cupid painted blind. [Ib.]

36 A part to tear a cat in. [I.2]

1 I will roar, that I will make the duke say, 'Let him roar again, let him roar again.' [Ib.]

2 I will roar you as gently as any sucking dove. [Ib.]

3 Ill met by moonlight, proud Titania. [II.1]

4 I'll put a girdle round about the earth / In forty minutes. [Ib.]

5 I know a bank whereon the wild thyme blows. [Ib.]

6 Night and silence — who is here? [II.2]

7 Bless thee, Bottom! bless thee! thou art translated. [III.1]

8 Lord, what fools these mortals be! [III.2]

9 She was a vixen when she went to school. [Ib.]

10 I have a reasonable good ear in music: let us have the tongs and bones. [IV.1]

11 I have had a dream, past the wit of man to say what dream it was. [Ib.]

12 The lunatic, the lover, and the poet, / Are of imagination all compact. [V.1]

13 The poet's eye, in a fine frenzy rolling, / Doth glance from heaven to earth, from earth to heaven; / And, as imagination bodies forth / The forms of things unknown, the poet's pen / Turns them to shapes, and gives to airy nothing / A local habitation and a name. [Ib.]

14 A tedious brief scene of young Pyramus / And his love Thisbe: very tragical mirth. [Ib.]

15 The best in this kind are but shadows, and the worst are no worse, if imagination amend them. [Ib.]

MUCH ADO ABOUT NOTHING

16 There was a star danced, and under that I was born. [II.1]

17 Is it not strange that sheep's guts should hale souls out of men's bodies? [II.3]

18 Sigh no more, ladies, sigh no more, / Men were deceivers ever. [Ib.]

19 Sits the wind in that corner? [Ib.]

20 The world must be peopled. [Ib.]

21 Comparisons are odorous. [III.5]

22 Patch grief with proverbs. [V.1]

OTHELLO

23 A fellow almost damned in a fair wife. [I.1]

24 Your daughter and the Moor are now making the beast with two backs. [Ib.]

25 Keep up your bright swords, for the dew will rust them. [I.2]

26 The wealthy curled darlings of our nation. [Ib.]

27 Rude am I in my speech. [I.3]

28 I will a round unvarnished tale deliver. [Ib.]

29 The Anthropophagi, and men whose heads / Do grow beneath their shoulders. [Ib.]

30 Virtue! a fig! 'tis in ourselves that we are thus, or thus. [Ib.]

31 Put money in thy purse. [Ib.]

32 I am nothing if not critical. [II.1]

33 Potations pottle-deep. [II.3]

34 O God! that men should put an enemy in their mouths to steal away their brains. [Ib.]

35 Excellent wretch! Perdition catch my soul / But I do love thee! and when I love thee not, / Chaos is come again. [III.3]

36 Who steals my purse steals trash; 'tis something, nothing; / 'Twas mine, 'tis his, and has been slave to thousands; / But he that filches from me my good name / Robs me of that which not enriches him, / And makes me poor indeed. [Ib.]

37 O! beware, my lord, of jealousy; / It is the green-ey'd monster which doth mock / The meat it feeds on. [Ib.]

38 For I am declined / Into the vale of years. [Ib.]

39 Trifles light as air / Are to the jealous confirmation strong / As proofs of holy writ. [Ib.]

40 Othello's occupation's gone! [Ib.]

41 Be sure of it; give me the ocular proof. [Ib.]

42 But yet the pity of it, Iago! O! Iago, the pity of it, Iago! [IV.1]

1 Goats and monkeys! [Ib.]

2 He hath a daily beauty in his life / That makes me ugly. [V.1]

3 It is the cause, it is the cause, my soul. [V.2]

4 Put out the light and then put out the light. [Ib.]

5 I have done the state some service and they know't. [Ib.]

6 Then, must you speak / Of one that lov'd not wisely but too well. [Ib.]

7 One whose hand, / Like the base Indian, threw a pearl away / Richer than all his tribe. [Ib.]

PERICLES

8 *3rd Fisherman:* I marvel how the fishes live in the sea.
1st Fisherman: Why, as the men do a-land; the great ones eat up the little ones. [II.1]

RICHARD II

9 We are not born to sue but to command. [I.1]

10 Things sweet to taste prove in digestion sour. [I.3]

11 Teach thy necessity to reason thus; / There is no virtue like necessity. [Ib.]

12 O! who can hold a fire in his hand / By thinking on the frosty Caucasus? [Ib.]

13 This royal throne of kings, this scepter'd isle, / This earth of majesty, this seat of Mars, / This other Eden, demi-Paradise. [II.1]

14 This happy breed of men, this little world, / This precious stone set in the silver sea. [Ib.]

15 This blessed plot, this earth, this realm, this England, / This nurse, this teeming womb of royal kings. [Ib.]

16 I count myself in nothing else so happy / As in a soul remembering my good friends. [II.3]

17 The caterpillars of the commonwealth. [Ib.]

18 Let's talk of graves, of worms and epitaphs. [III.2]

19 For God's sake let us sit upon the ground / And tell sad stories of the death of kings. [Ib.]

20 What must the king do now? Must he submit? / The king shall do it. [III.3]

21 A little, little grave, an obscure grave. [Ib.]

22 I have been studying how I may compare / The prison where I live unto the world. [V.5]

RICHARD III

23 Now is the winter of our discontent / Made glorious summer by this sun of York. [I.1]

24 In this weak piping time of peace. [Ib.]

25 And therefore, since I cannot prove a lover,... / I am determined to prove a villain. [Ib.]

26 Was ever woman in this humour wooed? / Was ever woman in this humour won? [I.2]

27 Thou art a traitor: / Off with his head! [III.4]

28 I am not in the giving vein today. [IV.2]

29 A horse! a horse! my kingdom for a horse! [V.4]

ROMEO AND JULIET

30 A pair of star-crossed lovers. [Prologue]

31 The two hours' traffic of our stage. [Ib.]

32 And 'tis not hard, I think, / For men so old as we to keep the peace. [I.2]

33 O! then I see Queen Mab hath been with you. [I.4]

34 O! she doth teach the torches to burn bright. [I.5]

35 He jests at scars that never felt a wound. / But, soft! what light through yonder window breaks? / It is the east, and Juliet is the sun. [II.2]

36 O Romeo, Romeo! wherefore art thou Romeo? [Ib.]

37 What's in a name? that which we call a rose / By any other name would smell as sweet. [Ib.]

1 O swear not by the moon, the inconstant moon, / That monthly changes in her circled orb, / Lest that thy love prove likewise variable. [Ib.]

2 Good-night, good-night! parting is such sweet sorrow / That I shall say good-night till it be morrow. [Ib.]

3 These violent delights have violent ends. [II.6]

4 A plague o' both your houses! / They have made worms' meat of me. [III.1]

5 O! I am Fortune's fool. [Ib.]

6 Adversity's sweet milk, philosophy. [III.3]

7 Night's candles are burnt out, and jocund day / Stands tiptoe on the misty mountain tops. [III.5]

THE TAMING OF THE SHREW

8 Look in the chronicles; we came in with Richard Conqueror. [Induction]

9 Love in idleness. [I.1]

10 Nothing comes amiss, so money comes withal. [I.2]

11 Lead apes in hell. [II.1]

12 Kiss me, Kate. [Ib.]

13 This is the way to kill a wife with kindness. [IV.1]

14 Such duty as the subject owes the prince, / Even such a woman oweth to her husband. [V.2]

THE TEMPEST

15 The dark backward and abysm of time. [I.2]

16 You taught me language; and my profit on't / Is, I know how to curse. [Ib.]

17 Come unto these yellow sands, / And then take hands; / Curtsied when you have, and kissed, — / The wild waves whist. [Ib.]

18 Full fathom five thy father lies; / Of his bones are coral made. [Ib.]

19 They'll take suggestion as a cat laps milk. [II.1]

20 Misery acquaints a man with strange bedfellows. [II.2]

21 'Ban, 'Ban, Ca-Caliban, / Has a new master — Get a new man. [Ib.]

22 Thought is free. [Ib.]

23 Be not afeard: the isle is full of noises, / Sounds and sweet airs, that give delight and hurt not. [Ib.]

24 Our revels now are ended. These our actors, / As I foretold you, were all spirits and / Are melted into air, into thin air: / And, like the baseless fabric of this vision, / The cloud-capped towers, the gorgeous palaces, / The solemn temples, the great globe itself, / Yea, all which it inherit, shall dissolve / And, like this insubstantial pageant faded, / Leave not a rack behind. We are such stuff / As dreams are made on, and our little life / Is rounded with a sleep! [IV.2]

25 The rarer action is / In virtue than in vengeance. [V.1]

26 This rough magic / I here abjure. [Ib.]

27 Where the bee sucks, there suck I: / In a cowslip's bell I lie; / There I couch when owls do cry. [Ib.]

28 O brave new world, / That has such people in't. [Ib.]

TIMON OF ATHENS

29 He that loves to be flattered is worthy o' the flatterer. [I.1]

30 The strain of man's bred out / Into baboon and monkey. [I.2]

31 I wonder men dare trust themselves with men. [Ib.]

TITUS ANDRONICUS

32 What, man! more water glideth by the mill / Than wots the miller of. [I.2]

33 If one good deed in all my life I did, / I do repent it from my very soul. [V.3]

TROILUS AND CRESSIDA

34 Men prize the thing ungained more than it is. [I.2]

35 O! when degree is shaked, / Which is the ladder to all high designs, / The enterprise is sick. [I.3]

1 Take but degree away, untune that string, / And hark what discord follows. [Ib.]

2 'Tis mad idolatry / To make the service greater than the god. [II.2]

3 All the argument is a whore and a cuckold. [II.3]

4 This is the monstruosity in love, lady, that the will is infinite and the execution confined; that the desire is boundless, and the act a slave to limit. [III.2]

5 Time hath, my lord, a wallet at his back, / Wherein he puts alms for oblivion. [III.3]

6 Perseverance, dear my lord, / Keeps honour bright. [Ib.]

7 One touch of nature makes the whole world kin. [Ib.]

8 There's language in her eye, her cheek, her lip, / Nay, her foot speaks. [IV.5]

9 What a pair of spectacles is here! [IV.4]

10 Lechery, lechery; still wars and lechery; nothing else holds fashion. [V.2]

TWELFTH NIGHT

11 If music be the food of love, play on; / Give me excess of it, that, surfeiting, / The appetite may sicken, and so die. [I.1]

12 That strain again! it had a dying fall. [Ib.]

13 Is it a world to hide virtues in? [I.3]

14 Many a good hanging prevents a bad marriage. [I.5]

15 Not to be a-bed after midnight is to be up betimes. [II.3]

16 Journeys end in lovers meeting, / Every wise man's son doth know. [Ib.]

17 Youth's a stuff will not endure. [Ib.]

18 Dost thou think, because thou art virtuous, there shall be no more cakes and ale? [Ib.]

19 Come away, come away, death, / And in sad cypress let me be laid. [II.4]

20 Be not afraid of greatness: some are born great, some achieve greatness, and some have greatness thrust upon them. [II.5]

21 Remember who commended thy yellow stockings, and wished to see thee ever cross-gartered. [Ib.]

22 Love sought is good, but giv'n unsought is better. [III.1]

23 Why this is very midsummer madness. [III.4]

24 If this were played upon a stage now, / I could condemn it as an improbable fiction. [Ib.]

25 And thus the whirligig of time brings in his revenges. [V.1]

26 I'll be revenged on the whole pack of you. [Ib.]

THE TWO GENTLEMEN OF VERONA

27 Who is Silvia? What is she, / That all our Swains commend her? [IV.2]

THE WINTER'S TALE

28 A sad tale's best for winter. [II.1]

29 Exit, pursued by a bear. [III.3 (stage direction)]

30 Thou mett'st with things dying, I with things new-born. [III.3]

31 A snapper-up of unconsidered trifles. [IV.2]

32 For the life to come, I sleep out the thought of it. [Ib.]

33 Jog on, jog on, the foot-path way, / And merrily hent the stile-a: / A merry heart goes all the day, / Your sad tires in a mile-a. [Ib.]

34 This is an art / Which does mend nature — change it rather; but / The art itself is nature. [IV.4]

35 When you do dance I wish you / A wave o' the sea; that you might ever do / Nothing but that; move still, still so, / And own no other function. [Ib.]

36 Good sooth, she is / The queen of curds and cream. [Ib.]

37 The self-same sun that shines upon his court / Hides not his visage from our cottage, but / Looks on alike. [Ib.]

THE PASSIONATE PILGRIM

1 Crabbed age and youth cannot live together: / Youth is full of pleasance, age is full of care.

SONNETS

2 To the only begetter of these ensuing sonnets, Mr. W.H. [Dedication]

3 When forty winters shall besiege thy brow, / And dig deep trenches in thy beauty's field. [2]

4 Shall I compare thee to a summer's day? / Thou art more lovely and more temperate. / Rough winds do shake the darling buds of May / And summer's lease hath all too short a date. [18]

5 When in disgrace with Fortune and men's eyes, / I all alone beweep my outcast state. [29]

6 For the sweet love remembered such wealth brings / That then I scorn to change my state with kings. [Ib.]

7 When to the sessions of sweet silent thought / I summon up remembrance of things past. [30]

8 Full many a glorious morning have I seen. [33]

9 Roses have thorns, and silver fountains mud. [35]

10 Like as the waves make towards the pebbled shore, / So do our minutes hasten to their end. [60]

11 When I have seen by Time's fell hand defaced / The rich-proud cost of outworn buried age. [64]

12 No longer mourn for me when I am dead / Than you shall hear the surly sullen bell. [71]

13 That time of year thou mayst in me behold / When yellow leaves, or none, or few, do hang / Upon those boughs which shake against the cold, / Bare ruined choirs, where late the sweet birds sang. [73]

14 They that have power to do hurt and will do none, / That do not do the thing they most do show. [94]

15 Lilies that fester smell far worse than weeds. [Ib.]

16 The chronicle of wasted time. [106]

17 For we, which now behold these present days, / Have eyes to wonder, but lack tongues to praise. [Ib.]

18 Let me not to the marriage of true minds / Admit impediments. Love is not love / Which alters when it alteration finds. [116]

19 Love's not Time's fool. [Ib.]

20 If this be error, and upon me proved, / I never writ, nor no man ever loved. [Ib.]

21 The expense of spirit in a waste of shame / Is lust in action. [Ib. 129]

22 My mistress' eyes are nothing like the sun. [130]

23 Good friend, for Jesu's sake forbear / To dig the dust enclosèd here. / Blest be the man that spares these stones, / And curst be he that moves my bones. [Epitaph]

24 Item, I give unto my wife my second best bed. [Will]

Shankly, Bill (1914–1981)

25 Some people think football is a matter of life and death. I don't like that attitude. I can assure them it is much more serious than that. [Remark on BBC T.V.]

Shaw, George Bernard (1856–1950)

26 What Englishman will give his mind to politics as long as he can afford to keep a motor car? [*The Apple Cart*, I]

27 You can always tell an old soldier by the inside of his holsters and cartridge boxes. The young ones carry pistols and cartridges: the old ones, grub. [*Arms and the Man*, I]

28 You're not a man, you're a machine. [Ib. III]

29 He who has never hoped can never despair. [*Caesar and Cleopatra*, IV]

30 We have no more right to consume happiness without producing it than to consume wealth without producing it. [*Candida*, I]

31 It is easy — terribly easy — to shake a man's faith in himself. To take advantage of that to break a man's spirit is devil's work. [Ib.]

1 I'm only a beer teetotaller, not a champagne teetotaller. [Ib. III]

2 Man can climb to the highest summits, but he cannot dwell there long. [Ib.]

3 The British soldier can stand up to anything — except the British War Office. [*The Devil's Disciple*, III]

4 All professions are conspiracies against the laity. [*The Doctor's Dilemma*, I]

5 With the single exception of Homer, there is no eminent writer, not even Sir Walter Scott, whom I can despise so entirely as I despise Shakespeare when I measure my mind against his. [*Dramatic Opinions and Essays*]

6 It's all that the young can do for the old, to shock them and keep them up to date. [*Fanny's First Play*]

7 The one point on which all women are in furious secret rebellion against the existing law is the saddling of the right to a child with the obligation to become the servant of a man. [*Getting Married*]

8 If you will only take the trouble always to do the perfectly correct thing, and to say the perfectly correct thing, you can do just what you like. [*Heartbreak House*, I]

9 Do you think the laws of God will be suspended in favour of England because you were born in it? [Ib. III]

10 Money is indeed the most important thing in the world; and all sound and successful personal and national morality should have this fact for its basis. [*The Irrational Knot*, Preface]

11 Reminiscences make one feel so deliciously aged and sad. [Ib.14]

12 An Irishman's heart is nothing but his imagination. [*John Bull's Other Island*, I]

13 What really flatters a man is that you think him worth flattering. [Ib. IV]

14 The greatest of evils and the worst of crimes is poverty. [*Major Barbara*, Preface]

15 Cusins is a very nice fellow, certainly: nobody would ever guess that he was born in Australia. [Ib. I]

16 I am a Millionaire. That is my religion. [Ib. II]

17 Nothing is ever done in this world until men are prepared to kill one another if it is not done. [Ib. III]

18 The more things a man is ashamed of, the more respectable he is. [*Man and Superman*, I]

19 The true artist will let his wife starve, his children go barefoot, his mother drudge for his living at seventy, sooner than work at anything but his art. [Ib.]

20 There is no love sincerer than the love of food. [Ib.]

21 A lifetime of happiness! No man alive could bear it: it would be hell on earth. [Ib.]

22 Very nice sort of place, Oxford, I should think, for people who like that sort of place. [Ib. II]

23 It is a woman's business to get married as soon as possible, and a man's to keep unmarried as long as he can. [Ib.]

24 Hell is full of musical amateurs: music is the brandy of the damned. [Ib. III]

25 I am a gentleman: I live by robbing the poor. [Ib.]

26 An Englishman thinks he is moral when he is only uncomfortable. [Ib.]

27 This creature man, who in his own selfish affairs is a coward to the backbone, will fight for an idea like a hero. [Ib.]

28 At every one of those concerts in England you will find rows of weary people who are there, not because they really like classical music, but because they think they ought to like it. [Ib.]

29 There are two tragedies in life. One is not to get your heart's desire. The other is to get it. [Ib. IV]

30 Beware of the man whose god is in the skies. ['Maxims for Revolutionists']

31 Do not do unto others as you would they should do unto you. Their tastes may not be the same. [Ib.]

32 Marriage is popular because it combines the maximum of temptation with the maximum of opportunity. [Ib.]

1 Democracy substitutes election by the incompetent many for appointment by the corrupt few. [Ib.]

2 When domestic servants are treated as human beings it is not worth while to keep them. [Ib.]

3 If you strike a child, take care that you strike it in anger, even at the risk of maiming it for life. A blow in cold blood neither can nor should be forgiven. [Ib.]

4 The reasonable man adapts himself to the world: the unreasonable one persists in trying to adapt the world to himself. Therefore all progress depends on the unreasonable man. [Ib.]

5 Youth, which is forgiven everything, forgives itself nothing: age, which forgives itself anything, is forgiven nothing. [Ib.]

6 He who can, does. He who cannot teaches. [Ib.]

7 Activity is the only road to knowledge. [Ib.]

8 The golden rule is that there are no golden rules. [Ib.]

9 The populace cannot understand the bureaucracy: it can only worship national idols. [Ib.]

10 Every man over forty is a scoundrel. [Ib.]

11 Titles distinguish the mediocre, embarrass the superior, and are disgraced by the inferior. [Ib.]

12 In heaven an angel is nobody in particular. [Ib.]

13 Life levels all men: death reveals the eminent. [Ib.]

14 Decency is Indecency's Conspiracy of Silence. [Ib.]

15 Liberty means responsibility. That is why most men dread it. [Ib.]

16 There is no satisfaction in hanging a man who does not object to it. [*The Man of Destiny*]

17 There is only one universal passion: fear. [Ib.]

18 There is nothing so bad or so good that you will not find Englishmen doing it; but you will never find an Englishman in the wrong. He does everything on principle. He fights you on patriotic principles; he robs you on business principles; he enslaves you on imperial principles; he supports his king on royal principles and cuts off his king's head on republican principles. [Ib.]

19 The Gospel of Getting On. [*Mrs. Warren's Profession*, IV]

20 Man is a creature of habit. You cannot write three plays and then stop. [*Plays Pleasant*, Preface]

21 There is only one religion, though there are a hundred versions of it. [*Plays Unpleasant*, Preface]

22 The English have no respect for their language, and will not teach their children to speak it...It is impossible for an Englishman to open his mouth, without making some other Englishman despise him. [*Pygmalion*, Preface]

23 *Pickering:* Have you no morals, man?
Doolittle: Can't afford them, Governor. [Ib. II]

24 My aunt died of influenza: so they said...But it's my belief they done the old woman in. [Ib. III]

25 Gin was mother's milk to her. [Ib.]

26 Not bloody likely. [Ib.]

27 I have never sneered in my life. Sneering doesn't become either the human face or the human soul. [Ib. V]

28 Assassination is the extreme form of censorship. [*The Rejected Statement*]

29 An all-night sitting in a theatre would be at least as enjoyable as an all-night sitting in the House of Commons, and much more useful. [*St. Joan*, Preface]

30 Must then a Christ perish in torment in every age to save those that have no imagination? [Ib. Epilogue]

31 O God that madest this beautiful earth, when will it be ready to receive Thy saints? How long, O Lord, how long? [Ib.]

1 A day's work is a day's work, neither more nor less, and the man who does it needs a day's sustenance, a night's repose, and due leisure, whether he be painter or ploughman. [*An Unsocial Socialist*, 5]

2 We don't bother much about dress and manners in England, because as a nation we don't dress well and we've no manners. [*You Never Can Tell*, I]

3 The trouble is that you are only interested in art, and I am only interested in money. [Remark to Sam Goldwyn, quoted in Halliwell, *Filmgoers' Book of Quotes*]

Shawcross, Lord (1902-)

4 We are the masters at the moment, and not only at the moment, but for a very long time to come. [Speech, 1946]

Sheale, Richard (fl. 16th century)

5 For when his legs were smitten off, / He fought upon his stumps. ['Ballad of Chevy Chase']

Sheldon, A.F. (1868-1935)

6 He profits most who serves best. [Motto of International Rotary]

Shelley, Percy Bysshe (1792-1822)

7 It might make one in love with death, to think that one should be buried in so sweet a place. [*Adonais*, Preface]

8 I weep for Adonais — he is dead! [Ib. 1]

9 To that high Capital, where kingly Death / Keeps his pale court in beauty and decay. [Ib. 7]

10 Ah, woe is me! Winter is come and gone, / But grief returns with the revolving year. [Ib. 18]

11 Whence are we, and why are we? of what scene / The actors or spectators? [Ib. 21]

12 Why didst thou leave the trodden paths of men / Too soon? [Ib. 27]

13 Our Adonais has drunk poison — oh! / What deaf and viperous murderer could crown / Life's early cup with such a draught of woe? [Ib. 36]

14 From the contagion of the world's slow stain / He is secure. [Ib. 40]

15 He is a portion of the loveliness / Which once he made more lovely. [Ib. 43]

16 What Adonais is, why fear we to become? [Ib. 51]

17 The One remains, the many change and pass; / Heaven's light forever shines, Earth's shadows fly; / Life, like a dome of many-coloured glass, / Stains the white radiance of Eternity, / Until Death tramples it to fragments. [Ib. 52]

18 The fountains of divine philosophy / Fled not his thirsting lips. [*Alastor*, 4]

19 Day after day a weary waste of hours. [Ib. 7]

20 England, farewell! thou, who hast been my cradle, / Shalt never be my dungeon or my grave! [*Charles the First* (Hampden's speech)]

21 A widow bird sate mourning for her love / Upon a wintry bough; / The frozen wind crept on above, / The freezing stream below. / There was no leaf upon the forest bare, / No flower upon the ground, / And little motion in the air / Except the mill-wheel's sound. [Ib. (Fool's song)]

22 That orbèd maiden with white fire laden, / Whom mortals call the Moon. ['The Cloud']

23 I silently laugh at my own cenotaph, / And out of the caverns of rain, / Like a child from the womb, like a ghost from the tomb, / I arise and unbuild it again. [Ib.]

24 How wonderful is Death, / Death and his brother Sleep! [*The Daemon of the World*, I (also the opening of *Queen Mab*)]

25 My Song, I fear that thou will find but few / Who fitly shall conceive thy reasoning, / Of such hard matter dost thou entertain. [*Epipsychidion*, Advertisement]

26 My last delight! tell them that they are dull, / And bid them own that thou art beautiful. [Ib.]

27 We — are we not formed, as notes of music are, / For one another, though dissimilar? [Ib. 8]

1 I never was attached to that great sect, / Whose doctrine is, that each one should select / Out of the crowd a mistress or a friend, / And all the rest, though fair and wise, commend / To cold oblivion. [Ib. 9]

2 The breath of her false mouth was like faint flowers, / Her touch was as electric poison. [Ib. 13]

3 A ship is floating in the harbour now, / A wind is hovering o'er the mountain's brow; / There is a path on the sea's azure floor, / No keel has ever ploughed that path before. [Ib. 18]

4 One Heaven, one Hell, one immortality / And one annihilation. [Ib. 19]

5 Fame is love disguised. ['An Exhortation']

6 I hated thee, fallen tyrant! I did groan / To think that a most unambitious slave, / Like thou shouldst dance and revel on the grave / Of Liberty. ['Feelings of a Republican on the Fall of Bonaparte']

7 Virtue owns a more eternal foe / Than Force or Fraud: old Custom, legal Crime, / And bloody Faith the foulest birth of Time. [Ib.]

8 Youth will stand foremost ever. ['Goethe's Faust']

9 Good-night? ah! no; the hour is ill / Which severs those it should unite; / Let us remain together still, / Then it will be *good* night. ['Good Night']

10 Let there be light! said Liberty, / And like sunrise from the sea, / Athens arose! [*Hellas*, 'The Voices of War']

11 Heaven smiles, and faiths and empires gleam, / Like wrecks of a dissolving dream. [Ib. 'The Future']

12 Another Athens shall arise, / And to remoter time / Bequeath, like sunset to the skies, / The splendour of its prime. [Ib.]

13 Oh, cease! must hate and death return? / Cease! must men kill and die? / Cease! drain not to its dregs the urn / Of bitter prophecy. / The world is weary of the past, / Oh, might it die or rest at last! [Ib.]

14 The awful shadow of some unseen Power / Floats though unseen among us. ['Hymn to Intellectual Beauty']

15 Spirit of Beauty, that dost consecrate / With thine own hues all thou dost shine upon / Of human thought or form. [Ib.]

16 While yet a boy I sought for ghosts, and sped / Through many a listening chamber, cave and ruin, / And starlight wood, with fearful steps pursuing / Hopes of high talk with the departed dead. [Ib.]

17 Thou Paradise of exiles, Italy! [*Julian and Maddalo*]

18 Most wretched men / Are cradled into poetry by wrong: / They learn in suffering what they teach in song. [Ib.]

19 O world! O life! O time! / On whose last steps I climb, / Trembling at where I had stood before; / When will return the glory of your prime? / No more — Oh, never more! ['A Lament']

20 The self-impelling steam-wheels of the mind. ['Letter to Maria Gisborne']

21 London, that great sea, whose ebb and flow / At once is deaf and loud, and on the shore / Vomits its wrecks, and still howls on for more. [Ib.]

22 We'll have tea and toast; / Custards for supper, and an endless host / Of syllabubs and jellies and mince-pies, / And other such lady-like luxuries. [Ib.]

23 Alas, good friend, what profit can you see / In hating such a hateless thing as me? ['Lines to a Critic']

24 When the lamp is shattered / The light in the dust lies dead. ['Lines: When the Lamp']

25 O Love! who bewailest / The frailty of all things here, / Why choose you the frailest / For your cradle, your home, and your bier? [Ib.]

26 I met Murder on the way — / He had a mask like Castlereagh. [*The Mask of Anarchy*]

1 His big tears, for he wept well, / Turned to mill-stones as they fell. / And the little children, who / Round his feet played to and fro, / Thinking every tear a gem, / Had their brains knocked out by them. [Ib.]

2 Rise like Lions after slumber / In unvanquishable number, / Shake your chains to earth like dew / Which in sleep had fallen on you — / Ye are many — they are few. [Ib.]

3 Some say that gleams of a remoter world / Visit the soul in sleep, — that death is slumber. ['Mont Blanc']

4 Power dwells apart in its tranquillity, / Remote, serene, and inaccessible. [Ib.]

5 The flower that smiles to-day / To-morrow dies. ['Mutability']

6 O wild West Wind, thou breath of Autumn's being, / Thou, from whose unseen presence the leaves dead / Are driven, like ghosts from an enchanter fleeing. ['Ode to the West Wind']

7 Wild Spirit, which art moving every-where; / Destroyer and preserver; hear, oh, hear. [Ib.]

8 Oh, lift me as a wave, a leaf, a cloud! / I fall upon the thorns of life! I bleed! [Ib.]

9 O, Wind, / If Winter comes, can Spring be far behind? [Ib.]

10 My name is Ozymandias, king of kings: / Look on my works, ye Mighty, and despair! ['Ozymandias']

11 Hell is a city much like London — / A populous and a smoky city. [*Peter Bell the Third*]

12 Things whose trade is, over ladies / To lean, and flirt, and stare, and simper, / Till all that is divine in woman / Grows cruel, courteous, smooth, inhuman, / Crucified 'twixt a smile and whimper. [Ib.]

13 Cruel he looks, but calm and strong. / Like one who does, not suffers wrong. [*Prometheus Unbound,* I]

14 The heaven around, the earth below / Was peopled with thick shapes of human death, / All horrible, and wrought by human hands, / And some appeared the work of human hearts, / For men were slowly killed by frowns and smiles. [Ib.]

15 The good want power, but to weep barren tears. / The powerful goodness want: worse need for them. / The wise want love; and those who love want wisdom; / And all best things are thus confused to ill. [Ib.]

16 Peace is in the grave. / The grave hides all things beautiful and good: / I am a God and cannot find it there. [Ib.]

17 From the dust of creeds outworn. [Ib.]

18 On a poet's lips I slept / Dreaming like a love-adept / In the sound his breathing kept. [Ib.]

19 To know nor faith, nor love, nor law; to be / Omnipotent but friendless is to reign. [Ib. II.4]

20 He gave man speech, and speech created thought, / Which is the measure of the universe; / And Science struck the thrones of earth and heaven. [Ib.]

21 Fate, Time, Occasion, Chance, and Change? To these / All things are subject but eternal Love. [Ib.]

22 My soul is an enchanted boat, / Which, like a sleeping swan, doth float / Upon the silver waves of thy sweet singing. [Ib. II.5]

23 The soul of man, like unextinguished fire, / Yet burns towards heaven with fierce reproach. [Ib. III.1]

24 Death is the veil which those who live call life: / They sleep, and it is lifted. [Ib. III.3]

25 But what was he who taught them that the God / Of nature and benevolence hath given / A special sanction to the trade of blood? [*Queen Mab,* 2]

26 Many faint with toil, / That few may know the cares and woe of sloth. [Ib. 3]

27 Yet every heart contains perfection's germ. [Ib. 5]

28 But human pride / Is skilful to invent most serious names / To hide its ignorance. [Ib. 7]

29 Earth groans beneath religion's iron age, / And priests dare babble of a God of peace / Even whilst their hands are red with guiltless blood. [Ib.]

1 Rarely, rarely, comest thou, / Spirit of Delight! ['Song']

2 I love tranquil solitude, / And such society / As is quiet, wise, and good. [Ib.]

3 Men of England, wherefore plough / For the lords who lay you low? ['Song to the Men of England']

4 Lift not the painted veil which those who live / Call Life. ['Sonnet']

5 [Of George III] An old, mad, blind, despised, and dying king. ['Sonnet: England in 1819']

6 If I esteemed you less, Envy would kill / Pleasure. ['To Byron']

7 The worm beneath the sod / May lift itself in worship to the God. [Ib.]

8 Less oft is peace in Shelley's mind / Than calm in water seen. ['To Jane: The Recollection']

9 Music, when soft voices die, / Vibrates in the memory. ['To ——:' 'Music When Soft Voices']

10 Beware, O Man — for knowledge must to thee / Like the great flood to Egypt, ever be. ['To the Nile']

11 One word is too often profaned / For me to profane it, / One feeling too falsely disdained / For thee to disdain it. ['To ——:' 'One Word is too often Profaned']

12 The desire of the moth for the star, / Of the night for the morrow, / The devotion to something afar / From the sphere of our sorrow. [Ib.]

13 Hail to thee, blithe Spirit! / Bird thou never wert. ['To a Skylark']

14 And singing still dost soar, and soaring ever singest. [Ib.]

15 Like an unbodied joy whose race is just begun. [Ib.]

16 We look before and after / And pine for what is not: / Our sincerest laughter / With some pain is fraught; / Our sweetest songs are those that tell of saddest thought. [Ib.]

17 Teach me half the gladness / That thy brain must know, / Such harmonious madness / From my lips would flow / The world should listen then — as I am listening now. [Ib.]

18 In honoured poverty thy voice did weave / Songs consecrate to truth and liberty, — / Deserting these, thou leavest me to grieve, / Thus having been, that thou shouldst cease to be. ['To Wordsworth']

19 Poets are the unacknowledged legislators of the world. [*A Defence of Poetry*]

20 The rich have become richer, and the poor have become poorer. [Ib.]

21 Poetry is the record of the best and happiest moments of the happiest and best minds. [Ib.]

Shenstone, William (1714-1763)

22 Whoe'er has travell'd life's dull round, / Where'er his stages may have been, / May sigh to think he still has found / The warmest welcome, at an inn. ['At an Inn at Henley']

23 A fool and his words are soon parted; a man of genius and his money. [*Essays on Men and Manners*, 'On Reserve']

Sheridan, Philip Henry (1831-1888)

24 The only good Indian is a dead Indian. [Attr.]

Sheridan, Richard Brinsley (1751-1816)

25 No scandal about Queen Elizabeth, I hope? [*The Critic*, II.1]

26 I open with a clock striking, to beget an awful attention in the audience: it also marks the time, which is four o'clock in the morning, and saves a description of the rising sun, and a great deal about gilding the eastern hemisphere. [Ib. II.2]

27 All that can be said is, that two people happened to hit on the same thought — and Shakespeare made use of it first, that's all. [Ib. III.1]

28 I wish, sir, you would practise this without me. I can't stay dying here all night. [Ib.]

29 O Lord, sir, when a heroine goes mad she always goes into white satin. [Ib.]

30 I was struck all of a heap. [*The Duenna*, II.2]

1 'Tis safest in matrimony to begin with a little aversion. [*The Rivals*, I.2]

2 Madam, a circulating library in a town is as an evergreen tree of diabolical knowledge! It blossoms through the year! [Ib.]

3 If I reprehend anything in this world, it is the use of my oracular tongue, and a nice derangement of epitaphs! [Ib. III.3]

4 She's as headstrong as an allegory on the banks of the Nile. [Ib.]

5 Too civil by half. [Ib. III.4]

6 Our ancestors are very good kind of folks; but they are the last people I should choose to have a visiting acquaintance with. [Ib. IV.1]

7 No caparisons, miss, if you please. Caparisons don't become a young woman. [Ib. IV.2]

8 My valour is certainly going! — it is sneaking off! I feel it oozing out as it were at the palms of my hands! [Ib. V.3]

9 You shall see them on a beautiful quarto page, where a neat rivulet of text shall meander through a meadow of margin. [*The School for Scandal*, I.1]

10 Here is the whole set! a character dead at every word. [Ib. II.2]

11 Here's to the maiden of bashful fifteen; / Here's to the widow of fifty; / Here's to the flaunting, extravagant quean; / And here's to the housewife that's thrifty. [Ib. III.3]

12 An unforgiving eye, and a damned disinheriting countenance. [Ib. IV.1]

13 The Right Honourable gentleman is indebted to his memory for his jests, and to his imagination for his facts. [Speech in House of Commons]

14 I hate Novels, and love Romances. The Praise of the best of the former, their being *natural*, as it is called, is to me their greatest Demerit. [Letter, 1772]

Sherman, William Tecumseh (1820–1891)

15 There is many a boy here to-day who looks on war as all glory, but, boys, it is all hell. [Speech, 1880]

16 I will not accept if nominated, and will not serve if elected. [Telegram refusing Presidential nomination]

Shirley, James (1596–1666)

17 Death lays his icy hand on kings. [*The Contention of Ajax and Ulysses*, I.3]

18 Only the actions of the just / Smell sweet, and blossom in their dust. [Ib.]

19 I presume you're mortal, and may err. [*The Lady of Pleasure*, II.2]

20 How little room / Do we take up in death, that, living know / No bounds? [*The Wedding*, IV.4]

Sickert, Walter (1860–1942)

21 Nothing links man to man like the frequent passage from hand to hand of cash. [Quoted in Auden, *A Certain World*]

Sidgwick, Henry (1838–1900)

22 We think so because other people think so, / Or because — or because — after all we do think so, / Or because we were told so, and think we must think so, / Or because we once thought so, and think we still think so, / Or because having thought so, we think we will think so. ['Lines Composed in his Sleep']

Sidney, Sir Philip (1554–1586)

23 Who shoots at the mid-day sun, though he be sure he shall never hit the mark; yet as sure he is he shall shoot higher than who aims but at a bush. [*The Arcadia*, 2]

24 My true love hath my heart and I have his, / By just exchange one for the other giv'n; / I hold his dear, and mine he cannot miss, / There never was a better bargain driv'n. [Ib. 3]

25 'Fool,' said my Muse to me, 'look in thy heart and write!' [*Astrophel and Stella*, 1]

26 With how sad steps, O Moon, thou climb'st the skies! / How silently, and with how wan a face! [Ib. 31]

1 Come, Sleep! O Sleep, the certain knot of peace, / The baiting-place of wit, the balm of woe, / The poor man's wealth, the prisoner's release, / Th'indifferent judge between the high and low. [Ib. 39]

2 That sweet enemy, France. [Ib. 41]

3 I am no pick-purse of another's wit. [Ib. 74]

4 The poet,...lifted up with the vigour of his own invention, doth grow, in effect, into another nature. [*The Defence of Poesy*]

5 Nature never set forth the earth in so rich tapestry as divers poets have done;...her world is brazen, the poets only deliver a golden. [Ib.]

6 For whatsoever the philosopher saith should be done, [the poet] giveth a perfect picture of it in some one by whom he presupposeth it was done, so as he coupleth the general notion with the particular example. A perfect picture, I say; for he yieldeth to the powers of the mind an image of that whereof the philosopher bestoweth only a wordish description, which doth neither strike, pierce, nor possess the sight of the soul so much as that other doth. [Ib.]

7 With a tale, forsooth, he cometh unto you, with a tale which holdeth children from play, and old men from the chimney-corner. [Ib.]

8 I never heard the old song of Percy and Douglas, that I found not my heart moved more than with a trumpet. [Ib.]

9 Thy necessity is greater than mine. [On giving his water-bottle to a dying soldier on the battlefield of Zutphen, 1586]

Sieyès, Abbé Emmanuel Joseph (1748–1836)

10 *J'ai vécu.* I survived. [Reply when asked what he did during the French Revolution]

Simonides (c. 556–468 B.C.)

11 Go, tell the Spartans, thou who passest by, / That here, obedient to their laws, we lie. [Herodotus, *Histories*]

Simpson, N.F. (1919–)

12 Each of us as he receives his private trouncings at the hands of fate is kept in good heart by the moth in his brother's parachute, and the scorpion in his neighbour's underwear. [*A Resounding Tinkle*]

Sims, George R. (1847–1922)

13 It is Christmas Day in the Workhouse. [*Dagonet Ballads*]

Sitwell, Edith (1887–1964)

14 When / Sir / Beelzebub called for his syllabub in the hotel in Hell / Where Proserpine first fell. [*Façade*]

15 Still falls the Rain — / Dark as the world of man, black as our loss — / Blind as the nineteen hundred and forty nails / Upon the Cross. ['Still Falls the Rain']

16 Why not be oneself? That is the whole secret of a successful appearance. If one is a greyhound, why try to look like a Pekingese? ['Why I look as I do']

Sitwell, Sir Osbert (1892–1969)

17 The British Bourgeoisie / Is not born, / And does not die, / But, if it is ill, / It has a frightened look in its eyes. ['At the House of Mrs. Kinfoot']

Skelton, John (c. 1460–1529)

18 Vengeance I ask and cry, / By way of exclamation, / On the whole nation / Of cattes wild and tame: / God send them sorrow and shame. ['The Sparrow's Dirge']

19 And robin redbreast, / He shall be the priest / The requiem mass to sing, / Softly warbeling. [Ib.]

Skinner, B.F. (1904–)

20 Education is what survives when what has been learnt has been forgotten. [*New Scientist*, 1964]

Smart, Christopher (1722–1771)

1 For I will consider my Cat Jeoffry. / For he is the servant of the Living God, duly and daily serving Him. / For at the first glance of the glory of God in the East he worships in his way. / For this is done by wreathing his body seven times round with elegant quickness. [*Jubilate Agno*, 19]

2 For the English Cats are the best in Europe. [Ib.]

Smedley, Francis Edward (1818–1864)

3 You are looking as fresh as paint. [*Frank Fairleigh*]

Smiles, Samuel (1812–1904)

4 The shortest way to do many things is to do only one thing at once. [*Self-Help*, 9]

5 A place for everything, and everything in its place. [*Thrift*, 5]

Smith, Adam (1723–1790)

6 [Of the rich] They are led by an invisible hand to make nearly the same distribution of the necessities of life which would have been made, had the earth been divided into equal portions among all its inhabitants. [*Theory of Moral Sentiments*, IV]

7 No society can surely be flourishing and happy, of which the far greater part of the members are poor and miserable. [*Wealth of Nations*, I, 8]

8 With the greater part of rich people, the chief enjoyment of riches consists in the parade of riches. [Ib. I, 11]

9 To found a great empire for the sole purpose of raising up a people of customers, may at first sight appear a project fit only for a nation of shopkeepers. It is, however, a project altogether unfit for a nation of shopkeepers; but extremely fit for a nation that is governed by shopkeepers. [Ib. II, 4]

10 The discipline of colleges and universities is in general contrived, not for the benefit of the students, but for the interest, or more properly speaking, for the ease of the masters. [Ib. V, 1]

11 [Of the English universities] A sanctuary in which exploded systems and obsolete prejudices find shelter and protection after they have been hunted out of every corner of the world. [Ib.]

Smith, Alfred Emanuel (1873–1944)

12 The kiss of death. [Speech, 1926]

13 No matter how thin you slice it, it's still baloney. [Speech, 1936]

Smith, Joseph (1805–1844)

14 No man knows my history. [Self-written funeral sermon]

Smith, Logan Pearsall (1865–1946)

15 Most people sell their souls and live with a good conscience on the proceeds. [*All Trivia*]

16 There are two things to aim at in life: First, to get what you want; and after that to enjoy it. Only the wisest of mankind achieve the second. [Ib.]

17 People say that life is the thing, but I prefer reading. [Ib.]

18 How often my Soul visits the National Gallery, and how seldom I go there myself! [Ib.]

19 Married women are kept women, and they are beginning to find it out. [Ib.]

20 It is the wretchedness of being rich that you have to live with rich people. [Ib.]

21 I cannot forgive my friends for dying: I do not find these vanishing acts of theirs at all amusing. [Ib.]

22 I love money; just to be in the room with a millionaire makes me less forlorn. [Ib.]

23 Thank heavens, the sun has gone in, and I don't have to go out and enjoy it. [Ib.]

Smith, Samuel Francis (1808–1895)

24 My country, 'tis of thee, / Sweet land of liberty, / Of thee I sing. ['America']

Smith, Stevie (1902–1971)

1 Oh I am a cat that likes to / Gallop about doing good. ['The Galloping Cat']

2 I was much further out than you thought / And not waving but drowning. ['Not Waving But Drowning']

3 Private Means is dead, / God rest his soul, / Officers and fellow-rankers said. ['Private Means is dead']

Smith, Sydney (1771–1845)

4 One of the greatest pleasures in life is conversation. [*Essays*, 'Female Education']

5 This great spectacle of human happiness. [Ib. 'Waterton's Wanderings']

6 The moment the very name of Ireland is mentioned, the English seem to bid adieu to common feeling, common prudence, and common sense, and to act with the barbarity of tyrants, and the fatuity of idiots. [*Peter Plymley's Letters*]

7 Curate — there is something which excites compassion in the very name of a Curate!!! [Ib.]

8 Where etiquette prevents me from doing things disagreeable to myself, I am a perfect martinet. [*Letters*, To Lady Holland]

9 I look upon Switzerland as an inferior sort of Scotland. [Ib. To Lord Holland]

10 What would life be without arithmetic, but a scene of horrors. [Ib. To Miss——]

11 I am convinced digestion is the great secret of life. [Ib. To Arthur Kinglake]

12 I have no relish for the country; it is a kind of healthy grave. [Ib. To Miss G. Harcourt]

13 Daniel Webster struck me much like a steam engine in trousers. [Lady Holland, *Memoirs*, I]

14 Take short views, hope for the best, and trust in God. [Ib.]

15 Not body enough to cover his mind decently with; his intellect is improperly exposed. [Ib.]

16 There are three sexes — men, women, and clergymen. [Ib.]

17 It requires a surgical operation to get a joke well into a Scotch understanding. Their only idea of wit...is laughing immoderately at stated intervals. [Ib.]

18 [Scotland] That knuckle-end of England — that land of Calvin, oat-cakes, and sulphur. [Ib.]

19 Looked as if she had walked straight out of the Ark. [Ib.]

20 No furniture so charming as books. [Ib.]

21 I have, alas, only one illusion left, and that is the Archbishop of Canterbury. [Ib.]

22 Let onion atoms lurk within the bowl, / And, scarce suspected, animate the whole. [Ib. 'Recipe for Salad']

23 Deserves to be preached to death by wild curates. [Ib.]

24 Madam, I have been looking for a person who disliked gravy all my life; let us swear eternal friendship. [Ib.]

25 How can a bishop marry? How can he flirt? The most he can say is, 'I will see you in the vestry after service.' [Ib.]

26 Praise is the best diet for us, after all. [Ib.]

27 He [Macaulay] has occasional flashes of silence, that make his conversation perfectly delightful. [Ib.]

28 You find people ready enough to do the Samaritan, without the oil and twopence. [Ib.]

29 ——'s idea of heaven is, eating *pâtés de foie gras* to the sound of trumpets. [Pearson, *The Smith of Smiths*]

30 Death must be distinguished from dying, with which it is often confused. [Ib.]

31 I am just going to pray for you at St. Paul's, but with no very lively hope of success. [Ib.]

32 I never read a book before reviewing it; it prejudices a man so. [Ib.]

33 [Of William Whewell] Science is his forte, and omniscience his foible. [Ib.]

1 Poverty is no disgrace to a man, but it is confoundedly inconvenient. [*His Wit and Wisdom*]

Smith, Sir Sydney (1883-1969)

2 No child is born a criminal: no child is born an angel: he's just born. [Remark]

Smollett, Tobias (1721-1771)

3 To a man of honour (said I) the unfortunate need no introduction. [*Ferdinand Count Fathom*, 62]

4 Hark ye, Clinker, you are a most notorious offender. You stand convicted of sickness, hunger, wretchedness, and want. [*Humphrey Clinker*, Letter to Sir Watkin Phillips]

5 The painful ceremony of receiving and returning visits. [*Peregrine Pickle*, 5]

6 A mere index hunter, who held the eel of science by the tail. [Ib. 43]

7 Some folks are wise, and some are otherwise. [*Roderick Random*, 6]

8 He was formed for the ruin of our sex. [Ib. 22]

9 I consider the world as made for me, not me for the world. It is my maxim therefore to enjoy it while I can, and let futurity shift for itself. [Ib. 45]

10 True Patriotism is of no party. [*Sir Lancelot Greaves*, 9]

11 A seafaring man may have a sweetheart in every port; but he should steer clear of a wife as he would avoid a quicksand. [Ib. 21]

12 Too coy to flatter, and too proud to serve, / Thine be the joyless dignity to starve. ['Advice']

13 What foreign arms could never quell / By civil rage and rancour fell. ['The Tears of Scotland']

14 [Of Johnson] That great Cham of literature. [Letter, 1759]

Snow, C.P. (1905-1980)

15 The Corridors of Power [Title of novel]

16 The Two Cultures [Title of lecture series]

Socrates (469-399 B.C.)

17 The unexamined life is not worth living. [Plato, *Apology*]

18 [Looking at goods for sale] How many things I have no need of! [Diogenes Laertius, *Lives of the Eminent Philosophers*]

19 Crito, I owe a cock to Asclepius; will you remember to pay the debt? [Last words]

Solon (c. 638-c. 559 B.C.)

20 Laws are like spider's webs, which stand firm when any light, yielding object falls upon them, while a larger thing breaks through them and escapes. [Diogenes Laertius, *Lives of the Eminent Philosophers*]

21 Call no man happy until he is dead, but only lucky. [Herodotus, *Histories*]

Solzhenitsyn, Alexander (1918-)

22 If decade after decade the truth cannot be told, each person's mind begins to roam irretrievably. One's fellow countrymen become harder to understand than Martians. [*Cancer Ward*, II, 11]

23 You only have power over people so long as you don't take *everything* away from them. But when you've robbed a man of everything he's no longer in your power — he's free again. [*The First Circle*, 17]

Somerville, William (1675-1742)

24 My hoarse-sounding horn / Invites thee to the chase, the sport of kings; / Image of war, without its guilt. [*The Chase*, I]

25 Hail, happy Britain! highly favoured isle, / And Heaven's peculiar care! [Ib.]

Sontag, Susan (1933-)

26 Interpretation is the revenge of the intellect upon art. [*Against Interpretation*]

Sophocles (495-406 B.C.)

27 Life is short but sweet. [*Alcestis*]

28 Marvels are many, but man is the greatest. [*Antigone*]

1 Death is not the worst thing; rather, to wish in vain for death, and not compass it. [*Electra*]

2 Athens, nurse of men. [*Oedipus at Colonus*]

3 Not to be born is best. The second best is to have seen the light and then to go back quickly whence we came. [Ib.]

Soule, John Babsone Lane (1815–1891)

4 Go west, young man. [*Terre Haute* (Indiana) *Express*, 1851]

South, Robert (1634–1716)

5 An Aristotle was but the rubbish of an Adam, and Athens but the rudiments of Paradise. [*Sermons*, I]

Southerne, Thomas (1660–1746)

6 And when we're worn, / Hack'd, hewn with constant service, thrown aside / To rust in peace, or rot in hospitals. [*Loyal Brother*, I]

Southey, Robert (1774–1843)

7 'Now tell us all about the war, / And what they fought each other for.' ['The Battle of Blenheim']

8 But what they fought each other for, / I could not well make out. [Ib.]

9 'But what good came of it at last?' / Quoth little Peterkin. / 'Why, that I cannot tell,' said he, / 'But 'twas a famous victory.' [Ib.]

10 My name is Death: the last best friend am I. [*Carmen Nuptiale*]

11 Curses are like young chickens, they always come home to roost. [*The Curse of Kehama*, motto]

12 The arts babblative and scribblative. [*Colloquies on the Progress and Prospects of Society*]

13 The march of intellect. [Ib.]

14 Your true lover of literature is never fastidious. [*The Doctor*, 17]

15 Show me a man who cares no more for one place than another, and I will show you in that same person one who loves nothing but himself. Beware of those who are homeless by choice. [Ib. 34]

16 Live as long as you may, the first twenty years are the longest half of your life. [Ib. 130]

17 Till the vessel strikes with a shivering shock, — / 'O Christ, it is the Inchcape Rock!' ['The Inchcape Rock']

18 You are old, Father William, the young man cried, / The few locks which are left you are grey; / You are hale, Father William, a hearty old man, / Now tell me the reason, I pray. ['The Old Man's Comforts, and how he Gained them']

19 In the days of my youth I remembered my God! / And He hath not forgotten my age. [Ib.]

20 Their wintry garment of unsullied snow / The mountains have put on. [*The Poet's Pilgrimage*, I]

21 The death of Nelson was felt in England as something more than a public calamity; men started at the intelligence, and turned pale, as if they had heard of the loss of a dear friend. [*The Life of Nelson*, 9]

Southwell, Robert (1561–1595)

22 As I in hoary winter's night stood shivering in the snow, / Surprised I was with sudden heat which made my heart to glow; / And lifting up a fearful eye to view what fire was near, / A pretty Babe all burning bright did in the air appear. ['The Burning Babe']

Spark, Muriel (1918–)

23 If only you small girls would listen to me, I would make of you the crème de la crème. [*The Prime of Miss Jean Brodie*, 1]

24 There was a Miss Jean Brodie in her prime. [Ib. last sentence]

Spencer, Herbert (1820–1903)

25 Science is organized knowledge. [*Education*, 2]

26 The ultimate result of shielding men from the effects of folly, is to fill the world with fools. [*Essays*, 'The Americans']

1 The Republican form of Government is the highest form of government; but because of this it requires the highest type of human nature — a type nowhere at present existing. [Ib.]

2 The survival of the fittest. [*Principles of Biology*]

3 How often misused words generate misleading thoughts. [*Principles of Ethics*]

4 Opinion is ultimately determined by the feelings, and not by the intellect. [*Social Statics*]

5 No one can be perfectly free till all are free; no one can be perfectly moral till all are moral; no one can be perfectly happy till all are happy. [Ib.]

6 It was remarked to me...that to play billiards well was a sign of an ill-spent youth. [Duncan, *Life and Letters of Spencer*]

Spender, Stephen (1909–)

7 I think continually of those who were truly great — / The names of those who in their lives fought for life, / Who wore at their hearts the fire's centre. ['I Think Continually of Those']

8 Born of the sun they travelled a short while towards the sun, / And left the vivid air signed with their honour. [Ib.]

9 My parents kept me from children who were rough / Who threw words like stones and who wore torn clothes. [*Preludes*]

10 After the first powerful, plain manifesto / The black statement of pistons, without more fuss / But gliding like a queen, she leaves the station. [Ib. 'The Express']

Spenser, Edmund (c. 1522–1599)

11 The merry cuckoo, messenger of Spring, / His trumpet shrill hath thrice already sounded. [*Amoretti*, Sonnet 19]

12 Most glorious Lord of life, that on this day / Didst make thy triumph over death and sin: / And, having harrow'd hell, didst bring away / Captivity thence captive, us to win. [Ib. 68]

13 So let us love, dear love, like as we ought, / — Love is the lesson which the Lord us taught. [Ib.]

14 One day I wrote her name upon the sand / But came the waves and washed it away: / Again I wrote it with a second hand / But came the tide, and made my pains his prey. [Ib. 75]

15 My verse your virtues rare shall eternize, / And in the heavens write your glorious name, / Where when as death shall all the world subdue, / Our love shall live, and later life renew. [Ib.]

16 Of such deep learning little had he need, / Ne yet, of Latin, ne of Greek, that breed / Doubts 'mongst Divines, and difference of texts, / From whence arise diversity of sects, / And hateful heresies. [*Complaints*, 'Mother Hubbard's Tale']

17 What more felicity can fall to creature, / Than to enjoy delight with liberty. [Ib. 'Muiopotmos']

18 The woods shall to me answer and my echo ring. [*Epithalamion*]

19 Open the temple gates unto my love, / Open them wide that she may enter in. [Ib.]

20 Ah! when will this long weary day have end, / And lend me leave to come unto my love? [Ib.]

21 Fierce wars and faithful loves shall moralize my song. [*The Faerie Queen*, I]

22 A gentle knight was pricking on the plain. [Ib.]

23 But on his breast a bloody cross he bore, / The dear remembrance of his dying Lord. [Ib.]

24 Her angel's face / As the great eye of heaven shined bright, / And made a sunshine in the shady place. [Ib.]

25 The noble heart, that harbours virtuous thought, / And is with child of glorious great intent, / Can never rest, until it forth have brought / Th' eternal brood of glory excellent. [Ib.]

26 A cruel crafty Crocodile, / Which in false grief hiding his harmful guile, / Doth weep full sore, and sheddeth tender tears. [Ib.]

1 Sleep after toil, port after stormy seas, / Ease after war, death after life, does greatly please. [Ib.]

2 And all for love, and nothing for reward. [Ib. II]

3 The dunghill kind / Delights in filth and foul incontinence: / Let Grill be Grill, and have his hoggish mind. [Ib.]

4 Dan Chaucer, well of English undefiled, / On Fame's eternal beadroll worthy to be filed. [Ib. IV]

5 A monster, which the Blatant beast men call, / A dreadful fiend of gods and men ydrad. [Ib. V]

6 The gentle mind by gentle deeds is known. / For a man by nothing is so well bewray'd, / As by his manners. [Ib. VI]

7 What man that sees the ever-whirling wheel / Of Change, the which all mortal things doth sway / But that thereby doth find, and plainly feel, / How Mutability in them doth play / Her cruel sports, to many men's decay? [Ib. VII]

8 For all that moveth doth in Change delight: / But thenceforth all shall rest eternally / With Him that is the God of Sabbaoth hight: / O that great Sabbaoth God, grant me that Sabbaoth's sight. [Ib. VIII]

9 Calm was the day and through the trembling air, / Sweet breathing Zephyrus did softly play. ['Prothalamion']

10 With that, I saw two Swans of goodly hue, / Come softly swimming down along the Lee. [Ib.]

11 Sweet Thames, run softly, till I end my song. [Ib.]

12 So now they have made our English tongue a gallimaufry or hodgepodge of all other speeches. [*The Shepherd's Calendar*, Letter to Gabriel Harvey]

Spinoza, Baruch (1632–1677)

13 One and the same thing can at the same time be good, bad, and indifferent, for example, music is good to the melancholy, bad to those who mourn, and neither good nor bad to the deaf. [*Ethics*, IV]

14 We feel and know that we are eternal. [Ib. V]

Spooner, William (1844–1930)

15 Kinquering Congs their titles take. [Announcing hymn in chapel]

16 Let us drink to the queer old Dean. [Attr.]

17 Poor soul, very sad; her late husband, you know, a very sad death — eaten by missionaries — poor soul! [W. Hayter, *Spooner*]

Sprat, Thomas (1635–1713)

18 Poetry is the mother of superstition. [*History of the Royal Society*]

Spring-Rice, Arthur Cecil (1859–1918)

19 I vow to thee, my country — all earthly things above — / Entire and whole and perfect, the service of my love. ['Last Poem']

20 Her ways are ways of gentleness and all her paths are peace. [Ib.]

Squire, J.C. (1884–1958)

21 It did not last: the devil howling 'Ho! / Let Einstein be!' restored the status quo. ['Answer to Pope's Epitaph on Sir Isaac Newton']

Stalin, Joseph (1879–1953)

22 The Pope! How many divisions has *he* got? [Remark, 1935]

Stanley, Sir Henry Morton (1841–1904)

23 Dr. Livingstone, I presume? [*How I found Livingstone*, 2]

24 The Dark Continent [Africa] [Title of book]

Stanton, Edwin McMasters (1814–1869)

25 Now he belongs to the ages. [Remark on hearing of Lincoln's assassination]

Stark, John (1728–1822)

26 We beat them today or Molly Stark's a widow. [Remark before Battle of Bennington, 1777]

Steele, Sir Richard (1672-1729)

1 I have often thought that a story-teller is born, as well as a poet. [*The Guardian*, 24]

2 Women dissemble their Passions better than Men, but Men subdue their Passions better than Women. [*The Lover*, 9]

3 No Woman of spirit thinks a Man hath any Respect for her 'till he hath played the Fool in her Service. [Ib.]

4 There are so few who can grow old with a good grace. [*Spectator*, 263]

5 [Of Lady Hastings] Though her mien carries much more invitation than command, to behold her is an immediate check to loose behaviour; to love her was a liberal education. [*Tatler*, 49]

6 The insupportable labour of doing nothing. [Ib. 54]

7 Reading is to the mind what exercise is to the body. [Ib. 54]

8 Let your precept be, Be easy. [Ib. 196]

Steffens, Lincoln (1866-1936)

9 I have seen the future, and it works. [Remark after visiting Russia in 1919]

Stein, Gertrude (1874-1946)

10 Rose is a rose is a rose is a rose. [*Sacred Emily*]

11 What is the answer?... [On receiving no response] In that case, what is the question? [Last words]

Stendhal (1783-1842)

12 A novel is a mirror walking along the highway. [*Le Rouge et le Noir*, 49]

Stephen, James Kenneth (1859-1892)

13 Two voices are there: one is of the deep; / ...And one is of an old half-witted sheep / Which bleats articulate monotony, / ...And Wordsworth, both are thine. [*Lapsus Calami*, Sonnet; *see* Wordsworth, *Sonnets*, 'Two Voices are there']

Stephens, James (1882-1950)

14 I heard a sudden cry of pain! / There is a rabbit in a snare. ['The Snare']

15 Little One! Oh, Little One! / I am searching everywhere! [Ib.]

Sterne, Laurence (1713-1768)

16 They order, said I, this matter better in France. [*A Sentimental Journey*, first sentence]

17 As an Englishman does not travel to see Englishmen, I retired to my room. [Ib. 'Preface']

18 I pity the man who can travel from Dan to Beersheba, and cry, 'tis all barren. [Ib. 'In the Street. Calais']

19 There are worse occupations in the world than feeling a woman's pulse. [Ib. 'The Pulse']

20 'I can't get out, — I can't get out,' said the starling. [Ib. 'The Passport']

21 He gave a deep sigh — I saw the iron enter into his soul! [Ib. 'The Captive. Paris']

22 I think there is a fatality in it — I seldom go to the place I set out for. [Ib. 'The Address. Versailles']

23 God tempers the wind to the shorn lamb. [Ib. 'Maria']

24 So that when I stretched out my hand, I caught hold of the fille de chambre's [Ib. 'The Case of Delicacy', last words]

25 I live in a constant endeavour to fence against the infirmities of ill health, and other evils of life, by mirth; being firmly persuaded that every time a man smiles, — but much more so, when he laughs, it adds something to this Fragment of Life. [*Tristram Shandy*, Dedication]

26 I wish either my father or my mother, or indeed both of them, as they were in duty both equally bound to it, had minded what they were about when they begot me. [Ib. I, 1]

27 'Pray, my dear,' quoth my mother, 'have you not forgot to wind up the clock?' [Ib.]

1 So long as a man rides his hobby-horse peaceably and quietly along the king's highway, and neither compels you or me to get up behind him, — pray, Sir, what have either you or I to do with it? [Ib. I, 7]

2 Desire of knowledge, like the thirst of riches, increases ever with the acquisition of it. [Ib. II, 3]

3 Writing, when properly managed (as you may be sure I think mine is), is but a different name for conversation. [Ib. II, 11]

4 'I'll not hurt thee,' says my uncle Toby, rising from his chair, and going across the room, with the fly in his hand...'This world surely is wide enough to hold both thee and me.' [Ib. II, 12]

5 'Tis no extravagant arithmetic to say, that for every ten jokes, — thou hast got an hundred enemies. [Ib.]

6 'Tis known by the name of perseverance in a good cause, — and of obstinacy in a bad one. [Ib. II, 17]

7 Whenever a man talks loudly against religion, — always suspect that it is not his reason, but his passions which have got the better of his creed. [Ib.]

8 'I wish,' quoth my uncle Toby, 'you had seen what prodigious armies we had in Flanders.' [Ib. II, 18]

9 My uncle Toby would never offer to answer this by any other kind of argument, than that of whistling half a dozen bars of Lillabullero. [Ib. II, 21]

10 Digressions, incontestably, are the sunshine; — they are the life, the soul of reading! — take them out of this book for instance, — you might as well take the book along with them. [Ib. II, 22]

11 A man's body and his mind...are exactly like a jerkin and a jerkin's lining; — rumple the one, — you rumple the other. [Ib. III, 4]

12 Of all the cants which are canted in this canting world, — though the cant of hypocrites may be the worst, — the cant of criticism is the most tormenting! [Ib. III, 12]

13 All is not gain that is got into the purse. [Ib. III, 30]

14 Heat is in proportion to the want of true knowledge. [Ib. IV, Slawkenbergius's Tale]

15 The nonsense of the old women (of both sexes). [Ib. V, 16]

16 There is a North-west passage to the intellectual world. [Ib. V, 42]

17 You forget the great Lipsius, quoth Yorick, who composed a work the day he was born; — they should have wiped it up, said my uncle Toby, and said no more about it. [Ib. VI, 2]

18 Ask my pen, — it governs me, — I govern not it. [Ib. IV, 6]

19 The excellency of this text is that it will suit any sermon, — and of this sermon, — that it will suit any text. [Ib. VI, 11]

20 'A soldier,' cried my uncle Toby, interrupting the corporal, 'is no more exempt from saying a foolish thing, Trim, than a man of letters.' — 'But not so often, an' please your Honour,' replied the corporal. [Ib. VIII, 19]

21 Love, an' please your Honour, is exactly like war, in this; that a soldier, though he has escaped three weeks complete o' Saturday night, — may, nevertheless, be shot through his heart on Sunday morning. [Ib. VIII, 21]

22 Honours, like impressions upon coin, may give an ideal and local value to a bit of base metal; but Gold and Silver will pass all the world over without any other recommendation than their own weight. [Ib. IX, Dedication]

23 Said my mother, 'what is all this story about?' — 'A Cock and a Bull', said Yorick. [Ib. IX, 33]

24 This sad vicissitude of things. [*Sermons*, 15]

Stevens, Wallace (1879–1955)

25 The only emperor is the emperor of ice-cream. ['The Emperor of Ice-Cream']

26 Poetry is the supreme fiction, madame. ['A High-Toned old Christian Woman']

27 Oh! Blessed rage for order, pale Ramon. ['The Idea of Order at Key West']

1 They said, 'You have a blue guitar, / You do not play things as they are.' / The man replied, 'Things as they are / Are changed upon a blue guitar.' [*The Man with the Blue Guitar*]

2 Complacencies of the peignoir, and late / Coffee and oranges in a sunny chair. ['Sunday Morning']

3 I do not know which to prefer, / The beauty of inflections / Or the beauty of innuendoes, / The blackbird whistling / Or just after. ['Thirteen Ways of Looking at a Blackbird']

Stevenson, Adlai (1900–1965)

4 A lie is an abomination unto the Lord , and a very present help in trouble. [Speech, 1951]

5 An editor is one who separates the wheat from the chaff and prints the chaff. [Quoted in *The Stevenson Wit*]

6 Making peace is harder than making war. [Address, 1946]

7 [Of Eleanor Roosevelt] She would rather light a candle than curse the darkness. [Speech, 1962]

Stevenson, Robert Louis (1850–1894)

8 In winter I get up at night / And dress by yellow candle-light. / In summer, quite the other way, — / I have to go to bed by day. [*A Child's Garden of Verses*, 'Bed in Summer']

9 A child should always say what's true, / And speak when he is spoken to, / And behave mannerly at table: / At least as far as he is able. [Ib. 'Whole Duty of Children']

10 When I am grown to man's estate / I shall be very proud and very great, / And tell the other girls and boys / Not to meddle with my toys. [Ib. 'Looking Forward']

11 The pleasant land of counterpane. [Ib. 'The Land of Counterpane']

12 O Leerie, I'll go round at night and light the lamps with you. [Ib. 'The Lamplighter']

13 The world is so full of a number of things, / I'm sure we should all be as happy as kings. [Ib. 'Happy Thought']

14 A birdie with a yellow bill / Hopped upon the window-sill. / Cocked his shining eye and said: / 'Ain't you 'shamed, you sleepy-head?' [Ib. 'Time to Rise']

15 All I seek, the heaven above / And the road below me. [*Songs of Travel*, 'The Vagabond']

16 Be it granted to me to behold you again in dying, / Hills of home! [Ib. 'To S.R. Crockett']

17 Trusty, dusky, vivid, true, / With eyes of gold and bramble-dew, / Steel-true and blade-straight, / The great artificer / Made my mate. ['My Wife']

18 There's nothing under Heav'n so blue / That's fairly worth the travelling to. [Ib. 'A Song of the Road']

19 Of all my verse, like not a single line; / But like my title, for it is not mine, / That title from a better man I stole; / Ah, how much better, had I stol'n the whole! [*Underwoods*, Foreword]

20 Under the wide and starry sky / Dig the grave and let me lie / Glad did I live and gladly die, / And I laid me down with a will. / This be the verse you grave for me: / 'Here he lies where he longed to be; / Home is the sailor, home from sea, / And the hunter home from the hill.' [Ib. 'Requiem']

21 'It's gey an' easy spierin',' says the beggar-wife to me. [Ib. 'The Spaewife']

22 The harmless art of knucklebones has seen the fall of the Roman Empire and the rise of the United States. [*Across the Plains*, 'The Lantern-Bearers']

23 The bright face of danger. [Ib.]

24 Everyone lives by selling something. [Ib. 'Beggars']

25 Surely we should find it both touching and inspiriting, that in a field from which success is banished, our race should not cease to labour. [Ib. 'Pulvis et Umbra']

1 To be honest, to be kind — to earn a little and to spend a little less, to make upon the whole a family happier for his presence, to renounce when that shall be necessary and not be embittered, to keep a few friends, but these without capitulation — above all, on the same grim condition, to keep friends with himself — here is a task for all that a man has of fortitude and delicacy. [Ib. 'A Christmas Sermon']

2 These are my politics: to change what we can; to better what we can; but still to bear in mind that man is but a devil weakly fettered by some generous beliefs and impositions; and for no word however sounding, and no cause however just and pious, to relax the stricture of these bonds. [*The Dynamiter*]

3 Politics is perhaps the only profession for which no preparation is thought necessary. [*Familiar Studies of Men and Books*]

4 'Am I no a bonny fighter?' [*Kidnapped*, 10]

5 'I've a grand memory for forgetting, David.' [Ib. 18]

6 Is there anything in life so disenchanting as attainment? [*New Arabian Nights*, 'The Adventure of the Hansom Cab']

7 I regard you with an indifference closely bordering on aversion. [Ib. 'The Rajah's Diamond']

8 For my part, I travel not to go anywhere, but to go. I travel for travel's sake. The great affair is to move. [*Travels with a Donkey*]

9 Fifteen men on the dead man's chest / Yo-ho-ho, and a bottle of rum! / Drink and the devil had done for the rest — / Yo-ho-ho, and a bottle of rum. [*Treasure Island*, 1]

10 Tip me the black spot. [Ib. 3]

11 Pieces of eight! [Ib. 10]

12 Many's the long night I've dreamed of cheese — toasted, mostly. [Ib. 15]

13 In marriage, a man becomes slack and selfish, and undergoes a fatty degeneration of his moral being. [*Virginibus Puerisque*, 1]

14 Even if we take matrimony at its lowest, even if we regard it as no more than a sort of friendship recognized by the police. [Ib.]

15 Lastly (and this is, perhaps, the golden rule), no woman should marry a teetotaller, or a man who does not smoke. [Ib.]

16 Marriage is like life in this - that it is a field of battle and not a bed of roses. [Ib.]

17 Times are changed with him who marries; there are no more by-path meadows, where you may innocently linger, but the road lies long and straight and dusty to the grave. [Ib.]

18 To marry is to domesticate the Recording Angel. Once you are married, there is nothing left for you, not even suicide, but to be good. [Ib.]

19 Man is a creature who lives not upon bread alone, but principally by catchwords. [Ib.]

20 Old and young, we are all on our last cruise. [Ib.]

21 Youth is the time to go flashing from one end of the world to the other both in mind and body; to try the manners of different nations; to hear the chimes at midnight; to see sunrise in town and country; to be converted at a revival; to circumnavigate the metaphysics, write halting verses, run a mile to see a fire, and wait all day long in the theatre to applaud 'Hernani'. [Ib.]

22 To love playthings well as a child, to lead an adventurous and honourable youth, and to settle when the time arrives, into a green and smiling age, is to be a good artist in life and deserve well of yourself and your neighbour. [Ib.]

23 It is better to be a fool than to be dead. [Ib.]

24 There is no duty we so much underrate as the duty of being happy. [Ib. 3]

25 By the time a man gets well into the seventies his continued existence is a mere miracle. [Ib. 5]

26 To travel hopefully is a better thing than to arrive, and the true success is to labour. [Ib. 6]

1 Though we are mighty fine fellows nowadays, we cannot write like Hazlitt. [Ib. 10]

2 Between the possibility of being hanged in all innocence, and the certainty of a public and merited disgrace, no gentleman of spirit could long hesitate. [*The Wrong Box*, 10 (with Lloyd Osbourne)]

Stone, Samuel John (1839–1900)

3 The Church's one foundation / Is Jesus Christ her Lord. [Hymn]

4 Though with a scornful wonder / Men see her sore oppressed, / By schisms rent asunder, / By heresies distressed, / Yet saints their watch are keeping, / Their cry goes up, 'How long?' [Ib.]

Stoppard, Tom (1937–)

5 We do on the stage the things that are supposed to happen off. Which is a kind of integrity, if you look on every exit being an entrance somewhere else. [*Rosencrantz and Guildenstern Are Dead*, I]

6 To sum up: your father, whom you love, dies, you are his heir, you come back to find that hardly was the corpse cold before his younger brother popped on to his throne and into his sheets, thereby offending both legal and natural practice. Now why exactly are you behaving in this extraordinary manner? [Ib.]

7 The bad end unhappily, the good unluckily. That is what tragedy means. [Ib. II]

8 [After BBC-type sea sounds] We're on a boat! [Ib. III]

Stowe, Harriet Beecher (1812–1896)

9 'Who was your mother?' 'Never had none!' said the child, with another grin. 'Never had any mother? What do you mean? Where were you born?' 'Never was born!' persisted Topsy. [*Uncle Tom's Cabin*, 20]

10 'Do you know who made you?' 'Nobody, as I knows on,' said the child, with a short laugh...'I 'spect I grow'd.' [Ib.]

11 ''Cause I's wicked — I is. I's mighty wicked, any how. I can't help it.' [Ib.]

Stowell, Lord (1745–1836)

12 The elegant simplicity of the three per cents. [Campbell, *Lives of the Lord Chancellors*, X]

Stubbes, Philip (fl. c. 1580)

13 Football...causeth fighting, brawling, contention, quarrel picking, murder, homicide and great effusion of blood, as daily experience teacheth. [*Anatomy of Abuses*]

Suckling, Sir John (1609–1642)

14 Her feet beneath her petticoat, / Like little mice, stole in and out, / As if they fear'd the light. ['Ballad upon a Wedding']

15 I prithee send me back my heart, / Since I cannot have thine: / For if from yours you will not part, / Why then shouldst thou have mine? ['Song']

16 Out upon it, I have lov'd / Three whole days together; / And am like to love three more, / If it prove fair weather. ['Song']

17 Why so pale and wan, fond lover? / Prithee, why so pale? / Will, when looking well can't move her, / Looking ill prevail? ['Song']

18 'Tis love in love that makes the sport. [Sonnet]

Suetonius (fl. A.D. 75–150)

19 *Festina lente.* Hasten slowly. [*Divus Augustus*]

20 *Ave, Imperator, morituri te salutant.* Hail, Emperor, those about to die salute thee. [*Life of Claudius*]

Sullivan, Sir Arthur (1842–1900)

21 [Accused of plagiarism] We all have the same eight notes to work with. [Attr.]

Sully, Duc de (1559–1641)

22 *Les Anglais s'amusent tristement, selon l'usage de leur pays.* The English enjoy themselves sadly, after the custom of their country. [*Memoirs*]

Surrey, Henry Howard, Earl of (c. 1517–1547)

1 My friend, the things for to attain / The happy life be these, I find: / The riches left, not got with pain; / The fruitful ground, the quiet mind. ['The Happy Life']

Surtees, Robert Smith (1803–1864)

2 The only infallible rule we know is, that the man who is always talking about being a gentleman never is one. [*Ask Mamma*]

3 Where the M.F.H. dines he sleeps, and where the M.F.H. sleeps he breakfasts. [*Handley Cross*, 15]

4 It ar'n't that I loves the fox less, but that I loves the 'ound more. [Ib. 16]

5 Champagne certainly gives one werry gentlemanly ideas, but for a continuance, I don't know but I should prefer mild hale. [*Jorrocks's Jaunts and Jollities*, 9]

6 These sort of boobies think that people come to balls to do nothing but dance; whereas everyone knows that the real business of a ball is either to look out for a wife, to look after a wife, or to look after somebody else's wife. [*Mr. Facey Romford's Hounds*]

7 There is no secret so close as that between a rider and his horse. [*Mr. Sponge's Sporting Tour*]

Swift, Jonathan (1667–1745)

8 Satire is a kind of glass, wherein beholders do generally discover everybody's face but their own. [*Battle of the Books*, Preface]

9 Instead of dirt and poison we have rather chosen to fill our hives with honey and wax; thus furnishing mankind with the two noblest of things, which are sweetness and light. [Ib.]

10 It is the folly of too many to mistake the echo of a London coffee-house for the voice of the kingdom. [*The Conduct of the Allies*]

11 Big-endians and small-endians. [*Gulliver's Travels*, 'Lilliput']

12 I cannot but conclude the bulk of your natives to be the most pernicious race of little odious vermin that nature ever suffered to crawl upon the surface of the earth. [Ib. 'Brobdignag']

13 And he gave it for his opinion, that whoever could make two ears of corn or two blades of grass to grow upon a spot of ground where only one grew before, would deserve better of mankind, and do more essential service to his country than the whole race of politicians put together. [Ib.]

14 I said the thing which was not. [Ib. 'The Houyhnhnms']

15 My horses understand me tolerably well; I converse with them at least four hours every day. They are strangers to bridle or saddle; they live in great amity with me, and friendship to each other. [Ib.]

16 Will she pass in a crowd? Will she make a figure in a country church? [*Journal to Stella*, 1711]

17 He showed me his bill of fare to tempt me to dine with him; poh, said I, I value not your bill of fare, give me your bill of company. [Ib.]

18 Monday is parson's holiday. [Ib. 1712]

19 Proper words in proper places, make the true definition of a style. ['Letter to a Young Clergyman']

20 I have been assured by a very knowing American of my acquaintance in London, that a young healthy child, well nursed, is, at a year old, a most delicious, nourishing, and wholesome food, whether stewed, roasted, baked, or boiled; and I make no doubt that it will equally serve in a fricassee, or a ragout. [*A Modest Proposal*]

21 Promises and pie-crust are made to be broken. [*Polite Conversation*, 1]

22 Bachelor's fare; bread and cheese, and kisses. [Ib.]

23 Why, every one as they like; as the good woman said when she kissed her cow. [Ib.]

24 I won't quarrel with my bread and butter. [Ib.]

25 Faith, that's as well said, as if I had said it myself. [Ib. 2]

1 Books, like men their authors, have no more than one way of coming into the world, but there are ten thousand to go out of it, and return no more. [*A Tale of a Tub*, Dedication]

2 Satire, by being levelled at all, is never resented for an offence by any. [Ib. Preface]

3 What though his head be empty, provided his commonplace book be full. [Ib. 'Digression in Praise of Digression']

4 Last week I saw a woman flayed, and you will hardly believe how much it altered her person for the worse. [Ib. 9]

5 This is the sublime and refined point of felicity, called, the possession of being well deceived; the serene peaceful state of being a fool among knaves. [Ib.]

6 When a true genius appears in the world, you may know him by this sign, that the dunces are all in confederacy against him. ['Thoughts on Various Subjects']

7 What they do in heaven we are ignorant of; what they do *not* we are told expressly, that they neither marry, nor are given in marriage. [Ib.]

8 No wise man ever wished to be younger. [Ib.]

9 I never wonder to see men wicked, but I often wonder to see them not ashamed. [Ib.]

10 We have just enough religion to make us hate, but not enough to make us love one another. [Ib.]

11 Every man desires to live long; but no man would be old. [Ib.]

12 When men grow virtuous in their old age, they only make a sacrifice to God of the devil's leavings. [Ib.]

13 The stoical scheme of supplying our wants by lopping off our desires is like cutting off our feet when we want shoes. [Ib.]

14 So, naturalists observe, a flea / Hath smaller fleas that on him prey; / And these have smaller fleas to bite 'em, / And so proceed *ad infinitum*. [*On Poetry: A Rhapsody*]

15 As learned commentators view / In Homer more than Homer knew. [Ib.]

16 In all distresses of our friends, / We first consult our private ends; / While nature, kindly bent to ease us, / Points out some circumstance to please us. ['Verses on the Death of Dr. Swift']

17 Yet malice never was his aim; / He lash'd the vice, but spared the name; / No individual could resent, / Where thousands equally were meant. [Ib.]

18 He gave the little wealth he had / To build a house for fools and mad; / And show'd, by one satiric touch, / No nation wanted it so much. [Ib.]

19 I've often wish'd that I had clear, / For life, six hundred pounds a year, / A handsome house to lodge a friend, / A river at my garden's end, / A terrace walk, and half a rood / Of land, set out to plant a wood. ['Imitation of Horace, Satires II, 6']

20 I have ever hated all nations, professions and communities, and all my love is towards individuals...But principally I hate and detest that animal called man; although I heartily love John, Peter, Thomas, and so forth. [Letter, 1725]

21 Not die here in a rage, like a poisoned rat in a hole. [Letter, 1729]

22 [Of *A Tale of a Tub*] Good God! what a genius I had when I wrote that book. [Scott, *Life of Swift*]

23 *Ubi saeva indignatio ulterius cor lacerare nequit.* Where fierce indignation can no longer tear his heart. [Epitaph]

Swinburne, Algernon Charles (1837–1909)

24 When the hounds of spring are on winter's traces, / The mother of months in meadow or plain / Fills the shadows and windy places / With lisp of leaves and ripple of rain. [*Atalanta in Calydon*, Chorus]

25 And time remembered is grief forgotten, / And frosts are slain and flowers begotten. [Ib.]

26 For words divide and rend; / But silence is most noble till the end. [Ib.]

1 For a day and a night and a morrow, / That his strength might endure for a span / With travail and heavy sorrow, / The holy spirit of man. [Ib.]

2 Now all strange hours and all strange loves are over, / Dreams and desires and sombre songs and sweet. ['Ave atque Vale']

3 Sleep; and if life was bitter to thee, pardon, / If sweet give thanks; thou hast no more to live; / And to give thanks is good, and to forgive. [Ib.]

4 Villon, our sad bad glad mad brother's name. ['Ballad of François Villon']

5 But sweet as the rind was the core is; / We are fain of thee still, we are fain, / O sanguine and subtle Dolores, / Our Lady of Pain. [*Dolores*]

6 The delight that consumes the desire, / The desire that outruns the delight. [Ib.]

7 For the crown of our life as it closes / Is darkness, the fruit thereof dust; / No thorns go as deep as a rose's, / And love is more cruel than lust. [Ib.]

8 Come down and redeem us from virtue, / Our Lady of Pain. [Ib.]

9 In a coign of the cliff between lowland and highland, / At the sea-down's edge between windward and lee, / Walled round with rocks as an inland island, / The ghost of a garden fronts the sea. ['The Forsaken Garden']

10 Stretched out on the spoils that his own hand spread, / As a god self-slain on his own strange altar, / Death lies dead. [Ib.]

11 Pale, beyond porch and portal, / Crowned with calm leaves, she stands / Who gathers all things mortal / With cold immortal hands. ['The Garden of Proserpine']

12 We thank with brief thanksgiving / Whatever gods may be / That no man lives forever, / That dead men rise up never; / That even the weariest river / Winds somewhere safe to sea. [Ib.]

13 Glory to Man in the highest! for Man is the master of things. ['Hymn of Man']

14 Thou has conquered, O pale Galilean; the world has grown grey from Thy breath; / We have drunken of things Lethean, and fed on the fullness of death. ['Hymn to Proserpine']

15 A little soul for a little bears up this corpse which is man. [Ib.]

16 I have lost, you have won this hazard; yet perchance / My loss may shine yet goodlier than your gain, / When time and God give judgement. [*Marino Faliero*, 5]

17 I will go back to the great sweet mother, / Mother and lover of men, the sea. / I will go down to her, I and no other, / Close with her, kiss her and mix her with me. ['The Triumph of Time']

Symonds, John Addington (1840–1893)

18 These things shall be — a loftier race / Than e'er the world hath known shall rise, / With flame of freedom in their souls, / And light of knowledge in their eyes. ['The Days that Are to Be']

Synge, J. M. (1871–1909)

19 A man who is not afraid of the sea will soon be drownded, he said, for he will be going out on a day he shouldn't. But we do be afraid of the sea, and we do only be drownded now and again. [*The Aran Islands*]

20 I have put away sorrow like a shoe that is worn out and muddy, for it is I have had a life that will be envied by great companies. [*Deirdre of the Sorrows*, III]

21 Drink a health to the wonders of the western world, the pirates, preachers, poteen-makers, with the jobbing jockies; parching peelers, and the juries fill their stomachs selling judgements of the English law. [*The Playboy of the Western World*, II]

22 A daring fellow is the jewel of the world, and a man did split his father's middle with a single clout should have the bravery of ten, so may God and Mary and St. Patrick bless you, and increase you from this mortal day. [Ib. III]

1 I've lost the only playboy of the western world. [Ib., final words]

2 Lord, confound this surly sister, / Blight her brow with blotch and blister, / Cramp her larynx, lung and liver, / In her guts a galling give her. ['The Curse' (to the sister of an enemy who disapproved of his play)]

Syrus, Publilius (fl. 1st century B.C.)

3 *Bis dat qui cito dat.* He gives twice who gives soon. [Attr. proverb]

4 *Necessitas non habet legem.* Necessity has no law. [Ib.]

Tacitus (A.D. c. 55–c. 120)

5 *Omne ignotum pro magnifico est.* Everything unknown is regarded as magnificent. [*Agricola*]

6 *Ubi solitudinem faciunt pacem appellant.* They create desolation, and call it peace. [Ib.]

7 *Tu vero felix, Agricola, non vitae tantum claritate, sed etiam opportunitate mortis.* You were lucky, Agricola, not only in the brilliance of your life, but also in the opportune timing of your death. [Ib.]

8 [Petronius] *Elegantiae arbiter.* Arbiter of taste. [*Annals*]

9 [Of the Emperor Galba] *Capax imperii nisi imperasset.* Suited for office if only he had not had to hold it. [*Histories*, I]

10 *Etiam sapientibus cupido gloriae novissima exuitur.* The desire for fame is the last thing to be put aside, even by wise men. [Ib. IV]

Talleyrand, Charles-Maurice de (1754–1838)

11 *Voilà le commencement de la fin.* This is the beginning of the end. [Comment on Napoleon's defeat at Borodino, 1812]

12 *Pas trop de zèle.* Not too much zeal. [Attr.]

13 *Quelle triste vieillesse vous vous préparez.* How sad an old age you are preparing for yourself. [Attr. remark to young man who boasted that he did not play whist]

14 *Ils n'ont rien appris, ni rien oublié.* They have learnt nothing, and forgotten nothing. [Comment on exiled French aristocrats]

15 War is much too serious to be left to the generals. [Attr.]

Tarkington, Booth (1869–1946)

16 An ideal wife is any woman who has an ideal husband. [Attr.]

Tate, Nahum (1652–1715) and Brady, Nicholas (1659–1726)

17 As pants the hart for cooling streams / When heated in the chase. [*New Versions of the Psalms*]

18 Through all the scenes of changing life. [Ib.]

19 While shepherds watch'd their flocks by night, / All seated on the ground, / The Angel of the Lord came down, / And glory shone around. [Ib.]

Tawney, R. H. (1880–1962)

20 It is a commonplace that the characteristic virtue of Englishmen is their power of sustained practical activity, and their characteristic vice a reluctance to test the quality of that activity by reference to principles. [*The Acquisitive Society*]

21 As long as men are men, a poor society cannot be too poor to find a right order of life, nor a rich society too rich to have need to seek it. [Ib.]

Taylor, Ann (1782–1866) and Jane (1783–1824)

22 I thank the goodness and the grace / Which on my birth have smiled, / And made me, in these Christian days, / A happy English child. [*Hymns for Infant Minds*]

23 Twinkle, twinkle, little star, / How I wonder what you are! / Up above the world so high, / Like a diamond in the sky. ['The Star' (by Jane Taylor)]

Taylor, Bishop Jeremy (1613–1667)

24 As our life is very short, so it is very miserable, and therefore it is well it is short. [*Holy Dying*]

25 Every school boy knows it. [*On the Real Presence*]

1 The union of hands and hearts. [*Sermons*, 'The Marriage Ring']

Taylor, John (1580–1653)

2 'Tis a mad world, my masters. [*Western Voyage*, 1]

Temple, Sir William (1628–1699)

3 When all is done, human life is, at the greatest and the best, but like a froward child, that must be play'd with and humoured a little to keep it quiet till it falls asleep, and then the care is over. ['Of Poetry']

Tenniel, John (1820–1914)

4 Dropping the pilot. [Caption to cartoon (1890) depicting Wilhelm II dispensing with Bismarck's services]

Tennyson, Alfred, Lord (1809–1892)

5 Cleave ever to the sunnier side of doubt. ['The Ancient Sage']

6 Cophetua sware a royal oath: / 'This beggar maid shall be my queen!' ['The Beggar Maid']

7 Break, break, break, / On thy cold grey stones, O Sea! / And I would that my tongue could utter / The thoughts that arise in me. ['Break, Break, Break']

8 But O for the touch of a vanish'd hand, / And the sound of a voice that is still! [Ib.]

9 I come from haunt of coot and hern, / I make a sudden sally / And sparkle out among the fern, / To bicker down a valley. ['The Brook']

10 For men may come and men may go, / But I go on for ever. [Ib.]

11 You praise when you should blame / The barbarism of wars. / A juster epoch has begun. ['The Charge of the Heavy Brigade', Epilogue]

12 The song that nerves a nation's heart, / Is in itself a deed. [Ib.]

13 Half a league, half a league, / Half a league onward, / All in the valley of Death / Rode the six hundred. ['The Charge of the Light Brigade']

14 'Forward the Light Brigade!' / Was there a man dismay'd? / Not tho' the soldier knew / Some one had blunder'd: / Their's not to make reply, / Their's not to reason why, / Their's but to do and die. [Ib.]

15 Cannon to the right of them / Cannon to the left of them / Cannon in front of them / volley'd and thunder'd. [Ib.]

16 Sunset and evening star, / And one clear call for me! / And may there be no moaning of the bar / When I put out to sea. ['Crossing the Bar']

17 Then she rode forth, clothed on with chastity. ['Godiva']

18 But thro' all this tract of years / Wearing the white flower of a blameless life, / Before a thousand peering littlenesses, / In that fierce light which beats upon a throne. [*The Idylls of the King*, Dedication]

19 We needs must love the highest when we see it. [Ib. 'Guinevere']

20 'God make thee good as thou art beautiful,' / Said Arthur, when he dubb'd him knight. [Ib. 'The Holy Grail']

21 He is all fault who hath no fault at all: / For who loves me must have a touch of earth. [Ib. 'Lancelot and Elaine']

22 His honour rooted in dishonour stood, / And faith unfaithful kept him falsely true. [Ib.]

23 He makes no friend who never made a foe. [Ib.]

24 It is the little rift within the lute, / That by and by will make the music mute, / And ever widening slowly silence all. [Ib. 'Merlin and Vivien']

25 Where blind and naked Ignorance / Delivers brawling judgements, unashamed, / On all things all day long. [Ib.]

26 Man dreams of fame while woman wakes to love. [Ib.]

27 So all day long the noise of battle roll'd / Among the mountains by the winter sea. [Ib. 'The Passing of Arthur']

28 An arm / Clothed in white samite, mystic, wonderful. [Ib.]

1 The days darken round me, and the years, / Among new men, strange faces, other minds. [Ib.]

2 And slowly answer'd Arthur from the barge: / 'The old order changeth, yielding place to new, / And God fulfils himself in many ways, / Lest one good custom should corrupt the world.' [Ib.]

3 More things are wrought by prayer / Than this world dreams of. [Ib.]

4 I have lived my life, and that which I have done / May He within Himself make pure! [Ib.]

5 The island-valley of Avilion; / Where falls not hail, or rain, or any snow, / Nor ever wind blows loudly; but it lies / Deep-meadow'd, happy, fair, with orchard lawns / And bowery hollows crown'd with summer sea. [Ib.]

6 Believing where we cannot prove. [*In Memoriam*, Prologue]

7 Men may rise on stepping-stones / Of their dead selves to higher things. [*In Memoriam*]

8 For words, like Nature, half reveal / And half conceal the Soul within. [Ib.]

9 Never morning wore / To evening, but some heart did break. [Ib.]

10 Dark house, by which once more I stand / Here in the long unlovely street, / Doors, where my heart was used to beat / So quickly, waiting for a hand. [Ib.]

11 And ghastly thro' the drizzling rain / On the bald streets breaks the blank day. [Ib.]

12 I envy not in any moods / The captive void of noble rage, / The linnet born within the cage, / That never knew the summer woods. [Ib.]

13 I hold it true, whate'er befall; / I feel it, when I sorrow most, / 'Tis better to have loved and lost / Than never to have loved at all. [Ib.]

14 How fares it with the happy dead? [Ib.]

15 How many a father have I seen, / A sober man, among his boys, / Whose youth was full of foolish noise. [Ib.]

16 An infant crying for the light: / And with no language but a cry. [Ib.]

17 Who trusted God was love indeed / And love Creation's final law — / Tho' Nature, red in tooth and claw / With ravine, shrieked against his creed. [Ib.]

18 So many worlds, so much to do, / So little done, such things to be. [Ib.]

19 There lives more faith in honest doubt, / Believe me, than in half the creeds. [Ib.]

20 Ring out, wild bells, to the wild sky, / The flying cloud, the frosty light: / The year is dying in the night; / Ring out, wild bells, and let him die. [Ib.]

21 Ring out the old, ring in the new / ...Ring out the false, ring in the true. [Ib.]

22 Ring out the feud of rich and poor, / Ring in redress to all mankind. [Ib.]

23 One God, one law, one element, / And one far-off divine event, / To which the whole creation moves. [Ib.]

24 The gardener Adam and his wife / Smile at the claims of long descent. ['Lady Clara Vere de Vere']

25 Kind hearts are more than coronets, / And simple faith than Norman blood. [Ib.]

26 On either side the river lie / Long fields of barley and of rye, / That clothe the wold and meet the sky; / And thro' the field the road runs by / To many-tower'd Camelot. ['The Lady of Shalott']

27 But who hath seen her wave her hand? / Or at the casement seen her stand? / Or is she known in all the land, / The Lady of Shalott? [Ib.]

28 'I am half sick of shadows' said / The Lady of Shalott. [Ib.]

29 'Tirra lirra,' by the river / Sang Sir Lancelot. [Ib.]

30 She left the web, she left the loom, / She made three paces thro' the room. [Ib.]

31 The mirror crack'd from side to side; / 'The curse is come upon me,' cried / The Lady of Shalott. [Ib.]

32 He said, 'She has a lovely face; / God in his mercy lend her grace, / The Lady of Shalott.' [Ib.]

1 In the Spring a young man's fancy lightly turns to thoughts of love. [*Locksley Hall*]

2 Cursed be the social wants that sin against the strength of youth! / Cursed be the social lies that warp us from the living truth. [Ib.]

3 He will hold thee, when his passion shall have spent its novel force, / Something better than his dog, a little dearer than his horse. [Ib.]

4 Men, my brothers, men the workers, ever reaping something new: / That which they have done but earnest of the things that they shall do: / For I dipt into the future, far as human eye could see, / Saw the Vision of the world, and all the wonder that would be; / Saw the heavens fill with commerce, argosies of magic sails, / Pilots of the purple twilight, dropping down with costly bales. [Ib.]

5 Till the war-drum throbb'd no longer, and the battle-flags were furl'd / In the Parliament of man, the Federation of the world. [Ib.]

6 Forward, forward let us range, / Let the great world spin for ever down the ringing grooves of change. [Ib.]

7 Better fifty years of Europe than a cycle of Cathay. [Ib.]

8 Music that gentlier on the spirit lies, / Than tir'd eyelids upon tir'd eyes. ['The Lotos-Eaters']

9 Surely, surely, slumber is more sweet than toil, the shore / Than labour in the deep mid-ocean, wind and wave and oar; / Oh rest ye, brother mariners, we will not wander more. [Ib.]

10 The rise / And long roll of the Hexameter. ['Lucretius']

11 She only said, 'My life is dreary, / He cometh not,' she said; / She said, 'I am aweary, aweary, / I would that I were dead!' ['Mariana']

12 I hate that dreadful hollow behind the little wood. [*Maud*, I, 1]

13 Faultily faultless, icily regular, splendidly null. [Ib. I, 2]

14 Gorgonized me from head to foot / With a stony British stare. [Ib. I, 13]

15 Come into the garden, Maud, / For the black bat, night, has flown. / Come into the garden, Maud, / I am here at the gate alone. [Ib. I, 22]

16 O that 'twere possible / After long grief and pain / To find the arms of my true love / Round me once again! [Ib. II, 4]

17 My life has crept so long on a broken wing / Thro' cells of madness, haunts of horror and fear, / That I come to be grateful at last for a little thing. [Ib. III, 6]

18 Doänt thou marry for munny, but goä wheer munny is! ['Northern Farmer. New Style']

19 The last great Englishman. ['Ode on the Death of the Duke of Wellington']

20 For this is England's greatest son, / He that gain'd a hundred fights, / Nor ever lost an English gun. [Ib.]

21 Not once or twice in our rough island story, / The path of duty was the way to glory. [Ib.]

22 The splendour falls on castle walls / And snowy summits old in story: / The long light shakes across the lakes, / And the wild cataract leaps in glory.
Blow, bugle, blow, set the wild echoes flying, / Blow, bugle; answer, echoes dying, dying, dying.
O hark, O hear! how thin and clear, / And thinner, clearer, farther going! / O sweet and far from cliff and scar / The horns of Elfland faintly blowing! [*The Princess*, IV]

23 Tears, idle tears, I know not what they mean, / Tears from the depth of some divine despair. [Ib.]

24 Dear as remembered kisses after death, / And sweet as those by hopeless fancy feign'd / On lips that are for others. [Ib.]

25 Man is the hunter; woman is his game: / The sleek and shining creatures of the chase, / We hunt them for the beauty of their skins; / They love us for it, and we ride them down. [Ib. V]

26 Man to command and woman to obey; / All else confusion. [Ib.]

27 The moan of doves in immemorial elms, / And murmuring of innumerable bees. [Ib. VII]

1 At Flores in the Azores Sir Richard Grenville lay. ['The Revenge']

2 Let us bang these dogs of Seville, the children of the devil, / For I never turn'd my back on Don or devil yet. [Ib.]

3 Sink me the ship, Master Gunner — sink her, split her in twain! / Fall into the hands of God, not into the hands of Spain! [Ib.]

4 And the little Revenge herself went down by the island crags / To be lost evermore in the main. [Ib.]

5 Battering the gates of heaven with storms of prayer. ['St. Simeon Stylites']

6 My strength is as the strength of ten, / Because my heart is pure. ['Sir Galahad']

7 It little profits that an idle king, / By this still hearth, among these barren crags, / Match'd with an aged wife, I mete and dole / Unequal laws unto a savage race. ['Ulysses']

8 I will drink / Life to the lees: all times I have enjoy'd / Greatly, have suffer'd greatly. [Ib.]

9 I am become a name. [Ib.]

10 Far on the ringing plains of windy Troy. [Ib.]

11 How dull it is to pause, to make an end, / To rust unburnished, not to shine in use! / As tho' to breathe were life. [Ib.]

12 To follow knowledge like a sinking star, / Beyond the utmost bound of human thought. [Ib.]

13 Some work of noble note may yet be done, / Not unbecoming men that strove with Gods. [Ib.]

14 Come, my friends, / 'Tis not too late to seek a newer world. / Push off, and sitting well in order smite / The sounding furrows. [Ib.]

15 That which we are, we are; / One equal temper of heroic hearts, / Made weak by time and fate, but strong in will / To strive, to seek, to find, and not to yield. [Ib.]

16 Every moment dies a man, / Every moment one is born. [*The Vision of Sin*]

17 O plump head-waiter at the Cock, / To which I must resort, / How goes the time? 'Tis five o'clock. / Go fetch a pint of port. ['Will Waterproof's Lyrical Monologue']

18 [Of a critic] A louse in the locks of literature. [Charteris, *Life of Gosse*]

Terence (c. 190–159 B.C.)

19 *Id arbitror / Adprime in vita esse utile, ut nequid nimis.* My view is that the most important thing in life is never to have too much of anything. [*Andria*]

20 *Amantium irae amoris integratio est.* The quarrels of lovers are the renewal of love. [Ib.]

21 *Hinc illae lacrimae.* Hence these tears. [Ib.]

22 *Modo liceat vivere, est spes.* While there's life, there's hope. [*Heauton Timoroumenos*]

23 *Homo sum; humani nil a me alienum puto.* I am a man, I count nothing human indifferent to me. [Ib.]

24 *Quot homines tot sententiae.* So many men, so many opinions. [*Phormio*]

25 *Fortis fortuna adiuvat.* Fortune helps the brave. [Ib.]

Tertullian (c. A.D. 160–c. 225)

26 *Semen est sanguis Christianorum.* The blood of the martyrs is the seed of the church. [*Apologeticus*]

27 *O testimonium animae naturaliter Christianae.* O witness of a naturally Christian soul. [Ib.]

28 *De calcaria in carbonarium.* Out of the frying pan into the fire. [*De Carne Christi*]

29 *Certum est quia impossibile est.* It is certain because it is impossible. [Ib.]

Thackeray, William Makepeace (1811–1863)

30 He who meanly admires mean things is a Snob. [*The Book of Snobs*]

31 It is impossible, in our condition of Society, not to be sometimes a Snob. [Ib.]

1 'Tis not the dying for a faith that's so hard, Master Harry — every man of every nation has done that — 'tis the living up to it that is difficult. [*Henry Esmond*, 6]

2 'Tis strange what a man may do, and a woman yet think him an angel. [Ib. 7]

3 There are a thousand thoughts lying within a man that he does not know till he takes up the pen to write. [Ib. 15]

4 The leopard follows his nature as the lamb does, and acts after leopard law; she can neither help her beauty, nor her courage, nor her cruelty; nor a single spot on her shining coat; nor the conquering spirit which impels her; nor the shot which brings her down. [Ib. 36]

5 Remember, it is as easy to marry a rich woman as a poor woman. [*Pendennis*, 28]

6 The *Pall Mall Gazette* is written by gentlemen for gentlemen. [Ib. 32]

7 'No business before breakfast, Glum!' says the King. 'Breakfast first, business next.' [*The Rose and the Ring*, 11]

8 And this I set down as a positive truth. A woman with fair opportunities, and without an absolute hump may marry *whom she likes*. [*Vanity Fair*, 4]

9 Some cynical Frenchman has said that there are two parties to a love transaction; the one who loves and the other who condescends to be so treated. [Ib. 13]

10 Whenever he met a great man he grovelled before him, and my-lorded him as only a free-born Briton can do. [Ib.]

11 Them's my sentiments! [Ib. 21]

12 Darkness came down on the field and city: and Amelia was praying for George, who was lying on his face, dead, with a bullet through his heart. [Ib. 32]

13 I think I could be a good woman if I had five thousand a year. [Ib. 36]

14 When you think that the eyes of your childhood dried at the sight of a piece of gingerbread, and that a plum-cake was a compensation for the agony of parting with your mamma and sisters; O my friend and brother, you need not be too confident of your own fine feelings. [Ib. 56]

15 Ah! *Vanitas Vanitatum!* Which of us is happy in this world? Which of us has his desire? or, having it, is satisfied? — Come, children, let us shut up the box and the puppets, for our play is played out. [Ib. 67]

16 Werther had a love for Charlotte / Such as words could never utter; / Would you know how first he met her? / She was cutting bread and butter. ['The Sorrows of Werther']

Thatcher, Margaret (1925-)

17 [Of her economic policy] There is no alternative. [Said on several occasions]

Thayer, W.M. (c. 1820-1898)

18 From Log Cabin to White House [Title of biography of President Garfield]

Thomas à Kempis, *see* KEMPIS.

Thomas, Brandon (1856-1914)

19 I'm Charley's aunt from Brazil — where the nuts come from. [*Charley's Aunt*, I]

Thomas, Dylan (1914-1953)

20 ...the hockey-legged girls who laughed behind their hands. [*Adventures in the Skin Trade*]

21 Though lovers be lost love shall not; / And death shall have no dominion. ['And death shall have no dominion']

22 Do not go gentle into that good night, / Old age should burn and rave at close of day; / Rage, rage against the dying of the light. ['Do not go gentle']

23 Now as I was young and easy under the apple boughs / About the lilting house and happy as the grass was green. ['Fern Hill']

1 The force that through the green fuse drives the flower / Drives my green age; that blasts the roots of trees / Is my destroyer. ['The force that through the green fuse drives the flower']

2 It was my thirtieth year to heaven / Woke to my hearing from harbour and neighbour wood / And the mussel pooled and the heron / Priested shore. ['Poem in October']

3 After the first death, there is no other. ['A refusal to mourn the death, by fire, of a child in London']

4 And I must enter again the round / Zion of the water bead / And the synagogue of the ear of corn. [Ib.]

5 To begin at the beginning: It is spring, moonless night in the small town, starless and bible-black, the cobblestreets silent and the hunched, courters'-and-rabbits' wood limping invisible down to the sloe-black, slow, black, crowblack, fishing-boat-bobbing sea. [*Under Milk Wood*]

6 And before you let the sun in, mind it wipes its shoes. [Ib.]

7 Nothing grows in our garden, only washing. And babies. [Ib.]

8 You just wait. I'll sin till I blow up! [Ib.]

9 Praise the Lord! We are a musical nation. [Ib.]

10 Organ Morgan, you haven't been listening to a word I said. It's organ organ all the time with you... [Ib.]

11 Seventeen and never been sweet in the grass ho ho. [Ib.]

12 These poems, with all their crudities, doubts, and confusions, are written for the love of Man and in praise of God, and I'd be a damn' fool if they weren't. [*Collected Poems*, note]

Thomas, Edward (1878–1917)

13 Yes, I remember Adlestrop — / The name, because one afternoon / Of heat the express train drew up there / Unwontedly. It was late June. ['Adlestrop']

14 I have come to the borders of sleep, / The unfathomable deep / Forest where all must lose / Their way. ['Lights Out']

15 All was foretold me; naught / Could I foresee; / But I learned how the wind would sound / After these things should be. ['The New House']

16 As well as any bloom upon a flower / I like the dust on the nettles, never lost / Except to prove the sweetness of a shower. ['Tall Nettles']

17 Choose me, / You English words. ['Words']

Thomas, R.S. (1913–)

18 An impotent people, / Sick with inbreeding, / Worrying the carcase of an old song. ['Welsh Landscape']

Thompson, Francis (1859–1907)

19 And I look through my tears on a soundless clapping host / As the run-stealers flicker to and fro, / To and fro: / O my Hornby and my Barlow long ago! ['At Lord's']

20 Nothing begins and nothing ends / That is not paid with moan; / For we are born in others' pain, / And perish in our own. ['Daisy']

21 I fled Him, down the nights and down the days; / I fled Him, down the arches of the years; / I fled Him, down the labyrinthine ways / Of my own mind; and in the mist of tears / I hid from Him, and under running laughter. [*The Hound of Heaven*]

22 But with unhurrying chase, / And unperturbèd pace, / Deliberate speed, majestic instancy, / They beat — and a Voice beat / More instant than the Feet — / 'All things betray thee, who betrayest Me.' [Ib.]

23 'Tis ye, 'tis your estrangèd faces, / That miss the many-splendoured thing. / But, when so sad thou canst not sadder, / Cry — and upon thy so sore loss / Shall shine the traffic of Jacob's ladder / Pitched betwixt Heaven and Charing Cross. ['In No Strange Land']

24 Summer set lip to earth's bosom bare, / And left the flushed print in a poppy there. ['The Poppy']

25 Look for me in the nurseries of Heaven. ['To my Godchild']

Thompson, Hunter S. (1939–)

1 Fear and Loathing in Las Vegas [Title of book]

Thompson, William Hepworth (1810–1886)

2 We are none of us infallible — not even the youngest. [Comment on Junior Fellow of Trinity]

3 What time he can spare from the adornment of his person he devotes to the neglect of his duties. [Remark on colleague]

Thomson, James (1700–1748)

4 Rule, Britannia, rule the waves; / Britons never will be slaves. [*Alfred: a Masque*, II]

5 Delightful task! to rear the tender thought, / To teach the young idea how to shoot. [*The Seasons*, 'Spring']

6 An elegant sufficiency, content, / Retirement, rural quiet, friendship, books. [Ib.]

7 While listening senates hang upon thy tongue. [Ib. 'Autumn']

8 Poor is the triumph o'er the timid hare! [Ib.]

9 There studious let me sit, / And hold high converse with the mighty dead. [Ib. 'Winter']

10 Oh! Sophonisba! Sophonisba! oh! [*Sophonisba*, III.2]

Thomson, James (1834–1882)

11 ...to cure the pain / Of the headache called thought in the brain. ['L'Ancien Régime']

12 The City is of Night; perchance of Death, / But certainly of Night; for never there / Can come the lucid morning's fragrant breath / After the dewy dawning's cold grey air. [*The City of Dreadful Night*, I]

13 The City is of Night, but not of Sleep; / There sweet sleep is not for the weary brain; / The pitiless hours like years and ages creep, / A night seems termless hell. [Ib.]

14 The vilest thing must be less vile than Thou / From whom it had its being, God and Lord! [Ib. VIII]

15 I find no hint throughout the universe / Of good or ill, of blessing or of curse; / I find alone Necessity Supreme. [Ib. XIV]

16 Speak not of comfort where no comfort is. [Ib. XVI]

17 The gracious power / Of sleep's fine alchemy. ['Insomnia']

18 Some dark Presence watching by my bed, / The awful image of a nameless dread. [Ib.]

19 Those pale and languid rich ones / Who are always and never free. [*Sunday at Hampstead*, 1]

20 For thirty generations of my corn / Outlast a generation of my men, / And thirty generations of my men / Outlast a generation of their gods. ['A Voice from the Nile']

21 For verily the Tribe is all, and we / Are nothing singly save as parts of it. [*Weddah and Om-el-Bonain*, 2]

Thomson, Roy, Lord (1894–1977)

22 [Commercial television] A licence to print your own money. [Attr.]

Thoreau, Henry David (1817–1862)

23 The mass of men lead lives of quiet desperation. [*Walden*, 'Economy']

24 It is true, I never assisted the sun materially in rising, but, doubt not, it was of the last importance only to be present at it. [Ib.]

25 It is a characteristic of wisdom not to do desperate things. [Ib.]

26 I have lived some thirty years on this planet, and I have yet to hear the first syllable of valuable or even earnest advice from my seniors. [Ib.]

27 Our life is frittered away by detail...Simplify, simplify. [Ib. 'Where I lived, and what I lived for']

28 I would rather sit on a pumpkin and have it all to myself than be crowded on a velvet cushion. [Ib.]

29 Things do not change; we change. [Ib. conclusion]

30 Poetry is nothing but healthy speech. [Journal, 1841]

31 Some circumstantial evidence is very strong, as when you find a trout in the milk. [Ib. 1850]

Thorpe, Jeremy (1929-)

1 Greater love hath no man than this, that he lay down his friends for his life. [Remark on Macmillan's Cabinet purge, 1962]

Thucydides (c. 460-c. 395 B.C.)

2 To great men the whole world is a sepulchre. [*History of the Peloponnesian War*, II]

Thurber, James (1894-1961)

3 It is not so easy to fool little girls today as it used to be. [*Fables for Our Time*]

4 There is no safety in numbers, or in anything else. [Ib.]

5 He knows all about art, but he doesn't know what he likes. [Cartoon caption]

6 Well, if I called the wrong number, why did you answer the phone? [Cartoon caption]

7 Perhaps *this* will refresh your memory. [Cartoon caption; remark by lawyer producing kangaroo in court]

8 Where did you get those big brown eyes and that tiny mind? [Cartoon caption]

9 It's a naïve domestic Burgundy, without any breeding, but I think you'll be amused by its presumption. [Cartoon caption]

10 All right, have it your way — you heard a seal bark. [Cartoon caption]

11 You wait here and I'll bring the etchings down. [Cartoon caption]

12 Progress was all right; only it went on too long. [Attr.]

Thurlow, Edward, First Baron (1731-1806)

13 Did you ever expect a corporation to have a conscience, when it has no soul to be damned, and no body to be kicked? [Attr.]

Tickell, Thomas (1686-1740)

14 There taught us how to live; and (oh! too high / The price for knowledge) taught us how to die. ['On the Death of Mr. Addison']

Titus Vespasianus (A.D. 39-81)

15 [On realizing that he had not done anything to help anybody that day] *Amici, diem perdidi.* Friends, I have lost a day. [Suetonius, *Life*]

Tobin, John (1770-1804)

16 The man that lays his hand upon a woman, / Save in the way of kindness, is a wretch / Whom 't were gross flattery to name a coward. [*The Honeymoon*, II]

Tocqueville, Alexis de (1805-1859)

17 I sought the image of democracy, in order to learn what we have to fear and to hope from its progress. [*Democracy in America*]

Tolkien, J.R.R. (1892-1973)

18 One Ring to rule them all, One Ring to find them, / One Ring to bring them all and in the darkness bind them. [*The Lord of the Rings*, I, 2]

Tolstoy, Leo (1828-1910)

19 All happy families resemble one another, but each unhappy family is unhappy in its own way. [*Anna Karenina*; trans. Maude]

20 All, everything that I understand, I understand only because I love. [*War and Peace*, VII, 16; trans. Maude]

21 Pure and complete sorrow is as impossible as pure and complete joy. [Ib. XV, 1]

22 Art is a human activity having for its purpose the transmission to others of the highest and best feelings to which men have risen. [*What is Art?*]

23 Art is not a handicraft, it is a transmission of feeling the artist has experienced. [Ib.]

24 I sit on a man's back, choking him and making him carry me, and yet assure myself and others that I am very sorry for him and wish to ease his lot by all possible means — except by getting off his back. [*What Then Must We Do?*]

Toplady, Augustus Montague (1740-1778)

25 Rock of Ages, cleft for me, / Let me hide myself in Thee. [Hymn]

1 Nothing in my hand I bring, / Simply to Thy Cross I cling; / Naked, come to Thee for dress; / Helpless, look to Thee for grace; / Foul, I to the fountain fly; / Wash me, Saviour, or I die. [Ib.]

Tourneur, Cyril (c. 1575–1626)

2 Were't not for gold and women, there would be no damnation. [*The Revenger's Tragedy*, II.1]

3 Does the silk-worm expend her yellow labours / For thee? for thee does she undo herself? [Ib. III.5]

Traherne, Thomas (c. 1637–1674)

4 You never enjoy the world aright, till the sea itself flows in your veins, till you are clothed with the heavens, and crowned with the stars: and perceive yourself to be sole heir of the whole world. [*Centuries of Meditations*, I, 29]

Trapp, Joseph (1679–1747)

5 The king, observing with judicious eyes, / The state of both his universities, / To Oxford sent a troop of horse, and why? / That learned body wanted loyalty; / To Cambridge books, as very well discerning, / How much that loyal body wanted learning. [Epigram on George I's donation of Bishop Ely's Library to Cambridge University; *see* Sir William Browne's reply]

Tree, Herbert Beerbohm (1853–1917)

6 My poor fellow, why not carry a watch? [Remark to a man carrying a grandfather clock in the street]

7 He is an old bore; even the grave yawns for him. [Attr.]

Trench, Archbishop Richard (1807–1886)

8 England, we love thee better than we know. ['Gibraltar']

Trevelyan, George Macaulay (1876–1962)

9 Disinterested intellectual curiosity is the life blood of real civilization. [*English Social History*]

10 Education...has produced a vast population able to read but unable to distinguish what is worth reading. [Ib.]

Trilling, Lionel (1905–1981)

11 I asked them to look into the Abyss, and, both dutifully and gladly, they have looked into the Abyss, and the Abyss has greeted them with the grave courtesy of all objects of serious study; saying: 'Interesting, am I not? And *exciting*, if you consider how deep I am and what dread beasts lie at my bottom.' [*Beyond Culture*]

Trollope, Anthony (1815–1882)

12 He must have known me had he seen me as he was wont to see me, for he was in the habit of flogging me constantly. Perhaps he did not recognize me by my face. [*Autobiography*, 1]

13 Three hours a day will produce as much as a man ought to write. [Ib. 15]

14 Of all the needs a book has the chief need is that it be readable. [Ib. 19]

15 'Unhand it, sir!' said Mrs. Proudie. [*Barchester Towers*, 11]

16 It is a comfortable feeling to know that you stand on your own ground. Land is about the only thing that can't fly away. [*The Last Chronicle of Barset*, 58]

17 It's dogged as does it. It ain't thinking about it. [Ib. 61]

18 It is because we put up with bad things that hotel-keepers continue to give them to us. [*Orley Farm*, 18]

19 It has been the great fault of our politicians that they have all wanted to do something. [*Phineas Finn*, 13]

20 Never think that you're not good enough yourself. A man should never think that. My belief is that in life people will take you very much at your own reckoning. [*The Small House at Allington*, 32]

21 The tenth Muse, who now governs the periodical press. [*The Warden*, 14]

Trotsky, Leon (1879–1940)

1 Marxism is above all a method of analysis. [*Permanent Revolution*]

Truman, Harry S. (1884–1972)

2 A statesman is a politician who's been dead ten or fifteen years. [Attr.]

3 The buck stops here. [Sign on his desk]

4 It's a recession when your neighbour loses his job: it's a depression when you lose yours. [*Observer*, 'Sayings of the Week', 1958]

Trumbull, John (1750–1831)

5 But optics sharp it needs I ween, / To see what is not to be seen. [*McFingal*]

Tucker, Sophie (1884–1966)

6 The Last of the Red-Hot Mamas. [Publicity self-description]

7 [Asked, when 80, the secret of longevity] Keep breathing. [Attr.]

8 I've been poor and I've been rich. Rich is better. [Quoted in Cowan, *The Wit of Women*]

Tupper, Martin (1810–1889)

9 Well-timed silence hath more eloquence than speech. [*Proverbial Philosophy*, 'Of Discretion']

10 A good book is the best of friends, the same today and for ever. [Ib. 'Of Reading']

Turgenev, Ivan (1818–1883)

11 I submit to no man's opinion; I have opinions of my own. [*Fathers and Sons*, 13]

12 The boldness to believe in nothing. [Ib. 14]

13 Whatever a man prays for, he prays for a miracle. Every prayer reduces itself to this: 'Great God, grant that twice two be not four.' ['Prayer']

Turner, W.J.R. (1889–1946)

14 Chimborazo, Cotopaxi, / They had stolen my soul away. ['Romance']

Tusser, Thomas (c. 1524–1580)

15 A fool and his money be soon at debate. [*Five Hundred Points of Good Husbandry*]

16 Make hunger thy sauce, as a medicine for health. [Ib.]

17 At Christmas play and make good cheer, / For Christmas comes but once a year. [Ib.]

18 Feb, fill the dyke / With what thou dost like. [Ib.]

19 Who goeth a borrowing / Goeth a sorrowing. / Few lend (but fools) / Their working tools. [Ib.]

Twain, Mark (1835–1910)

20 I have been told that Wagner's music is better than it sounds. [*Autobiography*]

21 I don't see no p'ints about that frog that's any better'n any other frog. ['The Celebrated Jumping Frog']

22 You tell me whar a man gets his corn pone, en I'll tell you what his 'pinions is. ['Corn Pone Opinions']

23 [Definition of a classic] Something that everybody wants to have read and nobody wants to read. ['The Disappearance of Literature']

24 Man is the only animal that blushes. Or needs to. [*Following the Equator*]

25 Persons attempting to find a motive in this narrative will be prosecuted; persons attempting to find a moral in it will be banished; persons attempting to find a plot in it will be shot. [*Huckleberry Finn*, Introduction]

26 There was things which he stretched, but mainly he told the truth. [Ib. 1]

27 You feel mighty free and easy and comfortable on a raft. [Ib. 18]

28 All kings is mostly rapscallions. [Ib. 23]

29 Hain't we got all the fools in town on our side? and ain't that a big enough majority in any town? [Ib. 26]

30 Lump the whole thing! say that the Creator made Italy from designs by Michael Angelo! [*Innocents Abroad*, 27]

1 When angry count four; when very angry swear. [*Pudd'nhead Wilson's Calendar*]

2 The English are mentioned in the Bible: Blessed are the meek for they shall inherit the earth. [Ib.]

3 Don't part with your illusions. When they are gone, you may still exist, but you have ceased to live. [Ib.]

4 As to the Adjective: when in doubt, strike it out. [Ib.]

5 The holy passion of Friendship is of so sweet and steady and loyal and enduring a nature that it will last through a whole lifetime, if not asked to lend money. [Ib.]

6 When in doubt, tell the truth. [*Pudd'nhead Wilson's New Calendar*]

7 Work consists of whatever a body is obliged to do...Play consists of whatever a body is not obliged to do. [*Tom Sawyer*, 2]

8 To promise not to do a thing is the surest way in the world to make a body want to go and do that very thing. [Ib. 22]

9 There ain't a-going to *be* no core. [*Tom Sawyer Abroad*, 1]

10 The cross of the Legion of Honour has been conferred upon me. However, few escape that distinction. [*A Tramp Abroad*, 8]

11 This poor little one-horse town. ['The Undertaker's Story']

12 There was worlds of reputation in it, but no money. [*A Yankee at the Court of King Arthur*, 9]

13 The report of my death was an exaggeration. [Cable, 1897]

14 Heaven for climate, hell for society. [Attr.]

15 I can live for two months on a good compliment. [Attr.]

16 Most people are bothered by those passages in Scripture which they cannot understand; but as for me, I always noticed that the passages in Scripture which trouble me most are those that I do understand. [Quoted in Simcox, *Treasury of Quotations on Christian Themes*]

17 When I was a boy of 14 my father was so ignorant I could hardly stand to have the old man around. But when I got to be 21, I was astonished at how much he had learned in 7 years. [Quoted in Mackay, *The Harvest of a Quiet Eye*]

Twells, Henry (1823–1900)

18 At even, when the sun was set, / The sick, O Lord, around Thee lay; / O in what divers pains they met! / O with what joy they went away! [Hymn]

19 Thy touch has still its ancient power; / No word from thee can fruitless fall. [Ib.]

Tynan, Kenneth (1927–1980)

20 What, when drunk, one sees in other women, one sees in Garbo sober. [Quoted in Halliwell, *Filmgoer's Book of Quotes*]

21 High-definition performance. [*Observer* review]

Ulpian, Domitius (d. c. A.D. 228)

22 *Volenti non fit iniuria.* To one who wishes it, no injustice is done. [*Corpus Iuris Civilis*]

Unamuno, Miguel de (1864–1937)

23 Faith which does not doubt is dead faith. [*The Agony of Christianity*]

24 Man, by the very fact of being man, by possessing consciousness, is, in comparison with the ass or the crab, a diseased animal. Consciousness is a disease. [*The Tragic Sense of Life*, 1]

25 It is not usually our ideas that make us optimists or pessimists, but it is our optimism or pessimism, of physiological or pathological origin...that makes our ideas. [Ib.]

26 To believe in God is to yearn for His existence and, furthermore, it is to act as if He did exist. [Ib. 8]

Upton, W. (fl. 18th century)

27 I'd crowns resign to call thee mine, / Sweet lass of Richmond Hill. ['The Lass of Richmond Hill']

Urey, Harold (1893-1981)

1 The next war will be fought with atom bombs and the one after that with spears. [*Observer*, 'Sayings of the Week', 1946]

Ussher, James (1581-1656)

2 The world was created on 22nd October, 4004 B.C. at 6 o'clock in the evening. [*Chronologia Sacra*]

Ustinov, Peter (1921-)

3 As for being a General, well, at the age of four with paper hats and wooden swords we're all Generals. Only some of us never grow out of it. [*Romanoff and Juliet*, I]

4 A diplomat these days is nothing but a head-waiter who's allowed to sit down occasionally. [Ib.]

5 ...the great thing about history is that it is adaptable. [Ib. II]

Valéry, Paul (1871-1945)

6 A poem is never finished, only abandoned. [Quoted in Auden, *A Certain World*]

7 A man is infinitely more complicated than his thoughts. [Ib.]

8 Consciousness reigns but does not govern. [Ib.]

Vanbrugh, Sir John (1664-1726)

9 Jealousy's a city passion; 'tis a thing unknown amongst people of quality. [*The Confederacy*, I.2]

10 The want of a thing is perplexing enough, but the possession of it is intolerable. [Ib.]

11 Much of a muchness. [*The Provok'd Husband*, I.1]

12 *Belinda:* Ay, but you know we must return good for evil.
Lady Brute: That may be a mistake in the translation. [Ib.]

13 Thinking is to me the greatest fatigue in the world. [*The Relapse*, II.1]

Vanderbilt, William H. (1821-1885)

14 The public be damned! I'm working for my stockholders. [Remark, 1883]

Vanzetti, Bartolomeo (1888-1927)

15 Never in our full life could we hope to do such work for tolerance, for justice, for man's understanding of man as now we do by accident. Our words — our lives — our pains — nothing! The taking of our lives — lives of a good shoemaker and a poor fish-pedlar — all! That last moment belongs to us — that agony is our triumph. [Statement after receiving death sentence]

Vaughan, Charles J. (1816-1897)

16 Must you go? Can't you stay? [Remark designed to conclude visits by schoolboys too embarrassed to leave]

Vaughan, Henry (1622-1695)

17 They are all gone into the world of light! / And I alone sit lingering here. [*Silex Scintillans*, 'Ascension-Hymn']

18 Dear, beauteous death! the Jewel of the Just. [Ib.]

19 And yet, as angels in some brighter dreams / Call to the soul when man doth sleep, / So some strange thoughts transcend our wonted themes, / And into glory peep. [Ib.]

20 Man is the shuttle, to whose winding quest / And passage through these looms / God order'd motion, but ordain'd no rest. [Ib. 'Man']

21 Wise Nicodemus saw such light / As made him know his God by night. [Ib. 'The Night']

22 Dear Night! this world's defeat; / The stop to busy fools; care's check and curb. [Ib.]

23 My soul, there is a country / Far beyond the stars, / Where stands a winged sentry / All skilful in the wars. [Ib. 'Peace']

24 Happy those early days! when I / Shin'd in my Angel-infancy. [Ib. 'The Retreat']

25 And in those weaker glories spy / Some shadows of eternity. [Ib.]

1 O how I long to travel back, / And tread again that ancient track! / That I might once again reach that plain, / Where first I left my glorious train; / From whence th'enlightened spirit sees / That shady city of palm-trees. [Ib.]

2 I saw Eternity the other night, / Like a great ring of pure and endless light, / All calm, as it was bright. [Ib. 'The World']

Vaughan Williams, Ralph (1872–1958)

3 [Asked what he thought about music] It's a Rum Go! [Quoted in Wintle and Kenin, *Dictionary of Biographical Quotations*]

Veblen, Thorstein (1857–1929)

4 Conspicuous consumption of valuable goods is a means of reputability to the gentleman of leisure. [*The Theory of the Leisure Class*, 4]

5 The requirement of conspicuous wastefulness is not commonly present, consciously, in our canons of taste, but it is none the less present as a constraining norm selectively shaping and sustaining our sense of what is beautiful. [Ib. 6]

Vegetius Renatus, Flavius (fl. c. A.D. 375)

6 *Qui desiderat pacem, praeparet bellum.* Let him who desires peace, prepare for war. [*Epitome Institutionum Rei Militaris*]

Venantius Fortunatus (c. 530–c. 610)

7 *Pange, lingua, gloriosi / Proelium certaminis.* Sing, tongue, of battle in the glorious conflict. [Hymn]

Vergniaud, Pierre (1753–1793)

8 It was possible to fear that the Revolution might, like Saturn, devour each of her children one by one. [Remark, attr. at his trial, 1793]

Verlaine, Paul (1844–1896)

9 *Prends l'éloquence et tords-lui son cou!* Take eloquence and wring its neck. ['L'Art poétique']

10 *Et tout le reste est littérature.* And all the rest is mere literature. [Ib.]

11 *Les sanglots longs / Des violons / De l'automne / Blessent mon coeur / D'une langueur / Monotone.* The long sobbings of autumn violins wound my heart with a monotonous languor. ['Chanson de l'automne']

12 *Et, O ces voix d'enfants chantants dans la coupole!* And oh those voices of children, singing in the cupola! ['Parsifal, A Jules Tellier']

13 *Il pleure dans mon coeur / Comme il pleut sur la ville.* There is weeping in my heart as it rains on the city. ['Romances sans paroles']

Vespasian (A.D. 9–79)

14 *Vae, puto deus fio.* Oh dear, I must be turning into a god. [Last words]

Victoria, Queen (1819–1901)

15 I will be good. [Remark, 1830]

16 The Queen is most anxious to enlist every one who can speak or write to join in checking this mad, wicked folly of 'Women's Rights', with all its attendant horrors. [Letter, 1870]

17 [Of Gladstone] He speaks to me as if I was a public meeting. [Attr.]

18 We are not amused. [Attr.]

19 We are not interested in the possibilities of defeat. [Attr. remark to A.J. Balfour, 1899]

Vidal, Gore (1925–)

20 He will lie even when it is inconvenient, the sign of the true artist. [*Two Sisters*]

21 American writers want to be not good but great; and so are neither. [Ib.]

Vigny, Alfred de (1797–1863)

22 *Dieu! que le son du cor est triste au fond des bois!* Oh God, how sad is the sound of the horn from the depths of the woods! ['Le Cor']

23 *Seul le silence est grand; tout le reste est faiblesse.* Silence alone is great; everything else is weakness. ['La Mort du Loup']

Villiers de l'Isle-Adam, Philippe-Auguste (1838–1889)

1 *Vivre? les serviteurs feront cela pour nous.* Live? Our servants will do that for us. [*Axel*, IV, 2]

Villon, François (1431–c. 1484)

2 *Mais où sont les neiges d'antan?* But where are the snows of yesteryear? ['Ballade des Dames du Temps Jadis'; trans. D.G. Rossetti]

3 *Frères humains qui après nous vivez, / N'ayez les cuers contre nous endurcis.* Brother humans who live after us, do not harden your hearts against us. ['Ballade des pendus']

4 *Mais priez Dieu que tous nous veuille absouldre!* But pray to God that he may absolve us all. [Ib.]

Vincent, St. (d. 450)

5 *Quod semper, quod ubique, quod ab omnibus creditum est.* What is believed always, everywhere, and by everybody. [*Commonitorium*]

Virgil (70–19 B.C.)

6 *Arma virumque cano.* Arms and the man I sing. [*Aeneid*, I, opening words]

7 *Tantaene animis caelestibus irae?* Why such great anger in heavenly minds? [Ib.]

8 *Forsan et haec olim meminisse iuvabit.* Perhaps some day even these things will be pleasant to remember. [Ib.]

9 *Sunt lacrimae rerum.* Events have tears. [Ib.]

10 *Mens sibi conscia recti.* A mind conscious of the right. [Ib.]

11 *Infandum, regina, iubes renovare dolorem.* You bid me renew, O queen, an unspeakable grief. [Ib. II]

12 *Quidquid id est, timeo Danaos et dona ferentis.* Whatever it is, I fear the Greeks even when they bring gifts. [Ib.]

13 *Quantum mutatus ab illo / Hectore qui redit exuvias indutus Achilli.* How greatly changed from that Hector who returned dressed in the armour stripped from Achilles. [Ib.]

14 *Dis aliter visum.* Heaven thought otherwise. [Ib.]

15 *Auri sacra fames!* Detestable desire for gold! [Ib. III]

16 *Varium et mutabile semper / Femina.* Woman is always fickle and changeable. [Ib. IV]

17 *Sic, sic, iuvat ire sub umbras.* Thus, thus, it is joy to pass to the world below. [Ib.]

18 *Facilis descensus Averni: / Noctes atque dies patet atri ianua Ditis; / Sed revocare gradum superasque evadere ad auras, / Hoc opus, hic labor est.* The way to Hell is easy: night and day the gates of black Dis stand open; but to retrace the step and reach the breezes above, this is the task, and in it the labour. [Ib. VI]

19 *Procul, o procul este, profani.* Far, far from me, let all profane ones be. [Ib.]

20 *Fidus Achates.* Faithful Achates. [Ib.]

21 *O mihi praeteritos referat si Iuppiter annos.* Would only Jupiter give me back my lost years. [Ib. VIII]

22 *Macte nova virtute, puer, sic itur ad astra.* Good luck to your young ambition, lad, that is the way to the stars. [Ib. IX]

23 *Experto credite.* Believe one who knows by experience. [Ib. XI]

24 *Deus nobis haec otia fecit.* A god has made this peace for us. [*Eclogues*, I]

25 *Habitarunt di quoque silvas.* Gods have also lived in the woods. [Ib. II]

26 *Latet anguis in herba.* A snake lurks in the grass. [Ib. III]

27 *Paulo maiora canamus!* Let us sing of somewhat greater things! [Ib. IV]

28 *Magnus ab integro saeclorum nascitur ordo. / Iam redit et virgo, redeunt Saturnia regna, / Iam nova progenies caelo demittitur alto.* The great cycle of the ages begins again. Now too the maiden returns, and the kingdom of Saturn returns, and a new race descends from on high. [Ib.]

29 *Non omnia possumus omnes.* We are not all able to do everything. [Ib. VIII]

1 *Omnia vincit Amor: et nos cedamus Amori.* Love conquers all: and we succumb to love. [Ib. X]

2 *Ultima Thule.* Farthest Thule. [*Georgics*, I]

3 *Labor omnia vincit.* Work conquers all. [Ib.]

4 *Imponere Pelio Ossam.* To heap Ossa on Pelion. [Ib.]

5 *O fortunatus nimium, sua si bona norint, / Agricolas!* Ah how fortunate are farmers, if only they knew their good fortune. [Ib. II]

6 *Felix qui potuit rerum cognoscere causas.* Happy the man who could understand the causes of things. [Ib.]

7 *Fortunatus et ille deos qui novit agrestis.* Happy too is he who knows the country gods. [Ib.]

8 *Sed fugit interea, fugit inreparabile tempus.* Time meanwhile flies, flies never to return. [Ib.]

9 *Hi motus animorum atque haec certamina tanta / Pulveris exigui iactu compressa quiescent.* These soul-stirrings and great conflicts are contained and quelled by throwing a little dust. [Ib. IV]

10 *Si parva licet componere magnis.* If one may compare small things with great. [Ib.]

Voltaire (1694–1778)

11 *Tout est pour le mieux dans le meilleur des mondes possibles.* All is for the best in the best of all possible worlds. [*Candide*, 1 (and elsewhere)]

12 *Dans ce pays-ci il est bon de tuer de temps en temps un amiral pour encourager les autres.* In this country [England] it is considered good to kill an admiral from time to time, to encourage the others. [Ib. 23]

13 *Il faut cultiver notre jardin — Quand l'homme fut mis dans le jardin d'Eden, il y fut mis pour qu'il travaillât; ce qui prouve que l'homme n'est pas né pour le repos.*
— Travaillons sans raisonner, c'est le seul moyen de rendre la vie supportable. We must cultivate our garden. When man was put in the garden of Eden, he was put there to work; that proves that man was not born for rest. Let us work without question, that is the only way to make life tolerable. [Ib. 30]

14 *Ils ne servent de la pensée que pour autoriser leurs injustices, et n'emploient les paroles que pour déguiser leurs pensées.* People exploit thought only to validate their injustices, and they use words only to disguise their thoughts. ['Dialogue du Chapon et de la Poularde']

15 *Le mieux est l'ennemi du bien.* The best is the enemy of the good. [*Dictionnaire philosophique*, 'Art dramatique']

16 *Si Dieu n'existait pas, il faudrait l'inventer.* If God did not exist, it would be necessary to invent him. [*Epîtres*, 96]

17 *Ce corps qui s'appelait et qui s'appelle encore le saint empire romain n'était en aucune manière ni saint, ni romain, ni empire.* This body, which was called and still calls itself the Holy Roman Empire was not Holy, nor Roman, nor an Empire. [*Essai sur les Moeurs*]

18 *En effet, l'histoire n'est que le tableau des crimes et des malheurs.* Indeed, history is nothing but a tableau of crimes and misfortunes. [*L'Ingénu*, 10]

19 All the ancient histories, as one of our wits said, are just fables that have been agreed upon. [*Jeannot et Colin*]

20 *La Liberté est née en Angleterre des querelles des tyrans.* Liberty was born in England from the quarrels of tyrants. [*Lettres philosophiques*]

21 The most amazing and effective inventions are not those which do most honour to the human genius. [Ib.]

22 No one will ever make me believe that I think all the time. [Ib.]

1 *On doit des égards aux vivants; on ne doit aux morts que la vérité.* We owe respect to the living; to the dead we owe nothing but truth. [*Lettres sur Oedipe*, 1]

2 *Divisés d'intérêts, et pour le crime unis.* Divided by interests, and united by crime. [*Mérope*, 1]

3 *Le sombre Anglais, même dans ses amours, / Veut raisonner toujours. / On est plus raisonnable en France.* The gloomy Englishman, even in his loves, always wants to reason. We are more reasonable in France. [*Les Originaux, Entrée des Diverses Nations*]

4 *La crainte suit la crime, et c'est son châtiment.* Fear follows crime, and is its punishment. [*Semiramis*, V]

5 *Le secret d'ennuyer est...de tout dire.* The secret of being boring is to say everything. ['Sept Discours en verse sur l'Homme']

6 *Si Dieu nous a fait à son image, nous le lui avons bien rendu.* If God has created us in his image, we have repaid him well. [*Le Sottisier*]

7 *La lâche fuit en vain; la mort vole à sa suite. / C'est en la défiant que le brave l'évite.* The coward flies in vain, death follows close behind. It is by defying it that the brave escapes. [*Le Triumvirat*, IV]

8 *Dieu n'est pas pour les gros bataillons, mais pour ceux qui tirent le mieux.* God isn't on the side of the big batallions, but of the best marksmen. [*Notebooks*]

9 *Ecrasez l'infâme.* Wipe out the infamous. [Letter to d'Alembert, 1760 (Voltaire's motto)]

10 I have never made but one prayer to God, a very short one: 'O Lord, make my enemies ridiculous.' And God granted it. [Letter, 1767]

11 I am very fond of truth, but not at all of martyrdom. [Letter to d'Alembert, 1776]

12 I disapprove of what you say, but I will defend to the death your right to say it. [Attr.]

Vulgate

13 *Dominus illuminatio mea.* The Lord is my light. [Psalms, 26:1]

14 *Asperges me hyssopo, et mundabor.* You will sprinkle me with hyssop, and I shall be clean. [Ib. 50:9]

15 *Cantate Dominum canticum novum.* Sing unto the Lord a new song. [Ib. 97:1]

16 *Non nobis, Domine, non nobis.* Not unto us, Lord, not unto us. [Ib. 113:9]

17 *Laudate Dominum, omnes gentes.* Praise the Lord, all nations. [Ib. 116:1]

18 *De profundis clamavi ad te, Domine.* Out of the depths I have cried to thee, Lord. [Ib. 129:1]

19 *Vanitas vanitatum, et omnia vanitas.* Vanity of vanities, and all things are vanity. [Ecclesiastes, 1:2]

20 *Magnificat anima mea Dominum.* My soul magnifies the Lord. [Luke, 1:46]

21 *Nunc dimittis servum tuum, Domine, secundum verbum tuum in pace.* Lord, now lettest thou thy servant depart in peace: according to thy word. [Ib. 2:29; trans. Book of Common Prayer]

22 *Pax Vobis.* Peace be unto you. [Ib. 24:36]

23 *Quo vadis?* Where are you going? [John, 16:5]

24 *Ecce homo.* Behold the man. [Ib. 19:5]

25 *Consummatum est.* It is finished. [Ib. 19:30]

26 *Noli me tangere.* Do not touch me. [Ib. 20:17]

Waley, Arthur (1889-1966)

27 What is hard today is to censor one's own thoughts — / To sit by and see the blind man / On the sightless horse, riding into the bottomless abyss. ['Censorship']

Wallace, Henry (1888-1965)

28 The century on which we are entering — the century which will come out of this war — can be and must be the century of the common man. [Speech, 1942]

Wallace, William Ross (c. 1819–1881)

1 The hand that rocks the cradle / Is the hand that rules the world. [*John o' London's Treasure Trove*]

Wallas, Graham (1858–1932)

2 The little girl had the makings of a poet in her who, being told to be sure of her meaning before she spoke, said: 'How can I know what I think till I see what I say?' ['The Art of Thought']

Waller, Edmund (1606–1687)

3 Poets that lasting marble seek / Must carve in Latin or in Greek. ['Of English Verse']

4 Poets lose half the praise they should have got, / Could it be known what they discreetly blot. ['On Roscommon's Translation of Horace']

5 Every conqueror creates a Muse. ['Panegyric to My Lord Protector']

6 Go, lovely Rose! / Tell her, that wastes her time and me, / That now she knows, / When I resemble her to thee, / How sweet and fair she seems to be. ['Song']

7 How small a part of time they share, / That are so wondrous sweet and fair. [Ib.]

8 Others may use the ocean as their road, / Only the English make it their abode. ['Of a War with Spain']

Walpole, Horace (1717–1797)

9 Lord Rochester's poems have much more obscenity than wit, more wit than poetry, more poetry than politeness. [*Catalogue of Royal and Noble Authors*]

10 William Kent leapt the fence, and saw that all Nature was a garden. [*On Modern Gardening*]

11 Our supreme governors, the mob. [Letter, 1743]

12 One of the greatest geniuses that ever existed, Shakespeare, undoubtedly wanted taste. [Letter, 1764]

13 The works of Richardson...are pictures of high life as conceived by a bookseller, and romances as they would be spiritualized by a Methodist preacher. [Letter, 1764]

14 It is charming to totter into vogue. [Letter, 1765]

15 Everybody talks of the constitution, but all sides forget that the constitution is extremely well, and would do very well, if they would let it alone. [Letter, 1770]

16 [Of the East] It was easier to conquer it than to know what to do with it. [Letter, 1772]

17 Old age is no such uncomfortable thing if one gives oneself up to it with a good grace, and don't drag it about 'To midnight dances and the public show'. [Letter, 1774]

18 By the waters of Babylon we sit down and weep, when we think of thee, O America! [Letter, 1775]

19 This world is a comedy to those that think, and a tragedy to those that feel. [Letter, 1776]

20 The wisest prophets make sure of the event first. [Letter, 1785]

21 [Of Sir Joshua Reynolds] All his own geese are swans, as the swans of others are geese. [Letter, 1786]

22 They who cannot perform great things themselves may yet have a satisfaction in doing justice to those who can. [Attr.]

Walpole, Sir Robert (1676–1745)

23 Madam, there are fifty thousand men slain this year in Europe, and not one Englishman. [Remark to the Queen, 1734]

24 They now ring the bells, but they will soon wring their hands. [Remark on declaration of war with Spain, 1739]

25 The balance of power. [Speech, House of Commons, 1741]

26 [On being asked whether he would like to be read to] Anything but history, for history must be false. [Attr.]

27 All those men have their price. [Attr.]

Walsh, William (1663–1708)

1 In love alone we hate to find / Companions of our woe. ['Of All the Torments']

2 I can endure my own despair, / But not another's hope. [Ib.]

Walton, Izaak (1593–1683)

3 As no man is born an artist, so no man is born an angler. [*The Compleat Angler*, Epistle to the Reader]

4 Angling is somewhat like poetry, men are to be born so. [Ib.]

5 An excellent angler, and now with God. [Ib. 4]

6 We may say of angling as Dr. Boteler said of strawberries: 'Doubtless God could have made a better berry, but doubtless God never did'; and so (if I might be judge) God never did make a more calm, quiet, innocent recreation than angling. [Ib.]

7 I love such mirth as does not make friends ashamed to look upon one another next morning. [Ib. 5]

8 This dish of meat is too good for any but anglers, or very honest men. [Ib. 8]

9 Look to your health; and if you have it, praise God, and value it next to a good conscience; for health is the second blessing that we mortals are capable of; a blessing money cannot buy. [Ib. 21]

10 All that are lovers of virtue, and dare trust in His providence; and be quiet; and go a-Angling. [Ib.]

Warburton, William (1698–1779)

11 Orthodoxy is my doxy; heterodoxy is another man's doxy. [Remark]

Ward, Artemus (1834–1867)

12 I now bid you a welcome adoo. [*Artemus Ward His Book*]

13 N.B. This is rote Sarcasticul. [Ib.]

14 I girdid up my Lions & fled the Seen. [Ib.]

15 He [Brigham Young] is dreadfully married. He's the most married man I ever saw in my life. [*Artemus Ward's Lecture*]

16 Why is this thus? What is the reason of this thusness? [Ib.]

17 Why care for grammar as long as we are good? ['Pyrotechny']

18 Let us all be happy, and live within our means, even if we have to borrer the money to do it with. ['Science and Natural History']

Ward, Nathaniel (1578–1652)

19 The world is full of care, and much like unto a bubble; / Women and care, and care and women, and women and care and trouble. [Epigram]

Warhol, Andy (1931–1987)

20 In the future everyone will be famous for fifteen minutes. [Attr. remark]

Warner, Anna (1820–1915)

21 Jesus loves me! this I know, / For the Bible tells me so; / Little ones to Him belong, / They are weak, but He is strong. [Hymn]

Warner, Susan (1819–1885)

22 Jesus bids us shine / With a pure, clear light, / Like a little candle / Burning in the night. / In this world is darkness; / So let us shine, / You in your small corner, / And I in mine. [Hymn]

Washington, George (1732–1799)

23 Few men have virtue to withstand the highest bidder. [*Moral Maxims*]

24 To persevere in one's duty and be silent is the best answer to calumny. [Ib.]

25 Influence is not government. [*Political Maxims*]

26 Associate yourself with men of good quality if you esteem your own reputation; for 'tis better to be alone than in bad company. [*Rules of Civility*]

27 The very idea of the power and the right of the People to establish Government, presupposes the duty of every individual to obey the established Government. [Farewell Address, 1796]

1 'Tis our true policy to steer clear of permanent alliances, with any portion of the foreign world. [Ib.]

2 It is not a custom with me to keep money to look at. [Letter, 1780]

3 Be courteous to all, but intimate with few, and let those few be well tried before you give them your confidence. True friendship is a plant of slow growth, and must undergo and withstand the shocks of adversity before it is entitled to the appellation. [Letter, 1783]

4 Mankind, when left to themselves, are unfit for their own government. [Letter, 1786]

5 Liberty, when it begins to take root, is a plant of rapid growth. [Letter, 1788]

6 [On being accused of chopping down a cherry tree] Father, I cannot tell a lie; I did it with my little hatchet. [Attr., probably apocryphal]

7 Put none but Americans on guard tonight. [Attr. order, 1777]

Watkyns, Rowland (fl. 1660)

8 I love him not, but shew no reason can / Wherefore, but this, I *do not love* the man. [*Flamma sine fumo*, 'Antipathy']

Watson, Sir William (1858–1936)

9 Too long, that some may rest, / Tired millions toil unblest. ['New National Anthem']

10 The staid conservative, / Came-over-with-the-Conqueror type of mind. [*A Study in Contrasts*]

Watts, Isaac (1674–1748)

11 Let dogs delight to bark and bite, / For God hath made them so. [*Divine Songs for Children*, 'Against Quarrelling']

12 Birds in their little nests agree / And 'tis a shameful sight, / When children of one family / Fall out, and chide, and fight. [Ib. 'Love between Brothers and Sisters']

13 How doth the little busy bee / Improve each shining hour, / And gather honey all the day / From every opening flower! [Ib. 'Against Idleness and Mischief']

14 For Satan finds some mischief still / For idle hands to do. [Ib.]

15 'Tis the voice of the sluggard; I heard him complain, / 'You have wak'd me too soon, I must slumber again.' [*Moral Songs*, 'The Sluggard']

16 Time, like an ever-rolling stream, / Bears all its sons away; / They fly forgotten, as a dream / Dies at the opening day. [Psalm 90]

17 Jesus shall reign where'er the sun / Does his successive journeys run; / His Kingdom stretch from shore to shore, / Till moons shall wax and wane no more. [Hymn]

18 Blessings abound where'er He reigns; / The prisoner leaps to lose his chains. [Ib.]

19 When I survey the wondrous Cross / On which the Prince of Glory died, / My richest gain I count but loss, / And pour contempt on all my pride. [Hymn]

Waugh, Evelyn (1903–1966)

20 I expect you'll be becoming a schoolmaster, sir. That's what most of the gentlemen does, sir, that gets sent down for indecent behaviour. [*Decline and Fall*]

21 That's the public-school system all over. They may kick you out, but they never let you down. [Ib.]

22 We can trace almost all the disasters of English history to the influence of Wales. [Ib.]

23 I came to the conclusion many years ago that almost all crime is due to the repressed desire for aesthetic expression. [Ib.]

24 Feather-footed through the plashy fen passes the questing vole. [*Scoop*, I, 1]

25 When Lord Copper was right he said, 'Definitely, Lord Copper'; when he was wrong, 'Up to a point'. [Ib.]

26 All this fuss about sleeping together. For physical pleasure I'd sooner go to my dentist any day. [*Vile Bodies*]

Weatherly, Frederic Edward (1848–1929)

1 Where are the boys of the old Brigade, / Who fought with us side by side? ['The Old Brigade']

2 The gallant boys of the old Brigade, / They sleep in old England's heart. [Ib.]

Webb, Sidney (1859–1947)

3 Marriage is the waste-paper basket of the emotions. [Bertrand Russell, *Autobiography*]

Webster, Daniel (1782–1852)

4 The past, at least, is secure. [Speech, 1830]

5 The people's government, made for the people, made by the people, and answerable to the people. [Speech, 1830]

6 Inconsistencies of opinion, arising from changes of circumstances, are often justifiable. [Speech, 1846]

7 I was born an American; I will live an American; I shall die an American. [Speech, 1850]

8 Fearful concatenation of circumstances. ['Argument on the murder of Captain White']

9 There is always room at the top. [Remark]

Webster, John (c. 1580–1625)

10 I am Duchess of Malfi still. [*The Duchess of Malfi*, IV.2]

11 Glories, like glow-worms, afar off shine bright, / But, looked too near, have neither heat nor light. [Ib.]

12 I know death hath ten thousand several doors / For men to take their exits. [Ib.]

13 Cover her face; mine eyes dazzle; she died young. [Ib.]

14 Physicians are like kings — they brook no contradiction. [Ib. V.2]

15 We are merely the stars' tennis-balls, struck and bandied, / Which way please them. [Ib. V.4]

16 Is not old wine wholesomest, old pippins toothsomest? Does not old wood burn brightest, old linen wash whitest? Old soldiers, sweethearts, are surest, and old lovers are soundest. [*Westward Hoe*, II.2]

17 I saw him even now going the way of all flesh. [Ib.]

18 A mere tale of a tub, my words are idle. [*The White Devil*, II.1]

19 Call for the robin redbreast and the wren, / Since o'er shady groves they hover, / And with leaves and flowers do cover / The friendless bodies of unburied men. [Ib. V.4]

20 But keep the wolf far thence that's foe to men, / For with his nails he'll dig them up again. [Ib.]

21 My soul, like to a ship in a black storm, / Is driven, I know not whither. [Ib. V.6]

22 Prosperity doth bewitch men, seeming clear; / As seas do laugh, show white, when rocks are near. [Ib.]

23 I have caught / An everlasting cold; I have lost my voice / Most irrecoverably. [Ib.]

Wedgewood, Cicely Veronica (1910–)

24 ...truth can neither be apprehended nor communicated...history is an art like all other sciences. [*Truth and Opinion*]

Wedgwood, Josiah (1730–1795)

25 Am I not a man and a brother? [Motto adopted by Anti-Slavery Society]

Weiss, Peter (1916–1982)

26 *Denn was wäre schon dies Revolution / ohne eine allgemeine Kopulation.* What's the use of a revolution without general copulation! [*Marat/Sade*, II]

Welles, Orson (1915–1985)

27 In Switzerland they had brotherly love, five hundred years of democracy and peace, and what did they produce? The cuckoo clock! [*The Third Man*]

1 He has Van Gogh's ear for music. [Variously attr.]

Wellington, Arthur Wellesley, Duke of (1769–1852)

2 The battle of Waterloo was won on the playing fields of Eton. [Attr.]

3 Up guards and at 'em! [Attr. remark during Battle of Waterloo (but see below)]

4 What I must have said and possibly did say was, Stand up, Guards! and then gave the commanding officers the order to attack. [Letter to J.W. Croker]

5 It has been a damned nice thing — the nearest run thing you ever saw in your life. [Remark on Waterloo]

6 The next greatest misfortune to losing a battle is to gain such a victory as this. [Ib.]

7 Nothing except a battle lost can be half so melancholy as a battle won. [Despatch from Waterloo]

8 I hate the whole race...There is no believing a word they say — your professional poets, I mean — there never existed a more worthless set than Byron and his friends for example. [Remark, 1833]

9 Publish and be damned. [Attr.]

10 [On his troops] I don't know what effect these men will have on the enemy, but, by God, they frighten me. [Attr.]

11 The mere scum of the earth. [Remark, on his troops]

12 [To a man who approached him saying, 'Mr. Jones, I believe?'] If you believe that, you'll believe anything. [Attr.]

Wells, H.G. (1866–1946)

13 Every time Europe looks across the Atlantic to see the American eagle, it observes only the rear end of an ostrich. [*America*]

14 How d'you like her? Puts old Velasquez in his place. A young mistress is better than an old master, eh? [*Autocracy of Mr. Parham*, 3]

15 In the Country of the Blind the One-eyed Man is King. ['The Country of the Blind']

16 They feared the 'low' and they hated and despised the 'stuck up' and so they 'kept themselves to themselves', according to the English ideal. [*Kipps* I, 1]

17 I tell you, we're in a blessed drain-pipe, and we've got to crawl along it till we die. [Ib. I, 2]

18 There's no social differences — till women come in. [Ib. II, 4]

19 I don't 'old with Wealth. What *is* Wealth? Labour robbed out of the poor. [Ib.]

20 I was thinking jest what a Rum Go everything is. [Ib. III, 3]

21 [Of the British officer] He muffs his real job without a blush, and yet he would rather be shot than do his bootlaces up criss-cross. [*Mr. Britling Sees It Through*, II, 4]

22 Human history becomes more and more a race between education and catastrophe. [*The Outline of History*]

23 Moral indignation is jealousy with a halo. [*The Wife of Sir Isaac Harman*, 9]

24 In England we have come to rely upon a comfortable time-lag of fifty years or a century intervening between the perception that something ought to be done and a serious attempt to do it. [*Work, Wealth and Happiness of Mankind*]

25 The Shape of Things to Come [Title of book]

Wesley, Charles (1707–1788)

26 Gentle Jesus, meek and mild, / Look upon a little child. [Hymn]

27 Jesu, lover of my soul, / Let me to thy bosom fly, / While the nearer waters roll, / While the tempest still is high. [Hymn]

28 Hark! the herald angels sing, / 'Glory to the new-born King. / Peace on earth, and mercy mild, / God and sinners reconciled!' [Hymn]

29 O for a thousand tongues, to sing / My great Redeemer's praise. [Hymn]

30 Jesus! the Name that charms our fears, / That bids our sorrows cease; / 'Tis music in the sinner's ears, / 'Tis life, and health, and peace. [Ib.]

1 Hear Him, ye deaf; His praise, ye dumb, / Your loosened tongues employ; / Ye blind, behold your Saviour come; / And leap, ye lame, for joy! [Ib.]

2 Vain the stone, the watch, the seal; / Christ has burst the gates of hell. [Hymn]

Wesley, John (1703–1791)

3 Let it be observed, that slovenliness is no part of religion; that neither this, nor any text of Scripture, condemns neatness of apparel. Certainly this is a duty, not a sin. 'Cleanliness is, indeed, next to godliness.' [Sermon No. 93, 'On Dress' (phrase not original to Wesley)]

4 I look upon all the world as my parish. [*Journal*, 1739]

5 Though I am always in haste, I am never in a hurry. [Letter, 1777]

Wesley, Samuel (1662–1735)

6 The poet's fate is here in emblem shown, / He asked for bread, and he received a stone. ['Epigram on Butler's Monument in Westminster Abbey']

7 Style is the dress of thought; a modest dress, / Neat, but not gaudy, will true critics please. ['Epistle to a Friend concerning Poetry']

West, Mae (1892–1980)

8 Beulah, peel me a grape. [*I'm No Angel*]

9 Is that a gun in your pocket or are you just pleased to see me? [*My Little Chickadee*]

10 'Goodness, what beautiful diamonds!' 'Goodness had nothing to do with it!' [*Night After Night*]

11 Come up and see me sometime. [*She Done Him Wrong* (attr. version)]

Westcott, E.N. (1846–1898)

12 A reasonable amount o' fleas is good fer a dog — keeps him from broodin' over *bein'* a dog. [*David Harum*]

Wever, Robert (fl. 1550)

13 In youth is pleasure, in youth is pleasure. ['Lusty Juventus']

Wharton, Edith (1862–1937)

14 Mrs. Ballinger is one of the ladies who pursue Culture in bands, as though it were dangerous to meet it alone. [*Xingu*, 1]

Whately, Richard (1787–1863)

15 Happiness is no laughing matter. [*Apophthegms*]

16 It is a folly to expect men to do all that they may reasonably be expected to do. [Ib.]

17 Honesty is the best policy, but he who is governed by that maxim is not an honest man. [Ib.]

18 Preach not because you have to say something, but because you have something to say. [Ib.]

Whewell, William (1794–1866)

19 Hence no force, however great, can stretch a cord, however fine, into a horizontal line which is accurately straight. [*Elementary Treatise on Mechanics* (often cited as instance of accidental metre and rhyme)]

Whistler, James McNeil (1834–1903)

20 I am not arguing with you — I am telling you. [*The Gentle Art of Making Enemies*]

21 [To a lady who said that a landscape reminded her of his work] Yes, madam, Nature is creeping up. [D.C. Seitz, *Whistler Stories*]

22 You shouldn't say it is not good. You should say, you do not like it; and then, you know, you're perfectly safe. [Ib.]

23 [To a lady who said the two greatest painters were himself and Velasquez] Why drag in Velasquez? [Ib.]

24 [Replying to the question 'For two days' labour, you ask two hundred guineas?'] No, I ask it for the knowledge of a lifetime. [Ib.]

25 *Oscar Wilde:* I wish I had said that. *Whistler:* You will, Oscar, you will. [Ingleby, *Oscar Wilde*]

White, William Allen (1868–1944)

1 All dressed up with nowhere to go. [Remark, 1916]

Whitefield, George (1714–1770)

2 I had rather wear out than rust out. [Attr.]

Whitehead, A.N. (1861–1947)

3 It is more important that a proposition be interesting than that it be true. [*Adventures of Ideas*]

4 It is the essence of life that it exists for its own sake. [*Nature and Life*]

5 The history of Western philosophy is, after all, no more than a series of footnotes to Plato's philosophy. [Attr.]

6 The systematic thought of ancient writers is now nearly worthless; but their detached insights are priceless. [Quoted in Flesch, *The Book of Unusual Quotations*]

Whitehead, William (1715–1785)

7 An old tale, which every schoolboy knows. [*The Roman Father*, Prologue]

Whiting, William (1825–1878)

8 Eternal Father, strong to save, / Whose arm hath bound the restless wave / ...O hear us when we cry to Thee / For those in peril on the sea. [Hymn]

Whitman, Walt (1819–1892)

9 Women sit or move to and fro, some old, some young. / The young are beautiful — but the old are more beautiful than the young. ['Beautiful Women']

10 Silent and amazed even when a little boy, / I remember I heard the preacher every Sunday put God in his statements, / As contending against some being or influence. ['A Child's Amaze']

11 If anything is sacred the human body is sacred. ['I Sing the Body Electric']

12 O Captain! My Captain! our fearful trip is done. ['O Captain! My Captain!']

13 But O heart! heart! heart! / O the bleeding drops of red, / Where on the deck my Captain lies, / Fallen cold and dead. [Ib.]

14 Out of the cradle endlessly rocking, / Out of the mocking bird's throat, the musical shuttle. ['Out of the Cradle endlessly Rocking']

15 Camerado, this is no book, / Who touches this touches a man, / (Is it night? Are we here alone?) / It is I you hold and who holds you. ['So Long!']

16 Where the populace rise at once against the never-ending audacity of elected persons. ['Song of the Broad Axe, 5']

17 Where women walk in public processions in the streets the same as the men, / Where they enter the public assembly and take places the same as the men; / Where the city of the faithfullest friends stands, / Where the city of the cleanliness of the sexes stands... / ...There the great city stands. [Ib.]

18 I celebrate myself, and sing myself, / And what I assume you shall assume. [*Song of Myself*]

19 I loafe and invite my soul. [Ib.]

20 Has anyone supposed it lucky to be born? / I hasten to inform him or her, it is just as lucky to die and I know it. [Ib.]

21 I believe a leaf of grass is no less than the journey-work of the stars. [Ib.]

22 [Of animals] They do not sweat and whine about their condition, / They do not lie awake in the dark and weep for their sins, / They do not make me sick discussing their duty to God, / Not one is dissatisfied, not one is demented with the mania of owning things, / Not one kneels to another, nor to his kind that lived thousands of years ago. [Ib.]

23 Behold, I do not give lectures or a little charity, / When I give I give myself. [Ib.]

24 Do I contradict myself? / Very well then I contradict myself / (I am large, I contain multitudes). [*Song of Myself*]

1 I sound my barbaric yawp over the roofs of the world. [Ib.]

2 The earth, that is sufficient, / I do not want the constellations any nearer, / I know they are very well where they are, / I know they suffice for those who belong to them. ['Song of the Open Road']

3 That shadow my likeness that goes to and fro seeking a livelihood, chattering, chaffering, / How often I find myself standing and looking at it where it flits, / How often I question and doubt whether that is really me. ['That Shadow My Likeness']

4 The earth does not argue, / Is not pathetic, has no arrangements, / Does not scream, haste, persuade, threaten, promise, / Makes no discriminations, has no conceivable failures, / Closes nothing, refuses nothing, shuts none out. ['To the Sayers of Words']

5 When lilacs last in the dooryard bloom'd, / And the great stars early droop'd in the western sky in the night, / I mourn'd, and yet shall mourn with ever-returning spring. ['When Lilacs Last in the Dooryard Bloom'd']

6 Youth, large, lusty, loving — youth full of grace, force, fascination, / Do you know that Old Age may come after you with equal grace, force, fascination? ['Youth, Day, Old Age and Night']

7 I no doubt deserved my enemies, but I don't believe I deserved my friends. [Bradford, *Biography and the Human Heart*]

Whittier, John Greenleaf (1807–1892)

8 'Shoot if you must, this old grey head, / But spare your country's flag,' she said. ['Barbara Frietchie']

9 'Who touches a hair of yon grey head / Dies like a dog! March on!' he said. [Ib.]

10 For all sad words of tongue or pen, / The saddest are these: 'It might have been!' ['Maud Muller']

11 The Indian Summer of the heart. ['Memories']

12 Dear Lord and Father of mankind, / Forgive our foolish ways. [Hymn]

13 Take from our souls the strain and stress, / And let our ordered lives confess / The beauty of Thy peace. [Ib.]

Whittington, Robert (fl. 1520)

14 [Of Sir Thomas More] As time requireth, a man of marvellous mirth and pastimes, and sometimes of as sad gravity, as who say: a man for all seasons. [*Vulgaria*, II]

Whurr, Cornelius (1782–1853)

15 But lasting joys the man attend / Who has a polished female friend. ['The Accomplished Female Friend']

Whyte-Melville, George (1821–1878)

16 Then drink, puppy, drink, and let ev'ry puppy drink, / That is old enough to lap and swallow. ['Drink, Puppy, Drink']

Wilberforce, Bishop Samuel (1805–1873)

17 If I were a cassowary / On the plains of Timbuctoo, / I would eat a missionary, / Cassock, band, and hymn-book too. [Attr. impromptu]

Wilbur, Richard (1921–)

18 We milk the cow of the world, and as we do / We whisper in her ear, 'You are not true.' ['Epistemology']

Wilcox, Ella Wheeler (1855–1919)

19 Laugh and the world laughs with you; / Weep, and you weep alone; / For the sad old earth must borrow its mirth, / But has trouble enough of its own. ['Solitude']

20 So many gods, so many creeds, / So many paths that wind and wind. ['The World's Need']

Wilde, Oscar (1854–1900)

21 At least / I have not made my heart a heart of stone, / Nor starved my boyhood of its goodly feast, / Nor walked where Beauty is a thing unknown. ['Apologia']

22 That little tent of blue / Which prisoners call the sky. [*The Ballad of Reading Gaol*, I]

1 Yet each man kills the thing he loves, / By each let this be heard, / Some do it with a bitter look, / Some with a flattering word, / The coward does it with a kiss, / The brave man with a sword! [Ib.]

2 For Man's grim Justice goes its way, / And will not swerve aside: / It slays the weak, it slays the strong, / It has a deadly stride. [Ib. III]

3 For he who lives more lives than one / More deaths than one must die. [Ib.]

4 There is no chapel on the day / On which they hang a man. [Ib. IV]

5 I know not whether Laws be right, / Or whether Laws be wrong; / All that we know who lie in gaol / Is that the wall is strong; / And that each day is like a year, / A year whose days are long. [Ib. V]

6 Each passion being loth / For love's own sake to leave the other's side / Yet killing love by staying. ['The Burden of Itys']

7 Sing on! sing on! I would be drunk with life, / Drunk with the trampled vintage of my youth. [Ib.]

8 As for modern journalism, it is not my business to defend it. It justifies its own existence by the great Darwinian principle of the survival of the vulgarest. [*The Critic as Artist*, I]

9 To give an accurate description of what has never occurred is not merely the proper occupation of the historian, but the inalienable privilege of any man of parts and culture. [Ib.]

10 Education is an admirable thing, but it is well to remember from time to time that nothing that is worth knowing can be taught. [Ib.]

11 For there is no art where there is no style, and no style where there is no unity, and unity is of the individual. [Ib.]

12 Movement, that problem of the visible arts, can be truly realized by Literature alone. It is Literature that shows us the body in its swiftness and the soul in its unrest. [Ib. II]

13 Ah! don't say that you agree with me. When people agree with me I always feel that I must be wrong. [Ib.]

14 As long as war is regarded as wicked, it will always have its fascination. When it is looked upon as vulgar, it will cease to be popular. The change will, of course, be slow, and people will not be conscious of it. [Ib.]

15 I became the spendthrift of my own genius and to waste an eternal youth gave me a curious joy. [*De Profundis*]

16 Most people are other people. Their thoughts are someone else's opinions, their lives a mimicry, their passions a quotation. [Ib.]

17 Art never expresses anything but itself. [*The Decay of Lying*]

18 Everybody who is incapable of learning has taken to teaching. [Ib.]

19 The final revelation is that Lying, the telling of beautiful untrue things, is the proper aim of Art. [Ib.]

20 [Of Wordsworth] He found in stones the sermons he had already hidden there. [Ib.]

21 No, my Lord Cardinal, I weary of her! / Why, she is worse than ugly, she is good. [*The Duchess of Padua*, II]

22 We are each our own devil, and we make / This world our hell. [Ib. V]

23 And down the long and silent street, / The dawn, with silver-sandalled feet, / Crept like a frightened girl. ['The Harlot's House']

24 Ah! somehow life is bigger after all / Than any painted Angel. ['Humanitad']

25 Men can be analysed, women...merely adored. [*An Ideal Husband*, I]

26 Questions are never indiscreet. Answers sometimes are. [Ib.]

27 Morality is simply the attitude we adopt towards people whom we personally dislike. [Ib. II]

28 To love oneself is the beginning of a lifelong romance, Phipps. [Ib. III]

1 Really, if the lower orders don't set us a good example, what on earth is the use of them? They seem, as a class, to have absolutely no sense of moral responsibility. [*The Importance of Being Earnest*, I]

2 The truth is rarely pure and never simple. Modern life would be very tedious if it were either, and modern literature a complete impossibility. [Ib.]

3 You don't seem to realize, that in married life three is company and two is none. [Ib.]

4 To lose one parent, Mr. Worthing, may be regarded as a misfortune; to lose both looks like carelessness. [Ib.]

5 All women become like their mothers. That is their tragedy. No man does. That's his. [Ib.]

6 The good ended happily, and the bad unhappily. That is what Fiction means. [Ib. II]

7 I never travel without my diary. One should always have something sensational to read in the train. [Ib.]

8 *Cecily:* When I see a spade I call it a spade.
Gwendolen: I am glad to say that I have never seen a spade. It is obvious that our social spheres have been widely different. [Ib.]

9 On an occasion of this kind it becomes more than a moral duty to speak one's mind. It becomes a pleasure. [Ib.]

10 In matters of grave importance, style, not sincerity, is the vital thing. [Ib. III]

11 Three addresses always inspire confidence, even in tradesmen. [Ib. III]

12 Never speak disrespectfully of Society, Algernon. Only people who can't get into it do that. [Ib.]

13 Untruthful! My nephew Algernon? Impossible! He is an Oxonian. [Ib.]

14 Please do not shoot the pianist. He is doing his best. [*Impressions of America*, 'Leadville']

15 It is absurd to divide people into good and bad. People are either charming or tedious. [*Lady Windermere's Fan*, I]

16 I couldn't help it. I can resist everything except temptation. [Ib.]

17 He thinks like a Tory, and talks like a Radical, and that's so important nowadays. [Ib. II]

18 *Cecil Graham:* What is a cynic?
Lord Darlington: A man who knows the price of everything and the value of nothing. [Ib.]

19 We are all in the gutter, but some of us are looking at the stars. [Ib. III]

20 There is no such thing as a moral or an immoral book. Books are well written or badly written. [*Picture of Dorian Gray*, Preface]

21 The nineteenth century dislike of Realism is the rage of Caliban seeing his own face in the glass. [Ib.]

22 There is only one thing in the world worse than being talked about, and that is not being talked about. [Ib.]

23 A man cannot be too careful in the choice of his enemies. [Ib.]

24 The only way to get rid of a temptation is to yield to it. [Ib. 2]

25 A cigarette is the perfect type of a perfect pleasure. It is exquisite, and it leaves one unsatisfied. What more can one want? [Ib. 6]

26 It is better to be beautiful than to be good. But...it is better to be good than to be ugly. [Ib. 17]

27 And out of the bronze of the image of *The Sorrow that endureth for Ever* he fashioned an image of *The Pleasure that abideth for a Moment.* [*Poems in Prose*, 'The Artist']

28 Wickedness is a myth invented by good people to account for the curious attractiveness of others. [*Phrases and Philosophies for the Use of the Young*]

29 Nothing that actually occurs is of the smallest importance. [Ib.]

30 If one tells the truth, one is sure, sooner or later, to be found out. [Ib.]

31 The old believe everything: the middle-aged suspect everything: the young know everything. [Ib.]

32 It is only by not paying one's bills that one can hope to live in the memory of the commercial classes. [Ib.]

1 The only way to atone for being occasionally a little over-dressed is by being always absolutely over-educated. [Ib.]

2 In examinations the foolish ask questions that the wise cannot answer. [Ib.]

3 If property had simply pleasures, we could stand it; but its duties make it unbearable. In the interest of the rich we must get rid of it. [*The Soul of Man under Socialism*]

4 We are often told that the poor are grateful for charity. Some of them are, no doubt, but the best amongst the poor are never grateful. They are ungrateful, discontented, disobedient, and rebellious. They are quite right to be so. [Ib.]

5 As for the virtuous poor, one can pity them, of course, but one cannot possibly admire them. They have made private terms with the enemy, and sold their birthright for very bad pottage. [Ib.]

6 Most personalities have been obliged to be rebels. [Ib.]

7 The Lords Temporal say nothing, the Lords Spiritual have nothing to say, and the House of Commons has nothing to say and says it. We are dominated by Journalism. [Ib.]

8 Let God or the Czar look to it. [*Vera, or The Nihilists*]

9 Experience, the name men give to their mistakes. [Ib.]

10 One should never trust a woman who tells one her real age. A woman who would tell one that would tell one anything. [*A Woman of No Importance*, I]

11 It is not customary in England, Miss Worsley, for a young lady to speak with such enthusiasm of any person of the opposite sex. English women conceal their feelings till after they are married. [Ib.]

12 It is the problem of slavery. And we are trying to solve it by amusing the slaves. [Ib.]

13 The English country gentleman galloping after a fox — the unspeakable in full pursuit of the uneatable. [Ib.]

14 Twenty years of romance make a woman look like a ruin; but twenty years of marriage make her something like a public building. [Ib.]

15 Children begin by loving their parents. After a time they judge them. Rarely, if ever, do they forgive them. [Ib.]

16 Nothing is so aggravating as calmness. There is something positively brutal about the good temper of most modern men. [Ib. II]

17 You should study the Peerage, Gerald. It is the one book a young man about town should know thoroughly, and it is the best thing in fiction the English have done. [Ib. III]

18 Moderation is a fatal thing, Lady Hunstanton. Nothing succeeds like excess. [Ib.]

19 Those things which the English public never forgives — youth, power, and enthusiasm. [Lecture, 'The English Renaissance']

20 I must decline your invitation owing to a subsequent engagement. [Attr.]

21 Frank Harris is invited to all the great houses in England — once. [Attr.]

22 George Meredith is a prose Browning, and so is Browning. [Attr.]

23 Work is the curse of the drinking classes. [Pearson, *Life of Wilde*]

24 [Of Bernard Shaw] He hasn't an enemy in the world, and none of his friends like him. [Shaw, *Sixteen Self Sketches*]

25 [Wilde was to be charged a large fee for an operation] 'Ah, well, then,' said Oscar, 'I suppose that I shall have to die beyond my means.' [R.H. Sherard, *Life of Oscar Wilde*]

26 [At the New York Customs] I have nothing to declare except my genius. [F. Harris, *Oscar Wilde*]

27 A thing is not necessarily true because a man dies for it. [*Sebastian Melmoth* and *Oscariana*]

Wilder, Billy (1906–)

1 France is a country where the money falls apart in your hands and you can't tear the toilet paper. [Quoted in Halliwell, *Filmgoer's Book of Quotes*]

Wilhelm II, Kaiser (1859–1941)

2 You will be home before the leaves have fallen from the trees. [Remark to troops leaving for the Front, August 1914]

3 A contemptible little army. [Of the British Expeditionary Force in 1914]

Wilkes, John (1727–1797)

4 The chapter of accidents is the longest chapter in the book. [Quoted in Southey, *The Doctor*, IV]

5 [Told by Lord Sandwich that he would die either on the gallows or of the pox] That must depend on whether I embrace your lordship's principles or your mistress. [Attr.]

William III (1650–1702)

6 [On his country, Holland] There is one way never to see it lost, and that is to die in the last ditch. [Burnet, *History of his own Times*]

7 Every bullet has its billet. [Remark, quoted by John Wesley]

Williams, Harry (1874–1924) and Judge, Jack (1878–1938)

8 Good-bye Piccadilly, Farewell Leicester Square; / It's a long, long way to Tipperary, but my heart's right there. ['It's a Long Way to Tipperary']

Williams, Tennessee (1911–1983)

9 Knowledge—Zzzzzp! Money — Zzzzzzp! — Power! That's the cycle democracy is built on! [*The Glass Menagerie*]

10 I have always depended on the kindness of strangers. [*A Streetcar Named Desire*, II]

Williams, William Carlos (1883–1963)

11 Of Asphodel, that greeny flower, / ...I come, my sweet, / to sing to you. ['Asphodel, that Greeny Flower']

12 ...no ideas but in things. [*Paterson*, I, 1]

13 In old age / the mind / casts off / rebelliously / an eagle / from its crag. [Ib. V, 1]

14 no woman is virtuous / who does not give herself to her lover / — forthwith. [Ib. VI, 3]

15 so much depends / upon / a red wheel / barrow / glazed with rain / water / beside the white / chickens. ['The Red Wheelbarrow']

Willkie, Wendell (1892–1944)

16 The Constitution does not provide for first and second class citizens. [*An American Program*]

Wilson, Charles E. (1890–1961)

17 What is good for the country is good for General Motors, and vice versa. [Remark to Congressional Committee, 1953]

Wilson, Harold (1916–)

18 The little gnomes of Zurich. [Speech, 1956]

19 After half a century of democratic advance, the whole process has ground to a halt with a 14th Earl. [Speech, 1963]

20 It does not mean, of course, that the pound here in Britain, in your pocket or purse or in your bank, has been devalued. [T.V. broadcast, 1967]

21 A week is a long time in politics. [Remark, 1965]

Wilson, Harriette (1789–1846)

22 I shall not say why and how I became, at the age of fifteen, the mistress of the Earl of Craven. [*Memoirs*, first sentence]

Wilson, Woodrow (1856–1924)

23 Generally young men are regarded as radicals. This is a popular misconception. The most conservative persons I ever met are college undergraduates. [Address, 1905]

1 America lives in the heart of every man everywhere who wishes to find a region where he will be free to work out his destiny as he chooses. [Speech, 1912]

2 The history of liberty is a history of resistance. [Speech, 1912]

3 I fancy that it is just as hard to do your duty when men are sneering at you as when they are shooting at you. [Speech, 1914]

4 No nation is fit to sit in judgement upon any other nation. [Address, 1915]

5 There is such a thing as a man being too proud to fight. [Address, 1915]

6 Character is a by-product; it is produced in the great manufacture of daily duty. [Address, 1915]

7 We have stood apart, studiously neutral. [Address, 1915]

8 There is a price which is too great to pay for peace, and that price can be put in one word. One cannot pay the price of self-respect. [Speech, 1916]

9 Armed neutrality. [Address, 1917]

10 It must be a peace without victory. [Address, 1917]

11 The world must be made safe for democracy. [Address, 1917]

12 The right is more precious than peace. [Ib.]

13 Open covenants of peace, openly arrived at, after which there shall be no private international understandings of any kind, but diplomacy shall proceed always frankly and in the public view. [Speech ('Fourteen Points'), 1918]

14 America is the only idealistic nation in the world. [Speech, 1919]

Winchilsea, Anne Finch, Lady (1661–1720)

15 We faint beneath the aromatic pain. ['The Spleen']

Windsor, Duchess of (1896–1986)

16 One can never be too rich. One can never be too thin. [Quoted in Sontag, *Illness as Metaphor*]

Wister, Owen (1860–1938)

17 When you call me that, *smile*! [*The Virginian*, 2]

Wither, George (1588–1667)

18 Hang sorrow, care will kill a cat, / And therefore let's be merry. ['Christmas']

19 Shall I, wasting in despair, / Die because a woman's fair? ['Sonnet']

Wittgenstein, Ludwig (1889–1951)

20 The solution of the problem of life is seen in the vanishing of the problem. [*Tractatus Logico-Philosophicus*]

21 Whereof one cannot speak, thereon one must be silent. [Ib.]

22 The world is everything that is the case. [Ib.]

23 Everything that can be said can be said clearly. [Ib.]

24 Ethics does not treat of the world. Ethics must be a condition of the world, like logic. [Quoted in Auden, *A Certain World*]

Wodehouse, P.G. (1881–1975)

25 He spoke with a certain what-is-it in his voice, and I could see that, if not actually disgruntled, he was far from being gruntled. [*The Code of the Woosters*]

26 She had a penetrating sort of laugh. Rather like a train going into a tunnel. [*The Inimitable Jeeves*]

27 She fitted into my biggest armchair as if it had been built round her by someone who knew they were wearing armchairs tight about the hips that season. ['Jeeves and the Unbidden Guest']

28 I spent the afternoon musing on Life. If you come to think of it, what a queer thing Life is! So unlike anything else, don't you know, if you see what I mean. ['Rallying Round Old George']

29 'That,' I replied cordially, 'is what it doesn't do anything else but.' [*Ukridge*]

Wolfe, Charles (1791-1823)

1 Not a drum was heard, not a funeral note, / As his corse to the rampart we hurried. ['The Burial of Sir John Moore at Corunna']

2 We buried him darkly at dead of night, / The sods with our bayonets turning. [Ib.]

3 But he lay like a warrior taking his rest, / With his martial cloak around him. [Ib.]

4 We carved not a line, and we raised not a stone — / But we left him alone in his glory. [Ib.]

Wolfe, Humbert (1886-1940)

5 You cannot hope / to bribe or twist, / thank God! the / British journalist. / But, seeing what / the man will do / unbribed, there's / no occasion to. [*The Uncelestial City*]

Wolfe, James (1727-1759)

6 The General...repeated nearly the whole of Gray's Elegy...adding, as he concluded, that he would prefer being the author of that poem to the glory of beating the French tomorrow. [Robinson, *Biographical Account*]

Wolfe, Tom (1931-)

7 Radical chic. [Title of essay]

Wollstonecraft, Mary (1759-1797)

8 [Of women] I do not wish them to have power over men; but over themselves. [*A Vindication of the Rights of Women*, 4]

9 When a man seduces a woman, it should, I think, be termed a *left-handed* marriage. [Ib.]

Wolsey, Thomas, Cardinal (c. 1475-1530)

10 Father Abbot, I am come to lay my bones amongst you. [Remark at Leicester Abbey, 1529]

11 Had I but served God as diligently as I have served the King, he would not have given me over in my grey hairs. [Attr.]

Wood, Mrs. Henry (1814-1887)

12 Dead! and...never called me mother. [*East Lynne* (stage adaptation)]

Woodroofe, Lt. Comdr. Thomas (1899-1978)

13 The Fleet's lit up. [Broadcast commentary on Spithead Naval Review, 1937]

Woolf, Virginia (1882-1941)

14 In or about December, 1910, human character changed. ['Mr. Bennett and Mrs. Brown']

15 I have lost friends, some by death...others through sheer inability to cross the street. [*The Waves*]

16 A Room of One's Own [Title of essay]

17 [Of Joyce's *Ulysses*] Merely the scratching of pimples on the body of the bootboy at Claridge's. [Letter, 1922]

Wordsworth, Elizabeth (1840-1932)

18 If all the good people were clever, / And all clever people were good, / The world would be nicer than ever / We thought that it possibly could. But somehow, 'tis seldom or never / The two hit it off as they should; / The good are so harsh to the clever, / The clever so rude to the good. ['Good and Clever']

Wordsworth, William (1770-1850)

19 Suffering is permanent, obscure, and dark, / And shares the nature of infinity. [*The Borderers*]

20 Who is the happy Warrior? Who is he / That every man in arms should wish to be? ['Character of the Happy Warrior']

21 I wandered lonely as a cloud / That floats on high o'er vales and hills, / When all at once I saw a crowd, / A host of golden daffodils. ['Daffodils']

22 For oft when on my couch I lie / In vacant or in pensive mood, / They flash upon that inward eye / Which is the bliss of solitude; / And then my heart with pleasure fills, / And dances with the daffodils. [Ib.]

1 The gleam, / The light that never was, on sea or land, / The consecration, and the Poet's dream. ['Elegiac Stanzas']

2 On Man, on Nature and on Human Life, / Musing in solitude. [*The Excursion*, Preface]

3 Oh! many are the Poets that are sown / By Nature; men endowed with highest gifts, / The vision and the faculty divine; / Yet wanting the accomplishment of verse. [Ib. I]

4 Wisdom is ofttimes nearer when we stoop / Than when we soar. [Ib. III]

5 'Tis a thing impossible, to frame / Conceptions equal to the soul's desires; / And the most difficult of tasks to *keep* / Heights which the soul is competent to gain. [Ib. IV]

6 The wiser mind / Mourns less for what age takes away / Than what it leaves behind. ['The Fountain']

7 The moving accident is not my trade; / To freeze the blood I have no ready arts. ['Hart-Leap Well']

8 I travelled among unknown men / In lands beyond the sea; / Nor, England! did I know till then / What love I bore to thee. ['I Travelled among Unknown Men']

9 The gods approve / The depth, and not the tumult, of the soul. ['Laodamia']

10 In that sweet mood when pleasant thoughts / Bring sad thoughts to the mind. ['Lines Written in Early Spring']

11 Feelings too / Of unremembered pleasure; such, perhaps, / As may have had no trivial influence / On that best portion of a good man's life; / His little, nameless, unremembered acts / Of kindness and of love. ['Lines composed a few miles above Tintern Abbey']

12 That blessed mood, / In which the burthen of the mystery, / In which the heavy and the weary weight / Of all this unintelligible world, / Is lightened. [Ib.]

13 We are laid asleep / In body, and become a living soul /...We see into the life of things. [Ib.]

14 The sounding cataract / Haunted me like a passion. [Ib.]

15 I have learned / To look on nature, not as in the hour / Of thoughtless youth; but hearing often-times / The still, sad music of humanity. [Ib.]

16 And I have felt / A presence that disturbs me with the joy / Of elevated thoughts; a sense sublime / Of something far more deeply interfused, / Whose dwelling is the light of setting suns, / And the round ocean and the living air, / And the blue sky, and in the mind of man, / A motion and a spirit, that impels / All thinking things, all objects of all thought, / And rolls through all things. [Ib.]

17 Nature never did betray / The heart that loved her. [Ib.]

18 My heart leaps up when I behold / A rainbow in the sky. ['My heart leaps up']

19 The Child is father of the Man; / And I could wish my days to be / Bound each to each by natural piety. [Ib.]

20 There was a time when meadow, grove, and stream, / The earth, and every common sight, / To me did seem / Apparelled in celestial light, / The glory and the freshness of a dream. ['Ode: Intimations of Immortality']

21 There hath passed away a glory from the earth. [Ib.]

22 Whither is fled the visionary gleam? / Where is it now, the glory and the dream? / Our birth is but a sleep and a forgetting. [Ib.]

23 Not in entire forgetfulness, / And not in utter nakedness, / But trailing clouds of glory do we come / From God, who is our home: / Heaven lies about us in our infancy! / Shades of the prison house begin to close / Upon the growing boy. [Ib.]

24 At length the man perceives it die away, / And fade into the light of common day. [Ib.]

25 High instincts before which our mortal nature / Did tremble like a guilty thing surprised. [Ib.]

26 Though nothing can bring back the hour / Of splendour in the grass, of glory in the flower. [Ib.]

1 To me the meanest flower that blows can give / Thoughts that do often lie too deep for tears. [Ib.]

2 A primrose by a river's brim / A yellow primrose was to him / And it was nothing more. [*Peter Bell*, I]

3 A reasoning, self-sufficing thing, / An intellectual All-in-all! ['A Poet's Epitaph']

4 But who is He, with modest looks, / And clad in homely russet brown? / He murmurs near the running brooks / A music sweeter than their own. [Ib.]

5 The harvest of a quiet eye, / That broods and sleeps on his own heart. [Ib.]

6 Fair seed-time had my soul, and I grew up / Fostered alike by beauty and by fear. [*The Prelude*, I]

7 Dust as we are, the immortal spirit grows / Like harmony in music; there is a dark / Inscrutable workmanship that reconciles / Discordant elements, makes them cling together / In one society. [Ib.]

8 Where the statue stood / Of Newton, with his prism and silent face, / The marble index of a mind for ever / Voyaging through strange seas of Thought, alone. [Ib. III]

9 The unfetter'd clouds, and region of the Heavens, / Tumult and peace, the darkness and the light / Were all like workings of one mind, the features / Of the same face, blossoms upon one tree, / Characters of the great Apocalypse, / The types and symbols of Eternity, / Of first and last, and midst, and without end. [Ib. VI]

10 Bliss was it in that dawn to be alive, / But to be young was very heaven. [Ib. XI]

11 There is / One great society alone on earth: / The noble living and the noble dead. [Ib.]

12 Instruct them how the mind of man becomes / A thousand times more beautiful than the earth / On which he dwells. [Ib. XIV]

13 I thought of Chatterton, the marvellous boy, / The sleepless soul that perished in his pride. ['Resolution and Independence']

14 We poets in our youth begin in gladness; / But thereof comes in the end despondency and madness. [Ib.]

15 Choice words, and measured phrase, above the reach / Of ordinary men; a stately speech; / Such as grave livers do in Scotland use, / Religious men, who give to God and Man their dues. [Ib.]

16 We feel that we are greater than we know. ['The River Duddon']

17 She dwelt among the untrodden ways / Beside the springs of Dove, / A maid whom there were none to praise / And very few to love. ['She Dwelt among the Untrodden Ways']

18 But she is in her grave, and, oh, / The difference to me! [Ib.]

19 For still, the more he works, the more / Do his weak ankles swell. ['Simon Lee']

20 She was a phantom of delight / When first she gleamed upon my sight. ['She was a Phantom of Delight']

21 A slumber did my spirit seal; / I had no human fears: / She seemed a thing that could not feel / The touch of earthly years.
No motion has she now, no force; / She neither hears nor sees; / Rolled round in earth's diurnal course, / With rocks, and stones, and trees. ['A Slumber did My Spirit Seal']

22 Behold her, single in the field, / Yon solitary Highland lass! ['The Solitary Reaper']

23 Some natural sorrow, loss, or pain / That has been, and may be again. [Ib.]

24 The music in my heart I bore, / Long after it was heard no more. [Ib.]

25 Earth has not anything to show more fair; / Dull would he be of soul who could pass by / A sight so touching in its majesty. [*Sonnets*: 'Sonnet composed upon Westminster Bridge']

26 Dear God! the very houses seem asleep; / And all that mighty heart is lying still. [Ib.]

27 It is a beauteous evening, calm and free, / The holy time is quiet as a nun, / Breathless with adoration. [Ib. 'It is a beauteous evening']

1 God being with thee when we know it not. [Ib.]

2 Nuns fret not at their convent's narrow room; / And hermits are contented with their cells. [Ib. 'Nuns fret not']

3 Surprised by joy — impatient as the Wind / I turned to share the transport — Oh! with whom / But Thee, deep buried in the silent tomb. [Ib. 'Surprised by joy']

4 Thy friends are exultations, agonies, / And love, and man's unconquerable mind. [Ib. 'To Toussaint L'Ouverture']

5 Two Voices are there; one is of the sea, / One of the mountains; each a mighty Voice, / In both from age to age thou didst rejoice, / They were thy chosen music, Liberty! [Ib. 'Thought of a Briton on the Subjugation of Switzerland'; *see also* J.K. Stephen, 'Two voices are there']

6 The world is too much with us; late and soon, / Getting and spending, we lay waste our powers. [Ib. 'The world is too much with us']

7 Wisdom doth live with children round her knees. [*Sonnets Dedicated to Liberty*, 4]

8 Happy is he, who, caring not for Pope, / Consul, or King, can sound himself to know / The destiny of Man, and live in hope. [Ib. 5]

9 Once did she hold the gorgeous East in fee, / And was the safeguard of the West. [Ib. 6, 'On the Extinction of the Venetian Republic']

10 Men are we, and must grieve when even the Shade / Of that which once was great is pass'd away. [Ib.]

11 Milton! thou should'st be living at this hour: / England hath need of thee. [Ib. 14]

12 We must be free or die, who speak the tongue / That Shakespeare spake; the faith and morals hold / Which Milton held. [Ib. 16]

13 What, you are stepping westward? ['Stepping Westward']

14 Strange fits of passion have I known: / And I will dare to tell, / But in the lover's ear alone, / What once to me befell. ['Strange Fits of Passion']

15 'O mercy!' to myself I cried, / 'If Lucy should be dead!' [Ib.]

16 Books! 'tis a dull and endless strife: / Come, hear the woodland linnet, / How sweet his music! on my life, / There's more of wisdom in it. ['The Tables Turned']

17 One impulse from a vernal wood / May teach you more of man, / Of moral evil and of good, / Than all the sages can. [Ib.]

18 Sweet is the lore which Nature brings; / Our meddling intellect / Misshapes the beauteous forms of things: / We murder to dissect. [Ib.]

19 I've measured it from side to side; / 'Tis three feet long, and two feet wide. ['The Thorn']

20 Sweet childish days, that were as long / As twenty days are now. ['To a Butterfly']

21 O cuckoo! Shall I call thee bird, / Or but a wandering voice? ['To the Cuckoo']

22 A simple child, / That lightly draws its breath, / And feels its life in every limb, / What should it know of death? ['We are Seven']

23 I take my little porringer / And eat my supper there. [Ib.]

24 I have said that poetry is the spontaneous overflow of powerful feelings: it takes its origin from emotion recollected in tranquillity: the emotion is contemplated till, by a species of reaction, the tranquillity gradually disappears, and an emotion, kindred to that which was before the subject of contemplation, is gradually produced, and does itself actually exist in the mind. [*Lyrical Ballads*, Preface]

25 Every great and original writer, in proportion as he is great and original, must himself create the taste by which he is to be relished. [Letter, 1807]

Wotton, Sir Henry (1568–1639)

26 Lord of himself, though not of lands, / And having nothing, yet hath all. ['The Character of a Happy Life']

1 He first deceased; she for a little tried / To live without him: liked it not, and died. ['Death of Sir Albertus Morton's Wife']

2 You meaner Beauties of the Night, / That poorly satisfy our Eyes. ['On his Mistress, the Queen of Bohemia']

3 Virtue is the roughest way, / But proves at night a bed of down. ['Upon the Imprisonment of the Earl of Essex']

4 Well building hath three conditions: Commodity, Firmness, and Delight. [*Elements of Architecture*, I]

5 *Legatus est vir bonus peregrare missus ad mentiendum rei publicae causae.* An ambassador is an honest man sent to lie abroad for the good of the state. [Written in the Album of Christopher Fleckamore, 1604]

Wren, Sir Christopher (1632–1723)

6 *Si monumentum requiris, circumspice.* If you would see his monument look around. [Inscription, St. Paul's Cathedral, London]

Wright, Frank Lloyd (1869–1959)

7 Give me the luxuries of life and I will willingly do without the necessities. [Attr.]

8 The truth is more important than the facts. [Quoted in Simcox, *Treasury of Quotations on Christian Themes*]

Wyatt, Sir Thomas (c. 1503–1542)

9 They flee from me, that sometime did me seek / With naked foot, stalking in my chamber. ['They flee from me']

10 When her loose gown from her shoulders did fall, / And she me caught in her arms long and small, / Therewith all sweetly did me kiss / And softly said, 'Dear heart how like you this?' [Ib.]

11 Whoso list to hunt, I know where is an hind. ['Whoso list to hunt']

12 There is written her fair neck round about: / *Noli me tangere*, for Caesar's I am; / And wild for to hold, though I seem tame. [Ib.]

Wycherley, William (c. 1640–1716)

13 Go to your business, I say, pleasure, whilst I go to my pleasure, business. [*The Country Wife*, II]

14 With faint praises one another damn. [*The Plain Dealer*, Prologue]

Wyntoun, Andrew (c. 1350–c. 1420)

15 Quhen Alysandyr oure King wes dede / That Scotland led in luve and lé, / Away wes sons of Ale and Brede, / Of wyne and wax, of gamyn and glé, / Oure gold wes changyd into lede. / Chryst, born into Virgynyté, / Succour Scotland, and remede / That stad in perplexyté. [*Oryginale Cronykille of Scotland*]

Xenophon (c. 430–355 B.C.)

16 The sea! The sea! [*Anabasis*]

Yeames, W.F. (1835–1918)

17 And when did you last see your father? [Title of painting]

Yeats, W. B. (1865–1939)

18 A line will take us hours may be; / Yet if it does not seem a moment's thought, / Our stitching and unstitching has been naught. ['Adam's Curse']

19 For it is a ghost's right, / His element is so fine / Being sharpened by his death, / To drink from the wine-breath / While our gross palates drink from the whole wine. ['All Souls' Night']

20 O chestnut-tree, great-rooted blossomer, / Are you the leaf, the blossom or the bole? / O body swayed to music, O brightening glance, / How can we know the dancer from the dance? ['Among School Children']

21 And God-appointed Berkeley that proved all things a dream. ['Blood and the Moon', II]

22 This pragmatical, preposterous pig of a world. [Ib.]

23 The fury and the mire of human veins. ['Byzantium']

1 Before me floats and image, man or shade, / Shade more than man, more image than a shade; / For Hades' bobbin bound in mummy-cloth / May unwind the winding path. [Ib.]

2 That dolphin-torn, that gong-tormented sea. [Ib.]

3 The intellect of man is forced to choose / Perfection of the life, or of the work. ['The Choice']

4 Now that my ladder's gone, / I must lie down where all the ladders start, / In the foul rag-and-bone shop of the heart. ['The Circus Animals' Desertion']

5 I made my song a coat / Covered with embroideries / Out of old mythologies. ['A Coat']

6 Song, let them take it, / For there's more enterprise / In walking naked. [Ib.]

7 Now I may wither into the truth. ['The Coming of Wisdom with Time']

8 But Love has pitched his mansion in / The place of excrement. / For nothing can be sole or whole / That has not been rent. ['Crazy Jane talks with the Bishop']

9 He knows death to the bone — / Man has created death. ['Death']

10 Only the dead can be forgiven; / But when I think of that my tongue's a stone. ['A Dialogue of Self and Soul', I]

11 I am content to live it all again / And yet again, if it be life to pitch / Into the frog-spawn of a blind man's ditch, / A blind man battering blind men. [Ib. II]

12 Down by the salley gardens my love and I did meet; / She passed the salley gardens with little snow-white feet. / She bid me take love easy, as the leaves grow on the tree; / But I, being young and foolish, with her would not agree. ['Down by the Salley Gardens']

13 He, too, has resigned his part / In the casual comedy; / He, too, has been changed in his turn, / Transformed utterly. ['Easter 1916']

14 Too long a sacrifice / Can make a stone of the heart. [Ib.]

15 And what if excess of love / Bewildered them till they died? [Ib.]

16 MacDonagh and MacBride / And Connolly and Pearse / Now and in time to be, / Wherever green is worn, / Are changed, changed utterly: / A terrible beauty is born. [Ib.]

17 Before I am old / I shall have written him one / Poem maybe as cold / And passionate as the dawn. ['The Fisherman']

18 Locke sank into a swoon; / The Garden died; / God took the spinning-jenny / Out of his side. ['Fragments', I]

19 The second best's a gay goodnight and quickly turn away. ['From "Oedipus at Colonus"']

20 I have spread my dreams under your feet; / Tread softly because you tread on my dreams. ['He wishes for the Cloths of Heaven']

21 The light of evening, Lissadell, / Great windows open to the south, / Two girls in silk kimonos, both / Beautiful, one a gazelle. ['In Memory of Eva Gore-Booth and Con Markiewicz']

22 Those that I fight I do not hate, / Those that I guard I do not love; / My country is Kiltartan Cross, / My countrymen Kiltartan's poor, / No likely end could bring them loss / Or leave them happier than before. ['An Irish Airman Foresees his Death']

23 The years to come seemed waste of breath, / A waste of breath the years behind / In balance with this life, this death. [Ib.]

24 I will arise and go now, and go to Innisfree, / And a small cabin build there, of clay and wattles made. ['The Lake Isle of Innisfree']

25 And I shall have some peace there, for peace comes dropping slow. [Ib.]

26 All men have aimed at, found and lost; / Black out; Heaven blazing into the head: / Tragedy wrought to its uttermost. ['Lapis Lazuli']

27 A shudder in the loins engenders there / The broken wall, the burning roof and tower / And Agamemnon dead. ['Leda and the Swan']

1 O heart, we are old; / The living beauty is for younger men: / We cannot pay its tribute of wild tears. ['The Living Beauty']

2 *Like a long-legged fly upon the stream / His mind moves upon silence.* ['Long-legged fly']

3 *When I was a boy with never a crack in my heart.* ['The Meditation of the Old Fisherman']

4 We had fed the heart on fantasies, / The heart's grown brutal from the fare; / More substance in our enmities / Than in our love. ['Meditations in Time of Civil War', VI]

5 All men are dancers and their tread / Goes to the barbarous clangour of a gong. ['Nineteen Hundred and Nineteen', II]

6 Why should I blame her that she filled my days / With misery, or that she would of late / Have taught to ignorant men most violent ways, / Or hurled the little streets upon the great, / Had they but courage equal to desire? ['No Second Troy']

7 Why, what could she have done, being what she is? / Was there another Troy for her to burn? [Ib.]

8 A statesman is an easy man, / He tells his lies by rote; / A journalist makes up his lies / And takes you by the throat; / So stay at home and drink your beer / And let the neighbours vote, / *Said the man in the golden breastplate / Under the old stone Cross.* ['The Old Stone Cross']

9 If Folly link with Elegance / No man knows which is which. [Ib.]

10 I think it better that in times like these / A poet's mouth be silent, for in truth / We have no gift to set a statesman right; / He has had enough of meddling who can please / A young girl in the indolence of her youth, / Or an old man upon a winter's night. ['On being Asked for a War Poem']

11 Where, where but here have Pride and Truth, / That long to give themselves for wage, / To shake their wicked sides at youth / Restraining reckless middle-age? ['On Hearing that the Students of our New University have joined the Agitation against Immoral Literature']

12 How can I, that girl standing there, / My attention fix / On Roman or on Russian / Or on Spanish politics? ['Politics']

13 In courtesy I'd have her chiefly learned; / Hearts are not had as a gift but hearts are earned / By those that are not entirely beautiful. ['A Prayer for My Daughter']

14 An intellectual hatred is the worst, / So let her think opinions are accursed. [Ib.]

15 That is no country for old men. ['Sailing to Byzantium']

16 An aged man is but a paltry thing, / A tattered coat upon a stick, unless / Soul clap its hands and sing / For every tatter in its mortal dress. [Ib.]

17 Lord, what would they say / Did their Catullus walk that way? ['The Scholars']

18 Turning and turning in the widening gyre / The falcon cannot hear the falconer; / Things fall apart; the centre cannot hold; / Mere anarchy is loosed upon the world, / The blood-dimmed tide is loosed, and everywhere / The ceremony of innocence is drowned; / The best lack all conviction, while the worst / Are full of passionate intensity. ['The Second Coming']

19 And what rough beast, its hour come round at last, / Slouches towards Bethlehem to be born? [Ib.]

20 Far-off, most secret, and inviolate Rose. ['The Secret Rose']

21 A woman of so shining loveliness / That men threshed corn at midnight by a tress. [Ib.]

22 Was it for this the wild geese spread / The grey wing upon every tide; / For this that all that blood was shed... / All that delirium of the brave? / Romantic Ireland's dead and gone, / It's with O'Leary in the grave. ['September, 1913']

1 You think it horrible that lust and rage / Should dance attention upon my old age; / They were not such a plague when I was young; / What else have I to spur me into song? ['The Spur']

2 We Irish, born into that ancient sect / But thrown upon this filthy modern tide / And by its formless spawning fury wrecked, / Climb to our proper dark, that we may trace / The lineaments of a plummet- measured face. ['The Statues']

3 Those dancing days are gone. ['Those Dancing Days are Gone']

4 Know, that I would accounted be / True brother of a company / That sang, to sweeten Ireland's wrong, / Ballad and story, rann and song. ['To Ireland in the Coming Times']

5 But was there ever dog that praised his fleas? ['To a Poet, who would have me Praise certain Bad Poets, Imitators of His and Mine']

6 Come near; I would, before my time to go, / Sing of old Eire and the ancient ways: / Red Rose, proud Rose, sad Rose of all my days! ['To the Rose upon the Rood of Time']

7 And I may dine at journey's end / With Landor and with Donne. ['To a Young Beauty']

8 What shall I do with this absurdity — / O heart, O troubled heart — this caricature, / Decrepit age that has been tied to me / As to a dog's tail? ['The Tower', I]

9 It seems that I must bid the Muse go pack, / Choose Plato and Plotinus for a friend / Until imagination, ear and eye, / Can be content with argument and deal / In abstract things; or be derided by / A sort of battered kettle at the heel. [Ib.]

10 Death and life were not / Till man made up the whole, / Made lock, stock and barrel / Out of his bitter soul. [Ib. III]

11 Odour of blood when Christ was slain / Made all Platonic tolerance vain / And vain all Doric discipline. ['Two Songs from a Play', II]

12 Irish poets, learn your trade, / Sing whatever is well made, / Scorn the sort now growing up / All out of shape from toe to top, / Their unremembered hearts and heads / Base-born products of base beds. ['Under Ben Bulben' V]

13 Cast your mind on other days / That we in coming days may be / Still the indomitable Irishry. [Ib.]

14 *Cast a cold eye / On life, on death. / Horseman, pass by!* [Ib. VI (Yeats' epitaph)]

15 Why should not old men be mad? ['Why Should not Old Men be Mad?']

16 [Ireland] This blind bitter land. ['Words']

17 The years like great black oxen tread the world, / And God the herdsman goads them on behind, / And I am broken by their passing feet. [*The Countess Cathleen*, IV]

18 Twelve pennies! What better reason for killing a man? [*The Death of Cuchulain*]

19 A good writer should be so simple that he has no faults, only sins. ['The Death of Synge']

20 We have no longer in any country a literature as great as the literature of the old world, and that is because the newspapers, all kinds of second rate books, the preoccupation of men with all kinds of practical changes, have driven the living imagination out of this world. [*Samhain*, 1904]

21 Out of the quarrel with others we make rhetoric; out of the quarrel with ourselves we make poetry. [Essay]

Young, Andrew (1807–1889)

22 There is a happy land, / Far, far away, / Where saints in glory stand, / Bright, bright as day. [Hymn]

Young, Edward (1683–1765)

23 Be wise today; 'tis madness to defer. [*The Complaint: Night Thoughts*, I]

24 Procrastination is the thief of time. [Ib.]

25 All men think all men mortal, but themselves. [Ib.]

1 Lean not on Earth; 'twill pierce thee to the heart; / A broken reed at best. [Ib. III]

2 Man wants but little; nor that little long. [Ib. IV]

3 A God all mercy, is a God unjust. [Ib.]

4 By night an atheist half believes a God. [Ib. V]

5 Devotion! daughter of astronomy! / An undevout astronomer is mad. [Ib. IX]

6 You are so witty, profligate, and thin, / At once we think thee Milton, Death and Sin. [Epigram on Voltaire]

7 Some, for renown, on scraps of learning dote, / And think they grow immortal as they quote. [*Love of Fame*, I]

8 Be wise with speed; / A fool at forty is a fool indeed. [Ib. II]

9 One to destroy, is murder by the law; / And gibbets keep the lifted hand in awe; / To murder thousands, takes a specious name, / War's glorious art, and gives immortal fame. [Ib. VII]

Young, George W. (1846–1919)

10 The lips that touch liquor must never touch mine! [Temperance verse]

Young, Michael (1915-   )

11 The Rise of the Meritocracy [Title of book]

Zangwill, Israel (1864–1926)

12 Let us start a new religion with one commandment, 'Enjoy thyself.' [*Children of the Ghetto*]

13 America is God's Crucible, the great Melting-Pot where all the races of Europe are melting and re-forming! [*The Melting Pot*]

Zanuck, Darryl F. (1902–1979)

14 For God's sake, don't say yes until I've finished talking. [Quoted in Colombo, *Wit and Widsom of the Moviemakers*}

Zola, Emile (1840–1902)

15 *J'accuse.* I accuse. [Title of open letter to the President of the Republic, 1898 (on the Dreyfus Affair)]

16 *La vérité est en marche; rien ne peut plus l'arrêter.* The truth is on the move and nothing can stop her now. [Article on the Dreyfus affair]

Zukor, Adolph (1873–1976)

17 The public is never wrong. [Quoted in Halliwell, *Filmgoers' Book of Quotes*]

INDEX

end of life is...A. 143:14
good a. by stealth 161:16
I prefer thought to a. 19:1
Thought is the child of A. 97:27
tragedy...the imitation of an a. 8:27
actions: a. are my ministers' 72:16
a. are what they are 59:13
Activity: A. is the only road 240:7
actor: a....ain't listening 46:3
fault and not the a. 232:34
see he is an a. 114:10
world plays the a. 7:14
actors: a. are cattle 136:13
a. most often get asked 105:3
A. speak of things imaginary 25:7
of what scene / The a. 241:11
actresses: a. excite my amorous 147:25
adage: poor cat i' the a. 231:32
Adam: A.'s dream — he awoke 156:9
A. was a gardener 229:10
A. was not Adamant 138:10
Aristotle...rubbish of an A. 250:5
flower of A.'s bastards 62:11
gardener A. and his wife 263:24
When A. delved 7:25
Adamant: Adam was not A. 138:10
adamantine: God put His a. fate 48:2
adapt: persists in trying to a. the world 240:4
adaptable: history is that it is a. 273:5
added: things shall be a. unto you 35:29
adder: day that brings forth the a. 229:25
address: a. will soon be Annihilation 90:15
addresses: Three a. always inspire 287:11
adieu: bid a. to common feeling 248:6
Bidding a. 154:31
eternal a. to all the pains 58:12
Que signifie a. 19:2
Adjective: A.: when in doubt, strike it out 272:4
Adlestrop: Yes, I remember A. 267:13
administer'd: best a. is best 206:22
admiral: kill an a. from time to time 276:12
admiration: from a. to love 12:25
admire: Not to a., is all the art 206:32
admired: a. through being misunderstood 80:16
all who understood a. 209:6
admires: meanly a. mean things 265:30
Adonais: weep for A. — he is dead 241:8
adoo: bid you a welcome a. 279:12
adoration: Breathless with a. 293:27
adored: women...merely a. 286:25
adorn: a. a tale 147:19
adornment: time he can spare from the a. 268:3
adulteration: Not quite adultery, but a. 63:14
adultery: a., / Is much more common 62:16
Do not a. commit 79:21
Not quite a., but adulteration 63:14
Thou shalt not commit a. 26:22
advance: a. or die 61:27
look divine as you a. 191:1
retrograde if it does not a. 121:23
advantage: a. both of Eyes and Voice 177:7
A. rarely comes of it 79:21
takes a. that get 106:14
when to forego an a. 98:13
Adventure: A. must be held in delicate 104:9
awfully big a. 20:7
adventures: a. of his soul among masterpieces 117:5
adversary: disturb their a.'s convictions 104:11
Your a. the devil 40:27
Adversity: A. doth best discover Virtue 14:10
A. is not without comforts 14:9
A.'s sweet milk, philosophy 236:6
bread of a. 33:12
uses of a. 225:6
withstand the shocks of a. 280:3
advertisement: a. that will take in 142:20
Advertisements: A. contain the only truths 145:12
Advertising: A....arresting the...intelligence 164:2
spend on a. is wasted 165:9
Advice: A. is seldom welcome 75:14
A. to persons about to marry 211:13
A.: The smallest current coin 41:12
ask a. is...to tout for flattery 83:6
even earnest a. from my seniors 268:26
adviser: good political a. 106:3
aere: *a. perennius* 140:12
aesthetic: crime...desire for a. expression 280:23
high a. band 123:9
aesthetics: long-haired a. 123:7
affair: never had a love a. 162:23
affairs: Nothing in the a. of men 202:28
Affectation: for Ornament, is A. 15:13
affection: a. beaming in one eye 95:3
more a. than she feels 13:12
affections: history of the a. 144:3
affinity: betray a secret a. 131:21
affliction: waters of a. 33:12
Affluent: A. Society 119:17
afford: a. to keep a motor car 238:26
morals...Can't a. them 240:23
parties could any way a. it 105:15
afire: common bush a. with God 49:15
afraid: a. of death, as ashamed 49:6
be not a. 36:18
But Were A. to Ask 213:19
do what you are a. to do 110:8
many are a. of God 167:24
not afraid of God, a. of me 207:8
not a. of the sea 260:19
they were sore a. 37:12
Who's A. of Virginia Woolf 3:3
Africa: change is blowing through [A.] 173:21
Ex A. semper aliquid novi 203:5
something new out of A. 203:5
After: A. us the flood 203:23
A. you, Claude 153:4
Brother humans who live a. us 275:3
afternoon: At five in the a. 120:1
one a. / Of heat 267:13
again: And all's to do a. 140:21
not pass this way a. 128:4
ye no come back a. 137:8

Look homeward, A., now 182:32
man an ape or an a. 98:5
no child is born an a. 249:2
Than any painted A. 286:24
woman yet think him an a. 266:2
wrote like an a. 120:4
Angel-infancy: Shin'd in my A. 273:24
Angels: A. affect us oft, and worship'd 98:21
a. all are Tories 64:13
A. and ministers of grace 226:14
A. came and ministered 35:15
A. fear to tread 206:6
a. of God ascending 26:5
a. on the walls of heaven 176:11
A. would be Gods 206:13
entertained a. unawares 40:18
Four a. to my bed 6:8
give his a. charge 30:12
herald a. sing 282:28
little lower than the a. 29:16
on the side of the a. 98:5
Tears such as A. weep 183:22
they have the countenance of a. 128:2
'twixt Air and A.' purity 98:22
ye A., Progeny of Light 184:22
Anger: A. is a brief madness 139:16
A. is one of the sinews 119:9
mistress some rich a. shows 154:30
monstrous a. of the guns 197:22
strike it in a. 240:3
such great a. in heavenly 275:7
telegrams and a. 116:19
angler: a., and now with God 279:5
no man is born an a. 279:3
anglers: a., or very honest men 279:8
Angles: they were called A. 128:2
Angli: *A. vocarentur* 128:2
Angling: A. is somewhat like poetry 279:4
innocent recreation than a. 279:6
Anglo-Saxon: A. Messenger 70:9
angry: a. at a slander 150:15
a. man...thinks he can do more 2:25
a. with my friend 43:23
Be ye a., and sin not 39:19
When a. count four 272:1
anguis: *a. in herba* 275:26
animal: a. is very wicked 5:2
detest that a. called man 259:20
Man is...a political a. 9:1
Man is a tool-using a. 68:16
man is the superior a. 208:21
only a. that blushes 271:24
poor, bare, forked a. 230:32
romantic a., that may be adorned 2:13
tool-making a. 117:31
animals: All a. are equal 196:20
[a.] do not sweat and whine 284:22
distinguish us from the other a. 21:7
Wild a. never kill for sport 118:21
animate: scarce suspected, a. the whole 248:22
animation: constitutional a. never failed to carry 80:13
Animula: *A. vagula blandula* 128:16
anither: ne'er made a. 55:20
ankles: his weak a. swell 293:19
Anna: great A.! whom three realms obey 207:18
Annabel Lee: By the name of A. 203:13
annals: Happy the people whose a. 67:23
short and simple a. 127:12
War's a. will cloud 130:7
Annan: A. water's wading deep 17:1
Annihilating: A. all that's made 177:14
Annihilation.: A. As for my name 90:15
a. after such long-continued slow progress 90:17
annoy: He only does it to a. 69:10
annuity: a. is a very serious business 13:6
Anointed: Hail to the Lord's A. 188:3
I am your a. Queen 108:24
anointest: a. my head with oil 29:20
another: damned thing after a. 141:10
Answer: A. a fool 31:35
a. and my echo ring 251:18
a. came there none 221:13
a. is blowin' in the wind 105:6
dusty a. gets the soul 179:23
man's waitin' for a a. 93:25
more than the wisest man can a. 83:17
not stay for an a. 13:28
soft a. turneth 31:26
What is the a. 253:11
wrong number, why did you a. 269:6
answerable: a. to the people 281:5
answered: father a. never a word 168:24
I came, and no one a. 92:18
Answers: A. sometimes [indiscreet] 286:26
ant: a....cannot philosophize 143:8
Go to the a. thou sluggard 31:18
antan: *neiges d'a.* 275:2
ante: *qui a. nos* 98:20
ant-hill: epoch of the a. 4:6
Anthropophagi: A., and men whose heads 234:29
antic: dance the a. hay 175:17
put an a. disposition 226:21
anti-Caledonian: essentially a. 161:7
anti-everythings: hungry, savage a. 137:17
antipathies: a....betray a secret affinity 131:21
antipathy: strong a. of good to bad 207:7
Antipodes: like A. in shoes 177:24
Antiquities: A. are history defaced 13:22
antiquity: finisht piece of all a. 1:20
ants: If a. are such busy workers 102:9
anvil: a. unto sorrow 175:15
England's on the a. 158:18
anxiety: Nothing...worthy of great a. 202:28
anybody: Is there a. there 92:17
Then no one's a. 122:12
anyone: a. lived in a pretty how 89:11
anything: cocksure of a. as...Macaulay 179:3
doesn't do a. else but 290:29
Rembering him like a. 76:17
you'll believe a. 282:12
ape: caravans, but never an a. 208:14
degenerate from the a. 142:18
How like us is the a. 112:1
Jesus and a nameless a. 172:17
man an a. or an angel 98:5
Naked A. 189:9
apes: a. and peacocks 178:10
Lead a. in hell 236:11
pride that a. humility 81:24
aphrodisiac: Power...ultimate a. 160:5

A. but the rudiments of Paradise 250:5
A., nurse of men 250:2
Maid of A., ere we part 63:30
sunrise from the sea, / A. arose 242:10
Atlantic: A. wall / Off 'Sconset 170:1
atom bombs: a. and the one after 273:1
Atoms: A. of Democritus 43:1
attack: situation excellent. I shall a. 115:17
with his plan of a. 220:24
attacked: When...a. it defends 5:2
attainment: so disenchanting as a. 256:6
attempted: Something a., something done 168:22
attendre: *J'ai failli a.* 169:3
attention: a. must finally be paid 181:6
very *A.* a *Stretching-to* 68:17
withdrew my a. 149:32
attentive: want a. and favourable hearers 138:14
Attic: A. shape 154:24
little brain a. 101:13
attire: Her rich a. creeps 153:27
attitude: Fair a. 154:24
attitudes: Anglo-Saxon a. 70:9
attractiveness: account for the curious a. 287:28
Auchtermuchty: Tak' A. for a name 172:13
auctoritee: Experience though noon a. 73:29
audace: *a., et toujours de l'audace* 90:14
audacity: command her with a. 173:9
never-ending a. of elected 284:16
audience: awful attention in the a. 244:26
aught: while a. remains to do 214:25
augury: we defy a. 227:26
Aulder: A. than mammoth or than mastodon 172:20
aunts: dull a., and croaking rooks 205:11
Auri: *A. sacra fames* 275:15
Austen: A....prettiest, silliest 186:10
favourite, Miss A., is my country-woman 186:10
Australia: guess that he was born in A. 239:15
Austrian: A. army, awfully arrayed 4:21
author: asked by an a. what he thinks 149:25
a. and giver of all good 209:27
a. as you choose a friend 216:16
a. of peace 209:16
authority: little brief a. 232:35
authors: damn those a. whom they never read 77:8
scorn of A. 83:2
We a., Ma'am 98:11
autobiography: arist writes his own a. 109:15
automatic: hair with a. hand 108:17
autres: *encourager les a.* 276:12
Autumn: thou breath of A.'s being 243:6
Autumnal: seen in one A. face 99:4
availeth: struggle naught a. 80:1
avant-garde: a. bias against the great public 23:18
Avarice: A., the spur of industry 142:4
Valour bleed / While A. 185:26
Ave: *A., Imperator* 257:20
frater, a. atque vale 71:9
Avenge: A., O Lord, thy slaughtered 185:21
Averni: *Facilis descensus A.* 275:18
Avernus: fair are gone down to A. 208:22
aversion: a.; pleasure was his business 105:16
indifference closely bordering on a. 256:7
matrimony to begin with...a. 245:1
aversions: a. of their temporal masters 180:11
aves: thousand a. told 153:31
avoiding: superstition in a. superstition 14:22
Avon: Sweet Swan of A. 150:31
awake: man will lie a. thinking 217:25
one must stay a. all day 193:4
sleeping while a. 187:19
Smiles a. you when 92:11
trying to a. 151:20
awaked: he sleepeth, and must be a. 28:15
a-waltzing: You'll come a., Matilda 199:19
away: and quickly turn a. 296:19
a., / Down and away below 9:10
Keep well a. from here 197:11
awe: even kings in a. 90:22
power to keep them all in a. 136:19
aweary: I am aweary, a. 264:11
awful: Anything a. makes me laugh 161:20
God! this is an a. place 221:9
nobody goes, it's a. 21:20
awkward: Don't let the a. squad 58:19
awoke: a. and found it truth 156:9
a. one morning and found myself famous 65:2
a-wooing: frog he would a. go 194:1
Laird o' Drum is a. 17:21
axe: a.'s edge did try 177:15
Lizzie Borden took an a. 6:6
axioms: not a. until they are proved 156:14
axis: a. of the earth sticks out 137:13
Azores: Flores in the A. 265:1
Baa: B.! Baa! Baa 159:5
babblative: arts b. and scribblative 250:12
babbled: b. of green fields 228:29
Babe: B. all burning bright 250:22
naked new-born b. 231:30
Babes: B. reduced to misery, / Fed with 43:22
mouth of b. and sucklings 29:14
babies: bit the b. in the cradles 51:24
only washing. And b. 267:7
baboon: bred out / Into b. and monkey 236:30
baby: Bye, b. bunting 194:6
come from, b. dear 173:2
Hush-a-bye, b. 194:15
When the first b. laughed 20:5
Babylon: B. is fallen 41:2
By the rivers of B. 31:9
By the waters of B. 278:18
How many miles to B. 194:13
Bacchus: B. and his pards 155:3
Bachelor: B.'s fare 258:22
bachelors: All reformers are b. 188:8

reasons for b. to go out 106:24
back: b. the masses against 124:1
b. the world 152:21
except by getting off his b. 269:24
go b. quickly whence we came 250:3
I go, I come b. 153:5
those before cried 'B.!' 171:7
ye no come b. again 137:8
backbone: b. of the Army 159:1
backs: b. to the wall 129:1
beast with two b. 234:24
backward: b. and abysm of time 236:15
backwards: memory that only works b. 70:4
only be understood b. 157:26
bad: altogether irreclaimably b. 68:15
antipathy of good to b. 207:7
b. die late 91:19
b. end unhappily 257:7
b. in the best 7:12
b. men combine 54:15
b. she was horrid 168:8
come to a b. end 22:11
[Cromwell] a brave b. man 79:6
good, b., and indifferent 252:13
isolated way of having a b. time 75:3
put up with b. things 270:18
Some of them are b. 126:11
so sublimely b. 205:3
two legs b. 196:19
Badge: B. of Men 91:2
badinage: *mariage, Agnès, n'est pas un b.* 186:17
badly: worth doing b. 77:3
badness: b. of a bad one 89:23
badness of her b. 20:9
baffled: are b. to fight better 52:13
Bainters: all Boets and B. 121:3
bairn: bonnie broukit b. 172:3
Baker Street: B. irregulars 101:18
balance: b. of power 278:25
redress the b. of the Old 67:1
balances: weighed in the b. 34:16
bald: b. and discontented 64:15
Go up, thou b. head 28:19
otherwise b. and unconvincing narrative 123:3
bales: dropping down with costly b. 264:4
Balfour: Mr. B.'s poodle 167:14
Ball: B. no question makes 114:24
sweetness up into one b. 177:23
ballad: b. of Sir Patrick Spence 81:20
ballads: better than all the b. 168:4
make all the b. 115:12
ballet: Unearthly b. of bloodless 45:17
ballot: b. is stronger than the bullet 166:5
balls: b. to do nothing but dance 258:6
elliptical billiard b. 123:1
balm: b. upon the world 153:34
no b. in Gilead 34:4
baloney: it's still b. 247:13
Banbury: cock-horse to B. Cross 195:11
bandied: struck and b., / Which way please 281:15
banditti: black b., / The City Guard 113:14
bands: pursue Culture in b. 283:14
Bandusiae: *O fons B.* 140:10
baneful: Ten thousand b. arts combined 125:13
bang: *b.* — went saxpence 211:17
big b. does come 197:5
Not with a b. but a whimper 107:25
bang-up: in a b. chariot 95:30
banish: b. all the world 227:41
I b. you 225:26
night that should b. all sin 124:7
bank: cried all the way to the b. 165:18
I know a b. where 234:5
well-regarded at the b. 179:14
bankrupt: our penurious b. age 67:2
banks: Ye b. and braes 58:10
banner: b. with the strange device 168:6
star-spangled b. 157:22
banners: Confusion on thy b. 127:6
banquet: but your b. that is eloquent 176:28
bar: Get up and b. the door 17:13
Barabbas: B. was a publisher 66:15
crowd will always save B. 80:18
Barbara Allen: Her name was B. 17:3
Barbarian: Dancing...a B. exercise 55:8
Barbarians: B., Philistines, and Populace 10:8
Barbaric: B. Pearl and Gold 183:27
I sound my b. yawp 285:1
barbarism: blame / The b. of wars 262:11
directly from b. to degeneration 79:12
barbarity: Sooner b. than boredom 120:12
barbarous: b. clangour of a gong 297:5
Invention of a b. Age 183:6
Bard: If the B. was weatherwise 81:20
Bards: B. of Passion 154:19
bare: child she b. 87:19
one b. hour to live 175:9
barefooted: b. friars were singing 121:13
bargain: Bad is our b. 50:30
Necessity never made a good b. 117:12
never was a better b. 245:24
bargains: the rule, for b. 95:5
barge: answer'd Arthur from the b. 263:2
b. she sat in 224:24
Baring: Wing-Commander Maurice B. 23:12
bark: dogs delight to b. and bite 280:11
Barkis: B. is willin' 93:24
barley: A-shearing at her b. 17:21
fields of b. and of rye 263:26
barley-bree: taste the b. 58:8
Barlow: Hornby and my B. long ago 267:19
Baronet: B.'s rank is exceedingly nice 123:20
baronets: All b. are bad 123:16
barrel: b. of a gun 174:21
barren: cry, 'tis all b. 253:18
destined to a b. strand 147:19
barrenest: b....is the sentimentalist 67:12
barricade: At some disputed b. 223:9
bars: through the same b. 162:12
barty: Vhere ish dat b. now 164:20
base: All that is b. shall die. 52:24
b. degrees / By which 229:28
b. uses we may return 227:23
Base-born: B. products of base beds 298:12

bashfulness: in England a particular b. 2:7
basia: *Da mi b. mille* 71:4
Basil-pot: steal my B. away 154:14
basking: sunny Eyes does b. play 86:20
bassoon: heard the loud b. 81:3
bastard: daddy, you b., I'm through 202:16
knocked the b. off 136:7
bastards: flower of Adam's b. 62:11
gods, stand up for b. 230:20
Bastille: [Fall of B.]...greatest event 117:1
bat: black b., night 264:15
bataillons: *pas pour les gros b.* 277:8
batallions: side of the big b. 277:8
bathing: caught the Whigs b. 98:3
baths: Two walking b. 88:22
bathtub: As a b. lined with white 208:7
bâton: *b. de maréchal de France* 190:12
marshal's b. in his knapsack 190:12
Batter: B. my heart 99:27
Batteries: B. of alluring Sense 177:6
Battering: B. the gates of heaven 265:5
battle: b. and not a bed of roses 256:16
b. of Britain 77:26
best trousers to go out to b. 143:21
In a b., a great 167:8
Lord mighty in b. 29:25
melancholy as a b. won 282:7
noise of b. roll'd 262:27
nor the b. to the strong 32:13
seemed that out of b. 197:24
Sing, tongue, of b. 274:7
battles: blood and b. is my age 9:31
Instead of by b. 116:24
bauble: do with the b. 89:5
bawdy-house: keeping a b. 149:22
bay: like a green b. tree 29:26
bayonets: throne of b. 144:1
Bays: Oak, or B. 177:9
be: It must b. 22:14
not mean / But b. 173:16
rather see than b. one 53:30
To b., or not to be 226:37
tree / Continues to b. 160:11
beaches: fight on the b. 77:24
Beachy Head: Birmingham by way of B. 76:14
beadroll: Fame's eternal b. 252:4
beak: He can take in his b. 180:1
Take thy b. from out my heart 203:18
be-all: b. and the end-all 231:29
beaming: affection b. in one eye 95:3
beamish: my arms, my b. boy 69:29
beams: Dim, as the borrowed b. 103:20
bear: b. all naked truths 154:8
B. of Very Little Brain 181:12
b. with a sore head 176:19
Exit, pursued by a b. 237:29
gave pain to the b. 171:16
How a b. likes honey 181:10
never an ape or a b. 208:14
oft outwatch the B. 182:8
Silly old B. 181:11
still less the b. 118:4
bear-baiting: Puritan hated b. 171:16
beard: b. full of butterflies 120:2
Old Man with a b. 164:4
singeing of the King of Spain's B. 101:26
Beareth: B. all things 39:7
beast: any b. of the field 25:18
b., but a just beast 4:14
b. in view 103:25
Blatant b. men call 252:5
life of his b. 31:23
magnificent blond b. 193:1
making the b. with two backs 234:24
maw-crammed b. 51:32
what rough b. 297:19
wild B., or a God 15:4
beastie: cow'rin', tim'rous b. 57:24
beasties: ghosties and long leggety b. 5:15
beastly: b. the bourgeois is 163:14
b. to the Germans 86:16
beasts: these b. do live at jar 100:21
beat: b. time, out of time 120:7
hearts that b. as one 169:12
They b. — and a Voice beat 267:22
We b. them today 252:26
beaten: b. till they know / What wood 59:23
beating: hear the b. of his wings 46:18
Beats: B. my approach 158:3
Nobody ever b. Wales at rugby 190:3
Beauties: B. in vain their pretty eyes 207:24
meaner B. of the Night 295:2
spoils of meaner B. 169:11
beautiful: All that is b. shall abide, 52:24
b. and therefore to be woo'd 229:8
b. is as useful as 141:19
B. Railway Bridge 173:6
b. than to be good 287:26
believe to be b. 189:11
good is the b. 202:22
more b. than the earth 293:12
most b. and most brittle 55:12
not entirely b. 297:13
old are more b. 284:9
own that thou art b. 241:26
Oysters are more b. 219:13
sense of what is b. 274:5
Small is B. 221:6
When a woman isn't b. 74:29
Beauty: B. and Truth, though never found 52:28
b....best thing God invents 50:28
b. in all things 156:19
B. in things exists in the mind 142:5
B. is nature's coin 182:1
B. is the child of love 109:16
B. is the lover's gift 84:31
B. is truth 154:26
B. of face is a frail 186:19
b. of inflections 255:3
B., that dost consecrate 242:15
B. that must die 154:31
b. without a fortune 112:27
b. / Of an aged face 65:23
daily b. in his life 235:2
dreamed that life was B. 138:16
England, home and b. 46:1
Everything has its b. 84:13
first in b. should be 154:9
flaw in b. 109:13
Fostered alike by b. 293:6
ghosts of b. glide 204:29
hearts is their own b. 197:15
Isle of B., Fare thee well 21:2
like to hear their b. praised 197:12
living b. is for younger 297:1
no b. that we should desire him 33:24
no Excellent B. 15:11

No Spring, nor Summer B. 99:4
relationship with b. and truth 156:3
soon as b. dies 99:1
Teaches such b. as a woman's 231:12
terrible b. is born 296:16
thing of b. is a joy 153:15
trenches in thy b.'s field 238:3
walks in b., like the night 64:6
where B. is a thing unknown 285:21
beaver: Harry with his b. on 228:5
Became: B. him like the leaving it 231:23
because: b. — after all we do think 245:22
Becket: [B.] this turbulent priest 133:14
becomes: woman, one b. one 21:19
bed: And so to b. 200:18
B. be blest that I lie on 6:8
Creep into thy narrow b. 9:17
Early to b. 117:24
Every b. is narrow 181:4
go to b. by day 255:8
go to b. in another world 134:3
grave as little as my b. 157:14
home and die — in b. 220:21
I in my b. again 7:19
make my b. soon 17:23
my second best b. 238:24
newly gone to b. 183:5
remember thee upon my b. 30:5
take up thy b. 38:3
used to go to b. early 211:8
Welcome to your gory b. 57:14
bedfellows: strange b. 236:20
beds: products of base b. 298:12
bed-time: b., Hal, and all well 228:8
bee: b. sucks, there suck I 236:27
How doth the little busy b. 280:13
like a b., / Doth suck 167:26
sting like a b. 3:15
beef: island of b. flesh 174:19
roast b. of England 113:20
bee-hive: not good for the b. 12:3
Beelzebub: B. called for his syllabub 246:14
been: b. and gone and done 122:5
beer: all b. and skittles 141:13
drink b. will think beer 144:5
like thine inspirer, B. 204:11
only a b. teetotaller 239:1
Beer-sheba: Dan even to B. 27:23
bees: murmuring of innumerable b. 264:27
Beethoven: B.'s Fifth Symphony...most sublime 116:18
before: I have been here b. 217:7
not dead — but gone b. 214:26
Not lost but gone b. 193:17
said our remarks b. us 98:20
those b. cried 'Back!' 171:7
what went on b. this life 21:24
beg: law...forbids the rich...to b. 117:3
begat: fathers that b. us 35:3
begetter: only b. of these ensuing 238:2
beggar: b. maid shall be my queen 262:6
Patience, the b.'s virtue 178:23
beggar'd: b. all description 224:25
beggar-wife: says the b. to me 255:21
beggary: b. in the love 224:19
begged: Homer b. his Bread 6:26
Begin: B. at the beginning 69:25
b. with a single step 162:21
b. with doubts 13:15
to b. with the beginning 62:15
vee may perhaps to b. 217:13
beginning: b. and the ending 40:30
b. and the decline of love 160:18
b. of wisdom 30:21
b. of the end 261:11
difficult as a b. / In poesy 63:2
In my b. is my end 107:15
In the b. 25:11
In the b. was the Word 37:36
more than his b. 29:12
not even the b. of the end 78:7
Or never had b. 134:19
was in the b. 209:10
beginnings: b....a realm of the fantastic 100:26
great things in their b. 162:17
Begone: B., dull Care 4:26
begot: when they b. me 253:26
begotten: b. by despair 177:4
beguile: lady to b. 18:1
beguiled: serpent b. me 25:21
begun: end, where I b. 100:24
behaving: b. in this extraordinary manner 257:6
behind: led his regiment from b. 122:6
those b. cried 'Forward!' 171:7
true of most we leave b. 80:3
Behold: B. her, single in the field 293:22
granted to me to b. you 255:16
thou mayst in me b. 238:13
being: have our b. 38:27
Belgrade: by battery besieged B. 4:21
Belgrave: May beat in B. Square 122:19
Belial: Sons / Of B. 183:19
belief: all b. is for it 149:17
b. is not true 4:8
b., no less than action and passion 67:21
b. of Truth 14:1
once we choose b. 50:3
beliefs: contradictory b. in one's mind 197:1
some generous b. and impositions 256:2
believe: b. and rejoice in Christ 170:18
b., because they so were bred 103:12
b. in God, believe also 38:11
B. it or not 214:15
B. one who knows by experience 275:23
b. only possibilities 49:4
b. that what is true for you 110:11
boldness to b. in nothing 271:12
I b. in God the Father 209:14
I don't b. in fairies 20:6
If you b. that 282:12
If you don't b. it 11:26
I will not b. 38:17
Lord, I b. 37:7
man does practically b. 68:1
men will b. more than they need 103:22
Men willingly b. what they wish 65:7
must b. in God 151:7
must b. what you ought 192:8
one *can't* b. impossible things 70:6
reasons for what we b. 45:16
Thou shalt b. in Milton 62:21
to b. concerning God 70:17
undesirable to b. a proposition 218:19
believed: and yet have b. 38:18
understood, and not be b. 43:8

What is b. always 275:5
Who hath b. our report 33:23
believer: sounds / In a b.'s ear 192:15
believers: earnest b. in the world 16:12
believes: atheist half b. a God 299:4
b. he shall ever die 131:16
man wishes he generally b. 92:23
yet each b. his own 205:25
Believing: B. where we cannot prove 263:6
no b. a word they say 282:8
torture them, into b. 192:4
Bell: B., book, and candle 230:14
for whom the *b.* tolls 98:28
I shall b. the cat 101:2
sexton toll'd the b. 138:5
surly sullen b. 238:12
Who will b. the cat 93:11
Bellamy: eat one of B.'s veal pies 202:11
belle: b. Dame sans Merci 153:13
bells: b. of Hell go ting 6:14
b. of St. Clement's 195:7
b. were ringing the Old Year 124:7
From the b., bells 203:15
liked the ringing of church b. 75:2
Ring out, wild b. 263:20
ring the b. of Heaven 137:1
They now ring the b. 278:24
bellum: *praeparet b.* 274:6
belly: fain have filled his b. 37:28
fellow with the great b. 228:15
God is their b. 39:25
Jonah was in the b. 34:24
something of a round b. 228:14
bellyful: Rumble thy b. 230:26
belong: b. to any club 177:27
so many of my readers b. 76:26
belongs: he b. to the ages 252:25
beloved: Dearly b. 210:11
Luke, the b. physician 40:2
thy b. more than another beloved 32:24
below: Down and away b. 9:10
joy to pass to the world b. 275:17
belt: b. without hitting below 10:20
belts: Fasten your seat b. 91:13
bely: wombe! O b.! O stynking cod 74:5
Ben Adhem: B.'s name led all the rest 142:10
bend: b. and do not break 115:19
bends: Though she b. him, she obeys 168:19
benevolence: question whether the b. of mankind 16:15
Berkeley: God-appointed B. 295:21
Berliner: *Ich bin ein B.* 157:17
Bermudas: remote B. ride 177:1
Berries: pluck your B., harsh and crude 182:19
berry: better b., but doubtless God never 279:6
sweeter than the b. 120:15
beset: Who so b. him round 53:26
best: All is for the b. 276:11
bad in the b. 7:12
b. and distinguished above 138:1
b. and happiest moments 244:21
b. day in the year 111:17
best ends by the b. means 142:15
b. is the best 212:8
b. is the enemy of the good 276:15
b. is yet to be 51:31
b. of men cannot suspend 91:19
b. which has been thought and said 10:3
b. words in their best 83:1
better than any other person's b. 131:9
criticism...to learn and propagate the b. 10:10
how much the b. 117:1
In art the b. is good enough 124:17
It was the *b.* butter 69:17
It was the b. of times 96:18
live in the b. of all possible worlds 65:3
prayeth b., who loveth best 81:16
times I've done my b. 140:21
worst, and we will do our b. 78:3
best-regulated: b. families 94:6
bestride: Why, man, he doth b. 229:20
Bethlehem: B. Ephratah, though thou be little 34:25
Slouches towards B. 297:19
betimes: to be up b. 237:15
betray: b. thee, who betrayest Me 267:22
guts to b. my country 116:22
never did b. / The heart 292:17
betray'd: b. me into common sense 204:5
better: b. day, the worse deed 133:16
b. one than you 47:20
b. than it sounds 271:20
can make b. chairs 110:25
even from worse to b. 138:15
far, far b. rest 96:19
for b. for worse 210:14
getting b. and better 86:5
knows of a b. 'ole 16:18
nae b. than he should be 56:3
no b....much the same 13:13
no b. than you should be 21:10
one way be b. than another 8:23
Rich is b. 271:8
still the b. for them 125:16
title from a b. man I stole 255:19
to b. what we can 256:2
where it's likely to go b. 118:6
You're a b. man 159:8
bettre: b. than wisdom? Womman 74:6
Between: B. the idea / And the reality 107:24
'ouses in b. 20:19
betwixt: day that comes b. / A Saturday 67:11
Beware: B. of the dog 201:12
B., O Man 244:10
B. the Ides of March 229:18
Bewildered: excess of love / B. them 296:15
bewray'd: b., / As by his manners 252:6
Bezonian: Under which king, B. 228:23
Bible: B. made England 141:22
B. tells me so 279:21
English are mentioned in the B. 272:2
English B., a book which 171:10
bible-black: starless and b. 267:5
bibles: b., billet-doux 207:14
Novels are as useful as B. 109:20
biblia: *b. a-biblia* 161:14
bicker: b. down a valley 262:9
bicycle: question then / Why we lean our b. 118:23
bidder: withstand the highest b. 279:23
bidding: Thousands at his b. speed 185:23
big: b. lie than to a small 136:14
never use a b., big D 122:16

thought of b. men and little 148:20
Big-endians: B. and small-endians 258:11
bigger: b. they come 115:5
bigoted: more b., more gloomy 191:24
Big-Sea-Water: shining B. 168:17
bill: your b. of company 258:17
billboard: b. lovely as a tree 190:25
billet: Every bullet has its b. 289:7
billet-doux: patches, bibles, b. 207:14
billiards: to play b. well 251:6
bills: not paying one's b. 287:32
Billy: B., in one of his nice 126:14
way for B. and me 137:6
binds: tie that b. / Our hearts 113:9
Bind-their-kings-in-chains: Obadiah B. 171:2
Binnorie: B., O Binnorie 17:6
biographers: Boswell...first of b. 171:23
Biography: [B.] One of the new terrors 8:6
b. of great men 68:5
B. / Is different from Geography 24:12
no history; only b. 110:9
birches: swinger of b. 118:7
Bird: B. of Time 114:14
B. thou never wert 244:13
crop-full b. 51:32
forgets the dying b. 198:8
hear the b.'s song without attempting 111:15
immortal B. 155:6
No b. soars too high 43:5
rare b. upon the earth 152:12
shall I call thee b. 294:21
Sweet b., that shunn'st 182:4
What b. so sings 170:21
widow b. sate mourning 241:21
birdie: b. with a yellow bill 255:14
birds: all the b. are flown 72:13
And no b. sing 153:11
B. in their little nests 280:12
b. without are desperate to get in 187:20
late the sweet b. sang 238:13
Birmingham: no great hopes from B. 12:10
Birnam: Fear not, till B. wood 232:29
Birth: B., and copulation and death 108:11
b. is but a sleep 292:22
hour of our b. 107:4
no cure for b. and death 220:12
Whom long descent of b. 185:12
birthright: b. for a mess of potage 5:11
sold his b. 26:2
Bis: *B. dat qui cito dat* 261:3
Bishop: another B. dead 179:5
How can a b. marry 248:25
No b., no king 144:15
bisier: seemed b. than he was 73:11
bisy: b. larke, messeger of day 73:22
Nowher so b. a man as he 73:11
bitch: old b. gone in the teeth 208:18
bitch-goddess: b., Success 143:3
b., Success 145:5
bite: *b.* some of my other generals 121:4
man recover'd of the b. 125:15
smaller fleas to b. 'em 259:14
bites: man b. a dog that is news 89:24
bitter: b. to thee, pardon 260:3
no b. springs 158:24
This blind b. land 298:16
bitterness: no hatred or b. towards anyone 71:11
black: b. man there is only one destiny 112:22
B.'s not so black 66:25
colour, so long as it's b. 116:12
I am b., but comely 32:19
I am b., but O 43:31
Take them down in b. 60:24
Tip me the b. spot 256:10
Black out: B.; Heaven blazing 296:26
Black Widow: B., death 169:25
black-a-moor: leave the b. alone 137:3
blackbird: b. whistling / Or just after 255:3
blackbirds: Four and twenty b. 195:15
full of b. than of cherries 2:10
black-eyed: landlord's b. daughter 193:22
blacks: poor are the b. of Europe 72:5
blade: magic b., begins to rust 91:7
blame: Nobody dast b. this man 181:5
not b. an epoch 80:17
past, it is needless to b. 83:26
poor wot gets the b. 6:3
Why should I b. her 297:6
blameless: white flower of a b. life 262:18
blaming: b. it on you 159:10
blanca: *trajo la b. s 'abana* 120:1
blank: streets breaks the b. day 263:11
whose annals are b. 67:23
blankets: rough male kiss of b. 48:6
Blatant: monster, which the B. beast 252:5
blaze: amid the b. of noon 185:11
blazing: Heaven b. into the head 296:26
bleed: prick us, do we not b. 233:14
thorns of life! I b. 243:8
bleibt: *b. sie immer neu* 132:13
Bless: B. relaxes 43:13
B. the Lord, O my soul 30:17
except thou b. me 26:7
God b. Captain Vere 179:8
God b. us every one 93:23
Lord b. you real good. 126:13
Blessed: B. are the meek 35:17
b. be the name 28:32
children...call her b. 32:3
I b. them unawares 81:12
it is twice b. 233:19
more b. than to cast cares aside 71:5
blessedness: work; let him ask no other b. 68:13
blessing: b. this smoking is 132:20
dismiss us with thy b. 53:4
health is the second b. 279:9
(no harm in b.) the Pretender 60:25
blessings: all b. flow 157:15
first of earthly b., independence 121:14
blest: always to be b. 206:12
Bed be b. that I lie on 6:8
b. by the suns of home 48:13
blew: hotch'd and b. 57:19
blin': ane of tham is b. 45:14
blind: among the b. the one-eyed man 112:4
b. from sheer supremacy 154:7
b. lead the blind 36:20
b. man battering blind men 296:11
b. man / On the sightless 277:27
B. mouths 182:28

B. the One-eyed Man 282:15
eyes to the b. 29:7
halt, and the b. 37:26
old, mad, b., despised and dying 244:5
Poet b., yet bold 177:16
right to be b. sometimes 191:9
Three b. mice 195:25
Ye b., behold your Saviour 283:1
blindness: 'eathen in 'is b. 159:1
blinked: other fellow just b. 218:3
Bliss: B. was it in that dawn 293:10
ignorance is b. 127:23
moment may with b. repay 66:11
mutual and partak'n b. 182:1
Now leiff thi b. 44:3
sum of earthly b. 184:26
virtue only makes our b. 206:30
blithe: Hail to thee, b. Spirit 244:13
block: big black b. 122:28
blockhead: b.'s insult points the dart 147:5
bookful b., ignorantly read 206:5
but a b. ever wrote 149:14
blocks: You b., you stones 229:17
blond: magnificent b. beast 193:1
Blondes: Gentlemen Prefer B. 168:25
blood: 'Let there be b.!' says man 63:9
all that b. was shed 297:22
b. and iron 41:23
b. of a British man 230:35
b. of the martyrs 265:26
b., toil, tears, and sweat 77:23
flesh and b. so cheap 138:11
freeze the b. 292:7
full of b. and battles 9:31
his b. for the country 216:7
make haste to shed innocent b. 33:28
pure and eloquent b. / Spoke 100:13
reaped in b. 43:19
red with guiltless b. 243:29
sanction to the trade of b. 243:25
so much b. in him 232:22
summon up the b. 228:30
Tiber foaming with much b. 209:4
wash this b. / Clean 232:3
with the b. of patriots 145:9
bloody: b., but unbowed 133:6
Not b. likely 240:26
What b. man is that 231:21
where's the b. horse 66:1
wipe a b. nose 120:25
bloom: [Charm] a sort of b. 20:10
bloomin': 'is b. lyre 160:1
blossom: b. as the rose 33:13
b. in their dust 245:18
hundred flowers b. 174:20
blossoms: b. through the year 245:2
blot: art to b. 207:4
I will not b. out his name 40:33
what they discreetly b. 278:4
blotted: each loved one b. 61:17
never b. out a line 151:3
blow: b. and swallow at the same 203:2
B., blow, thou winter wind 225:17
B. out, you bugles 47:21
B., winds 230:25
b. your own trumpet 123:17
b. / Your trumpets, Angels 99:22
sin till I b. up 267:8
blowin': b. in the wind 105:6
blubber'd: how b. is that pretty face 210:25
blude-red: Drinking the b. wine 18:9
Blue: B. as a vein 50:7
China that's ancient and b. 162:8
Little Boy B. 194:24
little tent of b. 285:22
bluid: brand sae drap with b. 17:12
blunder: it is a b. 45:10
man only a b. of God 193:5
Youth is a b. 97:18
blunder'd: Some one had b. 262:14
blunders: escaped making the b. 132:21
one of Nature's agreeable b. 87:3
blush: b. is beautiful, but 124:25
b. is no language 106:17
b. to find it fame 207:6
born to b. unseen 127:17
would it bring a b. to 95:26
young man b. than turn pale 70:23
blushes: only animal that b. 271:24
blushful: b. Hippocrene 154:35
blushing: b. to the very whites 96:9
blynde: b. world, O blynde entencioun 74:19
Board: wasn't any B.; and now 134:14
Boast: B. not thyself of to morrow 31:37
boasteth: then he b. 31:31
boastings: b. as the Gentiles use 159:26
boat: beautiful pea-green b. 164:10
soul is an enchanted b. 243:22
We're on a b. 257:8
boating: Jolly b. weather 86:4
boats: leathern b. begin to hoist 177:24
messing about in b. 126:15
bobbin: b. bound in mummy-cloth 296:1
bocks: drink our b. 108:7
bodies: friendless b. of unburied men 281:19
rough notes and our dead b. 221:11
bodkin: bare b. 226:38
body: a b. like mine 8:1
Absent in b. 39:4
b. gets its sop 49:26
b. in its swiftness 286:12
b. is his book 99:13
b. of a weak 109:1
Gin a b. meet a body 55:22
healthy mind in a healthy b. 152:18
her b. thought 100:13
human b. is sacred 284:11
man's b. and his mind 254:11
Selling one's b. to keep 173:14
whatever a b. is not obliged 272:7
Boets: I hate all B. 121:3
bog: This Bolshevik b. 173:1
To an admiring b. 97:1
Bogs: Fens, B., Dens 184:8
boil: b. along there till the floodgates 58:14
boiling: b. oil in it, I fancy 123:2
Boire: *B. sans soif* 21:7
bois: *au fond des b.* 274:22
n'irons plus aux b. 6:12
bok: Go litel b. 74:25
bokes: old b., in good feith, / Cometh 74:15
bold: b. as a lion 31:39
drunk hath made me b. 232:2
Poet blind, yet b. 177:16
boldest: b. measures are the safest 167:9
Boldness: B. and more boldness 90:14
B. be my friend 225:29
b. to believe in nothing 271:12

borrower: Neither a b. 226:11
borrowing: b. only lingers 228:16
b. / Goeth a sorrowing 271:19
goes a b. goes a sorrowing 117:21
bosom: every b. returns an echo 147:1
in my b., like a bee 167:26
lip to earth's b. bare 267:24
not a b. to repose upon 94:25
to thy b. fly 282:27
bosoms: silk stockings and white b. 147:25
Boston: B., / The home of the bean 45:8
Boswell: B. is the first of biographers 171:23
botched: b. civilization 208:18
Bother: B. Mrs. Harris 95:9
botté: *toujours b.* 187:12
Bottom: Bless thee, B. 234:7
b. not her own 113:15
bottomless: pit that is b. 144:13
To b. perdition 183:11
boue: *nostalgie de la b.* 11:18
Bough: beneath the B. 114:15
on a wet, black b. 208:20
boughs: b. which shake against the cold 238:13
bought: politician...when he is b. 65:22
bound: made a sudden b. 81:14
bounden: our b. duty 210:9
bounds: living, know no b. 245:20
Bountiful: My Lady B. 112:25
bourgeois: beastly the b. is 163:14
B....is an epithet 138:21
épater le b. 20:25
Bourgeoisie: British B. / Is not born 246:17
bourgeois-smug: trend is towards the b. 126:22
bourn: from whose b. / No traveller 226:39
see beyond our b. 153:22
boutique: *réserver une arrière b.* 187:14
Bow: B., bow, ye lower middle classes 122:18
b. of burning gold 42:27
drew a b. at a venture 28:18
not b. down thyself 26:29
unto the b. the cord 168:19
bowels: in the b. of Christ 89:3
Bowery: B., / Hoppy, Croppy 109:10
Bowl: inverted B. they call the Sky 114:26
Love in a golden b. 42:7
Morning in the B. of Night 114:13
bows: never b. its head to the force 90:13
Bow-Wow: Big B. strain 223:2
not for his *b. way* 200:15
Box: B. about: 'twill come 11:2
b. is only temporary 202:14
to no B. his being owes 88:28
boy: b. as he really is 164:1
b. my greatness 224:31
b. playing on the seashore 192:11
b. stood on the burning deck 133:1
b.'s will is the wind's 168:11
can't expect a b. to be vicious 219:7
Chatterton, the marvellous b. 293:13
mad about the b. 86:17
Speak roughly to your little b. 69:10
Than when I was a b. 138:7
That every b. and every gal 122:20
What a good b. am I 194:25
when I was a b. 23:17
boyhood: starved my b. 285:21
Boys: B. and girls come out 194:5
b. get at one end 149:8
b. of the old Brigade 281:2
B. will be boys 138:20
Christian b. I can scarcely hope 10:16
Old b. have their playthings 117:20
bracelet: b. of bright hair 100:8
braces: Damn b. 43:13
Bradshaw: vocabulary of B. is nervous 101:24
braes: b. o' bonny Doon 58:10
brag: b., th'other to pray 88:23
braided: b. her yellow hair 18:11
Brain: Bear of Very Little B. 181:12
b. in a dry season 107:22
from the heat-oppressèd b. 231:36
harmful to the b. 144:13
little b. attic stocked 101:13
More b., O Lord 179:22
my teeming b. 155:25
brains: b. knocked out by them 243:1
b. out of a brass knob 94:27
girl with b. ought 168:27
mix them with my b. 196:16
steal away their b. 234:34
brainwork: *fundamental b.*, is what makes 217:9
Branch: B. shall grow 33:5
b. that might have grown 175:14
brandy: get me a glass of b. 121:6
hero must drink b. 149:21
brass: as sounding b. 39:7
brains out of a b. knob 94:27
brave: b. bad man 79:6
B. New-nothing-very-much 197:5
b. new world 236:28
b.! that are no more 87:25
b. towards God 14:3
delirium of the b. 297:22
Fortune helps the b. 265:25
home of the b. 157:22
How sleep the b. 83:9
I'm very b. generally 70:3
Johnny was as b. 17:18
None but the b. 102:24
passing b. to be a King 176:5
young, the proud, the b. 61:6
braver: b. who overcomes his desires 8:19
bravery: should have the b. of ten 260:22
bravest: seem the b., but to be it 2:21
brazen: her world is b. 246:5
Brazil: B. — where the nuts come from 266:19
breach: b. than the observance 226:13
Once more unto the b. 228:30
bread: asked for b., and he received 283:6
bit of butter to my b. 181:19
b. and circuses 152:17
b. of adversity 33:12
b. should be so dear 138:11
b. upon the waters 32:14
cutting b. and butter 266:16
did eat of my b. 29:28
in breaking of b. 37:35
like b. in a besieged town 149:6
lives not upon b. alone 256:19

not live by b. only 27:6
not live by b. alone 35:13
quarrel with my b. and butter 258:24
taste of another's b. 90:11
this day our daily b. 35:24
break: bend and do not b. 115:19
b. a man's spirit 238:31
B., break, break, / On thy 262:7
b. off this last lamenting 99:12
some heart did b. 263:9
breakfast: b., dinner, lunch, and tea 23:4
B. first, business next 266:7
doth but b. here 134:3
Hope is a good b. 13:26
six impossible things before b. 70:6
Where shall we our b. take 18:15
breakfasts: M.F.H. sleeps he b. 258:3
breaking: b. of windows 189:2
in b. of bread 37:35
breaks: b. just like a little girl 105:9
larger thing b. through 249:20
breamis: brook was full of b. 104:18
breast: b. a bloody cross 251:23
calms the troubled b. 192:16
see my baby at my b. 225:2
vein o'er the Madonna's b. 50:7
breastie: panic's in thy b. 57:24
breasts: she hath no b. 32:25
breath: grown grey from thy b. 260:14
hear her tender-taken b. 155:17
lords are but the b. of kings 56:1
May my last b. 161:23
waste of b. the years 296:23
breathe: figures seem to b. 113:25
yearning to b. free 163:24
breathed: b. upon dead bodies 111:1
Breathes: B. there the man 222:1
breathing: Keep b. 271:7
bred: believe, because they so were b. 103:12
B. en bawn in a brier-patch 130:20
strain of man's b. out 236:30
breeches: hand in its b. pocket 156:20
breed: happy b. of men 235:14
more careful of the b. 200:17
breeds: lesser b. without the Law 159:26
breeze: battle and the b. 66:13
Breezy: B., Sneezy, Freezy 109:10
Breitmann: Hans B. gife a barty 164:20
Brekekekex: B. 8:15
Brer Fox: B., he lay low 130:21
brethren: for we be b. 25:28
brevity: b., and wit its soul 81:25
B. is the soul of wit 226:24
bribe: cannot hope / to b. 291:5
brick: 'Eave 'arf a b. at 'im 211:16
found it b. and left it marble 65:4
half b., carries better 164:3
bricks: Throw b. at your father instead 22:16
bridal-cakes: and of their b. 135:19
Bride: but a barren B. 204:25
darknss as a b. 232:37
ser' him for a b. 172:12
unravish'd b. of quietness 154:20
bridge: b. of asses 112:13
keep the b. with me 171:6
London B. is falling down 195:1
bridle: strangers to b. 258:15
brief: struggle to be b. 139:5
brier: out of the other a b. 18:4
brier-patch: bawn in a b. 130:20
briers: full of b. is this working-day 225:5
Brigade: boys of the old B. 281:1
bright: All things b. and beautiful 3:9
b. book of life 163:22
B. star, would I were 155:16
Keeps honour b. 237:6
Myriads though b. 183:13
torches to burn b. 235:34
Brightness: B. falls from the air 191:2
brilliant: envy of b. men 22:11
far less b. pen than mine 22:6
brillig: b., and the slithy toves 69:28
brim: but sparkles near the b. 61:19
winking at the b. 154:35
bringing: b. me up by hand 94:16
brioche: *Qu'ils mangent de la b.* 175:1
brisk: spoke a b. little somebody 49:25
bristles: my skin b. 141:4
Britain: battle of B. 77:26
B. a fit country 167:16
[B.]...club for mutual flattery 81:27
B. has lost an Empire 1:2
B. is going to make war 25:1
Graces do not seem...natives of...B. 75:19
happy B.! highly favoured isle 249:25
Britannia: B., rule the waves 268:4
Ocean Queen, the free B. 61:13
brithers: b. be for a' that 56:23
British: blood of a B. man 230:35
B. Public, ye who like me not 52:3
B. subject, in whatever land 198:14
ridiculous as the B. public 171:20
stony B. stare 264:14
Briton: grovelled...as only a free-born B. 266:10
Britons: B. never will be slaves 268:4
brittle: most b. of all human things 55:12
broad: b. of mind 25:6
brocade: or her new b. 207:17
broken: argument of the b. pane 198:17
b. heart lies here 171:3
b. limbs of a poet 140:17
b. reed at best 299:1
sound of b. glass 23:11
broken-hearted: bind up the b. 33:29
ne'er been b. 55:17
Bromides: B. and sulphites 54:3
bronze: more lasting than b. 140:12
brood: eternal b. of glory excellent 251:25
broodin': b. over *bein'* a dog 283:12
brooks: crystal b. 98:24
murmurs near the running b. 293:4
brothels: b. with bricks of Religion 43:6
Brother: Big B. is watching you 196:23
B. humans who live after us 275:3
b., or I kill you 72:6
man and a b. 281:25
moth in his b.'s parachute 246:12
my b.'s keeper 25:23
True b. of a company 298:4
Turk a man and a b. 112:7
white man's b., not 158:7
brotherhood: Love the b. 40:25
brother-in-law: not his b. 158:7
brotherly: Let b. love continue 40:17
brothers: men will be b. 220:28
we band of b. 229:3
brow: bleeding b. of labour 52:19
winters shall besige thy b. 238:3
browes: With scalled b. blake 73:16

brown: old b. hills 178:14
Browning: Meredith is a prose B. 288:22
Brüder: *Menschen werden B.* 220:28
Brute: B. heart of a brute 202:15
Et tu, B. 65:12
Et tu, B. 229:31
Feed the b. 104:16
brutish: nasty, b., and short 136:20
Brutus: B. is an honourable man 230:2
bubble: b. on the fountain 221:18
b. winked at me 135:18
now a b. burst 206:11
world...like unto a b. 279:19
world's a b. 15:25
bubbles: With beaded b. 154:35
buck: b. stops here 271:3
Buck Mulligan: Stately, plump B. 151:14
bud: nip him in the b. 214:17
Buddha: Jesus and Mary and B. 190:7
budding: b. morrow in midnight 155:19
buds: shake the darling b. of May 238:4
bug: b. with gilded wings 205:8
snug / As a b. in a rug 117:27
Bugger: B. Bognor 121:8
bugle: Blow, b., blow 264:22
wind like a b. 96:26
bugles: b., over the rich Dead 47:21
build: b. your ship of death 163:15
Except the Lord b. 31:8
think that we b. for ever 218:10
builders: stone which the b. refused 31:2
building: b. hath three conditions 295:4
Light...principal beauty of b. 119:8
no looking at a b. 55:9
something like a public b. 288:14
built: almost lost that b. it 48:26
Love b. on beauty 99:1
we have b. Jerusalem 42:28
Bull: Cock and a B. 254:23
milk the b. 148:14
peculiarity of the Irish b. 105:17
bullet: ballot is stronger than the b. 166:5
b. through his heart 266:12
Every b. has its billet 289:7
bullets: b. than pointed speeches 41:20
bullocks: yoke of b. at Stamford Fair 228:20
bulls: Strong b. of Bashan 29:24
bully: Like a tall b. 205:15
bumbast: b. out a blank verse 128:1
bump: not to b. into the furniture 170:14
things that go b. 5:15
bumpy: going to be a b. night 91:13
bundle: b. of contradictions 83:18
b. of prejudices 161:5
bunk: History is b. 116:11
bunting: wrap the baby b. 194:6
burden: carry the heavy b. of responsibility 106:1
terrible b. of having nothing to do 44:12
White Man's B. 160:2
bureaucracy: cannot understand the b. 240:9
Burg: *Ein feste B.* 170:15
Burgundy: naïve domestic B. 269:9
buried: b. him darkly at dead 291:2
b. in Marie's kirk 18:4
b. in so sweet a place 241:7
But Thee, deep b. 294:3
Burke: [B.] rose like a rocket 198:7
burn: another Troy for her to b. 297:7
I'll b. my books 175:13
marry than to b. 39:5
We b. daylight 233:27
Burn'd: B. on the water 224:24
burned: few of you are b. 215:12
give my body to be b. 39:7
men too are eventually b. 132:14
burning: Babe all b. bright 250:22
boy stood on the b. deck 133:1
b. fiery furnace 34:14
plucked out of the b. 34:22
Tiger! b. bright 43:24
burnish'd: like a b. throne 224:24
burns: b. towards heaven with fierce 243:23
You canna gang to a B. supper 172:7
burnt: b. the Temple of Diana 48:26
b. the topless towers 175:7
Christians have b. each other 62:18
burnt-out: b. ends of smoky days 108:6
burrs: like b. where they walk 118:17
burst: first that ever b. 81:5
suddenly b. out singing 220:25
burthen: b. of the mystery 292:12
Bury: B. my heart at Wounded Knee 23:23
come to b. Caesar 230:1
dead b. their dead 36:8
disposed to b. for nothing 95:6
We will b. you 157:25
bus: not even a b., I'm a tram 130:15
bush: aims but at a b. 245:23
b. burned with fire 26:15
common b. afire with God 49:15
business: about my Father's b. 37:16
B. as usual 77:21
b. in great waters 30:20
b., I say, pleasure 295:13
b. of America 85:17
b. of consequence, do it yourself 19:15
B. was his aversion 105:16
Christianity; it is good b. 167:18
gang about his b. 137:9
involved in this b. 187:1
No b. before breakfast 266:7
No praying, it spoils b. 197:10
real b. of a ball 258:6
Treasury is the spring of b. 15:28
true b. precept 95:5
bustle: b. of the busy 58:13
Busy: B. old fool 100:16
b. world and I 86:25
English are b. 188:1
little b. bee / Improve 280:13
thou knowest how b. 10:21
but: 'b.' in this imperfect world 47:3
doesn't do anything else b. 290:29
butler: inspired b. 131:13
butlers: we have friends and no b. 208:13
butt: with the b. end of it 125:29
butter: b. in a lordly dish 27:15
b. will only make us fat 124:8
cutting bread and b. 266:16
It was the *best* b. 69:17
like a little bit of b. 181:19
buttered: always on the b. side 200:4
butterflies: beard full of b. 120:2
butterfly: breaks a b. upon a wheel 205:7
Float like a b. 3:15

button: don't care a b. 164:9
undo this b. 231:8
buttress: regarded as a b. of the church 179:7
buy: b. repentance at the cost 92:22
Do not b. what you want 70:26
Vintners b. / One half so precious 115:1
buyer: naught, saith the b. 31:31
buying: b. — it's men's lives 222:14
reading, it is worth b. 218:7
buys: b. its opinions as it buys 60:10
Byron: [B.] Mad, bad and dangerous 161:1
B. they drew a system 171:22
Close thy B. 68:19
more worthless set than B. 282:8
C major: C. of this life 49:22
write / Even yet in C. 172:21
cabbages: Of c. — and kings 70:2
cabin: c. build there, of clay 296:24
Log C. to White House 266:18
cabin'd: now I am c. 232:12
Cabots: C. talk only to God 45:8
Ca-Caliban: 'Ban, 'Ban, C. 236:21
cackle: cut / The c. and pursue real ends 172:26
don't c. w'en he fine a wum 130:24
cackling: c. save the monarchy 204:6
cacoethes: *Scribendi c.* 152:14
cadence: harsh c. of a rugged line 103:29
caecos: *inter c. luscum* 112:4
Caelum: *C. non animum* 139:18
Caesar: *C. aut nihil* 45:2
C.'s I am 295:12
C.'s self is God's 88:24
C.'s wife must be above suspicion 65:8
loved C. less 229:33
that C. might be great 66:10
things which are C.'s 36:31
where some buried C. bled 114:17
Cage: C. / Puts all Heaven 42:3
Iron bars a C. 169:7
Cain: and the first city C. 86:22
Had C. been Scot 79:14
cake: Let them eat c. 175:1
Cakes: Hear, Land o' C. 57:11
manufacture of little c. 116:24
no more c. and ale 237:18
Calais: find 'C.' lying in my heart 178:8
calamity: more than a public c. 250:21
calculating: desiccated c. machine 25:9
calculation: c. shining out the other 95:3
Caledonia: C.! stern and wild 222:3
Caledonian: erect the C. stood 137:23
calf: fatted c., and kill 37:29
Caliban: C. casts out Ariel 208:17
rage of C. seeing 287:21
Call: C. me Ishmael 179:10
c. me that, *smile* 290:17
C. of the Wild 168:2
C. yet once 9:11
c. ye upon him 33:26
come when you do c. for 228:2
Go, for they c. you 9:22
one clear c. for me 262:16
Callay: Callooh! C. 69:29
called: many are c., but 36:29
never c. me mother 291:12
calling: how to live is all my c. 187:16
calm: c. and classical 95:20
c. of mind 185:17
c. the rage of thundering Jupiter 176:10
C. was the day 252:9
for a c. unfit 102:15
Music...c. the troubled mind 84:22
calme: *Luxe, c. et volupté* 20:22
calmness: so aggravating as c. 288:16
calms: Wisdom c. the mind 147:21
calumny: silent is the best answer to c. 279:24
Calvin: land of C., oat-cakes 248:18
cam': c. wi' a lass 144:11
Cambridge: C. books, as very well discerning 270:5
C. people rarely smile 48:3
C. science and a sausage 6:17
put back at Oxford or C. 22:8
came: I c., and no one answered 92:18
I c., I saw, I conquered 65:11
camel: easier for a c. 37:9
swallow a c. 36:30
Camelot: many-tower'd C. 263:26
Came-over-with-the-Conqueror: C. type of mind 280:10
camera: I am a c. 144:7
camp: weakest c....strongest school 76:24
Campbell: do not Maister or C. me 222:25
can: He who c., does 240:6
You c., for you must 124:21
Can't: It C. Happen Here 165:15
cancel: back to c. half a Line 114:25
cancers: because women have c. 156:15
candid: be c. where we can 206:9
save me, from the c. friend 66:26
candle: Bell, book, and c. 230:14
c. burns at both ends 181:3
c. in the sun 59:7
c. to the sun 115:11
light such a c. 163:11
Like a little c. / Burning 279:22
little c. throws his beams 233:26
Out, out, brief c. 232:28
rather light a c. 255:7
white c. / In a holy place 65:23
candle-light: Colours seen by c. 49:16
get there by c. 194:13
sit in the c. 215:11
candlelights: stately and daintily as c. 13:29
candles: Night's c. are burnt out 236:7
candlestick-maker: baker, / The c. 195:13
Candy: C. / Is dandy 190:23
canem: *Cave c.* 201:12
canker: joy without c. or cark 162:8
worm, the c., and the grief 64:3
cannikin: why clink the c. 50:26
Cannon: C. to the right of them 262:15
Even in the c.'s mouth 225:14
cannon-ball: c. took off his legs 138:4
canoe: paddle his own c. 176:23
canoes: shod their heads in their c. 177:24
cant: Clear your *mind* of c. 149:27
Cantabit: *C. vacuus* 152:16
Cantate: *C. Dominum* 277:15
canting: canted in this c. world 254:12
cursed the c. moralist 91:6
cants: Of all the c. 254:12
capability: world of c. / For joy 50:16
capacity: Genius...c. of taking trouble 67:22

infinite c. for taking pains 139:4
caparisons: No c., miss 245:7
Capax: *C. imperii* 261:9
Cape St. Vincent: nobly C. to the North-west 51:1
capitaine: *Mort, vieux c.* 20:24
Capital: high C., where kingly Death 241:9
capitalism: unacceptable face of c. 132:6
Capitol: ruins of the C. 121:13
capitulate: I will not c. 149:29
capta: *Graecia c. ferum* 139:21
Captain: C.! My Captain 284:12
c. of my soul 133:7
on the deck my C. lies 284:13
captains: All my sad c. 224:27
C. and the Kings depart 159:24
c. couragious 18:3
C. of industry 68:14
Capten: C., art thou sleepin' 191:19
captives: liberty to the c. 33:29
Captivity: bring away / C. thence captive 251:12
caravans: c., but never an ape 208:14
carbonarium: *De calcaria in c.* 265:28
carcase: c. of an old song 267:18
card: cheery old c.,' grunted Harry 220:24
Cardinal: sat on the C.'s chair 19:17
cards: Campaspe play'd / At c. 170:20
old age of c. 204:29
patience, and shuffle the c. 71:20
Care: Begone, dull C. 4:26
c. and women 279:19
c.'s check and curb 273:22
c. whether Mister John Keats 156:10
c. will kill a cat 290:18
don't c. a button 164:9
don't c. what is written about me 134:4
foregather wi' Sorrow and C. 55:23
full of c., / We have no 91:12
Irks c. the crop-full bird 51:32
neither c. nor know 140:25
ravell'd sleave of c. 232:1
Take c. of the sense 69:21
Teach us to c. 107:6
took c. of number one 176:16
weary fu' o' c. 58:10
wrinkled C. derides 182:12
career: c. open to talents 190:14
nothing which might damage his c. 20:12
careful: c. indeed what we say 84:12
carelessly: time c., as they did 225:4
carelessness: lose both looks like c. 287:4
cares: blessed than to cast c. aside 71:5
c. that infest the day 168:5
no one c. for me 41:10
what I am, none c. or knows 79:3
Carew: grave of Mad C. 131:7
cargo: c. of ivory 178:10
caricature: c. are the most penetrating 142:22
this c., / Decrepit age 298:8
carlin: ilka c. swat and reekit 57:18
carnal: heathen in the c. part 204:24
wun at times in c. states 172:15
carolings: little cause for c. 129:19
Carpe: *C. diem* 139:28
carpet: figure in the c. 144:24
carpets: long c. rose 153:30
spreading it with c. 2:17
carrière: *c. ouverte aux talentes* 190:14
carries: half brick, c. better 164:3
carry: c. off the latter 200:11
small head could c. all he knew 125:9
cars: giant finned c. 169:24
Carthage: C. must be destroyed 70:22
To C. I came 11:19
carve: c. him as a dish 229:27
carved: c. not a line 291:4
carver: c. happy while he was 218:9
case: c. will be closed 140:18
everything that is the c. 290:22
heard only one side of the c. 60:5
nothing to do with the c. 123:4
casement: at the c. seen her stand 263:27
c. ope at night 155:9
Full on this c. 153:29
casements: Charm'd magic c. 155:6
Cash: C. payment is not the sole nexus 68:12
hand to hand of c. 245:21
take the C. in hand 114:16
Cassock: C., band, and hymn-book 285:17
cassowary: If I were a c. 285:17
cast: c. (of which we rather boast) 177:3
die is c. 65:10
castle: c. hath a pleasant seat 231:27
house...is...as his c. 80:24
king of the c. 194:17
Castlereagh: had a mask like C. 242:26
castles: c. I have, are built with air 150:20
casualty: first c. when war comes 146:7
cat: bell the c. 93:11
care will kill a c. 290:18
c. and the fiddle 194:11
c. may look at a king 69:16
c.'s averse to fish 127:20
c. that likes to / Gallop 248:1
C., the Rat, and Lovell 83:4
[C.] walked by himself 159:14
College, or a C. 205:13
consider my C. Jeoffry 247:1
Had Tiberius been a c. 9:18
I play with my c. 187:18
I shall bell the c. 101:2
on little c. feet 220:5
poor c. i' the adage 231:32
see how the c. jumps 223:3
suggestion as a c. laps milk 236:19
swing a c. 94:8
to tear a c. in 233:36
Touch not the c. 222:16
ways of killing a c. 158:16
would have made a c. laugh 202:13
cataract: sounding c. / Haunted me 292:14
wild c. leaps in glory 264:22
catastrophe: c. of the old comedy 230:22
race between education and c. 282:22
catch: c. a falling star 100:14
Catch-22: C., which specified 132:17
catched: wise, and not be c. 201:4
catchwords: Man...lives...by c. 256:19
Catechisms: To know but C. 100:12
categories: ballet of bloodless c. 45:17
caterpillars: c. of the commonwealth 235:17
two religious c. 175:27

catharsis: c. of such emotions 8:27
Cathay: cycle of C. 264:7
Catherine the Great: illegitimate child of...C. 10:22
Catiline: How long, O C. 78:24
Cats: C. is 'dogs' 211:18
English C. are the best 247:2
wild c. in a red-hot iron cage. n 50:11
cattes: nation / Of c. wild and tame 246:18
cattle: actors are c. 136:13
these who die as c. 197:22
women are mostly troublesome c. 169:14
Catullus: Did their C. walk that way 297:17
Caucasus: thinking on the frosty C. 235:12
caught: c. hold of the fille 253:24
Scotchman, if he be *c.* young 148:27
small flies were c. 13:27
cauldron: Fire burn and c. bubble 232:15
causas: *rerum cognoscere c.* 276:6
cause: armour of a righteous c. 52:20
believing in the justice of our c. 129:1
c. is just 97:2
c. of dullness in others 116:8
c. that perishes with them 79:17
c. we believe to be just 166:8
effect, / Whose c. is God 88:12
it is the c., my soul 235:3
kings can c. or cure 125:23
Obstinacy in a bad c. 49:3
one can discover the c. 203:20
what great c. is he identified with 24:1
causes: any good, brave c. left 197:5
flowers, as in their c., sleep 67:6
understand the c. of things 276:6
cautious: c. seldom err 83:27
cavalier: c. who loves honour 221:12
cavaliero: perfect c. 60:27
Cavaliers: C. (Wrong but Wromantic) 223:23
Cave: *C. canem* 201:12
on the opposite wall of the c. 202:26
caverns: c. measureless to man 82:3
caves: c. for thousands of years 192:24
caviare: c. to the general 226:32
cease: c. along the whole front 115:18
C.! must men kill 242:13
day and night shall not c. 25:27
that I may c. to be 155:25
thou shouldst c. to be 244:18
whether you are happy, and you c. 180:7
Wonders will never c. 104:7
ceasing: Pray without c. 40:3
Cedant: *C. arma togae* 78:19
cedar: c. in Lebanon 30:14
Cedite: *C. Romani* 211:4
celebrate: c. myself, and sing 284:18
celebrity: c....for his well-knownness 44:19
celibacy: c. has no pleasures 147:11
cellar: Born in a c. 116:7
cells: contented with their c. 294:2
pedant colleges and c. 103:6
cena: *c. diserta tua est* 176:28
cenotaph: laugh at my own c. 241:23
censor: c. one's own thoughts 277:27
censorship: Assassination...extreme form of c. 240:28
censure: c. freely who have written well 205:26
hope from c. or praise 146:10
No man can justly c. 49:7
centre: c. cannot hold 297:18
c. gives way 115:17
visibly through the c. 137:13
centuries: forty c. look down upon you 190:10
century: c. of the common man 277:28
cerebration: well of unconscious c. 144:17
ceremonious: Nerves sit c., like Tombs 96:20
ceremony: painful c. of receiving...visits 249:5
Ceres: laughing C. reassume the land 205:18
certain: A lady of a 'c. age,' 63:7
c. because it is impossible 265:29
However c. our expectation 108:4
nothing can be said to be c., except 117:29
certainties: begin with c. 13:15
hot for c. 179:23
Certum: *C. est* 265:29
cesspool: c. into which all the loungers 101:22
chaff: c. is printed 141:12
chain: flesh to feel the c. 47:15
chains: c. and calls them Liberty 52:27
everywhere is in c. 217:16
leaps to lose his c. 280:18
nothing to lose but their c. 178:1
Shake your c. to earth 243:2
sons in servile c. 57:15
chair: *La c. est triste* 174:12
chaise-longue: hurly-burly of the c. 65:24
Cham: great C. of literature 249:14
chamber: in my lady's c. 194:10
chambermaid: c. as of a Duchess 149:18
chambre: *demeurer en repos dans une c.* 199:6
Champagne: C. certainly gives one werry gentlemanly 258:5
c. teetotaller 239:1
Chance: await / No gifts from C. 9:20
care o' th' main c. 59:26
c., direction which thou canst not see 206:17
c. favours only the prepared 199:13
C. is perhaps God's pseudonym 117:2
in nativity, c. or death 233:33
marriage...a matter of c. 12:24
now to prove our c. 102:5
right, by c. 87:9
Under the bludgeonings of c. 133:6
chang'd: c. / From him who 183:13
loves are but c. sorts of meat 98:26
change: cannot c. from black to white 137:3
C. is not made without 138:15
c., now thou art gone 182:21
c. of heart 11:13
c. takes place in the fundamental 180:8
c. their clime 139:18
c. their faces wi' their clo'es 113:13
courage to c. the things 192:19
ever-whirling wheel / Of C. 252:7
I would c. still less 49:24
more things c. 152:24
moveth doth in C. delight 252:8
nous avons c. tout cela 187:2

c. look makes a dish 135:16
God loveth a c. giver 39:14
Lord with c. voice 157:20
sometimes far more c. 137:19
cheerfulness: c. was always breaking in 106:2
cheering: great cause of c. us 24:1
cheese: dreamed of c. — toasted, mostly 256:12
Chelsea: dressed up as people in C. 190:7
cheque: Bringing the c. 11:11
Chequer-board: C. of Nights and Days 114:23
Chequer'd: Dancing in the C. shade 182:16
cherche: *Je ne c. pas* 201:23
Cherchez: *C. la femme* 104:13
cherish: c. pity, lest you drive 43:29
love, c. and to obey 210:15
cherries: full of blackbirds than of c. 2:10
Cherry: 'C. ripe' themselves do cry 66:18
c. was her cheek 17:2
ruddier than the c. 120:15
cherry-ripe: c. themselves do cry 3:16
C., ripe, ripe I cry 135:21
chess-board: We called the c. white 50:2
chest: men on the dead man's c. 256:9
chestnut: c. casts his flambeaux 140:20
Under the spreading c. tree / The 168:21
chestnut-tree: c., great-rooted blossomer 295:20
Chevalier: the young C. 55:21
young C. 137:7
chewing: c. little bits of string 23:3
chic: Radical c. 291:7
Chicagoan: as a C., I am rather skeptical 23:20
chicken: c. in his pot every Sunday 133:13
Some c.! Some neck 78:5
chickens: young c., they always come home 250:11
Chief: bloated C.'s unwholesome reign 61:6
Hail to the C. 221:17
chieftain: c. o' the puddin'-race 57:22
chield: c.'s amang you taking notes 57:12
Child: C.! Do not throw this book 22:23
c. imposes on the man 103:12
C. is father of the Man 292:19
c. should always say what's true 255:9
c., / That lightly draws 294:22
every formal visit a c. 13:7
father than knows his own c. 233:10
happy English c. 261:22
healthy c....is...wholesome food 258:20
If you strike a c. 240:3
life is...like a froward c. 262:3
no c. is born a criminal 249:2
saddling of the right to a c. 239:7
towards the c. she bare 87:19
Train up a c. 31:32
Tuesday's c. is full of grace 6:9
unto us a c. is born 33:4
wild went o'er his c. 66:7
with a sprightly and forward c. 75:13
with c. of glorious great intent 251:25
Childhood: C. is the kingdom 181:2
c. shews the man 185:6
c. used to know 130:8
eyes of your c. dried 266:14
childish: Sweet c. days 294:20
childishness: Second c. and mere oblivion, / 225:16
children: c. are a kind of Discipline 14:14
C. are dumb to say 127:2
C. begin by loving 288:15
c. cried in the streets 189:20
C. dear, was it yesterday 9:11
c. died in the streets 11:4
c. fear to go in the dark 14:4
c....hostages to fortune 14:12
c. of a larger growth 75:18
c. of a larger growth 103:3
c. of one family / Fall out 280:12
c. round her knees 294:7
c., singing in the cupola 274:12
c. who were rough 251:9
devour each of her c. 274:8
dogs than of their c. 200:17
family of ten c. 12:18
had so many c. 195:22
Her c. arise up 32:3
not much about having c. 167:25
Old men are c. 8:14
Parents...last people...to have c. 60:9
stars...are my c. 156:19
Suffer the little c. 37:8
tale which holdeth c. from play 246:7
chill: bitter c. it was 153:23
chilly: room grows c. 126:14
Chimborazo: C., Cotopaxi 271:14
chimes: heard the c. at midnight 228:21
CHIMNEY: HORSES WEDGED IN A C. 189:18
chimney-corner: old men from the c. 246:7
chimney-sweeps: c., come to dust 225:32
China: C. that's ancient and blue 162:8
though C. fall 204:30
treads the Wall / Of C. 200:3
Chinee: scrunt o' a knock-knee / C. 172:7
chivalrie: He loved c. 73:3
chivalry: age of c. is gone 54:7
save fallen C. 61:7
choice: careful in the c. of his enemies 287:23
in the worth and c. 150:17
just the terrible c. 52:8
no c. / To the citizen 11:14
you takes your c. 7:27
choirs: Bare ruined c. 238:13
choking: c. her with cream 158:16
sit on a man's back, c. him 269:24
choose: can believe what you c. 192:8
c. a member indeed 54:16
c. between betraying my country 116:22
C. me, / You English words 267:17
c. who will be crucified 80:18
c. / Perfection of the life 296:3
means just what I c. 70:7
woman can hardly ever c. 106:18
chooses: destiny as he c. 290:1
chopcherry: c. ripe within 200:13
chord: struck one c. 211:3
chore: c. done by the gods 111:18
chosen: few are c. 36:29
Christ: all things through C. 40:1
C. cannot save thy soul 175:6

C. perish in torment in every age 240:30
C. the tiger 107:20
C. were to come to-day 68:26
in the bowels of C. 89:3
Odour of blood when C. 298:11
See see where C.'s blood 175:11
Christe: C. receive thy saule 18:2
Christendom: wisest fool in C. 133:11
Christian: C. can die 2:15
C. ideal has not been tried 77:2
forgive them as a C. 13:3
naturally C. soul 265:27
Onward! C. soldiers 19:19
sad, good C. at her heart 204:24
to form C. men 10:16
Christianity: C. is part of the Common Law 129:2
decay of C. 219:14
local cult called C. 130:3
loving C. better than Truth 82:12
not merely sound C. 167:18
Christians: C. have burnt each other 62:18
Christmas: C. brought his sports 222:9
C. comes but once a year 271:17
C. Day in the Workhouse 246:13
C....in the middle of Winter 2:4
C. is coming 5:4
happens very well that C. 2:4
Happy C. to all 188:6
night before C. 188:5
chronicle: c. of wasted time 238:16
chronicles: Look in the c. 236:8
Chryst: C., born into Virgynyté 295:15
Chuck: C. it, Smith 76:4
Church: army / Moves the C. 19:20
As some to c. repair 206:1
Broad of C. 25:6
buttress of the c. 179:7
C. as his mother 89:20
C.'s one foundation / Is Jesus 257:3
c. without pulling off 148:12
figure in a country c. 258:16
free C. in a free State 71:12
In c. with saints 90:7
I will build my c. 36:21
martyrs is the seed of the c. 265:26
nearer the C. 4:12
no salvation outside the c. 11:24
no salvation outside the C. 89:21
silent c. before the service 110:16
churches: chapels had been c. 233:4
C. built to please the priest 57:5
cigar: good c. is a Smoke 158:21
good five-cent c. 176:24
cigarette: c. is the perfect type 287:25
Cinara: dear C. was my queen 140:14
cinco: *a las c. de la tarde* 120:1
cinders: Sat among the c. 194:27
Cinema: C. is truth twenty-four times 124:5
Cinna: I am C. the poet 230:7
circenses: *Panem et c.* 152:17
circle: firmness makes my c. just 100:24
God...a c. of which the centre 7:11
circle-citadels: c. there 139:1
Circumlocution: C. Office was beforehand 94:23
circumnavigate: c. the metaphysics 256:21
circumscrib'd: c. / In one self place 175:5
circumspice: *requiris, c.* 295:6
circumstance: envisage c., all calm 154:8
fell clutch of c. 133:6
pomp and c., has more attraction 131:8
some c. to please us 259:16
very slave of c. 64:5
Circumstances: C. beyond my individual 94:9
concatenation of c. 281:8
trust...not in c. 111:4
circuses: Bread and c. 152:17
cities: flour of c. all 104:25
hum / Of human c. torture 61:26
saw the c. of many 138:2
citizen: c. of no mean city 38:29
c. of the world 14:19
c. of the world 97:10
humblest c. of all the land 52:20
I am a Roman c. 78:26
requisite of a good c. 216:6
citizens: fat and greasy c. 225:7
first and second class c. 289:16
To arms, c. 217:15
city: and the first c. Cain 86:22
as it rains on the c. 274:13
c. 'half as old as Time' 54:4
C. is of Night 268:12
crowded c.'s horrible street 50:25
day in the c. square 52:15
long in c. pent 155:24
long in populous C. pent 184:28
no continuing c. 40:19
no mean c. 38:29
not to see Thy Holy C. 214:9
populous and a smoky c. 243:11
second grandest c. 173:5
There the great c. stands 284:17
Unreal C. 108:14
City-builder: whom they name the C. 68:22
civil: By c. rage and rancour fell 249:13
Too c. by half 245:5
civilities: sees / Cities and their c. 200:3
civilization: botched c. 208:18
can't say c. don't advance 215:2
C. degrades the many 2:27
C. is paralysis 120:10
c....not yet exhausted 123:28
elements of modern c. 67:20
life blood of real c. 270:9
usual interval of c. 79:12
[Western c.] an excellent idea 119:20
civilized: force another to be c. 180:19
last thing c. by Man 179:24
Machines...distinguish the c. man 80:7
civilizes: sex whose presence c. 87:11
Civis: *C. Romanus sum* 78:26
when he could say *C. Romanus* 198:14
clamour: c. of the crowded street 168:12
Clan: C. Alpine's warriors true 221:19
clangour: trumpet's loud c. 103:27
clanjamfrie: droun / The haill c. 172:3
clap: If you believe, c. 20:8
Soul c. its hands 297:16
Claret: C. is the liquor for boys 149:21
[c.] would be port 24:17
clarion: Sound, sound the c. 189:1
class: c. struggle necessarily leads 178:6

Every c. is unfit to govern 1:4
Like many of the upper c. 23:11
not that of any one c. 202:25
While there is a lower c. 91:17
classes: divisible into two great c. 22:9
maintaining...privileged c. 85:16
masses against the c. 124:1
ye lower middle c. 122:18
classic: [c.] nobody wants to read 271:23
on C. ground 204:17
tread on c. ground 1:15
classical: c., that's it 95:20
really like c. music 239:28
Classicism: C. is health 124:22
classics: Dryden and Pope are not c. 10:15
Claude: After you, C. 153:4
claw: red in tooth and c. 263:17
claws: ragged c. / Scuttling across 107:32
clay: c. mix with the earth 64:26
clay-cauld: c. were her rosy lips 17:2
clean: I shall be c. 277:14
one more thing to keep c. 118:25
Cleanliness: C. is, indeed, next to godliness 283:3
cleanly-wantonness: sing of c. 135:20
Cleanse: C. the thoughts of our hearts 210:6
clear: deep yet c. 92:25
in life than a c. conscience 219:8
clearly: can be said c. 290:23
clears: c. us of this deed 232:4
cleft: who c. the Devil's foot 100:14
clémence: *c. est la plus belle* 85:20
Clemency: C. is also a revolutionary measure 93:12
Cleopatra: C. strikes me as the epitome 64:16
If C.'s nose had been shorter 199:7
some squeaking C. 224:31
Clercs: *Trahison des C.* 23:21
clergy: in spite of what the c. 151:7
clergyman: c. with a one-storey 137:12
Once a c. always 6:15
clergymen: sexes — men, women, and c. 248:16
Cleric: C. before, and Lay behind 59:22
Clerk: C. ther was of Oxenford 73:9
clerkes: c. been noght the wysest 73:26
clever: c., but is it Art 158:26
c. people were good 291:18
let who will be c. 158:8
like all very c. people, could not 62:19
vera c. chiel 46:4
very c. woman to manage 159:30
cliffs: those white c. I never 171:3
climate: Heaven for c. 272:14
climb: best to c. and get to him 51:20
Fain would I c. 212:25
Man can c. to the highest 239:2
road is hard to c. 211:5
clime: Ambition...growth of every c. 42:18
clock: c. at ten to three 48:5
c. is always slow 224:6
c. struck one 194:12
c. will strike 175:10
forgot to wind up the c. 253:27
open with a c. striking 244:26
clod: soul is not a c. 153:33
cloistered: fugitive and c. virtue 186:5
Clootie: Satan, Nick, or C. 55:14
close: c. behind him tread 81:15
closed: c. twice before its close 96:24
closer: for a c. walk with God 87:17
closet: in the world, and not in a c. 75:7
one by one back in the C. 114:23
Cloth'd: C. with transcendent brightness 183:13
clothed: arm c. in white samite 174:16
C., and in his right mind 37:5
c. on with chastity 262:17
c. with the heavens 270:4
Naked and ye c. me 36:35
clothes: Kindles in c. a wantonness 135:24
liquefaction of her c. 135:28
Loves but their oldest c. 100:20
walked away with their c. 98:3
cloud: c. of witnesses 40:15
lonely as a c. 291:21
pillar of a c. 26:20
cloud-capped: c. towers 236:24
Cloudcuckooland: How do you like 'C.' 8:13
clouds: trailing c. of glory 292:23
clown: emperor and c. 155:6
clownage: conceits as c. keeps 176:2
club: any c. that would have me 177:27
best c. in London 95:28
most exclusive c. there is 190:19
clubs: philosophy...to dwell in c. 1:23
Clun: Clungunford and C. 141:1
clutching: alien people c. their gods 107:27
coach: c. and six horses through 214:6
coal: whole world turn to c. 135:13
coals: Heap c. of fire 31:34
coarse: what c. hands he has 94:17
coarsened: Action is but c. thought 4:5
coat: c. of many colours 26:8
my c. from the tailor 125:30
song a c. / Covered 296:5
tattered c. upon a stick 297:16
cobbler: c. should not judge beyond 203:7
cobwebs: laws were like c. 13:27
Cocaine: C. isn't habit-forming 19:8
Cock: C. and a Bull 254:23
c. who thought the sun 106:15
C. with lively din 182:14
owe a c. to Asclepius 249:19
cock-horse: c. to Banbury Cross 195:11
Cockney: C. impudence before now 218:4
piper is a C. 172:7
cocksure: I was as c. of anything 179:3
cocktail: weasel under the c. cabinet 202:2
coffee: c., I want tea 211:23
C., (which makes the politician wise 207:20
life with c. spoons 107:31
o'er cold c. trifle 205:12
coffee-house: c. for the voice of the kingdom 258:10
Cogito: *C., ergo sum* 93:9
cognisance: such c. of men and things 50:12
coherence: all c. gone 99:16
coil: shuffled off this mortal c. 226:37
coin: Beauty is nature's c. 182:1
smallest current c. 41:12

coined: c. my cheek to smiles 61:28
coitum: *Post c. omne animal* 6:20
cok: This gentil c. 74:8
cold: blow in c. blood 240:3
called a c. a cold 23:25
Cast a c. eye 298:14
caught / An everlasting c. 281:23
c. comfort 230:17
c. coming we had of it 107:26
C. Pastoral 154:25
Europe catches c. 180:2
How c. my toes 181:9
neither c. nor hot 40:34
cold war: midst of a c. 20:18
Coldness: Wisdom, C., or deep Pride 61:22
Cole: Old King C. 195:5
Coleridge: [C.] Archangel a little damaged 161:21
C. lull the babe 63:26
[C.] talked on for ever 131:12
Cultivate simplicity, C. 161:17
Thou shalt not set up...C. 62:21
Coliseum: stands the C., Rome shall 62:6
collective: vast c. madness 163:17
College: endow a C., or a Cat 205:13
colleges: discipline of c. 247:10
pedant c. and cells 103:6
colonnade: whispering sound of the cool c. 87:27
Colossus: world / Like a C. 229:20
colour: any c., so long as it's black 116:12
he who c. loves 100:20
Colourless: C. green ideas 77:7
colours: All c. will agree 14:7
coat of many c. 26:8
coltes: I hadde alwey a c. tooth 73:31
column: fifth c. 186:11
London's c., pointing at the skies 205:15
combat: c. of the brain 103:8
combine: bad men c. 54:15
combustion: hideous ruin and c. 183:11
come: ain't much dat don't c. out 130:19
Cannot c., lie follows 211:10
C. up and see me 283:11
c. when you do call 228:2
men may c. and men may go 262:10
Shape of Things to C. 282:25
slow, or c. he fast 222:7
things to c. 38:38
ve must all c. to it 96:15
whistle, and I'll c. 58:7
comedies: c. are ended by a marriage 62:30
C. of manners swiftly become obsolete 86:15
comedy: All I need to make a c. 72:9
catastrophe of the old c. 230:22
C. is medicine 128:8
c. is over 165:4
c. to those that think 278:19
dressed for this short c. 7:22
In the casual c. 296:13
comedye: myght to make in som c. 74:25
comeliness: no form nor c. 33:24
comely: I am black, but c. 32:19
cometh: He c. not,' she said 264:11
no man c. unto the Father 38:13
comets: Ye country c. 177:17
comfort: a' the c. we're to get 58:4
Be of good c., Master Ridley 163:11
carry their c. about 106:22
cold c. 230:17
c. me with apples 32:20
C.'s a cripple 102:2
c. where no comfort is 268:16
love of c....not...a scholar 84:7
naught for your c. 76:6
speeches / That c. cruel 76:12
comfortable: baith grand and c. 20:4
something more c. 130:17
comfortably: should have liv'd c. so long 120:16
comforting: cloud of c. convictions 218:20
comforts: Adversity is not without c. 14:9
comic: c. romance is a comic epic-poem 113:24
coming: as their c. hither 231:5
cold c. they had 4:13
cold c. we had 107:26
gude time c. 222:24
I was c. to that 127:4
There's a good time c. 173:11
command: Man to c. and woman 264:26
not in mortals to c. success 1:11
Through obedience learn to c. 202:21
to sue but to c. 235:9
to sue than to c. 221:15
commandment: one c., 'Enjoy thyself' 299:12
commandments: c. were, to hate 171:22
perfectly to keep the c. 70:20
commedia: c. é finita 165:4
commemorative: cold c. eyes 217:4
commencement: *c. de la fin* 261:11
commend: thy hands I c. my spirit 37:34
Comment: C. is free 221:8
commentators: c. view / In Homer 259:15
Commerce: C. its god 167:3
equal to the whole of that c. 54:21
heavens fill with c. 264:4
honour sinks where c. 125:24
commercial: memory of the c. classes 287:32
commercing: looks c. with the skies 182:6
commit: c. his body to the ground 210:21
loves to c. eating 218:1
Commodity: C., Firmness, and Delight 295:4
c. of good names 227:32
stranger c....than books 166:1
common: century of the c. man 277:28
c. as the air 126:21
c. cry of ours 225:26
c. task 157:6
hard to say c. things 139:7
He nothing c. did 177:15
Horse Guards and still be c. 213:8
light of c. day 292:24
not already c. 167:20
one want for a c. good 175:25
saying in c. talk 1:18
commonplace: c. a crime is, the more difficult 101:7
c. things and characters interesting 223:2

c. book be full 259:3
conformers to c. 180:17
Commons: C., faithful to their system 173:15
common sense: betray'd me into c. 204:5
c. and plain dealing 110:4
C. is the collection of prejudices 106:12
English...bid adieu to...c. 248:6
organized c. 143:11
commonwealth: caterpillars of the c. 235:17
commune: werche and wysse / To c. profit 74:16
communion: fall lost c. with God 70:19
Communism: C. is the illegitimate child 10:22
spectre of C. 177:28
communist: c.? One who hath yearnings 109:9
community: c. has a right to force 180:19
part of the c. of Europe 219:18
companions: Shun evil c. 198:13
company: alone than in bad c. 279:26
bear him c. 168:23
C., villainous company 228:3
Crowds without c. 121:12
except the present c. 196:15
good c. improves a woman 113:2
I see an innumerable c. 44:1
three is c. and two 287:3
tone of the c. you are in 75:9
your bill of c. 258:17
compare: c. small things with great 276:10
c. thee to a summer's day 238:4
c. / The prison where I live 235:22
not Reason and C. 42:13
Comparisons: C. are odorous 234:21
compassion: c. in the very name of a Curate 248:7
compensation: plum-cake was a c. 266:14
competition: Approves all forms of c. 79:23
c. and mutual envy 136:23
c., the laws of death 218:13
Complacencies: C. of the peignoir 255:2
complain: c. of the age 54:13
Never c., never explain 98:9
complained: c. he had not enough time 111:13
complains: c. of his memory 163:5
complete: most c....of all antiquity 1:20
Pure and c. sorrow 269:21
complexion: Mislike me not for my c. 233:9
putting on a false c. 113:15
compliance: by a timely c., prevented 113:21
complicated: more c. than his thoughts 273:7
complies: c. against his will 59:28
compliment: two months on a good c. 272:15
composed: Lipsius...who c. a work 254:17
composition: mad c. 230:13
comprehend: not c. the heav'n 206:14
compromise: his idea of a c. 141:14
compromises: one finds certain c. 187:6
compulsion: fools by heavenly c. 230:21
comrade: stepping where his c. stood 222:13
concatenation: Fearful c. of circumstances 281:8
conceal: woman...should c. 12:20
Conceit: Riches...but C. 15:8
conceited: pity for c. people 106:22
conceits: best c. do prove the greatest 102:4
c. as clownage keeps 176:2
Words are the tokens...for c. 13:23
concentrates: c. his mind wonderfully 149:15
concentred: wretch, c. all in self 222:2
Conception: C., my boy, *fundamental* 217:9
Conceptions: C. equal to the soul's 292:5
concerts: c. in England you will find 239:28
conclusion: could but spot a c. 190:18
hasten to a c. 15:3
conclusions: art of drawing sufficient c. 60:14
comin' to c. 172:16
jump to c. rarely alight 128:10
Concordia: *C. discors* 139:19
concubines: Twenty-two acknowledged c. 121:19
Condemn: C. the fault 232:34
nor the years c. 41:18
condemned: c. to be free 220:16
condemns: freedom with which Dr. Johnson c. 55:13
condescends: loves and the other who c. 266:9
condition: Ethics must be a c. 290:24
observe the c. of the people 152:2
conditions: sorts and c. of men 209:23
conduct: characters...result of our c. 8:25
c....Three fourths of life 10:13
C....to the prejudice 5:5
confederacy: dunces are all in c. 259:6
conference: naked into the c. chamber 25:8
confess: c. our manifold sins 209:7
confidence: addresses always inspire c. 287:11
greatest success is c. 109:20
confident: Never glad c. morning 51:9
confin'd: cabin'd, cribb'd, c. 232:12
conflict: c. of opinions and sentiments 150:4
field of human c. 77:27
in armed c. 105:13
conflicts: great c. are contained 276:9
conform: to God they would either c. 201:4
conformers: c. to commonplace 180:17
Confound: C. their politics 67:8
confounded: Confusion worse c. 184:10
confus'd: harmoniously c. 207:26
confused: best things are thus c. 243:15
Confusion: C. now hath made 232:7
C. worse confounded 184:10
obey; / All else c. 264:26
congratulates: not blame an epoch; one c. 80:17

congregation: face of this c. 210:11
latter has the largest c. 92:1
Congress: C....dances 166:3
Congs: Kinquering C. 252:15
conjuring: Parson left c. 223:15
connect: Only c. 116:20
conquer: c. it than to know what 278:16
c. without danger 85:19
In this sign thou shalt c. 85:11
Like Douglas c. 137:22
never c. that kingdom 146:6
You cannot c. America 202:6
conquered: Chance, have c. Fate 9:20
c. and peopled half the world 223:10
c., O pale Galilean 260:14
I came, I saw, I c. 65:11
I will be c. 149:29
not yet c. one 203:11
perpetually to be c. 54:22
You have c., Galilaean 151:23
conquering: c. spirit which impels 266:4
lawfulness of their c. America 148:16
See, the c. hero comes 189:7
Conqueror: came in with Richard C. 236:8
c. creates a Muse 278:5
fame of a c.; a cruel 76:1
Greece subdued her fierce c. 139:21
hero the C. Worm 203:16
they name C. or City-burner 68:22
Conquerors: madmen...C. and Kings 61:23
conquers: Love c. all 276:1
Conquest: Roman C. was, however, a *Good* 223:21
subdue / By C. far and wide 185:5
To joy in c. 162:18
conquests: carnage and his c. 61:2
conscience: catch the c. of the king 226:36
c. that it is wrong 16:12
c. doth make cowards 226:40
c., when it has no soul 269:13
good c. on the proceeds 247:15
Help us to save free C. 185:28
Science without c. 187:22
than a clear c. 219:8
uncreated c. of my race 151:13
conscientious: c. man, when I throw rocks 190:20
Consciousness: C. is a disease 272:24
C. reigns but does not govern 273:8
consecrate: c. / With thine own hues 242:15
consecrates: Time c. 221:2
consecration: c., and the Poet's dream 292:1
consent: 'I will ne'er c.' — consented 62:20
consented: 'I will ne'er consent' — c. 62:20
consenting: c. language of the heart 120:22
Consents: brow / C. to death 62:3
consequence: business of c., do it yourself 19:15
consequences: c. of them will be 59:13
damn the c. 181:21
there are c. 144:2
consequentially: who reasoned or acted c. 75:18
conservation: without the means of its c. 54:8
Conservatism: C. discards Prescription 97:15
Conservative: C. government...Tory men and Whig measure 97:16
C. government is an organized hypocrisy 98:2
c. when old 118:14
else a little C. 122:20
most c....undergraduates 289:23
staid c. 280:10
Tory...called the C. 89:2
Conservatives: C....the stupidest party 180:9
consider: c. the end 116:5
considerations: no personal c. 126:19
considérer: *c. la fin* 116:5
consistency: c. is the hobgoblin 110:14
consolation: one c., as they always says 96:1
suicide is a great c. 192:20
conspicuous: c. by its presence 218:23
C. consumption 274:4
c. wastefulness 274:5
conspiracies: c. against the laity 239:4
conspiracy: concerning Catiline's c. 149:32
Indecency's C. of Silence 240:14
conspire: you and I with Fate c. 115:2
constancy: but c. in a good 49:3
c. to a bad, ugly woman 64:12
constant: c. as the northern star 229:30
often change who would be c. 84:14
constellations: want the c. any nearer 285:2
constitution: c. is extremely well 278:15
C. does not provide for 289:16
election...very essence of the c. 152:3
Every country has its own c. 4:22
genius of the C. 202:7
higher law than the C. 224:9
principle of the English c. 41:25
principles of a free c. 121:17
watchdog of the c. 167:14
constitutional: c. monarchy such as ours 16:5
constrained: by violence c. to do 108:24
construct: c. the socialist order 164:21
construction: mind's c. in the face 231:24
construe: c. things after their own fashion 229:24
consuls: Let the c. see to it 5:1
consume: c. happiness without 238:30
consumed: bush was not c. 26:15
consummation: And c. comes 129:18
Consummatum: *C. est* 277:25
consumption: Conspicuous c. 274:4
this c. of the purse 228:16
contact: c. of two skins 72:4
contagion: c. of the world's slow stain 241:14
contain: I c. multitudes 284:24
contemplate: Let us c. existence 95:4
sometimes would c., sometimes do 100:3
contemporaries: we shall all of us be c. 2:12
contempt: pour c. on all my pride 280:19
Silence is the supreme c. 219:5
contemptible: c. little army 289:3

contend: schools of thought c. 174:20
contending: c. against some being 284:10
Content: C. to breathe his native 207:10
has eneuch that is c. 105:1
lot is happy if you are c. 44:7
Contented: C. wi' little 55:23
contentment: c. depends not on what we have 83:23
contests: mighty c. rise from trivial 207:13
Continent: Dark C. 252:24
continents: and three separate c. 101:17
Continual: C. drips hollow 170:9
continuance: for a c....prefer mild hale 258:5
continuation: c. of politics 79:9
Contract: C. into a span 135:8
verbal c. isn't worth 126:5
contradict: Do I c. myself? / Very well then 284:24
contradiction: Physicians...brook no c. 281:14
without fear of c. 173:5
contradictions: bundle of c. 83:18
contradictories: either of two c. 106:17
contraries: Without c. is no progression 42:20
Contrariwise: C.,' continued Tweedledee 70:1
contrary: Mary, quite c. 195:3
contrive: head to c. 121:21
contrived: cunning passages, c. corridors 107:21
control: beyond my individual c. 94:9
Fate, which God...doth not c. 100:7
controversy: c. is either superfluous 192:5
conturbat: *Timor Mortis c. me* 104:24
conveniences: c. of common life 146:15
convent: c.'s narrow room 294:2
Convention: C. is the dwarfish demon 61:4
Conventionality: C. is not morality 47:5
Convents: C., bosom'd deep in vines 204:16
conversation: best of life is c. 109:20
c. in a mixed company 75:25
c. with the finest men 93:10
c. avec les plus honnêtes gens 93:10
ignorance cramps my c. 138:22
pleasures in life is c. 248:4
silence that makes his c. 248:27
war: it ruins c. 116:6
Writing...different name for c. 254:3
conversations: without pictures or c. 69:3
converse: high c. with the mighty dead 268:9
converted: c. at a revival 256:21
converts: women can true c. 113:4
convicted: c. of sickness, hunger 249:4
conviction: best lack all c. 297:18
convictions: cloud of comforting c. 218:20
convince: persuading others, we c. ourselves 152:5
convinced: not those which have c. themselves 180:17
Cook: C. is a little unnerved 25:2
c. was a good cook 219:15
cookery: c. do 179:26
cooks: literary c. / who skim the cream 189:3
Many excellent c. are spoiled 120:9
cool: c. repentance came 222:23
Cool'd: C. a long age 154:34
cooling: slow c. of our chivalrous passion 208:7
coompaignye: Withouten oother c. in youthe 73:13
cooperation: c....the laws of life 218:13
coot: haunt of c. and hern 262:9
Cophetua: C. sware a royal oath 262:6
copia: *Inopem me c. fecit* 197:17
copier: c....never produce anything great 214:2
mere c. of nature 214:2
Copper: Definitely, Lord C. 280:25
copulation: Birth, and c. and death 108:11
Let c. thrive 230:39
revolution without general c. 281:26
coquette: death and I will c. 176:14
coquettish: c. to the last 64:16
cor: *son du c. est triste* 274:22
coral: bones are c. made 236:18
India's c. strand 132:8
corbies: I heard twa c. 18:16
cord: unto the bow the c. is 168:19
core: ain't a-going to *be* no c. 272:9
cormorant: c. devouring Time 231:10
corn: amid the alien c. 155:6
make two ears of c. 258:13
man gets his c. pone 271:22
raise the price of c. 60:26
treadeth out the c. 27:8
corner: only one c. of the universe 143:6
Sits the wind in that c. 234:19
world in ev'ry c. sing 134:22
You in your small c. 279:22
cornfield: c. where Troy once was 197:16
Cornishmen: twenty thousand C. 131:5
Coromandel: coast of C. 164:6
coronets: Kind hearts are more than c. 263:25
corporation: expect a c. to have a conscience 269:13
corpse: c. which is man 260:15
frozen c. was he 168:24
hardly was the c. cold 257:6
make a lovely c. 95:7
correct: All present and c. 4:18
do the perfectly c. thing 239:8
corridors: contrived c. / And issues 107:21
C. of Power 249:15
corriger: *c. le monde* 187:3
corroborative: Merely c. detail 123:3
corrupt: appointment by the c. few 240:1
moth and rust doth c. 35:25
Power tends to c. 1:3
Corruption: C., the most infallible symptom 121:20
corse: As his c. to the rampart 291:1
Cortez: like stout C. 155:22
cosmopolitan: c. in the end 188:10
cost: not to count the c. 170:3
Costly: C. thy habit 226:10

cracker-barrel: mirth of c. men 23:24
crackling: c. of thorns under a pot 32:9
cradle: Between the c. and the grave 105:5
bough breaks the c. will fall 194:15
c. endlessly rocking 284:14
c., / Shalt never be my dungeon 241:20
rocks the c....rules the world 278:1
cradled: c. into poetry by wrong 242:18
craft: c. so long to lerne 74:14
Crafticant: Written by C. 153:14
craftiness: cunning c. 39:17
Crafty: C. men contemn Studies 15:14
crainte: *c. suit la crime* 277:4
crammed: Earth's c. with heaven 49:15
crape: saint in c. is twice 205:19
Cras: *C. amet qui nunquam amavit* 5:6
crawl: c. along it till we die 282:17
slimy things did c. 81:8
crazier: World is c. 174:4
cream: choking her with c. 158:16
queen of curds and c. 237:36
create: must himself c. the taste 294:25
my business is to C. 42:13
created: all men are c. equal 166:10
C. sick, commanded 128:6
God c. the heaven and the earth 25:11
Man has c. death 296:9
men are c. free 166:7
Nothing can be c. from nothing 170:8
world was c. on 22nd October 273:2
Creation: consulted me...upon C. 3:13
c....of the non-absolute 82:21
greatest week...since the c. 193:9
love C.'s final law 263:17
opposition / To the facts of c. 118:24
To which the whole c. moves 263:23
creations: acts his own c. 51:18
creator: [Disraeli]...worships his c. 46:20
for the glory of the C. 13:16
Remember now thy C. 32:15
creature: c.'s at his dirty work 204:32
Not a c. was stirring 188:5
creatures: All c. great and small 3:9
all c. here below 157:15
credideritis: *Nisi c.* 11:26
credit: an't much c. in that 95:1
some c. in being jolly 95:2
Creditors: C. have better memories 117:25
creditum: *ab omnibus c.* 275:5
credulities: miseries or c. of mankind 85:8
creed: church c. which he professes 68:1
c. of slaves 202:8
got the better of his c. 254:7
make himself a c. 103:22
shrieked against his c. 263:17
creeds: dust of c. outworn 243:17
our casual c. 9:25
so many c. 285:20
strewn with c. 16:13
Vain are the thousand c. 47:14
creep: ambition can c. as well as soar 54:5
C. into thy narrow bed 9:17
make your flesh c. 95:34
Creeps: C. in this petty pace 232:28
crème: c. de la crème 250:23
crept: c. silently to Rest 114:18
crew: admit me of thy c. 182:13
cribb'd: c., confin'd, bound in 232:12
cricket: [c.] more than a game 141:15
c. on the hearth 182:5
cried: c. all the way to the bank 165:18
when he c. the little children died 11:4
crime: c.; it is a mistake 116:23
c....desire for aesthetic expression 280:23
c. of being a young man 202:3
c. so shameful as poverty 112:26
c. to love too well 204:20
Fear follows c. 277:4
featureless and commonplace a c. 101:7
Lady, were no c. 177:19
Napoleon of c. 101:12
old Custom, legal C. 242:7
punishment fit the c. 122:29
united by c. 277:2
worse than a c. 45:10
crimes: c., follies, and misfortunes 121:18
C., like virtues 113:5
liberty! what c. are committed 215:9
tableau of c. and misfortunes 276:18
tissue of c., follies 125:2
worst of c. is poverty 239:14
criminal: c. class I am of it 91:17
No child is born a c. 249:2
crimson-dyed: Albion's sins are c. 42:19
cripple: Comfort's a c. 102:2
Crispian: feast of C. 229:1
Crispin: upon Saint C.'s Day 229:4
criterion: c. of goodness 58:15
critic: attribute of a good c. 169:22
C. and whippersnapper 49:25
[c.] louse in the locks 265:18
good c. is one who recounts 117:5
Jonson knew the c.'s part 83:11
not too inquiring c. 142:20
critical: nothing if not c. 234:32
that word again — c. 95:20
criticism: cant of c. is the most 254:12
c.; a disinterested endeavour 10:10
c. is applied only 144:21
father of English c. 146:22
People ask you for c. 178:25
criticisms: most penetrating of c. 142:22
most penetrating of c. 142:22
criticize: don't c. / What you can't understand 105:11
criticizing: c. takes away from us 160:20
critics: c. are? The men who have failed 97:22
C. like me shall make it Prose 204:15
lot of c. is to be remembered 188:11
therefore they turn c. 82:19
Turn'd C. next 205:27
Crocodile: cruel crafty C. 251:26
Cromwell: [C.] a brave bad man 79:6
C., damn'd to everlasting fame 206:27
C. guiltless of his country's 127:13
C. knocked about 167:10
crooked: c. shall be made straight 33:16
should I strive to set the c. 189:12
There was a c. man 195:20
cross: breast a bloody c. 251:23
survey the wondrous C. 280:19
to Thy C. I cling 270:1

cross-bow: With my c. / I shot 81:4
crosses: c., row on row 171:26
cross-gartered: see thee ever c. 237:21
crossing: while c. a river 166:12
crow: to hear him c. 106:15
crowd: c. flowed over London Bridge 108:14
crucified, the c. will always save 80:18
I hate the common c. 140:5
madding c.'s ignoble strife 127:18
Out of the c. a mistress 242:1
who in the midst of the c. 110:18
Will she pass in a c. 258:16
crowded: busy scenes of c. life 147:17
c. on a velvet cushion 268:28
One c. hour of glorious life 189:1
Crowdieknowe: men o' C. 172:5
Crowds: C. without company 121:12
Crown: C. Him with many crowns 46:11
c. is merely a hat that 118:2
C....the fountain of honour 15:28
fruition of an earthly c. 176:7
head that wears a c. 228:18
my verse is not a c. 135:10
Crown'd: C. and again discrown'd 146:8
hollows c. with summer sea 263:5
crowning: c. mercy 89:4
crowns: are c. to be broke 221:12
c. are empty things 92:5
c. resign to call thee mine 272:27
Crucible: America is God's C. 299:13
Crucified: C. 'twixt a smile and whimper 243:12
crucify: c. mankind upon a cross 52:19
cruel: 'For c. 'tis,' 154:14
C. he looks, but calm 243:13
c., not unnatural 227:11
c., only to be kind 227:16
love is more c. than lust 260:7
more c. the pen is 59:2
speeches / That comfort c. men 76:12
cruellest: c. month, breeding / Lilacs 108:12
cruelty: Fear is the parent of c. 118:22
full / Of direst c. 231:26
cruise: all on our last c. 256:20
little oil in a c. 28:13
crumb: craved no c. 123:25
crumbs: picker up of learning's c. 50:21
Crusoe: Robin C.? Where are you 92:6
crust: water and a c. 154:16
cry: c. goes up, 'How long?' 257:4
heard my c. 29:27
infant's c. of fear 43:25
make 'em c. 213:11
Need a body c. 55:22
no language but a c. 263:16
too old to c. 166:19
crying: no use c. over spilt milk 178:27
one c. in the wilderness 35:10
We came c. hither 231:2
Crystal: Ring out ye C. spheres 183:2
cuccu: Lhude sing c. 7:4
cuckold: whore and a c. 237:3
Cuckoo: C., jug-jug 191:3
c.! Shall I call thee bird 294:21
c. shouts all day 140:24
c.: O word of fear 231:16
merry c., messenger of Spring 251:11
rainbow and a c.'s song 91:11
what did they produce? The c. clock 281:27
Cui: *C. bono* 78:28
culpa: *felix c.* 186:9
Mea c. 178:16
cult: c. of cheeriness 196:22
local c. called Christianity 130:3
Cultivate: C. simplicity, Coleridge 161:17
cultivated: land is c. entirely 180:22
cultiver: *c. notre jardin* 276:13
Culture: C....best which has been thought 10:3
great aim of c. 10:5
hear anyone talk of C. 124:9
ladies who pursue C. 283:14
men of c. are the true apostles 10:6
Cultures: Two C. 249:16
cunctando: *c. restituit rem* 112:2
cunningly: little world made c. 99:21
Cup: Ah, fill the C. 114:20
Come, fill the C. 114:14
let this c. pass 36:36
Life's enchanted c. 61:19
my c. runneth over 29:20
cupboard: c. was bare 195:6
Cupid: C. and my Campaspe 170:20
wing'd C. painted blind 233:35
cupiditas: *Radix malorum est c.* 74:3
cups: c., / That cheer but not inebriate 88:10
Curate: compassion in the very name of a C. 248:7
sit upon the c.'s knee 76:11
curates: preached to death by wild c. 248:23
curd: mere white c. of ass's milk 205:7
curds: Eating her c. and whey 194:26
queen of c. and cream 237:36
cure: c. it but the scratching 169:13
kings can cause or c. 125:23
labour against our own c. 49:9
no c. for birth and death 220:12
curfew: c. tolls the knell 127:9
Curiosa: *C. felicitas* 201:15
curiosities: c. would be quite forgot 11:1
curiosity: Disinterested intellectual c. 270:9
curious: c. habits of man 208:21
c. incident of the dog 101:21
Tammie glowr'd, amaz'd, and c. 57:18
Curiouser: C. and curiouser 69:4
curl: had a little c. 195:21
currency: Debasing the moral c. 107:3
current: hoarded, / But must be c. 182:1
currite: *c., noctis equi* 175:10
curs: common cry of c. 225:26
c. of low degree 125:14
curse: bless them that c. 35:20
C. God, and die 28:34
c. Him on His throne 48:2
c. is come upon me 263:31
c. of the drinking classes 288:23
c. the darkness 255:7
I know how to c. 236:16
Curses: C. are like young chickens 250:11
C., not loud but deep 232:26
c. which the Furies breathe 176:9
curst: c. be he that moves my bones 238:23
curtain: Draw the c. 212:14

Iron C. has descended 78:10
curteisie: honour, fredom and c. 73:3
Curtsied: C. when you have 236:17
cushion: c. and soft Dean invite 205:17
Custards: C. for supper 242:22
custodiet: *quis c. ipsos / Custodes* 152:13
Custom: C....guide of human life 142:1
c. is no argument 130:9
c. loathesome to the eye 144:13
c. of one wife and hardly any 219:17
c. stale / Her infinite variety 224:26
C., that unwritten law 90:22
c. / More honoured 226:13
good c. should corrupt 263:2
old C., legal Crime 242:7
What c. hath endeared 16:16
Without the aid of...c. 131:17
customer: c. is always right 223:19
customers: raising up a people of c. 247:9
Cut: C. is the branch 175:14
most unkindest c. of all 230:6
cutting: c. all the pictures out 22:23
Cutty-sark: Weel done, C. 57:19
cycle: c. of the ages begins 275:28
Europe than a c. of Cathay 264:7
cycle-clips: c. in awkward reverence 163:8
cymbal: tinkling c. 39:7
cynic: c....knows the price 287:18
Cynicism: C. is intellectual dandyism 179:28
cypress: sad c. let me be laid 237:19
Czar: God or the C. look 288:8
D: big, big D. 122:16
Daddy: D., daddy, you bastard 202:16
Daffodil: D. bulbs instead of balls 108:20
daffodils: Fair d., we weep 135:23
host of golden d. 291:21
daft: thinks the tither d. 222:22
dagger: d. which I see 231:35
daggers: speak d. to her but use 227:11
daily: d. beauty in his life 235:2
Daily Mail: sandwich-men of the *D.* 76:19
dairy: nothing like a d. 107:1
daisies: must lie upon the d. 123:8
dalliance: silken d. in the wardrobe 228:28
dam: pretty chickens and their d. 232:20
damaged: Archangel a little d. 161:21
Dame: belle D. sans Merci 153:13
dance in the old d. yet 176:14
dammed: saved by being d. 138:13
Damn: D. braces 43:13
d.' fool if they weren't 267:12
d. the consequences 181:21
d. those authors 77:8
doesn't give a d. 6:25
I don't give a d. 119:13
like a parson's d. 130:10
praises one another d. 295:14
damnation: would be no d. 270:2
damn'd: d. be him that first cries 232:32
Faustus must be d. 175:10
foremost shall be d. to fame 204:10
damned: Better be d. than mentioned not 201:26
call me a d. nigger 176:18
D. from here to Eternity 159:5
d. if I see how the helican 180:1
d. in a fair wife 234:23
d. nice thing 282:5
must be d. perpetually 175:9
one d. thing after another 141:10
Out, d. spot 232:21
public be d. 273:14
Publish and be d. 282:9
damp: d. souls of housemaids 108:2
damsel: d. with a dulcimer 82:6
Dan: D. even to Beer-sheba 27:23
Danaos: *timeo D.* 275:12
dance: best d. e'er cam to the Land 56:4
could d. more skilfully 219:23
d. has begun 25:5
d. in the old dame yet 176:14
d. I wish you / A wave 237:35
dancer from the d. 295:20
easiest who have learn'd to d. 206:2
fallen was in loves d. 144:10
maids d. in a ring 191:3
will you join the d. 69:23
danced: d. by the light 164:12
David d. before the Lord 28:6
he d. his did 89:11
star d., and under that 234:16
dancer: know the d. from the dance 295:20
dancers: All men are d. 297:5
dances: all the modern d. 107:9
d. with the daffodils 291:22
getting nowhere; it d. 166:3
No sober man d. 78:29
dancing: d. days are gone 298:3
D....of savage origin 55:8
d. on a volcano 220:4
manners of a d. master 148:2
dandy: Candy / Is d. 190:23
dandyism: Cynicism is intellectual d. 179:28
danger: bright face of d. 255:23
conquer without d. 85:19
d. past, both are alike 151:5
life there is d. 111:21
Pleased with the d. 102:15
so much as to be out of d. 143:12
this nettle, d. 227:37
dangerous: bad, and d. to know 161:1
D. Dan McGrew 224:8
d. to meet it alone 283:14
Into the d. world 43:27
such men are d. 229:22
dangerously: Live d. 192:26
dangers: d. and diseases of the old 99:17
Daniel: D. come to judgement 233:22
Danny: hangin' D. Deever 158:27
danse: *ne marche pas, il d.* 166:3
dansons: *d. sur un volcan* 220:4
dappled: for d. things 138:27
dare: 'I d. not' wait upon 231:32
d. call it treason 130:16
d. do all that may 231:33
d. to be poor 121:1
d. to eat a peach 108:1
I d. say she will do 47:20
Love that d. not speak 101:1
dared: I have d. and done 49:22
dares: Who d. do more is none 231:33
wretch that d. not die 57:6
Darien: upon a peak in D. 155:22

daring: d. fellow is the jewel 260:22
d. is to know how far 80:14
d. young man 165:17
No crime's so great as d. 77:9
stole with subtle d. 23:12
dark: Climb to our proper d. 298:2
colours...agree in the d. 14:7
D. Continent 252:24
fear to go in the d. 14:4
fell of d., not day 138:25
go home in the d. 133:21
great leap in the d. 136:24
leap into the d. 48:17
O d., dark, dark 185:11
one stride comes the d. 81:9
darkeneth: this that d. counsel 29:8
darker: Do not let us speak of d. days 78:4
sky grows d. yet 76:6
darkest: d. just before the day 119:11
Darkling: D. I listen 155:5
on a d. plain 9:8
darkness: candle than curse the d. 255:7
cast away the works of d. 209:24
d. comprehended it not 37:37
d. deepens 170:22
d. falls at Thy behest 109:6
d. was upon the face of the deep 25:11
encounter d. as a bride 232:37
life as it closes / Is d. 260:7
Lighten our d. 209:19
lump bred up in d. 160:14
pass'd the door of D. through 114:22
people that walked in d. 33:3
prince of d. is a gentleman 230:34
rather d. visible 183:12
rear of d. thin 182:14
Universal D. buries All 204:19
world to d. and to me 127:9
darling: Charlie he's my d. 55:21
Charlie is my d. 137:7
D. of the Gods 177:18
darlings: wealthy curled d. 234:26
data: theorize before one has d. 101:15
date: keep them up to d. 239:6
dates: several d. of the tombs 2:12
daughter: d. of a fair mother 139:29
Don't put your d. 86:19
King of Spain's d. 194:16
landlord's d. 193:22
Marrying off your d. 219:3
O my d. 233:12
daughters: O ye d. of Jerusalem 32:19
your d. shall prophesy 34:20
dauntless: so d. in war 222:8
dauphin: daylight's d. 139:2
lichter nor a d. 45:14
David: D. danced before the Lord 28:6
D. his ten thousands 27:35
Davy: Humphrey D. / Abominated gravy 24:14
dawn: d. comes up like thunder 159:22
d., with silver-sandalled feet 286:23
passionate as the d. 296:17
Rosy-fingered d. 137:25
dawneth: darkest... before the day d. 119:11
day: best d. in the year 111:17
better d., the worse deed 133:16
d. is a miniature eternity 110:23
d. is for honest men 112:15
each d. is like a year 286:5
Every d., in every way 86:5
every dog has his d. 45:6
fell of dark, not d. 138:25
I consider that great d. 2:12
I have lost a d. 269:15
long weary d. have end 251:20
love but one d. 67:11
Not a minute on the d. 85:12
rave at close of d. 266:22
spent one whole d. well 157:13
Sufficient unto the d. 36:1
what a d. may bring 31:37
Without all hope of d. 185:11
dayesye: 'd.', or elles the 'ye of day' 74:13
daylight: man any good, d. 119:5
naked and open d. 13:29
We burn d. 233:27
days: As thy d., so 27:9
childish d., that were as long 294:20
come perfect d. 169:23
d. darken round me 263:1
d. may be long 26:34
d. of our glory 64:9
d. of wine and roses 101:6
For d. and days and days 181:16
lov'd / Three whole d. together 257:16
not dark d.; these are great 78:4
sad Rose of all my d. 298:6
Ten D. that Shook 213:15
Thirty d. hath November 126:12
daysyes: Swiche as men callen d. 74:11
day-to-day: in d. work, was certainty 66:21
dazzle: mine eyes d. 281:13
de'il: d.'s awa' wi' th'Exciseman 56:4
dead: an' I war d. 17:22
be a fool than to be d. 256:23
besides, the wench is d. 175:28
better than a d. lion 32:11
bugles over the rich D. 47:21
By the incurious d. 93:13
character d. at every word 245:10
cold, pure, and very d. 165:14
contend for Homer D. 6:26
converse with the mighty d. 268:9
D.! and...never called 291:12
d. art / Of poetry 208:15
d. bury their dead 36:8
d. can be forgiven 296:10
d. ere his prime 182:20
D. for a ducat 227:13
d. selves to higher things 263:7
d. we owe nothing but truth 277:1
Death lies d. 260:10
Down among the d. men 105:4
Either he's d. or my watch 177:25
frightful when one's d. 205:22
good Indian is a d. Indian 244:24
happy d. 263:14
happy until he is d. 249:21
hatred will be d. 141:17
I am d. and opened 178:8
If Lucy should be d. 294:15
long run...we are all d. 157:24
Mistah Kurtz — he d. 85:4
never know that he is d. 60:17
not d. — but gone before 214:26
not doubt is d. faith 272:23
number of the d. 91:1
one d. deathless hour 217:2
on his face, d., with a bullet 266:12
quick and the d. 209:14

saw a d. man win a fight 17:5
sea gave up the d. 41:3
sea shall give up her d. 210:22
she has been d. many times 199:14
simplify me when I'm d. 101:3
talk with the departed d. 242:16
There are no d. 174:7
when you're d. 135:18
you remind me of the d. 220:23
deadborn: fell *d. from the press* 142:3
deadly: more d. than the male 159:3
Dead Sea: D. fruits, that tempt 188:23
D.'s shore, / All ashes 61:30
deaf: Hear Him, ye d. 283:1
deal: new d. for the American people 215:14
square d. afterwards 216:7
dealer: d. in magic and spells 123:21
Dean: cushion and soft D. invite 205:17
dear: bread should be so d. 138:11
not need is d. at a farthing 70:26
Yes — oh d., yes — the novel 116:21
dearer: d. than his horse 264:3
dearth: inhuman d. / Of noble natures 153:16
death: abolish the d. penalty 152:25
afraid of d., as ashamed 49:6
angel of d. has been abroad 46:18
Any man's *d.* diminishes *me* 98:28
back resounded D. 184:9
Be absolute for d. 232:36
Birth and copulation and d. 108:11
Brought D. into the World 183:7
build your ship of d. 163:15
but D. who comes 222:7
come away, d. 237:19
competition, the laws of d. 218:13
cry'd out D. 184:9
Dear, beauteous d. 273:18
D. — / He kindly stopped 96:21
d. after life, does greatly please 252:1
D. and life were not 298:10
D., as the Psalmist saith 228:20
D. be not proud 99:24
d., but conquers agony 62:3
D. cometh soon or late 171:5
d. complete the same 52:2
D. does not surprise 116:1
D. goes dogging 133:8
d. had undone so many 108:14
D. has a thousand doors 178:24
d. hath ten thousand several doors 281:12
D. in the front 61:16
d. in the pot 28:20
D. is not the worst 250:1
d. is slumber 243:3
d. is the cure of all diseases 49:9
D. is the privilege 217:24
D. is the veil 243:24
d. itself be a farewell 19:2
d. I was to dee 18:6
D. lays his icy hand 245:17
d. lie heavily 224:5
D. lies dead 260:10
D....like a mole 135:4
D. must be distinguished from dying 248:30
d. of his saints 31:1
d. reveals the eminent 240:13
d. shall be no more 99:25
d. shall have no dominion 266:21
d., the destroyer of worlds 25:10
D. therefore is nothing 170:11
d. they were not divided 28:3
d. to the bone 296:9
D. tramples it to fragments 241:17
D., where is thy sting-a-ling-a-ling 6:14
d., where is thy sting 39:12
D.: the last best friend 250:10
eloquent, just and mighty D. 213:1
enemy is but D. 48:10
enormously improved by d. 219:10
envy of the devil came d. 34:30
except d. and taxes 117:29
Fear d.? — to feel the fog 51:29
fed on the fullness of d. 260:14
first d., there is no other 267:3
glad of another d. 107:27
half in love with easeful D. 155:5
have not hope of d. 90:3
immortal d. 170:12
in love with d., to think 241:7
kingly D. / Keeps his pale court 241:9
kiss of d. 247:12
last enemy...is d. 39:10
liberty, or give me d. 133:23
love thee better after d. 49:20
matter of life and d. 238:25
Men fear D. as children 14:4
million-murdering D. 216:21
my d. was an exaggeration 272:13
never taste of d. but once 229:29
new terrors of d. 8:6
not born for d. 155:6
opportune timing of your d. 261:7
Pale D., with impartial foot 139:25
parting...image of d. 106:25
perchance of D., / But certainly 268:12
possessed by d. 108:20
ranks of d. you'll find 188:21
remembered kisses after d. 264:24
rendezvous with D. 223:9
Revenge triumphs over D. 14:5
room / Do we take up in d. 245:20
sat on him was D. 40:37
shades of D. 184:8
stories of the d. of kings 235:19
swallow up d. in victory 33:11
swoon to d. 155:17
thick shapes of human d. 243:14
This fell sergeant, d. 227:28
This is d., / To die 169:25
Those by d. are few 145:11
till d. us do part 210:14
up the line to d. 220:20
valley of the shadow of d. 29:20
wages of sin is d. 38:35
way to dusty d. 232:28
we are in d. 210:20
What should it know of d. 294:22
with this life, this d. 296:23
wonderful is D. 241:24
death-bed: d. repentance 12:1
death-bill: d. must be passed off-hand 65:1
deathless: one dead d. hour 217:2
progress of a d. soul 100:7
deaths: More d. than one 286:3
Debasing: D. the moral currency 107:3
debonaire: kaught is d. 74:19
debt: life we are in d. 190:5
National D. is a very Good 224:1
paid the d. of nature 112:21
remember to pay the d. 249:19
Women hate a d. 51:3

pestilence, good Lord, d. us 191:4
deluding: deer, d. Woman 56:13
vain, d. joys 182:2
déluge: *Après nous le d.* 203:23
delusion: but under some d. 55:1
d. and a snare 85:10
demagogues: as d. and not as writers 23:18
demented: d. with the mania of owning 284:22
democracies: d. against despots — suspicion 92:24
democracy: cycle d. is built on 289:9
D....government by the uneducated 77:4
d. in order to have a revolution 76:27
D. passes into despotism 202:27
D. substitutes election by the incompetent 240:1
[d.] whole is equal to the scum 210:24
fear and hope from [d.'s] progress 269:17
five hundred years of d. 281:27
great arsenal of d. 215:20
made safe for d. 290:11
our d....most aristocratic 171:15
sought the image of d. 269:17
democratic: half a century of d. advance 289:19
Democritus: D. would laugh 139:22
demon: Convention is the dwarfish d. 61:4
demon-lover: wailing for her d. 82:4
demonstrandum: *Quod erat d.* 112:12
denied: Emma d. none of it aloud 12:11
denies: spirit that forever d. 124:12
Denmark: rotten in the state of D. 226:15
dentist: For physical pleasure...go to my d. 280:26
deny: d., or delay, right or justice 174:9
D. yourself 124:13
Room to d. ourselves 157:6
Depart: D., I say, and let us have done 89:6
I am ready to d. 162:2
servant d. in peace 37:15
servant d. in peace 277:21
To d. is to die 129:13
departed: glory is d. 52:17
Lord was d. from him 27:21
departing: God be...at my d. 5:17
depended: always d. on the kindness 289:10
dependent: d. on what happens 106:18
depends: d. a good deal on where 69:9
d. on what you mean by 146:5
d. upon the taste 96:8
so much d. / upon 289:15
depravity: stupidity than of d. 148:22
depression: it's a d. when you lose 271:4
deprived: d. of everlasting bliss 175:4
depth: But far beyond my d. 229:14
d., and not the tumult 292:9
depths: Out of the d. I have cried 277:18
derangement: nice d. of epitaphs 245:3
descended: desirable to be well d. 203:12
descensus: *Facilis d. Averni* 275:18
descent: claims of long d. 263:24
description: beggar'd all d. 224:25
d. of what has never occurred 286:9
saves a d. of the rising 244:26
descriptions: describe with his d. 12:16
desert: beyond High-Park's a d. 112:10
D. and reward...seldom keep company 214:11
d. shall rejoice 33:13
make straight in the d. 33:16
man after his d. 226:33
waste its sweetness on the d. 127:17
wide d. where no life 138:12
Deserting: D. these, thou leavest 244:18
deserts: his d. are small 188:4
deserve: success in war, but only d. it 78:12
we'll d. it 1:11
wicked to d. such pain 50:10
deserved: d. my enemies 285:7
deserves: government it d. 174:10
insulted, d. to be 85:21
desiccated: d. calculating machine 25:9
design: Acting without d. 162:17
his vast D. unfold 177:16
palpable d. upon us 156:20
design'd: d. yon lordling's slave 57:8
desire: courage equal to d. 297:6
d. is boundless 237:4
d. should so many years outlive 228:17
d. that outruns the delight 260:6
lineaments of gratified d. 43:3
my arrows of d. 42:27
no beauty that we should d. 33:24
not to get your heart's d. 239:29
to fill my heart's d. 23:8
what I've tasted of d. 118:10
Which of us has his d. 266:15
desired: More to be d. are they 29:23
desires: braver who overcomes his d. 8:19
doing what one d. 180:20
equal to the soul's d. 292:5
fondly flatter our d. 102:4
lopping off our d. 259:13
nurse unacted d. 43:14
desist: d. from the experiment 161:6
desk: Is but a d. to write upon 59:24
desolation: create d., and call it peace 261:6
despair: by d. / Upon Impossibility 177:4
D., law, chance, hath slain 99:23
endure my own d. 279:2
heaven in hell's d. 43:21
never hoped can never d. 238:29
No need to d. 139:27
none should d. 12:1
owner whereof was Giant D. 53:18
some divine d. 264:23
very life in our d. 61:21
within d. of getting out 187:20
ye Mighty, and d. 243:10
despairer: Too quick d. 10:1
desperandum: *Nil d.* 139:27
desperate: diseases require d. remedies 113:10
wisdom not to do d. things 268:25
desperation: lives of quiet d. 268:23
despicit: *Qui omnes d.* 2:26
despise: d. / This wrecched world 74:26
I d. Shakespeare 239:5
know them best, d. them most 57:13

pity his ignorance and d. him 95:14
some other Englishman d. him 240:22
despised: d. and rejected of men 33:24
d. as well as served it 60:12
despiseth: Who d. all, displeaseth 2:26
Despond: slough was D. 53:15
despondency: in the end d. and madness 293:14
despondently: Sprouting d. at area gates 108:2
despotism: crushes individuality is d. 180:16
Democracy passes into d. 202:27
d. tempered by epigrams 68:6
despots: democracies against d. — suspicion 92:24
Destiny: belief in a brute Fate or D. 111:9
Character is d. 193:18
d.. And it is white 112:22
D. with Men for Pieces plays 114:23
destroy: whom God wishes to d. 112:16
destroyed: once d., can never be supplied 125:4
very ruins have been d. 170:6
destroyer: death, the d. of worlds 25:10
D. and preserver; hear 243:7
destruction: All other things, to their d. 98:23
D. in the rear 61:16
D. with destruction to destroy 184:33
Pride goeth before d. 31:28
destructive: In the d. element immerse 85:6
detail: corroborative d., intended 123:3
frittered away by d. 268:27
detecting: d. what I think a cheat 148:29
determined: d. to prove a villain 235:25
detest: but they d. at leisure 63:15
d. that animal called man 259:20
detrimenti: *Caveant consules...res publici d.* 5:1
deus: *puto d. fio* 274:14
deviates: never d. into sense 103:18
device: banner with the strange d. 168:6
Devil: And the D. did grin 81:24
apology for the d. 60:5
A walking the D. is gone 81:23
children of the d. 265:2
D. always builds a chapel 92:1
d. a monk he'd be 190:2
d. can cite Scripture 233:7
d. damn thee black 232:24
d. howling 'Ho 252:21
d. is dead 213:10
d. should have all the good tunes 136:6
d.'s leavings 259:12
d. turned precisian 178:22
D. with Devil damn'd 184:6
do the d.'s work for nothing 113:27
each our own d. 286:22
envy of the d. came death 34:30
Frenchman as you hate the d. 191:14
how the D. they got there 205:2
man is but a d. weakly 256:2
renounce the d. and all his works 70:18
Resist the d. 40:22
who cleft the D.'s foot 100:14
world, the flesh and the d. 209:21
Your adversary the d. 40:27
devilish: most d. when respectable 49:14
Tough, and d. sly 94:11
Devils: at liberty when of D. 42:22
become d. in life 10:18
poor d. are dying 201:18
devoir: *Faites votre d. et laissez* 85:22
Devotion: D.! daughter of astronomy 299:5
d. throughout our land 144:6
d. to something afar 244:12
devour: d. each of her children 274:8
seeking whom he may d. 40:27
devourers: so great d., and so wild 189:4
devouring: cormorant d. Time 231:10
dew: d. on the mountain 221:18
d. will rust them 234:25
resolve itself into a d. 226:4
dewdrop: d. on its perilous way 155:10
deyntee: No d. morsel passed 74:7
diable: *d. est mort* 213:10
dialect: purify the d. of the tribe 107:18
diamond: Better a d. with a flaw 84:17
d. in the sky 261:23
d....lasts forever 168:26
D.! thou little knowest 192:14
rough than of polished d. 75:19
set with sixty d. minutes 174:18
Diana: burnt the Temple of D. 48:26
diapason: loud d. after dinner 19:14
diary: never travel without my d. 287:7
dice: never believe that God plays d. 106:11
dickens: cannot tell what the d. 233:30
Dicky-bird: D., why do you sit 123:5
dictatorship: d. of the proletariat 178:6
dictionary: but a walking d. 72:12
did: But he d. for them both 220:24
ever d. a wise one 214:19
die: advance or d. 61:27
and gladly d. 255:20
as natural to d. 14:6
bad d. late 91:19
being born, to d. 15:26
believes he shall ever d. 131:16
believe they d. to vex me 179:5
can't d., along the coast 94:7
Curse God, and d. 28:34
Death, thou shalt d. 99:25
depart is to d. a little 129:13
d....an awfully big adventure 20:7
d., and go we know not where 232:38
D. because a woman's fair 290:19
d. before they sing 81:26
d. beyond my means 288:25
d. for one's country 140:8
d. here in a rage 259:21
d. in a tavern 8:10
d. in earnest 7:23
d. in the last ditch 289:6
d. is cast 65:10
D., my dear Doctor 198:16
d. on your feet 143:18
d. young is our doom 19:5
do anything but d. 161:12
Ere their story d. 130:7
for to-morrow we shall d. 33:10
frogs do not d. in sport 41:17
I d. / As often as from thee 100:1
If I should d. 48:12
I shall d. an American 281:7

just as lucky to d. 284:20
know that he is going to d. 60:17
Let me d. eating ortolans 97:26
let us do or d. 66:3
Lives to d. another day 141:2
love one another or d. 11:14
not altogether d. 140:13
not d. when the trees 79:2
not so difficult to d. 64:2
should d. before I wake 6:13
someday d., which is not so 163:26
taught us how to d. 269:14
Their's but to do and d. 262:14
those about to d. salute thee 257:20
time to d. 32:7
To d. and know it 169:25
To d.: to sleep 226:37
we d. in earnest 212:23
We shall d. alone 199:9
who would wish to d. 45:3
you asked this man to d. 11:3
died: Bewildered them till they d. 296:15
d. the little children cried 189:20
dog it was that d. 125:15
he d. in a good old age 28:25
I had d. for thee 28:9
liked it not, and d. 295:1
Men have d. from time 225:19
millions d. — that Caesar 66:10
should have d. hereafter 232:28
when love for you d. 48:8
diem: *Carpe d.* 139:28
d. perdidi 269:15
dies: artist d. with me 191:15
d. to himself unknown 224:5
Every moment d. a man 265:16
gods love d. young 179:12
kingdom where nobody d. 181:2
king never d. 41:24
not necessarily true because a man d. 288:27
One d. but once 186:15
Who d. if England live 159:4
young person who...d. 12:7
diet: Praise is the best d. 248:26
diete: d. was accordant to hir cote 74:7
dieted: not be d. with praise 154:28
Dieu: *D. est mort* 191:16
D. et mon droit 214:8
Si D. n'existait pas 276:16
Verbe, c'est D. 141:16
differ: all things d., all agree 207:26
difference: grave, and, oh, / The d. 293:18
differences: no social d. — till women 282:18
different: something d. from either 108:13
differently: do things d. there 131:2
difficult: d.; and left untried 77:2
D. do you call it 150:2
D. things take a long time 5:8
it is d. to speak 55:2
not so d. to die 64:2
difficulties: In grave d. 167:9
Little local d. 174:2
Ten thousand d. do not make 192:2
Diffidence: wife, and her name was D. 53:19
Diffugere: *D. nives* 140:15
dig: d. the dust enclosèd 238:23
digest: d. it in company 75:23
learn and inwardly d. them 209:25
digestion: d. is the great secret of life 248:11
good d. wait upon appetite 232:13
prove in d. sour 235:10
dight: richly d. 182:10
dignitate: *Otium cum d.* 78:21
dignity: d. of thinking beings 146:18
joyless d. to starve 249:12
Leisure with d. 78:21
maintained the d. of history 44:15
Dignum: *D. laude virum* 140:16
Digressions: D., incontestably, are the sunshine 254:10
diligently: God as d. as I have served 291:11
dim: d. religious light 182:10
diminished: Hide their d. heads 184:11
diminishes: death d. me 98:28
dimittis: *Nunc d.* 277:21
din: Cock with lively d. 182:14
dine: d. at journey's end 298:7
gang and d. the day 18:16
going to d. with some men 24:15
I shall d. late 162:6
jury-men may d. 207:19
Ding: D., dong, bell 194:7
dining-room: d. will be well lighted 162:6
dinner: good d. and feasting reconciles 201:5
good d. enough 148:8
heard our fame before d. 64:20
pleased when he has a good d. 150:3
They would ask him to d. 68:26
want d. do not ring 16:10
we may make our d. sweet 18:16
dinner-bell: tocsin of the soul — the d. 63:5
Diogenes: D. struck the father 59:8
I would be D. 3:7
tub was large enough for D. 83:23
diplomacy: d. shall proceed always frankly 290:13
diplomat: d....nothing but a head-waiter 273:4
dire: *ennuyer est...de tout d.* 277:5
direct: all going d. the other way 96:18
direction: chance, d. which thou canst not see 206:17
directions: indirections find d. 226:23
rode madly off in all d. 163:25
direful: something d. in the sound 12:10
dirge: By forms unseen their d. 83:10
dirt: do d. on it 163:20
Huddled in d. 214:21
painted child of d. 205:8
dirty: at his d. work again 204:32
d. songs and dreary 48:11
Dis: *D. aliter visum* 275:14
disagree: men only d. / Of Creatures rational 184:6
disagreeable: Matrimony...always d. 12:4
things d. to myself 248:8
disagreeables: all d. evaporate 156:3
disappointed: he shall never be d. 207:30
disappointing: As for d. them 125:20
disapprove: d. of what you say 277:12
disapproves: condemns whatever he d. 55:13

disasters: guilty of our d. the sun 230:21
disbelief: d. in great men 68:4
willing suspension of d. 82:15
disc: round d. of fire 44:1
discharge: no d. in the war 158:23
discipline: order and military d. 5:5
vain all Doric d. 298:11
wife...a kind of D. 14:14
discommendeth: d. others obliquely commendeth 48:20
disconsolate: bereaved — the d. 191:17
discontent: d. / Made glorious summer 235:23
divine d. 158:10
discontented: bald and d. 64:15
make a hundred men d. 169:2
discord: d., harmony not understood 206:17
hark what d. follows 237:1
Harmony in d. 139:19
discords: dire effects from civil d. 1:14
discors: *Concordia d.* 139:19
discount: life / At a d. 118:26
discourse: child...provision for d. 13:7
d. than see a play 59:6
discoverers: ill d. that think 13:19
discoveries: d. made in this Voyage 85:14
discovery: d. of a new dish 46:23
discretion: Philosophy is nothing but d. 223:17
discretioun: In taking suld d. be 105:2
discriminate: Not to d. every moment 199:17
discrown'd: Crown'd, and again d. 146:8
disdain: little d. is not amiss 84:32
more love or more d. 67:5
disdained: feeling too falsely d. 244:11
disease: Confront d. at its first stage 201:11
Consciousness is a d. 272:24
d. is incurable 228:16
d. of modern life 9:26
this long d., my life 205:1
diseased: minister to a mind d. 232:27
diseases: death is the cure of all d. 49:9
d. require desperate remedies 113:10
disenchanting: so d. as attainment 256:6
disgrace: d. and ignominy of our natures 49:6
d. with Fortune 238:5
public and merited d. 257:2
disgruntled: if not actually d. 290:25
disguise: naked is the best d. 84:21
words only to d. 276:14
disguised: d. by sobriety 93:3
dish: dainty d., / To set before 195:15
d. fit for the gods 229:27
d. ran away with the spoon 194:11
makes a d. a feast 135:16
new d. does more for the happiness 46:23
Disiecti: *D. membra poetae* 140:17
disinheriting: damned d. countenance 245:12
Disinterested: D. intellectual curiosity 270:9
dislike: I, too d. it 188:12
like and d. the same 219:22
people whom we personally d. 286:27
disliked: get ourselves rather d. 208:24
dislikings: of likings and d. 161:5
Dismal: [Economics] The D. Science 68:10
With d. stories 53:26
dismayed: neither be thou d. 27:11
dismiss: d. it with frigid tranquillity 146:10
d. us with thy blessing 53:4
disobedience: By one man's d. lost 185:2
Of Man's First D. 183:7
disobey: Naughty girl to d. 195:4
disorder: sweet d. in the dress 135:24
displeaseth: despiseth all, d. all 2:26
displicet: *omnibus d.* 2:26
disposes: God d. 157:11
disposition: antic d. 226:21
dispraised: d., is the most perfect praise 150:16
dispute: humanity will one day d. 116:24
Scholars d. 139:6
disputed: Facts...downa be d. 56:6
Disraeli: [D.]...worships his creator 46:20
disreputable: telling the d. truth 23:24
disrespectfully: speak d. of Society 287:12
dissatisfied: Not one is d. 284:22
dissect: murder to d. 294:18
dissemble: right to d. your love 41:8
Women d. their Passions 253:2
dissent: protestantism...a sort of d. 54:25
dissidence: d. of dissent 54:25
dissimilar: For one another, though d. 241:27
dissipation: d. without pleasure 121:12
dissociation: d. of sensibility 108:22
dissolve: d., and quite forget 155:1
distance: d. lends enchantment to the view 66:8
distant: d. countrie I was born 17:17
distempered: questions the d. part 107:16
distinct: composed of two d. races 161:9
distinction: few escape that d. 272:10
distinctly: speaks all his words d. 114:10
distinguish: d. us from the other animals 21:7
d. what is worth reading 270:10
distinguished: best and d. above 138:1
d. thing 145:3
distressed: Art thou sore d. 191:5
distressful: most d. country 7:1
distribution: except it be in d. 15:8
same d. of the necessities 247:6
distrusting: heart d. asks 125:10
ditch: blind man's d. 296:11
die in the last d. 289:6
great d. from all the world 89:8
shall fall into the d. 36:20
diurnal: in earth's d. course 293:21
Diuturnity: D. is a dream 48:27
diver: Don't forget the d. 153:3
divide: absurd to d. people into good 287:15
D. and rule, a sound motto 124:18
join the regions they d. 207:29
divided: cease to be d. 166:6

doom: burden o' his people's d. 172:18
crack of d. 232:18
regardless of their d. 127:22
Doomsday: every day is D. 111:17
Doon: braes o' bonny D. 58:10
door: flies swiftly in through one d. 21:24
Get up and bar the d. 17:13
I stand at the d. 40:35
knock at the d. 161:10
out by the same D. 114:19
doorkeeper: rather be a d. 30:8
doors: d. of perception 43:15
d. to let out life 178:24
ten thousand several d. 281:12
ye everlasting d. 29:25
dormons: *veillants d.* 187:19
dotage: streams of d. flow 147:20
dots: those damned d. 77:19
double: deep peace of the d. bed 65:24
D., double, toil and trouble 232:15
double-bed: this d. of a world 119:4
Doublethink: D. means the power of holding 197:1
doubt: calls all in d. 99:15
difficulties do not make one d. 192:2
d. diversified by faith 50:2
D. everything at least once 166:2
d., to prove that faith exists 50:5
explain a thing till all men d. it 204:4
Frets d. the maw-crammed beast 51:32
in d. have a man...with a gun 72:8
mair I am in d. 104:26
more faith in honest d. 263:19
No possible d. whatever 122:7
not d. is dead faith 272:23
overcompensates a secret d. 143:2
resolution lies by d. 212:2
speak out and remove all d. 166:18
sunnier side of d. 262:5
troubled with religious d. 76:11
When in d., tell the truth 272:6
When in d., win 141:9
doubted: And heard Troy d. 63:3
Never d. clouds would break 52:13
Doubting-Castle: castle, called D. 53:18
doubts: end in d. 13:15
Greek, that breed / D. 251:16
Douglas: doughty D. 17:4
like D. die 137:22
dove: gently as any sucking d. 234:2
wings like a d. 30:2
doves: d. in immemorial elms 264:27
harmless as d. 36:11
down: at night a bed of d. 295:3
D. among the dead men 105:4
d. need fear no fall 53:24
d. to the seas again 178:11
for my coming d. 189:5
You must never go d. 181:18
downhearted: Are we d. 4:24
We are not d. 71:24
downhill: d. path is easy 216:22
downstairs: you kick me d. 41:8
downwards: look no way but d. 53:22
doxy: another man's d. 279:11
drag: don't d. it about 'To midnight 278:17
Why d. in Velasquez 283:23
drain-pipe: in a blessed d. 282:17
Drake: D. he's in his hammock 191:19
Drama: D. is life with the dull bits 136:11
d.'s laws the drama's patrons 147:7
dramatist: d. only wants more liberties 144:22
Dramatize: D., dramatize 145:2
Drang: *Sturm und D.* 153:1
drap: d. by drap / On the a'e nerve 172:14
drappie: d. in our e'e 58:8
draught: d. of vintage 154:34
such a d. of woe 241:13
draw: can ye d. but twenty miles 176:12
d. more than a hundred 141:6
D. near with faith 210:8
drawbacks: everything has its d. 145:20
drawers: d. of water 27:12
drawing-rooms: taste for d. has spoiled 22:4
dread: image of a nameless d. 268:18
I may d. / The grave 157:14
dreadful: d. is the check 47:15
Mighty and d., for thou art not 99:24
dreadfully: [Brigham Young] is d. married 279:15
Dreadnoughts: two D.; and dukes are 167:15
dream: behold it was a d. 53:21
beyond the shadow of a d. 153:18
but an empty d. 168:13
deep d. of peace 142:8
dream'd a dreary d. 17:5
d. that I am home 115:6
d. / Dies at the opening day 280:16
glory and the d. 292:22
if I d. I have you 99:5
If you can d. 159:12
I have a d. 158:5
imagination...compared to Adam's d. 156:9
Life...is not a d. 47:11
life to a d. 187:19
love's young d. 188:20
not d. them, all day 158:8
old men shall d. dreams 34:20
picture a beautiful, romantic d. 55:7
proved all things a d. 295:21
salesman is got to d. 181:5
say what d. it was 234:11
To sleep: perchance to d. 226:37
vision, or a waking d. 155:7
With the first d. 180:4
wrecks of a dissolving d. 242:11
dreamed: d. that life was Beauty 138:16
dreamer: d. of dreams 27:7
D. of dreams 189:12
poet and the d. 153:34
this d. cometh 26:9
dreams: angels in some brighter d. 273:19
based upon the d. of spinsters 218:18
d. under your feet 296:20
d., wherewith they weave 153:32
less than nothing, and d. 161:3
Real are the d. of Gods 154:15
stuff / As d. are made on 236:24
Than this world d. of 263:3
tread on my d. 296:20
dreamt: d. of in your philosophy 226:20
I d. that I dwelt 53:12
dreary: My life is d. 264:11
Dreary-mouthed: D., gaping wretches 142:11
dress: d. is so fit for his use 110:2

Einstein: Let E. be 252:21
Eisen: *Blut und E.* 41:23
elected: audacity of e. persons 284:16
not serve if e. 245:16
election: e. by the incompetent many 240:1
only during the e. 217:17
right of e. is the very essence 152:3
electric: e. tidings came 13:13
touch was as e. poison 242:2
electronic: new e. interdependence 173:18
Elegance: Folly link with E. 297:9
elegancies: wanted not only the e. 146:15
elegant: e. sufficiency 268:6
It's so e. / So intelligent 108:16
with e. quickness 247:1
Elementary: E.,' said he 101:11
elements: e. / So mix'd in him 230:12
framed us of four e. 176:6
elephant: e. by the hind leg 166:14
Th'unwieldy E. 184:17
elephants: women and e. never forget 219:16
elevates: e. above the vulgar herd 119:15
eleven: second e. sort of chap 20:2
Elfland: horns of E. faintly blowing 264:22
Elginbrodde: Here lie I, Martin E. 173:3
eliminated: e. the impossible 101:19
Elizabeth: perfidious Succubus was that Queen E. 58:16
scandal about Queen E. 244:25
elliptical: e. billiard balls 123:1
elocution: public demands e. rather than reason 199:3
eloquence: e. is that which gets 167:17
Prends l'é. 274:9
silence hath more e. 271:9
Take e. and wring its neck 274:9
eloquent: bite secretly at the e. 8:3
e., just and mighty Death 213:1
pure and e. blood 100:13
silence may be e. 84:27
your banquet that is e. 176:28
else: happening to someone e. 215:5
elsewhere: world e. 225:27
Elysium: *Tochter aus E.* 220:27
emancipate: e. or relieve, you hesitate 65:1
embarrassment: e. of riches 3:17
e. on being left alone together 160:18
embrace: none I think do there e. 177:22
time to e. 32:7
whether I e. your lordship's 289:5
embroideries: Covered with e. 296:5
eminent: death reveals the e. 240:13
emolument: positions of considerable e. 119:15
emotion: e. recollected in tranquillity 294:24
escape from e. 108:23
emotions: e. from A to B 198:22
kill the e. and so live 19:5
waste-paper basket of the e. 281:3
emperor: e. and clown 155:6
E. has nothing on 4:10
e. of ice-cream 254:25
E. or nothing 45:2
emphasis: e. of passionate love 162:4
Empire: all the loungers of the E. 101:22
Britain has lost an E. 1:2
e. is no more than power 102:18
found a great e. 247:9
How is the E. 121:7
liquidation of the British E. 78:8
Westward the course of e. 24:18
empires: earth's proud e. 109:7
e. of the mind 78:9
faiths and e. gleam 242:11
Hatching vain E. 184:4
Vaster than e., and more slow 177:20
employed: innocently e. than in getting 149:1
employment: man who gives me e. 121:9
pleasure of an e. 13:8
wealthy man / To give e. 23:9
emptiness: little e. of love 48:11
smiles his e. betray 205:9
empty: crowns are e. things 92:5
e. stomach is not a good political 106:3
enchantment: lends e. to the view 66:8
enchantress: tune the e. plays 140:23
encourage: to e. the others 276:12
encourager: *pour e. les autres* 276:12
encumbers: e. him with help 148:1
Encyclopaedia: whole E. behind the rest 161:8
end: all will e., knows God 122:2
an e. of ane old song 196:12
beginning of the e. 261:11
come to the e.: then stop 69:25
consider the e. 116:5
difficult as...the e. 63:2
e. in certainties 13:15
e. of all our exploring 107:19
e. of life is...Action 143:14
e. of the beginning 78:7
e., where I begun 100:24
get at one e. they lose 149:8
God be at my e. 5:17
In my beginning is my e. 107:15
lead you to the e. of the world 68:20
Man's chief e. is to glorify God 70:16
many books there is no e. 49:11
take account of the e. 6:21
there's an e. on't 148:19
waiting for the e. 111:24
world will e. in fire 118:10
world without e. 209:10
Yes, to the very e. 216:30
endearing: all those e. young charms 188:17
ended: good e. happily 287:6
endow: Die, and e. a College 205:13
ends: best e. by the best means 142:15
e. and the beginnings 100:26
Everything e. in songs 21:9
endure: better to e. it 147:22
e. my own despair 279:2
e. / Their going hence 231:5
from age to age e. 157:21
in thyn hous e., / Wel lenger 74:2
teach us to e. it 125:27
Youth's a stuff will not e. 237:17
endured: much is to be e. 147:10
enemies: choice of his e. 287:23
deserved my e. 285:7
from the hands of Thy e. 214:9
he smote his e. 30:6

judge me by the e. 215:21
Love your e. 35:20
Love your e. 37:18
make my e. ridiculous 277:10
one of my most intimate e. 217:1
overcomes his desires...than...e. 8:19
ten jokes...an hundred e. 254:5
enemy: best is the e. of the good 276:15
effect...on the e., but 282:10
e. in their mouths 234:34
e. you killed, my friend 198:1
gall and wormwood to an e. 61:22
He hasn't an e. 288:24
How goes the e. 213:20
last e. that shall be destroyed 39:10
Man is not the e. of Man 198:9
old e. the gout 138:8
O mine e. 28:17
see / No e. / But winter 225:9
spoils of the e. 174:23
sweet e., France 246:2
two points nearer the e. 21:4
with the wrong e. 45:18
worst friend and e. 48:10
energy: e. divine 207:3
E. is Eternal Delight 42:21
eneuch: has e. that is content 105:1
enfants: *ces voix d'e.* 274:12
Les e. terribles 120:13
engagement: owing to a subsequent e. 288:20
engenders: e. there / The broken wall 296:27
engendred: Of which vertu e. is the flour 73:1
engine: e. that moves 130:15
two-handed e. at the door 182:30
Wit's an unruly e. 134:25
engineer: e. is nobody 111:14
sometimes the e. 134:25
Engines: E. more keen than ever 177:8
England: always be an E. 199:1
arm of E. will protect 198:14
Bible made E. 141:22
bred in E., I can dare 121:1
concerts in E. you will find 239:28
dress and manners in E. 241:2
E. and Saint George 228:32
E. bore, shaped, made aware 48:13
E....comfortable time-lag of fifty 282:24
E. expects 191:11
E. has saved herself by 202:9
E....hast been my cradle 241:20
E. hath need of thee 294:11
E., home and beauty 46:1
E. is a nation of shopkeepers 190:16
E. is a paradise for women 59:9
E. is merely an island of beef 174:19
E. is not all the world 178:7
E. is the paradise of women 115:16
[E.] it is considered good to kill 276:12
E....mother of Parliaments 46:19
E....resembles a family 196:21
E.'s greatest son 264:20
E.'s green and pleasant 42:28
E.'s mountains green 42:25
E.'s on the anvil 158:18
E.'s roast beef 113:20
E. to itself do rest but true 230:18
E. was merry England 222:9
E., we love thee better 270:8
E. will have her neck wrung 78:5
E., with all thy faults 88:5
gentlemen in E. now a-bed 229:4
in E. a particular bashfulness 2:7
in E. hath a life to live 212:21
In E., justice is open 5:26
in favour of E. because you 239:9
King born of all E. 174:15
Liberty was born in E. 276:20
lost the last of E. 23:16
Men of E., wherefore plough 244:3
Nor, E.! did I know 292:8
not suffer E. to be the workshop 97:30
Oh, to be in E. 50:33
old E.'s winding sheet 42:5
only E. know 159:2
people of E. that never 76:16
perfidious E. 45:9
ride / Into E., to drive 17:4
road that leads him to E. 148:6
Rulen all E. under an Hog 83:4
Scotland...a worse E. 149:20
Slaves cannot breathe in E. 88:4
sleep in old E.'s heart 281:2
Speak for E. 4:4
That is for ever E. 48:12
That knuckle-end of E. 248:18
this realm, this E. 235:15
Who dies if E. live 159:4
Ye Mariners of E. 66:13
English: among the E. Poets 156:18
bones would not rest in an E. grave 64:26
breathing E. air 48:13
Choose me, you E. words 267:17
disasters of E. history 280:22
E....act with the barbarity 248:6
E. are busy 188:1
E. are mentioned in the Bible 272:2
E. Cats are the best 247:2
[E.] conquered...half the world 223:10
E. enjoy themselves sadly 257:22
E....least...philosophers 16:4
E....little...inferior to the Scotch 193:13
E. lord should lightly me 17:20
E. make it their abode 278:8
E....no respect for their language 240:22
E. people imagine themselves 217:17
E. public never forgives 288:19
E....rather a foul-mouthed 131:22
E. tongue a gallimaufry 252:12
E. winter — ending in July 63:16
E. women conceal their feelings 288:11
happy E. child 261:22
if he went among the E. 20:11
rolling E. road 76:13
Roman-Saxon-Danish-Norman E. 92:2
shed one E. tear 171:3
under an E. heaven 48:14
well of E. undefiled 252:4
Englishman: E. added the shirt 110:1
E. never enjoys himself except 134:17
E. as ever coveted 158:14
E. is to belong to 190:19
E. will give his mind 238:26
E. thinks he is moral 239:26
E. in the wrong 240:18
E. to open his mouth 240:22
E. does not travel to see Englishmen 253:17
E., even in his loves 277:3
in Europe, and not one E. 278:23
Jesus will not do...for E. 42:8
last great E. 264:19

ordinary young E. 10:7
remains an E. 122:17
rights of an E. 152:1
stirred the heart of every E. 221:11
vain, ill-natur'd thing, an E. 92:3
weet an E. to the skin 213:4
Englishmen: characteristic virtue of E. 261:20
E. act better than Frenchmen 24:2
proper drink of E. 45:5
we will be, / Honest E. 158:9
engulf: e. him in the mire 147:15
enigma: mystery inside an e. 77:22
enjoy: after that to e. it 247:16
better to e. life 147:22
don't have to go out and e. 247:23
English e. themselves sadly 257:22
e. it while I can 249:9
impossible to e. idling 145:16
not bring us to e. life 125:27
one commandment, 'E. thyself' 299:12
save to e. the interval 220:12
to e. him forever 70:16
enjoy'd: all times I have e. 265:8
To have e. the sun 9:9
warm and still to be e. 154:23
enjoyed: little to be e. 147:10
enjoyment: capacity for innocent e. 123:13
chief e. of riches 247:8
Was it done with e. 218:9
enjoys: Englishman never e. himself 134:17
enmities: More substance in our e. 297:4
ennuie: *On s'e. presque toujours* 163:3
Enoch: E. walked with God 25:24
enough: best is good e. 124:17
doesn't go far e. 95:15
never know what is e. 43:9
enoynt: face, as he hadde been e. 73:6
enrich'd: on every side e. 175:24
ensample: noble e. to his sheep 73:14
enslave: but impossible to e. 48:15
enslaved: e. by another Man's 42:13
pleasures without being e. 66:20
entangle: e. themselves with indissoluble 147:12
Entbehren: *E. sollst Du* 124:13
enterprise: e. is sick 236:35
entertain: forgetful to e. strangers 40:18
entertainment: knee...not an e. 129:10
enthusiasm: forgives — youth, power, and e. 288:19
entirely: not e. beautiful 297:13
entrance: exit being an e. somewhere else 257:5
envious: rent the e. Casca made 230:5
environed: e. with a great ditch 89:8
envy: e. not him whom they name 68:22
e. of brilliant men 22:11
e. of the devil came death 34:30
e., or resentment led, / They damn 77:8
E. would kill / Pleasure 244:6
mutual e. of the living 136:23
épater: *é. le bourgeois* 20:25
épée: *coups d'é.* 90:21
epic-poem: comic e. in prose 113:24
épiderme: *attaché qu'à la simple é.* 186:19
Epigram: E.? a dwarfish whole 81:25
epigrams: tempered by e. 68:6
épingle: *coups d'é.* 90:21
epitaphs: nice derangement of e. 245:3
of worms and e. 235:18
epitome: all mankind's e. 102:20
epoch: blame an e.; one congratulates 80:17
e....of life in multiplicity 4:6
Eppur: *E. si muove* 119:18
equal: all men are created e. 7:17
all men are created e. 166:10
America...e. to...that commerce 54:21
compel us to be e. upstairs 20:1
created free and e. 166:7
e. division of unequal 109:9
men are e. is a proposition 142:25
sees with e. eye as God 206:11
some animals are more e. than 196:20
equal'd: e. the most High 183:10
equality: e. in the servants' hall 20:1
Liberty! E.! Brotherhood 6:5
true apostles of e. 10:6
equally: all e. wise — equally foolish 106:10
equi: *noctis e.* 175:10
equivocate: I will not e. 120:5
Eremite: patient, sleepless E. 155:16
err: Better to e. with Pope 63:24
cautious seldom e. 83:27
e. as grossly as the few 102:23
e. in company with Abraham Lincoln 216:9
mortal, and may e. 245:19
prefer / to e. / with her 7:26
To e. is human 206:4
wise may e. 2:18
erred: have e. exceedingly 28:1
If I have e. 216:9
We have e. 209:8
error: all the hosts of e. 52:20
e., and upon me proved 238:20
e. is immense 44:16
inherent power denied to e. 180:14
errs: man aspires, he e. 124:11
Esau: E. my brother is a hairy 26:3
E. selleth his birthright 5:11
escalier: *esprit de l'e.* 97:5
escape: e. from emotion 108:23
few e. that distinction 272:10
no guilty man e. 126:19
escaped: out of battle I e. / Down 197:24
escapes: defying it that the brave e. 277:7
ese: hit dyde her e. 72:25
esprit: *e. de l'escalier* 97:5
essence: fellowship with e. 153:17
Establishment: ideals is not the E. 23:19
estate: e. without a man 1:21
fourth e. of the realm 171:12
relief of man's e. 13:16
esteemed: If I e. you less 244:6
Etat: *L'E. c'est moi* 169:1
etchings: I'll bring the e. down 269:11
eternal: e. in the human breast 206:12
e. triangle 7:9
e. vigilance 89:19
know that we are e. 252:14
pairt o' an e. mood 172:13
with th'E. to be deem'd / Equal 183:29
eternity: As doth e. 154:25
Damned from here to E. 159:5
day is a miniature e. 110:23
E. in an Hour 41:28

E. is in love 43:11
ha'e heard E. drip water 172:14
I saw E. the other night 274:2
liberty...worth a whole e. 1:12
Lovers' hours be full e. 100:1
Silence is deep as E. 67:18
small parenthesis in e. 48:21
Some shadows of e. 273:25
thoughts that wander through E. 184:1
types and symbols of E. 293:9
white radiance of E. 241:17
eternize: e., / And in the heavens write 251:15
etherized: e. upon a table 107:28
ethics: e., compounded of misanthropy 171:22
E. must be a condition 290:24
Ethiopian: E. change his skin 34:5
etiquette: e. prevents me from doing 248:8
Eton: playing fields of E. 282:2
Etrurian: E. shades / High overarch'd 183:17
Eureka: *E.* 8:9
Europe: fifty years of E. than 264:7
glory of E. is extinguished 54:7
make peace in E. possible 23:22
out all over E. 128:7
part of the community of E. 219:18
poor are the blacks of E. 72:5
regard the history of E. 125:2
save E. by her example 202:9
slain this year in E. 278:23
sneezes, E. catches cold 180:2
spectre is haunting E. 177:28
Eurydices: thou gane, my luve E. 133:24
evadere: *e. ad auras* 275:18
evaporate: all disagreeables e. 156:3
Eve: and E. span 7:25
close at the ear of E. 184:20
pensive E., to soothe thine ear 83:8
When E. upon the first of Men 138:10
even: At e., when the sun 272:18
evening: e. is spread out against 107:28
It is a beauteous e. 293:27
eventide: fast falls the e. 170:22
events: stride on before the e. 81:19
unimportance of e. 107:10
ever: I go on for e. 262:10
think that we build for e. 218:10
would you live for e. 118:3
everlasting: caught / An e. cold 281:23
damn'd to e. fame 206:27
e. No 68:18
first, last, e. day 98:23
perish, but have e. life 38:1
truly to know is e. life 210:3
underneath are the e. arms 27:10
way to the e. bonfire 232:6
evermore: I am alive for e. 40:32
name liveth for e. 35:5
ever-rolling: Time, like an e. stream 280:16
every: e. cry of every man 43:25
E. day, in every way 86:5
e. day is the best day 111:17
e. man against every man 136:19
everybody: Always suspect e. 95:21
didn't know that e. was gazing 96:9
says what e. is thinking 216:14
everyday: e. affair life is 160:21
familiar merely with the e. 100:26
Everyman: E., I will go 5:13
everyone: stop e. from doing 134:12
everything: against e. all the time 157:18
boring is to say e. 277:5
don't take e. away 249:23
E....happens as it should 12:2
e. that he wants and nothing 141:14
e. about something 143:16
E. has been said 160:19
e. in its place 247:5
e. that is the case 290:22
Time brings e. 202:20
everywhere: e. he is in chains 217:16
Out of the e. into here 173:2
evidence: e. of things not seen 40:14
Some circumstantial e. is very strong 268:31
evil: All government is e. 197:7
book is like a great e. 65:16
Every law is an e. 24:9
e. and on the good 35:21
E. be thou my Good 184:15
e. on the ground of expediency 216:1
e., that good may come 38:33
e. that men do lives 230:1
Government...a necessary e. 198:6
him who e. thinks 5:19
is the e. thereof 36:1
necessary for the triumph of e. 55:6
open and notorious e. liver 210:4
partial e., universal good 206:17
preserve thee from all e. 31:5
punishment in itself is e. 24:10
Religion...lead to...e. 170:7
root of all e. 40:7
them that call e. good 32:30
evils: business is the choice of e. 24:9
greatest of e....is poverty 239:14
make imaginary e. 125:17
exact: greatness not to be e. 54:17
exactly: e. in the right places 60:21
I do not think so, e. 79:16
exaggerated: e. stress on not changing 178:26
exaggeration: my death was an e. 272:13
exalted: Every valley shall be e. 33:16
exalts: what man does which e. him 52:10
Examinations: E. are formidable 83:17
In e. the foolish ask 288:2
examined: have his head e. 126:7
examining: e. his wives' mouths 218:17
example: e., as it is my theme 92:25
e. / To a' Thy flock 56:19
set us a good e. 287:1
exceedest: thou e. the fame 28:26
excel: as daring to e. 77:9
rather e. others in the knowledge 3:8
excellence: e. in the manufacture of little cakes 116:24
excellent: it would be an e. idea 119:20
knowledge of what is e. 3:8
situation e.. I shall attack 115:17
Excels: dunce...sent to roam / E. 87:26
Excelsior: strange device, / E. 168:6
except: always e. the present company 196:15
exceptionally: I do it e. well 202:17
excess: e. of it, that, surfeiting 237:11

fine e., and not by singularity 156:21
moderation even in e. 97:25
Nothing succeeds like e. 288:18
road of e. leads 43:10
exchange: just e. one for the other 245:24
Excise: *E.* A hateful tax 146:11
Exciseman: de'il's awa wi' th'E. 56:4
exciting: *films.* They are too e. 24:22
found it less e. 122:6
excludeth: that he e. Love 134:20
exclusive: most e. club there is 190:19
exclusively: they are e. in the right 142:26
excrement: place of e. 296:8
excuses: e. for what we want to think 173:13
execute: and a hand to e. 121:21
execution: e. confined 237:4
executioner: Revenge proves its own e. 116:14
executive: nominated by the e. 121:17
Exegi: *E. monumentum* 140:12
exercise: every faculty...strengthens by e. 47:4
mind what e. is to the body 253:7
exhalations: swim like e. 68:2
exhaled: e. in a pun 161:23
exhaust: e. the boundaries of possibility 201:25
exhibits: that which he e. 152:26
exile: e. / Hath emptied Heav'n 183:23
therefore I die in e. 128:3
exiles: Paradise of e., Italy 242:17
exist: act as if He did e. 272:26
If God did not e. 276:16
still e., but you have ceased 272:3
existence: e., and a name 161:3
Let us contemplate e. 95:4
struggle for e. 90:19
woman's whole e. 62:22
exists: life...e. for its own sake 284:4
exit: every e. being an entrance 257:5
E., pursued by a bear 237:29
exits: e. and their entrances 225:13
men to take their e. 281:12
expect: folly to e. men to do 283:16
expectation: folly of e. 48:27
expected: no reasonable man could have e. 134:18
expects: England e. every man 191:11
man who e. nothing 207:30
expediency: evil on the ground of e. 216:1
expellas: *Naturam e. furca* 139:17
expenditure: annual e. nineteen 94:2
expense: e. damnable 76:3
expensive: love fruit when it's e. 201:28
experience: Believe one who knows by e. 275:23
E. though noon auctoritee 73:29
E. is the child of Thought 97:27
e. of women which extends 101:17
E. keeps a dear school 117:15
E., the name men give 288:9
knowledge...beyond his e. 167:21
Travel...is a part of E. 14:23
triumph of hope over e. 148:23
worth a life's e. 137:18
experiment: desist from the e. 161:6
expert: e....has made all the mistakes 44:10
e....knows more and more 59:14
Experto: *E. credite* 275:23
expiate: have something to e. 163:16
expires: wretched child e. 23:4
explain: e. a thing till all men doubt 204:4
Never complain, never e. 98:9
way to e. it is to do it 69:6
would e. his explanation 62:14
explanation: inaccuracy...saves tons of e. 219:9
would explain his e. 62:14
explanations: I do loathe e. 20:3
exploration: shall not cease from e. 107:19
exposed: intellect is improperly e. 248:15
express'd: ne'er so well e. 205:29
expresses: Art never e. anything 286:17
expression: not the e. of personality 108:23
exquisitely: touch, how e. fine 206:16
exterminate: science to e. the human 200:8
extinction: e. of all privileged classes 85:16
extinguished: glory of Europe is e. 54:7
Nature is...seldom e. 15:9
extra: *Salus e. ecclesiam* 11:24
extraordinary: behaving in this e. manner 257:6
extravagant: something strange and e. 110:3
extreme: For e. illnesses 136:10
Extremes: aye be whaur / E. meet 172:8
e. appear like man and wife 77:16
Extremism: E. in the defence of liberty 126:1
exuberance: e. of his own verbosity 98:8
eye: beaming in one e., and calculation 95:3
Cast a cold e. 298:14
E. for eye 26:26
far as human e. could see 264:4
flash upon that inward e. 291:22
great e. of heaven shined 251:24
harvest of a quiet e. 293:5
He had but one e. 95:11
If thine e. offend thee 36:24
less in this than meets the e. 19:7
neither e. to see 165:2
with his keener e. 177:15
With my little e. 196:4
eye-ball: We're e. to eye-ball 218:3
Eyeless: E. in Gaza 185:9
eyelids: tir'd e. upon tir'd eyes 264:8
eyes: big brown e. and that tiny mind 269:8
Black E., red Lips 177:8
cold commemorative e. 217:4
e. more bright / Than stars 103:7
e., no eyes 160:13
e. to the blind 29:7
Fortune and men's e. 238:5
Have e. to wonder 238:17
looks through his eager e. 189:14
Love in her sunny E. 86:20
Love looks not with the e. 233:35
Mine e. have seen 141:5
My mistress' e. are nothing 238:22

night has a thousand e. 45:12
only with thine e. 150:27
proud of those two e. 135:26
right in his own e. 27:22
see the whites of their e. 211:24
things not seen with e. 189:8
upon her peerless e. 154:30
will lift up mine e. 31:4
women's e. this doctrine 231:11
fable: life's sweet f. ends 88:25
fables: f. that have been agreed upon 276:19
Old wives' f. 40:5
face: Beauty of f. is a frail 186:19
blubber'd is that pretty f. 210:25
bright f. of danger 255:23
construction in the f. 231:24
everybody's f. but their own 258:8
f. is my fortune 196:3
f. it with a sneer 216:3
f. made up 88:27
f. that launch'd a thousand 175:7
features / Of the same f. 293:9
garden in her f. 66:17
in the f. of this congregation 210:11
Look on her f. 207:16
Lord make his f. shine 27:3
not recognize me by my f. 270:12
one to f. the world with 51:16
own f. in the glass 287:21
plummet-measured f. 298:2
proper f. to scan 167:12
She has a lovely f. 263:32
transmitter of a foolish f. 220:26
your honest sonsie f. 57:22
faces: apparition of these f. 208:20
grind the f. of the poor 32:28
know the f. I shall see 217:3
old familiar f. 161:15
public f. in private 11:12
sighin', cantin', grace-proud f. 58:3
facility: fatal f. of the octo-syllabic 62:7
painstaking f. 201:15
facit: *f. indignatio versum* 152:9
fact: any irritable reaching after f. 156:4
find the historical f. 108:3
Here or nowhere is the whole f. 111:22
hypothesis by an ugly f. 143:10
judges of f., tho' not 211:12
Faction: grow up there / From F. 183:28
Facts: F. are chiels that winna ding 56:6
f. are sacred 221:8
F. do not cease to exist 143:1
imagination for his f. 245:13
more important than the f. 295:8
Now, what I want is, F. 94:21
report the f. 215:8
Teach...nothing but F. 94:21
fade: cheek that doth not f. 153:36
die away, / And f. 292:24
F. far away 155:1
faded: lovely companions / Are f. 188:22
Olympus' f. hierarchy 155:8
faery: f. lands forlorn 155:6
faiblesse: *reste est f.* 274:23
fail: probability that we may f. 166:8
we'll not f. 231:34
failure: no success like f. 105:10
failures: has no conceivable f. 285:4
fain: f. of thee still 260:5
faint: Damn with f. praise 205:4
F., yet pursuing 27:17
With f. praises 295:14
fair: brave deserves the f. 102:24
days when I was f. 215:11
Die because a woman's f. 290:19
F. is foul 231:20
F. is too foul an epithet 176:8
F. stood the wind for France 102:5
false because she's f. 99:6
Fat, f. and forty 196:14
find how to make it f. 49:28
God doth admit the f. 134:20
Going to the f. 195:14
love, and she be f. 154:22
made to keep f. play 42:6
negroid, as now he is f. 163:13
never yet f. woman but 230:27
woman true, and f. 100:15
faire: f. felde ful of folke 162:14
Laissez f. 212:5
fairer: f. daughter of a fair mother 139:29
f. than the evening's air 175:8
F. than whitest snow 176:3
say f. than that, can I 123:19
say no f. than that 94:10
Fairest: F. Isle 103:15
thou f. among women 32:24
fairies: beginning of f. 20:5
believe in f. 20:8
f. at the bottom of our garden 119:12
f. left off dancing 223:15
fairness: Nocht is your f. bot 134:1
fairy: f. somewhere that falls down dead 20:6
loveliest f. in the world 158:15
fairy tale: there is an old f. 132:12
f. written by God's fingers 4:11
Fais: *F. ce que voudras* 212:13
faith: Bad f. 220:15
bloody F. the foulest birth 242:7
break f. with us who die 172:1
doubt, to prove that f. exists 50:5
f....could remove mountains 39:7
f. diversified by doubt 50:2
F....illogical belief 179:16
F. is the substance of things 40:14
F.'s defying 19:23
f. shines equal 47:13
f. unfaithful 262:22
F. which does not doubt 272:23
F. without works is dead 40:21
just shall live by f. 38:32
Kept f. with me 130:6
life is a profession of f. 4:7
Life without f. is an arid 86:8
Modes of F. let graceless zealots 206:22
more f. in honest doubt 263:19
not f., but mere Philosophy 49:4
not found so great f. 36:7
not the dying for a f. 266:1
savage f. works woe 91:8
Sea of F. / Was once 9:6
shake a man's f. in himself 238:31
staff of f. to walk upon 212:24
thou of little f. 36:19
With Carthaginian f. 220:2
faithful: better to be f. than famous 216:13
F. Achates 275:20
F. are the wounds 31:38
f. to thee, Cynara 101:5

good and f. servant 36:34
hold the f. mirror 167:12
Faithless: F. as the winds 223:8
Human on my f. arm 11:9
faiths: f., and both are gone 9:12
f. and empires gleam 242:11
Falcon: dapple-dawn-drawn F. 139:2
f. cannot hear the falconer 297:18
fall: Another thing to f. 232:33
by their f. lost communion with God 70:19
cliffs of f. / Frightful 138:26
decline and f. of the city 121:13
dividing we f. 97:3
down need fear no f. 53:24
f., and leave their little lives 207:28
f. into the hands 40:13
F. of some sort 82:21
f. upon the thorns 243:8
f. was destined to a barren strand 147:19
harder they f. 115:5
haughty spirit before a f. 31:28
it had a dying f. 237:12
Nowhere to f. but off 158:2
shall not f. on the ground 36:12
Things f. apart 297:18
We all f. down 195:12
yet fear I to f. 212:25
fall'n: f. into the sear 232:25
O how f. 183:13
Fallacy: Pathetic F. 218:5
fallen: f., that great city 41:2
How art thou f. 33:8
mighty f. 28:5
they are f. themselves 30:3
though f., great 61:10
falls: And when he f. 229:15
f. not hail, or rain 263:5
sober, / F. still with the leaf 115:13
when Rome f. — the World 62:6
false: Beware of f. prophets 36:5
f. because she's fair 99:6
Fortune and hir f. wheel 73:19
some f. impossible shore 9:32
falsehood: f. would be more miraculous 142:6
smallest foundation to f. 125:28
falsely: kept him f. true 262:22
falseness: f. in all our impressions 218:5
falser: his f. tongue, / That utter'd 99:7
fame: damn'd to f. 204:10
dreams of f. while woman 262:26
f....instinct of all great souls 54:18
F. is a food that dead 98:16
F. is at best an unperforming 207:12
F. is like a river 15:19
F. is love disguised 242:5
F. is no plant that grows 182:26
f. is not won by 90:8
f. is the last thing 261:10
F. is the spur 182:24
F., like a wayward girl 155:20
F., like water 65:14
f., that arises from the destruction 76:1
grant an honest F. 207:25
love and f. to nothingness 155:26
nor yet a fool to f. 204:33
only pleasure of f. 64:20
rage for f. attends both 201:26
trump of future f. 63:25
trust a good deal to common f. 110:25
fames: *Auri sacra f.* 275:15
familiar: mine own f. friend 29:28
old f. faces 161:15
families: best-regulated f. 94:6
but two f. in the world 71:19
happy f. resemble one another 269:19
Murder...run in f. 165:12
secrets in all f. 113:1
family: called a fine f. 12:18
educate a whole f. 173:10
f. happier for his presence 256:1
f. pride is something inconceivable 122:23
heard my f. called decent 200:6
large f., did more service 125:25
rather stuffy Victorian f. 196:21
famous: better to be faithful than f. 216:13
found myself f. 65:2
future everyone will be f. 279:20
praise f. men 35:3
fanatic: f....overcompensates 143:2
Fanaticism: F. consists in redoubling 220:8
fanatics: Art has its f. 141:20
F. have their dreams 153:32
fancies: proud, and full of f. 156:2
Then f. flee away 53:27
fancy: Ever let the f. roam 153:35
f. does you good 167:11
f. is the sails 156:5
f. lightly turns to thoughts of love 264:1
F....no other counters 82:14
not to f. what were fair 49:28
Shakespeare, f.'s child 182:17
taste and f. of the speller 96:8
where is f. bred 233:15
fantasies: fed the heart on f. 297:4
love...exchange of two f. 72:4
fantastic: Giddy f. Poets 100:9
light f. round 181:23
light f. toe 182:12
realm of the f. 100:26
fantastical: joys are but f. 99:5
Far: F. and few 164:8
f., far better thing 96:19
f. from me, let all profane 275:19
f. one can go too far 80:14
so f. as it goes 95:15
far-away: quarrel in a f. country 72:1
farce: f. is over 212:14
fare: value not your bill of f. 258:17
fare-weel: f., and then for ever 55:16
farewell: brother, hail and f. 71:9
F., a long farewell 229:13
f. mean, if not death 19:2
live, forever saying f. 214:14
farm: snug little f. the Earth 81:23
farmers: how fortunate are f. 276:5
farms: lass wi' the weel-stockit f. 56:15
farrow: sow that eats her f. 151:11
farther: f. off from heav'n 138:7
farthest: next way home's the f. 212:2
farthing: sparrows sold for a f. 36:12
farts: smell of their own f. 11:17
fascinates: it f. me. I can sit 145:19
fascination: grace, force, f. 285:6
war...have its f. 286:14
Fascist: Every woman adores a F. 202:15
fashion: faithful to thee...in my f. 101:5
f.'s brightest arts decoy 125:10
God's gentleman from F.'s 110:10
nothing else holds f. 237:10
remain men in shape and f. 10:18
Fashioned: F. so slenderly 138:3

fast: grew f. and furious 57:18
run at least twice as f. 69:30
Fasten: F. your seat belts 91:13
faster: Will you walk a little f. 69:22
fastest: f. who travels alone 160:3
fasting: lives upon hope will die f. 117:22
Fat: F., fair and forty 196:14
f. of others' works 58:22
f. of the land 26:12
in every f. man a thin one 85:2
Jack Sprat could eat no f. 194:19
men about me that are f. 229:22
O f. white woman 86:1
Who's your f. friend 52:18
fatal: first strange and f. interview 99:8
fatality: there is a f. in it 253:22
Fate: belief in a brute F. or Destiny 111:9
F. and character are the same 193:18
f. of this country depends 98:6
F., Time, Occasion 243:21
F., which God made 100:7
fears his f. too much 188:4
have conquer'd F. 9:20
master of my f. 133:7
over-rul'd by f. 175:18
trouncings at the hands of f. 246:12
when f. summons 103:16
fates: silly horrors o' oor f. 172:15
Father: about my F.'s business 37:16
Child is f. of the Man 292:19
Diogenes struck the f. when 59:8
f., Harry, to that thought 228:22
f. have I seen, / A sober 263:15
f. of English criticism 146:22
f. was so ignorant 272:17
F. which art in heaven 35:24
fathom five thy f. lies 236:18
folly without f. bred 182:2
gave her f. forty-one 6:6
God as his f. 89:20
Honour thy f. 26:34
In my F.'s house 38:12
It is the f. with his child 124:10
last see your f. 295:17
Lord and F. of mankind 285:12
man did split his f.'s middle 260:22
no longer have a f. 191:16
Throw bricks at your f. instead 22:16
wise f. that knows 233:10
wise son maketh a glad f. 31:22
fathers: ashes of his f. 171:5
f., provoke not 39:21
God of your f. 26:18
iniquity of the f. 26:29
our f. that begat us 35:3
sons your f. got 140:27
fathom: Full f. five thy father 236:18
many f. deep I am in love 225:20
fatigue: Thinking...the greatest f. 273:13
fatted: Bring hither the f. calf 37:29
fatter: valley sheep are f. 200:11
fatty: f. degeneration of his moral being 256:13
fatuity: f. of idiots 248:6
fault: all f. who hath no fault 262:21
f. and not the actor 232:34
f., dear Brutus 229:21
Faultless to a f. 52:7
great f. of our politicians 270:19
happy f. 186:9
Through my f. 178:16
Faultless: F. to a fault 52:7
faults: all thy f., I love 88:5
f. are such that one loves 125:16
f. they commit, the earth 212:4
never see such f. 230:9
no f., only sins 298:19
Not for thy f. but mine 62:2
Faustus: F. must be damn'd 175:10
faute: *c'est une f.* 116:23
crime, c'est une f. 45:10
fav'rite: f. has no friend 127:21
favour: to this f. she must come 227:22
Favours: F. to none 207:15
fear: Adonais is, why f. we to 241:16
arousing pity and f. 8:27
down need f. no fall 53:24
F. and Loathing in Las Vegas 268:1
F. follows crime 277:4
f. in a handful of dust 108:13
F. is an instructor 110:5
F. is the parent of cruelty 118:22
f. it would make me conservative 118:14
F. no more the heat 225:31
f. of little men 4:1
f. of the Lord 30:21
f. the Greeks even 275:12
hate whom they f. 112:3
have to f. is fear itself 215:15
I f. thee, ancient Mariner 81:10
Job f. God for naught 28:31
love casteth out f. 40:29
Men f. Death 14:4
one universal passion: f. 240:17
so long as they f. 1:1
soul that knew not f. 91:5
will not we f. 30:1
with f. and trembling 39:24
feared: f. above all gods 30:16
fearful: facing f. odds 171:5
f. thing to fall 40:13
frame thy f. symmetry 43:24
lovely and a f. thing 62:27
fears: f. may be liars 80:2
f. that I may cease 155:25
feast: called the f. of Crispian 229:1
great f. of learning 231:13
Liberty's a glorious f. 57:5
makes a dish a f. 135:16
feather: lying on a f. bed 90:8
Stuck a f. in his cap 19:6
feather'd: f. race with pinions skim 118:4
Feather-footed: F. through the plashy 280:24
feathers: owl, for all his f. 153:23
feats: What f. he did that day 229:2
Fed: F. with cold and usurous 43:22
Sheep look up, and are not f. 182:29
Federation: F. of the world 264:5
feeble: by f. sense, / But trust 87:22
f. God has stabb'd 120:14
feed: f. deep, deep 154:30
F. the brute 104:16
feel: tragedy to those that f. 278:19
feeling: f. the artist has experienced 269:23
f. too falsely disdained 244:11
man is as old as he's f. 83:7
feelings: confident of your own fine f. 266:14
f. till after they are married 288:11
highest and best f. 269:22
Opinion...determined by the f. 251:4

find: f. out what everyone is doing 134:12
f. their like agen 222:6
happiness she does not f. 147:21
I f. 201:23
not be able to f. my way 131:17
returns home to f. it 188:9
fine: except to bring in f. things 53:1
Grave's a f. and private 177:22
mighty f. fellows nowadays 257:1
Not to put too f. a point 93:21
particularly f., strike it out 148:28
finem: *respice f.* 6:21
finest: This was their f. hour 77:25
finger: Better a f. aff 213:5
f. into the print 38:17
Moving F. writes 114:25
fingernails: paring his f. 151:12
fingers: f. wandered idly 211:2
work of thy f. 29:15
finished: don't say yes until I've f. 299:14
f. my course 40:11
finita: *commedia é f.* 165:4
Finite: cannot quite bury under the F. 68:23
finned: giant f. cars 169:24
fire: awkward squad f. over me 58:19
chariot of f. 42:27
element of f. is quite put out 99:15
F. and fleet and candle-lighte 18:2
F. and people do in this agree 128:5
f. is dying in the grate 179:20
f. of life 162:2
f. until you see the whites 211:24
frighted with false f. 227:8
frying pan into the f. 265:28
Heap coals of f. 31:34
hold a f. in his hand 235:12
hold with those who favour f. 118:10
Lord was not in the f. 28:16
Luve is ane fervent f. 221:7
play with f. openly 215:12
wheel of f. 231:4
Years steal / F. from the mind 61:19
Your house is on f. 194:21
firebrand: Ye were as a f. 34:22
fired: f. another Troy 103:2
fire-folk: f. sitting in the air 139:1
firmament: f. sheweth his handiwork 29:22
spacious f. on high 2:8
streams in the f. 175:11
Firmness: Commodity, F., and Delight 295:4
f. in the right 166:13
f. makes my circle just 100:24
first: After the f. death 267:3
f. by whom the new 205:31
f. in beauty 154:9
f. in the hearts 164:16
f. shall be last 36:28
f. that ever burst 81:5
I f. adventure, follow me 129:8
loved not at f. sight 175:19
morning were the f. day 25:12
rather be f. in a village 65:9
which came f., the Greeks or 98:14
With the f. dream 180:4
first-rate: calling it a f. work 24:5
fish: f. out of the water 224:15
f. that *talks* 92:13
no f. ye're buying 222:14
no more land, say f. 48:7
weed instead of a f. 112:23
wives...f. from a private pond 219:4
fished: f. by obstinate isles 208:16
Fisher King: Shiva and the F. all chasing 190:7
Fishers: F. of men 35:16
Fishes: F., that tipple in the deep 169:6
how the f. live in the sea 235:8
fish-knives: Phone for the f. 25:2
fit: f. for the kingdom of God 37:19
only the F. survive 224:7
Why then I'll f. you 160:15
fits: periodical f. of morality 171:20
Strange f. of passion 294:14
Fittest: Survival of the F. 90:20
survival of the f. 251:2
five: at f. in the afternoon 120:1
F. minutes! Zounds 87:2
five-cent: good f. cigar 176:24
fixities: f. and definites 82:14
flag: hoist the black f. 179:13
one f., the Stars and Stripes 215:24
shall not f. or fail 77:24
spare your country's f. 285:8
flagons: Stay me with f. 32:20
flag-signal: dubious f. which may mean either 106:17
flambeaux: chestnut casts his f. 140:20
flame: sinking f. of hilarity 95:19
so in a shapeless f. 98:21
this hard, gemlike f. 199:16
Flamens: Here lie two F. 67:3
Flanders: armies we had in F. 254:8
In F. fields 171:26
flannelled: With the f. fools 159:13
Flask: F. of Wine 114:15
flat: Very f., Norfolk 86:12
flatten: His hide is sure to f. 'em 23:2
flatter: Too coy to f. 249:12
flattered: that loves to be f. 236:29
flatterer: worthy o' the f. 236:29
flattering: f. with delicacy 12:13
f. hopes 13:30
Lay not that f. unction 227:15
you think him worth f. 239:13
flatters: What really f. a man 239:13
flattery: [Britain]...club for mutual f. 81:27
f. lost on poet's ear 221:23
F. wearis ane furrit 104:22
sincerest form of f. 83:16
to tout for f. 83:6
Flaubert: His true Penelope was F. 208:16
flavour: f. of mild decay 137:16
flaw: beauty is itself a f. 109:13
Better a diamond with a f. 84:17
f. / In happiness 153:22
flayed: saw a woman f. 259:4
flea: f. in his ear 9:2
literature's performing f. 196:9
very f. of his dog 150:24
with a f. in's ear 21:13
fleas: dog that praised his f. 298:5
f. is good fer a dog 283:12
f. that tease 23:15
flea / Hath smaller f. 259:14
fled: all but he had f. 133:1
f. Him, down the nights 267:21
F. is that music 155:7
f. the Seen 279:14
flee: f. from me, that sometime 295:9
f. from the wrath 35:11

they f., howling in terror 208:25
wicked f. when no man 31:39
fleece: f. was white as snow 195:2
Fleet: F.'s lit up 291:13
fleeting: f. years are slipping by 140:3
flesh: All f. is grass 33:17
Art is science in the f. 80:19
f. is bruckle 104:23
f. is sad 174:12
f. is weak 36:37
F. to feel the chain 47:15
f. what dost thou know 100:11
going the way of all f. 281:17
make your f. creep 95:34
my f. longeth for thee 30:4
natural shocks / That f. is heir to 226:37
pound of f. 233:17
sinful lusts of the f. 70:18
soul to feel the f. 47:15
this too too solid f. 226:4
thorn in the f. 39:15
way of all f. 84:30
way of all f. 224:13
Word was made f. 37:38
world, the f. and the devil 209:21
flies: f. to wanton boys 230:38
He f. through the air 165:17
keeps a wife, / And f. 143:8
One catches more f. 133:9
small f. were caught 13:27
Time meanwhile f. 276:8
flight: f. beyond ordinary mortals 80:13
on tip-toe for a f. 154:12
flim-flam: pretty f. 21:11
Flinders: Little Polly F. 194:27
fling: Who doth not f. away 98:26
flippant: f., vain, / Inconstant 156:2
flirt: How can he f. 248:25
flirtation: innocent f., / Not quite adultery 63:14
most significant word, f. 76:2
Float: F. like a butterfly 3:15
flock: Fed the same f. 182:22
shall feed his f. 33:18
flocks: My f. feed not 19:23
watch'd their f. by night 261:19
flogging: habit of f. me constantly 270:12
less f. in our great schools 149:8
flood: After us the f. 203:23
Land of the mountain and the f. 222:3
race before the f. 103:9
taken at the f. 230:10
floor: along the gusty f. 153:30
fell upon the sanded f. 200:4
flotte: *Elle f., elle hésite* 212:18
flour: f. of cities all 104:25
floures: Of al the f. in the mede 74:11
flow: All things f. 134:5
could I f. like thee 92:25
F., Welsted, flow 204:11
f. / Of Iser, rolling 66:4
flower: as a f. of the field 30:18
Asphodel, that greeny f. 289:11
f. is born to blush unseen 127:17
f. of Adam's bastards 62:11
f. that smiles to-day 243:5
glory in the f. 292:26
goodliness...as the f. of the field 33:17
Heaven in a Wild F. 41:28
meanest f. that blows 293:1
white f. of a blameless life 262:18
flowers: Earth laughs in f. 110:20
f. at his feet 24:8
f. of the forest 109:8
f. that bloom in the spring 123:4
hundred f. blossom 174:20
mouth was like fruit f. 242:2
No road of f. leads to glory 116:2
flowing: f. with milk and honey 26:17
flown: soul but f. beyond the Alps 175:21
flung: f. himself upon his horse 163:25
f. the Stone that puts 114:13
flushed: f. print in a poppy 267:24
Flushing: F. his brow 153:28
flushpots: f. of Euston 151:10
flutter: f. of the gay 58:13
fly: as pigs have to f. 69:18
Do not all charms f. 154:17
f. from, need not be to hate 61:25
f., may fight again 59:29
f. sat upon the axletree 15:18
he will f. from you 40:22
I heard a F. buzz 96:22
I will f. to thee 155:3
ladybird, / F. away home 194:21
Like a long-legged f. 297:2
man is not a f. 206:15
only thing that can't f. 270:16
spider to a f. 141:8
flying: whither art thou f. 128:16
foaming: f. tho' not full 204:11
Fodder: F. comes first 46:10
foe: angry with my f. 43:23
another to let in the f. 185:13
friend or f. that spread 217:1
make one worthy man my f. 205:6
no friend who never made a f. 262:23
robbing of a f. 77:13
that's f. to men 281:20
wisdom even from a f. 8:12
foemen: f. worthy of their steel 221:20
fog: feel the f. in my throat 51:29
f. of the mind 161:11
London particular... A f. 93:20
The f. comes 220:5
yellow f. that rubs 107:30
foi: *Mauvaise f.* 220:15
foible: omniscience his f. 248:33
foiled: f. by woman's arts 43:16
folke: felde ful of f. 162:14
folkes: yonge, fresshe f. 74:27
folks: because other f. have 114:3
follies: f. and misfortunes of mankind 121:18
follow: fears to f. / Where airy 153:20
f. me and leave 90:12
followers: runs will never lack f. 104:10
follows: draws him, yet she f. 168:19
folly: according to his f. 31:35
brood of f. 182:2
dream and a f. of expectation 48:27
f. of the Great 116:4
f. of the wise 150:7
f. to be wise 127:23
from the effects of f. 250:26
If F. link with Elegance 297:9
lovely woman stoops to f. 108:17
wicked f. of 'Women's Rights' 274:16
folwed: taughte, but first he f. it 73:15
fond: Ae f. kiss 55:16
grow too f. of it 164:19
some are f. of Spanish wine 178:9
That f. impossibility 169:10

fonder: Absence makes the heart grow f. 21:2
fons: *O f. Bandusiae* 140:10
Food: F. for powder 228:6
f. that dead men eat 98:16
healthy child...is...wholesome f. 258:20
I live on good f. 186:18
Nothing to eat but f. 158:2
sincerer than the love of f. 239:20
What is f. to one 170:13
fool: being a f. among knaves 259:5
better to be a f. than 256:23
clever woman to manage a f. 159:30
f. according to his folly 31:35
f. and his money 271:15
f. and his words are soon parted 244:23
f. at forty 299:8
f. at least in every married 113:18
f. for the rest of his life 170:19
f. hath said in his heart 29:17
f., in whom these beasts 100:21
f. i' the forest 225:11
f. may ask more than the wisest 83:17
f. must now and then be right 87:9
f. returneth to his folly 31:36
f. some of the people 166:4
I am Fortune's f. 236:5
I have played the f. 28:1
Love's not Time's f. 238:19
not so easy to f. little girls 269:3
played the F. in her Service 253:3
silent and be thought a f. 166:18
wisdom of the f. 150:7
Wise man or a F. 42:14
wisest f. in Christendom 133:11
fooled: f. with hope 103:5
foolish: did anything very f. except 179:6
disguises from the f. 41:14
f. preparation 12:9
Forgive our f. ways 285:12
never said a f. thing 214:19
Soldier...saying a f. thing 254:20
transmitter of a f. face 220:26
women are f. 106:16
fools: all the f. in town 271:29
fill the world with f. 250:26
flannelled f. 159:13
f. and knaves 53:3
F. are my theme 63:21
f. by heavenly compulsion 230:21
F.! For I also had my hour 76:8
f. of time and terror 63:33
F. rush in 206:6
f., who came to scoff 125:7
Fortune, that favours f. 150:13
great stage of f. 231:3
honest Nature made you f. 56:9
human bodies are sic f. 58:6
incredulity! the wit of f. 72:10
prov'd plain f. at last 205:27
Silence is the virtue of f. 13:17
two f., I know, / For loving 100:18
what f. these mortals be 234:8
wise are greatest f. 3:12
foot: man's naked f. on the shore 92:7
suffer thy f. to be moved 31:4
Football: F....causeth fighting 257:13
f. is a matter of life 238:25
Foot-in-the-grave: F. young man 123:10
footnotes: f. to Plato's philosophy 284:5
Footprints: F. on the sands of time 168:15
footsteps: our f. guideth 16:21
forbear: scarce f. to cheer 171:9
forbearance: f. ceases to be a virtue 54:6
Forbidden: that F. Tree, whose mortal 183:7
forbids: Heaven f. certain pleasures 187:6
Muse f. to die 140:16
force: f. alone is but *temporary* 54:22
F., and fraud, are in war 136:21
F. is not a remedy 46:21
f. that through the green 267:1
no f. but argument 49:10
no f., however great 283:19
who overcomes / By f. 183:24
forefathers: rude f. of the hamlet 127:11
forego: when to f. an advantage 98:13
foreign: any portion of the f. world 280:1
f. arms could never quell 249:13
past is a f. country 131:2
Foreign Secretary: F....naked 25:8
foresee: naught / Could I f. 267:15
foreseen: f. may be unexpected 108:4
forest: fool i' the f. 225:11
f. are a' wede awae 109:8
unfathomable deep / F. 267:14
foretold: All was f. me 267:15
forever: diamond and safire bracelet lasts f. 168:26
no man lives f. 260:12
forget: conversing I f. all time 184:19
do not thou f. me 10:21
Don't f. the diver 153:3
f. because we must 9:5
f. so much 91:9
F. the spreading of the hideous town 189:13
forgive if I f. thee 47:16
half f. what world 155:18
Half to f. the wandering 115:6
hateful art, how to f. 158:4
if thou wilt, f. 216:29
lest we f. 159:25
ne'er f. the People 56:5
nor worms f. 95:10
Old men f. 229:2
should f. and smile 216:26
unforgetful to f. 217:6
you'll f. 'em all 207:16
forgetfulness: Not in entire f. 292:23
forgets: f. the dying bird 198:8
f. the flowers at his feet 24:8
forgetting: grand memory for f. 256:5
sleep and a f. 292:22
world f. 204:22
forgive: far as one woman can f. another 120:17
Father, f. them 37:33
f. if I forget thee 47:16
F. our foolish ways 285:12
f. some sinner 179:17
f. them as a Christian 13:3
f. us our debts 35:24
f. us our trespasses 209:9
if ever, do they f. them 288:15
lambs could not f. 95:10
to f., divine 206:4
Wilt thou f. that sin 99:30

forgiven: age...is f. nothing 240:5
Only the dead can be f. 296:10
forgiveness: such knowledge, what f. 107:21
forgives: never f. — youth, power 288:19
Youth...f. itself nothing 240:5
forgot: auld acquaintance be f. 55:18
curiosities would be quite f. 11:1
f. to wind up the clock 253:27
forgotten: f. even by God 51:19
Has God then f. 169:4
learnt has been f. 246:20
learnt nothing, and f. nothing 261:14
not f. my age 250:19
third — and I have f. 198:15
forked: poor, bare, f. animal 230:32
forlorn: faery lands f. 155:6
form: no f. nor comeliness 33:24
formal: great pain, a f. feeling 96:20
formed: f., as notes of music 241:27
Former: poetry? The feeling of a F. world 64:21
forms: f., measured forms 179:9
Fornication: Thou hast committed — F. 175:28
forsaken: why hast thou f. me 37:1
forsaking: f. all other 210:13
Forsan: *F. et haec olim* 275:8
forsworn: so sweetly were f. 232:40
Fortis: *F. fortuna adiuvat* 265:25
fortiter: *pecca f.* 170:18
fortress: my f., and my deliverer 29:19
fortuna: *Fortis f. adiuvat* 265:25
fortunate: f....to have found Homer 3:6
fortunatus: *f. nimium* 276:5
F. et ille deos 276:7
fortune: beauty without a f. 112:27
do F. what she can 102:3
face is my f. 196:3
F. and hir false wheel 73:19
F. and men's eyes 238:5
f. by way of marriage 114:9
F....friendly to the young 173:9
F. helps the brave 265:25
F., that favours fools 150:13
great, ere f. made him so 103:11
Health and high f. till 222:4
hostages to f. 14:12
I am F.'s fool 236:5
single man in possession of a good f. 12:23
sphere of f. raises 185:12
trails our f. in 175:24
woman's f. more or less 130:5
Fortunes: F....come tumbling 13:21
Love...troubleth Men's F. 14:15
forty: about the earth / In f. minutes 234:4
at f. is a fool indeed 299:8
Fat, fair and f. 196:14
f. winters shall besiege 238:3
From f. to fifty a man 201:29
hopeful than to be f. years old 137:19
man over f. is a scoundrel 240:10
forty-three: very well pass for f. 123:22
Forward: those behind cried 'F.!' 171:7
forwards: must be lived f. 157:26
Foster: Doctor F. went to Gloucester 194:8
foster-child: f. of silence 154:20
Fostered: F. alike by beauty 293:6
fou: f., we're sometimes capernoity 113:14
some are f. o' brandy 56:17
wasna f., but just had plenty 56:2
we're nae that f. 58:8
I amna' f. sae muckle 172:6
fought: f. a good fight 40:11
f. each other for 250:7
men f. upon the earth 222:11
what they f. each other for 250:8
foul: doubt some f. play 226:9
Fair is too f. an epithet 176:8
f. is fair 231:20
Murder most f. 226:17
foul-mouthed: rather a f. nation 131:22
found: f. himself out 20:14
fun where I f. it 159:19
Hast thou f. me 28:17
hast thou to say of 'Paradise f.' 109:18
while he may be f. 33:26
foundation: Church's one f. 257:3
smallest f. to falsehood 125:28
foundations: when I laid the f. 29:9
fountain: Foul, I to the f. fly 270:1
f. of honour 15:28
f. of the water of life 41:5
perpetual f. of good sense 104:4
fountains: f. fraught with tears 160:13
life, whose f. are within 81:21
silver f. mud 238:9
two faithful f. 88:22
Four: F. legs good 196:19
F. things greater than all 158:20
Fourscore: F. and seven years ago 166:10
reason of strength they be f. 30:11
Fourteen: bores me with his F. Points 79:13
fourth: f. estate of the realm 171:12
fox: f. obscene to gaping tombs 207:27
[F.] talked to me 149:32
gentleman galloping after a f. 288:13
loves the f. less, but 258:4
foxes: And f. stunk 127:19
f. grow grey 117:17
little f., that spoil the vines 32:22
frabjous: O f. day 69:29
fractus: *Si f. illabatur orbis* 140:9
fragile: f. dewdrop on its perilous 155:10
Fragment: this F. of Life 253:25
fragments: f. have I shored 108:19
frailest: f. / For your cradle 242:25
Frailty: F., thy name is woman 226:6
noblest f. of the mind 103:14
noblest f. of the mind 224:14
frame: bears in his bodily f. 90:16
heavens, a shining f. 2:8
universal f. began 103:26
France: Fair blows the wind for F. 175:16
Fair stood the wind for F. 102:5
F. has more need of me 190:11
[F.] money falls apart 289:1
F. was long a despotism 68:6
F. will say that I am a German 106:9
more reasonable in F. 277:3
slain me you will conquer F. 146:6
sweet enemy, F. 246:2
this matter better in F. 253:16
frankincense: gold, and f. 35:9
Frankly: F., my dear 119:13
frantic: f. for my Gaveston 175:15
Fraternité: *Liberté! Egalité! F.* 6:5
fraud: Force, and f., are in war 136:21
fredome: f. is a noble thing 19:9

think f. mar to pryss 19:11
free: always and never f. 268:19
But they shall be f. 57:15
Comment is f. 221:8
condemned to be f. 220:16
created f. and equal 166:7
f. as the road 135:1
f. Church in a free State 71:12
freedom to the f. 166:9
f. man addressing free 220:19
Greece might still be f. 62:34
imagine themselves to be f. 217:17
in your power — he's f. 249:23
know our will is f. 148:19
land of the f. 157:22
Man is born f. 217:16
mighty f. and easy 271:27
mind is f., whate'er afflict 102:3
never be f. until 97:4
our air, that moment they are f. 88:4
perfectly f. till all are free 251:5
region where he will be f. 290:1
soul in prison, I am not f. 91:17
sweet God, I will set them f. 202:14
Thou art f. 9:28
Thought is f. 236:22
truth shall make thee f. 38:5
we are f. to act 8:24
We must be f. or die 294:12
wholly slaves or wholly f. 103:13
Who would be f. themselves 61:15
yearning to breath f. 163:24
free verse: f. is like playing tennis 118:19
free-born: only a f. Briton can do 266:10
freedom: battle for f. and truth 143:21
every infringement of human f. 202:8
fight, but for F. only 5:14
flame of f. in their souls 260:18
F. and whisky gang 55:19
f., but the unfettered use 81:22
f....for man who lives by his own work 83:5
F. has a thousand charms 87:31
F. is the recognition of necessity 111:27
f. to the free 166:9
f. to use them 143:24
life for f. — This I know 112:19
live in f. everich in his kind 144:8
man might find f. 23:20
most dangerous foe to...f. 143:20
only one subjct — f. 220:19
service is perfect f. 209:16
What stands if F. fall 159:4
French: Every F. soldier carries 190:12
F. women better than English 24:2
some are fond of F. 178:9
Frenchman: F. invented the ruffle 110:1
hate a F. as you hate 191:14
Frenchmen: Fifty million F. can't be wrong 128:11
Frenssh: F. she spak ful faire 73:5
frenzy: in a fine f. rolling 234:13
frequent: when young did eagerly f. 114:19
frère: *mon semblable, — mon f.* 20:20
Sois mon f. 72:6
Frères: *F. humains* 275:3
fresh: f. Woods, and Pastures new 182:33
keep the passion f. 179:29
looking as f. as paint 247:3
freshness: f. of a dream 292:20
fresshe: yonge, f. folkes 74:27
fret: fever and the f. 155:1
Freude: *F., schöner Götterfunken* 220:27
fricassee: will equally serve in a f. 258:20
Friday: F. fil al this meschaunce 74:9
who laughs on F. 212:20
friend: author as you choose a f. 216:16
choose between...betraying my f. 116:22
communicating...to his F. 15:5
Death: the last best f. 250:10
ease some f., not wife 205:1
fav'rite has no f. 127:21
f.? A single soul dwelling in two 8:18
f....masterpiece of Nature 110:6
f. of every country but 66:24
f. or foe that spread 217:1
F. we have in Jesus 223:5
guide, philosopher, and f. 206:29
loss of a dear f. 250:21
no f. who never made a foe 262:23
polished female f. 285:15
portrait I lose a f. 220:14
save me, from the candid f. 66:26
should rejoin its f. 110:7
Who's your fat f. 52:18
worst f. and enemy is but Death 48:10
wounds of a f. 31:38
friendless: Omnipotent but f. 243:19
friendly: f. eye could never see 230:9
hostile, nor yet is it f. 137:11
friends: All thy f. are lapp'd 19:22
believe I deserved my f. 285:7
book is the best of f. 271:10
cheating of our f. 77:13
city of the faithfullest f. 284:17
distresses of our f. 259:16
forgive my f. for dying 247:21
F. are all that matter 54:2
f. I am quite forlorn 17:17
F. who set forth 9:21
his life for his f. 38:14
house of my f. 34:27
keep f. with himself 256:1
laughter and the love of f. 23:7
lay down his f. for his life 269:1
lost f., some by death 291:15
merely comes to meet one's f. 55:11
none of his f. like him 288:24
not in the multitude of f. 150:17
Old f. are best 223:13
old f., old times 125:19
remembering my good f. 235:16
they had been f. in youth 81:18
Thy f. are exultations 294:4
truth above our f. 8:22
we have f. and no butlers 208:13
Friendship: F. often ends in love 83:19
f. in constant repair 148:4
F. is of so sweet and steady 272:5
f. is a plant of slow 280:3
indeed true f. 219:22
In f. false 102:16
let us swear eternal f. 248:24
sort of f. recognized by the police 256:14
True f.'s laws 207:9
with the wing of f. 95:19
frighted: f. with false fire 227:8
frighten: by God, they f. me 282:10
frightened: ill, / It has a f. look 246:17

frightful: sure, be f. when one's dead 205:22
fringe: lunatic f. in all reform 215:22
frisson: *L'air est plein du f.* 20:21
frivolity: gay without f. 9:14
frog: better'n any other f. 271:21
f. he would a-wooing go 194:1
like a f. / To tell your name 97:1
frogs: throw stones at f. 41:17
frog-spawn: pitch into the f. 296:11
frolics: youth of f. 204:29
fromage: big f. in this family 190:21
front: Death in the f. 61:16
frontier: edge of a new f. 157:16
frost: f. performs its secret ministry 81:29
frosty: stern in f. nicht 104:18
froth: Life is mostly f. and bubble 126:9
frowning: Behind a f. providence 87:22
frowns: slowly killed by f. and smiles 243:14
frozen: Architècture is f. music 124:23
f. corpse was he 168:24
torrid or the f. zone 67:5
frugal: She had a f. mind 87:16
Fruit: F. / Of that Forbidden Tree 183:7
I love f. when it's expensive 201:28
Much f. of sense 205:30
fruitful: Be f., and multiply 25:15
f. ground, the quiet mind 258:1
fruitfulness: mellow f. 153:8
fruition: sweet f. of an earthly crown 176:7
fruits: By their f. ye shall know 36:6
Dead Sea f. 188:23
first partaker of the f. 40:10
f. of the Spirit 209:22
frying: f. pan into the fire 265:28
fudge: two-fifths sheer f. 169:17
fugaces: *Eheu f.* 140:3
fugit: *f. inreparabile tempus* 276:8
Führer: *Ein F.* 5:10
fule: Whilst I, pure f. 172:10
fules: verray naturall f. 167:2
Fulfilled: F. of dong 74:5
So shall they be f. 2:16
full: f. of days, riches and honour 28:25
fulness: f. thereof 29:21
fum: Fie, foh, and f., / I smell 230:35
fun: and make f. of it 68:26
I rhyme for f. 56:12
my f. where I found it 159:19
not here for f. 134:16
thought *What Jolly F.* 213:2
funeral: f. baked meats 226:7
misbehaved once at a f. 161:20
not a f. note 291:1
funny: Everything is f. as long as 215:5
funny-ha-ha: or f. 131:6
Funny-peculiar: F. or funny-ha-ha 131:6
fur: Oh my f. and whiskers 69:7
on some other f. 7:26
Furies: curses which the F. breathe 176:9
furious: grew fast and f. 57:18
furiously: green ideas sleep f. 77:7
he driveth f. 28:23
furnace: burning fiery f. 34:14
furnish: You f. the pictures 132:4
furniture: f. so charming as books 248:20
not to bump into the f. 170:14
furor: *Ira f. brevis* 139:16
furrow: f. followed free 81:5
furrows: smite / The sounding f. 265:14
further: f. one goes 162:19
f. out than you thought 248:2
nearer the Church...f. from God 4:12
seen f. it is by standing 192:13
shalt thou go and no f. 199:4
Fury: Comes the blind F. 182:25
full of sound and f. 232:28
f. and the mire 295:23
Nor Hell a f., like a woman 84:26
fuse: through the green f. drives 267:1
future: dipt into the f. 264:4
empires of the f. 78:9
extravagant hopes of the f. 54:13
fight against the f. 124:3
f....comes soon enough 106:7
greatness of its f. being 81:28
if you would divine the f. 84:6
love must have some f. 66:22
never think of the f. 106:7
prevail on our f. masters 169:15
seen the f., and it works 253:9
time f. contained in time past 107:11
futurity: let f. shift for itself 249:9
no reference to f. 149:11
Gaels: great G. of Ireland 76:7
gage: thou sall loss a g. 44:3
gai: toujours g. 176:14
gaiety: eclipsed the g. of nations 147:4
gain: All is not g. that is got 254:13
g. the whole world 36:23
weaker g. 103:8
gain'd: g. a hundred fights 264:20
gained: g. both the Wind and Sun 177:7
gains: Light g. make heavy purses 15:17
gait: musing g. 182:6
gaiters: gas and g. 95:17
galanterie: *n'ont jamais eu de g.* 162:23
galère: *dans cette g.* 187:1
gales: cool g. shall fan 207:11
Galilean: conquered, O pale G. 260:14
You have conquered, G. 151:23
Galilee: Ye men of G. 38:20
gall: wormwod and the g. 34:10
gallant: brake that g. ship 17:10
very g. gentleman 4:16
gallantry: men call g., and gods adultery 62:16
galleon: ghostly g. tossed upon 193:21
Gallia: *G. est omnis divisa* 65:6
gallimaufry: English tongue a g. 252:12
Gallop: likes to / G. about 248:1
galloped: we g. all three 51:2
gambler: g., by the state / Licensed 42:5
game: and play the g. 191:21
g....never lost till won 88:18
more than a g. 141:15
plenty of time to win this g. 102:1
Games: Winning G. without actually Cheating 208:4
Gamesmanship: G. or, The Art 208:4
gamut: whole g. of the emotions 198:22
gander: Goosey, goosey g. 194:10
gaol: know who lie in g. 286:5
gape: Ugly hell, g. not 175:13
Garbo: one sees in G. sober 272:20

garden: all Nature was a g. 278:10
Come into the g., Maud 264:15
cultivate our g. 276:13
don't go into Mr. McGregor's g. 208:3
first g. made, and the first city 86:22
g. full of flowers 162:10
g. in her face 66:17
g. is a lovesome thing 48:19
ghost of a g. fronts 260:9
Glory of the G. 159:7
God Almighty first planted a G. 15:12
How does your g. grow 195:3
I value my g. more 2:10
large g. have 87:1
loves a g. loves a greenhouse 88:9
nearer God's Heart in a g. 128:14
Nothing grows in our g. 267:7
river at my g.'s end 259:19
gardener: Adam was a g. 229:10
g. Adam and his wife 263:24
gardens: imaginary g. with real toads 188:13
in trim G. takes 182:7
passed the salley g. 296:12
garland: green willow is my g. 136:2
garret: living in a g. 116:7
garrison: hath friends in the g. 129:3
garters: g. to be bonds 14:13
gas: g. and gaiters 95:17
gate: at one g. to make defence 185:13
g. of the year 131:4
here at the g. alone 264:15
gates: heads, O ye g. 29:25
iron g. of life 177:23
temple g. unto my love 251:19
Gath: Tell it not in G. 28:2
gathered: two or three are g. 36:25
we are g. together 210:11
Gat-tothed: G. I was 73:31
Gaudeamus: *G. igitur* 5:16
gaudent: *g. tamen esse rogatae* 197:13
Gaul: G. is divided into three parts 65:6
Gaunt: seige of the city of G. 18:3
gave: g. my life for freedom 112:19
Lord g., and 28:32
gavest: day Thou g. 109:6
Gaveston: frantic for my G. 175:15
gay: gallant, g. Lothario 217:22
g. without frivolity 9:14
I'm a g. deceiver 83:13
gaz'd: Too much g. at 153:36
Gaza: Eyeless in G. 185:9
gaze: g. for long into an abyss 192:21
gazelle: both / Beautiful, one a g. 296:21
gazing: didn't know that everybody was g. at him 96:9
g. up into heaven 38:20
geese: for this the wild g. spread 297:22
g. are getting fat 5:4
his own g. are swans 278:21
Geist: *G. der stets verneint* 124:12
gem: many a g. of purest ray 127:16
gemlike: this hard, g. flame 199:16
gender: she's of the feminine g. 196:13
general: caviare to the g. 226:32
coupleth the g. notion 246:6
G. Good is the plea 42:16
G., well, at the age of four 273:3
General Motors: country is good for G. 289:17
generals: *bite*...my other g. 121:4
G. Janvier and Février 192:17
left to the g. 261:15
generation: best minds of my g. 123:26
g. of leaves 137:28
last representative of the pre-war g. 23:22
pride in this coming g. 215:12
generations: g. of the living 170:10
hungry g. tread thee 155:6
thirty g. of my men 268:20
three g. of a house 208:10
Genius: 'G.' (which means transcendent capacity 67:22
Consult the g. of the place 205:16
declare except my g. 288:26
Eccentricities of g. 96:5
G....a greater aptitude for patience 53:6
g. and his money 244:23
G. does what it must 179:30
g. I had when I wrote that book 259:22
g....infinite capacity for 139:4
G. is one per cent inspiration 105:18
g. of the Constitution 202:7
models destroy g. 131:19
spendthrift of my own g. 286:15
talent instantly recognizes g. 101:25
Three-fifths of him g. 169:17
true for all men — that is g. 110:11
unseen G. of the Wood 182:9
was g. found respectable 49:13
When a true g. appears 259:6
works of g. are the first 156:11
gentil: parfit g. knyght 73:4
pitee renneth soon in g. herte 73:25
gentle: Do not go g. 266:22
G. and low, an excellent 231:7
g. mind by gentle deeds 252:6
gentleman: first true g. that ever breath'd 92:10
g....never inflicts pain 192:3
g.: I live by robbing 239:25
God's g. from Fashion's 110:10
Once a g. 94:29
prince of darkness is a g. 230:34
talking about being a g. never is 258:2
very gallant g. 4:16
Who was then a g. 7:25
Gentleman-Rankers: G. out on the spree 159:5
Gentlemen: G. Prefer Blondes 168:25
g....sent down for indecent 280:20
g. were not seamen 171:17
Not a religion for g. 72:18
while the G. go by 159:27
written by g. for gentlemen 266:6
gentleness: ways are ways of g. 252:20
gently: g. as any sucking dove 234:2
shall g. lead those 33:18
genug: *Beste gut g.* 124:17
geographical: Italy is a g. expression 180:3
Geography: G. is about Maps 24:12
geology: what happens to the world's g. 172:24
geometric: by g. scale, / Could take the size 59:18
geometrical: increases in a g. ratio 174:17
looking so g. 119:1
Geometrician: God is like a skilful G. 49:5
geometry: no royal road to g. 112:11

George: [G. III] despised, and dying king 244:5
King G. will be able to read 129:11
George the First: G. was always reckoned 162:1
George the Third: Any good of G. 162:1
G. — ['Treason,' cried 133:22
Georges: praised, the G. ended 162:1
Georgics: [G.]...most complete, elaborate and finisht 1:20
Georgie: G. Porgie, pudding and pie 194:9
German: G. army was stabbed 136:8
wee G. lairdie 89:16
Germans: beastly to the G. 86:16
Germany: G. will claim me as a German 106:9
Offering G. too little 191:18
Get: G. you the sons 140:27
other is to g. it 239:29
therefore g. wisdom 31:16
Getting: G. and spending 294:6
Gospel of G. On 240:19
with all thy g. 31:16
Ghost: G. in the Machine 219:2
g. of a garden fronts 260:9
it is a g.'s right 295:19
some old lover's g. 100:2
thought to please my g. 179:17
ghosties: From ghoulies and g. 5:15
ghosts: [g.] All argument is against 149:17
g. from an enchanter 243:6
G. glut the throat 42:12
Wining the g. of yester-year 209:1
yet a boy I sought for g. 242:16
giant: g. race before the flood 103:9
g.'s shoulder to mount on 82:18
owner whereof was G. Despair 53:18
giants: g. in the earth 25:25
on the shoulders of g. 192:13
Gibbon: scribble! Eh! Mr. G. 124:4
Giddy: G. fantastic Poets 100:9
Gift: G., like genius 139:4
hate a debt as men a g. 51:3
your g. survived it all 11:6
giftie: some Power the g. gie us 57:23
gifts: presented unto him g. 35:9
when they bring g. 275:12
gild: g. refined gold 230:15
gilded: bug with g. wings 205:8
gilding: great deal about g. the eastern 244:26
Gilead: no balm in G. 34:4
Gin: G. was mother's milk 240:25
Giotto: G. and Cimabue showed 143:5
gipsy: prefer a g. by Reynolds 171:21
girdid: g. up my Lions 279:14
girdle: I'll put a g. round 234:4
girl: breaks just like a little g. 105:9
Crept like a frightened g. 286:23
find some g. perhaps 47:20
g. with brains ought 168:27
that g. standing there 297:12
There was a little g. 195:21
wink your eye at some homely g. 179:17
girls: Dear to g.' hearts 197:15
not so easy to fool little g. 269:3
prevent g. from being girls 138:20
Gitche Gumee: By the shores of G. 168:17
give: Don't g. up the ship 163:23
g. me back my heart 63:30
I g. myself 284:23
to g. than to receive 38:28
given: g. to government 94:15
giver: author and g. of all good 209:27
cheerful g. 39:14
gives: blesseth him that g. 233:19
He g. twice who gives soon 261:3
giving: not in the g. vein 235:28
Glad: G. did I live 255:20
g. of another death 107:27
g. when they said 31:6
some folks would be g. of 114:3
gladly: g. wolde he lerne 73:10
gladness: begin in g. 293:14
g. of her gladness 20:9
Teach me half the g. 244:17
Without g. availis no tresour 104:21
Gladstone: [G.] grand old man 193:16
[G.] old man in a hurry 77:18
glance: brightening g. 295:20
Glasgow: Beautiful city of G. 173:5
glass: broken pane of g. 198:17
clearer than g. 140:10
Drink not the third g. 134:24
Get thee g. eyes 231:1
g., wherein beholders do generally 258:8
mouths in a g. 230:27
sound of broken g. 23:11
glasses: girls who wear g. 198:19
glaze: g. and the mark 162:8
glean'd: g. my teeming brain 155:25
glee: laugh'd with counterfeited g. 125:8
glide: sunny beams did g. 43:20
glisters: g. is not gold 233:11
glittering: beard and g. eye 81:1
gloat: g. on the glaze 162:8
global: image of a g. village 173:18
globe: great g. itself 236:24
gloire: *g. des grands hommes* 163:1
jour de g. est arrivé 217:14
gloom: amid the encircling g. 192:6
gloria: *dat mihi g. vires* 211:5
Sic transit g. mundi 157:12
Glories: G., like glow-worms 281:11
in those weaker g. spy 273:25
glorify: Man's chief end is to g. God 70:16
gloriosus: *Miles g.* 203:4
glorious: Belial had a g. time 102:21
crowded hour of g. life 189:1
g. than those of war 42:17
it is a g. thing 123:11
many a g. morning 238:8
glory: And into g. peep 273:19
count the g. of my crown 109:2
duty was the way to g. 264:21
g. among the heathen 30:16
g. and good of Art 52:9
g. and the freshness 292:20
g. belongs to our ancestors 203:12
g. from the earth 292:21
g. gives me strength 211:5
g. is departed from Israel 27:26
g. is departed 52:17
g. is their shame 39:25
g., jest, and riddle 206:19
g. of beating the French 291:6
g. of great men 163:1
g. of the coming 141:5
G. of the Garden 159:7
g. of the Lord shone round 37:12
g. of the world passes 157:12

g., or the grave 66:5
g. that shall be revealed 209:26
g. that was Greece 203:19
G. to God in the highest 37:14
greater g. of God 4:17
I felt it was g. 64:10
left him alone in his g. 291:4
love, and I felt it was g. 64:10
name of G. were they proud 154:13
No road of flowers leads to g. 116:2
paths of g. lead 127:15
return the g. of your prime 242:19
sea of g. 229:14
Sudden g. is the passion 136:18
this King of g. 29:25
to g. we steer 216:23
triumph without g. when 85:19
war as all g., but, boys 245:15
glotoun: g. of wordes 162:15
Gloucester: Doctor Foster went to G. 194:8
glove: cat but a g. 222:16
iron hand in a velvet g. 72:23
gloves: walk through the fields in g. 86:1
glowr'd: Tammie g., amaz'd, and curious 57:18
glow-worms: g., afar off shine 281:11
glum: whose glance was g. 123:25
glut: g. thy sorrow 154:30
gluttons: in taverns with g. 90:7
Glyn: With Elinor G. / On a tiger-skin 7:26
gnat: strain at a g. 36:30
gnomes: g. of Zurich 289:18
go: as cooks g. 219:15
either g. or hang 41:16
I g., I come back 153:5
In the name of God, g. 89:6
I shall g. to him 28:8
It's a Rum G. 274:3
Must you g. 273:16
not let thee g., except 26:7
ought to g. from here 69:9
Time stays, *we* g. 98:17
goal: grave is not its g. 168:14
slacken my pace when approaching the g. 97:12
Goats: G. and monkeys 235:1
God: afraid of G. — / And more of 167:24
all mercy, is a G. unjust 299:3
am a jealous G. 26:29
angler, and now with G. 279:5
as it were, G.'s grandchild 90:5
atheist, thank G. 53:13
Beast, or a G. 15:4
Before G. we are all equally 106:10
Beware of the man whose g. 239:30
brave towards G. 14:3
by searching find out G. 29:3
Cabots talk only to G. 45:8
Caesar's self is G.'s 88:24
Chance is perhaps G.'s pseudonym 117:2
crieth out for the living G. 30:7
Curse G., and die 28:34
denied to G. 2:22
Doubtless G. could have made 279:6
Fall into the hands of G. 265:3
fed and watered / By G.'s 79:8
flood, leads — G. knows where 63:6
For G.'s sake look after 221:10
for G. took him 25:24
forgotten even by G. 51:19
further from G. 4:12
G. Almighty first planted a Garden 15:12
G. Almighty has only ten 79:13
[G.]...an under-achiever 3:19
G. as his father 89:20
G. being with thee 294:1
G. be in my head 5:17
G. be with you till 213:6
G. created the heaven 25:11
G. disposes 157:11
G. doth admit the fair 134:20
G. erects a house of prayer 92:1
G. fulfils himself in many 263:2
G. gives skill 107:2
g. has made this peace 275:24
G. has written all the books 60:5
G. is a circle 7:11
G. is a jealous God 27:5
G. is an unutterable sigh 109:12
G. is a Spirit 38:2
G. is dead 191:16
G. is dead 192:24
G. is forgotten 151:5
G. is his own interpreter 87:23
G. is in heaven, and thou 32:8
G. is like a skilful Geometrician 49:5
G. is love 40:28
G. is Love, I dare say 60:7
G. is no respecter of persons 38:24
G. is not mocked 39:16
G. is our refuge 30:1
G. is their belly 39:25
G. is the perfect poet 51:18
G. is thy refuge 27:10
G. is with thee 27:11
G. is working His purpose out 2:23
G. made him 233:5
G. made the country 88:2
G....merciful to the birds 7:18
G. moves in a mysterious 87:21
G. of Isaac 26:18
G. only a blunder of man 193:5
G. or the Czar look 288:8
G. saw that it was good 25:13
g. self-slain on his own strange 260:10
G.'s gentlemen from Fashion's 110:10
G.'s in his heaven 51:27
G.'s no blate gin he stirs up 172:5
G.'s own country 5:18
G. that he may absolve us 275:4
G. the first garden made 86:22
G. the herdsman goads 298:17
G., thou art my God 30:4
G. through the wrong end 172:22
G. took the spinning-jenny 296:18
G. was all negroid 163:13
G. wasn't too bad a novelist 20:17
G. will pardon me 132:16
G. will save the Queen 140:27
G. would make a man miserable 72:17
G., / Or something very like 79:20
greater glory of G. 4:17
great g. Pan is dead 203:10
Has G. then forgotten 169:4
I am a G. and cannot find 243:16
If G. be for us 38:37
If G. did not exist 276:16
If G. has created us 277:6
immensities, I found G. 50:13
I must be turning into a g. 274:14
I wad do, were I Lord G. 173:3
I who saw the face of G. 175:4
kills the image of G. 186:2
know his G. by night 273:21

Evil be thou my G. 184:15
evil, that g. may come 38:33
fancy does you g. 167:11
foxes...few grow g. 117:17
Gallop about doing g. 248:1
go about doing g. 88:30
God saw that it was g. 25:13
g. action by stealth 161:16
G. and bad are but names 110:17
g. as thou art beautiful 262:20
g., bad, and indifferent 252:13
g. ended happily 287:6
g. [end] unluckily 257:7
g. for the bees 12:3
g. for the country is good 289:17
g. in the worst 7:12
g. is oft interred 230:1
g. is the beautiful 202:22
g. Judge too 123:23
g. men to do nothing 55:6
g. morrow to our waking souls 99:20
g. must associate 54:15
g. people were clever 291:18
g., she was very, very good 195:21
g. than to be ugly 287:26
g. time coming, boys 173:11
g. time that was had by all 91:14
g. to be merry 6:2
g. woman if I had five thousand 266:13
grammar as long as we are g. 279:17
greatest g. 78:18
If one g. deed 236:33
I'm as g. as you be 111:8
I will be g. 274:15
loves what he is g. at 224:16
means up to no g. 119:5
must return g. for evil 273:12
my religion is to do g. 198:10
never had it so g. 173:20
nor g. / Compensate bad 52:8
not g. but great 274:21
nothing either g. or bad 226:28
shouldn't say it is not g. 283:22
them that call evil g. 32:30
Truth...the sovereign g. 14:1
what g. came of it 250:9
what is g. for them 89:10
When she was g. 168:8
work together for g. 38:36
worse than ugly, she is g. 286:21
would do g. to another 42:16
you're not g. enough yourself 270:20
Good Thing: Conquest was, however, a *G.* 223:21
good will: peace, g. toward men 37:14
goodness: criterion of g. 58:15
g. and mercy shall follow me 29:20
G. had nothing to do 283:10
g. in removing it from them 113:23
g. of a good egg 89:23
g. springs from a man's own heart 83:24
If g. lead him not 135:9
powerful g. want 243:15
thirst for g. as for drink 113:13
whose g. faileth never 16:19
Good-night: G.? ah! no; the hour is ill 242:9
His happy g. air 129:19
second best's a gay g. 296:19
to all a g. 188:6
goods: he's got the g. 133:20
paid for only with g. 193:12
with all my worldly g. 210:16
goose: but every g. can 203:9
every g. a swan 158:11
Goosey: G., goosey gander 194:10
gorgeous: g. East with richest hand 183:27
g. East in fee 294:9
Gorgon: myself as the G. Zola 190:21
Gorgonized: G. me from head to foot 264:14
Gormed: I'm G. — and I can't 94:10
Gospel: G. is their maw 185:28
G. of Getting On 240:19
G. of spilt milk 215:23
G.'s pearls upon our coast 177:3
g. / Of the radio-phonograph 11:8
preach the g. to every creature 37:10
gossip: known / More than the g. 118:23
to the town g. 215:7
got: he's g. the goods 133:20
Gotham: G.'s three Wise Men 200:12
Gothic: more than G. ignorance 114:7
Gottbetrunkener: *Ein G. Mensch* 193:19
gout: old enemy the g. 138:8
govern: Consciousness reigns but does not g. 273:8
difficult to drive; easy to g. 48:15
Every class is unfit to g. 1:4
g. according to the common weal 144:14
He that would g. others 178:21
Syllables g. the world 80:22
governans: in thee was g. 44:4
governaunce: cok hadde in his g. 74:8
governed: g. by shopkeepers 247:9
many are g. by the few 142:2
nation is not g. 54:22
not so well g. as they ought 138:14
government: best g....governs least 197:7
erected into a system of g. 123:27
false system of g. 198:9
Forms of G. let fools 206:22
given to g. 94:15
g. as with medicine 24:9
g. shall be upon his shoulder 33:4
G....contrivance of human wisdom 54:9
g. by the badly educated 77:4
g. of the people 166:11
g. it deserves 174:10
G....a necessary evil 198:6
g. to suffer so much poverty 200:16
G....the laws of life 218:13
Influence is not g. 279:25
just watch the g. 215:8
Monarchy is a strong g. 16:2
No G. can be long secure 97:14
obey the established G. 279:27
oppressive g. is more to be feared 83:25
people's g., made for the people 281:5
Republican...highest form of g. 251:1
right...to establish G. 279:27
unfit for their own g. 280:4
governors: supreme g., the mob 278:11
governs: pen, — it g. me 254:18
woman g. America 174:6
Gower: O moral G. 74:24
gown: loose g. from her shoulders 295:10
grace: all g. of ease 144:23
But for the g. of God there goes 45:15
equal g., force, fascination 285:6
g. of our Lord Jesus Christ 41:7
G. under pressure 133:4

grow old with a good g. 253:4
inward and spiritual g. 70:21
Thy g. is great and ample 56:19
Tuesday's child is full of g. 6:9
Will is to g. 11:27
graceful: g. action seldom fail 102:22
gracefulness: air of g. 1:19
Graces: G. do not seem to be natives of Great Britain 75:19
half mile g. 58:3
gracious: God save our g. king 67:7
grain: With a g. of salt 203:8
grammar: care for g. as long as 279:17
heedless of g. 19:16
grammarians: inquisitive tribe of g. 8:3
grammars: What sairs your g. 56:9
Grammatici: *G. certant* 139:6
Grammere: G., that grounde is of alle 162:16
gramophone: record on the g. 108:17
grand: baith g. and comfortable 20:4
g. seigneur...grand génie 21:8
g. style...serious subject 10:14
That g. old man 193:16
grandchild: Art...God's g. 90:5
grandeur: g. he derived from Heaven 103:11
g. of God 138:24
g. that was Rome 203:19
precepts with a kind of g. 1:19
grandfather: who my g. was 166:15
grandmother: walk over my g. 83:14
grandson: what his g. will be 166:15
grange: at the moated g. 232:39
grano: *Cum g. salis* 203:8
granted: g.,' said, and died 135:11
Grape: G. that can with Logic 114:21
peel me a g. 283:8
grapes: eaten sour g. 34:11
g. of wrath 141:5
grapeshot: whiff of g. 68:7
Grasp: G. it like a man 136:4
reach should exceed his g. 49:23
grass: believe a leaf of g. 284:21
g. below 79:4
g. comes again 140:15
his days are as g. 30:18
snake lurks in the g. 275:26
spears are like the summer g. 43:17
splendour in the g. 292:26
sweet in the g. ho ho 267:11
two blades of g. to grow 258:13
grasses: presage the g.' fall 177:17
Grate: G. on their scrannel 182:29
grateful: told that the poor are g. 288:4
gratuit: *acte g.* 122:3
gratuitous: g. action 122:3
grave: ayont the g., man 58:4
baith in ae g. 17:22
Between the cradle and the g. 105:5
bore; even the g. yawns 270:7
dark inn, the g. 222:5
dread / The g. as little 157:14
glory lead but to the g. 127:15
glory, or the g. 66:5
g., and, oh, / The difference 293:18
g. hides all things beautiful 243:16
g. is not its goal 168:14
G.'s a fine and private place 177:22
g., where is thy victory 39:12
kind of healthy g. 248:12
little, little g. 235:21
my dungeon or my g. 241:20
not rest in an English g. 64:26
O G., thy victoree 6:14
pot of honey on the g. 179:21
with sorrow to the g. 26:11
grave-digger: if I were a g. 146:1
graven: any g. image 26:29
graves: Let's talk of g. 235:18
gravis: *Illi mors g.* 224:5
gravity: alters the centre of g. 68:24
G. is only the bark of wisdom's 84:3
gravy: gulf stream of g. 174:19
person who disliked g. 248:24
Gray: [G.] dull in a new way 149:5
Gray's Elegy: prefer being the author of [G.] 291:6
grease: slides by on g. 169:24
greasy: fat and g. citizens 225:7
g. Joan doth keel 231:17
grey-green, g. Limpopo 159:15
great: age of g. men is going 4:6
battle, a g. battle 167:8
but g.; and so are neither 274:21
cannot perform g. things 278:22
compare small things with g. 276:10
disbelief in g. men 68:4
folly of the G. 116:4
glory of g. men 163:1
g. brake through 13:27
g., ere fortune made him so 103:11
g. has been done by youth 97:17
g. man...keeps...independence 110:18
g. men all remind us 168:15
G. things are done 42:9
history...biography of g. men 68:5
History of the G. Men 67:24
judge g. and lofty matters 187:15
Men in G. Place 14:16
nothing g. but mind 129:9
once was g. is pass'd 294:10
people think him *g.* 149:5
rising to G. Place 14:17
seekest thou g. things 34:8
they are all g. 126:11
To g. men...world is a sepulchre 269:2
who were truly g. 251:7
Greater: G. love hath no man 269:1
g. prey upon the less 127:27
g. than we know 293:16
necessity is g. than mine 246:9
sing of somewhat g. things 275:27
Something g. than the Iliad 211:4
greatest: g. event it is 117:1
g. good 78:18
g. happiness of the greatest number 24:11
g. happiness of the greatest 142:16
g. of these is charity 39:8
I am the g. 3:14
to live as the g. he 212:21
greatness: Be not afraid of g. 237:20
farewell, to all my g. 229:13
G. consists in bringing...mischief 113:23
g. not to be exact 54:17
g. thrust upon them 237:20
Greece: glory that was G. 203:19
G. might still be free 62:34
G.! Sad relic of departed worth 61:10
G. subdued her fierce 139:21
isles of G., the isles 62:31
Greedy: G. for others' possessions 219:21
G. for quick returns 50:30
Greek: a G. / In pity and mournful awe 9:12
G. to me, except 118:27

it was G. to me 229:23
small Latin, and less G. 150:28
study of G. literature 119:15
when his wife talks G. 150:3
Greeks: first, the G. or the Romans 98:14
G. even when they bring gifts 275:12
G. joined Greeks 164:17
green: All a g. willow 136:2
am'rous as this lovely g. 177:10
babbled of g. fields 228:29
dye one's whiskers g. 70:11
England's g. and pleasant 42:28
G. grow the rashes O 56:14
G. grow the rushes O 5:24
G. I love you green 120:3
g. Thought in a green Shade 177:14
I was g. in judgement 224:23
laid him on the g. 17:8
lamps in a g. light 177:2
Making the g. one red 232:3
There is a g. hill 3:11
tree of life is g. 124:14
trees were g., / For he loved 79:2
wearin' o' the G. 7:1
Wherever g. is worn 296:16
greenery-yallery: g., Grosvenor Gallery 123:10
green-ey'd: g. monster 234:37
greenhouse: loves a garden loves a g. 88:9
Greenland: G.'s icy mountains 132:8
green-rob'd: Those g. senators 154:4
greenwood: Under the g. tree 225:9
greet: g., an' in your tears 172:3
g., upon some well-fought field 9:29
How should I g. thee 64:14
Grenville: Sir Richard G. lay 265:1
grey: foxes grow g. 117:17
given me over in my g. hairs 291:11
old g. head, / But spare 285:8
theory...is g. 124:14
grey-green: great, g., greasy Limpopo 159:15
greyhound: If one is a g. 246:16
greyhounds: stand like g. in the slips 228:31
grief: acquainted with g. 33:24
false g. hiding his harmful 251:26
G. brought to numbers 100:19
g. in wine we steep 169:6
G. is itself a med'cine 87:6
g. is like a summer storm 16:17
g.! It blows a man 227:40
G. never mended no broken bones 96:17
g. returns with the revolving 241:10
heart which g. hath cankered 65:17
my distracting g. 137:20
Patch g. with proverbs 234:22
renew, O queen, an unspeakable g. 275:11
time remembered is g. forgotten 259:25
Was ever g. like mine 135:12
worm, the canker, and the g. 64:3
Griefs: cutteth G. in halves 15:5
grieve: g., / Thus having been 244:18
Men are we, and must g. 294:10
than a nation g. 102:19
grieving: Margaret, are you g. 138:28
grievous: my most g. fault 178:16
Grill: Let G. be Grill 252:3
grimaces: g. called laughter 136:18
grin: How cheerfully he seems to g. 69:5
one universal g. 114:11
grind: g. slow, but they grind 168:1
g. the faces of the poor 32:28
one demd horrid g. 95:18
grinning: such g. honour as Sir Walter 228:10
groan: hear each other g. 155:1
groan'd: My mother g. 43:27
Grocer: God made the wicked G. 76:18
grooves: predestinate g. 130:15
ringing g. of change 264:6
grope: We g. for Truth 90:23
ground: g. where only one grew before 258:13
holy g. 26:16
no g. whatever for supposing it true 218:19
stand on your own g. 270:16
grounde: Grammere, that g. is of alle 162:16
groundlings: split the ears of the g. 227:4
grounds: round the g. for the second time 200:9
grovelled: great man he g. before him 266:10
groves: feels as if it was g. 94:26
g. of Academe 139:23
grow: boys refuse to g. up 174:6
some of us never g. out of it 273:3
two blades of grass to g. 258:13
grow'd: I 'spect I g. 257:10
growing: close / Upon the g. boy 292:23
g., Jock, when ye're sleeping 222:19
g. up into a pretty woman 12:14
grows: power g. out of the barrel 174:21
grub: old ones, g. 238:27
grumbling: g. grew to a mighty rumbling 51:25
Grundy: more of Mrs. G. 167:24
Solomon G. 195:16
what will Mrs. G. zay 189:19
gruntled: far from being g. 290:25
guarantee: No one can g. success 78:12
guard: changing g. at Buckingham Palace 181:17
none but Americans on g. 280:7
who is to g. the guards 152:13
Guards: Stand up, G. 282:4
Up g. and at 'em 282:3
gud: symply g. man callyt 19:12
gude: g. time coming 222:24
guerre: *mais ce n'est pas la g.* 45:7
guess: dream of him, and g. 51:20
Guesses: G. at Heaven 153:32
guest: receive an honoured g. 11:7
speed the parting g. 207:9
guests: g. few and select 162:6
hosts and g. 22:9
guid: ony g. or ill, / They've done 56:18
guide: great g. of human life 142:1
g., philosopher, and friend 206:29
g., / in thy most need 5:13
probability is the very g. 59:12
guides: Ye blind g. 36:30
guiding-star: g. of a whole brave nation 189:20
guilt: Image of war, without its g. 249:24
upright life and free from g. 140:1

Guilty: G. of dust and sin 135:6
like a g. thing surprised 292:25
no g. man escape 126:19
scorn the g. bays 207:25
started like a g. thing 225:35
ten g. persons escape 41:26
guinea: somewhat like a g. 44:1
guineas: crowns and pounds and g. 140:28
guitar: sang to a small g. 164:10
You have a blue g. 255:1
gules: warm g. on Madeline's 153:29
gulf stream: swimming in a warm g. 174:19
gulfs: whelmed in deeper g. 87:5
gull: To the g.'s way 178:12
gun: come through a door with a g. 72:8
ever lost an English g. 264:20
Is that a g. in your pocket 283:9
out of the barrel of a g. 174:21
Gunga Din: than I am, G. 159:8
Gunpowder: G., Printing, and the Protestant 67:20
G., treason and plot 6:18
Guns: G. will make us powerful 124:8
like loaded g. with boys 88:17
gushed: love g. from my heart 81:12
gusty: along the g. floor 153:30
guts: g. a galling give her 261:2
g. to betray my country 116:22
I'll lug the g. 227:18
sheep's g. should hale souls 234:17
gutter: all in the g., but some 287:19
gutters: taste for g. 22:4
gypsies: Play with the g. 195:4
gypsy: to the vagrant g. life 178:12
gyre: turning in the widening g. 297:18
ha'penny: haven't got a h., God bless you! 5:4
habit: Costly thy h. as thy purse 226:10
H. with him was all the test 88:14
habitation: local h. and a name 234:13
habit-forming: Cocaine isn't h. 19:8
habits: curious h. of dogs 208:21
h. that carry them far apart 84:4
habitual: nothing is h. but indecision 145:4
hacked: h. him in pieces sma' 17:16
had: good time that was h. by all 91:14
Hades: H.' bobbin bound 296:1
Haggis: Him H. — velly goot 172:7
hail: brother, h. and farewell 71:9
H. to the Chief 221:17
hair: bright h. about the bone 100:8
false h. / Become a verse 135:5
h. of a woman can draw 141:6
h. of yon grey head 285:9
My h. is grey, but not with years 64:4
tangles of Neaera's h. 182:23
you have lovely h. 74:29
hairless: h. as an egg 135:25
hairs: bring down my gray h. 26:11
H. less in sight 207:22
ill white h. become 228:25
hairy: my brother is a h. man 26:3
halcyon: h. days 229:7
half: ae h. of the warld thinks 222:22
dearer h. 184:21
don't know which h. 165:9
h. of the world cannot understand 12:5
H. to remember days 115:6
h. was not told me 28:11
loves but h. of Earth 212:6
one h. of the greatness 28:26
overcome but h. his foe 183:24
Too civil by h. 245:5
half-a-dozen: h. of the other 176:22
half-and-half: No h. affair 122:8
half-free: half-slave and h. 166:6
half-human: h. cheer 91:5
half-pennyworth: monstrous! but one h. of bread 228:1
half-shut: through all things with his h. eyes 207:20
half-slave: endure permanently h. 166:6
Hallowed: H. be thy name 35:24
Halls: tap'stry H. / And Courts 181:26
your dreary marble h. 65:18
halo: h.? It's only one more 118:25
halt: h., and the blind 37:26
How long h. ye between 28:14
hame: h. in my ain countree 89:15
Hamlet: good juggler to a bad H. 80:11
I saw H....played 112:18
hammers: hear the h. ring 158:18
hammock: Drake he's in his h. 191:19
hand: bringing me up by h. 94:16
h. into the hand of God 131:4
handle toward my h. 231:35
H. that made us 2:9
h. that rocks the cradle 278:1
h. to execute 121:21
hat was in his h. 147:23
his h. to the plough 37:19
lays his h. upon a woman 269:16
led by an invisible h. 247:6
sweeten this little h. 232:23
This is the h. that wrote 88:19
times be in Thy h. 52:2
touch of a vanish'd h. 262:8
Whatsoever thy h. findeth 32:12
handful: fear in a h. of dust 108:13
Just for a h. of silver 51:7
handicraft: Art is not a h. 269:23
handicraftsmen: h. wore the mask / Of Poesy 155:13
handiwork: sheweth his h. 29:22
handkerchiefs: moral pocket h. 96:3
handle: h. toward my hand 231:35
polished up the h. 122:15
handmaid: philosophy...an h. to religion 13:25
Riches are a good h. 13:18
hands: at any h., however lowly 122:25
cold immortal h. 260:11
h. are red with guiltless 243:29
h. are the hands of Esau 26:4
h. of the living God 40:13
hath not a Jew h. 233:13
his h. formed the dry land 30:15
not into the h. of Spain 265:3
not without men's h. 107:2
Pale h. I loved 138:23
shook h. with time 116:15
soon wring their h. 278:24
their h. are blue 164:8
union of h. and hearts 262:1
handsaw: hawk from a h. 226:31
handwriting: sight of their own h. 11:17
hang: h. a man first 187:4
help us to h. ane 46:6
neither go nor h. 41:16

On which they h. a man 286:4
We must all h. together 117:30
will not h. myself today 76:5
wretches h. that jury-men 207:19
hang'd: h. my braw John Highlandman 57:2
hanged: h. in a fortnight 149:15
h. in all innocence 257:2
h. our harps 31:10
Harrison h., drawn and quartered 201:1
not h. for stealing horses 129:5
hanget: he was h. 46:7
hangin': h. Danny Deever in the mornin' 158:27
h. men an' women there 7:1
hanging: good h. prevents a bad marriage 237:14
h. garments of Marylebone 151:10
H. is too good for him 53:17
nane the waur o' a h. 46:4
no satisfaction in h. a man 240:16
hangman: if I were...a h. 146:1
these h.'s hands 231:37
hansel: h. of this guid new year 104:27
happen: h. / to somebody else 176:15
It Can't H. Here 165:15
happens: Everything that h. 12:2
h. anywhere 163:9
Nothing h., nobody comes 21:20
What h. to us 172:24
happier: leave them h. than before 296:22
middling zone, a h. state 220:11
happiest: h. and best minds 244:21
h. women, like the happiest nations 106:23
happiness: consume h. without producing it 238:30
Domestic h., thou only bliss 88:6
flaw / In h. 153:22
greatest h. of the greatest number 24:11
h. / Consists not in the multitude 150:17
h. destroyed by preparation 12:9
H. in marriage 12:24
H. is no laughing matter 283:15
h....no longer at school 22:8
h.! no man alive could bear it 239:21
h. of the greatest number 142:16
H.! our being's end 206:24
Knowledge is not h. 63:34
makes the h. 147:21
new dish does more for the h. 46:23
Nothing brings complete h. 140:4
only thing for h. 105:15
Perfect h....not common 12:8
pursuit of h. 7:17
result h. 94:2
so much h. is produced 149:9
spectacle of human h. 248:5
state is the greatest h. 202:25
substantial h., *to eat* 207:12
Wherein lies h. 153:17
Withdraws into its h. 177:13
happy: all be as h. as kings 255:13
all be h., and live within 279:18
duty of being h. 256:24
every lot is h. if 44:7
fares it with the h. dead 263:14
h., and you cease to be so 180:7
h. / As in a soul remembering 235:16
h. as the grass was green 266:23
h. could I be with either 120:20
h. English child 261:22
h. families resemble one another 269:19
h. in the arms of a chambermaid 149:18
h. land, / Far, far away 298:22
H. the man 207:10
H. the man 276:6
H. the man, and happy 103:30
h. until he is dead 249:21
h. while y'er leevin 4:25
I've had a h. life 132:3
keep me h., but wanting that 131:14
make men h., and to keep 206:32
misfortune is to have been h. 44:6
never so h. or so unhappy 162:22
O h. day, that fixed 98:18
perfectly h. till all are happy 251:5
policeman's lot is not a h. 123:14
See the h. moron 6:25
splendid and a h. land 125:11
Take my counsel, h. man 122:10
to attain / The h. life 258:1
was the carver h. while 218:9
Who is the h. Warrior 291:20
harbinger: morning Star, Day's h. 185:18
hard: chance to work h. 216:8
H. Rain's A-Gonna Fall 105:7
how h. is the way 90:11
more h. to please himself 103:4
hard-beaten: broad, h. road to his house 110:25
harder: h. they fall 115:5
hard-faced: lot of h. men 16:22
Hardly: *never?*' / 'H. ever!' 122:13
hardness: without h. will be sage 9:14
Hardy: H. became a sort of village atheist 77:1
Kiss me, H. 191:13
hare: triumph o'er the timid h. 268:8
hares: little hunted h. 137:1
Hark: H.! hark! the lark 225:30
harlot: h.'s cry from street 42:5
prerogative of the h. 160:4
harm: benevolence...does most...h. 16:15
No people do so much h. 88:30
harmless: h. as doves 36:11
h. drudge 148:10
harmonious: h. sisters, Voice and Verse 181:22
Such h. madness 244:17
harmoniously: world, h. confus'd 207:26
harmony: discord, h. not understood 206:17
From h., from heavenly harmony 103:26
H. in discord 139:19
h. is in immortal souls 233:24
spirit grows / Like h. 293:7
harness: joints of the h. 28:18
harp: h. that once through Tara's 188:19
h. with a solemn sound 30:13
heart and h. have lost a string 61:18
wild h. slung behind 188:21
harps: h. upon the willows 31:10
Harris: Frank H. is invited to all 288:21
harrow: toad beneath the h. 159:23
Harry: Cry 'God for H. 228:32
young H. with his beaver on 228:5
harsh: Berries, h. and crude 182:19
h. after the songs of Apollo 231:18
hart: As pants the h. 261:17

h.! heart! heart 284:13
h. in hiding 139:3
h. is an anvil 175:15
h. is deceitful above 34:6
h. is like Indian rubber 47:2
h., not in the knees 145:24
H. of Man...consists of four 46:16
h. of the matter 139:8
h. or in the head 233:15
H.'s denying 19:23
h.'s grown brutal from the fare 297:4
h.'s in the Highlands 57:9
h. to resolve 121:21
h. upon my sleeve 91:2
h. was going like mad 151:22
His h.... / Wax to receive 61:1
Indian Summer of the h. 285:11
in thy h. and write 245:25
In your h. you know 5:25
language of the h. 205:10
Let not your h. be troubled 38:11
Lord looketh on the h. 27:32
make a stone of the h. 296:14
maketh the h. sick 31:24
man after his own h. 27:29
mighty h. is lying still 293:26
more knowledge of the h. 148:25
My h. leaps up 292:18
my h. waketh 32:23
natural language of the h. 224:12
never a crack in my h. 297:3
no longer tear his h. 259:23
not to get your h.'s desire 239:29
not your h. away 140:28
Open my h. 50:20
private h. is true for all 110:11
rag-and-bone shop of the h. 296:4
send me back my h. 257:15
softer pillow than my h. 64:25
there will your h. be 35:26
true love hath my h. 245:24
weeping in my h. 274:13
wounds more deep the gen'rous h. 147:5
heart-ache: we end / The h. 226:37
heart-easing: tell the most h. things 155:15
hearth: By this still h. 265:7
cricket on the h. 182:5
hearths: their altars, and their h. 219:24
heart-quake: Each kiss a h. 62:28
hearts: all that human h. endure 125:23
do not harden your h. against 275:3
equal temper of heroic h. 265:15
first in the h. 164:16
H. are not had as a gift 297:13
H. just as pure and fair 122:19
Kind h. are more than coronets 263:25
Lift up your h. 178:18
Queen of H., she made 69:24
queen of H. / She made 195:19
their h. the fire's centre 251:7
Two h. that beat 169:12
unto whom all h. be open 210:6
Heat: H. is in proportion to the want 254:14
h. o' the sun 225:31
sudden h. which made my heart 250:22
heath: foot is on my native h. 222:25
heathen: h. in the carnal part 204:24
Why do the h. rage 29:13
Heav'n: against H.'s matchless King 184:12
Down from the verge of H. 184:24
make a H. of Hell 183:15
than serve in H. 183:16
Heav'n-borne: H. child 183:1
heav'ns: finds not h. to suit 188:24
Heaven: all going direct to H. 96:18
all H. in a Rage 42:3
all of h. we have below 1:17
All this and h. too 133:18
all we know of h. 96:25
Battering the gates of h. 265:5
do in h. we are ignorant 259:7
Earth's crammed with h. 49:15
earth was nigher h. 51:28
even from the gates of h. 53:20
farther off from h. 138:7
gazing up into h. 38:20
gentle sleep from H. 81:13
God's in his h. 51:27
Guesses at H. 153:32
h. above / And the road 255:15
h. an angel is nobody 240:12
H. and earth shall pass 36:33
H. and Earth have no pity 162:20
H. blazing into the head 296:26
H. cannot brook two suns 3:5
H. forbids certain pleasures 187:6
H. for climate 272:14
H. in a Wild Flower 41:28
h. in hell's despair 43:21
h. is, eating *pâtés* 248:29
H. is empty 191:16
H. lies about us 292:23
H.'s peculiar care 249:25
H. thought otherwise 275:14
H. views it with delight 177:6
H. vows to keep him 150:23
Joy shall be in h. 37:27
kingdom of h. is like 36:16
Lord made h. and earth 26:33
love is h., and heaven 221:22
more things in h. and earth 226:20
new h. and a new earth 41:4
not mad, sweet h. 230:24
nurseries of H. 267:25
One H., one Hell 242:4
open face of h. 155:24
some call it the road to h. 18:13
spark from h. 9:24
thankful thought raised to h. 165:5
then — what pleases H. 222:4
thirtieth year to h. 267:2
top of it reached to h. 26:5
what's a h. for 49:23
young was very h. 293:10
yourselves treasures in h. 35:25
heavenly: anger in h. minds 275:7
from h. harmony 103:26
heavens: h. declare the glory of God 29:22
h. fill with commerce 264:4
Hung be the h. with black 229:6
Let the h. be glad 28:24
spangled h. a shining frame 2:8
starry h. above me 152:22
though the h. fall 113:11
When I consider thy h. 29:15
heavy: h. and the weary weight 292:12
Lie h. on him, Earth 112:17
O the h. change 182:21
Hecuba: What's H. to him 226:35
heeded: heard it, but he h. not 62:4
heel: battered kettle at the h. 298:9
lifted up his h. against me 29:28

heels: Time wounds all h. 7:13
Heights: H. which the soul 292:5
heir: sole h. of the whole world 270:4
Helen: Dust hath closed H.'s eye 191:2
I were where H. lies 17:15
like another H. 103:2
Like H., in the night 217:23
Helicon: watered our horses in H. 72:11
hell: all we need of h. 96:25
ancient prince of h. 170:16
Better to reign in H. 183:16
boys, it is all h. 245:15
deepest pot of h. 104:17
England...h. of horses 115:16
go to h. like lambs 76:10
heaven? — Is he in h. 196:18
heaven in h.'s despair 43:21
Heaven, one H., one immortality 242:4
h., even from the gates of heaven 53:20
h. for society 272:14
H. is a city 243:11
H. is full of musical amateurs 239:24
H. is other people 220:17
H. of Heav'n 183:15
h. of this world 21:22
H. raised a hoarse 91:5
h. shall not prevail against 36:21
H. trembl'd at the hideous 184:9
h. / of a good universe 89:13
Italy...h. for women 59:9
Lead apes in h. 236:11
make / This world our h. 286:22
never mentions H. to ears polite 205:17
night seems termless h. 268:13
Nor H. a fury, like a woman 84:26
out of H. leads up 184:7
stirrup-pump / Will extinguish h. 213:13
this is h., nor am I out 175:4
Ugly h., gape not 175:13
way to H. is easy 275:18
where we are is H. 175:5
Which way I fly is H. 184:13
would be h. on earth 239:21
helm: Pleasure at the h. 127:7
help: encumbers him with h. 148:1
in whom there is no h. 31:13
My h. cometh from the Lord 31:4
Since there's no h. 102:8
very present h. in trouble 30:1
help meet: h. for him 25:16
helped: over, and can't be h. 96:1
Helpless: I leapt; / H. 43:27
hemispheres: jars two h. 129:18
hemlock: h. I had drunk 154:33
hen: h. is only an egg's way 60:3
nat of that text a pulled h. 73:7
hennes: in his governaunce / Sevene h. 74:8
herald: Hark! the h. angels 282:28
heralds: chosen h. of England's Marshal 76:19
herbs: dinner of h. where love is 31:27
h., and other country messes 182:15
herde: Oon ere it h. 74:23
herd-instinct: Morality is the h. 192:25
Here: H. or nowhere is the whole fact 111:22
Hereditary: H. Bondsmen 61:15
heresies: By h. distressed 257:4
new truths to begin as h. 143:13
sects, / And hateful h. 251:16
heritage: have a goodly h. 29:18
Our h. the sea 89:18
Hermes: thrice great H. 182:8
hermitage: take / That for an h. 169:7
hermits: h. are contented 294:2
hero: conquering h. comes 189:7
fight for an idea like a h. 239:27
h. becomes a bore 111:11
h. must drink brandy 149:21
h. the Conqueror Worm 203:16
h. to his valet 86:3
very valet seem'd a h. 60:27
Herod: It out-herods H. 227:5
heroes: And speed glum h. 220:20
fit country for h. 167:16
land that is in need of h. 46:9
heroic: finish'd / A life h. 185:14
h. poem of its sort 67:17
something more than h. 215:13
heroine: h. goes mad she always 244:29
heron: h. / Priested shore 267:2
Herostratus: H. lives that burnt 48:26
herts: Deep i' the h. o' a' men 172:20
Herveys: men, women, and H. 187:11
hesitates: She wavers, she h. 212:18
Hesperus: schooner H. 168:23
heterodoxy: h. is another man's doxy 279:11
heterogeneous: h. ideas are yoked 146:20
heureux: *jamais si h. ni si malheureux* 162:22
Hewers: H. of wood 27:12
Hexameter: long roll of the H. 264:10
Hey: H. diddle diddle 194:11
Hickory: H., dickory, dock 194:12
hid: mist of tears / I h. from Him 267:21
hide: Talent which is death to h. 185:22
world to h. virtues in 237:13
Youk'n h. de fier 130:26
hideous: h. ruin and combustion 183:11
hierarchy: Olympus' faded h. 155:8
High: equal'd the most H. 183:10
from h. life high characters 205:19
highbrow: h....looks at a sausage 134:9
highbrows: article denouncing 'h. 196:22
High-definition: H. performance 272:21
higher: dead selves to h. things 263:7
he shall shoot h. than 245:23
h. law than the Constitution 224:9
highest: h. summits, but he cannot 239:2
h. type of human nature 251:1
love the h. when we see it 262:19
Highland: solitary H. lass 293:22
Highlandman: hang'd my braw John H. 57:2
Highlands: heart's in the H. 57:9
H. and ye Lawlands 17:8
Highness: his H.' dog at Kew 205:23
high-rife: h. / With old Philosophy 154:18
highway: h. for our God 33:16
hilarity: flame of h. with the wing 95:19
hill: green h. far away 3:11
H. will not come to Mahomet 14:18
hunter home from the h. 255:20
On a huge h., / Cragged 100:10
one holier h. than Rome 76:20

Hills: H. of home 255:16
mine eyes unto the h. 31:4
Over the h. and far away 120:18
him: all cried, 'That's h.!' 19:16
Himself: H. is his own dungeon 181:27
loving h. better than all 82:12
Man was not born for h. 202:19
speaks so much of H. 15:7
superior man seeks is in h. 84:10
To be h. 143:22
hind: know where is an h. 295:11
hinder: in the h. parts 30:6
hindrances: h. to human improvement 181:1
hint: Just h. a fault 205:4
Hippocrene: blushful H. 154:35
Hippopotamus: shoot the H. 23:2
hire: labourer is worthy of his h. 37:20
hired: h. the money, didn't they 85:18
hireling: paw / Of h. wolves 185:28
hiss: dismal universal h. 184:32
h. in their hair 103:1
Historian: first an H. or a Traveller 130:18
h., and leave me to reason 41:27
h....wants more documents 144:22
proper occupation of the h. 286:9
historians: alter the past, h. can 59:31
historical: find the h. fact 108:3
histories: ancient h....fables...agreed upon 276:19
history: Anything but h. 278:26
dignity of h. 44:15
great deal of h. to produce 145:1
happiest women...have no h. 106:23
h....biography of great men 68:5
H. came to a 224:3
H. has many cunning passages 107:21
h. in all men's lives 228:19
h. is an art like all 281:24
H. is a nightmare 151:20
H. is bunk 116:11
h. is nothing but a tableau 276:18
h. is on our side 157:25
H. is past politics 223:11
H. is Philosophy teaching 44:13
h. is that it is adaptable 273:5
h. is the world's judgement 221:3
h. must be false 278:26
h. of revivals 60:19
H. of the Great Men 67:24
[H.] register of the crimes 121:18
H. tells me nothing 13:11
H. to the defeated 11:15
Human h....race between education 282:22
knowledge...a product of h. 67:21
never learned anything from h. 132:10
no h.; only biography 110:9
No man knows my h. 247:14
regard the h. of Europe 125:2
seems h. is to blame 151:18
some remnants of h. 13:22
War makes rattling good h. 130:4
what experience and h. teach 132:10
whole h. of civilization 16:13
whole h. of the world would 199:7
history-books: blank in h. 67:23
histrionem: *mundus agit h.* 7:14
hit: Don't h. at all if 216:12
h., a very palpable hit 227:27
hundred's soon h. 50:31
Hitler: H. has missed the bus 72:3
hoarded: Beauty...must not be h. 182:1
hobby-horse: rides his h. peaceably 254:1
hobgoblin: h. of little minds 110:14
Hobson: H. has supped 183:5
hockey-legged: h. girls who laughed 266:20
Hodge: H. for ever be 130:2
hodgepodge: h. of all other speeches 252:12
hoe: long row to h. 169:16
Hog: England under an H. 83:4
go the whole h. 176:17
hoggish: have his h. mind 252:3
Hoist: H. with his own petar 227:17
hold: forever h. his peace 210:12
h. the faithful mirror 167:12
H., / enough 232:32
Once did she h. 294:9
To have and to h. 210:14
holds: h. him with his glittering eye 81:2
hole: blasts a great big h. 165:16
holiday: Butcher'd to make a Roman h. 62:5
Change holds h. 91:8
Monday is parson's h. 258:18
holidays: year were playing h. 227:34
holier: one h. hill than Rome 76:20
Holiness: Go! put off H. 42:14
h. of the heart's affections 156:6
what he has lost in h. 60:16
Holland: H....lies so low 138:13
hollow: I hate that dreadful h. 264:12
We are the h. men 107:23
Hollywood: phony tinsel off H. 165:8
holy: everything that lives is h. 42:23
h. and good thought 35:6
h. ground 26:16
h. spirit of man 260:1
Is this a h. thing 43:22
to keep it h. 26:31
Holyday: Sunshine H. 182:16
Holy Roman Empire: H. was not Holy, nor Roman 276:17
homage: h. that vice pays 163:2
owes no h. unto the sun 49:8
home: best country ever is, at h. 125:22
blest by the suns of h. 48:13
burned / As h. his footsteps 222:1
but confined him h. 79:14
different from the h. life 5:21
dream that I am h. again 115:6
England, h. and beauty 46:1
go h. in the dark 133:21
Hills of h. 255:16
h. and friends...forlorn 17:17
H. is the sailor 255:20
h., I was in a better 225:8
H....they have to take you in 118:8
murder back into the h. 136:12
no place like h. 200:5
Pleasure never is at h. 153:35
returns h. to find it 188:9
sick for h. 155:6
till the cow comes h. 21:16
will be h. before the leaves 289:2
homeless: h. by choice 250:15
Homer: contend for H. Dead 6:26
H. as the herald 3:6
H. sometimes sleeps 63:1
man who has not read H. 16:9
more than H. knew 259:15

must not call it H. 24:16
single exception of H. 239:5
worthy H. nods 139:12
homes: stately h. of England 133:2
Homesickness: H. for the gutter 11:18
homeward: Look h., Angel 182:32
homines: *Quot h. tot sententiae* 265:24
hommage: *h. que le vice rend* 163:2
homo: *Ecce h.* 277:24
H. sum 265:23
honest: anglers, or very h. men 279:8
day is for h. men 112:15
good to be h. 6:2
h. by an act of parliament 150:19
h. Fame, or grant me none 207:25
h. God's the noblest work 60:2
h. man's the noblest work 56:1
h. Man's the noblest work 206:26
h. politician is one who 65:22
looking for an h. man 97:9
more faith in h. doubt 263:19
Necessity makes an h. man 92:8
not an h. man 283:17
honestly: If possible, make money h. 139:15
make money h. 139:15
Honesty: H. is praised and is neglected 152:8
H. is the best policy, but 283:17
honey: Eating bread and h. 195:15
eat our pot of h. 179:21
flowing with milk and h. 26:17
hives with h. and wax 258:9
h. still for tea 48:5
How a bear likes h. 181:10
spoonful of h. than 133:9
sweeter also than h. 29:23
took some h. 164:10
With milk and h. blest 24:19
honey-dew: on h. hath fed 82:7
Honi: *H. soit qui mal* 5:19
honied: h. indolence 154:27
honour: All is lost save h. 117:6
do h. the very flea 150:24
fountain of h. 15:28
greater share of h. 228:34
high h. / Bot wind 134:1
H. all men 40:25
h., it is no longer peace 218:22
H. pricks me on 228:9
h. rooted in dishonour 262:22
h. sinks where commerce 125:24
H. the greatest poet 90:6
H. thy father and 26:34
idiot race, to h. lost 57:13
Keeps h. bright 237:6
king delighteth to h. 28:29
leap / To pluck bright h. 227:35
Lov'd I not H. more 169:9
man of h....the unfortunate 249:3
most h. to the human genius 276:21
Or stain her h. 207:17
peace, I hope, with h. 98:7
peace with h. 72:2
places where their h. died 204:29
prophet is not without h. 36:17
sick hearts that h. could not 48:11
signed with their h. 251:8
sin to covet h. 228:35
such grinning h. 228:10
titles do not reflect h. 173:7
woman's h.; which is probably more 177:26
honour'd: for his h. bones 183:4
honourable: all h. men 230:2
strictly h., as the phrase is 114:9
honoured: Ambition's h. fools. 61:5
from these h. dead 166:11
more h. in the breach 226:13
honours: h. immediately from Almighty God 56:7
H., like impressions upon coin 254:22
men serve / Whom h. smokes 99:3
hook: leviathan with an h. 29:11
hooter: because the h. hoots 76:10
hope: Abandon h., all ye who enter 90:2
Because I do not h. 107:5
But not another's h. 279:2
fooled with h. 103:5
have not h. of death 90:3
h. beyond the shadow 153:18
H. deferred maketh 31:24
h. for the best 248:14
H. is a good breakfast 13:26
H. springs eternal 206:12
H., whereof he knew 129:19
life, there's h. 265:22
lives upon h. will die fasting 117:22
loving...when h. is gone 12:22
Never to h. again 229:15
sure and certain h. 210:21
triumph of h. over experience 148:23
unconquerable h. 9:27
While there's tea there's h. 201:27
without any h. of doing it well 77:5
hoped: never h. can never despair 238:29
hopefully: travel h. is a better 256:26
hopes: far-reaching h. 139:26
H. which obscure 47:16
If h. were dupes 80:2
no great h. from Birmingham 12:10
Hoping: H. it might be so 130:8
Horace: H.; whom I hated so 62:2
horizontal: best life is led h. 119:5
fine, into a h. line 283:19
horn: Come blow your h. 194:24
h. from the depths of 274:22
Horner: Little Jack H. 194:25
Hornie: Auld H., Satan, Nick 55:14
horns: h. of Elfland faintly blowing 264:22
Horny-handed: H. sons of toil 153:7
horreur: *h. d'une profonde nuit* 212:17
horrid: bad she was h. 168:8
bad, she was h. 195:21
horror: h. and fear 264:17
h. of a profoundly dark 212:17
h. that I writhe in 172:9
h.! The horror 85:5
horrors: silly h. o' oor fates 172:15
horse: behold a pale h. 40:37
between a rider and his h. 258:7
German to my h. 72:24
h. is to the rider 11:27
kingdom for a h. 235:29
like a pawing h. let go 81:14
little dearer than his h. 264:3
Never look a gift h. 145:23
strength of the h. 31:14
where's the bloody h. 66:1
Horse Guards: H. and still be common 213:8
Horseman: H., pass by 298:14
horses: All the king's h. 194:14
as fed h. in the morning 34:2
breed of their h. 200:17

No h. generations tread 155:6
hunt: country patriots born? / To h. 60:26
Whoso list to h. 295:11
hunted: h. out of every corner 247:11
little h. hares 137:1
others by their h. expression 165:13
hunter: hungry as a h. 161:18
h. home from the hill 255:20
Man is the h. 264:25
hunters: h. ben nat hooly men 73:7
hunting: call h. [pleasure] 150:1
huntress: Queen and h., 150:18
Hurl'd: H. headlong flaming 183:11
hurly-burly: h. of the chaise-longue 65:24
hurry: never in a h. 283:5
old man in a h. 77:18
hurt: h. too much to laugh 166:19
I'll not h. thee 254:4
lie that sinketh...doth the h. 14:2
power to do h. and will do 238:14
husband: bad h. and an ill provider 109:22
Chaste to her H. 204:25
good works in her H. 184:29
has an ideal h. 261:16
[H.] Feed the brute 104:16
h. is a whole-time job 24:7
husband-hunting: h. butterfly 186:10
husbandman: h. that laboureth 40:10
husbands: pushing their h. along 93:15
reasons for h. to stay 106:24
When h., or when lap-dogs 207:21
hush: breathless h. in the Close 191:20
husks: h. that the swine did eat 37:28
hut: Love in a h. 154:16
hydroptic: h. earth hath drunk 100:6
hymn-book: Cassock, band, and h. 285:17
hymns: sweet bird's marriage h. 106:20
hymself: ech man for h. 73:18
Hyphenated: H. Americans 215:25
hypocrisie: *h. est un hommage* 163:2
hypocrisy: Conservative government is an organized h. 98:2
H. is the homage 163:2
love is taught h. from youth 62:17
hypocrite: h. in his pleasures 149:28
H. lecteur 20:20
hypothesis: slaying of a beautiful h. 143:10
hyssop: h., and I shall be clean 277:14
Iacta: *I. alea est* 65:10
Iambics: I. march from short 82:8
you shall not escape my i. 71:10
ice: good to break the i. 14:25
Some say in i. 118:10
ice-cream: emperor of i. 254:25
Ichabod: I., Ichabod 52:17
named the child I. 27:26
icy: Death lays his i. hand 245:17
idea: Between the i. / And the reality 107:24
fight for an i. like a hero 239:27
pain of a new i. 16:14
would be an excellent i. 119:20
young i. how to shoot 268:5
ideal: i. reader suffering 151:9
i. wife...has...ideal husband 261:16
idealistic: America...only i. nation 290:14
idealize: struggles to i. and to unify 82:13
ideals: enemy of progressive i. 23:19
ideas: green i. sleep furiously 77:7
i. that make us optimists 272:25
invasion of i. 141:18
no i. but in things 289:12
scholars...who love i. 2:24
sound and original i. 174:1
trust in i. 111:4
Idem: *I. velle atque* 219:22
identity: find...i. by killing his oppressor 23:20
has no i. 156:16
sleep / Without i. 47:12
Ides: Beware the I. of March 229:18
idiot: law is a ass — a i. 95:25
Told by an i. 232:28
idle: i. as a painted ship 81:6
i. hands to do 280:14
less i. than when free from work 78:20
months the most i. and unprofitable 121:10
more or less i. people 16:6
my words are i. 281:18
profits that an i. king 265:7
such i. fellows as I 11:1
Tears, i. tears 264:23
Idleness: I. is only the refuge of weak 75:21
I passed a day in i. 70:25
Love in i. 236:9
unyoked humour of your i. 227:33
idlers: number of well-to-do i. 178:4
idling: impossible to enjoy i. thoroughly 145:16
idol: one-eyed yellow i. 131:7
idolatry: honour his memory, on this side i. 151:3
of the ancients without i. 75:15
If: I. you can fill 159:11
much virtue in 'i.' 225:24
ifs: If i. and ands were pots 200:10
ignoble: Counsel'd i. ease 184:2
doctrine of i. ease 216:5
Ignorance: blind and naked I. 262:25
i. cramps my conversation 138:22
i. is bliss 127:23
I., madam 148:9
I. of the law excuses 223:14
more than Gothic i. 114:7
names / To hide its i. 243:28
no sin but i. 175:22
pity his i. and despise him 95:14
putting us to i. again 50:15
science...exchange of i. 63:34
women in a state of i. 160:12
ignorant: father was so i. 272:17
Where i. armies clash 9:8
ignorantly: blockhead, i. read 206:5
ignored: cease to exist because...i. 143:1
Ignotus: *I. moritur sibi* 224:5
ignus: Reason, an *i. fatuus* 214:20
Iliad: greater than the I. is born 211:4
ill: every i., a woman is the worst 126:20
I. fares the land 125:3
Looking i. prevail 257:17
ony guid or i., / They've done 56:18
ill-born: i. mob began 92:3
ill-bred: i., as audible laughter 75:5
ill-contrived: singularly i. world 16:25
illegitimacy: stain of i. 12:12

ill-favoured: i. thing, sir, but mine own 225:23
ill-housed: one-third of a nation i. 215:18
ill-natur'd: vain, i. thing, an Englishman 92:3
illnesses: extreme i. extreme remedies 136:10
ill-nourished: ill-clad, i. 215:18
illogical: i. belief in the...improbable 179:16
ills: i. have not been done by woman 197:9
nae real i. perplex them 58:6
ill-spent: billiards well was a sign of an i. 251:6
illuminatio: *Dominus i. mea* 277:13
illusion: alas, only one i. left 248:21
only one i....the Archbishop 248:21
illusions: Don't part with your i. 272:3
Indulgin' in i. 172:16
Image: Best I. of my self 184:21
graven i., or any likeness 26:29
i. of that whereof the philosopher 246:6
in his i., we have repaid him 277:6
make man in our i. 25:14
Maker's i. through the land 102:12
more i. than a shade 296:1
images: i. which find a mirror 147:1
imaginary: as if they were i. 25:7
i. gardens with real toads 188:13
make i. evils 125:17
imagination: driven the living i. out 298:20
fight in his i. 151:4
heart is nothing but his i. 239:12
I. is more important than knowledge 106:6
I.'s struggles, far and nigh 153:19
i. the rudder 156:5
i. may be compared to Adam's 156:9
i....wings of an ostrich 171:11
i. bodies forth 234:13
i. amend them 234:15
i. for his facts 245:13
lady's i. is very rapid 12:25
literalists of the i. 188:13
of i. all compact 234:12
primary i. 82:13
save those that have no i. 240:30
sweeten my i. 230:40
truth of i. 156:6
Were it not for i. 149:18
imaginations: i. as one would 13:30
imagine: i. a vain thing 29:13
imagined: earth's i. corners 99:22
Imbrown: golden ear / I. the slope 205:18
Imitation: I. is the sincerest form 83:16
i. of an action 8:27
Immanent: I. Will that stirs 129:17
immensities: probing their i. 50:13
immerse: In the destructive element i. 85:6
Immodest: I. words admit of no defence 216:17
immoral: moral or an i. book 287:20
immortal: grow i. as they quote 299:7
His biting is i. 224:32
I. death 170:12
I. longings in me 225:1
I., though no more 61:10
in a long i. dream 154:15
Know thyself first i. 74:16
make me i. with a kiss 175:7
not search for i. life 201:25
To himself every one is an i. 60:17
What i. hand or eye 43:24
With cold i. hands 260:11
immortalis: *mors cum i.* 170:12
immortality: achieve i. through my work 3:22
admit the i. of the human 90:17
just Ourselves — / And I. 96:21
ne'er is crown'd / With i. 153:20
one Hell, one i. 242:4
Immortals: President of the I. 130:12
Imparadis'd: I. in one another's arms 184:14
impartial: Death, with i. foot 139:25
impatient: i. as the Wind 294:3
impediment: cause, or just i. 210:10
impediments: Admit i. 238:18
imperfect: 'but' in this i. world 47:3
imperfection: fatal i. of all the gifts 85:10
imperial: enslaves you on i. principles 240:18
i. theme 231:22
Imperialism: I. is a paper tiger 174:22
Imperially: think I. 71:23
imperii: *Capax i.* 261:9
impertinence: variety of matter to his i. 1:22
importance: matters of grave i., style 287:10
Nothing...of the smallest i. 287:29
important: more i. than the facts 295:8
imposes: child i. on the man 103:12
impossibile: *quia i. est* 265:29
Impossibility: by despair / Upon I. 177:4
That fond i. 169:10
impossible: believed as many as six i. things 70:6
certain because it is i. 265:29
eliminated the i. 101:19
i. takes a little longer 5:8
i. to be silent 55:2
i. to ravish me 115:14
I. venir, mensonge 211:10
I.! He is an Oxonian 287:13
not i. she 88:26
states that something is i. 79:7
wish it were i. 150:2
impotent: i. people 267:18
impoverished: i. the public stock 147:4
Plenty has i. me 197:17
imprecision: i. of feeling 107:17
imprison: i. me, for I / Except you enthrall 99:28
improbable: condemn it as an i. fiction 237:24
however i., must be the truth 101:19
illogical belief in the...i. 179:16
Impropriety: I. is the soul of wit 178:28
improved: enormously i. by death 219:10
Murderers are not i. by murdering 23:20
improvement: hindrances to human i. 181:1
political i. are very laughable 148:21
improvements: No great i. in the lot 180:8
improving: certain of i., and that's your own 143:6
impudence: Cockney i. before now 218:4

impulse: i. from a vernal wood 294:17
slave of circumstance / And i. 64:5
impune: *Nemo me i. lacessit* 6:11
impure: Puritan all things are i. 163:19
inability: i. to cross the street 291:15
inaccessible: Remote, serene, and i. 243:4
inaccuracy: i. sometimes saves tons 219:9
lying, but I hate i. 60:11
inactivity: masterly i. 173:15
inarticulate: raid on the i. 107:17
inbreeding: Sick with i. 267:18
incapacity: old maid courted by i. 43:7
incarnadine: multitudinous seas i. 232:3
Inchcape: it is the I. Rock 250:17
inch-rule: i. of taste 1:5
incident: i. but the illustration of character 144:20
That was the curious i. 101:21
inclination: read just as i. 148:13
inclined: he i. unto me 29:27
include: i. me out 126:2
income: Annual i. twenty pounds 94:2
live beyond its i. 60:15
moderate i. — such a one 161:24
source of the family i. 196:21
incomprehensible: more speakingly i. 12:15
Inconsistencies: I....are often justifiable 281:6
incontinence: filth and foul i. 252:3
inconvenience: i., even from worse to 138:15
inconvenient: blush...sometimes i. 124:25
i. to be poor 87:7
lie even when it is i. 274:20
Poverty...confoundedly i. 249:1
Incorrigibly: I. plural 174:4
Incorruptible: sea-green I. 68:8
increase: God gave the i. 39:3
i. / The number of the dead 91:1
increases: Population, when unchecked, i. 174:17
incredulity: i.! the wit of fools 72:10
increment: Unearned i. 180:23
incurable: Life is an i. disease 86:24
incurious: By the i. dead 93:13
Indecency: I.'s Conspiracy of Silence 240:14
indecent: sent down for i. behaviour 280:20
indecision: nothing is habitual but i. 145:4
indelible: i. stamp of his lowly 90:16
independence: all my boasted i. 58:18
essence of...American Declaration of I. 111:8
first of earthly blessings, i. 121:14
i. of solitude 110:18
independent: i. wish / E'er planted 57:8
poor and i. 80:5
index: mere i. hunter 249:6
Indian: I. Summer of the heart 285:11
Like the base I. 235:7
like the I., in another life 206:25
only good I. is a dead 244:24
indictment: i. against a whole people 54:24
indifference: cold i. came 217:21
i. closely bordering on aversion 256:7
indifferent: count nothing human i. 265:23
good, bad, and i. 252:13
universe...is i. 137:11
indignatio: *facit i. versum* 152:9
Ubi saeva i. 259:23
indignation: fierce i. can no longer 259:23
i. makes verses 152:9
Moral i. is jealousy 282:23
Indignor: *I. quandoque* 139:12
indirections: i. find directions 226:23
indiscreet: Questions are never i. 286:26
indissoluble: entangle themselves with i. compacts 147:12
inditing: My heart is i. 29:31
individual: man you educate an i. 173:10
not an i., but a species 114:1
not the i. but the species 147:9
program that every i. 145:15
property of every i. in it 111:7
individualism: Rugged i. 138:17
individuality: ceases to possess i. 180:15
crushes i. is despotism 180:16
individuals: love is towards i. 259:20
worth of the i. composing it 180:21
indivisible: Peace is i. 167:6
indolence: honied i. 154:27
indolent: readers to become more i. 125:1
indulge: i. in all the usual 66:20
i. somewhat in the luxury 180:18
industry: Avarice, the spur of i. 142:4
Captains of i. 68:14
I. and all the virtues 142:23
talents, i. will improve 214:1
War...national i. of Prussia 186:8
inebriate: cheer but not i. 88:10
inebriated: i. with the exuberance of 98:8
Ineluctable: I. modality of the visible 151:19
inexactitude: terminological i. 77:20
infallible: i. — not even the youngest 268:2
infâme: *Ecrasez l'i.* 277:9
infamous: Wipe out the i. 277:9
infancy: Nations...have their i. 44:14
Infandum: *I., regina* 275:11
infant: i. crying for the light 263:16
i. phenomenon 95:16
i.'s slumbers, pure and light 157:7
inferior: disgraced by the i. 240:11
inferiority: conscious of an i. 149:10
infini: *l'i. me tourmente* 190:8
infinis: *espaces i. m'effraie* 199:8
infinite: appear as it is, i. 43:15
i. deal of nothing 233:1
i. I AM 82:13
i. Majesty 209:11
i. number of worlds 203:11
I. riches in a little 175:23
i. spaces terrifies me 199:8
there is an I. in him 68:23
Though i. can never meet 177:5
infinite-resource-and-sagacity: man of i. 159:18
infinitum: And so proceed *ad i.* 259:14
Infinity: finite reason reach I. 103:21
Hold I. in the palm 41:28

i. still torments me 190:8
shares the nature of i. 291:19
infirmities: thine often i. 40:6
infirmity: last i. of Noble mind 182:24
inflames: i. the great 59:11
inflections: beauty of i. 255:3
influence: inevitable and silent i. 4:7
I. is not government 279:25
Win Friends and I. People 69:2
influenced: i. my vote 113:12
influenza: i.: so they said 240:24
no i. in my young days 23:25
information: can find i. upon it 149:7
more useful i. than...Thucydides 80:10
only ask for i. 94:4
informed: to be reminded than i. 147:8
ingenious: kind of i. nonsense 20:16
Inglese: *I. Italianato* 10:18
inglorious: not unworthy, not i. son 9:29
ingratitude: so unkind / As man's i. 225:17
inherit: shall i. the earth 35:17
inheritance: i., how wide and spacious 124:20
inhumanity: Man's i. to man 57:7
iniquity: i. of the fathers 26:29
laid on him the i. 33:25
loved justice and hated i. 128:3
measure of i. 58:15
injuries: adding insult to i. 188:7
injury: i. is much sooner forgotten 75:8
never forget an i. 219:16
injustice: i. of it is almost perfect 197:6
who wishes it, no i. 272:22
injustices: *autoriser leurs i.* 276:14
thought only to validate their i. 276:14
ink: all the sea were i. 5:23
buried in the i. that writes 79:5
inland: rocks as an i. island 260:9
inn: by a good tavern or i. 149:9
dark i., the grave 222:5
life...but an i. 141:7
Make my house / your i. 188:15
mine ease at mine i. 228:4
no room for them in the i. 37:11
warmest welcome, at an i. 244:22
Innisfree: go to I. 296:24
innocence: ceremony of i. 297:18
hanged in all i. 257:2
i. itself has many a wile 62:17
innocent: I am i. of the blood 36:39
i. sleep 232:1
than one i. suffer 41:26
innocently: more i. employed 149:1
innovator: Time is the greatest i. 15:2
inns: go to i. to dine 76:18
when you have lost your I. 23:16
innuendoes: beauty of i. 255:3
innumerable: i. company of the heavenly host 44:1
inops: *inter opes i.* 140:11
inquiring: not too i. critic 142:20
inscriptions: i. a man is not upon oath 149:3
insect: into a gigantic i. 152:19
this 'ere 'Tortis' is an i. 211:18
inside: attention to the i. of books 75:20
in your little i. 123:6
insight: moment's i. is sometimes worth 137:18
insights: detached i. are priceless 284:6
insolence: flown with i. and wine 183:19
insomnia: ideal i. 151:9
inspiration: Genius is one per cent i. 105:18
inspired: i. butler 131:13
inspiriting: both touching and i. 255:25
instinct: all healthy i. for it 60:8
i. for being unhappy 219:12
I. is a great matter 227:39
reasons is no less an i. 45:16
instincts: i. before which our mortal 292:25
institution: It's an i. 141:15
institutions: i. which were invaluable 16:13
instructing: delighting the reader while i. 139:11
instruction: horses of i. 43:12
instrument: i. of ten strings 30:13
instruments: i. to plague us 231:6
insufferable: Oxford that has made me i. 22:7
insufficient: from i. premises 60:14
insult: adding i. to injuries 188:7
blockhead's i. points the dart 147:5
much sooner forgotten than an i. 75:8
one more i. to God 51:8
insulted: i., deserves to be 85:21
i. in places where 91:16
insupportable: i. labour of doing nothing 253:6
insurrection: i. of the negroes 149:12
Integer: *I. vitae* 140:1
integrity: i., if you look on every exit 257:5
Intellect: And put on I. 42:14
i. is improperly exposed 248:15
i. of man is forced 296:3
march of i. 250:13
meddling i. / Misshapes 294:18
one-storey i. 137:12
Opinion...determined...not by the i. 251:4
revenge of the i. upon art 249:26
weakness of i., birdie 123:6
intellects: order of imperfect i. 161:7
intellectual: Cynicism is i. dandyism 179:28
Disinterested i. curiosity 270:9
i. All-in-all 293:3
i. hatred is the worst 297:14
murderer, / Yet being i. 65:20
passage to the i. world 254:16
tear is an i. thing 42:15
this i. being 184:1
intellectuals: literary i....avant-garde bias 23:18
treachery of the i. 23:21
intelligence: i. long enough to get money 164:2
intensity: art is its i. 156:3
full of passionate i. 297:18
intent: told with bad i. 41:29
Inter-assured: I. of the mind 100:23
interest: common i. always will prevail 102:22
O, I *du* in i. 169:21
sounds, exceed in i. 161:10
interested: not i. in the possibilities 274:19
you are only i. in art 241:3

not a j. woman 134:10
to the j. confirmation 234:39
jealousy: j.; / It is the green-ey'd 234:37
J.'s a city passion 273:9
j. with a halo 282:23
Jehu: driving of J. 28:23
jelly: Out, vile j. 230:36
Jenny: J. kissed me 142:12
Jericho: from Jerusalem to J. 37:21
jerkin: like a j. and a jerkin's lining 254:11
jerks: bring me up by j. 94:16
Jerusalem: due to the absence from J. 109:14
J. the golden 24:19
O ye daughters of J. 32:19
was J. builded here 42:26
Jesse: out of the stem of J. 33:5
jest: die...that's no j. 7:23
fellow of infinite j. 227:21
glory, j., and riddle 206:19
j.'s prosperity lies 231:15
Life is a j. 120:26
that's no j. 212:23
jests: j. at scars 235:35
memory for his j. 245:13
Jesus: call his name J. 35:7
Friend we have in J. 223:5
Gentle J., meek and mild 282:26
How sweet the Name of J. 192:15
J. and a nameless ape 172:17
J. calls us 3:10
J. loves me! this I know 279:21
J. shall reign where'er 280:17
J. wept 38:9
J. wept; Voltaire smiled 141:21
more popular than J. Christ 165:1
Shove J. and Judas equally 110:15
this J. will not do 42:8
jeunesse: *Si j. savoit* 112:8
Jew: declare that I am a J. 106:9
for Englishman or J. 42:8
Hath not a J. eyes 233:13
poor they call him a J. 132:15
Jewel: death! the J. of the Just 273:18
jewels: bosom to hang j. upon 94:25
Jewish: national home for the J. people 16:26
Jews: born King of the J. 35:8
To choose / The J. 112:20
jigging: j. veins of rhyming 176:2
Jill: Jack and J. went up 194:18
jilted: Better be courted and j. 66:6
jingo: by j. if we do 142:7
jo: John Anderson my j. 56:24
Joan Hunter Dunn: Miss J. 25:5
job: Doing one's j. well 66:21
fifth and lost the j. 151:21
husband is a whole-time j. 24:7
neighbour loses his j. 271:4
we will finish the j. 78:2
jocund: j. day / Stands tiptoe 236:7
jog: j. on, the foot-path way 237:33
man *might j. on with* 161:24
John Anderson: J. my jo 56:24
John Peel: D'ye ken J. 127:1
Johnny: Little J. Head-In-Air 137:4
Johnson: As Dr. J. never said 19:25
freedom with which Dr J. condemns 55:13
[J.] Cham of literature 249:14
J.'s...*bow-wow way* 200:15
no arguing with J. 125:29
join: j. house to house 32:29
seas but j. the regions 207:29
joined: whom God hath j. together 210:17
joint: time is out of j. 226:22
joke: Dullness ever loves a j. 204:7
j. well into a Scotch 248:17
Marriage, Agnès, is not a j. 186:17
jokes: accomplished at seeing / My j. 223:6
all his j., for many a joke 125:8
I don't make j. 215:8
ten j....an hundred enemies 254:5
jolly: serves us j. well right 159:20
some credit in being j. 95:2
Jonathan: Saul and J. were lovely 28:3
Jonson: [J.] a learned plagiary 104:2
learn'd J. 102:6
Too nicely J. knew the critic's 83:11
Joseph: Israel loved J. 26:8
jostling: not done by j. 42:9
journalism: j....survival of the vulgarest 286:8
We are dominated by J. 288:7
journalist: j. makes up his lies 297:8
thank God! the / British j. 291:5
Journalists: J. say a thing 24:6
journey: he is in a j. 28:15
jade on a j. 125:18
j.; but I like to go by myself 132:1
j. of a thousand 162:21
j. really necessary 6:1
j. take the whole long 216:30
worst time...For a j. 107:26
worst time...to take a j. 4:13
Journeys: J. end in lovers meeting 237:16
joy: good tidings of great j. 37:13
if this be j. 125:10
impossible as pure and complete j. 269:21
j. in the loss of human life 162:18
j. is ever on the wing 185:8
j. o' the worm 224:33
J. shall be in heaven 37:27
j. to pass to the world below 275:17
J., whose hand is ever 154:31
j. without canker or cark 162:8
let j. be unconfined 61:20
Like an unbodied j. 244:15
O J., lovely gift 220:27
reap in j. 31:7
sons of God shouted for j. 29:10
Surprised by j. 294:3
thing of beauty is a j. for ever 153:15
world of capability / For j. 50:16
joys: j. are but fantastical 99:5
j. to this are folly 58:21
redoubleth J. 15:5
vain, deluding j. 182:2
Judas: Jesus and J. equally aside 110:15
J. Iscariot was a sad dog 58:16
judge: After a time they j. them 288:15
and a j. over us 26:13
For now I am a J. 123:23
j. great and lofty matters 187:15
j. me by the enemies 215:21
J. not, that ye be not 36:2
J. not the Lord 87:22
J. not the play 91:10
J. not the play 212:3
not j. beyond his last 203:7
sober as a j. 113:19

judgement: at forty, the j. 117:14
Daniel come to j. 233:22
history is the world's j. 221:3
j. comes, we shall not be asked 157:9
J. in discerning what is true 15:6
j. of the world is sure 11:23
j. upon any other nation 290:4
make J. wholly by their rules 15:13
judgements: brawling j., unashamed 262:25
our j. as our watches 205:25
judges: hundred j. have declared 212:8
hungry j. soon the sentence sign 207:19
j. of fact 211:12
judgment: lawful j. of his peers 174:8
nobody [complains] of his j. 163:5
vulgarize the day of j. 146:3
judgments: diff'ring j. serve but to declare 87:14
Jug: 'J. Jug' to dirty ears 108:15
j., jug, tereu, she cries 170:21
loose from de j. 130:23
juger: *j. des choses grandes* 187:15
juggler: prefer a good j. 80:11
Juliet: J. is the sun 235:35
Jumblies: lands where the J. live 164:8
jump: j. the life to come 231:29
j. to conclusions rarely 128:10
jumps: Nature does not make j. 167:5
see how the cat j. 223:3
June: newly sprung in J. 57:10
rare as a day in J. 169:23
juniper: sat under a j. tree 107:7
Juno: J. when she walks 150:32
Jupiter: rage of thundering J. 176:10
vespers in the Temple of J. 121:13
juries: j. fill their stomachs selling 260:21
just: actions of the j. / Smell sweet 245:18
but a j. beast 4:14
cause is j. 97:2
cause we believe to be j. 166:8
chiefly on the j. 45:13
death! the Jewel of the J. 273:18
j. is as the shining light 31:17
j. men but little 217:19
j. shall live by faith 38:32
nor help the j. cause 189:2
over ninety and nine j. persons 37:27
rain on the j. 35:21
reflect that God is j. 145:7
sleep of the j. 212:16
this j. person: see ye 36:39
juste: *dans les vers une j. cadence* 44:11
juster: j. epoch has begun 262:11
justice: delay, right or j. 174:9
for j., for man's understanding 273:15
j., and leaving mercy to Heaven 114:6
j. is open to all 5:26
J. with Mercy 184:31
Let j. be done 113:11
loved j. and hated iniquity 128:3
Man's grim J. goes its way 286:2
mercy seasons j. 233:20
price of j. is eternal publicity 24:4
Revenge is...wild J. 14:8
satisfaction in doing j. 278:22
sword of j. first lay down 92:5
We love j. greatly 217:19
justified: no more j. in silencing 180:13
justify: j. the ways of God 183:9
justitia: *Fiat j. ruat* 113:11
juvescence: j. of the year 107:20
Kalends: At the Greek K. 65:5
kann: *Ich k. nicht anders* 170:17
kannst: *k., denn du sollst* 124:21
Kate: Kiss me, K. 236:12
Katherine: Her name was K. Janfarie 17:19
Keats: Who killed John K. 63:29
keel: No k. has ever ploughed 242:3
keener: k. with constant use 144:4
with his k. eye 177:15
keep: If you can k. your head 159:10
K. breathing 271:7
k. her in sickness and in health 210:13
k. on saying it long enough 24:6
many to k. 158:12
time to k. 32:7
keeper: k. is only a poacher turned 158:13
my brother's k. 25:23
ken: little did my mother k. 18:6
kept: k. the good wine until 37:40
Married women are k. women 247:19
That I k. my word 92:18
kernel: when he hath the k. eat 98:26
kettle: battered k. at the heel 298:9
How agree the k. 34:32
Kew: K. in lilac-time 193:20
key: out of k. with his time 208:15
keys: Over the noisy k. 211:2
Two massey K. he bore 182:27
Khatmandu: to the north of K. 131:7
kick: have Nixon to k. around 193:8
k. against the pricks 38:23
They may k. you out 280:21
kicked: many k. down stairs 129:7
no body to be k. 269:13
kid: lie down with the k. 33:6
kidlings: k. blithe and merry 120:15
kidney: man of my k. 233:32
kill: brother, or I k. you 72:6
charlatans k. 160:17
kill a man as k. a good book 186:2
k. a wife with kindness 236:13
k. one another if it is not done 239:17
k. sick people groaning 175:26
k. us for their sport 230:38
k. you a new way 215:2
not k.; but need'st not 79:22
Sharpens his pencil for the k. 53:7
Thou shalt not k. 26:21
Wild animals never k. for sport 118:21
would not mine k. you 52:12
killed: enemy you k., my friend 198:1
I'm k., Sire 51:5
snake, not k. it 232:10
Who k. Cock Robin 196:4
Who k. John Keats 63:29
killeth: letter k. 39:13
killing: k. love by staying 286:6
K. no Murder 224:10
reason for k. a man 298:18
ways of k. a cat 158:16
kills: k. me some six or seven dozen 227:38
k. the thing he loves 286:1
Kilmeny: K. had been she knew not 137:10
Kiltartan: country is K. Cross 296:22
kimonos: Two girls in silk k. 296:21
kin: little more than k. 226:2
makes the whole world k. 237:7
kind: cruel, only to be k. 227:16
K. hearts are more than coronets 263:25

less than k. 226:2
people will always be k. 220:22
Too k. — too kind 193:6
kindly: never lov'd sae k. 55:17
sure to be k. spoken of 12:7
kindness: any k. that I can show 128:4
depended on the k. 289:10
it is human k. 66:23
kill a wife with k. 236:13
k. does at last distinguish 110:10
K. in another's trouble 126:9
milk of human k. 231:25
repaying injury with k. 162:17
Save in the way of k. 269:16
shew forth thy loving k. 30:13
unrememberd acts / Of k. 292:11
kinds: two k. of people 198:18
king: all the k.'s men 194:14
cat may look at a k. 69:16
deil hae we got for a K. 89:16
despised, and dying k. 244:5
distinguish a true k. 85:20
divinity doth hedge a k. 227:19
fight for its K. and country 7:6
God save the k. 27:28
heart and stomach of a k. 109:1
Idea of a Patriot K. 44:17
kind of k. for me 122:11
K. born of all England 174:15
k. can do no wrong 41:25
k. delighteth to honour 28:29
K. George will be able to read 129:11
k. my father's death 108:18
k. never dies 41:24
K. of England cannot enter 202:4
K. of Love 16:19
k. of shreds and patches 227:14
k. of the castle 194:17
K. over the Water 7:10
K.'s a King 102:3
k. springs from a race of slaves 202:29
K. to have things done as cheap 201:3
K., / and ride in triumph 176:5
last k. is strangled 97:4
little profits that an idle k. 265:7
Long live our noble k.! 67:7
No bishop, no k. 144:15
no k. in Israel 27:22
not offended the k. 189:6
One-eyed Man is K. 282:15
Ozymandias, k. of kings 243:10
sea hath no k. but God 217:8
served my k., he would not 229:16
Under which k., Bezonian 228:23
unjust and wicked k. 224:4
What must the k. do now 235:20
who Pretender is, or who is K. 60:25
kingdom: enter into the k. 37:9
first the k. of God 35:29
In a k. by the sea 203:13
k. for a horse 235:29
k. for it was too small 228:11
k. is divided 34:17
K. stretch from shore 280:17
k. where nobody dies 181:2
such is the k. of God 37:8
thine is the k. 35:24
Thy k. come 35:24
voice of the k. 258:10
kings: accounted poet k. 155:15
all be as happy as k. 255:13
Beside the schemes of k. 130:5
Captains and the K. 159:24
change my state with k. 238:6
chase, the sport of k. 249:24
even k. in awe 90:22
for the sport of k. 91:1
hovels and the towers of k. 139:25
icy hand on k. 245:17
k. is mostly rapscallions 271:28
no k., though they possess the crown 92:5
part which laws or k. can 125:23
Physicians are like k. 281:14
politeness of k. 169:5
saddest of all K. 146:8
show to subjects, what they show to k. 88:15
stories of the death of k. 235:19
Kinquering: K. Congs 252:15
kinship: any k. with the stars 179:20
kirtle: kilted her green k. 18:11
kiss: Ae fond k. 55:16
coward does it with a k. 286:1
Gin a body k. a body 55:22
immortal with a k. 175:7
I saw you take his k. 200:1
k. may play, / Yet carry nothing 88:29
K. me, Hardy 191:13
K. me, Kate 236:12
k. my Julia's dainty leg 135:25
k. of death 247:12
k.'s strength...must be reckon'd 62:28
K. the book's outside 87:13
last lamenting k. 99:12
leave a k. but in the cup 150:27
let us k. and part 102:8
man may k. a bonny lass 223:1
never wholly k. you 89:14
swear to never k. the girls 50:29
sweetly did me k. 295:10
kissed: Jenny k. me 142:12
k. by a man who 159:28
K. the girls and made them cry 194:9
righteousness and peace have k. 30:9
when she k. her cow 258:23
kisses: bread and cheese, and k. 258:22
cards for k. 170:20
Give me a thousand k. 71:4
k. of his mouth 32:18
remembered k. after death 264:24
With k. four 153:12
Kissing: K. don't last 179:26
k. had to stop 52:14
K. your hand may make 168:26
kittens: Three little k. 196:1
knave: feed the titled k., man 58:4
honest man a k. 92:8
K. of Hearts / He stole 195:19
The K. of Hearts 69:24
knaves: calls the k., Jacks 94:17
fool among k. 259:5
fools and k. 53:3
knavish: Frustrate their k. tricks 67:8
knee: choose to bend / The supple k. 184:23
k. is a joint 129:10
Kneeling: K. ne'er spoil'd silk 134:27
knees: body between your k. 86:4
heart, not in the k. 145:24
live on your k. 143:18
knell: By fairy hands their k. 83:10
k. of parting day 127:9
knew: If youth only k. 112:8
k. almost as much at eighteen 147:24
K. only this 22:17
k. what it meant once 160:7
knife: War even to the k. 61:8

Lamb: L. of God 178:19
L. of God / On England's 42:25
l. was sure to go 195:2
Little L., who made thee 43:30
wolf...dwell with the l. 33:6
lambs: go to hell like l. 76:10
l. could not forgive 95:10
l. who've lost our way 159:5
lame: feet was I to the l. 29:7
L. dogs over stiles 158:9
lamenting: he was left l. 66:7
Lamp: Lady with a L. 168:16
l. unto my feet 31:3
When the l. is shattered 242:24
lampada: *vitai l. tradunt* 170:10
lamps: golden l. in a green light 177:2
l. are going out all over 128:7
light the l. with you 255:12
old l. for new 8:4
lance: l. a wand of the willow 17:20
land: before we were the l.'s 118:11
fat of the l. 26:12
half a rood / Of l. 259:19
Ill fares the l. 125:3
L....can't fly away 270:16
l. of the free 157:22
l. that is in need of heroes 46:9
new people takes the l. 76:15
no more l., say fish 48:7
plunder from a bleeding l. 61:13
think there is no l. 13:19
Where lies the l. 80:4
landmarks: hardly any l. from the wisdom 54:14
Landor: With L. and with Donne 298:7
land-rats: l. and water-rats 233:6
lands: though not of l. 294:26
lang: l. will his Lady / Look 17:9
language: bad l. disdain 198:13
best chosen l. 12:19
but one l., the English 215:24
consenting l. of the heart 120:22
dear l. which I spake 171:3
else in our l. should perish 171:10
l. all nations understand 22:21
l. charged with meaning 209:3
L. has not the power to speak 79:5
L....has its internal logic 165:11
l. in her eye 237:8
L. is a kind of human reason 165:11
L. is the dress of thought 146:21
l. of the age is never 127:25
l. of the unheard 158:6
l. of the tribe 174:13
l. sunk under him 2:5
L. was not powerful enough 95:16
No l., but 205:10
no l. but a cry 263:16
no respect for their l. 240:22
Sighs are the natural l. 224:12
sorry when any l. is lost 150:9
You taught me l. 236:16
languages: l. are the pedigree of nations 150:9
silent in seven l. 221:5
langueur: *D'une l. / Monotone* 274:11
languid: art thou l. 191:5
languor: heart with a monotonous l. 274:11
lank: long, and l., and brown 81:10
lap-dogs: when l. breathe their last 207:21
lapidary: l. inscriptions 149:3
lapidem: *l. cavat* 170:9
laps: Fortunes...into some men's l. 13:21
lard: l. their lean books 58:22
lards: l. the lean earth 227:36
large: l. as life and twice 70:8
Old Priest writ l. 185:24
largest: Shout with the l. 95:35
lark: l. at heaven's gate 225:30
l. shall sing me hame 89:15
l.'s on the wing 51:27
larke: bisy l., messeger of day 73:22
larks: mounting l. their notes prepare 207:28
Lars Porsena: L. of Clusium 171:4
larynx: Cramp her l., lung 261:2
Lasciva: *L. est nobis pagina* 176:25
lascivious: Poetry is...set to...l. music 179:15
lass: every l. a queen 158:11
gang wi' a l. 144:11
l. of Richmond Hill 272:27
l. that has acres o' charms 56:15
l. unparallel'd 225:3
lover and his l. 225:22
lasses: spent among the l. 56:14
last: all on our l. cruise 256:20
fame is the l. thing 261:10
held to the l. man 129:1
here it is at l. 145:3
Kissing don't l.: cookery do 179:26
l. act crowns the play 212:3
l. great Englishman 264:19
l. shall be first 36:28
l. territorial claim...in Europe 136:16
l. thing I shall do 198:16
l. through a whole lifetime 272:5
l. to lay the old aside 205:31
meets his Waterloo at l. 201:21
world's l. night 99:26
lasting: l. marble seek / Must carve 278:3
monument more l. than bronze 140:12
late: bad die l. 91:19
even that too l. 191:18
five minutes too l. all 87:2
never l. at meals 179:14
not too l. to seek 265:14
too l. after more than seven thousand 160:19
too l. or too early 220:18
later: l. than you think 224:6
latest: l. born and loveliest 155:8
Latin: carve in L. or in Greek 278:3
he speaks L. 229:11
small L., and less Greek 150:28
Latin-bred: L. woman 135:15
latter: blessed the l. end of Job 29:12
Laudant: *L. illa* 176:26
Laudate: *L. Dominum* 277:17
Laudator: *L. temporis acti* 139:10
laugh: awful makes me l. 161:20
closed with a l. 140:18
Democritus would l. 139:22
hurt too much to l. 166:19
I make myself l. 21:6
know when to l. 197:21
L. and be well 127:28
L. and the world laughs 285:19
l. at them in our turn 13:4
l....that I may not weep 63:4
L. where we must 206:9
loud l. that spoke 125:6
made a cat l. 202:13
Make 'em l. 213:11

penetrating sort of l. 290:26
sillier than a silly l. 71:6
time to l. 32:7
laugh'd: l. with counterfeited glee 125:8
laughable: very l. things 148:21
laughed: first baby l. for the first time 20:5
once heartily and wholly l. 68:15
laughing: Happiness is no l. matter 283:15
l. immoderately at stated intervals 248:17
Set the crew l. 115:9
shake the l. heart's long peace 48:10
You also, l. one 93:13
Laughing Water: Minnehaha, L. 168:18
laughs: Earth l. in flowers 110:20
when he l., it adds 253:25
who l. at anyone must be afraid 186:16
who l. on Friday 212:20
laughter: grimaces called l. 136:18
ill-bred, as audible l. 75:5
l. and the love of friends 23:7
L. holding both his sides 182:12
l., learnt of friends 48:14
l. of a fool 32:9
senators burst with l. 11:4
sincerest l. / With some pain 244:16
when her lovely l. shows 66:19
laughters: tears and l. for all time 49:21
launch'd: face that l. a thousand ships 175:7
laundry-list: l. and I will set 217:12
laurel: burnèd is Apollo's l. bough 175:14
laurels: l. all are cut 6:12
once more, O ye L. 182:19
lauriers: *l. sont coupés* 6:12
lave: Whistle owre the l. 57:3
Lavender: L.'s blue, diddle 194:22
law: army of unalterable l. 179:19
become a universal l. 152:23
built with stones of L. 43:6
by the l. of the land 174:8
Christianity is part of the Common L. 129:2
Ignorance of the l. excuses 223:14
I'll find them l. 46:8
L....built about...Reasonable Man 134:15
l. ends, there tyranny begins 202:5
L. ends, Tyranny begins 167:22
l. for the lion and ox 42:24
l., in its majestic equality 117:3
l. is a ass — a idiot 95:25
l. is an infraction of liberty 24:9
l. itself is nothing else but reason 80:21
lesser breeds without the L. 159:26
Love...l. unto itself 44:8
moral l. within me 152:22
Necessity has no l. 261:4
Necessity hath no l. 89:7
ought L. to weed it out 14:8
those by l. protected 57:5
ultimate l. 78:17
will is the man's l. 50:23
windward of the l. 77:12
lawe: Love is a gretter l. 73:20
lawful: that which is neither quite l. 60:16
lawfulness: l. of their conquering 148:16
Lawless: L. they lived 42:6
lawn: on the l. I lie 11:16
twice a saint in l. 205:19
laws: bad or obnoxious l. 126:18
breaking of l. 189:2
cooperation...the l. of life 218:13
L. are inoperative in war 78:27
L. are like spider's webs 249:20
l. of England are at my commandment 228:24
l. of the Persians 28:28
l. were like cobwebs 13:27
L. were made to be broken 193:15
Nature's l. lay hid in night 205:24
not care who should make the l. 115:12
nothing to do with the l. 140:19
not judges of l. 211:12
obedient to their l., we lie 246:11
That part which l. 125:23
Then l. were made 42:6
Unequal l. unto a savage race 265:7
whatever the l. permit 187:23
Lawsuit: *L.:* A machine 41:15
lawyers: l. too powerful 83:22
Lay: L. your sleeping head 11:9
one can l. it on so thick 60:21
lays: Freedom...which no good man l. down 5:14
ways of constructing tribal l. 159:9
Lazarus: Come forth, L. 151:21
Lazy: L. fokes' stummucks don't git tired 130:25
lea: and o'er the l. 137:6
lead: friends are lapp'd in l. 19:22
L., kindly Light 192:6
L. us, heavenly Father 105:19
Unite and l. a better 124:18
wond'rous life is this I l. 177:12
leader: one people, one l. 5:10
leadeth: l. me beside the still waters 29:20
leaf: power, thou cursed l. 56:26
yellow l. 232:25
leafy: In l. dells alone 140:24
league: Half a l. onward 262:13
leak: One l. will sink a ship 53:23
lean: lards the l. earth 227:36
l. and hungry look 229:22
wife could eat no l. 194:19
leap: giant l. for mankind 9:4
great l. in the dark 136:24
l. into the dark 48:17
l., ye lame, for joy 283:1
leaps: My heart l. up 292:18
Lear: pleasant to know Mr. L. 164:5
learn: cannot l. men from books 97:27
l. in suffering 242:18
l. so little 91:9
l. something about everything 143:16
masters to l. their letters 169:15
season for the old to l. 2:19
through so much to l. so little 96:4
we have to l. to do 8:26
We live and l. 203:22
who know how to l. 1:6
learned: how much he had l. in 7 years 272:17
l. body wanted loyalty 270:5
l., if they speak first 84:23
never l. anything from history 132:10
obscurity of a l. language 121:15
Learning: age saw L. fall, and Rome 206:7
All Classic l. lost 204:17
a' the l. I desire 56:10

deep l. little had he need 251:16
enough of l. to misquote 63:23
great feast of l. 231:13
incapable of l. 286:18
knew all that ever l. writ 22:17
l. doth make thee mad 38:30
L. hath gained most 119:10
L. is but an adjunct 231:12
l. is most excellent 116:9
l., like your watch 75:16
l....makes a silly man 1:22
L. without thought 84:9
little l. is a dang'rous thing 205:28
mad with much l. 201:14
on scraps of l. dote 299:7
picker up of l.'s crumbs 50:21
Swallow all your l. 75:23
Their l. is like bread 149:6
learnt: l. has been forgotten 246:20
l. nothing, and forgotten nothing 261:14
leave: how I l. my country 202:12
Intreat me not to l. thee 27:24
L. off first 35:2
l. the rest to the Gods 85:22
l. the trodden paths 241:12
love's own sake to l. 286:6
Oh, never l. me 5:9
leaves: As the generation of l. 137:28
home before the l. have fallen 289:2
l. on the trees 140:15
naturally as l. to a tree 156:22
Thick as Autumnal L. 183:17
what it l. behind 292:6
Words are like l. 205:30
leaving: like the l. it 231:23
leavings: devil's l. 259:12
Lebanon: cedar in L. 30:14
lechery: still wars and l. 237:10
lecteur: *Hypocrite l.* 20:20
lectures: I do not give l. 284:23
led: l. his regiment from behind 122:6
left: handful of silver he l. us 51:7
not thy l. hand know 35:23
She l. the web 263:30
leg: elephant by the hind l. 166:14
Julia's dainty l. 135:25
lege: *Tolle l.* 11:22
Legion: L. of Honour has been conferred 272:10
My name is L. 37:4
legislative: l. power is nominated by the executive 121:17
legislators: l. thought they could not well reform 115:12
unacknowledged l. of the world 244:19
legs: Does it matter? — losing your l. 220:22
Four l. good 196:19
his l., / So he laid down 138:4
l. enough for that number 12:18
l. of a man 31:14
l. were smitten off 241:5
see my l. when I take my boots 94:14
Walk under his huge l. 229:20
Leicester: Farewell L. Square 289:8
leiff: Now l. thi myrth 44:3
Leisure: L. with dignity 78:21
repent at l. 84:28
repose, and due l. 241:1
reputability to the gentleman of l. 274:4
retired L. 182:7
lemon: l. and a bit more 121:2
lemons: Oranges and l. 195:7
lend: Few l....their working tools 271:19
men who l. 161:9
not asked to l. money 272:5
lender: nor a l. be 226:11
length: reckon'd by its l. 62:28
value of life is not the l. 187:13
lengthen: l. thy life 117:10
Lenin: Unerringly as L. 172:26
lente: *Festina l.* 257:19
l., lente currite 175:10
leopard: l. follows his nature 266:4
l. his spots 34:5
l. shall lie down 33:6
leopards: Lady, three white l. 107:7
lerne: l. and gladly teche 73:10
lernis: l. ouir mekle at the sculis 167:2
Lesbia: *Vivamus, mea L.* 71:3
less: l. in this than meets the eye 19:7
L. is more 180:6
l. one has to do, the less time 75:26
more about less and l. 59:14
lesser: l. breeds without the Law 159:26
lesson: had a jolly good l. 159:20
Love is the l. 251:13
lessoun: Well koude he rede a l. 73:17
Lest: L. we forget 159:25
let: but they never l. you down 280:21
L. us go then, you and I 107:28
Lethe: no, go not to L. 154:29
letter: heart on one l. 148:25
l. killeth 39:13
only made this l. longer 199:5
wrote a l. 15:1
letters: foolish thing...than a man of l. 254:20
love the l. of his name 51:30
man of l....rich men hate 201:16
level: one dead l. ev'ry mind 204:13
levellers: l. wish to level *down* 148:15
levelling: cannot bear l. *up* 148:15
levels: Life l. all men 240:13
leviathan: Canst thou draw out l. 29:11
lex: *Salus populi suprema est l.* 78:17
Lexicographer: L.: a writer of dictionaries 148:10
liar: l. should have a good memory 212:10
sad eye that marks the perfect l. 23:24
liars: prove the greatest l. 102:4
libbaty: l.'s a kind o' thing 169:18
liberal: damned, compact l. majority 143:20
either a little L. 122:20
l. without the manual arts 146:15
Liberals: L. offer a mixture 174:1
Liberté: *L.! Egalité!* 6:5
l.! que de crimes 215:9
liberties: dramatist only wants more l. 144:22
people never give up their l. 55:1
Liberty: be light! said L. 242:10
cause of a single life, is L. 14:13
chains and calls them L. 52:27
consecrate to truth and l. 244:18
defence of l. is no vice 126:1
enjoy delight with l. 251:17
establish our own true l. 187:14
Give me l., or give 133:23
God hath given l. to man 89:19
Hard l. before the easy 184:3
hour of virtuous l. 1:12
I a man, and lackith l. 144:8

interfering with the l. 180:12
Know no such l. 169:6
lamp of l. will burn 166:7
land of l., / Of thee 247:24
law...an infraction of l. 24:9
L. consists in doing what 180:20
l. is a history of resistance 290:2
l....is eternal vigilance 89:19
l. is the love of others 132:2
L. is the right of doing 187:23
L. means responsibility 240:15
l. of the press 152:1
L....plant of rapid growth 280:5
L.'s a glorious feast 57:5
l. to the captives 33:29
L. was born in England 276:20
l.! what crimes 215:9
Licence they mean when they cry l. 185:20
life, l. and the pursuit 7:17
nation conceived in l. 166:10
people contend for their L. 129:6
revel on the grave / Of L. 242:6
seek Power and to lose L. 14:16
symptom of constitutional l. 121:20
thy chosen music, L. 294:5
tree of l. must be refreshed 145:9
yelps for l. among the drivers 147:16

Liberty-Hall: This is L. 125:21

library: circulating l. in a town 245:2
l. of sixty-two thousand 121:19
lumber-room of his l. 101:13
volumes which 'no gentleman's l. 161:14

libre: *L'homme est né l.* 217:16

licence: freedom of poetic l. 78:22
L. they mean when they cry liberty 185:20
l. to print your own money 268:22

licensing: do injuriously, by l. 186:6

licentious: poems are l. 176:25

Licht: *Mehr L.* 124:24

Licker: L. talks mighty loud 130:23

lie: big l. than to a small 136:14
Cannot come, l. follows 211:10
cannot tell a l. 280:6
fain wad l. doun 17:23
God's own name upon a l. 88:1
here let her l. 103:10
l....a very present help 255:4
l. even when it is inconvenient 274:20
l. for the good of the State 202:24
[L.]...help in time of trouble 4:19
l. is an abomination 255:4
l. shall rot 200:2
l.? 'Tis but / The truth in masquerade 63:10
l. usefully should lie seldom 136:1
no questions isn't told a l. 159:27
not the l. that passeth through 14:2
obedient to their laws, we l. 246:11
old L.: *Dulce et decorum* 197:23
saving l. 143:23
sent to l. abroad 295:5

lies: great l. about his wooden horse / 115:9
I were where Helen l. 17:15
l. you can invent 41:29
lifts the head, and l. 205:15
social l. that warp us 264:2
tells his l. by rote 297:8

lieth: man l....a coward 14:3

Life: afternoon musing on L. 290:28
All human l. is there 192:9
all I have, and take my l. 113:3
As our l. is very short 261:24
before this l., and what follows 21:24
better to enjoy l. 147:22
books...bring us to enjoy l. 125:27
bright book of l. 163:22
but have everlasting l. 38:1
cold eye / On l., on death 298:14
compared our l. to a dream 187:19
conduct...Three fourths of l. 10:13
crown / L.'s early cup 241:13
digestion...great secret of l. 248:11
disease of modern l. 9:26
drink / L. to the lees 265:8
end of l. is not Knowledge 143:14
Every man's l. is a fairy-tale 4:11
findeth his l. shall lose 36:13
For the l. to come 237:32
found that l. was Duty 138:16
Frail L. 90:23
give for his l. 28:33
giveth his l. for the sheep 38:8
glorious Lord of l. 251:12
good artist in l. 256:22
he is tired of l. 149:16
his friends for his l. 269:1
human l.: the war, the deeds 153:19
in l. people will take you 270:20
in the sea of l. enisled 9:15
into the l. of things 292:13
is a l. worthwhile 106:4
joy in the loss of human l. 162:18
large as l. and twice 70:8
lengthen thy l., lessen 117:10
l.? a play of passion 7:22
l. at best is but an inn 141:7
l. be without arithmetic 248:10
l. beyond life 186:3
L. can little more supply 206:8
L. can only be understood backwards 157:26
L....drawing sufficient conclusions 60:14
L. for life 26:26
L., friends, is boring 24:21
l. hovers like a star 63:20
L. I'm sure, was in the right 86:23
L. is a jest 120:26
L. is an incurable disease 86:24
l....is a poem 67:15
l. is a profession of faith 4:7
l. is but a day 155:10
L. is but an empty dream 168:13
l. is everywhere a state 147:10
L. is good only when 111:15
L. is just one damned thing 141:10
l. is...like a froward child 262:3
L. is mostly froth and bubble 126:9
L....is not a dream 47:11
L. is not living 176:27
L. is real 168:14
L. is short but sweet 249:27
l. is the other way 167:25
L. is very sweet 45:3
L. itself is but the shadow 48:22
l. just a stuff / To try 51:4
L. levels all men 240:13
L., like a dome 241:17
L....nothing much to lose 140:26
l. of a man...a heroic poem 67:17
l. of man, solitary, poor 136:20
l. of man / Less than a span 15:25
l. of sensations 156:8
L....process of getting tired 60:13
L.'s but a walking shadow 232:28
l.'s fitful fever 232:11

Rogues, would you l. 118:3
so long as ye both shall l. 210:13
strangely, I l. on 48:8
Teach me to l. 157:14
To l. is like love 60:8
To l. with thee, and be 212:22
tried / To l. without him 295:1
We l. and learn 203:22
we l., / Loathing our life 63:33
we that l. to please 147:7
whom you l. with, and I will tell 75:10
lived: Had we l. 221:11
I have l. my life 263:4
Only a life l. for others 106:4
livelihood: earned a precarious l. 127:5
liver: notorious evil l. 210:4
Liverpool: folk that live in L. 76:10
livers: grave l. do in Scotland 293:15
livery: shadowed l. 233:9
lives: Everyone l. by selling 255:24
everything that l. is holy 42:23
in their l. fought for life 251:7
it's men's l. 222:14
leave their little l. 207:28
l. more lives than one 286:3
L. of great men 168:15
l. of quiet desperation 268:23
L. to die another day 141:2
l. / Of those who ceased 129:16
One really l. nowhere 55:10
taking of our l. 273:15
their l. a mimicry 286:16
woman who l. for others 165:13
liveth: l. longest doth but sup 134:3
name l. for evermore 35:5
livin': brak' their l. tomb 172:18
living: become a l. soul 292:13
fever call'd 'L.' 203:17
hands of the l. God 40:13
l. dog is better 32:11
L. is an art 143:4
l. know / No bounds 245:20
l. to earn, poor fellows 104:12
l. up to it that is difficult 266:1
machine for l. in 164:15
mother I'm l. in sin 134:8
noble l. and the noble dead 293:11
respect to the l. 277:1
should'st be l. at this hour 294:11
ye are l. poems 168:4
Livingstone: Dr. L., I presume 252:23
Lizzie Borden: L. took an axe 6:6
Lloyd George: [L.] couldn't see a belt without hitting 10:20
load: Laid many a heavy l. 112:17
L. every rift 157:4
Loaf: Here with a L. of Bread 114:15
loafe: I l. and invite my soul 284:19
loathed: l. Melancholy 182:11
loathesome: custom l. to the eye 144:13
Loathing: Fear and L. in Las Vegas 268:1
we live, / L. our life 63:33
loathsome: more l. age 150:25
loaves: did eat of the l. 37:6
Lobster: voice of the L. 69:13
local: Little l. difficulties 174:2
Lochinvar: L. is come out of the West 222:8
Locke: L. sank into a swoon 296:18
locust: years that the l. hath eaten 34:19
locuta: *Roma l. est* 11:29
loftier: l. race / Than e'er 260:18
logic: as it isn't, it ain't. That's l. 70:1
condition of the world, like l. 290:24
l. of which man knows nothing 165:11
stank of L. 192:1
with L. absolute 114:21
logyk: unto l. hadde long ygo 73:9
loitered: l. my life away 131:14
loitering: and palely l. 153:11
London: broken arch of L. Bridge 171:14
crowd flowed over L. Bridge 108:14
dream of L., small and white 189:13
Hell...much like L. 243:11
I've been to L. to look 195:10
knowledge of L. was extensive 95:37
L. Bridge is falling down 195:1
[L.] Crowds without company 121:12
L. particular... A fog 93:20
L.! Pompous Ignorance sits 46:15
L., that great cesspool 101:22
L., that great sea 242:21
[L.] the great wen 80:9
L., thou art the flour 104:25
people of L. with one voice 78:3
tired of L. 149:16
vilest alleys of L. 101:10
Whittington, Lord Mayor of L. 7:15
lonely: l. sea and the sky 178:11
Lovely in a l. place 92:16
lonesome: on a l. road / Doth walk 81:15
long: crafte so l. to lerne 74:14
desires to live l. 259:11
How l., O Lord 240:31
In the l. run 157:24
Live as l. as you may 250:16
l., and two feet wide 294:19
l. life better than figs 224:21
l., long thoughts 168:11
l. / As twenty days 294:20
love me l. 6:7
nor that little l. 299:2
not too l. in coming 60:1
Progress...went on too l. 269:12
pull out, on the L. Trail 159:21
short and l. of it 233:29
that's for such a l. time 186:15
worst is not; / So l. 230:37
longed: lies where he l. to be 255:20
longen: l. folk to goon on pilgrimages 73:2
longest: loving l. 12:22
longevity: [secret of l.] Keep breathing 271:7
long-haired: l. aesthetics 123:7
longings: Immortal l. in me 225:1
longitude: l. with no platitude 119:2
long-legged: *l. fly upon the stream* 297:2
longtemps: *c'est pour si l.* 186:15
look: just to l. about us and to die 206:8
keep money to l. at 280:2
like the owner of the l. 80:12
l. after a wife 258:6
l. at the trees 46:14
l. before you ere you leap 59:26
l. into the Abyss 270:11
L., Ma! Top of the world 65:13
L. on my works 243:10
see his monument l. around 295:6
looked: his wife l. back 26:1
never have l. at me 50:17
looking: Here's l. at you, kid 44:9

l. alone we hate to find / Companions 279:1
l. and be loved by me 203:13
L. and do what you like 11:28
l. and good company improves 113:2
l. and murder will out 84:20
l. and to be wise 54:19
l. a place the less 12:21
L., as it exists in society 72:4
L. bade me welcome 135:6
L. built on beauty 99:1
l. casteth out fear 40:29
L. ceases to be a pleasure 22:18
L. conquers all 276:1
l. Creation's final law 263:17
l., devoid of art 120:22
L....exactly like war 254:21
l....exchange of two fantasies 72:4
L. forgive us 154:16
L. has pitched his mansion 296:8
L....hath friends in the garrison 129:3
l. her was a liberal education 253:5
L. in a golden bowl 42:7
L. in a hut 154:16
l. in friendship — never 83:19
L. in her sunny Eyes 86:20
L. in idleness 236:9
L., in my bosom 167:26
L. is a gretter lawe 73:20
l. is better than wine 32:18
L. is dying 19:23
L. is like a dizziness 137:9
L. is like the measles 145:17
l. is more cruel than lust 260:7
L. is of a birth as rare 177:4
L. is only chatter 54:2
l. is taught hypocrisy 62:17
L. is the great Asker 163:12
L. is the lesson 251:13
L....law unto itself 44:8
l., let us be true 9:7
L. looks not with the eyes 233:35
l. match...for happiness 105:15
L. means never having to say 223:12
L. me little, love me long 6:7
l. might take no end 134:19
l. must have some future 66:22
L. ne'er will from me flee 87:1
l. of money 59:30
l. of power...love of ourselves 132:2
l. one another or die 11:14
l. oneself is the beginning 286:28
l. prove likewise variable 236:1
l. remembered such wealth brings 238:6
L. rules the court 221:22
L. seeketh not itself to please 43:21
L.'s like the measles 146:2
L.'s mysteries in souls 99:13
L.'s not so pure 100:3
L.'s not Time's fool 238:19
L. sometimes would contemplate 100:3
L. sought is good 237:22
l.'s own sake to leave 286:6
l.'s the noblest frailty 103:14
L. still has something of the sea 223:7
l.'s young dream 188:20
l. that can be reckoned 224:19
L. that dare not speak 101:1
l. that makes the world go round 69:20
l. that makes the sport 257:18
L. that never told 43:2
l. thee better after death 49:20
L....the folly of the wise 150:7
L., the human form divine 43:28
L., thou art absolute sole Lord 88:20
l. thy neighbour as thyself 27:2
l. thy neighbour as thyself 36:26
l. to me was wonderful 28:4
L....troubleth Men's Fortunes 14:15
L.! who bewailest / The frailty 242:25
l. / Wi' a scunner in't 172:25
L. your enemies 35:20
L. your enemies 37:18
made wery fierce l. to me 96:11
makes l. just like a woman 105:9
making l. all year round 21:7
man moot nedes l., maugree 73:21
man must l. a thing very much 77:5
Man's l. is of man's life 62:22
meant I should not l. 50:17
Men l. in haste 63:15
mischievous devil L. is 60:7
monstruosity in l., lady 237:4
more l. or more disdain 67:5
needs must l. the highest 262:19
no l. sincerer than 239:20
Nor l., nor pity knew 67:4
not enough to make us l. 259:10
not l. Thee, if I love Thee not 134:21
not l. thee (Dear) so much 169:9
not l. / Which alters when 238:18
not l. wine, woman and song 170:19
off with the old l. 6:2
our l. hath no decay 98:23
Pity is but one remove from l. 214:12
right place for l. 118:6
right to dissemble your l. 41:8
see her is to l. her 55:20
sports of l. 151:2
subject but eternal L. 243:21
support of the woman I l. 106:1
survive of us is l. 163:7
tests of generous l. 58:11
that he excludeth L. 134:20
thee, and be thy l. 212:22
those who l. want wisdom 243:15
time to l. 32:7
'Tis l. in love 257:18
too ladylike in l. 134:11
true l. hath my heart 245:24
true l. never did run smooth 233:34
'Twixt women's l., and men's 98:22
two parties to a l. transaction 266:9
two passions, vanity and l. 75:22
understand only because I l. 269:20
unholy mantrap of l. 119:3
what if excess of l. 296:15
what l. indites 79:5
when I l. thee not 234:35
which was more than l. 203:14
will be l. without marriage 117:11
woman wakes to l. 262:26
written for the l. of Man 267:12
love-adept: Dreaming like a l. 243:18
loved: better to have l. and lost 60:22
l. by mony men 17:19
l. Caesar less 229:33
l. the youngest above a' thing 17:7
l. with a love 203:14
Nature I l. 162:2
never to have l. at all 263:13
nor no man ever l. 238:20
not l. the World 61:28
Pale hands I l. 138:23
place / And the l. one 51:14
Twice or thrice had I l. thee 98:21
Whoever l. that 175:19
who never l. before 5:6

love-knot: l. into her long black hair 193:22
loveless: diviner than a l. god 50:14
lovelier: l. than the love of Jove 176:3
loveliest: l. and best / That Time 114:18
loveliness: he who l. within 100:20
Its l. increases 153:15
portion of the l. 241:15
woman of so shining l. 297:21
lovely: always say, 'You have l. eyes 74:29
gives a l. light 181:3
l. and pleasant in their lives 28:3
L. in a lonely place 92:16
make a l. corpse 95:7
once he made more l. 241:15
She has a l. face 263:32
lover: Beauty is the l.'s gift 84:31
give herself to her l. / — forthwith 289:14
in the l.'s ear alone 294:14
Jesu, l. of my soul 282:27
l. and his lass 225:22
l. of concord 209:16
l.'s quarrel with the world 118:9
lunatic, the l., and the poet 234:12
pale and wan, fond l. 257:17
sighed as a l. 121:11
some old l.'s ghost 100:2
woman loves her l. 62:29
lovere: yeve a l. any lawe 73:20
lovers: Dull sublunary l. 100:22
law to l. 44:8
l. be lost love shall not 266:21
quarrels of l. are the renewal 265:20
So must pure l.' 99:14
loves: all strange l. are over 260:2
As Lines so L. 177:5
cauldron of unholy l. 11:19
Chang'd l. 98:26
easily deceived by what one l. 187:5
fallen was in l. dance 144:10
he who colour l. 100:20
kills the thing he l. 286:1
L. but half enough 212:6
l. him still the better 125:16
l. nothing but himself 250:15
l. the 'ound more 258:4
l. what he is good at 224:16
one that l. his fellow-men 142:9
one who l....other who condescends 266:9
plurality of l. 99:10
reigned with your l. 109:2
lovesome: garden is a l. thing 48:19
loveth: He that l. not knoweth not 40:28
Lord l. he chasteneth 40:16
prayeth best, who l. best 81:16
loving: l. Christianity better than Truth 82:12
l. longest 12:22
l. the land that has taught us 188:16
tired...of l. 20:21
Lowells: L. talk only to Cabots 45:8
lower: if the l. orders don't 287:1
l. class, I am in it 91:17
lowers: Dark l. the tempest 168:7
Lowliness: L. is young ambition's 229:28
lowly: at any hands, however l. 122:25
indelible stamp of his l. 90:16
loyal: l. body wanted learning 270:5
loyalties: impossible l. 10:9
loyalty: [l.]...to mak a man sa gud 19:12
lucid: fool, full of l. intervals 71:18
Lucifer: falls like L. 229:15
L., son of the morning 33:8
luck: awf'lly bad l. on Diana 25:3
Has he l. 190:15
lucky: no man happy...only l. 249:21
supposed it l. to be born 284:20
You were l., Agricola 261:7
Lucy: If L. should be dead 294:15
lug: I'll l. the guts 227:18
lugger: on board the l. 150:10
lukewarm: thou art l. 40:34
lumber: loads of learned l. 206:5
lumber-room: l. of his library 101:13
luminous: beating in the void his l. wings 10:11
Dong with the L. Nose 164:7
lump: l. bred up in darkness 160:14
L. the whole thing 271:30
Man is a l. 100:21
lunatic: l. fringe in all reform 215:22
l., the lover, and the poet 234:12
Lupus: *L. est homo homini* 203:1
lust: fashed wi' fleshly l. 56:20
Is l. in action 238:21
love is more cruel than l. 260:7
think it horrible that l. 298:1
lute: rift within the l. 262:24
Luve: L. is ane fervent fire 221:7
L.'s like a red red rose 57:10
lux: *l. perpetua* 178:17
Luxe: *L., calme et volupté* 20:22
luxuries: Give me the l. of life 295:7
Give us the l. of life 190:1
other such lady-like l. 242:22
luxury: I hate that Persian l., boy 140:2
To pamper l. 125:13
Lycidas: L. is dead 182:20
lyf: l. so short 74:14
lyfe: haif ane mirrie l. 167:1
lying: do not mind l. 60:11
l. on his face, dead 266:12
L., the telling of beautiful untrue 286:19
world is given to l. 228:12
lyked: al that l. him 72:25
lyre: smote 'is bloomin' l. 160:1
lyric: among the l. poets 139:24
Mab: see Queen M. hath been 235:33
Macaroni: called it M. 19:6
Macaulay: as Tom M. is of everything 179:3
M. is well for a while 68:27
[M.] occasional flashes of silence 248:27
Macduff: Lay on, M. 232:32
Macedonia: Come over into M. 38:25
Macgregor: and my name is M. 222:25
Machiavel: much beholden to M. 13:24
world think M. is dead 175:21
Machine: Ghost in the M. 219:2
m. for living in 164:15
m. unmakes the man 111:14
not a man, you're a m. 238:28
Machinery: Age of M. 67:14
m....increased...well-to-do 178:4
Machines: M. are the produce of the mind 80:7
M. are worshipped 218:21
M....loathed...impose slavery 218:21
m., wi'out souls to weary 94:22
mackerel: Not so the m. 118:4
mad: All poets are m. 59:1
dances, unless he...be m. 78:29
he first makes m. 112:16

heroine goes m. she always 244:29
Hieronymo's m. againe 160:16
house for fools and m. 259:18
learning doth make thee m. 38:30
Let me not be m. 230:24
M. about the boy 86:17
M., bad, and dangerous 161:1
M. dogs and Englishmen 86:18
M., is he 121:4
madman and me. I am not m. 89:22
m. with much learning 201:14
M. world! mad kings 230:13
m. world, my masters 262:2
men that God made m. 76:7
old, m., blind 244:5
old men be m. 298:15
professor, who became m. 198:15
sad bad glad m. brother's 260:4
Madam: M. Life's a piece in bloom 133:8
madder: I cried for m. music 101:5
madding: Far from the m. crowd's 127:18
made: know who m. thee 43:30
know who m. you 257:10
m. and loveth all 81:16
M. lock, stock and barrel 298:10
poet's m. as well as born 150:30
Sing whatever is well m. 298:12
madman: difference between a m. and me 89:22
m. who thought he was...Hugo 80:15
madmen: m....Conquerors and Kings 61:23
madness: Anger is a brief m. 139:16
destroyed by m. 123:26
fine m. still he did retain 102:7
in the end despondency and m. 293:14
m., yet there is method in it 226:27
Money is our m. 163:17
sure to m. near alli'd 102:15
that way m. lies 230:29
Thro' cells of m. 264:17
'tis m. to defer 298:23
very midsummer m. 237:23
magazines: women's m....may not be subtle 119:14
Magdalen: fourteen months at M. College 121:10
Maggots: M. half-form'd in rhyme 203:27
magic: dealer in m. and spells 123:21
relic of primitive word m. 196:11
rough m. / I here abjure 236:26
magistrate: m. as equally useful 121:16
tyranny of the m. 180:10
Magna: *M. est veritas* 34:29
Magnificat: *M. anima mea* 277:20
magnificent: m., but it is not war 45:7
unknown is regarded as m. 261:5
Magnificently: M. unprepared 86:2
magnifico: *ignotum pro m.* 261:5
magnifies: soul m. the Lord 277:20
magnifique: *m. mais ce n'est pas* 45:7
magnify: m. him for ever 209:13
Magnus: *M. ab integro* 275:28
Mahomet: M. will go to the Hill 14:18
maid: beggar m. shall be my queen 262:6
could not live a m. 200:13
m. and her wight / Come whispering 130:7
M. of Athens, ere we part 63:30
maiden: m. of bashful fifteen 245:11
m. / That is makeles 5:22
m. with white fire laden 241:22
use a poor m. so 5:9
maids: pretty m. all in a row 195:3
Three little m. from school 122:27
Mail: Night M. crossing the Border 11:11
Strong m. of craft 170:16
maimed: poor, and the m. 37:26
wants [anger] hath a m. mind 119:9
main: care o' th' m. chance 59:26
maiora: *Paulo m. canamus* 275:27
mair: m. that I remead have socht 104:26
Maisie: Proud M. is in the wood 222:20
maison: *m. est une machine-à-habiter* 164:15
Maister: do not M. or Campbell me 222:25
maistrie: been in m. hym above 73:28
majestic: long m. march 207:3
Majesty: his M.'s head on a sign-post 171:21
infinite M. 209:11
m. / That from man's soul 189:14
ride on in m. 181:8
rounded them with m. 129:16
so touching in its m. 293:25
majorem: *Ad m. Dei gloriam* 4:17
Major-General: model of a modern M. 123:12
majority: big enough m. in any town 271:29
compact m. 143:20
damns the vast m. o' men 172:8
God's side, is a m. 201:22
great silent m. of Americans 193:10
joined the great m. 201:13
Majors: live with scarlet M. 220:20
make: does not usually m. anything 201:17
don't m. them in the one pot 151:16
m. his opportunity 13:20
Scotsman on the m. 20:13
to offend and m. up at pleasure 214:13
makeles: maiden that is m. 5:22
maker: m. is hymself ybeten 74:20
M. of heaven and earth 209:14
Scatter'd his M.'s image 102:12
Malaria: [M.] million-murdering Death 216:21
male: more deadly than the m. 159:3
rough m. kiss of blankets 48:6
Malfi: Duchess of M. still 281:10
Malherbe: *Enfin M. vint* 44:11
malice: m. never was his aim 259:17
m. toward none 166:13
malignity: motiveless m. 82:20
malt: gud m. and makis ill drink 7:20
m. does more than Milton 141:3
Mamas: Last of the Red-Hot M. 271:6
mammon: serve God and m. 35:27
mammoth: Aulder than m. or than mastodon 172:20
man: Arms and the m. 275:6
become a m. 231:33
childhood shews the m. 185:6
Child is father of the M. 292:19
corpse which is m. 260:15
detest that animal called m. 259:20
Every m. has three characters 152:26
gently scan your brother m. 55:15
Glory to M. in the highest 260:13
grown to m.'s estate 255:10

holy spirit of m. 260:1
hour is come, but not the m. 222:18
image, m. or shade 296:1
let him pass for a m. 233:5
love is of m.'s life a thing apart 62:22
make m. in our image 25:14
m. and a brother 281:25
m., by possessing consciousness 272:24
M. dreams of fame 262:26
M. has his will 137:14
M. is all symmetry 135:7
M. is...a political animal 9:1
M. is a tool-making animal 117:31
M. is a tool-using animal 68:16
M....is a wicked creature 187:7
M. is a wolf to man 203:1
M. is born unto trouble 29:1
m. is but a devil weakly fettered 256:2
M. is condemned to be free 220:16
m. is infinitely more complicated 273:7
m. is not a fly 206:15
M. is not the enemy of Man 198:9
M. is only a reed 199:11
m. is *so* in the way 120:6
M. is something to be surpassed 193:3
M. is the master of things 260:13
M. is the measure of all 211:6
M. is the shuttle 273:20
m. is the superior animal 208:21
M. is what he eats 113:16
m. keip weil ane toung 166:20
M....lives...by catchwords 256:19
m. may kiss a bonny lass 223:1
m....more perfect creature 90:17
M....must get drunk 62:25
m. of sorrows 33:24
m. only a blunder of God 193:5
M. partly is 50:18
M. proposes 157:11
m.'s a man 56:22
M.'s as perfect as he ought 206:10
m.'s bred out / Into baboon 236:30
m.'s [business] to keep unmarried 239:23
m. should be alone 25:16
m.'s the gowd for a' that 56:21
m., take him for all 226:8
m. that lays his hand upon 269:16
M. to command and woman 264:26
M. wants but little 60:1
m. who wasn't there 179:1
m....will fight for an idea 239:27
m. will live 141:17
m. with all his noble qualities 90:16
m. without an estate 1:21
Marvels...m. is the greatest 249:28
no' a m. ava' 172:12
not a m., you're a machine 238:28
nothing great but m. 129:9
Nothing links m. to man 245:21
not m. for the sabbath 37:2
only m. is vile 132:9
piece of work is a m. 226:29
present life of m. 21:24
strange what a m. may do 266:2
This was a m. 230:12
Thou art the m. 28:7
to know / The destiny of M. 294:8
What is m. 29:15
you'll be a M., my son 159:11
manacles: mind-forged m. I hear 43:25
manage: m. a clever man 159:30
Mandalay: road to M. 159:22
mandrake: Get with child a m. root 100:14
mane: runs with all his m. 212:7
mangent: *Qu'ils m. de la brioche* 175:1
manger: rude m. lies 183:1
manhood: conspiracy against the m. 110:12
M. a struggle 97:18
manhoods: hold their m. cheap 229:4
manifesto: first powerful, plain m. 251:10
manifold: m. sins and wickedness 209:7
mankind: all m.'s epitome 102:20
and thin m. 125:13
deserve better of m. 258:13
giant leap for m. 9:4
If all m. minus one 180:13
justified in silencing m. 180:13
M....two great classes 22:9
M....unfit for their own government 280:4
M., when left to themselves 280:4
mass of m. understand 16:2
spectator of m. than as one 2:1
study of M. is Man 206:18
surpasses or subdues m. 61:24
Survey m., from China 147:17
manliness: m., beer and cricket 196:22
manly: m. part is to 109:23
Manna: his Tongue / Dropt M. 183:30
m. to the hungry soul 192:16
manner: all m. of things shall be well 151:24
m. rude and wild 23:1
marmalade and a m. 6:17
no m. of doubt 122:7
manners: bewray'd, / As by his m. 252:6
first for m.' sake 35:2
Good m. are made up 111:2
m. of a dancing master 148:2
m. of a Marquis 123:15
M. take a tincture 205:21
no longer any m. 86:15
not men, but m. 114:1
pots have morals and m. 130:9
we've no m. 241:2
mansion: pitched his m. in 296:8
mansions: many m. 38:12
mantrap: unholy m. of love 119:3
manure: its natural m. 145:9
many: ease with which the m. 142:2
m. still must labour for 62:8
shortest way to do m. things 247:4
wretched M. 82:10
Ye are m. — they are few 243:2
many-coloured: m. glass, / Stains 241:17
many-headed: m. monster of the pit 207:5
many-splendoured: miss the m. thing 267:23
map: Roll up that m. 202:10
Maps: Geography is about M. 24:12
Marathon: force upon the plain of M. 146:17
M. looks on the sea 62:34
marble: but this in m. 21:15
dwelt in m. halls 53:12
found it brick and left it m. 65:4
m. to retain 61:1
marbly: great smooth m. limbs 50:8
march: m. of intellect 250:13
m. of the human mind is slow 54:20
marche: *ne m. pas, il danse* 166:3

mare: *mutant qui trans m.* 139:18
margin: meadow of m. 245:9
Marie Hamilton: M.'s to the kirk 18:5
Mariner: M. hath his will 81:2
Mariners: M. of England 66:13
market: little pig went to m. 195:24
Marlb'rough: M.'s eyes the streams 147:20
Marlowe: M., bathed in the Thespian 102:7
marmalade: m. and a manner 6:17
marmoream: *gloriatus m. se relinquere* 65:4
Marquis: manners of a M. 123:15
marriage: after m., he'll fall asleep 217:25
comedies are ended by a m. 62:30
Courtship to m. 84:29
fortune by way of m. 114:9
frighten her into m. 150:10
furnish forth the m. tables 226:7
hanging prevents a bad m. 237:14
Happiness in m. 12:24
In m., a man becomes slack 256:13
M., Agnès, is not a joke 186:17
m....as a mere matter of sentiment 47:9
[m.] as with cages 187:20
M....field of battle 256:16
M. has many pains 147:11
M. is popular because 239:32
m. is rather permitted than approved 147:12
M. is the greatest earthly happiness 97:28
M. is the waste-paper basket 281:3
m. of true minds 238:18
m. than a ministry 16:1
M.: the deep, deep peace 65:24
speke of wo that is in m. 73:29
termed a *left-handed* m. 291:9
twenty years of m. make 288:14
Where there's m. without love 117:11
marriages: m....selling one's soul 173:14
married: conceal their feelings till...m. 288:11
delight we m. people have 201:6
fool at least in every m. couple 113:18
honest man who m. 125:25
if ever we had been m. 120:16
I have m. a wife 37:25
in m. life three is company 287:3
m. and gone to New Zealand 79:18
m. before three and twenty 13:2
m., but I'd have no wife 88:21
M. in haste 84:28
m. man, Samivel, you'll understand 96:4
m....nothing left...but to be good 256:18
m. to a poem 157:3
M. women are kept women 247:19
most m. man I ever saw 279:15
never m., and that's his hell 59:3
Reader, I m. him 47:6
strange as if we had been m. 84:34
thankfu' ye're no m. to her 46:5
Unpleasing to a m. ear 231:16
woman's business to get m. 239:23
marries: m.; there are no more by-path 256:17
young person, who either m. 12:7
marry: advise no man to m. 149:31
as easy to m. a rich 266:5
better to m. than to burn 39:5
Doänt thou m. for munny 264:18
every woman should m. — and no man 97:21
How can a bishop m. 248:25
hump may m. *whom she likes* 266:8
m. his daughter to an indigent man 1:21
m. is to domesticate the Recording 256:18
neither m., nor are given 259:7
no woman should m. a teetotaller 256:15
persons about to m. — 'Don't 211:13
why they m. them 168:10
Marrying: M. off your daughter 219:3
Mars: this seat of M. 235:13
marshal: French m.'s baton 190:12
Marshes: see to 'Ackney M. 20:19
martial: m. cloak around him 291:3
Martians: harder to understand than M. 249:22
Martin: Saint M.'s summer 229:7
martinet: I am a perfect m. 248:8
Martyr: M. of the People 72:14
martyrdom: m. of our passions 19:5
m. to live 48:23
not at all of m. 277:11
martyrs: blood of the m. is the seed 265:26
noble army of m. 209:12
marvel: m. and a mystery 168:10
Marvels: M. are many, but man 249:28
Marx: illegitimate child of Karl M. 10:22
Marxism: M....method of analysis 271:1
Mary: M. had a little lamb 195:2
M., quite contrary 195:3
mask: had a m. like Castlereagh 242:26
mass: Paris is well worth a m. 133:12
massa: like m. like man 176:18
masses: back the m. against the classes 124:1
huddled m. yearning 163:24
master: Has a new m. 236:21
Man is the m. of things 260:13
m. of himself 178:21
m. of my fate 133:7
mistress is better than an old m. 282:14
my m., let me call him 121:9
not make dreams your m. 159:12
masterly: m. inactivity 173:15
master-passion: m. is the love of news 88:16
masterpiece: made his m. 232:7
masterpieces: adventures of his soul among m. 117:5
masters: aversions of their temporal m. 180:11
both ill m. be 128:5
by their Victory but new m. 129:6
for the ease of the m. 247:10
future m. to learn 169:15
mad world, my m. 262:2
nor earth two m. 3:5
passions...bad m. 165:7
people are the m. 54:26
serve two m. 35:27
The Old M. 11:10
We are the m. 241:4
mastery: m. of the thing 139:3
Masturbation: [M.]...sex with someone you love 3:18
match: made 'em to m. the men 106:16

matched: m. us with His hour 48:9
mate: great artificer / Made my m. 255:17
lady's ta'en anither m. 18:16
Matilda: a-waltzing, M., with me 199:19
matrimonial: difference in m. affairs 13:1
matrimony: barrier against m. 156:19
joined together in holy M. 210:10
Man and this Woman in holy M. 210:11
M., as the origin of change 12:4
m....friendship recognized by the police 256:14
m. to begin with...aversion 245:1
never...much improved by m. 64:15
to m. in a moment 12:25
matter: Friends are all that m. 54:2
hard m. dost thou entertain 241:25
Meaning...no great m. 65:19
More m. with less art 226:25
not much m. which we say 179:4
this m. better in France 253:16
matters: Nobody that m. 181:2
Nothing m. very much 16:24
Matthew: M., Mark, Luke, and John 6:8
mature: lip m. is ever new 153:36
Maud: Come into the garden, M. 264:15
maugree: love, m. his heed 73:21
mawkish: sweetly m. 204:11
maxim: governed by that m. 283:17
m. by which I act 152:23
useless as a general m. 171:19
Maxim Gun: we have got / The M. 23:10
maxima: *mea m. culpa* 178:16
maximum: m. of temptation 239:32
May: darling buds of M. 238:4
finding first / What m. be 49:28
leads with her / The Flow'ry M. 185:18
merry month of M. 18:8
There was a M. 17:19
maybe: definite m. 126:4
Mayor: What did the M. do 127:4
May-poles: sing of M. 135:19
maze: mighty m.! but not without a plan 206:8
Mazes: pleasant M. of her Hair 86:20
through m. running 182:18
meadow: painted m. 1:16
time when m., grove 292:20
meals: lessen thy m. 117:10
mean: admires m. things is a Snob 265:30
depends on what you m. by 146:5
if you see what I m. 290:28
m. streets a man must go 72:7
m. / Upon that memorable 177:15
not m. / But be 173:16
virtuous person with a m. mind 16:11
meander: m. through a meadow of margin 245:9
meaner: m. Beauties of the Night 295:2
She must take m. things 106:18
meanest: life of even the m. 67:15
m. flower that blows 293:1
m. flowret of the vale 127:24
m. of his precepts 1:19
Meaning: M....no great matter 65:19
m.'s press and screw 82:9
m. to the utmost possible 209:3
some faint m. make pretence 103:18
words have a m. of their own 196:11
meanly: All m. wrapt 183:1
thinks m. of himself 149:13
means: best ends by the best m. 142:15
die beyond my m. 288:25
make it by any m. 139:15
m., even if we have to borrer 279:18
m. just what I choose 70:7
measured by the m. 163:1
Private M. is dead 248:3
meant: what it m. once 160:7
measles: Love is like the m. 145:17
Love's like the m. 146:2
Measure: M. not the work 49:12
m. of all things 211:6
m. of our torment 159:6
serves to grace my m. 210:27
measured: forms, m. forms 179:9
I have m. out 107:31
m. by the means 163:1
m. it from side to side 294:19
meat: chang'd sorts of m. 98:26
eater came forth m. 27:18
m. is too good for any but 279:8
Some have m. and cannot eat 56:25
mechanic: m. part of wit 112:9
méchant: *animal est très m.* 5:2
m. animal 187:7
mécontents: *cent m. et un ingrat* 169:2
med'cine: Grief is itself a m. 87:6
meddle: Wha daur m. wi' me 6:11
meddling: enough of m. who can please 297:10
médecins: *m. laissent mourir* 160:17
Medes: given to the M. and the Persians 34:17
Persians and the M. 28:28
medias: *In m. res* 139:8
medicine: Comedy is m. 128:8
good like a m. 31:29
government as with m. 24:9
hunger...m. for health 271:16
M. for the soul 97:6
M. is my lawful wife 75:1
[m.] so long to learn 136:9
use in m. for poison 109:21
medicines: worthlessness of the most m. 117:9
medieval: lily in your m. hand 123:9
mediocre: Titles distinguish the m. 240:11
Mediocrity: M. knows nothing higher 101:25
welcomes Pretentious M. 46:15
Mediterranean: see the shores of the M. 149:10
medium: m. is the message 173:19
meek: Blessed are the m. 35:17
Jesus, m. and mild 282:26
meet: If I should m. thee 64:14
It is very m., right 210:9
Though infinite can never m. 177:5
till we m. again 213:6
meeter: therefore deemed it m. 200:11
meeting: as if I was a public m. 274:17
Journeys end in lovers m. 237:16
Parliament is...a big m. 16:6
this m. is drunk 96:7
Mehr: *M. Licht* 124:24
meilleur: *m. des mondes possibles* 276:11
mekle: ouir m. at the sculis 167:2
Melancholy: Hail divinest M. 182:3

method: madness, yet there is m. in it 226:27
Methodist: morals of a M. 123:15
spiritualized by a M. 278:13
methods: know my m.. Apply them 101:20
métier: *bien faire son m.* 66:21
C'est son m. 132:16
m. et mon art, c'est vivre 187:16
Metre: and lame M. 183:6
metropolis: monster, called...'the m. 80:9
metuant: *Oderint dum m.* 1:1
metuunt: *Quem m., oderunt* 112:3
mezzo: *Nel m. del cammin* 90:1
M.F.H.: M. dines he sleeps 258:3
mice: Like little m., stole in 257:14
schemes o' m. an' men 58:2
three blind m. 195:25
Michael Angelo: Italy from designs by M. 271:30
Michelangelo: Talking of M. 107:29
micht: weel ye m. 172:19
microscopic: has not man a m. eye 206:15
mid-day: out in the m. sun 86:18
middle: die ere m. age 64:1
it was / The M. of Next Week 70:14
middle age: wives...companions for m. 14:11
Restraining reckless m. 297:11
middle-aged: m. maiden lady 213:9
m. suspect everything 287:31
midnight: after m. is to be up 237:15
and m. never come 175:9
blackest m. born 182:11
chimes at m. 228:21
m. oil 120:23
morrow in m. 155:19
my Lamp at m. hour 182:8
'Tis the year's m. 100:5
midst: In the m. of life 190:5
In the m. of life 210:20
there am I in the m. 36:25
midsummer: very m. madness 237:23
mid-winter: In the bleak m. 216:24
mieux: *Tout est pour le m.* 276:11
might: do it with thy m. 32:12
do with m. and main 109:23
It m. have been 285:10
m. half slumb'ring 155:14
only what m. have been 161:3
run with all your m. 212:7
should be first in m. 154:9
With all thy m. 187:9
mightier: pen is m. than the sword 53:10
mighty: How are the m. fallen 28:5
Look on my works, ye M. 243:10
quell the m. of the Earth 185:16
mild: should prefer m. hale 258:5
mildest: m. manner'd man 62:33
mile: compel thee to go a m. 35:19
Miles: *M. gloriosus* 203:4
m. to go before I sleep 118:16
Three score m. and ten 194:13
milk: drunk the m. of Paradise 82:7
find a trout in the m. 268:31
flowing with m. and honey 26:17
Gin was mother's m. 240:25
gone to m. the bull 148:14
Gospel of spilt m. 215:23
m. of human kindness 231:25
m. the cow of the world 285:18
sincere m. of the word 40:24
With m. and honey blest 24:19
Mill: at the M. with slaves 185:9
M., / By a mighty effort of will 24:13
Millennium: description of the *M.* 131:20
miller: Than wots the m. of 236:32
There was a jolly m. 41:9
million: high man, aiming at a m. 50:31
Millionaire: M. That is my religion 239:16
m. makes me less forlorn 247:22
millions: m. of ages before 161:3
mystery will lead m. 44:18
Tired m. toil unblest 280:9
What m. died 66:10
mills: dark Satanic m. 42:26
m. of God grind slow 168:1
mill-stones: Turned to m. as they fell 243:1
mill-wheel: Except the m.'s sound 241:21
Milo: I may be found a M. 62:12
Milton: believe in M., Dryden, Pope 62:21
language sunk under [M.] 2:5
M., Death and Sin 299:6
[M.] surly republican 147:3
M.! thou should'st be living 294:11
M. wrote in fetters 42:22
morals hold / Which M. held 294:12
more than M. can / To justify 141:3
mute inglorious M. 127:13
mimicry: their lives a m. 286:16
mimsy: All m. were the borogoves 69:28
mince-pies: syllabubs and jellies and m. 242:22
mind: and in the m. of man 292:16
Beauty...exists in the m. 142:5
brown eyes and that tiny m. 269:8
but with the m. 233:35
cannot get out of my m. 132:12
complicated state of m. 123:8
concentrates his m. wonderfully 149:15
dagger of the m. 231:36
don't m. if I do 153:6
duty to speak one's m. 287:9
empires of the m. 78:9
find the m.'s construction 231:24
fit of absence of m. 223:10
healthy m. in a healthy body 152:18
like workings of one m. 293:9
man's body and his m. 254:11
man's unconquerable m. 294:4
march of the human m. is slow 54:20
measure my m. against his 239:5
m. casts off rebelliously 289:13
m. conscious of the right 275:10
M., from pleasure less 177:13
m. has mountains 138:26
m., in Metaphysics at a loss 204:18
m. is free, whate'er 102:3
m. is its own place 183:15
m. is the man himself 78:23
m. of man becomes / A thousand 293:12
m., that very fiery particle 63:11
m. was still unpledged 112:14
minister to a m. diseased 232:27
nothing great but m. 129:9
one dead level ev'ry m. 204:13
or the m. to admire 100:4

m. law within me 152:22
m. pocket handkerchiefs 96:3
m. when he is only uncomfortable 239:26
perfectly m. till all are moral 251:5
persons attempting to find a m. 271:25
To point a m. 147:19
moralist: He cursed the canting m. 91:6
sturdy m. who does not love 146:16
moralitee: Goodbye, m. 134:13
morality: Conventiality is not m. 47:5
Fodder...then m. 46:10
Master m. 192:22
m., and some of religion 105:14
M....attitude we adopt 286:27
m. for morality's sake 86:6
M. is the herd-instinct 192:25
periodical fits of m. 171:20
successful personal and national m. 239:10
moralize: m. my song 251:21
moralizers: away from here, you m. 197:11
morals: Have you no m., man 240:23
m. of a Methodist 123:15
m. of a whore 148:2
poets have m. and manners 130:9
self-interest was bad m. 215:16
Why man of m. 86:21
more: Less is m. 180:6
M. light 124:24
[M.] man for all seasons 285:14
m. things change 152:24
M. will mean worse 4:9
Oliver Twist has asked for m. 95:22
what is m. than enough 43:9
mores: *tempora! O m.* 78:25
more-than-oriental-splendour: reflected in m. 159:16
mori: *pro patria m.* 140:8
moriar: *Non omnis m.* 140:13
morituri: *m. te salutant* 257:20
morn: m. and cold indifference 217:21
m., in russet mantle clad 226:1
m. to night, my friend 216:30
No sleep till m. 61:20
morning: Early one m., just as 5:9
Good m. to the day 151:1
Gregor Samsa awoke one m. 152:19
many a glorious m. 238:8
m. of the world 51:28
Never glad confident m. 51:9
Never m. wore / To evening 263:9
rainbow in the m. 4:15
moron: wish I were a m. 6:25
morrow: m. shall take thought 36:1
rose the m. morn 81:17
mors: *Nil igitur m.* 170:11
mort: *m. ne surprend* 116:1
M., vieux capitaine 20:24
mortal: all men m., but themselves 298:25
death will visit m. life 170:12
gathers all things m. 260:11
makes this m. spirit feel / The joy 81:28
soul we have is m. 170:11
tatter in its m. dress 297:16
tush, man, m. men 228:6
you're m., and may err 245:19
mortalis: *natura animi m.* 170:11
mortality: nothing serious in m. 232:8
smells of m. 230:41
mortals: fools these m. be 234:8
m. love the letters 51:30
Mortis: *Timor M. conturbat me* 104:23
morts: *Il n'y a pas de m.* 174:7
mosaics: stiffly, m. of pain 93:14
Moss: wilderness of M. 204:18
most: m. may err 102:23
moth: desire of the m. for the star 244:12
m. and rust doth corrupt 35:25
m. in his brother's parachute 246:12
mother: Church as his m. 89:20
dogs tonight / For m. will be 134:7
Don't tell my m. 134:8
England is the m. of Parliaments 46:19
gave her m. forty whacks 6:6
great sweet m. 260:17
Honour...thy m. 26:34
like saying, 'My m., drunk 76:22
M. and lover of men 260:17
m., do not cry 112:24
m. drudge for his living 239:19
m.?' 'Never had none 257:9
m., / Who'd give her booby 120:24
never called me m. 291:12
Never throw stones at your m. 22:16
rob his m., he will not hesitate 113:8
ten times our m. 227:10
mother-in-law: said when his m. died 145:20
mothers: women become like their m. 287:5
mother-wits: rhyming m. 176:2
motion: Between the m. / And the act 107:24
little m. in the air 241:21
m. and a spirit, that impels 292:16
No m. has she now 293:21
order'd m., but ordain'd no rest 273:20
motive: mercenary, and the prudent m. 13:1
Persons attempting to find a m. 271:25
motiveless: m. malignity 82:20
motor car: afford to keep a m. 238:26
motor-cycle: son would have his m. 108:8
mottoes: than the m. on sun-dials 208:16
motus: *Hi m. animorum* 276:9
mould: Nature...broke the m. 8:11
moulds: distain your m. frae mine 17:22
mountain: He who ascends to m. tops 61:24
Land of the m. and the flood 222:3
or steepy m. yields 176:1
tiptoe on the misty m. tops 236:7
mountains: beautiful upon the m. 33:22
faith...could remove m. 39:7
High m. are a feeling 61:26
men and m. meet 42:9
M. are...natural scenery 218:6
M. are the beginning 218:6
m. be carried into the midst 30:1
m. look on Marathon 62:34
m. will be in labour 139:9
One of the m. 294:5
mourn: Blessed are they that m. 35:17
Makes countless thousands m. 57:7
m. with ever-returning spring 285:5
music...bad to those who m. 252:13
No longer m. for me 238:12
mourner: Be ev'ry m.'s sleep 157:7
mournful: not, in m. numbers 168:13
mourning: in m. for my life 74:28

Mourns: M. less for what age takes 292:6
mouse: leave room for the m. 219:11
m. ran up the clock 194:12
not even a m. 188:5
ridiculous m. will be born 139:9
mouse-trap: In baiting a m. 219:11
moustache: didn't wax his m. 159:28
mouth: Englishman to open his m. 240:22
false m. was like faint flowers 242:2
mouths: Blind m. 182:28
made m. in a glass 230:27
m. to steal away 234:34
moutons: *Revenons à nos m.* 6:23
move: But it does m. 119:18
great affair is to m. 256:8
I will m. the earth 8:8
m. still, still so 237:35
stars m. still 175:10
moved: m. by some very fine 160:20
m. more than with a trumpet 246:8
Movement: M., that problem of the visible 286:12
moveth: all that m. doth in Change 252:8
movies: m. are the only business 215:6
movin': boots — m. up an' down 158:23
moving: m. accident 292:7
M. Finger writes 114:25
Much: M. of a muchness 273:11
never to have too m. 265:19
so m. to do 214:4
muchness: Much of a m. 273:11
Muchos: *M. pocos hacen* 71:16
muck: m., not good except it be spread 14:20
Muckle: M. he made o' that 46:7
muck-rake: with a m. in his hand 53:22
mud: no sluice of m. / With deeper 204:8
One sees the m. 162:12
silver fountains m. 238:9
muddied: m. oafs 159:13
muddy: m. vesture of decay 233:24
Muffet: Little Miss M. 194:26
muffs: m. his real job 282:21
Multiplication: M. is vexation 6:10
multiply: Be fruitful, and m. 25:15
multitude: cover the m. of sins 40:26
to persuade a m. 138:14
multitudes: I am large, I contain m. 284:24
multitudinous: m. seas incarnadine 232:3
mummy-cloth: bobbin bound in m. 296:1
munch: So m. on, crunch on 51:26
mundi: *peccata m.* 178:19
munny: goä wheer m. is 264:18
Murder: I met M. on the way 242:26
Killing no M. 224:10
love and m. will out 84:20
Macbeth does m. sleep 232:1
m. an infant in its cradle 43:14
m. back into the home 136:12
M., like talent 165:12
M. most foul 226:17
M....One of the Fine Arts 93:8
m. to dissect 294:18
once indulges himself in m. 93:6
One to destroy, is m. 299:9
war called m. It is not 173:4
What is slavery?...M. 211:7
murdered: Each one a m. self 217:3
m. both his parents 166:17
murderer: deaf and viperous m. 241:13
m., / Yet, being intellectual 65:20
murderers: mirth / Of thieves and m. 135:11
M. are not improved by murdering 23:20
m. make the first move 152:25
murmuring: m. of innumerable bees 264:27
Murray: slain the Earl of M. 17:8
Musa: *M. vetat mori* 140:16
Muse: bid the M. go pack 298:9
conqueror creates a M. 278:5
M. forbids to die 140:16
M. of fire 228:26
m. on Nature with a poet's 66:9
M., who now governs the periodical 270:21
no Mistress but their M. 100:3
with the worst-natur'd m. 214:18
music: Architecture is frozen m. 124:23
brave M. of a *distant* Drum 114:16
but the m. there 206:1
Fled is that m. 155:7
formed, as notes of m. are 241:27
how potent cheap m. 86:13
If m. be the food of love 237:11
I shall be made thy M. 99:29
know anything about m. 22:12
laundry-list...set it to m. 217:12
make the m. mute 262:24
merry when I hear sweet m. 233:25
M. alone with sudden charms 84:22
M. and women I cannot but 201:7
[m.] a Rum Go 274:3
M. has charms to soothe 84:25
M. helps not the toothache 135:17
m. in my heart I bore 293:24
m. in the sinner's ears 282:30
M. is essentially useless 220:10
m. is good to the melancholy 252:13
m. is the brandy of the damned 239:24
M. shall untune the sky 103:28
m. sweeter than their own 293:4
M. that gentlier on the spirit 264:8
m. that you made below 91:4
M., the greatest good 1:17
M., when soft voices die 244:9
m. wherever she goes 195:11
m., yearning like a God 153:26
Poetry is...set to...lascivious m. 179:15
read m. but can't hear 22:2
really like classical m. 239:28
sounds of m. / Creep in 233:23
still, sad m. of humanity 292:15
stops when the m. stops 132:18
towards the condition of m. 199:15
uproar's your only m. 156:12
Van Gogh's ear for m. 282:1
musical: more m. than any song 216:27
Most m. 182:4
none of us m. 120:7
We are a m. nation 267:9
musicologist: m. is a man who 22:2
musing: m. gait 182:6
M. in solitude 292:2
M. upon the king 108:18
Muss: *M. es sein* 22:14
must: forget because we m. 9:5
M.! Is must a word 109:5
M. it be 22:14

You can, for you m. 124:21
mustard: grain of m. seed 36:16
mustn't: tell her she m. 211:19
mutabile: *m. semper / Femina* 275:16
Mutability: M. in them doth play 252:7
mutantur: *brevi spatio m.* 170:10
Tempora m., et nos 7:5
mutatus: *Quantum m. ab illo* 275:13
mute: are not soon m. 162:4
hangs as m. on Tara's walls 188:19
muttering: m. grew to a grumbling 51:25
mutton: m. with the usual trimmings 96:12
Old was his m. 137:23
mutual: benefit-club for m. flattery 81:27
my-lorded: grovelled before him, and m. him 266:10
myriad-minded: m. Shakespeare 82:16
Myriads: outshine / M. though bright 183:13
myrrh: frankincense, and m. 35:9
Myrtles: Ye M. brown 182:19
myself: and sing m. 284:18
been one m. for years 119:6
less alone than when by m. 121:25
like to go by m. 132:1
m. am Hell 184:13
mysterious: m. way / His wonders 87:21
mystery: burthen of the m. 292:12
lose myself in a m. 49:2
m. will lead millions 44:18
shew you a m. 39:11
mystic: walk your m. way 123:8
white samite, m., wonderful 262:28
mythical: built about a m. figure 134:15
mythologies: Out of old m. 296:5
Nagasaki: ashamed of, even in...N. 47:1
nail: hit the n. on the head 203:3
want of a n., the shoe 117:23
nails: naebody's n. can reach 222:21
nineteen hundred and forty n. 246:15
print of the n. 38:17
with his n. he'll dig them up 281:20
naïve: n. domestic Burgundy 269:9
naked: enterprise / In walking n. 296:6
left me n. to mine enemies 229:16
N. and ye clothed me 36:35
n. into the conference chamber 25:8
n. is the best disguise 84:21
seek / With n. foot 295:9
starving hysterical n. 123:26
nakedness: not in utter n. 292:23
see the n. of the land 26:10
nakid: n. as a worm was she 74:18
Namby-Pamby: N., pilly-piss 67:9
name: Ben Adhem's n. led all the rest 142:10
committed in thy n. 215:9
dare not speak its n. 101:1
deed without a n. 232:17
I am become a n. 265:9
Jesus! the N. that charms 282:30
my good n. / Robs me 234:36
n., at which the world 147:19
n. great in story 64:9
n....in the Pantheon of History 90:15
n. liveth for evermore 35:5
n. was writ in water 157:5
our n. will be linked 197:14
spared the n. 259:17
Thou shalt not take the n. 26:30
to see one's n. in print 63:22
What's in a n. 235:37
wrote her n. upon the sand 251:14
named: You have n. him 212:19
nameless: image of a n. dread 268:18
little, n., unremembered acts 292:11
names: allow their n. to be mentioned 13:3
commodity of good n. 227:32
Good and bad are but n. 110:17
n. / To hide its ignorance 243:28
naming: we have n. of parts 213:14
Naples: [N.] negation of God erected 123:27
Napoleon: dog, every man is N. 143:7
N. of crime 101:12
Narr: *ein N. sein Leben lang* 170:19
narrative: bald and unconvincing n. 123:3
motive in this n. 271:25
narrow: Every bed is n. 181:4
two n. words, *Hic jacet* 213:1
yon n. road 18:13
nascitur: *maius n. Iliade* 211:4
saeclorum n. ordo 275:28
nasty: n., brutish, and short 136:20
n. in the woodshed 122:1
n. soup away 137:2
nation: boundary of the march of a n. 199:4
n. conceived in liberty 166:10
n. of amateurs 216:18
n. of men's...religion 68:1
n. of shopkeepers 190:16
n. of shopkeepers 247:9
n. shall not lift up sword 32:27
N. shall speak peace 213:18
nerves a n.'s heart 262:12
noble and puissant n. rousing 186:4
No n. is fit to sit in judgement 290:4
No n. was ever ruined 117:26
one suffer than a n. grieve 102:19
this n., under God 166:11
We are a musical n. 267:9
national: always be above n. prejudices 193:13
only worship n. idols 240:9
National Gallery: Soul visits the N. 247:18
nationalities: rights of the smaller n. 10:19
nations: belong to other n. 122:17
n. behave wisely after 105:12
N....have their infancy 44:14
Praise the Lord, all n. 277:17
Two N. 97:23
native: foot is on my n. heath 222:25
my own, my n. land 222:1
repossess their n. seat 183:23
nativity: in n., chance or death 233:33
Natura: *N. non facit saltus* 167:5
natural: as n. to die 14:6
N. Selection 90:18
Novels...being *n.*...greatest Demerit 245:14
'twas n. to please 102:13
naturaliter: *animae n. Christianae* 265:27
naturally: n. Christian soul 265:27
Nature: all N. was a garden 278:10
art itself is n. 237:34
better...is N.'s way 8:23
debt of n. 112:21

nettle: n. shall flourish on the gravel 108:9
Tender-hearted stroke a n. 136:4
nettles: dust on the n. 267:16
neutral: stood apart, studiously n. 290:7
neutrality: 'n.', a word which in wartime 25:1
Armed n. 290:9
neutralize: White shall not n. 52:8
never: but I n. can 109:3
n. had it so good 173:20
N. met — or never parted 55:17
N., never, never, never, never 231:8
N. the time 51:14
n. to have too much 265:19
n. turned his back 52:13
roses, / And n. a spray 9:19
this will n. do't, sir 94:22
This will n. do 145:14
What, n. 122:13
Nevermore: Quoth the Raven, 'N.' 203:18
never-sear: with Ivy n. 182:19
New Zealand: married and gone to N. 79:18
Some traveller from N. 171:14
new: always something n. out of Africa 203:5
ancient story, yet it is ever n. 132:13
first by whom the n. are tried 205:31
n. book is published 215:1
N. lamps for old 8:4
n. moon late yestreen 18:10
N. World into existence 67:1
n. world may be safer 99:17
not apply n. Remedies 15:2
on with the n. 6:2
pain of a n. idea 16:14
ring in the n. 263:21
unto the Lord a n. song 277:15
newborn: As n. babes 40:24
I with things n. 237:30
use of a n. child 117:32
newer: late to seek a n. world 265:14
newest: In science, read...the n. 53:9
new-found-land: my America! my n. 99:11
news: All the n. that's fit 196:10
Ill n. hath wings 102:2
master-passion is the love of n. 88:16
n. that STAYS news 209:2
not n., but when a man bites 89:24
newspaper: n....same number of words 114:5
relied on in a n. 145:12
newspapers: n., all kinds of second rate 298:20
Newspeak: N. was the official language 197:2
Newton: God said, *Let N. be!* 205:24
N.'s Particles of Light 43:1
N., with his prism 293:8
New Year: Old Year out, / And the N. in 124:7
next: happiness of the n. world 48:23
time n. year I shall be 213:12
nexus: Cash payment is not the sole n. 68:12
nez: *n. de Cléopâtre* 199:7
Niagara: wouldn't *live* under N. 68:27
Nice: N. but nubbly 159:17
nicht: efter sic a n. 172:19
nicht goon: In his n. 181:7
Nick: Auld Hornie, Satan, N. 55:14
Nicodemus: N. saw such light 273:21
nigger: call me a damned n. 176:18
niggers: don't agree with n. 169:18
night: acquainted with the n. 118:5
at n. a bed of down 295:3
black bat, n., has flown 264:15
Bowl of N. 114:13
bump in the n. 5:15
By n. an atheist half believes 299:4
Chaos and old N. 183:20
City is of N. 268:12
dangers of this n. 209:19
Dear N.! this world's defeat 273:22
Death, / But certainly of N. 268:12
forests of the n. 43:24
gaudy n. 224:27
know his God by n. 273:21
last n. I swore 169:10
long out-living n. 185:8
N. and silence 234:6
n.? Are we here alone? 284:15
n. cometh 38:6
N. descending, the proud scene 204:2
n. for thieves 112:15
n. has a thousand eyes 45:12
n. is far spent 39:2
n. seems termless hell 268:13
profoundly dark n. 212:17
real dark n. of the soul 115:3
Ships that pass in the n. 168:20
sound of revelry by n. 61:29
tender is the n. 155:4
through the n. and storm 124:10
Work, for the n. is coming 80:20
world's last n. 99:26
nightingale: ravish'd n. 170:21
spoils the singing of the n. 153:22
nightmare: n. from which I am trying 151:20
nihil: *Caesar aut n.* 45:2
N. est ab omni 140:4
Nil: *N. posse creari* 170:8
Nile: serpent of old N. 224:22
nimis: *ut nequid n.* 265:19
nine: published for n. years 139:14
Nixon: to get N. re-elected 83:14
won't have N. to kick 193:8
No: able to say N. 8:24
own Araminta, say 'N.!' 209:5
The everlasting N. 68:18
Noah: N. he often said 76:21
Nobilitas: *N. sola est* 152:15
Nobility: all were noble, save N. 61:7
N. has obligations 165:10
unbleached by n. 12:12
Virtue alone is true n. 152:15
nobis: *Non n., Domine* 277:16
noble: dearth / Of n. natures 153:16
Do n. things 158:8
except for a n. purpose 134:17
last infirmity of N. minds 182:24
man with all his n. qualities 90:16
n. living and the noble dead 293:11
n. mind is here o'erthrown 227:2
Noblesse: *N. oblige* 165:10
noblest: God's the n. work of man 60:2
honest man's the n. work 56:1
honest Man's the n. work of God 206:26
love's the n. frailty 103:14
n. prospect which a Scotchman 148:6
n. Roman of them all 230:11
Time's n. offspring 24:18

number one: care of n. 176:16
numbers: for the n. came 204:33
no safety in n. 269:4
numbness: drowsy n. pains / My sense 154:33
nun: quiet as a n. 293:27
nuncheon: take your n. 51:26
nunnery: Get thee to a n. 227:1
n. / Of thy chaste breast 169:8
nunquam: *qui n. amavit, quique amavit* 5:6
Nuns: N. fret not 294:2
nurse: Athens, n. of men 250:2
continues what the n. began 103:12
keep a hold of N. 23:5
n. for a poetic child 222:3
N., O! my love is slain 99:9
n. unacted desires 43:14
nursed: n. upon the self-same hill 182:22
nurseries: n. of all vice 114:2
n. of Heaven 267:25
nurses: wives...old men's n. 14:11
Nut-brown: Spicy N. Ale 182:16
nutmeg: But a silver n. 194:16
nuts: Brazil — where the n. come from 266:19
nymph: n. more bright 120:15
O: This wooden O. 228:27
oafs: muddied o. 159:13
oak: hollow o. our palace is 89:18
thunders from her native o. 66:14
oaks: Little strokes fell great o. 117:19
mighty woods, / Tall o. 154:4
oat-cakes: land of Calvin, o., and sulphur 248:18
oaten: If aught of o. stop 83:8
oath: man is not upon o. 149:3
Oaths: O. are but words 59:25
Oats: *O.* A grain, which in England 146:13
Obadiah: O. Bind-their-kings-in-chains 171:2
obedience: Through o. learn to command 202:21
obedient: o. to their laws, we lie 246:11
obey: Anna! whom three realms o. 207:18
individual to o. the established 279:27
laws but to o. them 140:19
love, cherish and to o. 210:15
monarchs must o. 103:16
o. is better than sacrifice 27:31
o., were she ten times 227:10
woman to o.; / All else 264:26
obeyed: o. as a son 121:11
obeys: bends him, she o. him 168:19
object: hanging a man who does not o. 240:16
love to be the o. of love 113:17
oblig'd: that he ne'er o. 205:5
oblige: *Noblesse o.* 165:10
obliged: not o. to speak the truth 149:25
whatever a body is o. to do 272:7
obliging: So o., that he ne'er oblig'd 205:5
oblique: As Lines so Loves *o.* 177:5
obliquely: o. commendeth himself 48:20
oblivion: alms for o. 237:5
commend / To cold o. 242:1
iniquity of o. 48:25
obscenity: more o. than wit 278:9
obscure: Hopes which o. 47:16
I become o. 139:5
obscurity: decent o. of a learned 121:15
observance: breach than the o. 226:13
observation: In the field of o. 199:13
o. with extensive view 147:17
observe: see, but you do not o. 101:16
observed: continue to be, / Since o. 5:7
observer: o. of human nature 95:32
obsolete: exploded systems and o. prejudices 247:11
Obstinacy: O. in a bad cause 49:3
o. in a bad one 254:6
obstruction: lie in cold o. 232:38
obtained: none could be o. 147:13
Occasion: O., Chance and Change 243:21
occupation: Othello's o.'s gone 234:40
occupations: worse o. in the world 253:19
occurred: description of what has never o. 286:9
occurs: o. is of the smallest importance 287:29
ocean: fall into the o. 175:12
great o. of truth lay 192:11
like O. on a western beach 162:11
Mind, that O. where 177:13
o. as their road 278:8
round o. and the living air 292:16
Upon a painted o. 81:6
who has not seen the o. 16:9
oceans: Portable, and compendious o. 88:22
October: leaf still in O. 115:13
octo-syllabic: fatal facility of the o. 62:7
ocular: o. proof 234:41
odd: divinity in o. numbers 233:33
How o. / Of God 112:20
Nothing o. will do long 149:4
think it exceedingly o. 160:11
odds: facing fearful o. 171:5
Ode on a Grecian Urn: 'O.' is worth any number 113:8
Oderint: *O. dum metuant* 1:1
Odi: *O. et amo* 71:8
Odious: O.! in woollen 205:20
race of little o. vermin 258:12
your o. provisoes 84:35
odium: lived in the o. 24:14
odorous: Comparisons are o. 234:21
Odyssey: surge and thunder of the O. 162:11
Odysseys: last of all our O. 23:8
o'erflowing: without o. full 92:25
o'erleaps: o. itself / And falls 231:31
o'erthrown: noble mind is here o. 227:2
Off: O. with his head 69:15
O. with his head — so much for 78:13
offence: Satire...never...an o. 259:2
offend: If thine eye o. thee 36:24
to o. and make up at pleasure 214:13
offended: hath not o. the king 189:6
offending: most o. soul alive 228:35
offends: never once o. 207:15
offensive: path o. to the gods 2:17
offer: o. he can't refuse 46:2
offertorie: alderbest he song an o. 73:17
office: Suited for o. if only 261:9
office boys: By o. for office boys 219:20

oppressive: o. government is more to be feared 83:25
oppressor: find freedom...by killing his o. 23:20
optics: o. sharp it needs 271:5
use, were finer o. 206:14
optimism: o....of physiological...origin 272:25
pessimism...as agreeable as o. 24:3
optimist: o. proclaims...best of all possible worlds 65:3
opus: *Hoc o., hic labor est* 275:18
orange: in shades the o. bright 177:2
Oranges: O. and lemons 195:7
orare: *Laborare est o.* 6:4
orator: o....says what he thinks 52:21
ordained: powers that be are o. 39:1
order: Blessed rage for o. 254:27
decently and in o. 39:9
not necessarily in that o. 124:6
old o. changeth 263:2
o. in variety we see 207:26
right o. of life 261:21
Set thine house in o. 33:15
subversion of good O. 160:10
They o., said I, this matter 253:16
upon the o. of your going 232:14
whence arises all that o. 192:10
ordered: let our o. lives confess 285:13
ore: your subject with o. 157:4
organ: organ o. all the time 267:10
Seated one day at the o. 211:2
organized: o. common sense 143:11
origin: stamp of his lowly o. 90:16
original: as he is great and o. 294:25
common things in an o. way 139:7
more o. than his originals 111:1
o. ideas is sound 174:1
Their great O. proclaim 2:8
originator: o. of a good sentence 110:27
orisons: patter out their hasty o. 197:22
ornament: ask, respecting all o. 218:9
still deceived with o. 233:16
orphan: grounds that he was an o. 166:17
Orpheus: harp of O. was not more charming 186:7
orthodox: prove their doctrine o. 59:19
Orthodoxy: O. is my doxy 279:11
Oscar: You will, O., you will 283:25
Ossa: heap O. on Pelion 276:4
ostentation: for use rather than for o. 121:19
ostrich: rear end of an o. 282:13
wings of an o. 171:11
Othello: O.'s occupation's gone 234:40
other: because o. people think so 60:18
Hear the o. side 11:25
I am not as o. men 37:30
I can do no o. 170:17
no o. world 111:22
o. also laughs at him 186:16
were saying the o. day 165:3
others: do not do to o. 84:2
Do not do unto o. 239:31
lived for o. is...worthwhile 106:4
misfortunes and pains of o. 54:12
not astuter than all the o. 163:4
see oursels as o. see us 57:23
to encourage the o. 276:12
woman who lives for o. 165:13
otherwise: Heaven thought o. 275:14
some are o. 249:7
otia: *haec o. fecit* 275:24
otiosus: *o., nec minus solum* 78:20
Otium: *O. cum dignitate* 78:21
oublié: *Dieu, a-t-il donc o.* 169:4
ni rien o. 261:14
ought: gods, but there o. to be 97:7
must believe what you o. 192:8
not what they o. to do 13:24
not what we o. to say 231:9
perception that something o. to be done 282:24
think they o. to like it 239:28
WHERE O. I TO BE 77:6
which we o. to have done 209:8
ound: loves the 'o. more 258:4
ours: The land was o. 118:11
oursels: see o. as others see us 57:23
ourselves: do with o. this afternoon 115:4
in o., are triumph 168:12
in o. that we are thus 234:30
love of power...love of o. 132:2
Truth is within o. 51:17
out: at other o. it wente 74:23
I can't get o. 253:20
out-argue: out-vote them we will o. 149:19
outcast: beweep my o. state 238:5
outgrabe: mome raths o. 69:28
outlive: desire...o. performance 228:17
shame of it to o. him 152:20
outruns: desire that o. the delight 260:6
Outshone: O. the wealth of Ormus 183:27
outside: contempt for the o. 75:20
I am just going o. 196:5
Kiss the book's o. 87:13
out-vote: o. them we will out-argue 149:19
outward: all o. loathes 100:20
from o. forms to win 81:21
looketh on the o. appearance 27:32
o. shows be least themselves 233:16
outwatch: oft o. the Bear 182:8
outworn: dust of creeds o. 243:17
over: But this is o. now 71:2
having it o. 138:9
oversexed, and o. here 6:16
overcomes: who o. his enemies 8:19
who o. / By force 183:24
over-dressed: occasionally a little o. 288:1
over-educated: always absolutely o. 288:1
overflow: o. of powerful feelings 294:24
Overpaid: O., overfed 6:16
overrated: much o. by the poets 104:12
over-rul'd: will in us is o. by fate 175:18
over-run: o. / Large Countries 185:5
overthrow: never can work war's o. 42:10
overtopped: o. in anything else 58:11
overwhelm: o. / Myself in poesy 155:11
ovo: *Ex o. omnia* 131:3
owed: o. by so many to so few 77:27
Owl: O. and the Pussy-Cat 164:10
o., for all his feathers 153:23
sings the staring o. 231:17
wise old o. lived 194:3
owls: couch when o. do cry 236:27
O. would have hooted 127:19

own: but mine o. 225:23
Room of One's O. 291:16
owner: like the o. of the look 80:12
ox: lion and o. is oppression 42:24
o. goeth to the slaughter 31:19
stalled o. and hatred 31:27
Thou shalt not muzzle the o. 27:8
oxen: see the o. kneel 130:8
than a hundred pair of o. 141:6
Oxenford: Clerk ther was of O. 73:9
Oxford: clever men at O. / Know 126:16
nice sort of place, O. 239:22
nonsense...put back at O. 22:8
O. gave the world marmalade 6:17
[O.] Home of lost causes 10:9
O....made me insufferable 22:7
To O. sent a troop 270:5
Oxonian: Impossible! He is an O. 287:13
oyster: unselfishness of an o. 219:13
world's mine o. 233:28
oysters: first ventured on eating of o. 119:7
Poverty and o. 95:38
Ozymandias: O., king of kings 243:10
p'ints: no p. about that frog 271:21
pace: *e nostra p.* 90:10
pacem: *Qui desiderat p.* 274:6
paces: three p. thro' the room 263:30
Pacific: star'd at the P. 155:22
pack: revenged on the whole p. 237:26
pack-horse: p. on the down 189:13
paddle: p. his own canoe 176:23
padlock: p. of silence 47:7
page: on a beautiful quarto p. 245:9
pageant: insubstantial p. faded 236:24
paid: attention must finally be p. 181:6
ez mine's p. punctooal 169:20
for kisses, Cupid p. 170:20
might as well get p. 105:3
p. for only with goods 193:12
pain: After great p. 96:20
aromatic p. 290:15
born in other's p. 267:20
heard a sudden cry of p. 253:14
like a God in p. 153:26
no p., dear mother 112:24
one who never inflicts p. 192:3
Our Lady of P. 260:5
owes its pleasures to another's p. 88:8
p. of a new idea 16:14
p. to the bear 171:16
Razors p. you 198:21
Sweet is pleasure after p. 102:25
Unnumbered hours of p. 66:11
wicked to deserve such p. 50:10
pains: infinite capacity for taking p. 139:4
in what divers p. they met 272:18
to the p. of hell for ever 70:19
paint: looking as fresh as p. 247:3
p. an inch thick 227:22
p. in the public's face 218:4
p. my picture freely like me 89:9
p. the lily 230:15
to p. the souls of men 50:27
painted: p. meadow 1:16
p. ship / Upon a painted 81:6
young as they are p. 22:5
painter: vast commendation of a p. 113:25
painters: bad p. vomit Nature 71:21
Light is the first of p. 111:5
painting: Poetry is like p. 139:13
pair: p. of spectacles is here 237:9
palace: hollow oak our p. is 89:18
p. and a prison on each 61:31
palaces: cottages princes' p. 233:4
palates: While our gross p. 295:19
pale: blush than turn p. 70:23
p., and spectre-thin 155:2
P. hands I loved 138:23
Prithee, why so p. 257:17
palely: Alone and p. loitering 153:11
Palestine: establishment in P. of a national home 16:26
Palladium: *P.* of all the civil 152:1
palliate: neither attempt to p. nor deny 202:3
Pallida: *P. Mors* 139:25
Pall Mall Gazette: *P.* is written by gentlemen 266:6
palm: bear the p. alone 229:19
sweating p. to palm 142:19
To win the P., the Oak 177:9
palms: p. before my feet 76:8
palm-tree: flourish like the p. 30:14
palm-trees: shady city of p. 274:1
palmy: many a p. plain 132:8
palpable: p. design upon us 156:20
very p. hit 227:27
Palsied: P. strikes the summer 42:1
pampered: p. jades of Asia 176:12
Pan: great god P. 49:17
great god P. is dead 203:10
Pandion: King P., he is dead 19:22
Panem: *P. et circenses* 152:17
Pange: *P., lingua* 274:7
pantaloon: lean and slipper'd p. 225:15
panteth: As the hart p. 29:29
Pantheon: P. of History 90:15
panting: For ever p. 154:23
pants: As p. the hart 261:17
deck your lower limbs in p. 191:1
Papa: P., potatoes, poultry 94:28
paper: for a scrap of p. 25:1
Imperialism is a p. tiger 174:22
p. it's written on 126:5
papers: got my p., this man 202:1
parachute: moth in his brother's p. 246:12
parade: p. of riches 247:8
Paradise: Athens but the rudiments of P. 250:5
England...p. of women 115:16
enjoy p. in the next 21:22
hast the keys of P. 93:5
milk of P. 82:7
p. for a sect 153:32
sing / Recover'd P. 185:2
To him are opening p. 127:24
Wilderness is P. enow 114:15
Paradise Lost: said much here of 'P.' 109:18
paradises: true p....we have lost 211:9
Parallel: ours so truly *P.* 177:5
paralysis: Civilization is p. 120:10
paramours: his sustres and his p. 74:8
Parcae: P. thought him one 150:22
parchment: black / Upon white p. 208:12
virtue of wax and p. 54:23
pardon: God may p. you 109:3
God will p. me 132:16
pardonnera: *Dieu me p.* 132:16
parent: object to an aged p. 94:20

p. who could see his boy 164:1
To lose one p. 287:4
parenthesis: small p. in eternity 48:21
parents: begin by loving their p. 288:15
murdered both his p. 166:17
My p. kept me from 251:9
P. are the last people 60:9
parfit: verray, p. gentil knyght 73:4
Paris: P. is well worth a mass 133:12
When P. sneezes, Europe 180:2
parish: deserved well of his p. 218:12
world as my p. 283:4
park: comedy is a p., a policeman 72:9
parliament: he is a member of *p.* 54:16
honest by the act of p. 150:19
Mob, P. 80:6
P. is...a big meeting 16:6
P....formidable...as an audience 64:22
p. men o' our ain 222:21
P. of man 264:5
Parliamentary: old P. hand 124:2
Parliaments: England...mother of P. 46:19
parlour: walk into my p. 141:8
parochial: p. in the beginning to be cosmopolitan 188:10
Parody: P. and caricature 142:22
parrot: sell the family p. 215:7
Parsee: P. from whose hat 159:16
parson: Monday is p.'s holiday 258:18
P. left conjuring 223:15
P. lost his senses 137:1
stealthily, like a p.'s damn 130:10
parsons: p. are very like other men 75:6
p. too lazy 83:22
part: from yours you will not p. 257:15
heart ay's the p. 56:8
let us kiss and p. 102:8
p. of it all the way 126:3
We p. with sadly 16:16
parterre: nod on the p. 205:18
partickler: your p. wanity 96:14
particle: mind, that very fiery p. 63:11
Particles: Newton's P. of Light 43:1
particular: Did nothing in p. 122:21
with the p. example 246:6
Particulars: must do it in Minute P. 42:16
parting: agony of p. with your mamma 266:14
P. is all we know of heaven 96:25
p. is such sweet sorrow 236:2
p. there is an image of death 106:25
Partir: *P. c'est mourir* 129:13
partitions: thin p. do their bounds divide 102:15
partout: *p. il est dans les fers* 217:16
partridge: p. sitteth on eggs 34:7
Parts: P. of it are excellent 211:22
sum of the p. 8:20
we have naming of p. 213:14
Parturient: *P. montes* 139:9
party: Conservatives...the stupidest p. 180:9
of the Devil's p. 42:22
p.'s call 122:14
Patriotism is of no p. 249:10
save the P. we love 119:16
Stick to your p. 98:10
parva: *Si p. licet* 276:10
Parys: Frenssh of P. was to hire unknowe 73:5
pasarán: *No p.* 143:17
pass: all ye that p. by 34:9
earth shall p. away 36:33
let him p. for a man 233:5
p. through this world but once 128:4
Ships that p. in the night 168:20
They shall not p. 143:17
They shall not p. 193:7
Try not the P. 168:7
passage: p. which you think is particularly fine 148:28
passed: p. away a glory 292:21
p. by on the other side 37:22
So he p. over 53:29
passengers: we the p. 141:7
passer: laissez p. 212:5
P. mortuus est 71:1
passeront: *Ils ne p. pas* 193:7
passes: Men seldom make p. 198:19
never p. a church without 148:12
passest: thou who p. by 246:11
passeth: p. all understanding 210:7
passing: p. brave to be a King 176:5
speak each other in p. 168:20
passing-bells: p. for these who die 197:22
passion: all p. spent 185:17
Haunted me like a p. 292:14
In her first p. woman 62:29
keep the p. fresh 179:29
not p.'s slave 227:7
one universal p.: fear 240:17
P. for fame 54:18
p. shall have spent 264:3
ruling P. conquers Reason 205:14
Strange fits of p. 294:14
tear a p. to tatters 227:4
tender p. is much overrated 104:12
passionate: some p. attitude 199:17
Passions: discolour'd thro' our P. shown 205:21
dissemble their P. better 253:2
martyrdom of our p. 19:5
not his reasons, but his p. 254:7
p. as it is with fire 165:7
p....bad masters 165:7
their p. a quotation 286:16
two p., vanity and love 75:22
various ruling p. find 204:27
past: alter the p., historians can 59:31
lament the p. 54:13
p., at least, is secure 281:4
p. is a foreign country 131:2
p., it is needless to blame 83:26
power to change the p. 2:22
remember the p. are condemned 220:7
remembrance of things p. 238:7
Study the p....divine the future 84:6
world is weary of the p. 242:13
Pastoral: Cold P. 154:25
Pastures: and P. new 182:33
lie down in green p. 29:20
pat: Now I might do it p. 227:12
P. he comes 230:22
patches: king of shreds and p. 227:14
paternal: few p. acres 207:10
pâtés: eating *p. de foie gras* to the sound 248:29
path: p. on the sea's azure floor 242:3
That is the p. of wickedness 18:13
Pathetic: P. Fallacy 218:5
That's what it is. P. 181:14

pelican: wonderful bird is the p. 180:1
Pelion: heap Ossa on P. 276:4
Pelting: P. each other for the public 87:8
pen: Ask my p., — it governs 254:18
know till he takes up the p. 266:3
less brilliant p. than mine 22:6
more cruel the p. is 59:2
my p. has glean'd 155:25
my tongue is the p. 29:31
p. is mightier than the sword 53:10
scratching of a p. 169:13
pence: loss of p. 87:15
pencil: Sharpens his p. for the kill 53:7
pendulum: ominous vibration of a p. 152:4
penetrated: ever p. into the ear 116:18
penetrating: p. sort of laugh 290:26
penitent: p. thief 12:1
pennies: Twelve p.! What better 298:18
penny: haven't got a p., a ha'penny 5:4
not a p. had in wolde 74:18
not a p. off the pay 85:12
To turn a p. 88:1
pennyworths: buying good p. 117:16
pens: Let other p. dwell on guilt 12:17
pensant: *roseau p.* 199:11
Penser: *P., c'est voir* 18:19
pension: p. from his parish 218:12
pent: long in city p. 155:24
peonies: wealth of globèd p. 154:30
people: but ye are the p. 29:4
government...made by the p. 281:5
government of the p. 166:11
has such p. in't 236:28
Hell is other p. 220:17
indictment against a whole p. 54:24
Let my p. go 26:19
look after our p. 221:10
makes the p.'s wrongs his own 102:22
Martyr of the P. 72:14
Most p. are other people 286:16
ne'er forget the P. 56:5
new p. takes the land 76:15
One fifth of the p. 157:18
one p., one leader 5:10
opium of the p. 178:3
p. are the masters 54:26
p. have nothing to do with 140:19
p., it appears, may be progressive 180:15
p. keep even kings in awe 90:22
p. never give up their liberties 55:1
p. perish 32:1
p. some of the time 166:4
p.'s voice is odd 207:2
p. will always be kind 220:22
Privileged and the P. 97:23
right of the P. to establish Government 279:27
thy p. shall be my people 27:24
two kinds of p. in the world 198:18
voice of the p. 3:2
We are for our own p. 119:19
we are the p. of England 76:16
welfare of the p. is the ultimate 78:17
peopled: world must be p. 234:20
Pequod: P.'s sea wings 170:1
peradventure: p. he sleepeth 28:15
per cents: elegant simplicity of the three p. 257:12
perception: doors of p. 43:15
Percy: old song of P. and Douglas 246:8
Perdition: P. catch my soul 234:35
To bottomless p. 183:11
perdu: *Tout est p. fors l'honneur* 117:6
père: *vous n'avez plus de p.* 191:16
Pereant: *P....qui ante nos* 98:20
perennially: p. hopeless 93:19
perfect: Be ye therefore p. 35:22
far more p. creature than 90:17
if ever, come p. days 169:23
machine is so p. 111:14
Man's as p. as he ought 206:10
One p. rose 198:20
P. happiness, even in memory 12:8
P. love casteth out fear 40:29
perfection: ascertain what p. is 10:5
attain to the divine p. 168:9
heart contains p.'s germ 243:27
let us speak of p. 208:24
P. of the life 296:3
pursuit of p. 10:4
perfectly: be p. free till all 251:5
perfidious: p. England 45:9
perform: cannot p. great things themselves 278:22
performance: desire...outlive p. 228:17
High-definition p. 272:21
performing: literature's p. flea 196:9
perfume: p. on the violet 230:15
perfumes: All the p. of Arabia 232:23
Perhaps: grand P. 49:27
seek a great p. 212:15
vee may p. to begin 217:13
peril: those in p. on the sea 284:8
perils: p. and dangers of this night 209:19
periodical: Muse, who now governs the p. 270:21
perish: many p. for a private man 175:25
not p. from the earth 166:11
pain, / And p. in our own 267:20
P. the thought 78:14
p. with the sword 36:38
wisdom shall p. with you 29:4
perished: We p., each alone 87:5
periwig-pated: robustious p. fellow 227:4
permis: *pas p. de s'ennuyer* 163:3
pernicious: most p. race 258:12
perpetual: p. light shine 178:17
perpetually: must be damned p. 175:9
p. to be conquered 54:22
perpetuity: merit of p. 48:25
perplexyté: remede / That stad in p. 295:15
persecutest: Saul, why p. thou 38:22
persecution: truth put down by p. 180:14
Persepolis: ride in triumph through P. 176:5
Perseverance: P., dear my lord 237:6
p. in a good cause 254:6
Persian: P. luxury 140:2
Persians: Medes and the P. 34:17
P. and the Medes 28:28
Persicos: *P. odi* 140:2
person: altered her p. for the worse 259:4
p. on business from Porlock 82:2
there's no sich a p. 95:9
personal: No p. considerations should stand 126:19
P. relations are the important 116:19
personalities: p. have been obliged to be rebels 288:6

Envy would kill / P. 244:6
Fame...paves the way to p. 64:20
For physical p....go to my dentist 280:26
gave p. to the spectators 171:16
go to my p., business 295:13
greatest p. I know 161:16
hatred...the longest p. 63:15
in youth is p. 283:13
It becomes a p. 287:9
little p. out of the way 72:17
Love ceases to be a p. 22:18
love of p. 204:27
no such p. in life 52:15
on p. she was bent 87:16
perfect p. It is exquisite 287:25
P. at the helm 127:7
p. is momentary 76:3
P. never is at home 153:35
p. of an employment 13:8
p. of being moved 160:20
p. of having it over 138:9
P. that abideth for a Moment 287:27
p. was his business 105:16
public stock of harmless p. 147:4
rich wot gets the p. 6:3
seize the p. at once 12:9
Sweet is p. after pain 102:25
Variety is the soul of p. 22:20
when Youth and P. meet 61:20
pleasure-dome: stately p. decree 82:3
pleasures: all the p. prove 176:1
cannot understand the p. 12:5
celibacy has no p. 147:11
Garden...purest of human P. 15:12
Heaven forbids certain p. 187:6
hypocrite in his p. 149:28
our p. with rough strife 177:23
paucity of human p. 150:1
p. are like poppies 57:17
P. are ever in our hands 206:21
p. in life is conversation 248:4
p. without being enslaved 66:20
schooling in the P. 179:18
unreproved p. free 182:13
pledge: I will p. with mine 150:27
plenty: Here is God's p. 104:3
P. has impoverished me 197:17
wasna fou, but just had p. 56:2
pleure: *Il p. dans mon coeur* 274:13
Pleurez: *P.! enfants* 191:16
plight: I p. thee my troth 210:14
plod: To p. on and still 179:29
plods: ploughman homeward p. 127:9
plot: blessed p., this earth 235:15
find a p. in it will be shot 271:25
now the p. thickens 53:2
What the devil does the p. signify 53:1
plough: his hand to the p. 37:19
p. my furrow alone 216:19
p. over the bones 43:4
We p. the fields 79:8
wherefore p. / For the lords 244:3
ploughed: p. that path before 242:3
p. with swords 43:19
ploughing: Is my team p. 140:29
plowshares: swords into p. 32:27
pluck: offend thee, p. it out 36:24
plucked: p. out of the burning 34:22
plum: give a sugar p. than my time 156:19
pulled out a p. 194:25
plumage: pities the p. 198:8
plumber: no God, but try getting a p. 3:21
plum-cake: p. was a compensation 266:14
plummet-measured: p. face 298:2
plump: Stately, p. Buck Mulligan 151:14
plunder: poor p. from a bleeding land 61:13
your ill-got p., and bury 191:22
plural: Incorrigibly p. 174:4
plurality: p. of loves no crime 99:10
plures: *Abiit ad p.* 201:13
Plus: *P. ça change* 152:24
P. peut-être 141:19
poacher: p. a keeper turned 158:13
pocket: not scruple to pick a p. 93:1
pound...in your p. 289:20
Poe: comes P. with his raven 169:17
poem: admitted into a serious p. 1:18
life...is a p. 67:15
life of a man...a heroic p. 67:17
long p. is a test 156:5
married to a p. 157:3
ought himself to be a true p. 186:1
p. is never finished 273:6
p. lovely as a tree 158:1
P. maybe as cold 296:17
p. may be worked over 118:18
p. should not mean 173:16
pretty p., Mr. Pope 24:16
poems: My p. are licentious 176:25
p., with all their crudities 267:12
ye are living p. 168:4
Poesie: P.! thou nymph reserv'd 57:16
poesis: *Ut pictura p.* 139:13
poesy: difficult as a beginning / In p. 63:2
overwhelm / Myself in p. 155:11
p.; 'tis the supreme of power 155:14
viewless wings of P. 155:3
wore the mask / Of P. 155:13
poet: accounted p. kings 155:15
business of a p. 147:9
consecration, and the P.'s dream 292:1
could not well reform...without...p. 115:12
flattery lost on p.'s ear 221:23
girl had the makings of a p. 278:2
God is the perfect p. 51:18
great p....profound philosopher 82:17
Honour the greatest p. 90:6
I am Cinna the p. 230:7
I was a p., I was young 115:10
limbs of a p. 140:17
lunatic, the lover, and the p. 234:12
must on Nature with a p.'s eye 66:9
never be a p. 104:5
no person can be a p. 171:18
p. and the dreamer 153:34
P. blind, yet bold 177:16
[p.] giveth a perfect picture 246:6
p. is the most unpoetical 156:16
p.,...lifted up with the vigour 246:4
p.'s fate is here 283:6
p.'s function is to describe 8:28
p.'s lips I slept 243:18
p.'s made as well as born 150:30
p.'s mouth be silent 297:10
p.'s pen / Turns them to shapes 234:13
Scottish p. maun assume 172:18
should possess a p.'s brain 102:7
true P., and of the Devil's 42:22
worst tragedy for a p. 80:16
poetic: constitutes p. faith 82:15
crawl upon p. feet 203:27

poodle: Mr. Balfour's p. 167:14
poor: dare to be p. 121:1
Decent means p. 200:6
greater part of the members are p. 247:7
grind the faces of the p. 32:28
inconvenient to be p. 87:7
Labour robbed out of the p. 282:19
live by robbing the p. 239:25
p. always ye have with 38:10
p. and independent 80:5
p. and I've been rich 271:8
p. are never grateful 288:4
p. are the blacks of Europe 72:5
p. have become poorer 244:20
p. man surrounded by riches 140:11
p.'s decay 125:11
p. they call him a Jew 132:15
p. wot gets the blame 6:3
p., yet hast thou golden slumbers 92:12
property of the p. 218:14
simple annals of the p. 127:12
space that many p. supplied 125:12
too p. to find a right order 261:21
virtuous p., one can pity 288:5
poorest: p. he that is in England 212:21
p. man may 202:4
poor-folk: p. maun be wretches 58:5
Pope: believe in Milton, Dryden, P. 62:21
Better to err with P. 63:24
caring not for P. 294:8
Dryden and P. are not classics 10:15
If P. be not a poet 147:2
P.! How many divisions 252:22
[P.] made poetry...mechanic 87:30
pretty poem, Mr. P. 24:16
poplars: p. are felled 87:27
poppies: p. blow / Between 171:26
p. grow / In Flanders fields 172:1
poppy: flushed print in a p. 267:24
oblivion blindly scattereth her p. 48:25
populace: p. cannot understand the bureaucracy 240:9
p. rise at once 284:16
popular: more p. than Jesus Christ 165:1
popularity: constant p. of dogs 143:7
Population: P., when unchecked, increases 174:17
talked of p. 125:25
populi: *Salus p. suprema* 223:16
Porlock: person on business from P. 82:2
Pornography: P. is the attempt to insult sex 163:20
porringer: take my little p. 294:23
port: fetch a pint of p. 265:17
Let him drink p. 137:23
p. after stormy seas 252:1
p. for men 149:21
sweetheart in every p. 249:11
would be p. if it could 24:17
portable: p. property 94:19
portentous: p. phrase, 'I told you so' 63:18
Portion: I become / P. of that around me 61:26
p. of that unknown plain 130:2
portrait: paint a p. I lose a friend 220:14
two styles of p. painting 95:13
posies: pocket full of p. 195:12
position: p. ridiculous 76:3
possess: to feel, and to p. 61:14
possession: just p. of truth as of a city 49:1
p. of it is intolerable 273:10
possibilities: believe only p. 49:4
not interested in the p. 274:19
possibility: exhaust the boundaries of p. 201:25
sceptic to deny the p. 143:15
possible: best of all p. worlds 276:11
Politics...art of the p. 41:22
Politics is the art of the p. 59:15
p. as being probable 8:28
p. you may be mistaken 89:3
states that something is p. 79:7
with God all things are p. 36:27
Possum: Said the Honourable P. 24:22
possumus: *Non omnia p.* 275:29
post-chaise: p. with a pretty woman 149:11
posterity: don't give a hoot about p. 86:10
p. done for us 214:16
see P. do something for us 2:11
Trustees of P. 97:24
postern: latched its p. behind 129:15
posthumously: some are born p. 192:23
Posthumus: Alas, P. 140:3
postscript: most material in the p. 15:1
pot: chicken in his p. every Sunday 133:13
death in the p. 28:20
deepest p. of hell 104:17
doth keel the p. 231:17
earthen p. together 34:32
flinging a p. of paint 218:4
It's a Useful P. 181:15
make them in the one p. 151:16
who the P. 114:27
potage: mess of p. 5:11
Potations: P. pottle-deep 234:33
potatori: *propitius isti p.* 8:10
poteen-makers: p., with the jobbing jockies 260:21
potent: how p. cheap music is 86:13
Potomac: All quiet along the P. 22:13
quiet along the P. 171:25
pots: ands were p. and pans 200:10
Potter: Who *is* the P. 114:27
pottle-deep: Potations p. 234:33
pound: p....in your pocket 289:20
P. notes is the best religion 22:15
p. of flesh 233:17
pounds: About two hundred p. a year 59:27
six hundred p. a year 259:19
pours: one p. out a balm 153:34
pouvoit: *si vieillesse p.* 112:8
poverty: crime so shameful as p. 112:26
hardest thing about the miseries of p. 152:10
P. and oysters 95:38
P. is an anomaly to rich people 16:10
P. is no disgrace 249:1
suffer so much p. and excess 200:16
worst of crimes is p. 239:14
worth by p. depress'd 147:6
powder: Food for p. 228:6
power: balance of p. 278:25
Corridors of P. 249:15
empire is no more than p. 102:18
excellent, than in the extent of my p. 3:8
good want p. 243:15

present: All p. and correct 4:18
behold these p. days 238:17
golden age never was the p. 117:18
last importance only to be p. 268:24
P. has latched its postern 129:15
p. in spirit 39:4
p. in time future 107:11
Presents: P....endear Absents 161:2
preserve: p. thee from all evil 31:5
(Whom God P.) 189:17
preserver: Destroyer and p.; hear 243:7
President: P. of the Immortals 130:12
rather be right than be P. 79:10
press: *deadborn from the p.* 142:3
Muse, who now governs...p. 270:21
p. is the *Palladium* 152:1
pressure: Grace under p. 133:4
presume: Dr. Livingstone, I p. 252:23
none should p. 12:1
presumption: amused by its p. 269:9
prêt: *p. à partir* 187:12
toujours p. à partir 116:1
Pretender: who P. is, or who is King 60:25
pretexts: Tyrants seldom want p. 55:5
pretio: *Romae / Cum p.* 152:11
pretty: all love a p. girl 41:11
Arguments out of a p. mouth 2:14
come to a p. pass when religion 179:2
growing up into a p. woman 12:14
more than a prophetess — a uncommon p. 106:13
p. how town 89:11
p. to see what money will do 201:8
prevail: cares whether it p. or not 200:2
not p. against thee 34:1
prevailing: p. opinion and feeling 180:10
pre-war: p. mentality into the grave 23:22
prey: greater p. upon the less 127:27
price: before they would give the p. 218:8
difference is only in p. 117:20
Everything in Rome is at a p. 152:11
high / The p. for knowledge 269:14
knows the p. of everything 287:18
peace at any p. 146:4
p. is far above rubies 32:2
p. which is too great to pay 290:8
those men have their p. 278:27
prices: stroke, reduce the rise of p. 132:5
prick: if honour p. me off 228:9
p. us, do we not bleed 233:14
pricking: knight was p. on the plain 251:22
p. of my thumbs 232:16
pricks: kick against the p. 38:23
Pride: but here have P. and Truth 297:11
He that is low no p. 53:24
kind of p. of stomach 58:17
perished in his p. 293:13
P. goeth before destruction 31:28
p. that apes humility 81:24
p. / Is skilful to invent 243:28
priest: entrails of the last p. 97:4
free me of this turbulent p. 133:14
my religion from the p. 125:30
Presbyter is but old P. 185:24
p. continues what the nurse 103:12
p. / The requiem mass to sing 246:19
the true God's P. 67:3
priestcraft: ere p. did begin 102:11
priests: or p. devise 102:14
p. are only men 52:4
p. dare babble of a God 243:29
prime: dead ere his p. 182:20
Jean Brodie in her p. 250:24
splendour of its p. 242:12
primrose: p. by a river's brim 293:2
The p. way 232:6
prince: ancient p. of hell 170:16
great P. in prison lies 99:14
I the P. of Love 43:20
p. of Aquitaine 191:17
P. of Peace 33:4
Who made thee a p. 26:13
princerple: *don't* believe in p. 169:21
princes: addressed to p. 109:5
Put not your trust in p. 31:13
principalities: nor angels, nor p. 38:38
Principle: Conservatism...shrinks from P. 97:15
does everything on p. 240:18
from some strong p. 179:6
rebels from p. 54:10
principles: activity by reference to p. 261:20
Damn your p. 98:10
die for our p. is heroic 215:13
P. are only excuses 173:13
p. or your mistress 289:5
shews that he has good p. 148:12
print: licence to p. your own money 268:22
monotony / Of ugly p. marks 208:12
p. of a man's naked foot 92:7
see one's name in p. 63:22
see their names in p. 108:10
printed: chaff is p. 141:12
printers: books by which the p. have lost 119:10
Printing: civilization, Gunpowder, P. 67:20
prints: p. the chaff 255:5
prism: prunes and p. 94:28
prison: great Prince in p. lies 99:14
in p., and ye came 36:35
palace and a p. on each 61:31
P. make / Nor Iron 169:7
p. where I live 235:22
Shades of the p. house 292:23
ship but a p. 59:4
soul in p., I am not free 91:17
prisoner: p. leaps to lose 280:18
p.'s release 246:1
prisoners: blue / Which p. call the sky 285:22
p. and I'll find them law 46:8
Prisons: P. are built with stones 43:6
prius: *Sed haec p. fuere* 71:2
private: agreed to none of it in p. 12:11
consult our p. ends 259:16
fine and p. place 177:22
invade the sphere of p. life 179:2
many perish for a p. man 175:25
P. faces in public 11:12
P. Means is dead 248:3
P. respects must yield 185:15
public zeal to cancel p. crimes 102:17
to serve our p. ends, / Forbids 77:13
privilege: Death is the p. 217:24
p. of any man of parts 286:9

privileged: position of certain p. classes 85:16
P. and the People 97:23
privit: To very p. uses 169:19
prize: leave so rich a p. as this 176:9
p. the thing ungained more 236:34
proba: *vita p.* 176:25
probability: p. is the very guide 59:12
probable: No p., possible shadow of doubt 122:7
possible as being p. 8:28
probing: p. their immensities 50:13
problem: quite a three-pipe p. 101:14
solution of the p. of life 290:20
problematical: undercuts / the p. world 118:26
Proboscis: wreath'd / His Lithe P. 184:17
proceedings: p. interested him no more 131:1
proceeds: good conscience on the p. 247:15
procrastinates: One yawns, one p. 75:26
procrastination: from that to incivility and p. 93:6
P. is the thief of time 298:24
procul: *p. este, profani* 275:19
P. hinc 197:11
prodigal: p. of his own 219:21
producing: happiness without p. it 238:30
productions: from the p. which he left 121:19
profane: far from me, let all p. ones be 275:19
profaned: word is too often p. 244:11
profani: *procul este, p.* 275:19
profanum: *Odi p. vulgus* 140:5
profession: It is his p. 132:16
not what I call religion, this p. 68:1
only p. for which no preparation 256:3
professions: Of the p. it may be said 83:22
p. are conspiracies 239:4
professors: American p. like their literature 165:14
profit: Greedy for quick returns of p. 50:30
language; and my p. on't 236:16
may p. by their example 133:22
p. with pleasure 139:11
profited: What is a man p. 36:23
profits: little p. that an idle king 265:7
p. most who serves best 241:6
profligate: witty, p. and thin 299:6
profonde: *horreur d'une p. nuit* 212:17
profound: vast p. 204:3
profundis: *De p.* 277:18
profusus: *sui p.* 219:21
progenies: *Iam nova p.* 275:28
Progress: 'P.' is the exchange of one nuisance 109:11
calls each fresh link P. 52:27
fear and to hope from its p. 269:17
p....beyond its income 60:15
p. depends on the unreasonable 240:4
P., man's distinctive mark 50:18
p. of a deathless soul 100:7
p. of the arts 174:20
P. was all right 269:12
progression: contraries is no p. 42:20
progressive: enemy of p. ideals 23:19
p. for a certain length 180:15
prohibiting: p. to misdoubt her strength 186:6
proletariat: dictatorship of the p. 178:6
prologue: witty p. to a very dull Play 84:29
prologues: p. to the swelling act 231:22
promiscuous: exhaust their strength in p. living 219:4
promise: To p. not to do 272:8
promises: I have p. to keep 118:16
P....made to be broken 258:21
rake the p. to himself 47:17
promising: destroy they first call p. 84:37
Promoted: P. everybody 122:11
proof: ocular p. 234:41
proofs: As p. of holy writ 234:39
propaganda: peace p. makes war 163:18
propagate: p. understanding 149:31
Proper: P. words in proper places 258:19
property: consider himself as public p. 145:13
give me a little snug p. 105:14
If p. had simply pleasures 288:3
large p. as hadn't a title 96:11
portable p. 94:19
P. has its duties 102:10
p. of the poor 218:14
What is p.?...Theft 211:7
prophecies: p., they shall fail 39:7
prophecy: urn / Of bitter p. 242:13
prophesy: daughters shall p. 34:20
eat exceedingly, and p. 150:14
prophesying: voices p. war 82:5
Prophet: great P. of Tautology 103:17
p. ill sustains his holy 188:24
p. is not without honour 36:17
there is a p. in Israel 28:21
prophetess: p.? Yea, I say unto 106:13
young wench, a p. 135:15
prophets: armed p. were victorious 173:8
false p., which come 36:5
p. make sure of the event 278:20
Saul also among the p. 27:27
proportion: strangeness in the p. 15:11
proportions: Full of p. 135:7
proposes: Man p. 157:11
proposition: p. when there is no ground 218:19
proprie: *p. communia dicere* 139:7
propriety: not always evince its p. 13:8
prosaic: proof of a man being p. 76:23
prose: classics of our p. 10:15
love thee in p. 210:26
Meredith is a p. Browning 288:22
moderate weight of p. 162:5
nearest p. 103:23
not p. is verse 186:14
p. is verse 63:27
p. run mad 205:3
p. = words in their best order 83:1
shall make it P. again 204:15
speaking p. without knowing it 186:13
unattempted yet in P. or Rhyme 183:8
prospect: Though every p. pleases 132:9
prosper: if it p., none dare call 130:16
prosperitee: man to have ben in p. 74:22

prosperitie: trouble efter great p. 133:26
Prosperity: P....not without...fears 14:9
P. doth best discover Vice 14:10
P. doth bewitch men 281:22
Prostitution: P. Selling one's body 173:14
protection: p. also against the tyranny 180:10
protest: lady doth p. too much 227:9
Protestant: civilizaton...Printing...P. Religion 67:20
I am the *P.* whore 128:15
protestantism of the P. 54:25
protestantism: p....a sort of dissent 54:25
proud: all the p. shall be 204:21
be not p. of those two eyes 135:26
Death be not p. 99:24
death p. to take us 224:29
I must be p. to see 207:8
kaught is p. 74:19
Man, p. man 232:35
play in each p. land 130:1
p., and full of fancies 156:2
P. as peacocks 224:11
p. company 90:7
Red Rose, p. Rose 298:6
too p. to fight 290:5
very p. and very great 255:10
Why were they p. 154:13
prove: Believing where we cannot p. 263:6
p. anything by figures 67:19
to p. it, I'm here 60:23
proved: p. to be / Much as 130:6
p. upon our pulses 156:14
something or other could be p. 119:1
Which was to be p. 112:12
proverbs: Patch grief with p. 234:22
P. are art — cheap art 85:3
Providence: assert Eternal P. 183:9
dare trust in His p. 279:10
frowning p. / He hides 87:22
Irony is...character of P. 18:18
P. their guide 185:1
p. in the fall of a sparrow 227:26
provincial: dull p. discipline 167:3
provisoes: your odious p. 84:35
provoke: p. not your children 39:21
'twould a saint p. 205:20
prow: Youth on the p. 127:7
Prudence: P. is a rich, ugly 43:7
prudent: o'er stocked with p. men 103:19
p. motive 13:1
prudenter: *Quidquid agas, p. agas* 6:21
prunes: especially p. and prism 94:28
Prussia: military domination of P. 10:19
War...national industry of P. 186:8
pryin': p., en betwixt en betweenst 130:19
psalmist: sweet p. of Israel 28:10
psalms: sadder than its p. 167:3
psaltery: upon the p. 30:13
pseudonym: God's p. when he does not want to sign 117:2
psychiatrist: goes to see a p. 126:7
public: as if I was a p. meeting 274:17
assumes a p. trust 145:13
British P., ye who like me not 52:3
How p., like a frog 97:1
in convartin' p. trusts 169:19
mass of p. wrongs 160:13
Pelting each other for the p. good 87:8
p. be damned 273:14
p. faces in private 11:12
p. is always right 92:21
p. is never wrong 299:17
p. zeal to cancel private crimes 102:17
to the p. good 185:15
uncritical buying p. 142:20
publicity: price of justice is eternal p. 24:4
p. rather than of poetry 164:14
public offices: longing eye on [p.] 145:10
public-school: That's the p. system all over 280:21
publish: I'll p., right or wrong 63:21
P. and be damned 282:9
p. it not in the streets 28:2
published: not be p. for nine years 139:14
p., read an old one 215:1
publisher: Barabbas was a p. 66:15
pudding: p. and pie, / Kissed the girls 194:9
puddin'-race: chieftain o' the p. 57:22
puddle: stepped in a p. 194:8
puerisque: *Virginibus p.* 140:6
puff: p. of vapour from his mouth 50:22
puffed: charity...is not p. up 39:7
Puffs: P., powders, patches 207:14
Pugna: *P. magna victi sumus* 167:8
puking: Mewling and p. 225:13
pulchrior: *pulchra filia p.* 139:29
Pull: P. down thy vanity 208:8
pulse: feeling a woman's p. 253:19
p. like a soft drum 158:3
pulses: proved upon our p. 156:14
pumpkin: Peter, p. eater 195:8
rather sit on a p. 268:28
pumpkins: early p. blow 164:6
pun: could make so vile a p. 93:1
exhaled in a p. 161:23
Punctuality: P. is the politeness of kings 169:5
Punica: *P. fide* 220:2
punish: believers...wish to p. 16:12
punished: not p. for their sins, but 141:11
punishment: All p. is mischief 24:10
crime, and is its p. 277:4
p. fit the crime 122:29
suffer first p. 88:19
punishments: neither rewards nor p. 144:2
puppets: shut up the box and the p. 266:15
puppy: let ev'ry p. drink 285:16
pur: *sens plus p. aux mots* 174:13
pure: Because my heart is p. 265:6
Be warm but p. 63:28
Blessed are the p. in heart 35:17
cannot have a p. mind 161:4
clear, cold, p. and very dead 165:14
my life is p. 176:25
p. all things are pure 40:12
p. and complete joy 269:21
P. eyes and Christian hearts 157:8
real Simon P. 71:13
truth is rarely p. 287:2
within Himself make p. 263:4
purer: give a p. meaning 174:13
purgatory: England...p. of men 115:16

no other p. but a woman 21:17
purify: p. the dialect of the tribe 107:18
Puritan: P. all things are impure 163:19
P. hated bear-baiting 171:16
purling: p. stream 1:16
Purple: never saw a P. Cow 53:30
p. tyrant fled 42:11
purpose: Clean from the p. 229:24
risen with p. fell 170:16
working His p. out 2:23
purse: consumption of the p. 228:16
not grain that is got into the p. 254:13
Put money in thy p. 234:31
silken, or in leathern p. retains 201:19
steals my p. steals trash 234:36
purses: Light gains make heavy p. 15:17
pursued: Exit, p. by a bear 237:29
pursuing: Faint, yet p. 27:17
pursuit: p. of perfection...of sweetness and light 10:4
Pussy: beautiful P. you are 164:10
P. cat, pussy cat 195:10
P.'s in the well 194:7
put: shall never be p. out 163:11
putting: it's for p. things in 181:15
puzzles: Nothing p. me more 161:19
puzzling: p. questions, are not beyond 48:24
This is a p. world 106:21
pyramids: from the summit of these p. 190:10
Pyrenees: tease in the high P. 23:15
Quad: always about in the Q. 5:7
no one about in the Q. 160:11
quaesiveris: *Nec te q. extra* 201:10
quaffing: q., and unthinking time 103:24
Quakers: beaten up by Q. 3:20
qualis: *Non sum q. eram* 140:14
qualities: defects of their q. 19:4
q. as would wear well 125:26
quality: reluctance to test the q. 261:20
unknown amongst people of q. 273:9
quarrel: hath his q. just 229:9
lover's q. with the world 118:9
q. with my bread and butter 258:24
q. with others we make rhetoric 298:21
Take up our q. 172:1
quarrels: q. of lovers are the renewal 265:20
who in q. interpose 120:25
Quarterly: 'I,' says the Q. 63:29
quarters: awful q. of an hour 217:11
quean: flaunting, extravagant q. 245:11
Québec: *Vive le Q. libre* 92:9
queen: every lass a q. 158:11
ev'ry Lady would be Q. 204:28
life of our own dear Q. 5:21
Ocean Q., the free Britannia 61:13
q. of curds and cream 237:36
regular Royal Q. 122:8
to look at the q. 195:10
Yestreen the Q. had four Maries 18:6
Queens: Q. have died young and fair 191:2
queer: even thou art a little q. 197:20
ill-tempered and q. 164:5
q. old Dean 252:16
q. thing Life is 290:28
Queer Street: Q. is full of lodgers 95:29
querelles: *q. des tyrans* 276:20
questing: passes the q. vole 280:24
question: In that case, what is the q. 253:11
Irish q. 98:1
Others abide our q. 9:28
that is the q. 226:37
Who shall q. / That coming out 118:23
questions: doubtful q. 'tis the safest 103:22
no q. isn't told a lie 159:27
Q. are never indiscreet 286:26
q. the distempered part 107:16
q. that the wise cannot answer 288:2
quibble: q. is to Shakespeare 147:15
quick: judge the q. and the dead 209:14
Too q. despairer 10:1
quickly: Behold, I come q. 41:6
'twere well / It were done q. 231:28
quiet: All q. along the Potomac 22:13
All Q. on the Western 213:16
Anythin' for a q. life 96:13
be q.; and go a-Angling 279:10
Fie upon this q. life 227:38
lives of q. desperation 268:23
q. along the Potomac 171:25
Serve thee with a q. mind 210:1
quietest: q. places / Under the sun 141:1
Quietly: Q. shining to the quiet moon 82:1
quietness: unravish'd bride of q. 154:20
quietus: might his q. make 226:38
quince: mince, and slices of q. 164:12
Quinquireme: Q. of Nineveh 178:10
quires: howlings fill the sacred q. 207:27
Q. and Places where they sing 209:17
quivered: q. through the grass 96:26
quoque: *Tu q.* 197:19
quotation: their passions a q. 286:16
quotations: furnishes no q. is...no book 200:7
uneducated man to read books of q. 78:11
quote: grow immortal as they q. 299:7
kill you if you q. it 54:1
quoter: first q. of it 110:27
quotidienne: *vie est q.* 160:21
rabbit: r. in a snare 253:14
Rabble: R., House of Commons 80:6
Rabelais: R. dwelling in a dry place 82:23
race: idiot r. 57:13
new r. descends 275:28
our r. should not cease to labour 255:25
r. is not to the swift 32:13
r. where that immortal garland 186:5
should r. to it 190:18
steady wins the r. 167:13
uncreated conscience of my r. 151:13
whose r. is just begun 244:15
races: composed of two distinct r. 161:9
Underlying all these noble r. 193:1
rack: Leave not a r. behind 236:24
r. of a too easy chair 204:14
radiant: By her own r. light 181:25
radical: never dared be r. 118:14
R. chic 291:7
r. is a man with both feet 215:19
talks like a R. 287:17
radicals: young...regarded as r. 289:23
radio: had the r. on 187:8

radio-phonograph: gospel of the r. 11:8
Radix: *R. malorum est cupiditas* 74:3
raft: comfortable on a r. 271:27
Rag: Shakespeherian R. — / It's so 108:16
rag-and-bone: r. shop of the heart 296:4
Rage: all Heaven in a R. 42:3
Blessed r. for order 254:27
captive void of noble r. 263:12
die here in a r. 259:21
hard-favour'd r. 228:30
heathen r. 29:13
I r., I melt, I burn, 120:14
r. against the dying 266:22
r. / Should dance attention 298:1
r. / To set things right 49:25
What r. for fame 201:26
ragged: heard a r. noise 135:11
pair of r. claws 107:32
rags: r. of time 100:17
raid: r. on the inarticulate 107:17
rail: Some folks r. against other 114:3
rain: droppeth as the gentle r. 233:19
Hard R.'s A-Gonna Fall 105:7
little morning r. / Foretells 47:11
r. is over and gone 32:21
r. it raineth on the just 45:13
r. on the just 35:21
Still falls the R. 246:15
rainbow: r. and a cuckoo's song 91:11
r. in the morning 4:15
r. of His will 170:2
r.'s lovely form / Evanishing 57:17
when I behold / A r. 292:18
rains: as it r. on the city 274:13
raison: *r. du plus fort* 115:21
r. ne connaît point 199:10
raisonnable: *plus r. en France* 277:3
raisons: *coeur a ses r.* 199:10
rake: r. among scholars 171:24
Woman is at heart a R. 204:28
Raleigh: [R.] being strangely surprised 11:2
Rampage: On the R. 94:18
rams: fat of r. 27:31
Randal: Lord R., my son 17:23
rank: marched, r. on rank 179:19
r. is but the guinea's stamp 56:21
some other badge of r. 180:18
ranks: even the r. of Tuscany 171:9
rap: To r. and knock and enter 50:1
rapidly: Works done least r. 51:15
Rapine: R. share the land 185:26
rapscallions: kings is mostly r. 271:28
rapture: first fine careless r. 50:34
r. on the lonely shore 62:1
Rara: *R. avis in terris* 152:12
rare: r. as a day in June 169:23
r. bird upon the earth 152:12
Rarely: R., rarely, comest thou 244:1
rarer: The r. action is 236:25
rascal: Get down, you dirty r. 194:17
rashes: Green grow the r. 56:14
rat: giant r. of Sumatra 101:23
How now! a r. 227:13
I smell a r. 214:17
poisoned r. in a hole 259:21
rather: r. be in Philadelphia 114:12
rationalist: r., but he had to confess 75:2
rats: let's sing of *r.* 126:17
R. / They fought the dogs 51:24
Rattlesnake: He thought he saw a R. 70:14
rave: let her r. 154:30
Raven: Quoth the R., 'Nevermore' 203:18
ravens: three r. sat on a tree 18:15
ravish: chaste, except you r. me 99:28
r. me / I'm so willing 115:14
ravished: at least would have r. 113:21
'tis thou has r. me 175:2
Rawness: R. of judgement 116:13
ray: gem of purest r. serene 127:16
razor: r. ceases to act 141:4
Satire...like a polished r. 187:10
Razors: R. pain you 198:21
reach: man's r. should exceed his grasp 49:23
r. for my revolver 124:9
read: but his books were r. 23:14
early years I r. very hard 147:24
have r., but what we have done 157:9
I can r. anything 161:14
If I could always r. 64:18
In science, r., by preference 53:9
King George will be able to r. 129:11
nobody wants to r. 271:23
r. all the books 174:12
r. an old one 215:1
r. a novel I write one 98:12
r. him for the sentiment 148:26
r. just as inclination 148:13
r. music but can't hear 22:2
r. nothing but the race 108:10
r. without pleasure 150:6
Some r. to think 83:21
Take up and r. 11:22
they r. something else 176:26
vast population able to r. 270:10
who runs may r. 157:8
readable: that it be r. 270:14
Reader: R., I married him 47:6
r. suffering from an ideal 151:9
readers: r. better to enjoy life 147:22
r. to become more indolent 125:1
readeth: he may run that r. 34:26
readiness: r. is all 227:26
reading: I prefer r. 247:17
life, the soul of r. 254:10
looking at mankind instead of r. 64:24
not walking, I am r. 161:13
Peace is poor r. 130:4
R. is sometimes an ingenious 132:19
R. is to the mind 253:7
r....I would not exchange 121:24
R. maketh a full man 15:16
r. of all good books 93:10
tough faculty of r. 68:25
worth r., it is worth buying 218:7
reads: Who now r. Cowley 207:1
ready: always r. to leave 116:1
be r. to go 187:12
r. to receive Thy saints 240:31
r. writer 29:31
real: bless you r. good 126:13
Life is r. 168:14
R. are the dreams of Gods 154:15
r. as if they were imaginary 25:7
r. tinsel underneath 165:8
so many r. ones to encounter 125:17
weary of the study of r. life 47:8
Realism: dislike of R. 287:21
Realist: except he was a R. 20:17

reality: Cannot bear very much r. 107:12
realm: safety, honour and welfare of this r. 72:15
turned out of the R. 108:24
realms: r. of gold 155:21
reap: r. the whirlwind 34:18
shall r. in joy 31:7
soweth, that shall he also r. 39:16
rear: Destruction in the r. 61:16
post lay in the r. 216:23
rearranging: merely r. their prejudices 145:6
reason: any other r. why 3:4
Englishman...always wants to r. 277:3
finite r. reach Infinity 103:21
for the wrong r. 108:5
human r. weak 16:3
Is r. to the soul 103:20
I will not R. 42:13
kills r. itself 186:2
Language is...human r. 165:11
love, all r. is against it 60:8
not his r., but his passions 254:7
public demands elocution rather than r. 199:3
reaching after fact and r. 156:4
R., an *ignus fatuus* 214:20
R. is the life of the law 80:21
r. of this thusness 279:16
r. to an *O altitudo* 49:2
r. to strengthen...prejudices 104:11
ruling Passion conquers R. 205:14
shew no r. can / Wherefore 280:8
Tam tint his r. 57:19
Their's not to r. why 262:14
Will know the r. why 131:5
worse appear / The better r. 183:30
Reasonable: figure of 'The R. Man' 134:15
more r. in France 277:3
r. / Is an invention of man 118:24
r. man adapts himself 240:4
What is r. is true 132:11
reasonably: may r. be expected to 283:16
reasoning: away with your r. 41:27
fitly shall conceive thy r. 241:25
r. and belief, no less 67:21
r. engine lies 214:21
r., self-sufficing thing 293:3
truth by consecutive r. 156:7
reasons: bad r. for what we believe 45:16
heart has its r. 199:10
r. are as two grains of wheat 233:1
rebel: to be Angels, Men r. 206:13
your r. sex 67:4
rebellion: little r. now and then 145:8
R. lay in his way 228:7
rebellious: r. They are quite right 288:4
rebelliously: casts off / r. / an eagle 289:13
rebels: obliged to be r. 288:6
subjects are r. from principle 54:10
recalled: cannot be r. 139:20
recapture: never could r. 50:34
receive: ask Him to r. me 191:6
give than to r. 38:28
receiver: r. is always thought as bad 75:4
r. of stolen goods 149:22
recession: r. when your neighbour loses 271:4
reckoning: much at your own r. 270:20
recognition: Freedom...r. of necessity 111:27
reconciled: God and sinners r. 282:28
reconciles: feasting r. everybody 201:5
record: r. on the gramophone 108:17
recording: r., not thinking 144:7
records: all trivial fond r. 226:18
recover: seldom or never r. 224:32
recreation: innocent r. than angling 279:6
recte: *Si possis r.* 139:15
rectitude: unctuous r. of my countrymen 214:3
red: like a r. red rose 57:10
never blows so r. 114:17
r. in tooth and claw 263:17
thin r. line 219:1
wine when it is r. 31:33
redbreast: Call for the robin r. 281:19
redeem: r. us from virtue 260:8
redeemer: my r. liveth 29:6
Red-Hot: Last of the R. Mamas 271:6
redit: *Iam r. et virgo* 275:28
redress: r. the balance of the Old 67:1
Ring in r. to all 263:22
reed: broken r. at best 299:1
Man is only a r. 199:11
reef: r. upon which...frail mystic ships 86:9
reekit: carlin swat and r. 57:18
refin'd: by a love, so much r. 100:23
refined: disgust this r. age 112:18
r. out of existence 151:12
reflect: my country when I r. 145:7
r. all objects without being sullied 84:8
reflection: I prefer...r. to activity 19:1
reformers: All r. are bachelors 188:8
refresh: Perhaps *this* will r. your memory 269:7
refreshment: r. at any hands 122:25
refuge: God is our r. 30:1
God is thy r. 27:10
last r. of a scoundrel 149:2
r. of weak minds 75:21
refusal: great r. 90:4
refuse: offer he can't r. 46:2
r. the rules of life 187:21
Refused: R. about the age of three 76:11
refuses: r. nothing, shuts none out 285:4
refute: I r. it *thus* 148:17
reg'latin': r. 'em as if they was figures 94:22
regardless: r. of their doom 127:22
Regiment: Monstrous R. of Women 160:9
register: r. of the crimes, follies 121:18
regret: I r. a little 49:24
Old Age a r. 97:18
vain r. / Go hand in hand 217:5
regular: faultless, icily r. 264:13
r. Royal Queen 122:8
Reich: *Ein R.* 5:10
reign: Better to r. in Hell 183:16
bloated Chief's unwholesome r. 61:6
Jesus shall r. where'er 280:17
Omnipotent but friendless is to r. 243:19
reigned: r. with your loves 109:2
reigneth: Lord r. 28:24
reigns: r. like Dunce the first 203:26

re-invent: r. the world 20:17
rejected: despised and r. of men 33:24
rejects: Oft she r. 207:15
rejoice: Amazed to find it could r. 91:5
R. with them that do rejoice 38:39
relation: just supply and all r. 99:16
relations: r. between the two sexes 181:1
relaxes: Bless r. 43:13
relic: Sad r. of departed worth 61:10
relief: this r. much thanks 225:34
religio: *Tantum r.* 170:7
Religion: brothels with bricks of R. 43:6
depth in Philosophy...to R. 14:21
enough r. to make us hate 259:10
every thing that regards r. 2:7
grey with age becomes r. 221:2
groans beneath r.'s iron age 243:29
man's r. is the chief fact 68:1
Millionaire. That is my r. 239:16
more fierce in its r. 191:24
my r. from the priest 125:30
my r. is to do good 198:10
new r. with one commandment 299:12
One r. is as true 59:10
Oysters...more beautiful than...r. 219:13
philosophy...an handmaid to r. 13:25
Pound notes is the best r. 22:15
r., as a mere sentiment 191:25
r., but give me a little snug 105:14
r. but a childish toy 175:22
r. for religion's sake 86:6
R. *is* knight-errantry 71:17
R....is the opium 178:3
R....lead to...evil 170:7
R. [not] proper subject of conversation 75:25
R.'s in the heart, not 145:24
r. teaches us content 103:6
reproach to r. and government 200:16
rum and true r. 62:26
Self-righteousness is not r. 47:5
talks loudly against r. 254:7
There is only one r., though 240:21
when r. is allowed to invade 179:2
religious: but not r. good 130:13
dim r. light 182:10
troubled with r. doubt 76:11
whole r. complexion 109:14
remain: let one r. above 208:22
remains: waste r. and kills 111:25
while aught r. to do 214:25
remarks: said our r. before us 98:20
remedies: extreme r. are most fitting 136:10
not apply new R. 15:2
require desperate r. 113:10
remedy: Force is not a r. 46:21
one unfailing r. — the Tankard 65:17
sovereign r. to all diseases 59:5
remember: cannot r. the past 220:7
he'll r. with advantages 229:2
if thou wilt, r. 216:29
I r., I remember 138:6
like to something I r. 116:16
Please to r. / The Fifth 6:18
R. me when I am gone 216:25
R. now thy Creator 32:15
R. the sabbath day 26:31
should r. and be sad 216:26
things will be pleasant to r. 275:8
To r. with tears 4:2
We will r. them 41:18
Yes, I r. Adlestrop 267:13
remember'd: r. for a very long time 173:6
remembered: God r. Noah 25:26
Remembering: R. him like anything 76:17
r. my good friends 235:16
remembrance: appear almost a r. 156:21
drive away / R. 156:1
r. of things past 238:7
r. of his dying Lord 251:23
rosemary, that's for r. 227:20
remembren: ben in prosperitee, / And it r. 74:22
remembreth: it r. me / Upon my yowthe 73:30
remind: great men all r. 168:15
reminded: to be r. than informed 147:8
Reminiscences: R. make one feel 239:11
Re-mould: R. it nearer to the Heart's Desire 115:2
remove: r. / Those things which elemented 100:22
removed: r. from all that glads 82:10
render: r. it into nouns and verbs 111:15
R. therefore unto Caesar 36:31
rendezvous: r. with Death 223:9
rendu: *lui avons bien r.* 277:6
renew: shall r. their strength 33:20
renewal: quarrels of lovers are the r. 265:20
renounce: r. the devil and all his works 70:18
r. when that shall be necessary 256:1
rent: r. the envious Casca 230:5
That has not been r. 296:8
repaid: image, we have r. him 277:6
repair: friendship in constant r. 148:4
repay: I will r., saith the Lord 38:40
repeal: r. of bad or obnoxious laws 126:18
repeat: condemned to r. it 220:7
repent: r. at leisure 84:28
r. it from my very soul 236:33
truly and earnestly r. you 210:8
weak alone r. 62:9
repentance: death-bed r. 12:1
decline to buy r. 92:22
morning cool r. came 222:23
sinners to r. 36:10
repented: never r. but of three things 70:25
repenteth: one sinner that r. 37:27
report: r. of my death 272:13
Who hath believed our r. 33:23
reporters: gallery in which the r. 171:12
reports: nothing but the race r. 108:10
repossess: r. their native seat 183:23
reprehend: If I r. anything in 245:3
representation: Taxation without r. 197:8
representations: just r. of general nature 147:14
reproach: towards heaven with fierce r. 243:23
reproche: *sans peur et sans r.* 5:3
reproduce: r. what we see 160:6
republican: acrimonious and surly r. 147:3
king's head on r. principles 240:18

R. form of Government is the highest 251:1
reputation: act is all, the r. nothing 124:15
bubble r. 225:14
delicate as the r. of a woman 55:12
esteem your own r. 279:26
r. like its shadow 166:16
r. in it, but no money 272:12
reputations: home of ruined r. 106:19
Requiem: *R. aeternam* 178:17
Requiescant: *R. in pace* 178:20
require: men in women do r. 43:3
required: can nothing be r. 113:26
rerum: *lacrimae r.* 275:9
res: *In medias r.* 139:8
resemblance: straight its own r. find 177:13
resemble: I r. her to thee 278:6
resent: No individual could r. 259:17
resented: never r. for an offence 259:2
residences: Inns are not r. 188:15
resignation: by r. none 145:11
resigned: He, too, has r. his part 296:13
resist: r. everything except temptation 287:16
R. the devil 40:22
resistance: liberty is a history of r. 290:2
r. against her is vain 177:7
resisting: not over-fond of r. temptation 21:23
resolution: native hue of r. 226:40
road to r. lies by doubt 212:2
resolve: heart to r. 121:21
ripple of a spring change my r. 62:10
resort: should not r. to the gods 203:20
resources: r. of civilization 123:28
respect: any nation except their r. 78:1
Man hath any R. for her 253:3
owe r. to the living 277:1
respectable: apply to what is r. 138:21
ashamed of, the more r. 239:18
most devilish when r. 49:14
nice, r., middle-class 213:9
R. means rich 200:6
suspicion in the minds of r. 143:9
was genius found r. 49:13
respecter: God is no r. of persons 38:24
respice: *r. finem* 6:21
responsibility: no sense of moral r. 287:1
Power without r. 160:4
r. is to his art 113:8
r....most men dread it 240:15
rest: all the r. is mere literature 274:10
evening's r. from labour 43:18
Grant them eternal r. 178:17
I will give you r. 36:14
Keep it now, and take the r. 63:30
lie abed and r. 140:21
man was not born for r. 276:13
May they r. in peace 178:20
motion, but ordain'd no r. 273:20
R. in peace — until 6:22
r. is silence 227:30
she's at r., and so am I 103:10
reste: *tout le r. est littérature* 274:10
rested: r. the seventh day 26:33
resting-place: r. is found 49:22
restraint: firm r. with which they write 66:1
result: r. happiness 94:2
Resurrection: R. to eternal life 210:21
resuscitate: r. the dead art 208:15
retain: marble to r. 61:1
retire: sign for him to r. 97:20
retired: r. Leisure 182:7
retreating: seen yourself r. 191:1
retrograde: r. if it does not advance 121:23
return: Books...r. no more 259:1
he shall not r. to me 28:8
I shall r. 171:1
unto dust thou shalt r. 25:22
returns: Greedy for quick r. 50:30
Not one r. to tell 114:22
reveal: half r. / And half conceal 263:8
revealed: glory that shall be r. 209:26
revelry: sound of r. by night 61:29
revels: r. now are ended 236:24
Revenge: little R. herself went down 265:4
R. is...wild Justice 14:8
R. proves its own executioner 116:14
study of r., immortal hate 183:14
wrong us, shall we not r. 233:14
revenged: r. on the whole pack 237:26
revenges: brings in his r. 237:25
Revenons: *R. à nos moutons* 6:23
reverence: cycle-clips in awkward r. 163:8
Reviewers: R. are usually people who 82:19
reviewing: before r. it; it prejudices 248:32
never read a book before r. 248:32
revivals: art is the history of r. 60:19
revolts: r. me, but I do it 122:24
revolution: *c'est une r.* 163:6
r. in order to establish a democracy 76:27
R. might, like Saturn 274:8
r. without general copulation 281:26
Sire, it is a r. 163:6
revolutionary: Clemency is also a r. measure 93:12
revolutionist: plagiarist or a r. 120:11
revolutions: herald of all r. 110:5
R. are not about trifles 8:29
Women hate r. 179:14
reward: Desert and r., I can assure 214:11
nothing for r. 252:2
not to ask for any r. 170:3
rewarded: of thee be plenteously r. 210:2
rewards: neither r. nor punishments 144:2
their own r. 113:5
Reynolds: gipsy by R. 171:21
[R.] his own geese are swans 278:21
Such Artists as R. 44:2
rhetoric: For r. he could not ope 59:16
quarrel with others we make r. 298:21
rhetorician: A sophistical r., inebriated 98:8
For all a r.'s rules 59:17
Rhodope: no voices, O R. 162:4
rhyme: I r. for fun 56:12
Maggots half-form'd in r. 203:27
R. being no necessary Adjunct 183:6
R.'s sturdy cripple 82:9
r. the rudder is 59:21
taen the fit o' r. 56:11

rhyming: veins of r. mother-wits 176:2
rib: r., which the Lord 25:17
riband: r. to stick in his coat. n 51:7
rich: anomaly to r. people 16:10
forbids the r. as well as the poor 117:3
kind that r. men hate 201:16
marry a r. woman as a poor 266:5
never be too r. 290:16
pale and languid r. ones 268:19
Respectable means r. 200:6
r. have become richer 244:20
r. have butlers and no friends 208:13
r. have no right 218:14
r. in things or 143:24
R. is better 271:8
[r.] make...same distribution 247:6
r. man's joys increase 125:11
r. man to enter 37:9
r. wot gets the pleasure 6:3
r., yet is thy mind perplexed 92:12
Sincerely Want to be R. 85:23
too r. to have need to seek 261:21
wretchedness of being r. 247:20
Richardson: one letter of R.'s 148:25
read R. for the story 148:26
R....pictures of high life 278:13
richer: for r. for poorer 210:14
R. than all his tribe 235:7
riches: embarrassment of r. 3:17
folk live that hae r. 58:5
getteth r., and not by right 34:7
Infinite r. in a little 175:23
poor man surrounded by r. 140:11
R. are a good handmaid 13:18
R. are needless then 185:4
r. consists in the parade of 247:8
r. left, not got 258:1
R., there is no real use 15:8
r., which dispersed lie 135:8
thirst of r., increases 254:2
Richesse: *Embarras de R.* 3:17
Richmond: Sweet lass of R. Hill 272:27
richt: curst conceit o' bein' r. 172:8
rickshaw: no go the r. 174:3
ridden: r. more in omnibuses 132:21
riddle: glory, jest, and r. of the world 206:19
r. wrapped in a mystery 77:22
ride: r. on in majesty 181:8
we r. them down 264:25
rideau: *Tirez le r.* 212:14
rider: between a r. and his horse 258:7
horse is to the r. 11:27
rideret: *r. Democritus* 139:22
rides: Who r. so late 124:10
ridiculous: make my enemies r. 277:10
makes men r. 152:10
no spectacle so r. 171:20
position r. 76:3
sublime and the r. 198:4
sublime to the r. 190:17
rien: *n'avoir r. à faire* 44:12
n'ont r. appris 261:14
riff-raff: epithet which the r. 138:21
rifiuto: *gran r.* 90:4
rift: Load every r. 157:4
r. within the lute 262:24
right: about as much r. 69:18
All's r. with the world 51:27
and in his r. mind 37:5
conscious of the r. 275:10
customer is always r. 223:19
delay, r. or justice 174:9
exclusively in the r. 142:26
God and my r. 214:8
hath the r. sow 133:15
know it about the r. person 190:6
Life...was in the r. 86:23
makes us r. or wrang 56:8
more attraction than abstract r. 131:8
noisy man is always in the r. 87:10
no r. to the property 218:14
now and then be r., by chance 87:9
one — of — them — is — r. 159:9
our country, r. or wrong 91:18
public is always r. 92:21
rage / To set things r. 49:25
rather be r. than be President 79:10
r. deed for the wrong reason 108:5
r. in his own eyes 27:22
r. is more precious than peace 290:12
r. is what is after my own 110:17
r. of doing whatever the laws permit 187:23
r. that these wants 54:9
r. to force another 180:19
Roundheads (R. but Repulsive) 223:23
than r. with such men 79:1
To do a great r. 233:21
to see the r. 166:13
Ulster will be r. 77:17
Whatever IS, is R. 206:17
what is r. and not to do 84:16
what thy r. hand doeth 35:23
you know he's r. 5:25
your r. to say it 277:12
righteous: armour of a r. cause 52:20
Be not r. over much 32:10
call the r. 36:10
r. are as bold 31:39
r. man regardeth the life 31:23
r. shall flourish 30:14
righteousness: I choose r. 216:2
path of r. 18:13
paths of r. 29:20
r. and peace have kissed 30:9
Sun of r. arise 34:28
thirst after r. 35:17
rights: certain unalienable r. 7:17
duties as well as its r. 102:10
essence of the Massachusetts Bill of R. 111:8
folly of 'Women's R.' 274:16
perpetuity the r. of the people 85:16
r. of an Englishman 152:1
Sovereign has...three r. 16:5
riled: no sense / In gittin' r. 130:27
rill: cool Siloam's shady r. 132:7
rind: sweet as the r. was 260:5
young 'neath wrinkled r. 162:9
ring: great r. of pure and endless 274:2
One R. to rule them 269:18
one shilling / Your r. 164:11
R. out the false 263:21
R. out, wild bells 263:20
They now r. the bells 278:24
With this R. I thee wed 210:16
ringing: confess that he liked the r. 75:2
Rings: R. on her fingers 195:11
Riot: sound / Of R. 181:24
Riots: R. are the language 158:6
ripe: Cherry r.' themselves do cry 66:18
to hour we r. and ripe 225:12
Ripeness: R. is all 231:5
ripest: reach the r. fruit 176:7

ripp'd: Untimely r. 232:31
rire: *Je me presse de r. de tout* 21:6
rise: dead men r. up never 260:12
risen: r. to hear him crow 106:15
rises: son-in-law also r. 160:8
rising: r. to Great Place 14:17
risu: *Nam r. inepto* 71:6
Ritz: all, like the R. Hotel 5:26
rival: not r. him / Save with my mind 142:18
river: either side the r. lie 263:26
even the weariest r. 260:12
Fame is like a r. 15:19
twice into the same r. 134:6
riverrun: r., past Eve and Adam's 151:8
road: hard-beaten r. to his house 110:25
high r. that leads him to England 148:6
no royal r. to geometry 112:11
ocean as their r. 278:8
only monument the asphalt r. 108:9
out on the r. 178:13
r. below me 255:15
r. is hard to climb 211:5
r. of our life 90:1
r., this simple Entepfuhl road 68:20
R., / Which to discover we 114:22
r. wind up-hill all the way 216:30
rolling English r. 76:13
that braid, braid r. 18:13
roads: How many r. must a man 105:6
roam: let the fancy r. 153:35
sent to r. / Excels 87:26
roamed: sweet I r. from field 43:20
roar: Let him r. again 234:1
r. you as gently 234:2
roast: r. beef of England 113:20
rob: r. a lady of her fortune 114:9
robb'd: 'Ye have r.,' said he 191:22
robbed: r. a man of everything 249:23
robber: sing openly at the r. 152:16
robbing: Forbids the r. of a foe 77:13
live by r. the poor 239:25
think little of r. 93:6
Robespierre: [R.] The sea-green Incorruptible 68:8
robin: And r. redbreast 246:19
I killed Cock R. 196:4
poor r. do then? / Poor thing 195:18
R. Redbreast in a Cage 42:3
R. sits in the bush 222:20
Robs: R. not one light seed 154:2
r. you on business principles 240:18
Rochester: R.'s poems have much more obscenity 278:9
Rock: it is the Inchcape R. 250:17
Lord is my r. 29:19
R. of Ages 269:25
r. of our salvation 30:15
upon this r. 36:21
rocket: rose like a r. 198:7
rocking: cradle endlessly r. 284:14
upon a r. horse 155:12
rocks: My love...resembles the eternal r. 47:18
R., Caves, Lakes 184:8
She is older than the r. 199:14
white, when r. are near 281:22
With r., and stones, and 293:21
rod: Oppression stretches his r. 43:19
spareth his r. hateth his son 31:25
there shall come forth a r. 33:5
Throw away thy r. 135:3
rode: r. madly off 163:25
rogue: r. and peasant slave 226:34
rogues: world cannot move without r. 109:21
roi: *Plus royaliste que le r.* 6:19
Roland: Child R. to the dark tower 230:35
role: not yet found a r. 1:2
roll: Let us r. all our strength 177:23
R. up that map 202:10
rolling: r. English drunkard 76:13
rolls: And r. through all things 292:16
Roman: Give way, R. writers 211:4
high R. fashion 224:29
I am a R. citizen 78:26
Like the R. I seem to see 209:4
noblest R. of them all 230:11
R. and his trouble 140:31
R. people had only one neck 65:15
R.'s life 171:8
romance: comic r. is a comic epic-poem 113:24
love oneself...lifelong r. 286:28
Twenty years of r. make 288:14
Romances: and love R. 245:14
r. as they would be spiritualized 278:13
Romans: Friends, R., countrymen 230:1
Romantic: R. Ireland's dead 297:22
romanticism: r. is sickness 124:22
Rome: comes round by R. 52:6
Everything in R. is at a price 152:11
falls the Coliseum, R. shall fall 62:6
grandeur that was R. 203:19
in R., live in the Roman 4:3
loved R. more 229:33
R. has spoken 11:29
R. in Tiber melt 224:20
R., on the 15th October 121:13
saw Learning fall, and R. 206:7
than second at R. 65:9
time will doubt of R. 63:3
Romeo: wherefore art thou R. 235:36
romps: *plie et ne r. pas* 115:19
Ronsard: R. sang of me 215:11
room: always r. at the top 281:9
coming to that Holy r. 99:29
find my way across the r. 131:17
no r. for them in the inn 37:11
riches in a little r. 175:23
r. in this country for but 215:24
R. of One's Own 291:16
r. to swing a cat 94:8
stay quietly in a r. 199:6
roost: always come home to r. 250:11
rooster: Hongry r. don't cackle 130:24
root: love of money is the r. 40:7
r. of all sins 144:12
roote: tikleth me about my herte r. 73:30
rope: Thy r. of sands 135:2
rose: blossom as the r. 33:13
English unofficial r. 48:4
Go, lovely R. 278:6
June is past, the fading r. 67:6
last r. of summer 188:22
like a full-blown r. 153:28
luck to get / One perfect r. 198:20
Luve's like a red red r. 57:10
Morning R.: / Which to no Box 88:28
most secret, and inviolate R. 297:20
never blows so red / The R. 114:17
R. is a rose is 253:10

r. / By any other name 235:37
sad R. of all my days 298:6
saw a wild r. growing 124:16
under the r. 41:11
roseau: *n'est qu'un r.* 199:11
rose-buds: Gather ye r. 135:27
rosemary: r., that's for remembrance 227:20
Rosencrantz: R. and Guildenstern are dead. n 227:31
rose-red: r. city 'half as old 54:4
roses: Marriage...not a bed of r. 256:16
Ring-a-ring o' r. 195:12
R. have thorns 238:9
r., roses, all the way 51:21
scent of the r. will hang 188:18
Strew on her r. 9:19
Röslein: *R. auf der Heiden* 124:16
Rosy-fingered: R. dawn 137:25
rot: cold obstruction and to r. 232:38
Here continueth to r. 8:7
to hour we r. and rot 225:12
rote: This is r. Sarcasticul 279:13
rotten: goodly apple r. at the heart 233:8
r. in the state of Denmark 226:15
rottenness: r. begins in his conduct 145:10
rotting: rosing reid to r. sall retour 134:1
rough: children who were r. 251:9
r. magic / I here abjure 236:26
r. places plain 33:16
r. than of polished diamond 75:19
Rough-hew: R. them how we will 227:25
round: trivial r. 157:6
roundabouts: r. we pulls up on the swings 71:22
Roundheads: R. (Right but Repulsive) 223:23
Rousseau: mock on, Voltaire, R. 42:29
rout: pleasures of having a r. 138:9
routine: r. acquisition of wealth 167:4
row: long r. to hoe 169:16
r. one way and look another 58:23
royal: no r. road to geometry 112:11
royalist: More r. than the King 6:19
Royalty: R. will be strong 16:3
ruat: *r. caelum* 113:11
rub: may r. off on you 218:2
r. up against money 218:2
there's the r. 226:37
rubber: heart is like Indian r. 47:2
rubbish: reasoning and your r. 41:27
rubies: price is far above r. 32:2
rudder: imagination the r. 156:5
rhyme the r. is of verses 59:21
ruddier: r. than the cherry 120:15
rude: manner r. and wild 23:1
R. am I in my speech 234:27
r. to him was courtesy 90:9
Society is all but r. 177:11
ruffian: menaces of a r. 148:29
r. on the stair 133:8
ruffle: Frenchman invented the r. 110:1
rug: As a bug in a r. 117:27
rugby: Nobody ever beats Wales at r. 190:3
rugged: harsh cadence of a r. line 103:29
R. individualism 138:17
unpolished r. verse 103:23
Ruhm: *nicht der R.* 124:15
ruin: r. of our sex 249:8
r. of the State 42:4
R. seize thee 127:6
to r. or to rule the state 102:16
woman look like a r. 288:14
ruinae: *Etiam periere r.* 170:6
ruination: eddication to his r. 52:26
ruined: ever r. by trade 117:26
plenty of r. buildings 172:23
r. by buying good pennyworths 117:16
ruins: I'm one of the r. 167:10
musing amidst the r. 121:13
r. would strike him unafraid 140:9
shored against my r. 108:19
very r. have been destroyed 170:6
rule: Divide and r., a sound motto 124:18
not a regular r. 69:26
One Ring to r. them all 269:18
ruin or to r. the state 102:16
R., Britannia, rule the waves 268:4
Woman to bear r. 160:10
ruled: little wisdom the world is r. 198:3
Ruler: R. of the Queen's Navee 122:15
soul...r. of the life 220:1
rulers: r. of the darkness 39:23
r. of the State are the only 202:24
rules: hand that r. the world 278:1
Love r. the court 221:22
rhetorician's r. / Teach nothing 59:17
R. and models destroy 131:19
[r.] established without their consent 187:21
there are no golden r. 240:8
ruling: r. Passion, be it what it will 205:14
Rum: It's a R. Go! 274:3
r. and true religion 62:26
what a R. Go everything 282:20
Yo-ho-ho, and a bottle of r. 256:9
Rumble: R. thy bellyful 230:26
rumour: nor in broad r. lies 182:26
rumours: wars and r. of wars 36:32
rumple: r. the one, — you rumple the other 254:11
run: best to let him r. 166:14
he may r. that readeth 34:26
I r., I am gathered 180:4
long r....we are all dead 157:24
r., and not be weary 33:20
r. at least twice as fast 69:30
r., though not to soar 171:11
Sweet Thames, r. softly 252:11
runcible: ate with a r. spoon 164:12
Runic: some fallen R. stone 9:12
running: If I were r. 97:12
runs: book, who r. may read 157:8
man that r. away 141:2
r. will never lack followers 104:10
r. with all his mane 212:7
Woman who r. 104:10
run-stealers: r. flicker to and fro 267:19
rural: lovely woman in a r. spot 142:13
Rus: *R. in urbe* 176:29
rushed: r. through life trying to save 215:3
rushes: Green grow the r. O 5:24
rushy: Down the r. glen 4:1
russet: morn, in r. mantle clad 226:1

S., the strongest 43:16
sana: *mens s. in corpore sano* 152:18
sancta: *s. simplicitas* 142:14
sanction: special s. to the trade of blood 243:25
sanctuary: s. in which exploded systems 247:11
sand: name upon the s. 251:14
s. against the wind 42:29
World in a Grain of S. 41:28
Sandalwood: S., cedarwood and sweet 178:10
sands: s. of time 168:15
Thy rope of s. 135:2
sandwich-men: s. of the *Daily Mail* 76:19
sane: no s. individual has ever 142:25
saner: s. politics, / Whereof we dream 130:1
sang: brother of a company / That s. 298:4
morning stars s. together 29:10
sanglots: *s. longs / Des violons* 274:11
sans: sans taste, s. everything 225:16
sap: world's whole s. is sunk 100:6
sapientibus: *s. cupido gloriae* 261:10
Sappho: Greece! / Where burning S. loved 62:31
Sarcasticul: This is rote S. 279:13
Sargent: sort of musical Malcolm S. 22:3
sark: linket at it in her s. 57:18
sat: we s. down, yea 31:9
You have s. too long here 89:6
Satan: Even S. glowr'd 57:19
Get thee behind me, S. 36:22
S. exalted sat 183:27
S. finds some mischief 280:14
S., Nick, or Clootie 55:14
S. trembles when he sees 87:20
Satanic: dark S. mills 42:26
Satans: Hired by the S. 44:2
satin: goes into white s. 244:29
satire: difficult not to write s. 152:7
s. be my song 63:21
S., by being levelled at all 259:2
s.... is aggression 165:16
S. is a kind of glass 258:8
S. or sense, alas 205:7
S. should, like a polished razor 187:10
satiric: show'd, by one s. touch 259:18
satirist: be the second English s. 129:8
satisfactory: praised but-not-altogether-s. lady 208:7
satisfied: having it, is s. 266:15
saturam: *s. non scribere* 152:7
Saturn: kingdom of S. returns 275:28
Revolution might, like S., devour 274:8
Sat gray-hair'd S. 154:1
satyr: either a stoic or a s. 201:29
satyrs: like s. grazing on the lawns 175:17
sauce: best s....is hunger 71:15
Make hunger thy s. 271:16
Saul: S. also among the prophets 27:27
S. and Jonathan were lovely 28:3
S. hath slain his thousands 27:35
saule: Christe receive thy s. 18:2
sausage: s. and thinks of Picasso 134:9
science and a s. 6:17
Savage: been in S.'s condition 146:19
exercise, and of s. origin 55:8
laws unto a s. race 265:7
s. faith works woe 91:8
s. servility 169:24
s. too / From...his sleep 153:32
soothe a s. breast 84:25
save: Christ cannot s. thy soul 175:6
himself he cannot s. 36:40
s. his people from their sins 35:7
s. my soul, if I have 213:17
time...trying to s. 215:3
To s. your world 11:3
Whenever you s. five shillings 157:23
saved: and we are not s. 34:3
do to be s. 38:26
England has s. herself 202:9
He s. others 36:40
only s. by being dammed 138:13
only s. the world 76:9
s. the sum of things 140:22
saving: s. lie 143:23
Saviour: S. of 'is country 159:31
Wash me, S., or I die 270:1
savoit: *Si jeunesse s.* 112:8
savour: salt have lost his s. 35:18
saw: I came, I s., I conquered 65:11
Saxon: S., — I am Roderick 221:19
saxpence: bang — went s. 211:17
say: careful indeed what we s. 84:12
Do as we s. 44:5
hard to s. common things 139:7
have to s. something 283:18
I'll fear not what men s. 53:27
must all s. *the same* 179:4
nothing to s. and says it 288:7
nothing to s., say nothing 83:15
s., not as I do 223:18
s. the perfectly correct thing 239:8
see what I s. 278:2
They are to s. what they please 118:1
your right to s. it 277:12
saying: As we were s. 165:3
for loving, and for s. so 100:18
it needs not s. 140:23
s. the same things over 105:3
something is not worth s. 21:5
says: orator...s. what he thinks 52:21
scabs: Make yourself s. 225:25
scallop-shell: s. of quiet 212:24
scan: gently s. your brother man 55:15
scandal: In s. as in robbery 75:4
Love and s. are the best sweeteners 114:4
No s. about Queen Elizabeth 244:25
no s. like rags 112:26
Retired to their tea and s. 84:18
scandalous: monarch, s. and poor 214:22
scapegoat: go for a s. 27:1
scarlet: His sins were s. 23:14
sins be as s. 32:26
scatter: s. / The good seed 79:8
Scatter'd: S. his Maker's image 102:12
scene: ask to see / The distant s. 192:7
of what s. / The actors 241:11
tedious brief s. 234:14
scenery: end of all natural s. 218:6
S. is fine 156:13
scenes: From s. like these 56:1
no more behind your s. 147:25
s. of changing life 261:18
watch the busy s. 147:17
scent: s. of the roses will hang 188:18
scepter'd: this s. isle 235:13
sceptic: s. could inquire for 59:20
s. to deny the possibility 143:15
scepticism: wise s. 169:22

Sceptre: S., oftest better miss'd 185:4
sceptred: avails the s. race 162:3
schemes: best laid s. o' mice an' men 58:2
schisms: By s. rent asunder 257:4
Scholar: humour of a S. 15:13
s. all Earth's volumes carry 72:12
s. among rakes 171:24
s. who cherishes the love of comfort 84:7
what ills the s.'s life 147:18
Scholars: S. dispute 139:6
S. get [knowledge] with conscientious 118:17
two kinds of s. 2:24
scholarship: s. for scholarship's sake 142:21
school: creeping like snail / Unwillingly to s. 225:13
followed her to s. one day 195:2
knocked out of them at s. 22:8
till he's been to a good s. 219:7
to be in the strongest s. 76:24
vixen when she went to s. 234:9
school boy: Every s. knows it 261:25
Every s. knows 171:13
every s. knows 284:7
s.'s tale 61:11
whining s., with his satchel 225:13
schoolboys: s. playing in the stream 200:13
schoolgirl: Pert as a s. 122:27
schooling: Than s. in the Pleasures 179:18
school-master: you'll be becoming a s. 280:20
schools: a' their colleges and s. 58:6
hundred s. of thought 174:20
jargon o' your s. 56:9
Public s. are the nurseries of all vice 114:2
science: Art is s. in the flesh 80:19
deepest search after s. 157:10
destiny of s. to exterminate 200:8
eel of s. by the tail 249:6
great tragedy of S. 143:10
In s., read...the newest 53:9
Politics is not an exact s. 41:21
Rather than...Physical S....the principal thing 10:17
relates to s. 161:8
s. and a sausage 6:17
s....exchange of ignorance 63:34
S. falsely so called 40:9
S. has nothing to be ashamed 47:1
S. is for those who learn 217:18
S. is his forte 248:33
S. is nothing but trained 143:11
S. is organized knowledge 250:25
S. struck the thrones of earth 243:20
S. without conscience 187:22
this magnificent applied s. 106:8
this newe s. that men lere 74:15
sciences: art like all other s. 281:24
in s. untaught 63:32
scientific: s. acquisition of knowledge 167:4
scientist: distinguished but elderly s. 79:7
scoff: s., remain'd to pray 125:7
scold: You may s. a carpenter 148:5
scolding: and s. fail 207:23
scoondrels: hang ane o' thae daamned s. 46:6
score: just s. more points 190:3
scorn: foul s. that Parma 109:1
little s. is alluring 84:32
sound / Of public s. 184:32
Talk not with s. of Authors 83:2
scorn'd: fury, like a woman s. 84:26
scorning: s. the base degrees 229:28
scorpion: s. in his neighbour's 246:12
scorpions: chastise you with s. 28:12
Scot: Had Cain been S. 79:14
Hauf his soul a S. maun use 172:16
sober, as a S. ne'er was 172:10
Scotch: joke well into a S. 248:17
little indeed inferior to the S. 193:13
scotch'd: s. the snake 232:10
Scotchman: Much may be made of a S. 148:27
S. ever sees, is the high 148:6
S. must be a very sturdy moralist 146:16
Scotchmen: to like S. 161:6
Scotia: old S.'s grandeur springs 56:1
Scotland: for poor auld S.'s sake 57:21
grave livers do in S. 293:15
in S. at the present day 173:5
in S. supports the people 146:13
lay the scene in S. 131:20
love S. better than truth 146:16
Prince Charlie / Than S. 172:4
S....a worse England 149:20
[S.] land of...oat-cakes, and sulphur 248:18
Stands S. where it did 232:19
Switzerland...inferior sort of S. 248:9
swordless S. 167:3
That S. led in luve 295:15
Scots: Cakes, and brither S. 57:11
S....attained the liberal arts 146:15
[S.] learning is like bread 149:6
S. mist will weet 213:4
S., wha hae wi' Wallace 57:14
Scotsman: any S. without charm 19:25
grandest moral attribute of a S. 20:12
S....let loose upon the world 20:11
S. on the make 20:13
Scott: S....an inspired butler 131:13
[S.]...his drooping style 131:20
[S.] his worst is better 131:9
S., whom I can despise so 239:5
Scottish: auld S. sang 55:23
S. poet maun assume 172:18
S. prejudice in my veins 58:14
scoundrel: last refuge of a s. 149:2
man over forty is a s. 240:10
Scourge: Tamburlaine, the S. of God 176:13
scrannel: s. Pipes of wretched straw 182:29
scrap: for a s. of paper 25:1
scraps: stolen the s. 231:13
Scratch: S. a Russian 174:11
scratchez: itchez, Ah s. 190:24
scratching: cure it but the s. 169:13
s. of pimples 291:17
screams: airs, and flights, and s. 207:23
scribblative: babblative and s. 250:12
scribble: Always scribble, s. 124:4
Scribendi: *S. cacoethes* 152:14
scrimp: For lack o' thee I s. 56:26
Scripture: devil can cite S. 233:7
S., condemns neatness 283:3
S. moveth us in sundry places 209:7
S. which they cannot understand 272:16
Scriptures: S. principally teach what man is to believe 70:17
scrotumtightening: s. sea 151:15

sculis: ouir mekle at the s. 167:2
scum: mere s. of the earth 282:11
whole is equal to the s. 210:24
scunner: love / Wi' a s. in't 172:25
sea: Alone on a wide, wide s. 81:11
blood!' says man, and there's a s. 63:9
cold grey stones, O S. 262:7
do be afraid of the s. 260:19
Down to a sunless s. 82:3
fishing-boat-bobbing s. 267:5
garden fronts the s. 260:9
gong-tormented s. 296:2
I beneath a rougher s. 87:5
in the s. of life enisled 9:15
Into that silent s. 81:5
into the midst of the s. 30:1
life's wild restless s. 3:10
lover of men, the s. 260:17
never sick at s. 122:13
not having been at s. 149:13
one is of the s. 294:5
Our heritage the s. 89:18
rush across the s. 139:18
s. and all that in them 26:33
s. gave up the dead 41:3
s. hath no king but God 217:8
s. is his, and he made it 30:15
s. itself flows in your veins 270:4
S. of Faith...at the full 9:6
s. of glory 229:14
s. shall give up her dead 210:22
s.! The sea 295:16
s. / From whence his mother 223:7
see nothing but s. 13:19
sent them o'er the s. 18:17
those in peril on the s. 284:8
unplumb'd, salt, estranging s. 9:16
wet sheet and a flowing s. 89:17
Winds somewhere safe to s. 260:12
wine-dark s. 137:27
seafaring: s. man may have a sweetheart 249:11
sea-green: s. Incorruptible 68:8
seal: opened the seventh s. 41:1
you heard a s. bark 269:10
sealed: My lips are s. 16:23
sealing: ships — and s. wax 70:2
seals: loose the s. thereof 40:36
Seamen: S. three! What men be 200:12
s. were not gentlemen 171:17
sear: s., the yellow leaf 232:25
search: deepest s. after science 157:10
I do not s. 201:23
world over in s. 188:9
searching: by s. find out God 29:3
I am s. everywhere 253:15
seas: floors of silent s. 107:32
guard our native s. 66:13
s. but join the regions 207:29
s. do laugh 281:22
strange s. of Thought, alone 293:8
sea-sand: As is the ribbed s. 81:10
seashore: boy playing on the s. 192:11
season: brain in a dry s. 107:22
Love, all alike, no s. knows 100:17
think on at another s. 60:24
To everything there is a s. 32:7
seasons: interested in the changing s. 220:11
man for all s. 285:14
mercy s. justice 233:20
S. of mists 153:8
Seat: have a private S. 203:21
second: first and s. class citizens 289:16
first in a village than s. 65:9
my s. best bed 238:24
round the grounds for the s. time 200:9
s. and sober thoughts 133:17
secret: ceases to be a s. 22:18
keep a s., if two of them 117:13
no s. so close 258:7
s., for it's whispered everywhere 84:24
s. ministry of frost 82:1
S. sits in the middle and knows 118:15
trusted a woman with a s. 70:25
we did in s. 215:12
secrets: from whom no s. are hid 210:6
s. in all families 113:1
S. with girls 88:17
sect: attached to that great s. 242:1
paradise for a s. 153:32
Slave to no s. 206:28
sects: diversity of s. 251:16
Two-and-Seventy jarring S. confute 114:21
secure: past, at least, is s. 281:4
Securus: *S. indicat orbis* 11:23
sedge: s. has wither'd 153:11
seduces: When a man s. a woman 291:9
see: can't s. what he sees in her 134:10
last s. your father 295:17
rather s. than be one 53:30
s., but you do not observe 101:16
s. her is to love her 55:20
s. oursels as others see us 57:23
s. what is not to be seen 271:5
Shall never s. so much 231:9
think till I s. what I say 278:2
To think is to s. 18:19
seed: light s. from the feather'd 154:2
s. o' a' the men 172:11
s. of the church 265:26
seed-time: Fair s. had my soul 293:6
s. and harvest 25:27
seeing: only one way of *s.* 218:11
seek: All I s., the heaven above 255:15
s., and ye shall find 36:4
S. ye first the kingdom 35:29
S. ye the Lord 33:26
to s., to find, and not 265:15
We s. him here 196:18
seeks: small man s. is in others 84:10
seem: in age we s. 179:11
not to s. the bravest 2:21
seemed: s. bisier than he was 73:11
seems: I know not 's.' 226:3
seen: s. what she could not declare 137:10
they that have not s. 38:18
seeth: Lord s. not as man 27:32
seges: *Iam s. est* 197:16
seggendo: *s. in piuma* 90:8
sein: *Es muss s.* 22:14
seize: Cruel! been content to s. 207:22
seizes: imagination s. as beauty 156:6
seldom: s. I go there myself 247:18
select: each one should s. 242:1
Selection: Natural S. 90:18
self: Each one a murdered s. 217:3
to thine own s. be true 226:12
self-impelling: s. steam-wheels of the mind 242:20
self-interest: s. was bad morals 215:16
selfish: s. affairs is a coward 239:27

s. being all my life 13:5
Self-love: S. and Social be the same 206:23
self-made: s. man, and worships 46:20
self-protection: sole end...is s. 180:12
self-reproach: not abolish, of bitter s. 93:4
self-respect: own s. to distinguish them 110:24
price of s. 290:8
Self-righteousness: S. is not religion 47:5
self-sufficing: reasoning, s. thing 293:3
sell: are you willing to s. 164:11
boards, or pigs, to s. 110:25
no good: I'll s. him 164:1
precious as the Goods they s. 115:1
selling: buying and the s. 52:25
Everyone lives by s. 255:24
s. one's soul to keep 173:14
semblable: *mon s., — mon frère* 20:20
semblance: Its s. in another's case 87:4
Semen: *S. est sanguis* 265:26
semper: *Quod s.* 275:5
senates: listening s. hang upon thy tongue 268:7
senators: green-rob'd s. 154:4
send: Here am I; s. me 33:2
seniors: earnest advice from my s. 268:26
sensation: first s. on entering a wood 110:22
sensational: something s. to read 287:7
sensations: s. rather than of thoughts 156:8
Sense: Batteries of alluring S. 177:6
echo to the s. 206:2
fountain of good s. 104:4
fruit of s. beneath 205:30
love / (Whose soul is s.) 100:22
Money speaks s. 22:21
Nature, for it is not s. 77:11
never deviates into s. 103:18
Satire or s., alas 205:7
s., and the sounds will take care 69:21
swerv'd / Frae Common S. 57:16
want of decency is want of s. 216:17
senselessness: s. of suffering 193:2
senses: Oot o' the way, my s. 172:2
power of our s. 146:18
sensibility: dissociation of s. 108:22
sentence: originator of a good s. 110:27
S. first — verdict afterwards 69:27
sententiae: *Quot homines tot s.* 265:24
sentiment: marriage...as a mere matter of s. 47:9
occasion to the s. 148:26
religion, as a mere s. 191:25
sentimental: pet-lamb in a s. farce 154:28
sentimentalist: barrenest...is the s. 67:12
sentimentality: s. that truth, merely 180:14
sentiments: s. to which every bosom 147:1
Them's my s. 266:11
sentinel: s. stars set their watch 66:12
sentinels: s. to warn th'immortal souls 176:11
sentry: Where stands a winged s. 273:23
separate: s. the wheat from the chaff 141:12
s. us from the love of God 38:38
separately: we shall all hang s. 117:30
separation: s., amicably if they can 212:9
sepulchre: whole world is a s. 269:2
sera: *Che s., sera* 175:3
serenity: s. to accept the things 192:19
sergeant: fell s., death 227:28
serious: grand style...s. subject 10:14
much more s. than that 238:25
nor trusts them with, s. matters 75:13
nothing s. in mortality 232:8
portrait painting; the s. and 95:13
s. attempt to do it 282:24
sermon: good, honest and painful s. 201:2
s., — that it will suit any text 254:19
who a s. flies 134:23
Sermons: S. and soda water 62:24
s. he had already hidden 286:20
serpent: s. beguiled me 25:21
s. of old Nile 224:22
s. subtlest beast 184:27
s. was more subtil 25:18
sharper than a s.'s tooth 230:23
serpents: wise as s. 36:11
servant: become the s. of a man 239:7
for thy s. heareth 27:25
good and faithful s. 36:34
s. depart in peace 277:21
s.'s too often a negligent elf 19:15
thy s. depart in peace 37:15
whose s. I am 165:2
servants: both good s. 128:5
good s., but bad masters 165:7
Live? Our s. will do that 275:1
Men in Great Place are thrice S. 14:16
never be equality in the s.' hall 20:1
s. are treated as human 240:2
serve: also s. who only stand 185:23
let me not s. so 99:3
not s. if elected 245:16
s. for meat and fee 17:18
s. two masters 35:27
than s. in Heav'n 183:16
too proud to s. 249:12
served: as I have s. the King 291:11
despised as well as s. it 60:12
Had I but s. my God 229:16
lad I s. a term 122:15
Youth will be s. 45:6
serves: profits most who s. best 241:6
service: constant s., thrown aside 250:6
done the public any s. 192:12
done the state some s. 235:5
more essential s. to his country 258:13
s. greater than the god 237:2
s. is perfect freedom 209:16
s. of my love 252:19
services: goods and s. can be paid for 193:12
servility: savage s. 169:24
s. of mankind towards 180:11
Sesame: Open S. 8:5
sessions: s. of sweet silent thought 238:7
set: Here is the whole s. 245:10
settled: matter is s. 11:29
seul: *On mourra s.* 199:9
seven: acts being s. ages 225:13

s. years were come and gane 18:14
Seventeen: S. and never been sweet 267:11
seventh: s. day is the sabbath 26:32
seventies: man gets well into the s. 256:25
seventy: s. years young 137:19
sever: kiss, and then we s. 55:16
severity: treats with...s. a serious subject 10:14
Sewers: S. annoy the Air 184:28
sex: attempt to insult s. 163:20
either S. assume, or both 183:18
ruin of our s. 249:8
s. and not...having children 167:25
s. whose presence civilizes 87:11
s. with someone you love 3:18
subordination of one s. 181:1
Wanted to Know About S. 213:19
women are a s. by themselves 22:10
your rebel s., / Nor love 67:4
sexes: cleanliness of the s. stands 284:17
old ladies of both s. 94:24
old women (of both s.) 254:15
three s. — men, women, and clergymen 248:16
sexton: s. toll'd the bell 138:5
shabby: s. equipment always deteriorating 107:17
shackles: country, and their s. fall 88:4
shade: Amaryllis in the s. 182:23
crowd into a s. 207:11
farewell to the s. 87:27
in a green S. 177:14
in the Chequer'd s. 182:16
old sit under the s. 94:13
S. more than man 296:1
shades: s. / High overarch'd imbower 183:17
shadow: awful s. of some unseen 242:14
Falls the S. 107:24
his s. will be seen 192:24
hope beyond the s. 153:18
light but the s. of God 48:22
possible s. of doubt 122:7
s. at morning striding 108:13
s. has fallen across the scenes 78:10
s. is what we think 166:16
That s. my likeness 285:3
valley of the s. of death 29:20
shadows: half sick of s. 263:28
see only their own s. 202:26
this kind are but s. 234:15
shadowy: I am the s. one 191:17
shady: Deep in the s. 154:1
Shake-scene: only S. in a country 128:1
Shakespeare: all that may be found in S. 83:20
despise S. when I measure 239:5
England made S. 141:22
S., fancy's child 182:17
If S.'s genius had been cultivated 75:17
[S.] is an upstart crow 128:1
S. led a life of allegory 156:23
S. made use of it first 244:27
[S.] most comprehensive soul 104:1
S....more original than 111:1
myriad-minded S. 82:16
S....never blotted out a line 151:3
S., on whose forehead climb 49:21
Playing S. is very tiring 141:23
quibble is to S. 147:15
reading S. by flashes 82:22
[S.] Thou smilest and art still 9:28
souls most fed with S.'s flame 76:17
stuff as great part of S. 121:5
tongue / That S. spake 294:12
S., undoubtedly wanted taste 278:12
We all talk S. 12:16
What needs my S. 183:4
Whaur's yer Wully S. 7:24
Shakespeherian: that S. Rag 108:16
shaking: s., crazy, cold 214:24
Shalimar: beside the S. 138:23
shallow: s. draughts intoxicate 205:28
Shalott: Lady of S. 263:27
shame: ashamed with the noble s. 158:10
glory is their s. 39:25
s. of it to outlive him 152:20
shameful: so s. as poverty 112:26
shape: Attic s. 154:24
out of s. from toe to top 298:12
S. of Things to Come 282:25
share the selfsame s. 172:17
share: s. of honour 228:34
strength without a double s. 185:10
sharp: s. the conqueryng 74:14
sharper: s. than a serpent's tooth 230:23
shatter: s. the vase, if you will 188:18
shaving: s. of a morning 141:4
Shaw: [S.] hasn't an enemy 288:24
shay: one-hoss s. 137:15
shears: abhorred s., / And slits 182:25
sheathe: We shall never s. the sword 10:19
sheds: found in lowly s. 181:26
sheep: All we like s. 33:25
Baa, baa, black s. 194:4
black s. who've gone astray 159:5
Bo-peep has lost her s. 194:23
ensample to his s. he yaf 73:14
giveth his life for the s. 38:8
hungry S. look up 182:29
in s.'s clothing 36:5
mountain s. are sweeter 200:11
old half-witted s. 253:13
s., that were wont to be so meek 189:4
ways like lost s. 209:8
Sheep-hook: how to hold / A S. 182:28
sheer: s. ignorance 148:9
sheet: wet s. and a flowing sea 89:17
sheets: cool kindliness of s. 48:6
Shelley: once see S. plain 51:10
peace in S.'s mind / Than calm 244:8
[S.] beautiful and ineffectual angel 10:11
shells: silver bells and cockle s. 195:3
sheltered: In youth it s. me 189:10
Shepherd: for they call you, S. 9:22
God of Love my S. 135:14
good s. giveth his life 38:8
King of Love my S. is 16:19
Lord is my s. 29:20
S.'s delight 4:15
shepherdess: s. of sheep 180:5
shepherds: While s. watch'd their flocks 261:19
shew: we will s. you a thing 27:30
shielding: result of s. men 250:26
shift: let me s. for myself 189:5
shilling: for one s. / Your ring 164:11
splendid s. 201:19
Shin'd: S. in my Angel-infancy 273:24
shine: make his face to s. 30:19

not to s. in use 265:11
s. / With a pure, clear 279:22
shines: s. a good deed 233:26
shineth: s. more and more 31:17
ship: built your s. of death 163:15
Don't give up the s. 163:23
land to which the s. 80:4
One leak will sink a s. 53:23
s. but a prison 59:4
s. have I got 17:14
s. in a black storm 281:21
Sink me the s., Master Gunner 265:3
ships: down to the sea in s. 30:20
frail mystic s. are wrecked 86:9
S. are but boards 233:6
S. that pass in the night 168:20
something wrong with our bloody s. 21:4
shipwreck: s. of time 13:22
shirt: Englishman added the s. 110:1
shoal: bank and s. of time 231:29
shock: for the old, to s. them 239:6
hum, the s. of men 61:14
short, sharp s. 122:28
strikes with a shivering s. 250:17
shoe: s. be Spanish or neats-leather 59:23
woman who lived in a s. 195:22
shoemaker: lives of a good s. 273:15
shoes: call for his old s. 223:13
Put off thy s. 26:16
shone: glory of the Lord s. round 37:12
Shook: Days that S. the World 213:15
shoon: balled, that s. as any glas 73:6
in her silver s. 92:20
shoot: do not s. the pianist 287:14
guns begin to s. 159:31
S. if you must 285:8
s. the way you shout 216:11
young idea how to s. 268:5
shooting: when they are s. at you 290:3
shoots: s. at the mid-day sun 245:23
shop: keep a little back s. 187:14
no other s. / Than what nature's 88:27
shopkeepers: nation of s. 190:16
nation of s. 247:9
shops: shun the awful s. 76:18
shore: Fast by their native s. 87:25
native s. / Fades o'er the waters 61:3
rapture on the lonely s. 62:1
s. / Of the wide world 155:26
some false impossible s. 9:32
shored: fragments have I s. 108:19
shores: earth's human s. 155:16
shorn: wind to the s. lamb 253:23
short: come s. of the glory 38:34
lyf so s. 74:14
s. and long of it 233:29
s., sharp shock 122:28
s., so it is very miserable 261:24
Take s. views 248:14
shorter: not had time to make it s. 199:5
shortest: s. way to do many things 247:4
shot: fired the s. heard 110:21
I s. an arrow 168:3
Sahib s. divinely 7:18
s. than do his bootlaces 282:21
s. through his heart on Sunday 254:21
s. which brings her down 266:4
should: nae better than he s. be 56:3
no better than you s. be 21:10
shoulder: government shall be upon his s. 33:4
shoulders: grow beneath their s. 234:29
old head on young s. 111:19
standing on the s. 192:13
shout: shoot the way you s. 216:11
s. about my ears 76:8
s. to him golden shouts 179:25
S. with the largest 95:35
shouteth: s. by reason of wine 30:6
shouting: tumult and the s. 159:24
Shove: S. Jesus and Judas equally 110:15
show: thing they most do s. 238:14
shower: drainless s. / Of light 155:14
sweetness of a s. 267:16
shows: my s. are great 126:11
shreds: thing of s. and patches 122:22
shrine: Open the s. that I may see 151:1
shrunken: poor s. things 13:30
shudder: s. in the loins 296:27
shuffle: patience, and s. the cards 71:20
Shun: S. what I follow 52:1
shut: One cannot s. one's eyes 189:8
S., shut the door, good John 204:31
shuttered: s. rooms let others grieve 91:2
shuttle: musical s. 284:14
s., to whose winding quest 273:20
sick: blood makes s. the heavens 42:12
but they that are s. 36:9
devil was s. 190:2
half s. of shadows 263:28
I am s., I must die 191:2
I'm s. of both 150:8
kill s. people groaning 175:26
maketh the heart s. 31:24
never s. at sea 122:13
on our hands a s. man 192:18
say I'm s., I'm dead 204:31
s., and ye visited me 36:35
s., commanded to be sound 128:6
s., O Lord, around Thee lay 272:18
s. that surfeit with too much 233:3
were you not extremely s. 211:1
sicken'd: s. at all triumphs save 77:14
sicklied: s. o'er with the pale cast 226:40
sickness: convicted of s., hunger 249:4
in s. and in health 210:14
Sidcup: could get down to S. 202:1
side: fools in town on our s. 271:29
on the s. of the angels 98:5
thrust my hand into his s. 38:17
sides: might be said on both s. 2:3
Sieve: went to sea in a S. 164:8
sigh: s., and so away 88:25
s. is the sword 42:15
S. no more, ladies 234:18
unutterable S. in the Human 109:12
sighed: s. as a lover 121:11
sighing: and s. shall flee 33:14
plague of s. 227:40
Sighs: S. are the natural language 224:12
Venice, on the Bridge of S. 61:31
sight: Hairs less in s. 207:22
in the s. of God 210:11
out of s. is out of mind 80:3
thousand years in thy s. 30:10
sign: In this s. thou shalt conquer 85:11
Never s. a walentine with 96:6
outward and visible s. 70:21
signal: do not see the s. 191:9

I have s. 190:9
More s. against than sinning 230:28
sinner: Be a s. and sin 170:18
one s. that repenteth 37:27
sinners: mercy upon us miserable s. 209:20
s. to repentance 36:10
sinning: sinned against than s. 230:28
sins: Albion's s. are crimson 42:19
for their s., but by them 141:11
His s. were scarlet 23:14
multitude of s. 40:26
no faults, only s. 298:19
s. be as scarlet 32:26
takest away the s. 178:19
sip: s. is the most 3:1
sipped: s. no sup 123:25
Sirens: Blest pair of S. 181:22
What song the S. sang 48:24
sister: confound this surly s. 261:2
ministering angel shall my s. 227:24
We have a little s. 32:25
sit: cannot s. and think 161:13
he'll s. there, hours 94:26
let us s. upon the ground 235:19
s. down, unless you're a King 141:23
Teach us to s. still 107:6
Though I s. down now 97:29
Sits: S. the wind in that corner 234:19
sitteth: s. on the right hand 209:14
sitting: all-night s. in the House 240:29
situation: retreats; s. excellent 115:17
Sitwells: S. belong to the history 164:14
six: s. days the Lord made 26:33
s. of one 176:22
six hundred: Rode the s. 262:13
sixpence: Sing a song of s. 195:15
skies: whose god is in the s. 239:30
skilfully: dance more s. than a virtuous 219:23
Skill: S. comes so slow 91:9
skin: brightness belonging to the s. 186:19
Ethiopian change his s. 34:5
in the lion's s., the ass 116:3
skull beneath the s. 108:20
skinny: I fear thy s. hand 81:10
skins: beauty of their s. 264:25
skipper: get a gude s. 18:9
s. had taken his little daughter 168:23
Skrymmorie: S. monsters few daur look upon 172:20
skull: s. beneath the skin 108:20
sky: Above, the vaulted s. 79:4
pie in the s. 136:5
prisoners call the s. 285:22
untune the s. 103:28
wide and starry s. 255:20
Skye: Beyond the Isle of S. 17:5
slain: can never do that's s. 59:29
Despair, law, chance, hath s. 99:23
fifty thousand men s. this year 278:23
love is s.; I saw him go 99:9
Saul hath s. his thousands 27:35
s. a thousand men 27:19
s. me you will conquer France 146:6
slander: angry at a s. makes it true 150:15
slandered: Truth was s. 76:20
slap-up: s. gal 95:30
slaughter: ox goeth to the s. 31:19
through s. to a throne 127:14
slaughter'd: have s. and made an end 191:22
slave: design'd yon lordling's s. 57:8
freedom to the s. 166:9
not passion's s. 227:7
s. has had kings among his ancestors 202:29
s. morality 192:22
very s. of circumstance 64:5
slavery: problem of s. 288:12
s. of waiting upon other people 173:12
What is s.?...Murder 211:7
slaves: Britons never will be s. 268:4
creed of s. 202:8
S. cannot breathe in England 88:4
s., howe'er contented, never know 87:31
wholly s. or wholly free 103:13
slavish: too s. knees 155:20
slays: s. the weak 286:2
sleekit: Wee, s., cow'rin' 57:24
Sleep: at eve the Prince of S. 92:16
borders of s. 267:14
but a s. and a forgetting 292:22
Death and his brother S. 241:24
Do I wake or s. 155:7
How s. the brave 83:9
I s., but my heart 32:23
lay me down to s. 6:13
miles to go before I s. 118:16
Night, but not of S. 268:13
One short s. past 99:25
rounded with a s. 236:24
Six hours in s. 80:23
S.; and if life was bitter 260:3
S. after toil 252:1
S. it is a gentle thing 81:13
s. like a top 90:24
s. may I nocht 104:26
S. no more 232:1
s. of the just 212:16
s. out the thought of it 237:32
s.'s fine alchemy 268:17
s. that knows not breaking 221:16
S., the certain knot of peace 246:1
s. / Without identity 47:12
To die, to s. 226:37
to give their readers s. 204:1
to s. before evening 199:17
Visit the soul in s. 243:3
We shall not all s. 39:11
We shall not s. 172:1
sleepers: great s. are incapable of doing 133:10
s. in that quiet earth 47:19
snorted we in the Seven S. 99:19
sleepeth: peradventure he s. 28:15
sleepin': Capten, art tha' s. there 191:19
sleeping: fuss about s. together 280:26
growing...when ye're s. 222:19
S. is no mean art 193:4
We are awake while s. 187:19
Sleepless: S. themselves 204:1
S. with cold commemorative 217:4
sleeps: M.F.H. s. he breakfasts 258:3
s. feels not the toothache 225:33
sleepy-head: Ain't you 'shamed, you s. 255:14
sleeve: heart upon my s. 91:2
slenderly: Fashioned so s. 138:3
sleping: nought good a s. hound 74:21
slept: thought he thought I s. 200:1
slice: how thin you s. it 247:13
slid: s. into my soul 81:13
slighted: our soldiers s. 151:5

slimy: legs / Upon the s. sea 81:8
slip: Excuse me while I s. into 130:17
gave us all the s. 52:16
Slit: S. your girl's, and swing 158:17
slits: s. the thin-spun life 182:25
sloe-black: s., slow, black 267:5
slop: Raineth drop and staineth s. 208:6
sloth: and peaceful s. 184:2
cares and woe of s. 243:26
too much Time in Studies is S. 15:13
Slouches: S. towards Bethlehem 297:19
Slough: fall on S. 25:4
s. was Despond 53:15
slovenliness: s. is no part of religion 283:3
Slow: S. and steady wins 167:13
S. rises worth by poverty 147:6
slowly: Hasten s. 257:19
S., silently, now 92:20
sluggard: foul s.'s comfort 67:16
Go to the ant thou s. 31:18
voice of the s. 280:15
slumb'ring: might half s. 155:14
slumber: affected s. more 66:16
I must s. again 280:15
keepeth thee will not s. 31:4
mind and character s. 111:3
s. did my spirit seal 293:21
s. is more sweet than toil 264:9
slumbers: Golden s. kiss your eyes 92:11
infant's s., pure and light 157:7
sly: Tough, and devilish s. 94:11
small: compare s. things with great 276:10
grind exceeding s. 168:1
How s., of all that human hearts 125:23
S. have suffered 116:4
S. is Beautiful 221:6
so s. a thing 9:9
smaller: rights of the s. nationalities 10:19
Smart: pray with Kit S. as anyone 148:11
smattering: s. of everything 96:16
Smell: actions of the just/ S. sweet 245:18
I s. the blood 230:35
s. far worse than weeds 238:15
s. of their own farts 11:17
smile: call me that, *s.* 290:17
Cambridge people rarely s. 48:3
kind of sickly s. 131:1
one vast substantial s. 93:22
should forget and s. 216:26
s., and be a villain 226:19
S. at us, pay us 76:16
somewhat undignified, to s. 197:21
vain tribute of a s. 221:23
smiled: Jesus wept; Voltaire s. 141:21
smiles: all s. stopped together 51:13
coined my cheek to s. 61:28
Eternal s. his emptiness 205:9
every time a man s. 253:25
flower that s. to-day 135:27
flower that s. to-day 243:5
S. awake you when you rise 92:11
to all she s. extends 207:15
Venus when she s. 150:32
smiling: by your s., you seem to say 226:30
hides a s. face 87:22
smirk: serious and the s. 95:13
smite: s. once, and smite no more 182:30
Smithfield: brings / The S. Muses 203:25
smithy: in the s. of my soul 151:13
village s. stands 168:21
smoke: do wid de s. 130:26
good cigar is a S. 158:21
horrible Stygian s. 144:13
man who does not s. 256:15
pipe...and s. it 19:18
six counties overhung with s. 189:13
smoorit them with s. 104:17
turn s. into gold 109:4
smoked: s. / And danced 107:9
smokes: honours s. at once fatten 99:3
smoking: blessing this s. is 132:20
smoorit: s. them with smoke 104:17
smooth: I am a s. man 26:3
never did run s. 233:34
smoothes: s. her hair with automatic 108:17
smote: he s. his enemies 30:6
When 'Omer s. 160:1
smug: generation of the thoroughly s. 208:23
smylere: s. with the knyf 73:23
snaffle: use the s. and the curb 66:1
snail: creeping like s. / Unwillingly 225:13
snake: scotch'd the s., not killed 232:10
s. lurks in the grass 275:26
snapper-up: s. of unconsidered trifles 237:31
snare: delusion and a s. 85:10
snarling: silver, s. trumpets 153:25
snatches: Of ballads, songs and s. 122:22
sneer: face it with a s. 216:3
Sneering: S. doesn't become...the...face 240:27
without s., teach the rest to sneer 205:4
sneers: ten thousand s. than one abiding pang 93:4
sneezed: Not to be s. at 83:12
sneezes: beat him when he s. 69:10
When Paris s. 180:2
snewed: s. in his hous of mete 73:12
Snob: admires mean things is a S. 265:30
Paradise for the s. 46:15
Society, not to be sometimes a S. 265:31
snorted: s. we in the Seven Sleepers 99:19
snotgreen: s. sea 151:15
snow: everywhere in their s. 104:2
garment of unsullied s. 250:20
never shall love the s. 46:12
rosebuds fill'd with s. 66:19
s. came flying 46:13
s. disfigured the public statues 11:5
we shall have s. 195:18
white as s. 32:26
snows: s. have scattered 140:15
where are the s. 275:2
Snowy: S., Flowy, Blowy 109:10
snuff'd: s. out by an article 63:11
snug: s. little Island 93:17
s. / As a bug 117:27
soap: used your s. two years 211:21
soar: ambition can creep as well as s. 54:5
run, but not to s. 171:11
stoop / Than when we s. 292:4

sore: bear with a s. head 176:19
sorowe: s., ywhet with fals plesaunce 72:26
sorrow: any s. like unto my sorrow 34:9
complete s. is as impossible 269:21
glut thy s. 154:30
Hang s. 290:18
knowledge increaseth s. 32:6
natural s., loss, or pain 293:23
parting is such sweet s. 236:2
S. and sighing shall flee 33:14
s. like a shoe 260:20
S. that endureth for Ever 287:27
with s. to the grave 26:11
Sorrowful: Knight of the S. Countenance 71:14
sorrowing: borrowing / Goeth a s. 271:19
sorrows: man of s. 33:24
s. strike him, / Inclines to think there is 79:20
sorry: having to say you're s. 223:12
s., now, I wrote it 54:1
s. Scheme of Things 115:2
very s. to say / That ninety 173:6
sottises: *s. des Grands* 116:4
sought: east, she s. him west 18:7
soul: become a living s. 292:13
Call to the s. 273:19
captain of my s. 133:7
from man's s. looks 189:14
half conceal the S. 263:8
Heights which the s. 292:5
his s. among masterpieces 117:5
if I have a s. 213:17
iron enter into his s. 253:21
iron has entered his s. 167:19
knock and enter in our s. 50:1
leaves s. free a little 49:26
lips suck forth my s. 175:7
loafe and invite my s. 284:19
Lord my s. to keep 6:13
lose his own s. 36:23
Medicine for the s. 97:6
most comprehensive s. 104:1
must have such a s. 187:15
my s. drew back 135:6
my s. is white 43:31
my s. thirsteth for thee 30:4
my unconquerable s. 133:5
naturally Christian s. 265:27
No coward s. is mine 47:13
O s., be changed 175:12
Out of his bitter s. 298:10
real dark night of the s. 115:3
reason to the s. 103:20
single s. dwelling in two 8:18
Sneering doesn't become...human s. 240:27
so panteth my s. 29:29
S. clap its hands 297:16
s. completes the triumph 146:14
s., do not search for immortal 201:25
s. for a little bears up 260:15
s. in its unrest 286:12
s. in prison, I am not free 91:17
s. is an enchanted boat 243:22
s. is not a clod 153:33
s. is the captain 220:1
s. lies buried in the ink 79:5
s., like to a ship 281:21
s. magnifies the Lord 277:20
s. of man, like unextinguished 243:23
s....should rejoin its friend 110:7
s. that flashed from out 91:7
s. that knew not fear 91:5
S. visits the National Gallery 247:18
s. we have is mortal 170:11
stolen my s. away 271:14
stormy working s. 134:26
sweet and virtuous s. 135:13
This horror...is my s. 172:9
thy s. shall be required of thee 37:24
to keep one's s. 173:14
try the s.'s strength on 51:4
tumult, of the s. 292:9
two to bear my s. away 6:8
vapour from his mouth, man's s. 50:22
What of s. was left 52:14
with s. so dead 222:1
Soul-making: vale of S. 157:1
souls: fame...instinct of all great s. 54:18
good morrow to our waking s. 99:20
hale s. out of men's bodies 234:17
Love's mysteries in s. 99:13
sell their s. and live 247:15
s. but the shadows 48:22
s. descend / T'affections 99:14
s. in heaven too 154:19
s. with but a single thought 169:12
times that try men's s. 198:5
to paint the s. 50:27
two s., and vapours both 99:12
soul-sides: creatures / Boasts two s. 51:16
sound: commanded to be s. 128:6
hath been no s. 138:12
s. ideas is original 174:1
s. must seem an echo 206:2
wind sould s. / After these things 267:15
sounds: better than it s. 271:20
Not many s. in life 161:10
S. and sweet airs 236:23
s. will take care of themselves 69:21
Soup: Beautiful S., so rich 69:14
clear s. was a more important 219:8
Take the s. away 137:2
soupe: *Je vis de bonne s.* 186:18
South Seas: before made to the S. 85:15
southern: much talk'd of s. Continent 85:14
Southey: Thou shalt not set up...S. 62:21
souvenirs: *J'ai plus de s.* 20:23
Sovereign: S. has...three rights 16:5
sovereignty: That is the top of s. 154:8
sovereynetee: Wommen desiren to have s. 73:28
sow: Ireland is the old s. 151:11
right s. by the ear 133:15
s. in tears 31:7
s., you are like to reap 59:26
soweth: s., that shall he also reap 39:16
sown: s. the wind 34:18
space: more than time and s. 161:19
S. may produce new Worlds 183:25
s. that many poor supplied 125:12
spacious: Man's life was s. 106:20
spade: cultivated entirely by the s. 180:22
never seen a s. 287:8
Spain: not into the hands of S. 265:3
spake: s. worse, 'twere better 150:16
span: Contract into a s. 135:8

Spaniards: thrash the S. too 102:1
Spare: S. all I have 113:3
S., woodman, spare 66:2
s. your country's flag 285:8
spareth: s. his rod 31:25
spark: ae s. o' Nature's fire 56:10
Nae s. of life 17:2
Waiting for the s. from heaven 9:24
sparkle: star-like s. in their skies 135:26
sparkles: s. that flash from 103:1
sparkling: Take a pair of s. eyes 122:9
sparks: as the s. fly upward 29:1
sparrer-grass: Hit look lak s. 130:22
sparrow: flight of a lone s. 21:24
My lady's s. is dead 71:1
providence in the fall of a s. 227:26
s. hath found an house 30:7
sparrows: two s. sold for a farthing 36:12
Spartans: Go, tell the S. 246:11
speak: did you s. to him again 51:10
it is difficult to s. 55:2
Let him now s. 210:12
S. for England, Arthur 4:4
S., Lord 27:25
s. out and remove all doubt 166:18
S. softly and carry 216:15
s. Spanish to God 72:24
s. the tongue / That Shakespeare 294:12
S. what we feel 231:9
s. when he is spoken to 255:9
S. when you're spoken to 70:12
time to s. 32:7
Whereof one cannot s. 290:21
speakers: not formidable as *s.* 64:22
speaking: forty years I have been s. prose 186:13
speaks: her foot s. 237:8
s. so much of Himself 15:7
spearmen: stubborn s. still made good 222:13
spears: s. are like the summer grass 43:17
[war] after that with s. 273:1
specialism: his s. is omniscience 101:8
species: female of the s. is 159:3
individual, but a s. 114:1
not the individual but the s. 147:9
speckl'd: s. vanity 183:3
spectacle: no s. so ridiculous 171:20
s. of human happiness 248:5
spectacles: pair of s. is here 237:9
spectator: rather as a s. of mankind 2:1
S. had stood godfather 143:9
spectators: actors or s. 241:11
philosophers / Beheld mankind as mere s. 62:12
pleasure to the s. 171:16
Spectatress: S. of the mischief 217:23
spectre: s. is haunting Europe 177:28
spectre-thin: s., and dies 155:2
speech: continuous s....mental deficiency 16:8
more eloquence than s. 271:9
Poetry is...healthy s. 268:30
Rude am I in my s. 234:27
Speak the s., I pray 227:3
s. created thought 243:20
s. impelled us 107:18
s. is shallow as Time 67:18
S. is the small change 179:27
tongue blossom into s. 50:9
speeches: bullets than pointed s. 41:20
speechless: receive fair s. messages 233:2
speech-mouthing: s., speech-reporting guild 81:27
speed: rather to put on s. 97:12
s. the parting guest 207:9
time shall teach me s. 230:16
speller: fancy of the s. 96:8
spending: Getting and s. 294:6
spendis: only that thou s. 104:20
spendthrift: s. of my own genius 286:15
spent: our life is s. trying 215:3
s. one whole day well 157:13
speranza: *Lasciate ogni s.* 90:2
spheres: ever-moving s. of heaven 175:9
hears / The music of forfended s. 200:3
music of the s. 91:4
Ring out ye Crystal s. 183:2
spice: Variety's the very s. of life 88:3
spider: said a s. to a fly 141:8
s.'s touch, how exquisitely fine 206:16
s., / Who sat down beside 194:26
spierin': gey an' easy s. 255:21
spies: Ye are s. 26:10
spilling: bent on s. it 178:27
spin: neither do they s. 35:28
spinach: rowley, powley, gammon and s. 194:1
Spinner: S. of the Years 129:18
spinning-jenny: God took the s. 296:18
spinsters: dreams of s. 218:18
Spirit: Ah fleeting S. 128:16
And with thy s. 178:15
be filled with the S. 39:20
Blessed are the poor in s. 35:17
blithe S. 244:13
body did contain a s. 228:11
break a man's s. 238:31
expense of s. 238:21
fruits of the S. 209:22
God is a S. 38:2
holy s. of man 260:1
I commend my s. 37:34
in the S. on the Lord's day 40:31
life-blood of a master s. 186:3
makes the wounded s. whole 192:16
no gentleman of s. 257:2
poison and his s. died 137:23
present in s. 39:4
s. giveth life 39:13
s. indeed is willing 36:37
S. of God moved 25:11
s. that forever denies 124:12
th'enlightened s. sees 274:1
worship him in s. 38:2
spirits: call s. from the vasty 228:2
S. when they please 183:18
s. / Of great events 81:19
spiritu: *Et cum s. tuo* 178:15
spit: s. on his hands 179:13
spitefully: pray for them which s. use 35:20
spits: soul s. lies and froth 134:26
splendid: Between a s. and a happy 125:11
our s. isolation 126:10
splendidly: s. null 264:13
splendour: Not in lone s. hung 155:16
s. falls on castle walls 264:22
s. in the grass 292:26
s. of a sudden thought 50:19
spliced: s. in the humdrum way 47:10

s....are my children 156:19
S. / Hide their diminished heads 184:11
s. in their courses 27:14
s. move still 175:10
s. rush out 81:9
s.' tennis-balls, struck 281:15
s. with my exalted head 139:24
way to the s. 275:22
star-spangled: s. banner 157:22
started: s. like a guilty thing 225:35
starv'd: s. / 'Mid a' thy favors 57:16
starve: joyless dignity to s. 249:12
Let not poor Nelly s. 72:20
s. with nothing 233:3
state: burden on the reeling s. 87:12
done the s. some service 235:5
foundation of every s. is the education 97:13
free Church in a free S. 71:12
I am the S. 169:1
lie for the good of the S. 202:24
lie...for the...s. 295:5
no harm come to the s. 5:1
object...of the s. is...happiness 202:25
ruin of the S. 42:4
s. is not abolished 111:26
s. without...means of...change 54:8
worth of a S. 180:21
stately: s. homes of England 133:2
S., plump Buck Mulligan 151:14
states: many goodly s. 155:21
statesman: constitutional s. 15:27
no gift to set a s. right 297:10
s. is a politician...dead 271:2
s. is an easy man 297:8
statesmen: ye s., who survey 125:11
statue: ask why I have no s. 70:24
statues: snow disfigured the public s. 11:5
staves: comest to me with s. 27:34
stay: Can't you s. 273:16
STAYS: news that S. news 209:2
Time s., *we* go 98:17
steadfast: s. as thou art 155:16
steadily: saw life s. 10:2
steady: Slow and s. wins 167:13
steaks: smells of s. in passageways 108:6
steal: as silently s. away 168:5
law...forbids the rich...to s. 117:3
s. my Basil-pot 154:14
s. my thunder 93:2
Thou shalt not s. 26:23
stealing: not hanged for s. horses 129:5
stealth: Do good by s. 207:6
s. and have it found out 161:16
stealthily: s., like a parson's damn 130:10
steam: All the s. in the world 1:8
s. engine in trousers 248:13
Steamers: all you Big S. 158:22
steam-wheels: self-impelling s. of the mind 242:20
steed: border his s. was the best 222:8
steel: Give them the cold s. 9:3
worthy of their s. 221:20
Steele: [S.] rake among scholars 171:24
steer: s. too nigh the sands 102:15
step: one s. enough for me 192:7
small s. for a man 9:4
To s. aside is human 55:15
with a single s. 162:21
stepping: you are s. westward 294:13
stepping-stones: s. / Of their dead selves 263:7
steps: hand in hand with wand'ring s. 185:1
how sad s., O Moon 245:26
sterner: let us rather speak of s. days 78:4
made of s. stuff 230:3
stick: carry a big s. 216:15
let what will s. to them 118:17
principles! S. to your party 98:10
sticking-place: courage to the s. 231:34
stiff: Keep a s. upper lip 70:15
stiles: Lame dogs over s. 158:9
still: nearer by not keeping s. 128:13
Sit thou s. when kings 222:15
S. falls the Rain 246:15
s. it is not we 76:15
s. point of a turning world 107:13
s., sad music of humanity 292:15
s. small voice 28:16
s. things to do 170:4
s. to be drest 150:21
stilly: Oft, in the s. night 188:25
sting: death, where is thy s. 39:12
lives into the s. 110:26
sting-a-ling-a-ling: Death, where is thy s. 6:14
stings: s. you for your pains 136:4
stinks and s. 205:8
stinking: Stinking'st of the s. 161:11
stinks: s. and stings 205:8
Stir: S. up, we beseech 210:2
Stirred: S. for a bird 139:3
stirrup: Betwixt the s. and the ground 65:21
I sprang to the s. 51:2
stirrup-pump: s. / Will extinguish hell 213:13
stitching: s. and unstitching has been naught 295:18
St. Ives: going to S., / I met 194:2
stocked: o'er s. with prudent men 103:19
stockholders: I'm working for my s. 273:14
stocking: spoil'd silk s. 134:27
stoic: either a s. or a satyr 201:29
stoical: s. scheme of 259:13
stol'n: better, had I s. the whole 255:19
stole: he s. those tarts 69:24
stolen: s. his wits away 92:14
s. my soul away 271:14
S. sweets are best 78:15
S. waters are sweet 31:21
stomach: army marches on its s. 4:20
heart and s. of a king 109:1
kind of pride of s. 58:17
s. thinks her throat is cut 217:26
wine for thy s.'s sake 40:6
stomachs: march on their s. 224:2
stone: bread, and he received a s. 283:6
first cast a s. 38:4
heart a heart of s. 285:21
hollow out a s. 170:9
Jackson standing like a s. wall 22:1
make a s. of the heart 296:14
my tongue's a s. 296:10
quiet as a s. 154:1
S. Walls do not 169:7
s. which the builders refused 31:2
sword of this s. 174:15
Vain the s., the watch 283:2

stronger: argument of the s. 115:21
strongest: s. lose 103:8
stronghold: safe s. our God 170:15
strongly: sin s. 170:18
strove: men that s. with Gods 265:13
s. with none; for none 162:2
struck: s. all of a heap 244:30
s. regularly, like gongs 86:14
s. the board, and cry'd 135:1
structure: good s. in a winding stair 135:5
struggle: class s. necessarily leads 178:6
contemptible s. 54:15
s. for existence 90:19
s. naught availeth 80:1
struggles: Imagination's s. 153:19
struggling: unconcern on a man s. 148:1
strumpet: transformed / Into a s.'s fool 224:18
struts: s. and frets his hour 232:28
stuck up: despised the 's.' 282:16
students: not for the benefit of the s. 247:10
studied: s. books than men 15:23
Studies: too much Time in S. 15:13
wise men use [S.] 15:14
study: much s. is the weariness of 32:16
proper s. of Mankind 206:18
s. but the way / To love 158:4
s. of mankind is books 142:17
stuff: s. / As dreams are made on 236:24
such s. as great part of Shakespeare 121:5
write such s. for ever 149:23
written such volumes of s. 164:5
stuffed: We are the s. men 107:23
stumble: do not s. 173:17
stummucks: s. don't git tired 130:25
stumps: fought upon his s. 241:5
Stung: S. by the splendour 50:19
stupidest: s. party 180:9
stupidity: no less a proof of s. 148:22
s. the very gods contend 221:1
Sturm: S. und Drang 153:1
style: grand s. arises in poetry 10:14
no s. where there is no unity 286:11
S. is the dress of thought 283:7
S. is the man 53:5
s., not sincerity, is the vital 287:10
support his drooping s. 131:20
true definition of a s. 258:19
styles: New s. of architecture 11:13
subdue: Men s. their Passions 253:2
subduing: remove the necessity of s. again 54:22
subject: grant the artist his s. 144:21
itself and not in its s. 220:9
subjects: good of s. is the end of kings 92:5
show to s., what they show to kings 88:15
sublime: elevated thoughts; a sense s. 292:16
make our lives s. 168:15
most s. noise 116:18
My object all s. 122:29
step from the s. 190:17
s. and the ridiculous 198:4
sublunary: Dull s. lovers 100:22
Submerged: S. Tenth 45:1
submission: Yielded with coy s. 184:16
submit: Must he s. 235:20
never to s. or yield 183:14
s. to no man's opinion 271:11
subsequent: owing to a s. engagement 288:20
s. proceedings interested 131:1
Subsistence: S. only increases 174:17
substantial: one vast s. smile 93:22
subtle: may not be s. but neither are men 119:14
subtlest: s. beast of all the field 184:27
subversion: s. of good Order 160:10
succeed: first you don't s. 136:3
him that shall s. me 53:28
succeeds: Nothing s. like excess 288:18
Success: bitch-goddess, S. 145:5
failure's no s. at all 105:10
field from which s. is banished 255:25
guarantee s. in war 78:12
not in mortals to command s. 1:11
no very lively hope of s. 248:31
road to s. is filled with women 93:15
s. and miscarriage are empty 146:10
S....demands strange sacrifices 143:3
s. depends upon previous preparation 84:11
s. is confidence 109:20
to maintain this ecstasy, is s. 199:16
true s. is to labour 256:26
wisdom to vulgar judgements — s. 55:4
suck: Doth s. his sweet 167:26
lips s. forth my soul 175:7
Suck-a-Thumb: naughty little S. 137:5
sucker: s. born every minute 19:24
sucklings: mouth of babes and s. 29:14
sucks: as a weasel s. eggs 225:10
s. the nurse asleep 225:2
s. two souls, and vapours 99:12
Sudden: S. glory is the passion 136:18
suddenness: what the hill's s. resists 100:10
sue: Less used to s. 221:15
to s. but to command 235:9
suffer: Better one s. than 102:19
nobler in the mind to s. 226:37
s. first punishment 88:19
S. the little children 37:8
suffer'd: have s. greatly 265:8
suffereth: Charity s. long 39:7
suffering: About s. they were never wrong 11:10
nothing but s. 12:21
one's indignation against s. 193:2
S. is permanent, obscure 291:19
s. what they teach 242:18
sufficiency: elegant s. 268:6
Sufficient: S. unto the day 36:1
sugar: I must s. my hair 69:13
suggestion: s. as a cat laps milk 236:19
suicide: not even s., but to be good 256:18
s. is a great consolation 192:20
war...is s. 173:4
suit: Your s. is granted 135:11
sulphites: Bromides and s. 54:3
sultry: more common where the climate's s. 62:16
sum: more than the s. 8:20
Sumatra: giant rat of S. 101:23
summer: compare thee to a s.'s day 238:4

dewy Eve, / A S.'s day 183:26
Indian S. of the heart 285:11
last rose of s. 188:22
Made glorious s. 235:23
Saint Martin's s. 229:7
S., come the sweet seasoun 144:9
s. is ended 34:3
S. is icumen in 7:4
S. set lip to earth's 267:24
s.'s lease hath all too short 238:4
with love in s.'s wonderland 193:20
summit: high a s. in Poetry 156:17
Summum: *S. bonum* 78:18
sun: assisted the s. materially in rising 268:24
Born of the s. they travelled 251:8
burnished s. 233:9
by this s. of York 235:23
candle to the s. 115:11
gained both the Wind and S. 177:7
going down of the s. 41:18
I will sing of the s. 208:9
Juliet is the s. 235:35
let not the s. go down 39:19
let the s. in, mind it wipes 267:6
maketh his s. to rise 35:21
nothing like the s. 238:22
on which the s. never sets 193:14
out of my s. 97:8
own place in the s. 53:8
palsied strikes the summer s. 42:1
quietest places / Under the s. 141:1
set a candle in the s. 59:7
shoots at the mid-day s. 245:23
S. of righteousness 34:28
s. rises, do you not see 44:1
s. that shines upon his court 237:37
s....the dark *simulacrum* 48:22
Thank heavens, the s. has gone 247:23
think that the S. went round the Earth 10:17
To have enjoy'd the s. 9:9
to the s. my little taper 63:13
unruly S., / Why dost thou 100:16
sunbeam: s. in a winter's day 105:5
Sunday: will weep on S. 212:20
Sun-flower: S.! weary of time 43:26
sung: life were said and s. 153:24
s. women in three cities 208:9
sunlit: One hour was s. 208:11
sunnier: s. side of doubt 262:5
sunrise: s. from the sea, / Athens 242:10
suns: dwelling is the light of setting s. 292:16
Heaven cannot brook two s. 3:5
Sunshine: On a S. Holyday 182:16
s. in the shady place 251:24
Sun-treader: S., life and light be thine 51:22
Supererogation: Works of S. 210:23
superesset: *dum quid s. agendum* 170:4
superexcellent: s. tobacco 59:5
Superior: S. people never make long visits 188:14
superman: teach you the s. 193:3
superstition: Poetry...mother of s. 252:18
s. in avoiding superstition 14:22
superstitions: to end as s. 143:13
superstitious: were it vastly more s. 191:24
supped: Hobson has s. 183:5
supper: eat my s. there 294:23
Hope...is a bad s. 13:26
supply: All just s. and all relation 99:16
support: deter us from the s. 166:8
I s. it from the outside 179:7
no invisible means of s. 52:23
s. of the woman I love 106:1
suppose: round in a ring and s. 118:15
suprema: *Salus populi s. est lex* 78:17
supremacy: blind from sheer s. 154:7
Supreme: find alone Necessity S. 268:15
Poetry is the s. fiction 254:26
public safety be the s. law 223:16
sure: wisest prophets make s. 278:20
surest: s. way in the world 272:8
surface: not for a fine glossy s. 125:26
surfeit: sick that s. with too much 233:3
surge: s. and thunder of the Odyssey 162:11
surgeon: wounded s. plies 107:16
surgical: s. operation to get a joke 248:17
surly: acrimonious and s. republican 147:3
hear the s. sullen bell 238:12
surmise: wild s. 155:22
surpassed: Man is something to be s. 193:3
surprise: Death does not s. 116:1
s. by a fine excess 156:21
Surprised: S. by joy 294:3
s. to find it done at all 148:7
surprises: light s. / The Christian 87:24
surquidrie: s. and foul presumpcion 74:19
surrender: we shall never s. 77:24
Sursum: *S. corda* 178:18
survey: monarch of all I s. 87:28
Survival: S. of the Fittest 90:20
s. of the fittest 251:2
s. of the vulgarest 286:8
survive: only the Fit s. 224:7
What will s. of us 163:7
survived: I s. 246:10
survives: Lord s. the rainbow 170:2
suspect: Always s. everybody 95:21
suspected: opinions are always s. 167:20
suspension: willing s. of disbelief 82:15
suspicion: against despots — s. 92:24
wife must be above s. 65:8
swagman: Once a jolly s. camped 199:19
swain: dispossess the s. 125:5
Swains: all our S. commend her 237:27
swallow: blow and s. at the same time 203:2
s. a camel 36:30
s. a nest for herself 30:7
s. down the very men 189:4
swan: every goose a s. 158:11
Sweet S. of Avon 150:31
very like a black s. 152:12
swans: s. of others are geese 278:21
S. sing before they die 81:26
two S. of goodly hue 252:10
swap: s. horses while crossing 166:12
swarry: A friendly s. 96:12
sway: love of s. 204:27

talk't: how it t. 21:18
talked: not being t. about 287:22
t. on for ever 131:12
talkin': wimmin, dey does de t. 130:19
talking: ain't t. about him, ain't listening 46:3
always t. about being a gentleman 258:2
T. of Michelangelo 107:29
talks: fish that *t.* 92:13
Minerva when she t. 150:32
t. like a Radical 287:17
t. when you wish him to listen 41:13
tall: ask is a t. ship 178:11
tame: not t. / When once it is within 134:24
though I seem t. 295:12
tames: t. it, that fetters it in verse 100:19
tangere: *Noli me t.* 277:26
Noli me t. 295:12
Tankard: one unfailing remedy — the T. 65:17
Tanqueray: The Second Mrs. T. 23:6
Tao: method of T. 162:17
taper: to the sun my little t. 63:13
tapestry: rich t. as divers poets 246:5
Tara: once through T.'s halls 188:19
Tar-baby: T. ain't sayin' nuthin' 130:21
tarde: *A las cinco de la t.* 120:1
target: great big blaring t. 165:16
tarry: why t. the wheels 27:16
Tartar: you will find a T. 174:11
Tartars: hath seen T. and Turks 151:4
tarts: Hearts, she made some t. 69:24
t., / And took them clean away 195:19
Tarzan: Me T., you Jane 58:20
task: reads as a t. 148:13
t., and in it the labour 275:18
the common t. 157:6
taste: Arbiter of t. 261:8
inch-rule of t. 1:5
matter o' t. 96:4
must himself create the t. 294:25
native tact and t. 143:4
Shakespeare, undoubtedly wanted t. 278:12
t. for gutters 22:4
t. of another's bread 90:11
t. prove in digestion 235:10
very much more to their t. 123:7
whose mortal t. / Brought Death 183:7
tastes: heav'ns to suit the t. of all 188:24
t. may not be the same 239:31
Tat: *T. ist alles* 124:15
tattle: t., and sometimes wit 75:18
taught: t. us how to live 269:14
Tortoise because he t. us 69:19
worth knowing can be t. 286:10
taughte: afterward he t. 73:14
He t., but first he folwed 73:15
Tautology: great Prophet of T. 103:17
tavern: by a good t. or inn 149:9
die in a t. 8:10
tavernes: He knew the t. wel 73:8
taverns: in t. with gluttons 90:7
tax: t. levied upon commodities 146:11
To t. and to please 54:19
Taxation: T. without representation 197:8
taxes: except death and t. 117:29
true...as t. is 94:5
Tay: Silv'ry T. 173:6
Tea: and sometimes T. 207:18
honey still for t. 48:5
makes t. I makes tea 151:16
Retired to their t. and scandal 84:18
spill her solitary t. 205:12
t., then I wish for coffee 211:23
While there's t. there's hope 201:27
teach: t. others who themselves excel 205:26
t. the young idea 268:5
T. us to care 107:6
t. you more of man 294:17
what they t. in song 242:18
teacher: precepts for the t.'s sake 113:4
teaches: He who cannot t. 240:6
teaching: taken to t. 286:18
Teacup: Storm in a T. 24:20
team: Is my t. ploughing 140:29
tear: can't t. the toilet paper 289:1
no longer t. his heart 259:23
part to t. a cat in 233:36
T. him for his bad verses 230:8
t. is an intellectual thing 42:15
t. our pleasures 177:23
Thinking every t. a gem 243:1
tears: all t. from their eyes 40:38
blood, toil, t., and sweat 77:23
fountains fraught with t. 160:13
Hence these t. 265:21
lies too deep for t. 293:1
lost that's wrought with t. 91:4
sheddeth tender t. 251:26
sow in t. 31:7
t. and laughters for all time 49:21
t. from off all faces 33:11
T. from the depth 264:23
T., idle tears 264:23
t., prepare to shed them 230:4
T. such as Angels weep 183:22
through my t. on a soundless 267:19
To remember with t. 4:2
tribute of wild t. 297:1
With silence and t. 64:14
tease: fleas that t. 23:15
t. us out of thought 154:25
teases: Because he knows it t. 69:10
teatray: Like a t. in the sky 69:11
teche: and gladly t. 73:10
tedious: either charming or t. 287:15
t. brief scene 234:14
teeming: t. Mistress 204:25
teeth: I set my t. in rascals 97:11
No t., no teeth 208:2
Sans t., sans eyes 225:16
t. are set on edge 34:11
Writers, like t. 16:7
teetotaller: beer t. 239:1
should marry a t. 256:15
telegrams: outer life of t. and anger 116:19
telescope: wrong end of a t. 172:22
television: see bad t. for nothing 126:6
T. has brought murder back 136:12
tell: How could they t. 198:23
Never seek to t. thy love 43:2
T. it not in Gath 28:2
T. me not 168:13
T. me not here 140:23
t. you what his 'pinions is 271:22
t. you what you are 46:22
t. you who you are 75:10
What I t. you three times 70:13
when or how I cannot t. 217:7

would t. one anything 288:10
teller: Truth never hurts the t. 50:24
telling: arguing with you — I am t. 283:20
temper: brutal about the good t. 288:16
good t. when he's well dressed 95:1
t. so / Justice with Mercy 184:31
temperament: artistic t. is a disease 76:25
temperance: t. would be difficult 150:5
temperate: more lovely and more t. 238:4
tempers: God t. the wind 253:23
tempest: lowers the t. overhead 168:7
t. still is high 282:27
tempestuous: world's t. sea 105:19
temple: t. half as old as time 214:27
very t. of Delight 154:32
temples: t. of his Gods 171:5
Tempora: *T. mutantur* 7:5
t.! O mores 78:25
temporary: box is only t. 202:14
force alone is but *t.* 54:22
temporis: *t. acti* 139:10
tempt: shalt not t. the Lord 35:14
temptation: insist on their resisting t. 160:12
lead us not into t. 35:24
maximum of t. 239:32
not over-fond of resisting t. 21:23
oughtn't to yield to t. 138:19
resist everything except t. 287:16
rid of a t. is to yield 287:24
Yield not to t. 198:12
temptations: t. / To belong to other nations 122:17
tempted: one thing to be t. 232:33
tempus: *fugit inreparabile t.* 276:8
T. edax 197:18
ten: God Almighty has only t. 79:13
O for t. years 155:11
tenant: She's the t. of the room 133:8
tender: t. is the night 155:4
woman's t. care 87:19
tenderly: Take her up t. 138:3
tenderness: Want of t. 148:22
tendresse: *c'est la t. humaine* 66:23
ténébreux: *Je suis le t.* 191:17
Tenets: some nice T. might / Be wrong 86:23
tennis: lobelias and t. flannels 108:9
playing t. with the net down 118:19
tennis-balls: merely the stars' t. 281:15
tent: inside the t. pissing out 146:9
Tenth: Submerged T. 45:1
tents: dwell in the t. of wickedness 30:8
fold their t. 168:5
Israel's t. do shine 43:1
terminological: t. inexactitude 77:20
tern: leave no t. unstoned 190:20
terrestrial: nocht t. can escape 172:17
terrible: t. beauty is born 296:16
whole worl's...in a t. state 196:7
terribles: *Les enfants t.* 120:13
terrifies: infinite spaces t. me 199:8
territorial: last t. claim which I have 136:16
territory: comes with the t. 181:5
terror: as great a t. 167:15
fools of time and t. 63:33
terrorist: t. and the policeman both come 85:9
terrors: new t. of death 8:6
test: t. of a first-rate work 24:5
testimony: No t. is sufficient 142:6
Tetigisti: *T. acu* 203:3
text: English t. is chaste 121:15
He yaf nat of that t. 73:7
neat rivulet of t. 245:9
t. is that it will suit any sermon 254:19
texts: difference of t. 251:16
Thames: Sweet T., run softly 252:11
T., / The King of Dykes 204:8
thankful: single t. thought raised 165:5
t. and has nobody to thank 217:10
thankit: let the Lord be t. 56:25
thankless: have a t. child 230:23
thanks: give t. is good 260:3
That: 1066, And All T. 223:20
theatre: all-night sitting in a t. 240:29
problems of the modern t. 213:9
Theft: What is property?...T. 211:7
theme: example as it is my t. 92:25
My t. is alwey oon 74:3
themselves: all men mortal, but t. 298:25
kept t. to themselves 282:16
theorize: mistake to t. before 101:15
theory: t., dear friend, is grey 124:14
there: Because it is t. 174:14
wasn't t. again to-day 179:1
Thick: T. as Autumnal Leaves 183:17
thickens: now the plot t. 53:2
thief: Opportunity makes a t. 15:21
penitent t. 12:1
Taffy was a t. 195:17
t. of time 298:24
thieves: fell among t. 37:21
night for t. 112:15
t. break through and steal 35:25
thin: can never be too t. 290:16
hear! how t. and clear 264:22
in every fat man a t. one 85:2
into t. air 236:24
t. red line 219:1
thing: nearest run t. 282:5
t. which was not 258:14
we will shew you a t. 27:30
things: After these t. should be 267:15
hend of all t. 95:8
many t. I have no need of 249:18
no ideas but in t. 289:12
rich in t. 143:24
T. are where things are 2:16
T. do not change; we change 268:29
think: believe that I t. all the time 276:22
comedy to those that t. 278:19
don't *t.* foolishly 149:27
drink beer will t. beer 144:5
I never t. about them 161:19
I t. continually of those 251:7
I t., therefore I am 93:9
know what I t. till 278:2
later than you t. 224:6
miserable unless you t. it 44:7
something with them besides t. 168:27
they appear to t. 113:25
t. only this of me 48:12
t. on these things 39:27
t. they are thinking 145:6
t. we must think so 245:22
To t. is to see 18:19
We t. as we do 60:18
thinking: but he is a t. reed 199:11

dignity of t. beings 146:18
It ain't t. about it 270:17
never thought of t. for myself 122:14
pleasure of t. 79:19
recording, not t. 144:7
t. about something you said 217:25
T. is to me the greatest fatigue 273:13
t. makes it so 226:28
t. on the frosty Caucasus 235:12
t. Thy thoughts after Thee 157:19
t. when...merely rearranging 145:6
what everybody is t. most often 216:14
thinks: that which he t. he has 152:26
t. like a Tory 287:17
thirst: t. for goodness as for drink 113:13
thirsting: philosophy / Fled not his t. 241:18
thirsty: Drinking when we are not t. 21:7
dry and t. land 30:4
thirtieth: my t. year to heaven 267:2
thirty: and the next t. years 115:4
T. days hath November 126:12
thorn: t. in the flesh 39:15
thorns: crackling of t. under 32:9
Roses have t. 238:9
upon the t. of life 243:8
thorough: t. an Englishman 158:14
thoroughly: t. smug and thoroughly 208:23
Thou: Book of Verse — and T. 114:15
T. also 197:19
thought: believe your own t. 110:11
device for avoiding t. 132:19
dress of t. 146:21
due to patient t. 192:12
father, Harry, to that t. 228:22
happened to hit on the same t. 244:27
headache called t. 268:11
her body t. 100:13
He t. he saw a Rattlesnake 70:14
He t. I thought he thought 200:1
holy and good t. 35:6
I prefer t. to action 19:1
I t. so once; but 120:26
no t. for the morrow 36:1
once you have t. of big 148:20
pale cast of t. 226:40
Perish the t. 78:14
rear the tender t. 268:5
she lived with no other t. 203:13
Sinking from t. to thought 204:3
souls with but a single t. 169:12
splendour of a sudden t. 50:19
strange seas of T. 293:8
tease us out of t. 154:25
their modes of t. 180:8
t. become concrete 4:5
t. came like a full-blown 153:28
T. is free 236:22
T. is the child of Action 97:27
t....measure of the universe 243:20
t. only to validate their injustices 276:14
t. without learning 84:9
t., word and deed 70:20
To a green T. 177:14
utmost bound of human t. 265:12
What oft was t. 205:29
thoughts: generate misleading t. 251:3
man of many t. 63:31
more complicated than his t. 273:7
my t. are not your thoughts 33:27
pleasant t. / Bring sad 292:10
second and sober t. 133:17
sensations rather than of t. 156:8
thinking Thy t. after Thee 157:19
t. are someone else's opinions 286:16
T. of a dry 107:22
t. of youth 168:11
t. that wander through Eternity 184:1
T. vagrant as the wind 116:13
thousand t. lying within a man 266:3
to disguise their t. 276:14
wording of his own highest t. 156:21
thousand: Give me a t. kisses 71:4
good woman if I had five t. 266:13
one ten t. of those men 228:33
that he had blotted a t. 151:3
t. miles must begin 162:21
t. years in thy sight 30:10
tormented with ten t. hells 175:4
thousands: slain his t. 27:35
t. equally were meant 259:17
To murder t. 299:9
thrall: Hath thee in t. 153:13
thrash: t. the Spaniards too 102:1
thread: Feels at each t. 206:16
t. of his verbosity finer 231:14
threaten: nose and chin they t. 58:9
three: tell you t. times is true 70:13
The night she'll hae but t. 18:6
T. bags full 194:4
t. is company and two 287:3
When shall we t. meet again 231:19
three o'clock: always t. in the morning 115:3
T. is always too late 220:18
three-pipe: quite a t. problem 101:14
threescore: our years are t. and ten 30:11
three-sided: he would be t. 187:24
threshed: t. corn at midnight 297:21
Thrice: T. is he arm'd 229:9
Thrift: T., thrift, Horatio 226:7
thrive: t. baith in ae year 213:3
throat: Poetry...taking life by the t. 118:20
scuttled ship or cut a t. 62:33
stomach thinks her t. is cut 217:26
t. 'tis hard to slit 158:17
throats: begin slitting t. 179:13
throne: Alp as on a t. 155:18
build himself a t. of bayonets 144:1
High on a T. of Royal State 183:27
light which beats upon a t. 262:18
slaughter to a t. 127:14
This royal t. of kings 235:13
Thy t. shall never 109:7
Thrones: T., Dominations, Princedoms 184:22
throng: Join our happy t. 19:21
plaudits of the t. 168:12
through: part of it all the way t. 126:3
Throw: T. away thy wrath 135:3
thrust: greatness t. upon them 237:20
Thucydides: more useful information than...T. 80:10
Thule: Ultima T. 276:2
thumbs: pricking of my t. 232:16
thunder: dawn comes up like t. 159:22
steal my t. 93:2
surge and t. of the Odyssey 162:11
t., lightning, or in rain 231:19
thundering: rage of t. Jupiter 176:10
thunders: t. from her native oak 66:14
thus: To be t. is nothing 232:9
thusness: reason of this t. 279:16

thyme: whereon the wild t. blows 234:5
thyrldome: cowpyt to foule t. 19:10
thyself: knowledge of t. 157:10
Tiber: O Tiber! father T. 171:8
Rome in T. melt 224:20
T. foaming with much blood 209:4
Tiberius: T. might have sat 9:18
tickle: t. us, do we not laugh 233:14
Tiddely pom: nobody knows / (T.) 181:9
tide: blood-dimmed t. 297:18
except when the t.'s pretty nigh out 94:7
this filthy modern t. 298:2
t. in the affairs of women 63:6
t. in the affairs of men 230:10
tidings: bringeth good t. 33:22
good t. of great joy 37:13
tie: Blest be the t. 113:9
tiger: Christ the t. 107:20
imitate the action of the t. 228:30
Imperialism is a paper t. 174:22
T.! burning bright 43:24
t.'s heart wrapped in a player's 128:1
t.'s heart wrapped 229:12
tigers: tamed and shabby t. 137:1
t. of wrath are wiser 43:12
tiger-skin: sin...on a t. 7:26
tight: armchairs t. about the hips 290:27
t. little Island 93:17
tikleth: t. me aboute my herte 73:30
timber: season'd t., never gives 135:13
time: aching t. 154:3
backward and abysm of t. 236:15
bank and shoal of t. 231:29
being wise in t. 216:10
believe that I think all the t. 276:22
Bird of T. has but a little way 114:14
but for all t. 150:29
city 'half as old as T.' 54:4
cormorant devouring T. 231:10
Fleet the t. carelessly 225:4
foulest birth of T. 242:7
Give peace in our t. 209:15
good t. coming 173:11
How goes the t. 265:17
It will last my t. 67:16
Keeping t., time, time 203:15
lang t. deid 4:25
last syllable of recorded t. 232:28
less t. one finds to do it 75:26
loss of t., / Although it griev'd 87:15
lost no T. 15:10
Love's not T.'s fool 238:19
may be some t. 196:5
North, where T. stands still 91:8
not enough t. 111:13
people all the t. 166:4
productions of t. 43:11
puzzles me more than t. 161:19
sands of t. 168:15
shipwreck of t. 13:22
shook hands with t. 116:15
silence and slow t. 154:20
silent, never-resting thing called T. 68:2
small a part of t. 278:7
something to do with the t. 215:3
speech is shallow as T. 67:18
spirit of the t. 230:16
temple half as old as t. 214:27
That t. may cease 175:9
That t. of year thou mayst 238:13
thief of t. 298:24
through t. time is conquered 107:14
t. and the place 51:14
T. brings everything 202:20
t. brings in his revenges 237:25
T. consecrates 221:2
T. for a little something 181:13
T. goes, you say 98:17
t. has come,' the Walrus said 70:2
t. has not yet come 192:23
T. hath, my lord, a wallet 237:5
t. is filched by toil and sleep 91:7
t. is money 117:7
T. is my inheritance 124:20
T. is on our side 124:3
t. is out of joint 226:22
T. is slipping underneath 114:20
T. is still a-flying 135:27
T. is the greatest innovator 15:2
T. is the great physician 97:19
T. is the reef 86:9
T., like an ever-rolling 280:16
T. meanwhile flies 276:8
T. present and time past 107:11
t. remembered is grief forgotten 259:25
T.'s fell hand defaced 238:11
T.'s noblest offspring 24:18
T. the devourer of all things 197:18
T., the subtle thief of youth 185:19
t. to begin a new 103:25
t. to every purpose 32:7
t. to stand and stare 91:12
t. will come when you will hear me 97:29
t. will doubt of Rome 63:3
T. will run back 183:3
T. wounds all heels 7:13
wastes her t. and me 278:6
We are the fools of t. 63:33
wisest of counsellors, T. 201:9
world enough, and t. 177:19
worst t....to take a journey 4:13
time-lag: comfortable t. of fifty years 282:24
times: best of t., it was the worst 96:18
Our t. are in His hand 51:31
praiser of t. past 139:10
t. are changing, and we 7:5
T. contains more useful information 80:10
T. has made many ministries 15:29
t. that try men's souls 198:5
T. wingèd Chariot 177:21
time-servers: t. for truth 180:17
timid: really a t. person 3:20
timing: opportune t. of your death 261:7
Timor: *T. Mortis conturbat me* 104:23
tinsel: real t. underneath 165:8
tintinnabulation: t. that so musically wells 203:15
Tipperary: long, long way to T. 289:8
tipple: Fishes, that t. in the deep 169:6
tip-toe: I stood t. 154:10
jocund day / Stands t. 236:7
on t. for a flight 154:12
tir'd: eyelids on t. eyed 264:8
tired: Give me your t. 163:24
long process of getting t. 60:13
t. — deid dune 172:6
T. millions toil unblest 280:9
t. of London 149:16
tirent: *ceux qui t. le mieux* 277:8
tires: sad t. in a mile-a 237:33
Tirez: *T. le rideau* 212:14
tiring: Shakespeare is very t. 141:23
Tirra: 'T. lirra,' by the river 263:29

tissue: t. of crimes, follies and misfortunes 125:2
title: large property as hadn't a t. 96:11
require to possess a t. 180:18
Thou! Whatever t. suit 55:14
t., for it is not mine 255:19
t.'s uncommonly dear at the price 123:20
Titles: T. are shadows 92:5
T. distinguish the mediocre 240:11
t. do not reflect honour 173:7
titwillow: Sang 'Willow, t. 123:5
Toad: As intelligent Mr. T. 126:16
let the t. *work* 163:10
Squat like a T. 184:20
t. beneath the harrow 159:23
t., ugly and venomous 225:6
toads: imaginary gardens with real t. 188:13
T. in a poisoned tank 50:11
to and fro: going t. in the earth 28:30
toast: never a piece of t. 200:4
We'll have tea and t. 242:22
toasted: dreamed of cheese — t., mostly 256:12
tobacco: in a t. trance 108:7
T., divine, rare 59:5
T., I / Would do any thing 161:12
t....remedy to all diseases. 59:5
tocsin: t. of the soul — the dinner-bell 63:5
today: Be wise t. 298:23
fret about them if T. 114:20
here t. and gone tomorrow 22:19
I have lived t. 103:30
in t. already walks to-morrow 81:19
Never do t. what 211:15
Snatch at t. 139:28
toddle: t. safely home and die 220:21
toe: light fantastic t. 182:12
looking to his great t. 151:4
taken him in t. 138:8
toes: How cold my t. 181:9
toga: Let arms yield to the t. 78:19
toil: ambition mock their useful t. 127:10
blood, t., tears, and sweat 77:23
Horny-handed sons of t. 153:7
Many faint with t. 243:26
Sleep after t. 252:1
slumber is more sweet than t. 264:9
they t. not 35:28
Tired millions t. unblest 280:9
T., envy, want 147:18
toilet: can't tear the t. paper 289:1
told: bade me fight had t. me 112:19
half was not t. me 28:11
portentous phrase, 'I t. you so'. 63:18
t. my wrath 43:23
t. the sexton 138:5
t. you from the beginning 33:19
what they do *not* we are t. 259:7
tolerance: do such work for t. 273:15
tolerate: egoist does not t. egoism 217:20
Toll: T. for the brave 87:25
toll'd: sexton t. the bell 138:5
tolle: *t. lege* 11:22
tollis: *t. peccata mundi* 178:19
tolls: It t. for *thee* 98:28
Tom: T., the piper's son 196:2
tomb: dee to brak' their livin' t. 172:18
this our living T. 100:11
This side the t. 91:11
Tom Jones: Richardson's than in all T. 148:25
Tommy: It's T. this 159:31
tomorrow: Boast not thyself of t. 31:37
for t. we shall die 33:10
here to-day, and gone t. 22:19
jam t. 70:5
put off till t. 211:15
T., and to-morrow 232:28
T. do thy worst 103:30
T. to fresh Woods 182:33
trust as little as you can in t. 139:28
Tom Thumb: thought about T. 149:32
tom-tit: by a river a little t. 123:5
tone: Take the t. of the company 75:9
tongs: have the t. and bones 234:10
tongue: his falser t., that utter'd 99:7
his T. / Dropt Manna 183:30
hold your t., and let me love 98:25
my oracular t. 245:3
my t. is the pen 29:31
my t.'s a stone 296:10
senates hang upon thy t. 268:7
sharp t. is the only edged 144:4
T.; well that's a wery good thing 95:36
t. blossom into speech 50:9
t. swore, but my mind 112:14
t. to speak in this place 165:2
t. / Of him that makes it 231:15
trippingly on the t. 227:3
would that my t. could utter 262:7
tongues: lack t. to praise 238:17
thousand t., to sing 282:29
t. of men and of angels 39:7
t., they shall cease 39:7
ye dumb, / Your loosened t. 283:1
to-night: world may end t. 51:6
tonne: than of the t. / She drank 73:32
took: 'E went an' t. 160:1
tool: t. that grows keener 144:4
tool-making: Man is a t. animal 117:31
tools: Give us the t., and 78:2
lend (but fools) / Their working t. 271:19
to name his t. 59:17
tool-using: Man is a t. animal 68:16
toord: rymyng is nat worth a t. 74:10
tooth: t. for tooth 26:26
toothache: Music helps not the t. 135:17
sleeps feels not the t. 225:33
Top: Look, Ma! T. of the world 65:13
room at the t. 281:9
sleep like a t. 90:24
topics: two t., yourself and me 150:8
topless: burnt the t. towers of Ilium 175:7
top-mast: strack the t. 17:10
torch: bright t. 155:9
t. of life 170:10
torches: teach the t. to burn 235:34
Tories: angels all are T. 64:13
save the monarchy of T. 204:6
T. own no argument 49:10
torment: our t. is the measure 159:6
tormenting: most t. are / Black Eyes 177:8
torments: idea of infinity t. me 190:8
torrid: t. or the frozen zone 67:5
Tortis: this 'ere 'T.' is an insect 211:18
Tortoise: T. because he taught us 69:19
torture: put to the t. 149:25
t. and death of his fellow creatures 118:21

t. them, into believing 192:4
Tory: thinks like a T. 287:17
T....called the Conservative 89:2
T. men and Whig measures 97:16
tory rory ranter: *cavaliers* and *t. boys* 113:22
toss: weariness / May t. him 135:9
tossed: t. to and fro 39:17
Tosser: T. of balls in the sun 93:13
totter: t. into vogue 278:14
touch: dare not put it to the t. 188:4
Do not t. me 277:26
mere t. of cold philosophy 154:17
must never t. mine 299:10
One t. of nature 237:7
t. has still its ancient power 272:19
T. not the cat 222:16
t. of a vanish'd hand 262:8
t. of earth 262:21
Wound with a t. 187:10
touches: Who t. this touches a man 284:15
tough: t. faculty of reading 68:25
t., ma'am, tough 94:11
toujours: *t. de l'audace* 90:14
t. gai 176:14
toung: ane t., / And everie woman 166:20
tour: *à la t. abolie* 191:17
tower: Be as a strong t. 90:13
burning roof and t. 296:27
in his ivory t. 219:6
towers: burnt the topless t. 175:7
to-witta-woo: pu-we, t. 191:3
town: centre of each and every t. 137:13
country in t. 176:29
end of the t. 181:18
little one-horse t. 272:11
man made the t. 88:2
Near some fair t. 203:21
toy: religion but a childish t. 175:22
toys: All is but t. 232:8
Not to meddle with my t. 255:10
trace: that we may t. 298:2
t. / Its semblance in another's 87:4
traces: on winter's t. 259:24
track: t. him everywhere in their snow 104:2
trade: half a t. and half an art 143:25
Irish poets, learn your t. 298:12
There isn't any t. 134:14
t. is, over ladies / To lean 243:12
T.'s unfeeling train 125:5
t. to make tables 148:5
was ever ruined by t. 117:26
trades: best of all t., to make songs 23:13
t. have their moments of pleasure 146:1
tradesmen: confidence, even in t. 287:11
traffic: latest t. of the drowsy town 46:13
two hours' t. of our stage 235:31
tragedies: t. are finish'd by a death 62:30
two t. in life 239:29
tragedy: great t. of Science 143:10
That is their t. 287:5
That is what t. means 257:7
t. is the noblest production 2:2
t. of a man who has found 20:14
t....the imitation of an action 8:27
t. to those that feel 278:19
T. wrought to its uttermost 296:26
tragedye: go, litel myn t. 74:25
tragic: bitterest t. element in life 111:9
t. dividing of forces 199:17
tragical: very t. mirth 234:14
Trahison: *T. des Clercs* 23:21
trail: t. that is always new 159:21
trailing: t. clouds of glory 292:23
trails: t. our fortune in 175:24
Train: T. up a child 31:32
trained: t. and organized common sense 143:11
traitor: Thou art a t. 235:27
tram: not even a bus, I'm a t. 130:15
trample: t. those same vices 11:30
trampled: t. edges of the street 108:2
trampling: t. out the vintage 141:5
tranquillity: emotion recollected in t. 294:24
frigid t. 146:10
transaction: great t.'s done 98:19
transcendent: Worship is t. wonder 68:3
transcendental: idle chatter of a t. kind 123:8
T. moonshine 68:11
transformed: himself t. in his bed 152:19
transit: *Sic t. gloria mundi* 157:12
transitory: fals world is but t. 104:23
translated: thou art t. 234:7
translation: mistake in the t. 273:12
translunary: those brave t. things 102:7
transmitter: No tenth t. 220:26
transport: to share the t. 294:3
trapeze: on the flying t. 165:17
trash: steals my purse steals t. 234:36
traurig: *ich so t. bin* 132:12
travel: long to t. back 274:1
never t. without my diary 287:7
not t. to see Englishmen 253:17
t. for travel's sake 256:8
t. from Dan to Beersheba 253:18
t. hopefully is a better 256:26
T....is a part of Education 14:23
travell'd: Much have I t. 155:21
t. life's dull round 244:22
travelled: I t. among unknown men 292:8
traveller: anybody there?' said the t. 92:17
bourn / No t. returns 226:39
empty-handed t. 152:16
Politician, except he be...a T. 130:18
Some t. from New Zealand 171:14
travellers: t. must be content 225:8
travelling: fairly worth the t. to 255:18
grand object of t. 149:10
T. is the ruin of all happiness 55:9
travels: old to go again to my t. 72:21
t. the fastest 160:3
t. the world over in search 188:9
treachery: even t. cannot trust 152:6
tread: Angels fear to t. 206:6
T. softly because 296:20
treading: he's t. on my tail 69:22
treason: Gunpowder, t. and plot 6:18
If *this* be t. 133:22
temptation is the greatest t. 108:5
t. doth but peep 227:19
T. doth never prosper 130:16
t. was no crime 102:21

treasure: t. is, there will your heart 35:26
treasures: t. upon earth 35:25
Treasury: T....the spring of business 15:28
Treaties: T. are but the combat 103:8
tree: ay sticking in a t. 222:19
billboard lovely as a t. 190:25
blossoms upon one t. 293:9
Fruit / Of that Forbidden T. 183:7
gave me of the t. 25:19
had a little nut t. 194:16
never see a t. at all 190:25
poem as lovely as a t. 158:1
to the top of every t. 122:11
t. is the real thing 166:16
t. of liberty must be refreshed 145:9
t. of life is green 124:14
Woodman, spare that t. 189:10
woodman, spare the beechen t. 66:2
trees: look at the t. 46:14
t. were bread and cheese 5:23
T., where you sit 207:11
Trelawney: shall T. die 131:5
tremble: I t. for my country 145:7
Let Sporus t. 205:7
t. like a guilty thing 292:25
trembling: t., shivr'ing, dying 128:16
tremulous: behind my t. stay 129:15
trend: t. is towards the bourgeois-smug 126:22
trespass: t. there and go 140:25
we forgive them that t. 209:9
tresses: cheek and t. grey 221:21
triangle: eternal t. 7:9
triangles: t. invented a god 187:24
tribal: ways of constructing t. lays 159:9
tribe: dialect of the t. 107:18
language of the t. 174:13
may his t. increase 142:8
verily the T. is all 268:21
tribes: mighty t., the *Bores* and *Bored* 63:17
tribute: t. of wild tears 297:1
vain t. of a smile 221:23
trick: in doubt, win the t. 141:9
pleasing to t. the trickster 115:20
when the long t.'s over 178:12
trickster: trick the t. 115:20
tried: t. / To live without him 295:1
trifle: cold coffee t. with the spoon 205:12
trifles: Revolutions...spring from t. 8:29
snapper-up of unconsidered t. 237:31
T. light as air 234:39
triggers: dror resolves an' t. 169:18
Trimmer: innocent word 'T.' signifies 129:4
trimmings: mutton with the usual t. 96:12
trip: fearful t. is done 284:12
t. it as ye go 182:12
trippingly: t. on the tongue 227:3
tristement: *Anglais s'amusent t.* 257:22
tristesse: *Adieu t.* 109:19
Tristram Shandy: *T.* did not last 149:4
triumph: in ourselves, are t. and 168:12
ride in t. through 176:5
that agony is our t. 273:15
t. o'er the timid hare 268:8
t. of hope over experience 148:23
t. without glory 85:19
triumphs: all t. but his own 77:14
trivial: all t. fond records 226:18
contests rise from t. things 207:13
The t. round 157:6
Trochee: T. trips from long 82:8
trodden: t. the winepress alone 33:30
Troia: *ubi T. fuit* 197:16
tromper: *t. le trompeur* 115:20
trope: out there flew a t. 59:16
trouble: double, toil and t. 232:15
full of t. 29:5
Genius...capacity of taking t. 67:22
Kindness in another's t. 126:9
Man is born unto t. 29:1
saves me the t. of liking 13:9
Scripture which t. me most 272:16
So little t. had been given 64:11
taken the t. to be born 21:8
t. efter great prosperitie 133:26
women and care and t. 279:19
wood's in t. 140:30
troubled: short and stout / And t. 76:11
troubles: arms against a sea of t. 226:37
nothing t. me less 161:19
t. of men are caused 199:6
wealth that brings more t. 140:7
trousers: bottoms of my t. rolled 108:1
never put on one's best t. 143:21
steam engine in t. 248:13
trout: find a t. in the milk 268:31
trouve: *je t.* 201:23
trovato: *molto ben t.* 6:24
trowel: lays it on with a t. 84:19
Troy: And heard T. doubted 63:3
another T. for her to burn 297:7
cornfield where T. once was 197:16
fired another T. 103:2
plains of windy T. 265:10
true: as long as it isn't t. 134:4
England to itself do rest but t. 230:18
her ear, 'You are not t.' 285:18
interesting than that it be t. 284:3
Judgement in discerning what is t. 15:6
long enough it *will* be t. 24:6
not necessarily t. because a man dies 288:27
not t. because it is useful 4:8
not t., it is a happy 6:24
One religion is as t. 59:10
philosophy to be substantially t. 220:13
ring in the t. 263:21
tell you three times is t. 70:13
they know isn't t. 24:6
to thine own self be t. 226:12
t....as taxes is 94:5
t. / To one another 9:7
what is t. is reasonable 132:11
woman t., and fair 100:15
true-fix'd: t. and resting quality 229:30
trump: speaking t. of future fame 63:25
trumpet: blow your own t. 123:17
moved more than with a t. 246:8
t. shrill hath thrice 251:11
t.'s loud clangour 103:27
trumpets: *foie gras* to the sound of t. 248:29
silver, snarling t. 153:25
t. sounded for him 53:29
trust: cheated, she will thenceforth t. nothing 68:21
even treachery cannot t. 152:6

in whom I will t. 29:19
never t. a woman who tells 288:10
no more than power in t. 102:18
public t....public property 145:13
Put not your t. in princes 31:13
t. in ideas 111:4
T. the tale 163:21
wealth is a sacred t. 68:28
wonder men dare t. themselves 236:31
Trustees: T. of Posterity 97:24
truth: Absolute t. belongs to Thee 165:6
and steep, T. stands 100:10
Art...one way possible / Of speaking t. 52:9
awoke and found it t. 156:9
battle for freedom and t. 143:21
beauty must be t. 156:6
dangerous foe to t. 143:20
dead we owe nothing but t. 277:1
decade the t. cannot be told 249:22
Great is T. 34:29
grope for T. 90:23
half t. in argument 164:3
however improbable, must be the t. 101:19
Is there in t. no beauty 135:5
lie? 'Tis but / The t. in masquerade 63:10
love Scotland better than t. 146:16
loving Christianity better than T. 82:12
mainly he told the t. 271:26
ocean of t. lay all undiscovered 192:11
Plain t. will influence 44:18
possession of t. as of a city 49:1
Pride and T., / That long 297:11
relationship with beauty and t. 156:3
so T. be in the field 186:6
telling the disreputable t. 23:24
tells the t....found out 287:30
test of t., / 'It must be right 88:14
time-servers for t. 180:17
t. above our friends 8:22
t. at all times firmly 157:21
t. beauty 154:26
t. by consecutive reasoning 156:7
t. can neither be apprehended 281:24
T. from his lips prevail'd 125:7
t., has any inherent power 180:14
t. in every shepherd's tongue 212:22
T....is daylight 13:29
t. is great, and shall prevail 200:2
T. is in wine 203:6
t. is more important 295:8
t. is on the move 299:16
t. is rarely pure 287:2
T. is within ourselves 51:17
t. lies somewhere, / If we knew 87:14
T. lies within a little 44:16
T. never hurts the teller 50:24
t. shall make thee free 38:5
T., Sir, is a cow 148:14
T. sits upon the lips of dying 9:30
T....so as to be understood 43:8
T. that peeps / Over the edge 49:26
t. that's told with bad 41:29
T., though never found 52:28
t. twenty-four times a second 124:5
t. universally acknowledged 12:23
T., which is the love-making 14:1
t.... / Stranger than fiction 63:19
very fond of t. 277:11
way, the t., and the life 38:13
What is T. 13:28
What is t. 38:15
When in doubt, tell the t. 272:6
when war comes is t. 146:7
wither into the t. 296:7
truths: Advertisements contain the only t. 145:12
bear all naked t. 154:8
new t. to begin as heresies 143:13
t. to be self-evident 7:17
try: times that t. men's souls 198:5
t. him afterwards 187:4
T., try, again 136:3
tu: *Et t. Brute* 65:12
Et t., Brute 229:31
T. quoque 197:19
tub: tale of a t. 281:18
Three men in a t. 195:13
t. was large enough for Diogenes 83:23
Tudor: infernal Bess T. 58:16
tue: *ou je te t.* 72:6
tuffet: Muffet / Sat on a t. 194:26
tug of war: then was the t. 164:17
tulip: streaks of the t. 147:9
tumbles: Andrew that t. for sport 57:1
tumbling: Jill came t. after 194:18
rats came t. 51:25
tumult: depth, and not the t. 292:9
t. and the shouting 159:24
t. of our life's 3:10
tune: I t. the Instrument here 99:29
sweetly play'd in t. 57:10
t. the enchantress plays 140:23
tunes: devil...all the good t. 136:6
tunnel: like a train going into a t. 290:26
some profound dull t. 197:24
turbot: price of a large t. 218:8
turbulent: free me of this t. priest 133:14
tureen: Waiting in a hot t. 69:14
Turk: T. a man and a brother 112:7
Turkey: [T.] a sick man 192:18
T., ven they cuts the wrong man's 96:1
turn: do not hope to t. 107:5
T. on, tune in 164:13
turned: In case anything t. up 94:1
once t. round walks on 81:15
t. every one to his own 33:25
turning: there's no t. back 216:22
Turns: T. into Miss T 92:19
turpissima: *quam similis t. bestia* 112:1
Turret: caught / The Sultan's T. 114:13
turtle: voice of the t. is heard 32:21
Tuscany: ranks of T. / Could scarce 171:9
tutissima: *consilia t. sunt* 167:9
twain: go with him t. 35:19
never the t. shall meet 158:19
tway: toung, / And everie woman t. 166:20
twelve: I'll sing you t. O 5:24
twentieth century: t., war will be dead 141:17
twenty: can ye draw but t. miles 176:12
first t. years are the longest 250:16
twenty-two: still alive at t. 158:17
twice: gives t. who gives soon 261:3
step t. into the same river 134:6
t. two be not four 271:13
twinkle: Than stars that t. 103:7
T., twinkle, little bat 69:11
T., twinkle, little star 261:23

left u. those things 209:8
Unearned: U. increment 180:23
Uneasy: U. lies the head 228:18
uneatable: pursuit of the u. 288:13
uneducated: government by the u. 77:4
u. man to read books of quotations 78:11
unequal: u. to that greatness 2:5
unespied: ocean's bosom u. 177:1
unexamined: u. life is not worth 249:17
unexpected: u. / When it arrives 108:4
unexpectedness: character, which I call *u.* 200:9
unfaithful: faith u. kept him falsely 262:22
unfettered: u. use / Of all the powers 81:22
unfold: could a tale u. 226:16
unforgetful: Teach the u. to forget 217:6
unforgiving: u. minute / With sixty 159:11
unfortunate: u. need no introduction 249:3
ungained: prize the thing u. more 236:34
ungrateful: and one u. 169:2
Unhand: U. it, sir 270:15
unhappily: bad [ended] u. 287:6
bad end u. 257:7
unhappiness: Man's u., as I construe 68:23
unhappy: family is u. in its own 269:19
instinct for being u. 219:12
so u. as one thinks 162:22
till his death / Be called u. 49:12
unheard: language of the u. 158:6
u. / Are sweeter 154:21
unhewn: u. marble of great sculpture 142:24
unholy: cauldron of u. loves 11:19
unhonour'd: Unwept, u. and unsung 222:2
unhurrying: But with u. chase 267:22
uniform: u. must work its way 96:10
unify: struggles to idealize and to u. 82:13
unimportance: u. of events 107:10
unintelligent: so u., so unapt to perceive 10:7
unintelligible: all this u. world 292:12
union: Our u. is complete 97:2
u. of hands and hearts 262:1
U. to be dissolved 166:6
unite: severs those it should u. 242:9
U. and lead a better 124:18
Workers of the world, u. 178:1
united: u. by crime 277:2
u. voice of myriads cannot 125:28
uniting: By u. we stand 97:3
unity: u. is of the individual 286:11
u. which is God 19:3
universal: become a u. law 152:23
one u. grin 114:11
one u. passion: fear 240:17
u. frame began 103:26
universe: no hint throughout the u. 268:15
only one corner of the u. 143:6
thought...measure of the u. 243:20
u. is not hostile 137:11
u. is the property 111:7
u. next door 89:13
u. were bent on spilling 178:27
universities: discipline of...u. 247:10
[English u.]...a sanctuary 247:11
state of both his u. 270:5
unjust: also on the u. fella 45:13
mercy, is a God u. 299:3
u. and wicked king 224:4
unkind: so u. / As man's ingratitude 225:17
(Sweet) I am u. 169:8
unkindest: most u. cut of all 230:6
unknown: dies to himself u. 224:5
safely into the u. 131:4
u. is regarded as magnificent 261:5
Unlearn'd: U., he knew no schoolman's 205:10
unleaving: Golden-grove u. 138:28
unlike: So u. anything else 290:28
unluckily: good [end] u. 257:7
unlucky: so u. / that he runs into 176:15
unmarried: keep u. as long as 239:23
unmetaphorical: u. style you shall in vain 68:17
unnatural: cruel, not u. 227:11
unofficial: English u. rose 48:4
unpleasing: things that are tender and u. 14:25
U. to a married ear 231:16
unplumb'd: u., salt, estranging sea 9:16
unpoetical: most u. of anything 156:16
unprepared: u. / For the long littleness 86:2
unprofitable: most idle and u. of my 121:10
stale, flat, and u. 226:5
unquiet: ever imagine u. slumbers 47:19
unravish'd: still u. bride 154:20
Unreal: U. City 108:14
unreasonable: progress depends on the u. 240:4
unremembered: Feelings too / Of u. pleasure 292:11
unreproved: u. pleasures 182:13
unrequited: some idea of what u. affection 94:14
unsatisfied: leaves one u. What more 287:25
unseen: Floats though u. among us 242:14
friend u., unborn 115:10
U. before 154:6
unselfishness: u. of an oyster 219:13
Unsex: U. me here 231:26
unsought: Love...u. is better 237:22
unsought-for: For aye u. 153:31
unsoundness: certain u. of mind 171:18
unspeakable: u. in full pursuit 288:13
unstoned: leave no tern u. 190:20
unsung: unhonour'd and u. 222:2
unsuspected: learn what u. ancients 103:22
untaught: years in sciences u. 63:32
unthinking: quaffing, and u. time 103:24
Untimely: mother's womb / U. ripp'd 232:31
untouch'd: long time lie u. 175:20
untried: difficult and left u. 77:2
untrodden: dwelt among the u. ways 293:17
untroubled: u. where I lie 79:4
untrue: telling of beautiful u. things 286:19

vécu: *J'ai v.* 246:10
Vega: V. conspicuous overhead 11:16
vegetable: in matters v., animal 123:12
v. love should grow 177:20
vegetate: v., and wish it all at an end 55:10
veil: painted v. which those who live 244:4
v. which those who live 243:24
veillons: *Nous v. dormants* 187:19
vein: Blue as a v. o'er the Madonna's 50:7
not in the giving v. 235:28
veins: drain our dearest v. 57:15
mire of human v. 295:23
Velasquez: Puts old V. in his place 282:14
Why drag in V. 283:23
velvet: crowded on a v. cushion 268:28
iron hand in a v. glove 72:23
vengeance: v. found the bed 42:11
V. is mine 38:40
V. I ask and cry 246:18
virtue than in v. 236:25
Veni: *V., vidi, vici* 65:11
Venice: V....throned on her hundred isles 61:32
Venienti: *V. occurrite morbo* 201:11
Venomous: V. Bead 223:22
venture: drew a bow at a v. 28:18
Venus: V. when she smiles 150:32
Verb: V. is God 141:16
verbal: v. contract isn't worth 126:5
Verbe: *mot, c'est le V.* 141:16
verbosity: exuberance of his own v. 98:8
thread of his v. finer 231:14
verdict: Sentence first — v. afterwards 69:27
Vere: God bless Captain V. 179:8
verify: never occurred to him to v. 218:17
verisimilitude: intended to give artistic v. 123:3
veritas: *In vino v.* 203:6
v. et praevalet 34:29
vérité: *v. est en marche* 299:16
vermin: little odious v. that nature 258:12
vero: *Se non è v.* 6:24
verray: v., parfit gentil knyght 73:4
Verse: Book of V. — and Thou 114:15
court others in v. 210:26
Curst be the v. 205:6
false hair / Become a v. 135:5
fetters it in v. 100:19
give up v., my boy 208:19
made v. flow smoothly 44:11
my v. is not a crown 135:10
not v. is prose 186:14
sisters, Voice and V. 181:22
Turn what they will to V. 204:15
unpolished rugged v. 103:23
v. is merely prose 63:27
v. may find him 134:23
v. your virtues rare 251:15
wanting the accomplishment of v. 292:3
verses: indignation makes v. 152:9
praise those v. but they read 176:26
rhyme the rudder is of v. 59:21
tear him for his bad v. 230:8
vertu: maken v. of necessitee 73:24
very: She was v., very good 168:8
vestry: in the v. after service 248:25
vesture: muddy v. of decay 233:24
veterans: world its v. rewards 204:29
vex: believe they die to v. me 179:5
enow themsels to v. them 58:6
vexation: Multiplication is v. 6:10
vanity and v. of spirit 32:5
vexes: other v. it 153:34
vexit: v. am with heavy thocht 104:26
viator: *coram latrone v.* 152:16
vibration: ominous v. of a pendulum 152:4
vice: lash'd the v. 259:17
Prosperity doth best discover V. 14:10
v. pays to virtue 163:2
vices: hate hym that my v. telleth 73:27
ladder of our v. 11:30
of our pleasant v. 231:6
vicious: expect a boy to be v. till 219:7
vicissitude: sad v. of things 254:24
Vicisti: *V., Galilaee* 151:23
victims: little v. play 127:22
victis: *Vae v.* 167:7
victor: To the v. belong 174:23
vanquished, not the v. 109:17
vanquished v. sunk 102:26
victorie: bed, / Or to v. 57:14
victories: v. / no less renowned 185:27
victorious: armed prophets were v. 173:8
victory: Another such v. and 211:25
gain such a v. as this 282:6
grave, where is thy v. 39:12
peace without v. 290:10
swallow up death in v. 33:11
'twas a famous v. 250:9
Westminster Abbey or v. 191:7
vicus: commodius v. of recirculation 151:8
vieille: *Quand vous serez bien v.* 215:11
vieillesse: *Quelle triste v.* 261:13
si v. pouvoit 112:8
view: lends enchantment to the v. 66:8
views: Take short v., hope for 248:14
vigilance: liberty...is eternal v. 89:19
Vigny: V....in his ivory tower 219:6
vigour: v. from the limb 61:19
vile: less v. than Thou 268:14
only man is v. 132:9
Out, v. jelly 230:36
V., but viler George 162:1
vilest: v. thing must be less vile 268:14
vileynye: no v. ne sayde 73:4
village: blaspheming over the v. idiot 77:1
first in a v. than second 65:9
image of a global v. 173:18
village-Hampden: Some v. 127:13
villain: determined to prove a v. 235:25
smiling, damned v. 226:19
villainous: v. company, hath been the spoil 228:3
villains: v. by necessity 230:21
Villon: V., our sad bad 260:4
vinces: *In hoc signo v.* 85:11
vincit: *Omnia v. Amor* 276:1
vindicate: v. the ways of God to man 206:9
vinegar: twenty casks of v. 133:9

weakest: w. camp is to be in the strongest 76:24
weakness: amiable w. 114:8
everything else is w. 274:23
w. of intellect, birdie 123:6
weal: according to the common w. 144:14
wealth: by any means get w. and place 206:31
consume w. without producing it 238:30
don't 'old with W. 282:19
man of w. and pride 125:12
no w. but life 218:15
routine acquisition of w. 167:4
unbleached by nobility or w. 12:12
w. he had / To build 259:18
w. is a sacred trust 68:28
w. that brings more troubles 140:7
Where w. accumulates 125:3
wealthy: business of the w. man 23:9
w. curled darlings 234:26
w. man of my creed 132:15
weapons: w. of war perished 28:5
wear: rather w. out than rust 284:2
weariness: w. of the flesh 32:16
w., the fever and the fret 155:1
w. / May toss him 135:9
weary: Art thou w. 191:5
plods his w. way 127:9
run, and not be w. 33:20
to the w. rest 192:16
weasel: w. under the cocktail cabinet 202:2
weather: and rough w. 225:9
different kinds of good w. 218:16
Jolly boating w. 86:4
no such thing as bad w. 218:16
three more, / If it prove fair w. 257:16
weatherwise: If the Bard was w. 81:20
Weave: W. the warp 127:8
web: tangled w. we weave 222:10
webs: Laws are like spider's w. 249:20
Webster: Daniel W....steam engine 248:13
W. was much possessed 108:20
wedded: Hail w. Love 184:18
wedding: wife, as she did her w. gown 125:26
Wedding-Guest: W. here beat his breast 81:3
wedlock: Consented together in holy w. 210:18
weed: Pernicious w.! whose scent the fair annoys 87:11
w.? A plant whose virtues 110:19
w. instead of a fish 112:23
weeds: buy yourself w., and be cheerful 120:19
smell far worse than w. 238:15
week: days that's in the w. 67:11
greatest w. in the history of the world 193:9
w. is a long time 289:21
weekends: getting a plumber on w. 3:21
weep: he should w. for her 226:35
in case I should have to w. 21:6
laugh...that I may not w. 63:4
smell onions; I shall w. 224:17
time to w. 32:7
W., and you weep alone 285:19
w. for Adonais 241:8
w. with them that weep 38:39
will w. on Sunday 212:20
women must w. 158:12
weeping: w. in my heart 274:13
weighed: w. in the balances 34:16
w., not counted 83:3
weight: heavy and the weary w. 292:12
willing to pull his w. 216:6
Wein: *liebt W., Weib und Gesang* 170:19
welcome: And yet be w. home 223:1
bid you a w. adoo 279:12
Love bade me w. 135:6
warmest w., at an inn 244:22
W., somer 74:12
W. the coming 207:9
welcomes: w. little fishes in 69:5
well: all shall be w. 151:24
And did it very w. 122:21
deep w. of unconscious 144:17
devil was w. 190:2
Faith, that's as w. said 258:25
Harris, I am not w. 121:6
It is not done w. 148:7
Laugh and be w. 127:28
not wisely but too w. 235:6
Pussy's in the w. 194:7
spent one whole day w. 157:13
w. of English undefiled 252:4
who can do all things w. 77:10
well-bred: w. as if we were not married 84:34
welle: ofter of the w....she drank 73:32
Wellington: [W.] last great Englishman 264:19
wells: go about and poison w. 175:26
to *poison the w.* 191:23
Well-timed: W. silence 271:9
well-to-do: increased the number of w. 178:4
well-written: w. Life 67:13
Welshman: Taffy was a W. 195:17
Weltgeschichte: *W. ist das Weltgericht* 221:3
wen: great w. of all 80:9
wench: besides, the w. is dead 175:28
wenche: joly w. in every toun 74:4
Wenlock: On W. Edge 140:30
went: as cooks go she w. 219:15
wept: Jesus w. 38:9
w. when we remembered Zion 31:9
Werther: W. had a love for Charlotte 266:16
West: Go W., young man 127:26
Go w., young man 250:4
W. is West 158:19
w. wind but tears 178:14
Western: Quiet on the W. Front 213:16
W. wind, when wilt thou blow 7:19
wonders of the w. world 260:21
Western Union: Messages are for W. 126:8
West Indies: negroes in the W. 149:12
Westminster: peerage or W. Abbey 191:8
W. Abbey or victory 191:7
Weston: Mr. W.'s good wine 12:6
westward: stepping w. 294:13
W. the course of empire 24:18
wether: tainted w. of the flock 233:18
whacks: gave her mother forty w. 6:6
whale-white: w. obscenity 172:9
whang: *w., goes the drum* 52:15
Whatsoever: W. things are true 39:27
wheat: w. from chaff 255:5

wheel: breaks a butterfly upon a w. 205:7
red w. / barrow 289:15
Upon a w. of fire 231:4
wheels: spoke among your w. 21:14
tarry the w. of his chariots 27:16
whelmed: w. in deeper gulfs 87:5
where: w. you want to get to 69:9
wherefore: every why he had a w. 59:20
w. art thou Romeo 235:36
whiff: w. of grapeshot 68:7
Whig: Tory men and W. measures 97:16
Whigs: caught the W. bathing 98:3
W. admit no force 49:10
W. *not* getting into place 63:12
whim: strangest w. has seized me 76:5
whimper: bang but a w. 107:25
'twixt a smile and w. 243:12
whimsies: they have my w. 210:26
whine: w. about their condition 284:22
whining: saying so / In w. Poetry 100:18
whippersnapper: Critic and w. 49:25
whipping: who would 'scape w. 226:33
whips: chastised you with w. 28:12
whirligig: w. of time brings 237:25
whirlwind: reap the w. 34:18
Rides in the w. 1:10
whiskers: dye one's w. green 70:11
Oh my fur and w. 69:7
whisky: Freedom and w. gang 55:19
Whisper: W. who dares 181:20
whispered: secret, for it's w. everywhere 84:24
whispering: w. tongues can poison truth 81:18
whistle: w., and I'll come 58:7
W. owre the lave 57:3
whistling: argument, than that of w. 254:9
white: boy brought the w. sheet 120:1
How ill w. hairs 228:25
nor w. so very white 66:25
W. as an angel is 43:31
w. man's brother 158:7
W. Man's Burden 160:2
White House: Log Cabin to W. 266:18
no whitewash at the W. 193:11
whites: see the w. of their eyes 211:24
whitewash: no w. at the White House 193:11
whither: w. thou goest, I will go 27:24
whiting: said a w. to a snail 69:22
Whitman: *viejo hermoso Walt W.* 120:2
Whittington: Turn again, W. 7:15
whole: greatest happiness of the w. 202:25
man made up the w. 298:10
nothing can be sole or w. 296:8
saw it w. 10:2
seeing the w. of them 218:11
They that be w. 36:9
to go the w. hog 176:17
w. I planned 51:31
w. is more than the sum 8:20
wholly: w. hopes to be 50:18
whooping: out of all w. 225:18
whore: argument is a w. 237:3
Protestant w. 128:15
teach the morals of a w. 148:2
why: could he see you now, ask w. 11:3
every w. he had a wherefore 59:20
wibrated: better not be w. 93:18
wicked: and desperately w. 34:6
animal is very w. 5:2
I's mighty w., any how 257:11
no peace...unto the w. 33:21
pomps and vanity of this w. world 70:18
shake their w. sides 297:11
Something w. this way comes 232:16
war...regarded as w. 286:14
w. flee when no man 31:39
w. in great power 29:26
w. to deserve such pain 50:10
wonder to see men w. 259:9
worse than w. 211:20
wickedness: spiritual w. in high places 39:23
tents of w. 30:8
That is the path of w. 18:13
w. is but little 35:1
W. is a myth invented 287:28
widdercock: sad as w. in wind 134:2
wide: Alone on a w., wide sea 81:11
w. enough to hold both 254:4
widow: Here's to the w. of fifty 245:11
or Molly Stark's a w. 252:26
w. bird sate mourning 241:21
widows: as other w. — buy yourself weeds 120:19
w....the most perverse creatures 2:6
wife: Caesar's w. 65:8
chose my w. 125:26
covet thy neighbour's w. 26:25
damned in a fair w. 234:23
extremes appear like man and w. 77:16
Here lies my w. 103:10
ideal w. is any woman who 261:16
if Laura had been Petrarch's w. 62:32
kill a w. with kindness 236:13
look after somebody else's w. 258:6
look out for a w. 258:6
love your neighbour's w. 171:22
married, but I'd have no w. 88:21
Match'd with an aged w. 265:7
Medicine is my lawful w. 75:1
neighed after his neighbour's w. 34:2
single man...in want of a w. 12:23
steer clear of a w. 249:11
when his w. talks Greek 150:3
w....a kind of Discipline 14:14
w. and couldn't keep her 195:8
w., and her name was Diffidence 53:19
w., and therefore I cannot come 37:25
wind is my w. 156:19
your w., under pretence 149:22
wigwam: Stood the w. of Nokomis 168:17
Wild: Call of the W. 168:2
manner rude and w. 23:1
shut her w., wild eyes 153:12
to the w. sky 263:20
waters w. went o'er 66:7
w. for to hold 295:12
with a w. surmise 155:22
Wilderness: Beside me singing in the W. 114:15
crieth in the w. 33:16
crying in the w. 35:10
scapegoat into the w. 27:1
w. of this world 53:14
wildest: w. peal for years 137:1
will: boy's w. is the wind's 168:11
complies against his w. 59:28

Do what you w. 212:13
fantastic w. is the man's law 50:23
His w. is our peace 90:10
Immanent W. that stirs 129:17
knowing that we do Thy w. 170:3
laid me down with a w. 255:20
Man has his w. 137:14
not according to the common w. 144:14
not my w., but thine 37:32
rainbow of His w. 170:2
strong in w. 265:15
that w. nocht when he may 133:25
Thy w. be done in earth 35:24
twenty years of age, the w. reigns 117:14
unconquerable W. 183:14
We *know* our w. is free 148:19
What w. be, shall be 175:3
w. for the deed 190:4
w. in us is over-rul'd by fate 175:18
w. is infinite 237:4
W. is to grace 11:27
W. you, won't you 69:23
You w., Oscar 283:25
William: You are hale, Father W. 250:18
You are old, Father W. 69:8
willin': Barkis is w. 93:24
When a man says he's w. 93:25
willing: ravish me / I'm so w. 115:14
w. suspension of disbelief 82:15
w. that the maxim 152:23
willow: All a green w. 136:2
willows: harps upon the w. 31:10
win: and the match to w. 191:20
Heads I w. 89:1
How to W. Friends 69:2
in doubt, w. the trick 141:9
Let the boy w. his spurs 105:20
To w. or lose it all 188:4
w. for our principles 215:13
wind: after the w. an earthquake 28:16
blowin' in the w. 105:6
durch Nacht und W. 124:10
every w. of doctrine 39:17
Fair blows the w. for France 175:16
Fair stood the w. for France 102:5
forgot to w. up the clock 253:27
Frosty w. made moan 216:24
gained both the W. and Sun 177:7
God tempers the w. 253:23
gone with the w. 101:4
honour / Bot w. inflate in other 134:1
I never hear the west w. 178:14
learned how the w. would sound 267:15
north w. doth blow 195:18
O wild West W. 243:6
Sits the w. in that corner 234:19
sown the w. 34:18
walks upon the w. 206:20
what w. is to fire 59:11
w. bloweth where it listeth 37:41
w. blows it back 42:29
w. blows the cradle 194:15
w. is my wife 156:19
w. like a bugle 96:26
w. of change 173:21
w. was a torrent of darkness 193:21
words but w. 59:25
written in w. and running water 71:7
winding: England's w. sheet 42:5
rising...by a w. stair 14:17
structure in a w. stair 135:5
winding-sheet: w. of Edward's race 127:8
window: light through yonder w. breaks 235:35
windows: breaking of w. 189:2
W. richly dight 182:10
windward: w. of the law 77:12
wine: Be not drunk with w. 39:20
come to drink the w. 17:11
days of w. and roses 101:6
doesn't get into the w. 76:21
drink from the whole w. 295:19
Drinking the blude-red w. 18:9
Flask of W. 114:15
flown with insolence and w. 183:19
fond of Spanish w. 178:9
good w. until now 37:40
I don't see any w. 69:12
I'll not look for w. 150:27
It wasn't the w. 95:33
Look not thou upon the w. 31:33
love is better than w. 32:18
mellow, like good w. 201:20
Mr. Weston's good w. 12:6
old books, old w. 125:19
pass the rosy w. 95:19
red / Sweet w. of youth 48:1
shouteth by reason of w. 30:6
thirsty grief in w. 169:6
Truth is in w. 203:6
w. and women, mirth and laughter 62:24
w. for thy stomach's sake 40:6
W. is a mocker 31:30
w. that maketh glad 30:19
w., woman and song 170:19
wine-dark: continents unkent / And w. oceans 172:10
w. sea 137:27
winepress: trodden the w. alone 33:30
wines: Abbots, purple as their w. 204:16
Wing: Bird is on the W. 114:14
joy is ever on the w. 185:8
so long on a broken w. 264:17
Winged: W. words 137:26
wings: beating...his luminous w. 10:11
healing in his w. 34:28
healing in His w. 87:24
Ill news hath w. 102:2
shade of your soft w. 220:28
soars with his own w. 43:5
viewless w. of Poesy 155:3
w. like a dove 30:2
Wining: W. the ghosts of yester-year 209:1
wink: w. your eye at some homely girl 179:17
Winkie: Wee Willie W. 181:7
winks: w. / At drunk men lurching 127:3
winners: In war...there are no w. 71:25
winning: nothing worth the wear of w. 23:7
wins: steady w. the race 167:13
winter: disappeared in the dead of w. 11:5
English w. — ending in July 63:16
fall out in the Middle of W. 2:4
For, lo, the w. is past 32:21
From w., plague and pestilence 191:4
If W. comes, can 243:9
I in hoary w.'s night 250:22
It was the W. wild 183:1
on w.'s traces 259:24
sad tale's best for w. 237:28

sing with us, away, W. 144:9
w. and rough weather 225:9
w. I get up at night 255:8
W. is come and gone 241:10
W. is icummen in 208:6
w. of our discontent 235:23
wintry: w. garment of unsullied snow 250:20
wipe: God shall w. away 40:38
God will w. away 33:11
Let me w. it first 230:41
wiped: should have w. it up 254:17
wipes: sun in, mind it w. its shoes 267:6
wirklich: *vernünftig ist, das ist w.* 132:11
wisdom: bark of w.'s tree 84:3
beginning of w. 30:21
bettre than w.? Womman 74:6
celestial W. calms the mind 147:21
criterion of w. to vulgar judgements 55:4
full of potential w. 142:24
Government...contrivance of human w. 54:9
greatness of thy w. 28:26
little w. the world is ruled 198:3
more of w. in it 294:16
palace of w. 43:10
realizes that his w. is worthless 202:18
therefore get w. 31:16
W. be put in a silver rod 42:7
W. denotes the pursuing 142:15
W. doth live with children 294:7
w. even from a foe 8:12
W. hath builded her house 31:20
w. is being wise in time 216:10
W. is humble 88:11
W. is ofttimes nearer 292:4
W. is the principal thing 31:16
W. makes him an Ark 100:21
w. not to do desperate things 268:25
w. of our ancestors 54:14
w. of the fool 150:7
w. shall perish with you 29:4
w. to distinguish the one 192:19
without a double share / Of w. 185:10
wise: consider her ways, and be w. 31:18
discloses to the w. 41:14
ever did a w. one 214:19
folly of the w. 150:7
folly to be w. 127:23
like that w. old bird 194:3
more w., and not be catched 201:4
put aside, even by w. men 261:10
questions that the w. cannot answer 288:2
Some folks are w. 249:7
so witty and so w. 214:21
talks, and is extremely w. 143:8
wisdom is being w. in time 216:10
w. are greatest fools 3:12
w. as serpents 36:11
w., like a mirror 84:8
w. man...always ready to leave 116:1
w. man, he speaks so much 15:7
w. men from the east 35:8
w. men use [Studies] 15:14
w. scepticism 169:22
w. son maketh a glad father 31:22
w. want love 243:15
wisely: nations behave w. once 105:12
not w. but too well 235:6
w. worldly, not worldly wise 212:1
wiser: not the w. grow 203:22
sadder and a w. man 81:17
w. than the horses 43:12
w. than we know 111:10
wisest: That man is w. who 202:18
w. fool in Christendom 133:11
w....may err 2:18
w. of mankind achieve 247:16
wish: I w. he'd stay away 179:1
w. I liked the way it walks 213:2
w. in vain for death 250:1
w. was father 228:22
wished: ever w. to be younger 259:8
you w. him to talk on 131:12
wishes: what a man w. he generally believes 92:23
who w. it, no injustice 272:22
w. that they had formed 147:13
wist: He w. not that 27:21
wit: at thirty, the w. 117:14
baiting-place of w. 246:1
brevity, and w. its soul 81:25
Brevity is the soul of w. 226:24
cause that w. is in other 228:13
Commendation of W. 15:6
dream, past the w. of man 234:11
Impropriety is the soul of w. 178:28
mechanic part of w. 112:9
Monarchy of w. 67:3
more w. than poetry 278:9
no pick-purse of another's w. 246:3
not his pointed w. 207:1
potential wisdom and w. 142:24
Staircase w. 97:5
Usurp the chair of w. 150:25
W. is Nature to advantage 205:29
w., it waukens lear 56:16
W.'s an unruly engine 134:25
w.'s the noblest frailty 224:14
w. was a long time in gaol 207:30
W. will shine / Through 103:29
witch: suffer a w. to live 26:27
wither: w. into the truth 296:7
wither'd: sedge has w. 153:11
withers: state...w. away 111:26
within: all that is w. me 30:17
moral law w. me 152:22
who ne'er look w. 87:13
whose fountains are w. 81:21
withstand: w. the highest bidder 279:23
witless: w. nature 140:25
witness: Thou shalt not bear false w. 26:24
witnesses: cloud of w. 40:15
Wits: first for W. then Poets 205:27
Great w. are sure to madness 102:15
stolen his w. away 92:14
witty: not only w. in myself 228:13
proud, so w. and so wise 214:21
so w., profligate, and thin 299:6
too w.; Anglicè too pert 214:10
wive: canna w. an' thrive baith 213:3
Wives: bow to the Gods of his W. 185:3
man with seven w. 194:2
Old w.' fables 40:5
w. are on hand from bridal night 219:4
W. are young men's mistresses 14:11
wo: To speke of w. 73:29
Wodehouse: [W.] performing flea 196:9

woe: and all our w. 183:7
balm of w. 246:1
find / Companions of our w. 279:1
W. to the vanquished 167:7
woes: In all the w. that curse 122:4
What is the worst of w. 61:17
wolf: keep the w. far thence 281:20
like the w. on the fold 62:13
Man is a w. to man 203:1
w. also shall dwell 33:6
Wolf's-bane: neither twist / W. 154:29
WOLVERHAMPTON: AM IN W. STOP 77:6
wolves: hireling w. whose Gospel 185:28
Irish w. against the moon 225:21
ravening w. 36:5
w. behind 112:5
woman: damnable, deceitful w. 197:9
dear, deluding W. 56:13
delicate as the reputation of a w. 55:12
divine in w. / Grows cruel 243:12
done the old w. in 240:24
everie w. tway 166:20
Every w. adores a Fascist 202:15
every w. should marry — and no man 97:21
far as one w. can forgive another 120:17
Fortune is a w. 173:9
Frailty, thy name is w. 226:6
from man, made he a w. 25:17
fury, like a w. scorn'd 84:26
good company improves a w. 113:2
good thing when it an't a w.'s 95:36
hair of a w. 141:6
ill, a w. is the worst 126:20
ills have not been done by w. 197:9
in a word, she is a w. 212:18
just like a w. 105:9
lays his hand upon a w. 269:16
Look for the w. 104:13
Love a w.? You're an ass 214:23
lovely w. in a rural spot 142:13
Man that is born of a w. 29:5
no other purgatory but a w. 21:17
nor w. neither 226:30
not born a w. 21:19
nothing lovelier can be found / In w. 184:29
No where / Lives a w. true 100:15
old w. who lived in a shoe 195:22
One to show a w. 51:16
post-chaise with a pretty w. 149:11
promote a W. to bear rule 160:10
rew up-on w. 19:13
silliest w. can manage 159:30
sort of bloom on a w. 20:10
than a virtuous w. need 219:23
trusted a w. with a secret 70:25
unto the man is w. 168:19
Was ever w. in this humour 235:26
weak and feeble w. 109:1
what's one w.'s fortune 130:5
white w. whom nobody loves 86:1
Who can find a virtuous w. 32:2
wickedness of a w. 35:1
w.? — only one of Nature's agreeable 87:3
w., — some strange influence 64:19
w. as a beautiful, romantic animal 2:13
w. as old as she looks 83:7
w. can hardly ever choose 106:18
w. governs America 174:6
w. had better show 13:12
w. has her way 137:14
W.! in our hours of ease 222:12
W. is always fickle 275:16
w. is at heart a Rake 204:28
w. is his game 264:25
w. is only a woman 158:21
w. loves her lover 62:29
w. oweth to her husband 236:14
w.'s business to get married 239:23
w.'s grief is like a summer storm 16:17
w....should conceal 12:20
w.'s preaching 148:7
w.'s whole existence 62:22
w.'s whole life 144:3
w. that deliberates is lost 1:13
w., therefore to be won 229:8
w. to obey 264:26
w. wakes to love 262:26
W.! when I behold thee 156:2
w. who has had only one 162:23
w. who lives for others 165:13
w. whom thou gavest 25:19
W. will be the last thing civilized 179:24
w. yet think him an angel 266:2
w. you educate a whole family 173:10
writing, and w. of loving 20:21
womankind: think better of w. 156:10
worst he can of w. 137:21
womb: from his mother's w. 232:31
in / My virgin w. 172:11
teeming w. of royal kings 235:15
wombe: w.! O bely! O stynking cod 74:5
wombs: mothers' w. the tiring houses 7:22
women: Alas! the love of w. 62:27
As w. wish to be 137:20
Bah! I have sung w. 208:9
can find w. who have 162:23
Certain w. should be struck 86:14
could but say so of w. too 64:17
England...paradise of w. 115:16
English w. conceal their feelings 288:11
experience of w. which extends 101:17
folly of 'W.'s Rights' 274:16
French w. better than English 24:2
hardly any w. at all 13:11
In the room the w. come 107:29
In w., two almost divide 204:27
Italy...hell for w. 59:9
keeping w. in a state of ignorance 160:12
Like untun'd...strings all w. are 175:20
men that w. marry 168:10
Monstrous Regiment of W. 160:9
Most w. are not so young 22:5
no social differences — till w. 282:18
not for gold and w. 270:2
old w. (of both sexes) 254:15
passing the love of w. 28:4
proper function of w. 106:24
tide in the affairs of w. 63:6
'Twixt w.'s love and men's 98:22
w. — who appear to me as children 156:19
W. and care 279:19
W. and elephants never forget 219:16
W. and Horses and Power 158:20
w. are a sex by themselves 22:10
w. are glad to have been asked 197:13
w. are in furious secret rebellion 239:7
W. are like the Arts 99:2
w. are mostly troublesome cattle 169:14
W. are much more like each other 75:22

w. become like their mothers 287:5
W....care...more for a marriage 16:1
W. dissemble their Passions better 253:2
w. do in men require 43:3
W. hate a debt 51:3
W. hate revolutions 179:14
w. have no characters 204:23
w. I cannot but give way to 201:7
[w.]...man of sense only trifles 75:13
w....married to a poem 157:3
w....merely adored 286:25
w. must weep 158:12
W....off the pedestal 214:5
[w.] power...over themselves 291:8
w. pushing their husbands 93:15
W.... refuse the rules of life 187:21
W....some old, some young 284:9
W., then, are only children 75:18
w. walk in public processions 284:17
W., when nothing else, beguil'd 185:3
Womman: bettre than wisdom? W. 74:6
in humblesse...As w. 74:1
Wommen: W. desiren to have sovereynetee 73:28
won: never lost till w. 88:18
woman, therefore to be w. 229:8
wonder: all the w. that would be 264:4
Have eyes to w. 238:17
I w. by my troth 99:18
still the w. grew 125:9
w. to see them not ashamed 259:9
w. why he does 181:10
wonderful: but she was a w. woman 98:14
w., and most wonderful 225:18
wondering: Gods or w. men 154:6
wonders: His w. to perform 87:21
w. in the deep 30:20
w. of the western world 260:21
W. will never cease 104:7
wond'rous: What w. life is this 177:12
won't: will you, w. you 69:23
woo'd: beautiful and therefore to be w. 229:8
wood: Genius of the W. 182:9
Hewers of w. 27:12
impulse from a vernal w. 294:17
w.'s in trouble 140:30
wooden: lies about his w. horse 115:9
Our w. walls 86:7
This w. O 228:27
woodman: w., spare the beechen tree 66:2
W., spare that tree 189:10
Wood-notes: native W. wild 182:17
Woods: fresh W., and Pastures new 182:33
lived in the w. 275:25
never knew the summer w. 263:12
pleasure in the pathless w. 62:1
senators of mighty w. 154:4
to the w. no more 6:12
w. are lovely, dark, and deep 118:16
w. shall to me answer 251:18
woodshed: nasty in the w. 122:1
wooed: in this humour w. 235:26
wooer: knight to be their w. 17:6
woof: weave the w. 127:8
wool: Have you any w. 194:4
Woolf: Who's Afraid of Virginia W. 3:3
woollen: Odious! in w. 205:20
Worchyng: W. and wandryng 162:14
word: cuckoo: O w. of fear 231:16
doers of the w. 40:20
every w. that proceedeth 27:6
for a w. — 'neutrality' 25:1
For one w. a man is 84:12
Give me the right w. 85:7
thought, w., and deed 70:20
Thy w. abideth 16:21
Thy w. is a lamp 31:3
w. flies 139:20
w. is the Verb 141:16
w. is too often profaned 244:11
w....means just what I choose 70:7
w. no man relies on 214:19
W. was made flesh 37:38
W. was with God 37:36
wordes: glotoun of w. 162:15
wording: w. of his own highest thoughts 156:21
wordish: only a w. description 246:6
words: belief that w. have a meaning 196:11
Choose me, you English w. 267:17
Deeds, not w. shall speak 21:12
fool and his w. are soon parted 244:23
He w. me 224:30
knowing the force of w. 84:15
let thy w. be few 32:8
misused w. generate misleading thoughts 251:3
not fine w. 186:18
Proper w. in proper places 258:19
sad w. of tongue or pen 285:10
threw w. like stones 251:9
two narrow w., *Hic jacet* 213:1
unfit choice of w. 15:20
very good w. for the lips 94:28
Winged w. 137:26
without the sword are but w. 136:22
W. are like leaves 205:30
w. are my own 72:16
W. are the physicians 2:20
W. are the tokens 13:23
W. are wise men's counters 136:17
w. but wind 59:25
w. divide and rend 259:26
w. in their best order 83:1
w., like Nature, half reveal 263:8
W. may be false 224:12
w. only to disguise 276:14
w. shall not pass away 36:33
w. without knowledge 29:8
W., words, words 226:26
Wordsworth: W., both are thine 253:13
W. chime his childish verse 63:26
[W.] did weave / Songs consecrate 244:18
[W.] found in stones 286:20
[W.] shows / That prose is verse 63:27
W. sometimes wakes 63:1
Thou shalt not set up W. 62:21
[W.] totally deficient in 131:11
W. was only a poet 60:4
work: as tedious as to w. 227:34
counsel — w., work, work 41:19
day's w. is a day's 241:1
Do the w. that's nearest 158:9
If any would not w. 40:4
I like w.; it fascinates 145:19
in England / That do no w. 228:33
I want w. 227:38
let the toad *w.* 163:10
life, or of the w. 296:3

lives by his own w. 83:5
man out of w. for a day 157:23
Measure not the w., / Until 49:12
men must w. 158:12
Nothing to do but w. 158:2
shalt not do any w. 26:32
some people I could w. for 146:1
sympathy because he has to w. 216:8
test of a first-rate w. 24:5
things w. together for good 38:36
too warm w., Hardy, to last 191:10
unless one has plenty of w. 145:16
when no man can w. 38:6
w.; let him ask no other blessedness 68:13
w. at anything but his art 239:19
W. conquers all 276:3
W. expands so as to fill 199:2
W. is prayer 6:4
W. is the curse 288:23
w. of noble note may yet 265:13
W. out your own salvation 39:24
w. the day he was born 254:17
W....whatever a body is obliged to do 272:7
w. without question 276:13
w. worth doing 216:8
wrought at one great w. 91:3
your w. shall be rewarded 28:27
worked: w. and sang from morn 41:9
workers: men the w., ever reaping 264:4
W. of the world, unite 178:1
Workhouse: Christmas Day in the W. 246:13
working-day: briers is this w. world 225:5
workmanship: dark / Inscrutable w. 293:7
works: Faith without w. is dead 40:21
fruit of good w. 210:2
man w. no more 80:20
more he w., the more 293:19
seen the future, and it w. 253:9
see the w. of the Lord 30:20
workshop: w. of the world 97:30
world: All's right with the w. 51:27
all the w. were paper 5:23
all to all the w. 135:7
and now a w. 206:11
back the w. 152:21
back upon the w. 168:9
bed in another w. 134:3
brave new w. 236:28
busy oneself putting the w. to rights 187:3
by the w. forgot 204:22
citizen of the w. 14:19
citizen of the w. 97:10
condition of the w., like logic 290:24
contagion of the w.'s slow stain 241:14
cow of the w. 285:18
Days that Shook the W. 213:15
England is not all the w. 178:7
enjoy the w. aright 270:4
flashing from one end of the w. 256:21
gain the whole w. 36:23
gleams of a remoter w. 243:3
gone into the w. of light 273:17
great w. spin for ever 264:6
had my w. as in my time 73:30
Had we but w. enough 177:19
In search of this new W. 184:5
in the w., and not in a closet 75:7
judgement of the w. 11:23
Let all the w. in ev'ry 134:22
little w. made cunningly 99:21
lover's quarrel with the w. 118:9
mad w., my masters 262:2
makes the w. go round 69:20
masques and mummeries...of the w. 13:29
My country is the w. 198:10
not loved the W. 61:28
Oh w., no world 160:13
only saved the w. 76:9
Other w. 111:22
O w.! O life! O time 242:19
peace which the w. cannot give 209:18
perceive how the w. is really going 10:7
preposterous pig of a w. 295:22
singularly ill-contrived w. 16:25
still point of a turning w. 107:13
This w. is a comedy 278:19
though the w. perish 113:11
way the w. ends 107:25
when Rome falls — the W. 62:6
Where in this small-talking w. 119:2
whole w. is a sepulchre 269:2
whole w. plays the actor 7:14
whole w. wants: power 45:11
wilderness of this w. 53:14
w. and I shall ne'er agree 86:25
w. and love were young 212:22
w. as made for me 249:9
w. as my parish 283:4
w. can never fill 87:18
w. elsewhere 225:27
w. has grown grey 260:14
W. in a Grain of Sand 41:28
w. is a fine place and worth 133:3
w. is an old woman 68:21
w. is but a small parenthesis 48:21
w. is charged with 138:24
W. is crazier 174:4
w. is everything that is the case 290:22
w. is full of care 279:19
w. is given to lying 228:12
w. is made up...of fools and knaves 53:3
w. is queer save thee and me 197:20
w. is so full of a number 255:13
w. is too much with us 294:6
w. itself could not contain 38:19
w. laughs with you 285:19
w. may end to-night 51:6
w. must be getting old 145:18
w. must be peopled 234:20
w.'s a bubble 15:25
w.'s as ugly 167:23
w.'s history is the world's 221:3
w. should crack and fall 140:9
w.'s mine oyster 233:28
w. surely is wide enough 254:4
W. was all before them 185:1
w. was created on 22nd October 273:2
w. was too little for Alexander 83:23
w. will end in fire 118:10
w. will...follow only 60:12
w. would be nicer 291:18
W., you have kept faith 130:6
worldling: world or w. meant 155:18
worldly: not w. wise 212:1
worlds: best of all possible w. 276:11
many w., so much to do 263:18
Space may produce new W. 183:25
such a vast multitude of w. 203:11
two w., one dead 9:13

Worm: hero the Conqueror W. 203:16
joy o' the w. 224:33
loving w. within its clod 50:14
nakid as a w. was she 74:18
rather tough w. 123:6
w. beneath the sod 244:7
w., the canker, and the grief 64:3
worm-eaten: want facts and w. parchments 131:20
worms: graves, of w. and epitaphs 235:18
made w.' meat of me 236:4
nor w. forget 95:10
or dirt, or grubs, or w. 205:2
w. have eaten them 225:19
wormwood: w. and the gall 34:10
worn: when we're w., / Hack'd, hewn 250:6
worried: poem...not be w. into being 118:18
worrit: w. to make the days pass 107:1
Worrying: W. the carcase of an old song 267:18
worse: better day, the w. deed 133:16
fear of finding something w. 23:5
More will mean w. 4:9
person for the w. 259:4
w. than a crime 45:10
w. than a crime 116:23
w. than being talked about 287:22
worship: come to w. him 35:8
dollar...object of w. 7:7
modes of w., which prevailed 121:16
they that w. him 38:2
with my body I thee w. 210:16
W. is transcendent wonder 68:3
worshipped: Fathers w. Stocks and Stones 185:21
w. something other than itself 143:5
worships: Everybody w. me, it's nauseating 86:11
he w. in his way 247:1
worst: Death is not the w. 250:1
do your w., and we 78:3
good in the w. 7:12
it was the w. of times 96:18
This is the w. 230:37
w. are no worse 234:15
w. friend and enemy is 48:10
w. he can of womankind 137:21
w. is better than any other 131:9
w. kinde of infortune 74:22
w. time of the year 107:26
worst-natur'd: with the w. muse 214:18
worth: fairly w. the travelling to 255:18
Slow rises w. by poverty 147:6
thing is w. doing 77:3
w. of the individuals 180:21
Worthington: on the stage, Mrs. W. 86:19
worthlessness: w. of the most medicines 117:9
worthy: foemen w. of their steel 221:20
make one w. man my foe 205:6
w. o' the flatterer 236:29
wot: lovesome thing, God w. 48:19
wotthehell: but w. 176:14
would: He w., wouldn't he 214:7
what a man w. do 52:10
wouldn't: would, w. he 214:7
wound: Earth felt the w. 184:30
never felt a w. 235:35
Willing to w., and yet 205:4
W. with a touch 187:10
wounded: 'You're w.!' 'Nay,' 51:5
w. in the house 34:27
w. surgeon plies 107:16
Wounded Knee: heart at W. 23:23
wounds: not to heed the w. 170:3
Time w. all heels 7:13
w. of a friend 31:38
Wrapped: W. up in a five-pound 164:10
wrapt: All meanly w. 183:1
wrath: Achilles' w., to Greece 137:24
children to w. 39:21
eternal w. / Burnt after them 184:24
grapes of w. 141:5
my w. did end 43:23
sun go down upon your w. 39:19
tigers of w. are wiser 43:12
turneth away w. 31:26
w. to come 35:11
wreathing: w. his body seven times round 247:1
wreck: my brother's w. 108:18
wrecked: formless spawning fury w. 298:2
wrecks: Vomits its w. 242:21
Wren: Four Larks and a W. 164:4
Sir Christopher W. / Said 24:15
wrestle: w. not against flesh and blood 39:23
wrestling: When I behold a prize / Worth w. 62:12
wretch: w. that dares not die 57:6
wretched: set off w. matter 183:6
wretchedness: w. of being rich 247:20
wretches: w. hang that jury-men 207:19
wring: soon w. their hands 278:24
wrinkle: stamps the w. deeper 61:17
writ: having w., / Moves on 114:25
name was w. in water 157:5
never w., nor no man ever loved 238:20
write: hope to w. well hereafter 186:1
in thy heart and w. 245:25
itch to w. 152:14
much as a man ought to w. 270:13
read a novel I w. one 98:12
we cannot w. like Hazlitt 257:1
w. about it, and about it 204:4
w. at any time 147:26
w. / Even yet in C major 172:21
w. for the general amusement 222:17
W. me as one 142:9
w. three plays and then stop 240:20
writer: Every great and original w. 294:25
good w. should be so simple 298:19
w., a free man 220:19
w. has to rob his mother 113:8
writers: American w. want to be not good 274:21
as demagogues and not as w. 23:18
w. become more numerous 125:1
W., like teeth 16:7
writing: fine w. is next to fine doing 157:2
man is tired of w. 20:21
only end of w. is 147:22
w. an exact man 15:16
w. comes from art, not chance 206:2
W....different name for conversation 254:3
W....mechanic part of wit 112:9
written: censure freely who have w. well 205:26

have w., I have written 38:16
until he has w. a book 151:6
well w. or badly written 287:20
what is w. about me 134:4
w. better than Savage 146:19
w. by gentlemen for gentlemen 266:6
w. by people who don't understand 166:1
w. in wind and running water 71:7
w. without effort 150:6
wroghte: That first he w. 73:14
Wrong: Cavaliers (W. but Wromantic) 223:23
country, right or w. 91:18
do a little w. 233:21
Englishman in the w. 240:18
feel that I must be w. 286:13
Fifty million Frenchmen can't be w. 128:11
king can do no w. 41:25
Kings to govern w. 204:12
One w. more to man 51:8
only w. what is against it 110:17
public is never w. 299:17
rather be w. with Plato 79:1
right deed for the w. 108:5
something w. with our bloody ships 21:4
suffer w. no more 171:4
sweeten Ireland's w. 298:4
who does, not suffers w. 243:13
W. dressed out in pride, pomp 131:8
w. number, why did you answer 269:6
w. people going hungry 197:6
w. us, shall we not revenge 233:14
w. war, at the wrong 45:18
wrongs: makes the people's w. his own 102:22
mass of public w. 160:13
W. / By man on man 82:11
wrote: genius I had when I w. that book 259:22
never w., except for money 149:14
w. it with a second hand 251:14
w. like an angel 120:4
wrought: More things are w. by prayer 263:3
What God hath w. 189:16
Wully: Whaur's yer W. Shakespeare 7:24
wyf: A w. wol laste 74:2
Wykehamist: rather dirty W. 25:6
wysest: clerkes been noght the w. 73:26
Xanadu: In X. did Kubla Khan 82:3
Yankee: Y. Doodle came to town 19:6
Yarrow: bonny banks o' Y. 17:11
found him drown'd in Y. 18:7
yawns: grave y. for him 270:7
yawp: barbaric y. over the roofs 285:1
ybeten: maker is hymself y. 74:20
ye: 'dayesye', or elles the 'y. of day' 74:13
yea: Let your y. be yea 40:23
year: book that is not a y. old 111:12
gate of the y. 131:4
Old Y. out, / And the New Year in 124:7
returns with the revolving y. 241:10
That time of y. thou mayst 238:13
'Tis the y.'s midnight 100:5
y. is dying in the night 263:20
y. whose days are long 286:5
yearn: y. for His existence 272:26
yearning: music, y. like a God 153:26
years: fleeting y. are slipping by 140:3
give me back my lost y. 275:21
moments big as y. 154:3
vale of y. 234:38
y. like great black oxen 298:17
y. that the locust hath eaten 34:19
y. to come seemed waste 296:23
young in y....old in hours 15:10
87 y. ago, I think 145:15
Yeats: William Y. is laid to rest 11:7
yell: such a y. was there 222:11
yellow: Come unto these y. sands 236:17
commended thy y. stockings 237:21
My days are in the y. leaf 64:3
sear, the y. leaf 232:25
When y. leaves, or none 238:13
Y. God forever gazes 131:7
y. primrose was to him 293:2
yelps: loudest y. for liberty 147:16
yerde: man maketh ofte a y. 74:20
Yes: able to say Y. 8:24
don't say y. until I've finished 299:14
y. I said yes I will Yes 151:22
yesterday: but as y. when it is past 30:10
Children dear, was it y. 9:11
yesterdays: all our y. 232:28
yesteryear: snows of y. 275:2
yew: Never a spray of y. 9:19
yield: find, and not to y. 265:15
temptation is to y. to it 287:24
Y. not to temptation 198:12
y....to the dominion of the English 5:14
Yielded: Y. with coy submission 184:16
Yo-ho-ho: Y., and a bottle of rum 256:9
yoke: How a good y. of bullocks 228:20
liberty before the easy y. 184:3
teach us to cast off this Y. 184:23
yoked: y. by violence together 146:20
Yonghy-Bonghy-Bó: Lived the Y. 164:6
Yorick: Alas! poor Y. 227:21
young: and we were y. 140:26
[Brigham Y.] most married man 279:15
Caparisons don't become a y. woman 245:7
cheek of a y. person 95:26
crime of being a y. man 202:3
die y. is our doom 19:5
Fortune...friendly to the y. 173:9
gods love dies y. 179:12
happy while we are y. 5:16
if he be *caught* y. 148:27
I was a poet, I was y. 115:10
let me perish y. 64:8
Man that is y. in years 15:10
not so y. as she has been 214:10
No y. man believes 131:16
radical when y. / For fear 118:14
seventy years y. 137:19
she died y. 281:13
to feel y., really young 197:4
world and love were y. 212:22
y. are beautiful 284:9
y. are generally thwarted 196:21
y. as they are painted 22:5
y. can do for the old 239:6
y. heart beating under fourscore 111:19
y. know everything 287:31
y. men are regarded as radicals 289:23
y. 'neath wrinkled rind 162:9
y. person who marries 12:7
y. was very heaven 293:10

younger: older we do not get any y. 213:12
wished to be y. 259:8
youngest: infallible — not even the y. 268:2
yourself: must deny y. 124:13
not want done to y. 84:2
youth: age approve of y. 52:2
and y. stone dead 220:21
blood and battles was my y. 9:31
days of thy y. 32:15
done it from my y. 88:14
great has been done by y. 97:17
If y. only knew 112:8
In y. is pleasure 283:13
In y. we are 179:11
measure of our y. 159:6
old in their y. 64:1
public never forgives — y. 288:19
red / Sweet wine of y. 48:1
sign of an ill-spent y. 251:6
thoughts of y. are long 168:11
Time, the subtle thief of y. 185:19
To y. I have but three words 41:19
trampled vintage of my y. 286:7
waste an eternal y. 286:15
when Y. and Pleasure meet 61:20
wicked sides at y. 297:11
y. are the days of our glory 64:9
y. grows pale 155:2
y. I remembered my God 250:19
Y. is a blunder 97:18
Y. is the time 256:21
Y., large, lusty, loving 285:6
Y. means love 52:4
Y. of a Nation 97:24
y. of England are on fire 228:28
Y. on the prow 127:7
Y.'s a stuff will not endure 237:17
Y. shows but half 51:31
y. was full of foolish 263:15
Y., which is forgiven everything 240:5
Y. will be served 45:6
Y. will stand foremost 242:8
Yukon: Law of the Y. 224:7
ywhet: sorowe, y. with fals plesaunce 72:26
zeal: holy mistaken z. in politics 152:5
Not too much z. 261:12
z. / I served my king 229:16
zealots: let graceless z. fight 206:22
zèle: *Pas trop de z.* 261:12
Zenith: Dropt from the Z. 183:26
Zenocrate: entertain divine Z. 176:11
fair Zenocrate, divine Z. 176:8
Zephyrus: Z. did softly play 252:9
Zion: wept when we remembered Z. 31:9
Z. of the water bead 267:4
zone: torrid or the frozen z. 67:5
Zurich: gnomes of Z. 289:18
Zzzzzp: Knowledge — Z.! — Money 289:9